WHO
WAS WHO
DURING THE
AMERICAN
REVOLUTION

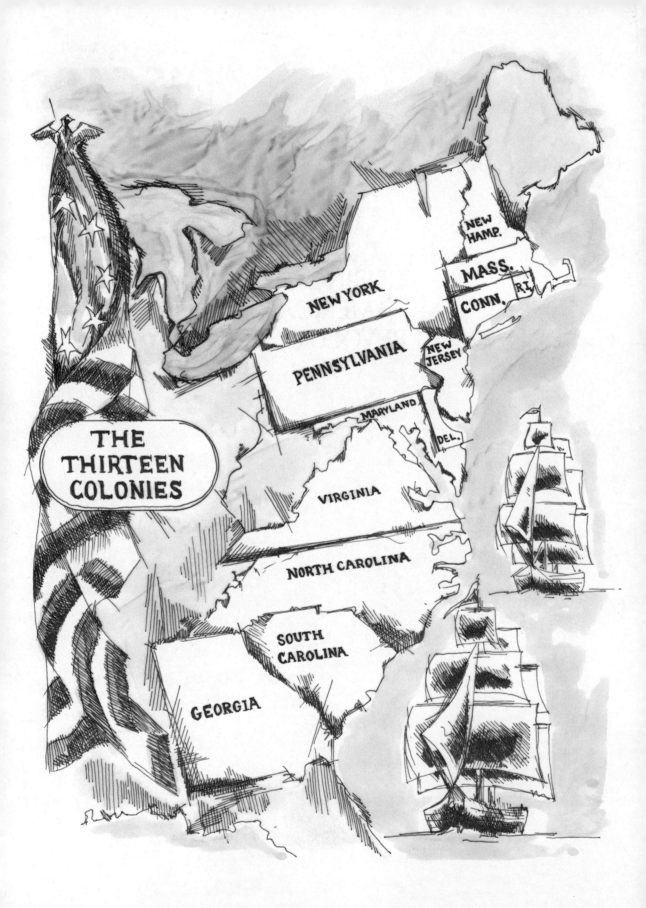

THE
THIRTEEN
COLONIES

NEW HAMP.

MASS.

CONN. R.I.

NEW YORK

PENNSYLVANIA

NEW JERSEY

MARYLAND

DEL.

VIRGINIA

NORTH CAROLINA

SOUTH CAROLINA

GEORGIA

WHO WAS WHO DURING THE AMERICAN REVOLUTION

Compiled by the editors of
WHO'S WHO IN AMERICA

with JERRY KAIL

THE BOBBS-MERRILL COMPANY, INC.
Indianapolis ★ New York

ISBN 0–672–52216–0
Library of Congress catalog card number 75–34514
Designed by Viki Webb
Illustrated by Ron McCorkle
Manufactured in the United States of America

First printing

12/76

CONTENTS

Introduction / vii

Connecticut / 1

Delaware / 37

Georgia / 47

Maryland / 63

Massachusetts / 91

New Hampshire / 167

New Jersey / 193

New York / 221

North Carolina / 279

Pennsylvania / 311

Rhode Island / 393

South Carolina / 409

Virginia / 437

Frontiersmen and Foreign Nationals / 493

INTRODUCTION

George Washington . . . Thomas Jefferson . . . James Madison . . . these are names that come to mind when one considers the period in history that saw one of the most notable occurrences of modern times—the American Revolution. These men and others of equal prominence stood as an inspiration to their fellows to make the final break with the mother country; upon the winning of independence, they proceeded to construct the framework for a new form of government. They are, in the true sense of the word, heroes.

However, during the American Revolution, as during any other epoch in history, the actions of a few heroic figures were abetted, supported, and at times even determined by that great mass of individuals often referred to as "common men"—the soldier in the ranks, the selectman of a provincial town, the proprietor of a small factory. Without these men there would have been no American Revolution, no "great experiment" in self-government. While the words and deeds of the great leaders provided rallying points for the cause of independence as a whole, it was left to the local leaders to mold these concepts and ideas into day-to-day reality. The Washingtons, Jeffersons, and Madisons have well earned their places in history, but it must not be forgotten that the American Revolution was a collective effort which saw heroic deeds at almost every turn.

This book contains biographical sketches not only of the great leaders of the Revolutionary era but of these men and women of lesser note who made important contributions to the Revolution. The nearly 1500 people described herein include several individuals—primarily members of the military and of various types of governmental bodies—who were intimately concerned with the planning and fighting of the Revolutionary War. Also included are others —bankers, printers, artists, storekeepers, even butchers and bakers—who, while not directly involved in the mechanics of the war, nevertheless had a hand in the winning of independence through the contribution of their skills and their spirit. Finally there are those—Loyalists, hostile Indians, frontier mercenaries—whose participation in the war took the form of opposition to the cause of independence. All of these people—the great, the near great, the infamous, the all-but-forgotten—make up the cast of characters of the drama known as the American Revolution.

INTRODUCTION

The scope of this book is not limited to the war years 1775–81, just as the American Revolution can be thought of as an ongoing process rather than an "event." A number of the men and women included here did not even live to see the Revolutionary War, but through their participation in early attempts at western migration (which contributed to a growing sense of separateness from the mother country) and their strenuous objections to the first instances of what they regarded as British tyranny, they laid the groundwork for the more organized resistance of the late 1760s and the early 1770s. In a sense, too, the Revolution did not end with the surrender of Cornwallis in 1781; the representative government established by the leaders of the new country in the late 1780s was as much a revolution as the act of breaking with England, and the men who formed and implemented that government were as much revolutionaries as were the men who faced the British at Bunker Hill, Saratoga, and Yorktown (indeed they were, in many cases, the same men). This book reaches beyond the war era into the first decades of the Government of the United States.

The biographies have been grouped according to the thirteen colonies in existence at the time of the Revolutionary War. There were, of course, other regions—Tennessee, Kentucky, Maine, Vermont—that by 1776 had been extensively settled but were not yet recognized as separate entities. For the purposes of this book, residents of these four regions are included in the colonies with which the regions were most closely identified during the Revolutionary era, i.e., Tennessee with North Carolina, Kentucky with Virginia, Maine with Massachusetts, and Vermont with New Hampshire. There were also several men and women—foreign nationals who volunteered their service in the war, frontier pioneers who operated on the perimeter of the colonial possessions, itinerant preachers, tradesmen, and artisans—who could call no colony their home. These people are included in a final section, "Frontiersmen and Foreign Nationals."

The American Revolution is now two hundred years past, but the work of the men and women of that era lives on, even though the memory of many of them does not. This book stands as a tribute to those people and as a reminder of an era that saw the ascendancy of the common man.

WHO
WAS WHO
DURING THE
AMERICAN
REVOLUTION

CONNECTICUT

"This day, one [Nathan] Hale, in New York, on suspicion of being a spy was taken up and dragged without ceremony to the execution post, and hung up."

—No source

ADAMS, Andrew: Continental congressman, jurist

Born Stratford, Connecticut, December 11,1736; son of Samuel and Mary (Fairchild) Adams; married Eunice Canfield; died November 26, 1797.

Adams earned a B.A. from Yale in 1760 and three years later was admitted to the Connecticut bar. He served in the upper house of the Connecticut General Assembly during the years 1776–77 and 1782–89. He was a member of the Connecticut Council of Safety and the state militia, receiving a commission as major and later becoming colonel. Appointed as a delegate to the Continental Congress in 1777, he was a signer of the Articles of Confederation.

Adams became associate judge of the Connecticut Superior Court in 1789 and rose to chief justice four years later, serving in that position until 1797. In 1796 Yale awarded him an honorary LL.D.

Adams died in Litchfield, Connecticut.

ARNOLD, Benedict: army officer

Born Norwich, Connecticut, January 14, 1741; son of Benedict and Hannah (Waterman) Arnold; married Margaret Mansfield, February 22, 1767; second marriage to Margaret Shippen, April 1779; father of eight children (including Benedict, Richard, and Henry); died June 14, 1801.

Arnold was commissioned a captain in the Connecticut militia and became a colonel in 1775. That same year he captured Fort Ticonderoga from the British but was defeated in his attack on Quebec. In 1776 he received the commission of brigadier general and twice stopped British forces who were attempting an expedition down Lake Champlain. Promoted to major general the next year, he played a major role in the defeat and surrender of Burgoyne at the Battle of Saratoga. He became military commander of Philadelphia in 1778 and commanded the American post at West Point, New York, two years later.

After experiencing a court-martial and some congressional slights, and after opposing the French Alliance, Arnold began corresponding with Sir Henry Clinton, British commander-in-chief in North America. Their correspondence culminated in 1780 in

1

Arnold's arrangement with Major John André of Clinton's staff to betray West Point. His treason discovered, Arnold fled to the British side. He became a brigadier general in the British Army in 1780 and led raids on Virginia in that year and on Connecticut the following year. He received a grant of land in Canada in 1797. He died in London, England.

★★★★★

BACKUS, Azel: clergyman, college president

Born near Norwich, Connecticut, October 13, 1765; son of Jabez and Deborah (Fanning) Backus; married Melicent Deming, February 7, 1791; died December 28, 1816.

Backus graduated from Yale in 1787 and was licensed to preach two years later. In 1791 he took on the pastorate at the First Congregational Church in Bethlehem, Connecticut. In 1798 he wrote *Absalom's Conspiracy,* a Federalist attack on Thomas Jefferson, and was consequently charged with, but not convicted of, libeling a President of the United States.

Backus earned a D.D. from the College of New Jersey (now Princeton) in 1810. He was the first president of Hamilton College, serving from 1812 until his death in 1816, in Clinton, New York.

BAILEY, Anna Warner

Born Groton, Connecticut, October 1758; married Captain Elijah Bailey, circa 1782; died January 10, 1851.

An orphan, Bailey lived in Groton with her uncle, Edward Mills, from her early childhood. On September 6, 1781, during the Battle of Groton Heights, she made her way to the battlefield and brought home her mortally wounded uncle, an event which was later celebrated in both poetry and legend. She was given the nickname "Mother Bailey" in 1813 when she gave her flannel petticoat to Groton soldiers to use in making cartridges in the War of 1812. She died and was buried in Groton. The local chapter of the D.A.R. is named in her honor.

BARLOW, Joel: poet, diplomat

Born Reading, Connecticut, March 24, 1754; son of Samuel and Esther (Hull) Barlow; married Ruth Baldwin, 1781; died December 14, 1812.

Barlow graduated from Yale in 1778 and participated in the American Revolution. He was the founder, with Elisha Babcock, of the *American Mercury* in 1784 and was a member of the Constitutional Society. He went to England in 1791, remaining until 1793, and was United States consul to Algiers in 1795. He effected treaties with Tunis, Algiers and Tripoli, closing one phase of the war with the Barbary States, although Barbary pirates continued their activities for several more years. In 1811 he became United States minister to France.

Barlow was a member of the United States Military Philosophical Society and the American Philosophical Society. He was director of the Bank of Washington, D.C., and the leading light of the so-called Hartford Wits. In 1812 he negotiated with Napoleon in Zarnavica, Poland, where he died from cold and privation.

Barlow was author of *The Vision of Columbus,* 1787; "Letter to the National Convention of France on the Defects in the Constitution of 1791," for which he received French citizenship, 1791; *Advice to the Privileged Orders,* 1792; *The Conspiracy of Kings,* 1792; *Hasty Pudding,* 1796; and *The Columbiad,* 1807.

BATES, Walter: Loyalist

Born Stamford, Connecticut, March 14, 1760; son of John and Sarah (Bostwick) Bates; married; died February 11, 1842.

In 1775 Bates was held in a stockade for his alleged loyalty to the British. After his release he joined the Tories in Long Island. In 1783 he settled in Nova Scotia and became the first man to be married there. He served for a time as sheriff of King's County, Nova Scotia. He was author of *The Mysterious Stranger,* 1816, and *Kingston and the Loyalists of the "Spring Fleet" of 1783,* published posthumously in 1889.

BOARDMAN, Elijah: senator

Born New Milford, Connecticut, March 7, 1760; father of at least one son (William Whiting); died October 8, 1823.

Educated by private tutors, Boardman served in Colonel Charles Webb's regiment in the Revolutionary War. After a time as clerk in a mercantile establishment, he himself became a merchant in 1781, retiring from the business in 1812.

Boardman was a member of the Connecticut House of Representatives in the years 1803–05 and 1816. From there he moved to the New York State Upper House, serving in 1817 and the following year. Having been elected to the New York State Senate for the period 1819–21, he then represented Connecticut as a Democrat in the United States Senate from 1821 until his death two years later, in Boardman, Ohio. He was buried in Center Cemetery in New Milford, the town of his birth.

BRACE, Jonathan: congressman, jurist, mayor

Born Harwinton, Connecticut, November 12, 1754; died August 26, 1837.

Brace graduated from Yale in 1779, studied law, and was admitted to the bar in Bennington, Vermont, the same year. He began his practice in Pawlet, Vermont, moving to Manchester three years later. As well as serving on the council of censors to revise the constitution, he was prosecuting attorney for Bennington County in 1784–85.

Brace moved to Glastonbury, Connecticut, in 1786 and was admitted to the Connecticut bar four years later. He participated in the state General Assembly in the years 1788, 1791–94, and 1798. He moved to Hartford, Connecticut, in 1794, where he became a judge in the City Court three years later. Except for a period of two years, he held this position until 1815. A Federalist, he served briefly in the United States House of Representatives, filling a vacancy on December 3, 1798, and resigning in 1800 (5th and 6th congresses).

Brace then returned to service of a more local nature. From prosecuting attorney of Hartford County (1807–09) he went on to hold the offices of judge of the county court from 1809 until 1821 and judge of probate from 1809 to 1824. He also found time to serve as mayor of Hartford during the period 1815 to 1824 and in the Connecticut Senate during 1819–20. He died at the age of eighty-two and was buried in Old North Cemetery, in Hartford.

BUELL, Abel: inventor, engraver, silversmith

Born Killingworth, Connecticut, February 1742; son of John Buell; married Mary Parker, 1762; second marriage to Aletta Devoe, 1771; third marriage to Mrs. Rebecca Parkman, 1779; fourth marriage to Sarah; died March 10, 1822.

After an apprenticeship to the silversmith Ebenezer Chittenden in Killingworth, Buell opened his own shop in 1762. The first signs of his ability were some Connecticut five-shilling notes which he artfully improved to five-pound notes, an indiscretion which cost him some months in jail plus branding and confiscation of property. Upon release from prison, he constructed a lapidary machine for cutting and finishing precious stones.

After learning the craft of type founding, in 1769 Buell produced the first known example of American type founding and was granted 100 pounds by the Connecticut Assembly to aid in establishing a type foundry in New Haven. The following year he began copperplate engraving. In 1784 he produced his chief engraving work, a map of the territories of the United States according to the Peace of 1783.

Remaining in New Haven, Buell extended his business to the operation of packet boats, the development of a marble quarry, and the ownership of two privateersmen. He also continued to fashion silver, cast type, and practice engraving. In 1785 he constructed a coining machine. After a trip to England in 1789, he worked at a New

York cotton manufacturing plant in 1793. Six years later he returned to Hartford, Connecticut, and continued silversmithing and engraving. He became a silversmith in Stockbridge, Massachusetts, in 1805.

Buell was a believer in the doctrines of Thomas Paine until 1813, when he embraced Christianity. He died nine years later in the New Haven Alms House.

BUSHNELL, David: inventor
Born Saybrook, Connecticut, 1742; died 1824.

A graduate of Yale in 1775, Bushnell designed and built a man-propelled submarine boat that year and was thus the originator of modern submarine warfare. He served as a captain-lieutenant in the Continental Army in 1779 and was a captain in 1781. He died in Warrenton, Georgia.

BUTLER, Zebulon: naval officer, army officer
Born Lyme, Connecticut, January 23, 1731; son of John and Hannah (Perkins) Butler; married Anna Lord, December 23, 1760; second marriage to Lydia Johnston, August 1775; third marriage to Phebe Haight, November 1781; died July 28, 1795.

Butler served as an ensign during the French and Indian War in 1757, then as a lieutenant and quartermaster in 1759, and finally as a captain in 1760. In 1769 he led a band of Connecticut settlers to the Wyoming Valley (now Luzerne County, Pennsylvania). As well as being director of Susquehanna County, he served as a member of the Connecticut Assembly from Wyoming during 1774–76. He was commissioned a lieutenant colonel in the Continental Army in 1776 and was promoted to colonel two years later. He died in Wilkes-Barre, Pennsylvania.

★★★★★

CHAMPION, Epaphroditus: congressman, businessman
Born Westchester Parish, Colchester, Connecticut, April 6, 1756; died December 22, 1834.

Champion attended common schools. During the Revolutionary War he served in the commissary and purchasing departments of the Continental Army. After moving to East Haddam, Connecticut, in 1782, he served as captain of the 24th Regiment of the Connecticut militia from 1784 to 1792; as major from 1793 to 1794; as lieutenant colonel from 1795 to 1798; and as brigadier general of the 7th Brigade from 1800 to 1803.

After his military service he became a merchant, shipowner, exporter, and importer. From 1791 to 1806 he was a member of the Connecticut Assembly. Elected as a Federalist to the United States House of Representatives, he served during the 10th through the 14th congresses, 1807–17.

Champion died in East Haddam and was buried in Riverview Cemetery.

CHAPIN, Clavin: clergyman
Born Chicopee, Massachusetts, July 22, 1763; son of Edward and Eunice (Cotton) Chapin; married Jerusha Edwards, February 2, 1795; died March 16, 1851.

After graduating from Yale in 1788, Chapin was licensed to preach by the Hartford North Association of Congregational Churches in 1791. He was a tutor at Yale from 1791 to 1794.

Chapin became pastor of Stepney Parish, Wethersfield (now Rocky Hill), Connecticut, in 1794, and served until his death. From 1805 to 1831 he was a trustee of the Missionary Society of Connecticut. He was a co-founder of the Connecticut Bible Society, 1809, and of the American Board of Foreign Missions, 1810; he served as recording secretary of the latter organization from 1810 to 1842.

In 1813 Chapin was a co-founder of the Connecticut Society for the Promotion of Good Morals. From 1816 to 1851, he was a member of the board of visitors of Andover Theological Seminary, serving as clerk of the board from 1816 to 1832. He was a member of the corporation of Yale University from 1820 to 1846.

CLAP, Thomas: clergyman, college president

Born Scituate, Massachusetts, June 26, 1703; son of Stephen and Temperance Clap; married Mary Whiting, November 23, 1727; second marriage to Mary Haynes, February 5, 1740; died January 7, 1767.

In 1726, four years after his graduation from Harvard, Clap was called to the Congregational Church in Windham, Connecticut, and was ordained that same year. He was elected rector of Yale College in 1739. Under his leadership the college drafted a more liberal charter, granted in 1745; he drew up a code of laws, which was also approved in 1745. From that year until 1766 he served as president of Yale.

Clap was the author of *Annals of Yale College,* which he wrote in 1766. He died in New Haven, Connecticut.

CLEAVELAND, Moses: army officer, pioneer

Born Canterbury County, Connecticut, January 29, 1754; son of Colonel Aaron and Thankful (Paine) Cleaveland; married Esther Champion, March 21, 1794; died November 16, 1806.

After graduating from Yale in 1777, Cleaveland was commissioned an ensign in the 2nd Connecticut Regiment of the Continental Army, later advancing to lieutenant. He served under Washington from 1777 to 1781. A member of the Connecticut Society of the Cincinnati, he was later commissioned a brigadier general in the Connecticut militia.

Cleaveland was a member of the Connecticut General Assembly, representing Canterbury, from 1787 to 1806. In 1788 he was a member of the Connecticut Convention which ratified the United States Constitution. In 1795 he became a director of the Connecticut Land Company and led a party to survey the Western Reserve Land Company land purchase. While involved in this venture, he founded Cleveland, Ohio, in 1796.

Cleaveland died in Canterbury, Connecticut.

COIT, Joshua: congressman

Born New London, Connecticut, October 7, 1758; died September 5, 1798.

Coit graduated from Harvard in 1776, later gaining admission to the bar and establishing a legal practice in New London. He was a member of the Connecticut House of Representatives in 1784–85, 1789–90, and 1792–93, serving as clerk for several terms and as speaker in 1793. A Federalist, he attended the United States House of Representatives for the 3rd–5th congresses (1793–September 5, 1798). He died in New London and was buried in Cedar Grove Cemetery.

COOK, Joseph Platt: Continental congressman

Born Stratford (now Bridgeport), Connecticut, January 4, 1730; died February 3, 1816.

Cook, a 1750 graduate of Yale, represented his town in about thirty sessions of the Connecticut General Assembly over a period of twenty years, 1763–83, also serving as a justice of the peace in 1764. In 1771 he was appointed colonel of the 16th Regiment of the Connecticut militia and accompanied General Wolcott's forces to New York in 1776. In command of the Continental forces when the British burned Danbury, Connecticut, in 1777, he resigned his commission the following year. He then became a member of the Council of Safety.

Cook was a member of the Connecticut House of Representatives in 1776, 1778, 1780–82, and 1784. From 1784 to 1788 he was a member of the Continental Congress. He was a judge in the Danbury district Probate Court for thirty-seven years, from 1776 to 1813. In 1803 he was a member of the Governor's Council.

Cook died in Danbury and was buried in Wooster Cemetery.

5

★★★★★

DABOLL, Nathan: mathematician, educator

Born Groton, Connecticut, April 24, 1750; son of Nathan and Anna (Lynn) Daboll; married Elizabeth Daboll; second marriage to "Widow Elizabeth Brown"; died March 9, 1818.

Daboll discovered errors in the almanac prepared by Clark Elliott and published by Timothy Green in 1770 and was employed to revise the calculations. He was responsible for the *New England Almanack by Nathan Daboll, Philomath,* published by Timothy Green, in 1773, 1774, and 1775.

Daboll was a professor of mathematics and astronomy at the Plainfield Academy in Connecticut from 1783 to 1788, and taught navigation aboard the frigate *President* in 1811. Besides the *Almanack,* he wrote *Daboll's Complete Schoolmaster's Assistant,* 1799, and *Daboll's Practical Navigator,* published posthumously in 1820.

DAGGETT, David: senator, jurist, mayor

Born Attleboro, Massachusetts, December 21, 1764; son of Thomas and Sibulah (Stanley) Daggett; married Wealthy Munson, September 10, 1786; second marriage to Mary Lines, March 4, 1840; died April 12, 1851.

Daggett graduated from Yale at the age of nineteen, and was admitted to the Connecticut bar in 1786. He was a member of the lower house of the Connecticut legislature, 1791–97 and 1805–09, serving as speaker from 1794 to 1797. He was a member of the Connecticut Council from 1797 to 1803 and from 1809 to 1813, and a member of the United States Senate from 1813 to 1819.

From 1826 to 1828 Daggett was associate justice of the Connecticut Superior Court. He was a Kent Professor of law at Yale for twenty-two years (1826–48) and mayor of New Haven, Connecticut, from 1828 to 1830. Chief justice of the Connecticut Supreme Court of Errors from 1832 to 1834, he upheld the right of the state legislatures to deprive free colored persons of school in-

struction, except by permission of the town selectmen, under the rule that they were not United States citizens. This was known as the Prudence Crandall case of 1833.

Daggett died in New Haven at the age of eighty-six.

DAGGETT, Naphtali: clergyman, college president

Born Attleboro, Massachusetts, September 8, 1727; son of Ebenezer and Mary (Blackington) Daggett; married Sarah Smith, December 19, 1753; died November 25, 1780.

Daggett was ordained as the first pastor of the Presbyterian Church of Smithtown, Long Island, New York, in 1741. He graduated from Yale in 1748 and eight years later became a professor of divinity there, remaining until 1766. He then served briefly as pastor of the Church of Christ at Yale before acceding to the presidency of the school. He remained in that position until 1777, when he resigned after the students petitioned for his removal. He then returned to his professorial post, serving until his death.

Daggett took part in the defense of New Haven in 1779, and was captured by the British. He was the author of *The Great Importance of Speaking in the Most Intelligible Manner in Christian Churches,* 1768; *The Excellency of a Good Name,* 1768; *The Testimony of Conscience, a Most Solid Foundation of Rejoicing,* 1773. He died in New Haven.

DANA, James: clergyman

Born Cambridge, Massachusetts, May 11, 1735; son of Caleb and Phoebe (Chandler) Dana; married Catherine Whittelsey, May 8, 1759; second marriage to Mrs. Abigail (Porter) Belden, July 10, 1796; third marriage to Mrs. Mary (Miles) Rice, September 14, 1798; father of Samuel Whittelsey; died August 18, 1812.

A graduate of Harvard, Dana later (1768) received an honorary D.D. from the University of Edinburgh in Scotland. He was called to the pastorate of the Congregational Church of Wallingford, Connecticut, in

1758, where he became involved in the "Wallingford Controversy," a theological-political dispute between two church factions (the "Old Lights," of which Dana was a member, and the "New Lights").

Dana became pastor of the First Congregational Church in New Haven, Connecticut, in 1789, and served until 1805, at which time he was dismissed. He wrote *An Examination of the Late Reverend President Edward's "Enquiry on Freedom of Will,"* published anonymously in 1770, and *"Examination . . ." Continued,* 1773. He died in New Haven.

DAVENPORT, James: congressman

Born Stamford, Connecticut, October 12, 1758; son of Abraham Davenport; died August 3, 1797.

Davenport, who graduated from Yale in 1777, served during the Revolutionary War in the commissary department of the Continental Army. He was later a judge in the Court of Common Pleas.

Davenport was a member of the Connecticut House of Representatives from 1785 to 1790 and of the Connecticut Senate from 1790 to 1797. He was a judge in the Fairfield County Court from 1792 to 1796. He filled a vacancy in the United States House of Representatives, from Connecticut, during the 4th and 5th congresses (December 5, 1796, to August 3, 1797).

Davenport died in Stamford and was buried in the North Field (Franklin Street) Cemetery.

DAVENPORT, John: congressman

Born Stamford, Connecticut, January 16, 1752; died November 28, 1830.

Davenport graduated from Yale in 1770, studied law, and was admitted to the bar in 1773. He taught at Yale in 1773 and 1774, then began to practice law in Stamford. During the Revolutionary War he served with the commissary department and, in 1777, was commissioned a major.

Davenport was a member of the Connecticut House of Representatives from 1776 to 1796. A Federalist, he served Connecticut in the United States House of Representatives during the 6th through the 14th congresses (1799–1817). He died in Stamford and was buried in North Field (now Franklin Street) Cemetery.

DEANE, Silas: Continental congressman

Born Groton, Connecticut, December 24, 1737; son of Silas and Sarah (Barker) Deane; married Mehitabel Webb, 1763; second marriage to Elizabeth Saltonstall, 1767; father of Jesse; died September 23, 1789.

Deane graduated from Yale in 1758 and received his A. M. five years later. He was admitted to the Connecticut bar in 1761.

A leader of the Revolutionary movement in Connecticut, Deane was a member of the Connecticut General Assembly in 1772, secretary of the Connecticut Committee of Correspondence in 1773, and a delegate to the First and Second Continental congresses, 1774–76.

In 1776 Deane was sent as a secret agent to France to seek aid and support for the American Revolution; he was the first American to represent the united colonies abroad. He secured eight shiploads of military supplies and commissioned several European military officers, including Lafayette, De Kalb, Von Steuben, and Pulaski. When he came before Congress, in 1780, to give a statement of his transactions in Europe, his report was deemed unsatisfactory, and he was sent back to France to obtain audits of accounts and vouchers. While in Europe, however, he lost faith in the American cause, a change of sentiment reflected in his letters to America urging reconciliation with England. The publication of these letters resulted in his being accused as a traitor and an embezzler. However, he was vindicated by Congress in 1842, long after his death.

Deane is known as the first American to use invisible ink in diplomatic correspondence. He died on shipboard outside of Deal, England, and was buried in Deal.

DOOLITTLE, Amos: engraver

Born Cheshire, Connecticut, May 18, 1754; son of Ambrose and Martha (Munson) Doolittle; married Sally; second marriage to Phebe Tuttle, November 8, 1797; died January 30, 1832.

Doolittle was apprenticed to a silversmith in Cheshire; he later turned to engraving and moved to New Haven. He was a member of the Governor's Foot Guards during the American Revolution.

Doolittle engraved four copper plates, titled "The Battle of Lexington and Concord," in 1775. He also engraved two maps printed in Jedidiah Morse's *Geography Made Easy,* in 1784. His other engravings include "Display of United States of America," in which Washington was the central figure, and two "New Displays," the first of which featured John Adams, the second, Thomas Jefferson.

Doolittle died in New Haven and was buried in the Grove Street Cemetery there.

DOUGLAS, William: army officer, naval officer

Born Plainfield, Connecticut, January 16, 1743; son of John and Olive (Spaulding) Douglas; married Hannah Manfield, July 5, 1767; father of William, John, Olive, and Hannah; died May 28, 1777.

Douglas was commissioned a major in the Connecticut militia in 1775. The following year he rose to major in a volunteer regiment and then to colonel under General Washington. He participated in the battles of Long Island, Philips Manor, Croton River, White Plains, and Harlem Heights. He was appointed commodore of vessels on Lake Champlain by the Continental Congress. In 1777 he was elected to the Connecticut Assembly. He died in Northford, Connecticut.

DUNBAR, Moses: Loyalist

Born Wallingford, Connecticut, June 14, 1746; son of John and Temperance (Hall) Dunbar; married Phebe Jerome, 1764; second marriage to Esther Adams; father of seven children; died March 19, 1777.

Dunbar, because of his Loyalist sympathies, joined the English at Long Island. There he was given the duty of encouraging enlistment in the King's Forces. He was betrayed, tried and sentenced to death by hanging in 1777, thus becoming the only person ever executed for treason in Connecticut.

DURKEE, John: army officer

Born Windham, Connecticut, December 11, 1728; son of William and Susannah (Sabin) Durkee; married Martha Wood, January 3, 1753; died May 29, 1782.

Durkee was an innkeeper and a justice of the peace in Norwich, Connecticut, and a member of the Connecticut General Assembly. He advanced from second lieutenant to major in the Connecticut militia during the French and Indian War.

Durkee was a founder of Fort Durkee, Pennsylvania, in 1769, although it was later renamed Wilkes-Barre for John Wilkes and Colonel Isaac Barre. He aided the patriot cause in a civilian capacity by serving on a committee to arrange a correspondence system between the Connecticut Sons of Liberty and those of other colonies, and on another to recommend Norwich's refraining from importation of some British manufacture.

Upon the outbreak of hostilities, Durkee became a major in the Continental Army, serving from 1775 to 1781. He then became a lieutenant colonel in the 3rd Connecticut Regiment, then a lieutenant colonel, and then a full colonel in the 20th Regiment. He later became a colonel in the 1st and 4th Connecticut regiments. He served with Sullivan's expedition against the Six Nations in 1779.

Durkee died in Norwich, Connecticut, near the end of the war.

DWIGHT, Timothy: college president, author

Born Northampton, Massachusetts, May 14, 1752; son of Major Timothy and Mary (Edwards) Dwight;

married Mary Woolsey, March 3, 1777; died January 11, 1817.

Dwight graduated from Yale in 1769, receiving an M.A. in 1772 and an honorary LL.D. from Harvard in 1810. He was headmaster of Hopkins Grammar School in New Haven from 1769 to 1771, then served as a tutor at Yale until 1777. In 1777 he was licensed to preach and became chaplain of General S. H. Parson's Connecticut Brigade, serving for two years.

Dwight was a member of the Massachusetts legislature in 1781 and 1782. The following year he was ordained to the ministry in the Congregational Church. He was president of Yale for twenty-two years (1795–1817), where he was a professor of theology and a founder of the medical department. He was a projector of the Andover Theological Seminary, a missionary for the Society of Connecticut, and a member of the American Board of Commissioners for Foreign Missions. He was also a member of a group called the "Hartford Wits."

Dwight wrote *The Conquest of Canaan* (the first American epic poem), 1785; *Greenfield Hill*, 1794; *Theology, Explained and Defended*, five volumes, 1818–19; and *Travels in New England and New York*, 1821. He died in New Haven.

DYER, Eliphalet: Continental congressman, jurist
Born Windham, Connecticut, September 14, 1721; son of Colonel Thomas and Lydia (Backus) Dyer; married Huldah Bowen; died May 13, 1807.

Dyer graduated with an A.B. and an A.M. from Yale in 1740 and received an honorary A.M. from Harvard in 1744. He was appointed a captain in the Connecticut militia in 1745 and rose to lieutenant colonel of his regiment in 1755.

In 1746 Dyer was admitted to the Connecticut bar and served as district representative to the Connecticut General Assembly from 1747 to 1762. He was the organizer of the Susquehanna Company in 1753, and the following year he purchased lands from the Six Nations. In 1774 he laid out the Connecticut Settlement in the Wyoming Valley, west of what was then New York Province. The title had been disputed with Pennsylvania in 1763, and, in 1782, Dyer argued the case before a congressional committee. However, he lost the title for Connecticut.

From 1762 to 1784 Dyer was a member of the Connecticut Governor's Council. In 1764 he was comptroller of the Port of New London, Connecticut. The following year he was Connecticut's delegate to the Stamp Act Congress, and, in 1766, he was an associate judge in the Connecticut Superior Court. In 1774 he represented Connecticut in the First Continental Congress. The following year he was a member of the Connecticut Committee of Safety. In 1780 he was the Connecticut commissioner at the Hartford Convention. From 1789 to 1793 he was chief justice of the Connecticut Supreme Court.

Dyer received an honorary LL.D. from Yale in 1787. He died in Windham at the age of eighty-five.

★★★★★

EARLE, Ralph: painter
Born Shrewsbury, Massachusetts, May 11, 1751; son of Ralph E. and Phebe (Whittemore) Earle; married Sarah Gates, 1774; second marriage to Anne Whitesides; father of four children, including Ralph E. W.; died August 16, 1801.

Earle was a portraitist in New Haven, Connecticut, and became known for his paintings of Revolutionary War battle scenes. In 1779 he left for London, where he became an established painter. While there, he had the honor of painting portraits of members of the royal family. Returning to America in the 1780s, he continued painting in Massachusetts, Connecticut, and New York City.

EATON, William: diplomat
Born Woodstock, Connecticut, February 23, 1764; son of Nathan and Sarah (Johnson) Eaton; married Eliza Sykes, August 22, 1792; died June 1, 1811.

After his graduation from Dartmouth in 1790, Eaton was commissioned a captain in the United States Army, serving initially in the Army of the West and later in Georgia (1792–95) and Philadelphia (1795–97). His diplomatic activities began in 1798, when he was appointed United States consul in Tunis. While there he acted as a navy agent to the Barbary States and was forced to return to America in 1804 because of his attempts to guide a faction in the Tripolitan civil war. He later served one term in the Massachusetts legislature.

Eaton died in Brimfield, Massachusetts.

EDMOND, William: congressman
Born Woodbury, Connecticut, September 28, 1755; died August 1, 1838.

Edmond served in the Continental Army during the Revolutionary War and was wounded in the Battle of Danbury (a town burned by the British). After the war he attended Yale, graduating in 1778, and began a long career in law and politics.

Edmond was admitted to the bar in 1780 and began practice in Newtown, Connecticut. He served in the Connecticut House of Representatives from 1791 to 1797 and again from 1801 to 1802, with an intervening term in the state senate (1797–99). During the same period he filled a Federalist vacancy in the United States House of Representatives, participating in the 5th and 6th congresses (1797–1801). For fourteen years (1805–19) he was an associate judge of the Connecticut Supreme Court.

Edmond died in Newtown, Connecticut, and was buried in the town cemetery.

EDWARDS, Pierpont: jurist
Born Northampton, Massachusetts, April 8, 1750; son of Jonathan and Sarah (Pierpont) Edwards; married Frances Ogden, May 1769; second marriage to Mary Tucker; died April 5, 1826.

Edwards was active in government on both the state and national levels. He graduated from the College of New Jersey (now Princeton) in 1768 and at the age of twenty-one began a legal practice in New Haven, Connecticut. A leader of Jefferson Republicans in Connecticut, he was a member of the lower house of the Connecticut legislature in 1777, from 1784 to 1785, and from 1787 to 1790, acting as speaker during the last term. Edwards served in the Continental Congress in 1787–88 and was a member of the Connecticut Convention which ratified the United States Constitution.

For twenty years (1806–26) Edwards was a judge of the United States District Court in Connecticut, his most well known case being his attempt to prosecute libel cases against certain newspapers in a grand jury charge. His decision against the papers was overturned by the U.S. Supreme Court in the case of *U.S. vs. Hudson and Goodwin,* 1812.

Edwards was a leading figure in the Connecticut Constitutional Convention of 1818, which drew up a new constitution that provided for the separation of church and state. Edwards died three days before his seventy-sixth birthday in Bridgeport, Connecticut. He was buried in the Grove Street Cemetery in New Haven.

ELLSWORTH, Oliver: chief justice of the United States Supreme Court
Born Windsor, Connecticut, April 29, 1745; son of Colonel David and Jemima (Leavitt) Ellsworth; married Abigail Wolcott, 1772; died November 26, 1807.

Credited in some circles with originating the term "United States," Ellsworth made an indelible mark on the structure of the legislative and judicial branches of the federal government.

Ellsworth graduated from Princeton in 1766. He served briefly in the Continental Congress, then became a delegate to the United States Constitutional Convention, where he took part in bringing about the Connecticut Compromise, which provided for equality of representation in the Senate. While serving as a United States Senator, he was chairman of the committee appointed

10

to bring in a bill organizing the federal judiciary; this work is still a part of the laws of the United States.

Ellsworth spent a long career in government service, beginning shortly after his admission to the Connecticut bar in 1771. He was a member of the Connecticut General Assembly from Windsor in 1775, a state's attorney for Hartford County, Connecticut, in 1777, and a member of the Connecticut Committee of the Pay Table during the Revolutionary War. He was also a member of the Connecticut Council of Safety in 1779, a member of the Governor's Council from 1780 to 1784, and a judge of the Superior Court from 1784 to 1789. As a member of the United States Senate from 1789 to 1796, he reported the first set of Senate rules, framed a measure admitting Rhode Island and North Carolina to the Union, and drew up the first bill regulating consular service.

Ellsworth was the second chief justice appointed to the United States Supreme Court, serving on the bench from 1796 to 1799. He was commissioner to France from February 1799 to November of that year. He then became a member of the Connecticut Governor's Council for a second time, serving from 1801 to 1807.

Ellsworth was awarded an honorary LL.D. from Yale in 1790 and from Princeton and Dartmouth in 1797. He died in Windsor, Connecticut, in 1807.

★★★★★

FANNING, Nathaniel: privateersman, naval officer
Born Stonington, Connecticut, May 31, 1755; son of Gilbert and Huldah (Palmer) Fanning; married Elizabeth Smith, November 21, 1784; father of six children; died September 30, 1805.

Nathaniel Fanning was a midshipman and private secretary to John Paul Jones on the ship *Bonhomme Richard;* his action in the fight with the *Serapis* on September 22, 1779, did much to bring about an American victory. He was a sea-fighting privateersman under Franco-American auspices at the time, continuing in this capacity until 1783. In 1804 he was commissioned a lieutenant in the United States Navy.

Fanning wrote *Narrative of the Adventures of an American Naval Officer,* published in 1801. He died in Charleston, South Carolina.

FITCH, Thomas: colonial governor
Born Norwalk, Connecticut, June 1700; son of Thomas and Sarah Fitch; married Hannah Hall, September 24, 1724; father of eight children; died July 18, 1774.

Fitch graduated from Yale in 1721. He entered public life in 1726 as deputy to the Connecticut General Assembly from Norwalk, serving for the next four years and again in 1732. He then served as an assistant to the Assembly in 1734 and 1735, and from 1740 to 1750. In 1749 he helped to complete the revision of the laws of Connecticut.

For four years (1750–54) Fitch was both chief justice of the Connecticut Superior Court and deputy governor of the state. He then became governor of Connecticut, an office he held until 1766. During his tenure as governor, he supported the British cause in the French and Indian War and, although he personally opposed it, strictly enforced the Stamp Act. His actions in these matters caused him to lose most of his political following.

Fitch was the author of *Reasons Why the British Colonies in America Should Not Be Charged with Internal Taxes, by Authority of Parliament, Humbly Offered for Consideration in Behalf of the Colony of Connecticut,* 1764. He died in Norwalk, the town of his birth, on the eve of the Revolution.

★★★★★

GALE, Benjamin: physician, author
Born Jamaica, Long Island, New York, December 14, 1715; son of John and Mary Gale; married Hannah Eliot, June 6, 1739; father of eight children; died May 6, 1790.

After obtaining an M.A. from Yale, Gale studied medicine and surgery with Dr. Jared

Eliot. He entered into the practice of medicine in Killingworth, Connecticut, circa 1739 and became highly respected for his abilities as a physician. A longtime member of the Connecticut General Assembly, in which he served from 1747 to 1767, he also helped devise the American Turtle, a depth bomb.

Gale wrote *The Present State of the Colony of Connecticut Considered* (1755); *Historical Memoirs, Relating to the Practice of Inoculation for the Small Pox, in the British American Provinces, Particularly in New England* (1765); and *A Brief Essay, or, An Attempt to Prove, from the Prophetick Writings of the Old and New Testaments, What Period of Prophecy the Church of God Is Now Under* (1788). The latter is his chief theological work.

Gale died in Killingworth.

GILBERT, Sylvester: congressman, lawyer
Born Hebron, Connecticut, October 20, 1755; died January 2, 1846.

Gilbert, a 1775 graduate of Harvard, studied law, was admitted to the bar in 1777, and began a practice in Hebron. He was a member of the Connecticut House of Representatives for many years, serving from 1780 to 1812 and again in 1826. After a long period as state's attorney of Tolland County (1786–1807), he served as chief judge of the county court and judge of the probate court (1807–18).

Gilbert was principal of a law school from 1810 until 1818. He served in the Connecticut Senate in 1815–16 and became a member of the United States House of Representatives on November 16, 1818, serving in the 15th Congress until 1819. From 1820 to 1825 he was a judge of the Tolland County Court.

Gilbert died in Hebron at the age of ninety and was buried in Old Cemetery.

GOODRICH, Chauncey: senator, congressman, mayor
Born Durham, Connecticut, October 20, 1759; son of the Reverend Elizur and Catharine (Chauncey) Goodrich; married Abigail Smith; second marriage to Mary Ann Wolcott, October 13, 1789; died August 18, 1815.

Goodrich graduated from Yale in 1776 and taught there from 1778 until 1781, when he was admitted to the Connecticut bar. After serving in the Connecticut House of Representatives (1793–94), he went as a Federalist to the United States House of Representatives during the 4th through the 7th congresses (1795–1801). In 1802 he returned to state politics, serving on the Connecticut Executive Council from 1802 to 1807. On October 25, 1807, he became a United States Senator; he held this position until May 1813. From 1813 to 1815 he served both as mayor of Hartford, Connecticut, and as lieutenant governor of the state, and in 1814 he was a delegate to the Hartford Convention.

Goodrich died in Hartford and was buried in Old North Cemetery there.

GOODRICH, Elizur: clergyman
Born Wethersfield, Connecticut, October 26, 1734; son of David and Hepzibah (Boardman) Goodrich; married Catharine Chauncey, February 1, 1759; father of seven children (including Chauncey, Elizur, and Chauncey Allen); died November 22, 1797.

Goodrich graduated from Yale in 1752 and was ordained to the ministry of the Congregational Church four years later. He became pastor of the Congregational Church in Durham, Connecticut, serving from 1756 until the year of his death. During the period 1766 to 1775 he was repeatedly chosen a member of the Conventions of Delegates from the Synod of New York and Philadelphia and the Association of Connecticut. He urged participation in the American Revolution as a religious duty. In 1776 he was elected to the Corporation of Yale College.

GREEN, Thomas: printer, editor
Born New London, Connecticut, August 25, 1735; son of Samuel and Abigail (Clark) Green; married Desire Sanford, September 1761; second marriage to Abigail Green; third marriage to Abigail Miles, 1782; father of two children; died May 1812.

In 1757 Green was employed by James Parker and Company, printers of the *Connect-*

icut *Gazette* in New Haven. From 1764 to 1767 he printed the *Connecticut Courant* in Hartford (the paper is now the *Hartford Courant*). Upon his return to New Haven in 1767 he began printing the *Connecticut Journal and New Haven Post Bay*, continuing until his retirement in 1809. He was conservative as an editor, and the paper had a slight Federalist bent after the American Revolution.

GRISWOLD, Matthew: governor of Connecticut, jurist

Born Lyme, Connecticut, March 25, 1714; son of John and Hannah (Lee) Griswold; married Ursula Wolcott, November 10, 1743; father of seven children (including Matthew and Robert); died April 28, 1799.

Griswold was admitted to the bar in 1743. From 1751 until 1759 he represented Lyme in the Connecticut General Assembly; he then was a member of the Connecticut Governor's Council from 1759 to 1766. He was a justice of the state superior court from 1766 to 1769; he then became chief justice of the court, a position he held from 1769 until 1784. He also served as deputy governor of Connecticut during the latter period. Yale awarded him an LL.D. in 1779.

Griswold was governor of Connecticut from 1784 until 1786. Two years later he presided over the Connecticut Convention which ratified the United States Constitution. He died in Lyme at the age of eighty-five.

★★★★★

HALE, Nathan: patriot

Born Coventry, Connecticut, June 6, 1755; son of Richard and Elizabeth (Strong) Hale; died September 22, 1776.

Hale, a graduate of Yale at the age of eighteen, taught school in East Haddam, Connecticut, in 1773 and 1774, and in New London, Connecticut, in 1774 and 1775. The latter year he was commissioned a lieutenant in the Continental Army and distinguished himself in the siege of Boston. The following year he was commissioned a captain in the army, and soon afterward he became captain of a company of Connecticut rangers known as Congress's Own, which served in the Battle of Long Island. He was with General Washington in the latter's retreat across the East River from Brooklyn.

Later in 1776 Hale became a captain in Knowlton's Rangers. Hale offered his services when Washington called for volunteers to gather intelligence concerning the condition and intentions of the British. He went from Harlem Heights to Long Island disguised as a schoolteacher, but he was captured on his return trip (September 21, 1776) and charged with spying. His execution was ordered by General Howe, and the order was carried out the next day. He is supposed to have said before being hanged: "I only regret that I have but one life to lose for my country."

HARDING, Seth: naval officer

Born Eastham, Massachusetts, April 17, 1734; son of Theodore and Sarah (Hamilton) Harding; married Abigail Doane, April 27, 1753; second marriage to Ruth Reed, November 23, 1760; died November 20, 1814.

In his youth, and during the French and Indian War, Harding served on merchant vessels to the West Indies. He assumed command of the Connecticut brig *Defence* at the start of the Revolutionary War. In 1776 he consummated the most brilliant American naval feat up to that time by forcing two British armed transports into Massachusetts Bay, where they surrendered. Two years later he commanded the Continental frigate *Confederacy*.

In 1781 Harding became the commander of the *Diana* and engaged in commerce raiding and convoy service between America and the West Indies until his capture late in 1781. He was exchanged in 1782 and became second in command of the ship *Alliance* under John Barry. He was in the merchant service after the war and retired on captain's half-pay in 1807. He died in Schoharie, New York.

CONNECTICUT

HARLAND, Thomas: watch and clock-maker, silversmith
Born England, 1735; married Hannah Leffingwell, 1779; died March 31, 1807.

Harland is supposed to have come to America in a tea ship. He opened a shop as a watch and clockmaker and silversmith in Norwich, Connecticut. He superintended the construction of a fire engine in Norwich in 1788. By 1790 he had become a master craftsman, and his shop produced some 200 \.atches and 40 clocks per year. He died in Norwich.

HERON, William: Revolutionary spy
Born Cork, Ireland, 1742; married Mary; father of eight children; died January 8, 1819.

Little is known about Heron before the Revolution in America, except that he was educated at Trinity College in Dublin, Ireland. He was a member of the Connecticut Assembly in 1778 and 1782. He was engaged in secret correspondence with Major Oliver De Lancey, head of the British secret service, from 1780 to 1782. Known as Hiram the Spy, he revealed to the British important facts about American forces, although he did some spying on the British for America also. His spying was done more out of self-interest than patriotism, and he was not suspected of treasonable activity until after his death. He was captured as a rebel by a band of Loyalists in 1781 and imprisoned for a short time.

Heron was a member of the Connecticut Assembly for several terms between 1784 and 1796. He died in Connecticut.

HILLHOUSE, James: senator
Born Montville, Connecticut, October 21, 1754; son of William and Sarah (Griswold) Hillhouse; married Sarah Lloyd, January 1, 1774; second marriage to Rebecca Woolsey, October 10, 1782; father of five children (including James Abraham); died December 29, 1832.

Hillhouse graduated from Yale in 1773, at which time he was admitted to the Connecticut bar. In 1776 he was a lieutenant in a company of New Haven (Connecticut) Volunteers, and in 1779 he was a captain in the Governor's Foot Guards when New Haven was attacked by the British under Tryon.

From 1778 to 1785 Hillhouse was a member of the Connecticut House of Representatives; from 1791 to 1796 he was a Connecticut delegate to the United States House of Representatives. He held a seat in the United States Senate from December 6, 1796, to June 10, 1810, serving as president pro tem from 1801 to 1810.

Hillhouse was commissioner of the Connecticut school funds from 1810 to 1825. For fifty years—from 1782 to 1832—he was the treasurer of Yale College. He was granted an honorary LL.D. from Yale in 1823. He died in New Haven and was buried in the Grove Street Cemetery there.

HILLHOUSE, William: Continental congressman, jurist
Born Montville, Connecticut, August 25, 1728; father of James; died January 12, 1816.

After studying law and gaining admission to the bar, Hillhouse established a legal practice. He was a member of the Connecticut House of Representatives from 1756 to 1760 and from 1763 to 1785. He served as a major in the 2nd Regiment of the Connecticut Cavalry during the Revolutionary War.

From 1783 to 1786 Hillhouse was a member of the Continental Congress, representing Connecticut. From 1784 to 1806 he was a judge in the Court of Common Pleas. He held a seat in the Connecticut Senate from 1785 to 1808, and from 1786 to 1807 he was a judge of probate for the New London, Connecticut, district.

Hillhouse died in Montville and was buried in Raymond Hill Cemetery there.

HINMAN, Elisha: naval officer
Born Stonington, Connecticut, March 9, 1734; son of Captain Andrew and Mary (Noble) Hinman; married Abigail Solbear, March 1, 1777; died August 29, 1805.

14

Hinman was commissioned a lieutenant in the Continental Navy and served as captain of the sloop *Cabot* and the frigate *Alfred* in 1777. The following year he was captured and imprisoned. He later became a privateer in command of the *Deane* and the *Marquis de Lafayette*. After the Revolutionary War he became a merchant. He died in Stonington, Connecticut.

HOPKINS, Lemuel: physician, satirist
Born Waterbury, Connecticut, June 19, 1750; son of Stephen and Dorothy (Talmadge) Hopkins; died April 14, 1801.

At the age of thirty-four Hopkins was awarded an honorary M. A. from Yale. He was the projector and associate editor of *The Anarchiad* and an honorary member of the Massachusetts Medical Society. A founder of the Connecticut Medical Society, he was one of a group called the "Hartford Wits." He was the author of *Hypocrite's Hope, The Echo, The Political Greenhouse,* and *The Guillotine.* He died in Hartford, Connecticut.

HOSMUS, Titus: jurist
Born Middletown, Connecticut, 1737; son of Stephen and Deliverance (Graves) Hosmus; married Lydia Lord, November 1761; father of seven children (including Stephen Titus); died August 4, 1780.

Hosmus received an A. B. from Yale in 1757. Between 1758 and 1772 he held several offices in Middletown, including justice of the peace. After being admitted to the Connecticut bar in 1760, he established a law practice in Middletown.

From 1773 to 1778 Hosmus was a member of the Connecticut General Assembly, serving as an assistant from 1778 to 1780. In 1777 he was speaker of the Connecticut House of Representatives and a member of the Connecticut Committee of Safety. In 1778 he was a member of the Continental Congress and a signer of the Articles of Confederation.

Hosmus was elected to the United States Maritime Court of Appeals, which was created by an act of Congress in 1780. He died later that year in Middletown.

HUMPHREYS, David: army officer, diplomat, writer
Born Derby, Connecticut, July 10, 1752; son of the Reverend Daniel and Sarah (Riggs) Humphreys; married Ann Frances Bulkeley, 1797; died February 21, 1818.

Humphreys received an A.B. from Yale in 1771 and an M.A. from that school in 1774. He served as a brigade major in 1777, and in 1780 he was a lieutenant colonel and aide-de-camp to General Washington. In 1784 he was appointed secretary of the Commission for Negotiating Treaties of Commerce with Foreign Powers. In 1786 he was a member of the Connecticut Assembly and a commandant of the new regiment for the operations against the Indians. The following year he was commander of the federal troops that suppressed Shays's Rebellion.

Humphreys, along with Barlow, Hopkins, and Trumbull, published *The Anarchiad,* a satirical essay, in 1786–87. A special agent to obtain information for the American government at London, Lisbon, and Madrid, Humphreys was also sole commissioner for Algerian affairs in 1793. Three years later he was Envoy Extraordinary and Minister Plenipotentiary to Spain. During the War of 1812 he was captain-general of the Veteran Volunteers.

A member of a group known as the "Hartford Wits," Humphreys wrote *A Poem Addressed to the Armies of the United States of America,* 1780; *The Happiness of America,* 1786; and *The Widow of Malabar: A Tragedy.* He also wrote the comedy *The Yankey in England,* 1815. He died in New Haven, Connecticut.

HUNTINGTON, Benjamin: congressman, mayor
Born Norwich, Connecticut, April 19, 1736; died October 16, 1800.

Huntington graduated from Yale at the age of twenty-five. He was appointed surveyor of lands in Windham County (Connecticut) in 1764. The following year he was admitted to the Connecticut bar and established a legal practice in Norwich.

Huntington was a member of the Connecticut House of Representatives from 1771 to 1780, serving as clerk in 1776 and 1777 and as speaker in 1778 and 1779. He was also a delegate to the Connecticut Provincial Congress in 1778. He served as a delegate from Connecticut to the Continental Congress from 1780 to 1788, and as a member of the Connecticut Senate from 1781 to 1790 and from 1791 to 1793. From 1784 to 1796 he was mayor of Norwich.

Huntington attended the 1st Congress of the United States House of Representatives (1789 to 1791). From 1793 to 1798 he was a judge in the Connecticut Superior Court. He died in Rome, New York, and was buried in the Norwichtown Cemetery in Norwich, Connecticut.

HUNTINGTON, Ebenezer: congressman
Born Norwich, Connecticut, December 26, 1754; son of General Jabez and Hannah (Williams) Huntington; died June 17, 1834.

A 1775 Yale graduate, Huntington served as a lieutenant colonel in the Continental Army during the Revolutionary War. He was commissioned a brigadier general in the United States Army in 1798 and discharged two years later. A Whig, he was a member of the United States House of Representatives for the 11th and 15th congresses (October 11, 1810, to 1811, and 1817 to 1819). He died in Norwich, Connecticut, and was buried in the Norwichtown Cemetery.

HUNTINGTON, Jabez: army officer, jurist
Born Norwich, Connecticut, August 7, 1719; son of Joshua and Hannah (Perkins) Huntington; married Elizabeth Backus, January 20, 1742; second marriage to Hannah Williams, 1746; father of Jedediah, Andrew, Joshua, and Ebenezer; died October 5, 1786.

After graduating from Yale in 1741, Huntington became a justice of the peace in New London, Connecticut. He represented Norwich in the Connecticut Assembly, serving as clerk in 1757. In 1760 he was speaker of the Connecticut House of Representatives. Thirteen years later he was appointed probate judge for the Norwich District. He was the moderator of a large meeting held in Norwich on June 6, 1774, which was assembled "to take into consideration the melancholy situation of our civil constitutional liberties, rights and privileges." From 1775 to 1779 he was a member of the Connecticut Council of Safety.

Huntington also had a distinguished military career. At the age of thirty-five he was commissioned captain of a troop of horse in the 3rd Regiment of the Connecticut militia. He was a lieutenant of the 1st Company of the 5th Regiment in 1760 and a captain in 1764; that same year he was made an assistant by the Connecticut Assembly. The following year he was a lieutenant colonel in the 3rd Regiment of the Connecticut militia. In 1776 he was appointed one of two major generals from Connecticut. He was major general of the entire Connecticut militia in 1777. He died at the age of sixty-seven.

HUNTINGTON, Jedediah: army officer
Born Norwich, Connecticut, August 4, 1743; son of General Jabez and Elizabeth (Backus) Huntington; married Faith Trumbull; second marriage to Ann Moore; father of Joshua and Daniel; died September 25, 1818.

Huntington, unlike his father and his brother Ebenezer, graduated from Harvard rather than Yale, in 1763. He followed in his famous father's footsteps, however, in that he had an extensive military career. At the age of twenty-six he was commissioned by the Connecticut Assembly as an ensign in the 1st Norwich Company. In two years he had become a lieutenant, and by 1774 he was a captain. The same year he rose to colonel of the 20th Regiment of the Connecticut militia. In 1775 he became a colonel in the 8th Regiment. A member of the 17th Infantry Regiment of the Continental Army in 1776, he fought at the Battle of Long Island. The following year he was a colonel in the 1st Connecticut Regiment. That same year he was also commissioned a brigadier general in the Continental Army. At the close of the Revolutionary War, he was brevetted a major general.

Huntington held several offices after leaving the military. He was sheriff of New London, Connecticut; delegate to the Connecticut Constitutional Convention; treasurer of Connecticut; the appointed collector of customs at the Port of New London, having been named by President Washington in 1789. He died in New London, Connecticut.

HUNTINGTON, Samuel: governor of Connecticut, president of the Continental Congress

Born Windham, Connecticut, July 3, 1731; son of Nathaniel and Mehetable (Thurston) Huntington; married Martha Devotion, 1761; died January 5, 1796.

Huntington was admitted to the Connecticut bar at the age of twenty-seven. He represented Norwich in the Connecticut General Assembly in 1765; that same year he was appointed King's attorney for Connecticut. From 1765 to 1775 he was a justice of the peace in New London, Connecticut. He served ten years—from 1773 to 1783—as a judge in the Superior Court of Connecticut. In 1775 he was appointed by the General Assembly to the committee for the defense of Connecticut.

Huntington represented Connecticut in the Continental Congress from 1775 to 1784, serving as president from 1779 to 1781. He was also a signer of the Declaration of Independence. In 1777 he was a member of a committee that met with representatives from Massachusetts, New Hampshire, Rhode Island, and New York to confer on the state of the currency of Springfield, Massachusetts. In 1784 he was chief justice of the Superior Court of Connecticut. In 1785 and 1786 he was lieutenant governor

of the state, and from 1786 to 1796 he was governor.

Huntington received LL.D.s from Dartmouth and Yale in 1785 and 1787, respectively. He died in Norwich.

★★★★★

JAVIS, Abraham: clergyman

Born Connecticut, May 5, 1740; son of Samuel and Naomi (Brush) Javis; married Ann Farmer, May 25, 1766; second marriage to Lucy Lewis, July 4, 1806; died May 3, 1813.

Javis, who graduated from Yale in 1761, sailed for England in 1763 and the following year was ordained a priest in the Episcopal Church by Charles Lyttelton, Bishop of Carlisle. Javis chaired the Convention of Episcopal Clergymen in New Haven in 1776. As an act of support for the revolutionary cause, he decided to suspend all public worship to avoid reading the prayer for the King.

In 1783 Javis was secretary for a secret meeting held in Woodbridge for the organization of the Episcopal Church in Connecticut; it was also decided at this meeting to send Samuel Seabury to England to be consecrated Bishop of Connecticut. In 1797 Javis was chosen to succeed Seabury and was consecrated Bishop of Connecticut at Trinity Church in New Haven, Connecticut.

Javis died two days before his seventy-third birthday.

JENKINS, John: pioneer, surveyor

Born East Greenwich, Connecticut, February 15, 1728; son of Lydia Alden; married Lydia Gardner, February 1751; father of at least one son (John); died November 1785.

Jenkins explored the Wyoming Valley in what is now Pennsylvania in 1753 and was the chief commissioner and leading spirit of the exploration. The following year he attended the Albany congress of the colonies. He obtained the deed to disputed lands on the Susquehanna River, including Wyoming and the country west of the Alleghenies, from the chief of the Six Nations. He began the settlement of Kingston, Pennsylvania, in 1769, and held all lands from the township line to Kingston and Exeter. He helped build Fort Jenkins.

In 1774, 1775, and again in 1777 Jenkins was a member of the Connecticut Assembly from Westmoreland County. He was the presiding judge of the first county court of Wyoming, Pennsylvania. He participated in the Pennamite war in Wyoming until he was driven out by the Pennamites in 1784. He died in Pennsylvania the following year.

JOHNSON, William Samuel: senator, jurist, college president

Born Stratford, Connecticut, October 7, 1727; son of Samuel and Charity (Floyd) Nicoll Johnson; married Anne Beach, November 5, 1749; second marriage to Mary (Brewster) Beach, December 11, 1800; died November 14, 1819.

Johnson received an A.B. from Yale in 1744 and an A.M. from Harvard in 1747. He served as an ensign in a Stratford company of the Connecticut militia in 1753, later advancing to higher ranks.

In 1761 and again in 1765 Johnson was a member of the Connecticut House of Representatives; also in 1765 he participated in the Stamp Act Congress. During the years 1766 to 1774 he served as either an assistant in or a member of the upper house of the state legislature. In 1766 he went to England, where he served briefly as a colonial agent in London and received a D.C.L. from Oxford. Returning to America, he became a member of the Governor's Council in 1766, serving until the next year and again in 1771. Also in 1771 he was chosen honorary judge of the Connecticut Superior Court.

Johnson refused an appointment to the Continental Congress in 1774, although he later signed the Declaration of Independence. Yale awarded him an honorary LL.D. in 1778. In 1784 he again was offered an appointment to the Continental Congress, which he accepted. He served in the Congress until 1787, chairing the "Grand Committee" which was appointed to frame the United States Constitution and proposing a measure for the formation of a separate legislative body, the Senate.

Johnson acted as a counselor in the Susquehanna case from 1784 to 1787. He was the first president of Columbia College, holding this office from 1787 to 1800. During his term in the United States Senate (1789–91) he was active in shaping the Judiciary Act of 1789. He died in Stratford at the age of ninety-two.

★★★★★

KIRBY, Ephraim: lawyer

Born Litchfield County, Connecticut, February 23, 1757; son of Abraham and Eunice (Starkweather) Kirby; married Ruth Marvin, March 17, 1784; father of eight children (including Frances); died October 20, 1804.

While a private in the Continental Army (1776–79) Kirby served in the battles of Brandywine, Monmouth, and Germantown. He spent a short time, 1782–83, as an ensign in the Rhode Island militia. Having at some point (probably after the Revolution) studied law under Reynold Marvin in Litchfield, he began a legal practice in the town. He was granted an honorary M.A. degree from Yale in 1787.

Kirby was active in several organizations. He helped found the Grand Lodge of Connecticut and the Grand Chapter of Royal Arch Masons in the United States. An original member of the Connecticut Society of the Cincinnati, he also was a delegate to the national meeting of the Society in 1796. He served in the Connecticut House of Representatives from 1791 until 1803, when he became United States commissioner on the Spanish Boundary. He remained in this post until his death the next year at Fort Stoddart, in the Mississippi Territory (now Mississippi).

★★★★★

LAW, Andrew: composer, author, clergyman

Born Milford, Connecticut, March 1749; son of Jahleel and Ann (Baldwin Hollingsworth) Law; died July 13, 1821.

Law graduated from Rhode Island College in 1775 and studied theology with the Reverend Levi Hart in Preston, Connecticut. In 1781 he successfully petitioned the Connecticut Assembly for the exclusive right to imprint and sell his tune collections.

In 1787 Law was ordained to the ministry of the Congregational Church in Hartford, Connecticut. He preached in Philadelphia and Baltimore and became a writer of tunes and hymns. He taught singing in Salem, Massachusetts, from 1795 to 1797.

One of Law's most notable achievements was his patenting of a new way to print music using four different note shapes. He was the author of *A Select Number of Plain Tunes Adopted to Congregational Worship,* 1767; *Select Harmony,* 1780; *The Musical Primer,* 1780; *Harmonic Companion,* 1807; and *Essays on Music,* Philadelphia, 1814. He died in Cheshire, Connecticut.

LAW, Richard: Continental congressman, jurist

Born Milford, Connecticut, March 7, 1733; son of Jonathan and Eunice (Hall) Law; married Ann Prentise, September 21, 1760; father of Lyman; died January 26, 1806.

After graduating from Yale in 1751, Law read law with Jared Ingersoll. Admitted to the Connecticut bar in 1753, he moved his practice to New London, Connecticut, four years later.

In 1765 Law served as justice of the peace of New London. The same year he was a member of the Connecticut General Court. He was chief judge of the New London County Court from 1773 to 1784, and from 1776 to 1786 he served on the Connecticut Governor's Council. He was a member of the Connecticut Council of Safety in 1776.

Law was a member of the Continental Congress from Connecticut in 1777 and in 1781–82. For twenty-two years—from 1784 to 1806—he served as mayor of New London. He was a judge of the Connecticut Supreme Court in 1784 and 1789 and chief justice in 1786. He was a delegate to the Connecticut Convention to ratify the United States Constitution in 1788 and was a member of the first electoral college. George Washington appointed Law United States district judge for Connecticut in 1789, a position he held until his death.

Law and Roger Sherman wrote a codification of Connecticut laws, titled *Acts and Laws of the State of Connecticut, in America,* which was published in 1784. In 1802 he was awarded an honorary LL.D. from Yale. He died in New London and was buried in the Cedar Grove Cemetery there.

LEARNED, Amasa: congressman

Born Killingly, Connecticut, November 15, 1750; died May 4, 1825.

Learned, a 1772 graduate of Yale, studied theology and law and taught at Union School in New London, Connecticut, before he was licensed to preach in 1773 by the Windham Association. He was a member of the Connecticut House of Representatives in 1779 and from 1785 to 1791. In 1788 he was a member of the Connecticut Convention that ratified the United States Constitution.

In 1791 Learned served in the Connecticut Upper House of Assistants. He was a delegate from Connecticut to the United States House of Representatives during the 2nd and 3rd congresses (1791 to 1795).

Learned served as a delegate to the Connecticut Constitutional Convention in 1818. He became a land speculator before his death in New London. He was buried in the Cedar Grove Cemetery there.

LEDYARD, John: explorer

Born Groton, Connecticut, 1751; son of John and

Abigail (Hempstead) Ledyard; died January 10, 1789.

Ledyard, who studied divinity at Dartmouth, served as a corporal in the marines and accompanied Captain Cook on his third expedition through the northern Pacific from 1776 to 1780. In 1788 he was arrested as a spy at Irkutsk, Russia, while attempting to reach the west coast of America by crossing the Bering Straits and going through Alaska.

In 1783 Ledyard wrote *A Journal of Captain Cook's Last Voyage to the Pacific Ocean.* He died in Cairo, Egypt, during an exploratory voyage to Central Africa, undertaken under the patronage of the African Association.

LEDYARD, William: army officer

Born Groton, Connecticut, December 6, 1738; son of John and Deborah (Youngs) Ledyard; married Ann Williams, January 1761; father of nine children; died September 6, 1781.

Ledyard served as a member of the Committee of Correspondence and in 1776 was commissioned a captain of artillery in the Continental Army. He fought against Benedict Arnold's British troops at Fort Griswold, Connecticut, in 1781. The British suffered heavy losses but won the battle. After the surrender, the British massacred the Revolutionaries, including Ledyard.

LYMAN, Samuel: congressman

Born Goshen, Connecticut, January 25, 1749; died June 5, 1802.

Lyman attended Goshen Academy and in 1770 graduated from Yale. He studied law in Litchfield, Connecticut, and in 1773 was admitted to the Connecticut bar. He established a practice in Hartford and in 1784 moved to Springfield, Massachusetts.

Lyman was a member of the Massachusetts House of Representatives from 1786 to 1788 and a member of the Massachusetts Senate from 1790 to 1793. He was a justice of the Hampshire County Court of Common Pleas from 1791 to 1800. He served as a delegate from Massachusetts to the United States House of Representatives 4th and 6th congresses (1795 to November 6, 1800).

Lyman died in Springfield and was buried in Goshen.

★★★★★

MANSFIELD, Richard: clergyman

Born New Haven, Connecticut, October 1, 1723; son of Jonathan and Sarah (Alling) Mansfield; married Anna Hull, October 10, 1751; father of thirteen children; died April 12, 1820.

After his graduation from Yale, Mansfield became rector of Hopkins Grammar School, where he served from 1742 to 1747. He was ordained deacon and priest of the Episcopal Church in England in 1748 and served as a missionary and a rector to Derby, Connecticut, for seventy-two years (1748–1820).

Mansfield was a Loyalist during the Revolution but remained in America. He received a D.D. from Yale in 1792. He died in Derby at the age of ninety-six and was buried there.

MEIGS, Josiah: lawyer, editor, educator

Born Middletown, Connecticut, August 21, 1757; son of Return and Elizabeth (Hamlin) Meigs; married Clara Benjamin, January 21, 1782; father of two children; died September 4, 1822.

A graduate of Yale in 1778, Meigs was elected a tutor at Yale in 1781. He was admitted to the Connecticut bar in 1783 and became city clerk of New Haven, Connecticut, serving from 1784 to 1789. He opened a printing office, establishing the *New Haven Gazette* in 1784. Meigs returned to Yale as a professor of mathematics and natural philosophy from 1794 to 1800. He was named president of the University of Georgia in 1800, also serving as a professor. Appointed surveyor general of the United States in 1812, Meigs was commissioner of the General Land Office of the United States in Washington, D.C., in 1814. He served as president of the Columbian Institute from 1819 to 1822 and was an original corporator and trustee of Columbian College (now

George Washington University). He died in Washington.

MEIGS, Return Jonathan, Jr.: army officer, Indian agent

Born Middletown, Connecticut, December 17, 1740; son of Return Jonathan and Elizabeth (Hamlin) Meigs; married Joanne Winborn, February 14, 1764; second marriage to Grace Starr, December 22, 1774; died January 28, 1823.

Meigs was commissioned a lieutenant in the 6th Connecticut Regiment in 1772 and became a captain in 1774. He was a major when he served with Arnold at Quebec (he recorded the campaign in his *Journal*) and was captured by the British in Canada.

Commissioned a colonel in the 6th Connecticut Infantry (Leather-Cap Regiment) at Peekskill, New York, in 1777, Meigs was appointed a surveyor of the Ohio Company. He landed with other New Englanders at the mouth of the Muskingum River in 1788. He drew up a code of rules which was later adopted by the colony. Appointed Indian agent to the Cherokees in 1801, he was commissioned to negotiate treaties in 1805, 1806, and 1807 and was given the authority to negotiate a convention between Tennessee and the Cherokees in 1808. He died at the Cherokee Agency in Tennessee.

MITCHELL, Stephen Mix: senator

Born Wethersfield, Connecticut, December 9, 1743; son of James and Rebecca (Mix) Mitchell; married Hannah Grant, August 2, 1796; father of six sons and five daughters; died September 30, 1835.

Mitchell was a Yale graduate in 1763 and a postgraduate (Berkeley scholar) from 1763 to 1766; he later (1807) was awarded an honorary LL.D. A teacher at Yale from 1766 to 1769, Mitchell was admitted to the Connecticut bar in 1770 and became a member of the Connecticut General Assembly, serving from 1778 to 1784. He served as a member of the Congress of Confederation from 1783 to 1785 and participated in the Connecticut Convention which ratified the United States Constitution in 1788. An associate judge of the Hartford County (Connecticut) Court from 1779 to 1790, he was presiding judge from 1790 to 1793.

Mitchell was elected to the United States Senate from Connecticut, serving during the 3rd Congress (1793–95). He was judge of the Connecticut Supreme Court from 1795 to 1807 and chief justice from 1807 to 1814. He was a member of the Connecticut Constitutional Convention in 1818. He died in Wethersfield and was buried in the Wethersfield Cemetery.

★★★★★

NOTT, Samuel: clergyman

Born Saybrook (now Essex), Connecticut, January 23, 1754; son of Stephen and Deborah (Selden) Nott; married Lucretia Taylor, February 14, 1782; father of eleven children; died May 26, 1852.

Nott was a blacksmith's apprentice in Connecticut from 1762 to 1766. After studying under the Reverend Daniel Welch in Mansfield, Connecticut (1775–76), he graduated from Yale (1780). He was licensed to preach by the New Haven Association of Ministers in 1781 and was ordained to the ministry of the Congregational Church in Connecticut the following year. He served as pastor of the Second Parish Congregational Church in Norwich (now Franklin), Connecticut, for seventy years—from 1782 to 1852, the year of his death.

Nott was director of the Missionary Society of Connecticut for eighteen years and served as president of the Connecticut Bible Society and the Norwich Foreign Missionary Society. He was the author of *The Sixtieth Anniversary Sermon* (1842), which is considered his best work. He died in Franklin at the age of ninety-eight.

★★★★★

OCCOM, Samson: Indian clergyman

Born Mohegan, Connecticut, 1723; married Mary Fowler, 1751; father of ten children; died July 14, 1792.

Occom studied theology under the Reverend Eleazar Wheelock from 1743 to 1747.

He was teacher and minister to the Montauk tribe on Long Island from 1749 to 1764, also serving as a missionary to the Oneida tribe in 1761 and 1763. He was ordained to the ministry by the Long Island Presbytery in 1759. In 1765 he went to England and spent three years raising funds for Eleazor Wheelock's Indian Charity School.

From 1768 to 1789 Occom was an itinerant preacher in New England. He was the founder of the Indian settlement of Brothertown, New York, in 1784, and served as a pastor there from 1789 until his death in 1792. He was the author of *Sermon Preached at the Execution of Moses Paul, an Indian*, 1772, and *A Choice Selection of Hymns*, 1774.

OLCOTT, Simeon: senator

Born Bolton, Connecticut, October 1, 1735; died February 22, 1815.

Olcott graduated from Yale in 1761, then studied law. He was admitted to the New Hampshire bar and began his practice in Charlestown. He was selectman for Charlestown from 1769 to 1771. In 1772 and 1773 he was a member of the New Hampshire Provincial General Assembly, also serving the latter year as judge of probate for Cheshire County, New Hampshire.

Olcott was appointed chief justice of the New Hampshire Court of Common Pleas in 1784. He was named judge of the New Hampshire Superior Court in 1790, serving as chief judge in 1795. A member of the Federalist party, he served New Hampshire in the United States Senate from June 17, 1801, to 1805.

Olcott died in Charlestown and was buried in Forest Hill Cemetery in Charlestown.

OLMSTED, Gideon: naval officer

Born East Hartford, Connecticut, February 12, 1749; son of Jonathan and Hannah (Meakins) Olmsted; married Mabel Roberts, 1777; died February 8, 1845.

Olmsted was master of the sloop *Seaflower* from 1776 to 1778. In 1778, while captain of the French ship *Polly*, he was captured as a privateer and taken prisoner. He captured the sloop *Active* with the support of other prisoners and sailed to America. He served as a privateer around the New York harbor from 1779 to 1782, and served as a French privateer from 1793 to 1795. He then became a merchant in East Hartford, where he died.

★★★★★

PARSONS, Samuel Holden: Revolutionary patriot

Born Lyme, Connecticut, May 14, 1737; son of Jonathan and Phebe (Griswold) Parsons; married Mehetable Mather, September 1761; father of eight children; died November 17, 1789.

After graduation from Harvard in 1756 and receiving his Master's degree three years later, Parsons was admitted to the Connecticut bar. He served as a member of the Connecticut General Assembly from 1762 to 1774 and was active on the Connecticut Committee of Correspondence.

Parsons was commissioned a colonel in the 6th Regiment of the Connecticut militia in 1775 and served during the taking of Fort Ticonderoga. In 1776 he was commissioned a brigadier general in the Continental Army and given the responsibility of defending Connecticut. He was in charge of an important secret service post and was promoted to commander of the Connecticut division in 1779, advancing to major general a year later.

On September 22, 1785, Congress named Parsons commissioner to deal with Indian claims to the territory northwest of the Ohio River. He became a promoter and a director of the Ohio Company in 1787. In that year he also became the first judge of the Northwest Territory.

Parsons was the author of the essay "Antiquities of the Western States." He drowned in the Big Beaver River in Ohio.

PERKINS, Elisha: physician

Born Norwich, Connecticut, January 27, 1742; son of Joseph and Mary (Bushnell) Perkins; married

22

Sarah Douglass, September 23, 1762; father of ten children (including Benjamin Douglas); died September 6, 1799.

Perkins attended Yale, then began a medical practice in Plainfield, Connecticut. In 1792 he was an incorporator of the Connecticut Medical Society and later served as chairman of the Windham County Medical Society.

In 1796 Perkins patented his invention known as a "tractor," a U-shaped piece of metal applied to affected parts of the body to ease pain and cure disorders. It was popular in the United States, England, and parts of Europe until 1800.

After his expulsion from the Connecticut Medical Society in 1798, Perkins devised a remedy composed of vinegar and muriate of soda. The next year he went to New York City during a yellow fever outbreak to test the remedy. However, he contracted the disease and died there.

PETERS, Samuel Andrew: clergyman
Born Hebron, Connecticut, November 31, 1735; son of John and Mary (Marks) Peters; married Hannah Owen, February 14, 1760; second marriage to Abigail Gilbert, June 25, 1769; third marriage to Mary Birdseye, April 21, 1773; father of at least two children; died April 19, 1826.

In 1757 Peters received a B.A. degree from Yale, completing his M.A. three years later. After his ordination as deacon and priest of the Anglican Church in 1759, he became rector of the Anglican Church in Hebron, where he preached against Revolutionary activities. He served the Hebron church until 1774, when he was attacked twice by mobs of the Sons of Liberty and fled to England. Twenty years later he was elected bishop of Vermont but was not allowed to take office because Parliament had prohibited the Archbishop of Canterbury from consecrating American bishops.

Peters returned to the United States in 1805 as a land agent for the heirs of Jonathan Carver. In 1781 his *A General History of Connecticut* was published. He also wrote "A Letter to the Reverend John Tyler, A.M.; Concerning the Possibility of Eternal Punishments, and the Improbability of Universal Salvation"; and, in 1807, *A History of the Reverend Hugh Peters, A.M.* He died in New York City and was buried in Hebron.

PITKIN, William: jurist, manufacturer
Born Hartford, Connecticut, 1725; son of William and Mary (Woodbridge) Pitkin; married Abigail Church; died December 12, 1789.

Pitkin owned several power sites and mills. He was commissioned captain of the 3rd Militia Company of Hartford in 1756. He became major-commander of the 1st Regiment of the Connecticut militia in 1758 and lieutenant colonel four years later.

From 1766 to 1785 Pitkin served as an assistant to the Connecticut Governor's Council. During the American Revolution he was a member of the Council of Safety. In 1784 he was elected to the United States Congress but did not serve.

Pitkin was a delegate from East Hartford to the Connecticut convention that ratified the United States Constitution. He was judge of the Superior Court from 1769 to 1789 and chief justice during the last two years of his tenure. He died in Hartford.

PUTNAM, Israel: army officer
Born Salem Village (now Danvers), Massachusetts, January 7, 1718; son of Joseph and Elizabeth (Porter) Putnam; married Hannah Pope, July 19, 1739; second marriage to Deborah (Lothrop) Gardiner, June 3, 1767; father of ten children; died May 29, 1790.

In 1754 Putnam was commissioned a second lieutenant in the Connecticut militia. A year later he was promoted to captain and in 1758 to major. He became a lieutenant colonel in 1759 and served in the French and Indian War. After becoming a major and then a lieutenant colonel in 1764, he served in Pontiac's War.

Putnam was an organizer of the Sons of Liberty and was a delegate to warn Governor Fitch of Connecticut that he could not enforce the Stamp Act. In 1773 he was a member of the exploration expedition to discover the possible values of West Florida. He cruised through the West Indies and through the Gulf of Mexico up to the Mississippi River.

After serving as a lieutenant colonel in the 11th Regiment of the Connecticut militia and as a brigadier general, Putnam became a major general in the Continental Army in 1775. He was a leader in planning for the Battle of Bunker Hill. He was chief in command of New York before Washington arrived in 1776. After the retreat of 1776 he was in charge of the removal of all troops and stores from New York City. He then had command of Philadelphia.

As commander in the Highlands (upper New York State), Putnam twice delayed in obeying orders from General Washington; a court of inquiry later acquitted him of a charge of insubordination. From 1778 to 1779 he was in charge of the recruiting service in Connecticut.

Putnam was the author of *Two Putnams— in the Havana Expedition 1762 and in the Mississippi River Exploration 1772–73*, published in 1931. He died in Brooklyn, Connecticut.

★★★★★

REEVE, Tapping: jurist, educator
Born Brookhaven, Long Island, New York, October 1744; son of Abner Reeve; married Sally Burr; second marriage to his former housekeeper, 1799; father of Aaron Burr Reeve; died December 13, 1823.

At the age of nineteen Reeve graduated from the College of New Jersey (now Princeton). He returned to his alma mater as a tutor in 1769, serving for one year. In 1772 he was admitted to the Connecticut bar.

In 1776 Reeve was appointed by the Connecticut Assembly to a committee charged with arousing interest in the Revolution. He served as state's attorney in 1788, also serving as a member of the Connecticut legislature and of the Connecticut Council. He was a Federalist.

A frequent contributor to the Litchfield (Connecticut) *Monitor,* Reeve wrote under the names "Phocion" and "Asdrubal." In 1806 he was indicted by a federal grand jury for libeling President Jefferson in the *Monitor.* In 1784 he was a founder of the Litchfield Law School, the first independent law school in the United States. Reeve was its sole teacher until 1798.

Reeve served as a judge in the Connecticut Superior Court from 1798 to 1814. He was an agent in Litchfield for the Connecticut Bible Society. In 1812 he was chairman of a meeting in New Haven to found a society for the suppression of vice and the promotion of good morals. He was chief justice of the Connecticut Supreme Court of Errors from 1814 to 1816.

Reeve wrote *The Law of Baron and Femme . . . ,* four editions, in 1816. *A Treatise on the Law of Descents in the Several United States of America* was published in 1825, two years after his death in Litchfield.

RIPLEY, Ezra: clergyman
Born Woodstock, Connecticut, May 1, 1751; son of Noah and Lydia (Kent) Ripley; married Phoebe Bliss; father of three children; died September 21, 1841.

Ripley graduated from Harvard in 1776. Two years later he was ordained and installed as pastor of First Church in Concord, Massachusetts, where he served until 1814.

Ripley was a member of the school committee at Concord and drew up a constitution for the Concord Library in 1784. In 1836 he gave land for a battle monument. He established one of the first temperance societies and was a member of the Massachusetts Temperance Society.

Ripley received an honorary D.D. from Harvard in 1818. He was the author of *History of the Fight at Concord* (1827) and "Half Century Discourse Delivered November 16, 1828." He died in Concord.

ROOT, Jesse: Continental congressman, jurist
Born Coventry, Connecticut, January 8, 1737; son of

Ebenezer and Sarah (Strong) Root; married Mary Banks, May 18, 1758; father of nine children; died March 29, 1822.

At the age of nineteen Root graduated from Princeton, later earning an LL.D. from Yale. In 1757 he was licensed to preach by the Hartford South Association, and six years later he was admitted to the Connecticut bar.

Root became a member of the Connecticut Council of Safety. He was commissioned a captain in the Connecticut militia in 1776, then a lieutenant colonel, and in 1777 an adjutant general. From 1778 to 1783 he served as a member of the Continental Congress. He was chairman of the Connecticut Council from 1780 to 1789 and state's attorney during the last half of that term. In 1789 he became an assistant judge in the Connecticut Superior Court and served as chief justice from 1796 to 1807. He was a member of the Connecticut House of Representatives in 1807 and 1809. In 1808 he served as a presidential elector. Ten years later he was a delegate to the Connecticut Constitutional Convention.

Root was a school visitor in Coventry, Connecticut, and a member of the American Academy of Arts and Sciences. He was the author of *Reports of Cases Adjudged in the Superior Court of Errors of Connecticut, 1789–93*, which was published in 1798. He died in Coventry and was buried in the Nathan Hale Memorial Cemetery in South Coventry, Connecticut.

★★★★★

SALTONSTALL, Dudley: naval officer

Born New London, Connecticut, September 8, 1738; son of General Gurdon and Rebecca (Winthrop) Saltonstall; married Frances Babcock, 1765; father of seven children; died 1796.

During the French and Indian War, Saltonstall was a privateersman. In 1775 he commanded the fort at New London and then was given command of the *Alfred,* the flagship of Commodore Esek Hopkins. The

next year, 1776, he was appointed fourth on the list of captains.

Having been placed in command of the expedition to Bagaduce (now Castine), in Penobscot Bay, Maine, he arrived in the bay in 1779, fleeing upon the arrival of the British fleet. He was dismissed from the navy after losing two ships to the British. He then became a successful privateer and merchant. He died in Môle St. Nicolas, Haiti.

SEABURY, Samuel: clergyman

Born Groton, Connecticut, November 30, 1729; son of the Reverend Samuel and Abigail (Mumford) Seabury; married Mary Hicks, October 12, 1756; father of at least six children; died February 25, 1796.

Seabury, who earned a B.A. from Yale in 1748, was a catechist in Huntington, Long Island, New York, from 1748 to 1752. After attending the University of Edinburgh in Scotland in 1752 and 1753, he was ordained a deacon in the Protestant Episcopal Church in 1753 and then was licensed to preach by the Bishop of London in 1754. From that year until 1757 he was a missionary in New Brunswick, Canada. In 1767 he was transferred to Jamaica, Long Island. During 1766–67 he served as secretary of the Convention of New York, which was composed of Anglican clergy, and in 1767 he became a rector in Westchester, New York.

Seabury wrote pamphlets urging the colonies to remain loyal to the Crown, the most important of which were signed A. W. Farmer. In 1775 he entered the Loyalists' campaign to prevent the election of committees and delegates to Provincial and Continental Congresses and to nullify the measures enacted by these bodies. Having gone into hiding on April 29, 1775, he was taken prisoner on November 22 of that year but released on December 23. In 1776 he served as a guide to the British Army. The following year he was appointed chaplain at the Provincial Hospital of New York.

In 1784 Seabury was consecrated a bishop

by nonjuring Scottish prelates, and from 1785 until 1796 he was rector of St. James' Church in New London and bishop of Connecticut and Rhode Island; he was the first Episcopalian bishop in America.

In addition to numerous collections of sermons, Seabury wrote *Discourses on Several Subjects,* two volumes (1793), and *Discourses on Several Important Subjects* (1798). He held an honorary D.D. from Oxford. He died in New London and was buried beneath the altar of St. James' Church.

SHAW, Nathaniel: merchant, naval agent
Born December 5, 1735; son of Nathaniel and Temperance (Harris) Shaw; married Lucretia (Harris) Rogers; died April 15, 1782.

A merchant in West Indian trade in the early 1760s, Shaw participated in various colonial actions against British restrictive measures between 1765 and 1775. The Connecticut General Assembly appointed him a negotiator for the purchase of powder in 1774. He acted as an agent for provisioning ships for the Colony of Connecticut and was designated by the Continental Congress as agent in Connecticut to supervise prize vessels and purchase stores in 1775. He also acted as an agent for the exchange of naval prisoners.

Shaw was appointed by the Connecticut General Assembly as director of all armed ships belonging to Connecticut in 1778, and he served as a deputy in the Connecticut Assembly for two terms. His wharves and warehouses were destroyed by Benedict Arnold's attack on New London, Connecticut, in 1781. He died in Connecticut.

SHERMAN, Roger: Continental congressman, senator, congressman
Born Newton, Massachusetts, April 19, 1721; son of William and Mehetabel (Wellington) Sherman; married Elizabeth Hartwell, November 17, 1749; second marriage to Rebecca (or Rebekah) Prescott, May 12, 1763; father of fifteen children; died July 23, 1793.

Sherman was the only member of the Continental Congress who signed all four of the great national documents: the Declaration of 1774, the Declaration of Independence, the Articles of Confederation, and the United States Constitution.

Surveyor of New Haven County, Connecticut, from 1745 to 1752, and of Litchfield County, Connecticut, from 1752 to 1758, Sherman published a series of almanacs between the years 1750 and 1761 and was admitted to the Litchfield County bar in 1754. He served in the Connecticut General Assembly in 1755 and 1756, from 1758 to 1761, and from 1764 to 1766. He moved to New Haven in 1761 and later, in 1768, received an honorary M.A. degree from Yale. He was elected to the Connecticut Senate, serving from 1766 to 1785, and served as judge of the Superior Court of Connecticut in the years 1766–67 and 1773–88. He was a member of the Council of Safety of Connecticut from 1777 to 1779 and again in 1782. With Richard Law, he revised the statutory law of Connecticut, and he served as mayor of New Haven for nine years, from 1784 to 1793.

A signer of the Articles of Association of 1774, he was a member of the committee on the declaration of rights of the First Continental Congress in 1774 and was also a member of the committee appointed to draft the Declaration of Independence. In addition, he sat on the committee concerned with the Articles of Confederation in 1774. A member of the Continental Congress from 1774 to 1781 and in 1783–84, he was one of the leaders in shaping the laws of the Congress.

Sherman was a leading member of the compromise group of the United States Constitutional Convention in Philadelphia in 1787 and introduced the Connecticut Compromise. He was elected to the 1st Congress of the United States House of Representatives (1789–91), and he served in the United States Senate (from Connecticut) from June 13, 1791, to July 12, 1793.

Sherman died in New Haven and was buried in the Grove Street Cemetery there.

SPENCER, Joseph: Continental congressman, army officer

Born Haddam, Connecticut, October 3, 1714; son of Isaac and Mary (Selden) Spencer; married Martha Brainerd, August 2, 1738; second marriage to Hannah Brown Southmayd, 1756; father of thirteen children; died January 13, 1789.

Smith was commissioned a lieutenant in the Connecticut militia in 1747, a major in 1757, a lieutenant colonel in 1759, and a colonel in 1766. Commissioned a brigadier general in the Connecticut militia, Continental Army, in 1775, he resigned after the Continental Congress promoted Israel Putnam over him. However, he returned to service with the Continental Army in Boston and New York State later that year.

Named major general in 1776, Spencer served in Providence, Rhode Island, in 1777, where he attempted an unsuccessful move against the enemy. He was investigated by a special court of inquiry and cleared. He resigned from the Continental Army in 1778 and the following year became a delegate to the Continental Congress from Connecticut.

Spencer was also active in Connecticut politics throughout his life, spending sixteen years (1750–66) as a deputy to the Connecticut Assembly and thirty-six years (1753–89) as probate judge in Haddam. He served as a member of the Connecticut Committee of Safety in 1780 and 1781. He died in East Haddam, where he was buried.

STILES, Ezra: clergyman, college president

Born North Haven, Connecticut, November 29, 1727 (old-style calendar); son of Isaac and Keziah (Taylor) Stiles; married Elizabeth Hubbard, February 10, 1757; second marriage to Mary (Cranston) Checkley, October 17, 1782; father of eight children (including Ezra, Isaac, and Ruth); died May 12, 1795.

Stiles graduated from Yale in 1746 and was a tutor at that school from 1749 to 1755.

He engaged in some of the first electrical experiments in New England when Benjamin Franklin sent an electrical apparatus to Yale in 1749.

Stiles was licensed to preach by the New Haven Association of Ministers in 1749. He was ordained to the ministry of the Congregational Church in 1755 and served as pastor of the Congregational Church in Newport, Rhode Island, that year.

Elected a member of the American Philosophical Society in 1768, Stiles was also a councilor in 1781. He was a founder of Rhode Island College (now Brown University) in 1763 and president of Yale in 1777, becoming a professor of ecclesiastical history there the next year. Late in his life (in 1783), he was admitted to the Connecticut bar.

Stiles was awarded a number of honorary degrees: a D.D. from the University of Edinburgh (Scotland), 1765; a D.D. from Dartmouth, 1780; a D.D. and an LL.D. from the College of New Jersey (now Princeton), 1784. He was president of a society for the abolition of slavery formed in Connecticut in 1790. He was the author of a *History of Three of the Judges of King Charles I,* 1794.

Stiles died in New Haven.

STRONG, Jedediah: Continental congressman, lawyer

Born Litchfield, Connecticut, November 7, 1738; died August 21, 1802.

Strong studied law, was admitted to the bar in 1764, and established a legal practice in Litchfield. He served as a member of the Connecticut House of Representatives from 1771 to 1801 and was Litchfield town clerk from 1773 to 1789. A member of the Committee of Inspection in 1774 and 1775, he was commissary of supplies for the Continental Army in 1775. Strong declined election to the Continental Congress in 1779 and instead became clerk of the Connecticut House of Representatives, serving from 1779 to 1788.

Strong was associate judge of the Litchfield County Court from 1780 to 1791 and was a delegate to the Continental Congress from Connecticut from 1782 to 1784. He was later (1788) a delegate to the Connecticut Convention to ratify the United States Constitution and in 1789 and 1790, a member of the Governor's Council.

Strong died in Litchfield and was buried in the West Burying Ground.

STURGES, Jonathan: congressman
Born Fairfield, Connecticut, August 23, 1740; father of at least one son (Lewis Burr); died October 4, 1819.

Sturges graduated from Yale in 1759, was admitted to the bar, and began to practice law in Fairfield. He served in the Connecticut House of Representatives in 1772, from 1773 to 1784, and in 1786. He was a justice of the peace in 1773 and a delegate to the Continental Congress from Connecticut from 1774 to 1787.

A judge of the probate court for the district of Fairfield in 1775, Sturges was elected to the United States House of Representatives from Connecticut for the 1st–2nd congresses (1789–93). He was an associate justice of the Connecticut Supreme Court from 1793 to 1805 and was a Federalist presidential elector in 1796 and 1804.

Sturges died in Fairfield and was buried in the Old Burying Ground there.

SWIFT, Zephaniah: congressman, jurist
Born Wareham, Massachusetts, February 27, 1759; son of Roland and Mary (Dexter) Swift; married Jerusha Watrous before 1792; second marriage to Lucretia Webb, March 14, 1795; father of eight children (including Mary A.); died September 27, 1823.

Swift was awarded a B.A. from Yale in 1778 and an M.A. from there three years later. After his admission to the Connecticut bar, he served in the Connecticut General Assembly from 1787 to 1793. He was clerk of the lower house for four sessions and speaker in 1792. He was elected to the United States House of Representatives

from Connecticut for the 3rd and 4th congresses (1793–97).

After serving as secretary to Oliver Ellsworth on his mission to France in 1800, Swift returned to Connecticut to become a member of the Connecticut General Assembly. A vigorous opponent of slavery, he was judge of the Connecticut Supreme Court from 1801 to 1810 and chief justice from 1806 to 1819. A supporter of the Hartford Convention of 1814, he also served in the Connecticut House of Representatives from 1820 to 1822.

Swift was the author of *Oration of Domestic Slavery*, 1791, and the *System of the Laws of Connecticut*, 1795–96. He died in Warren, Ohio, and was buried in Oakwood Cemetery there.

★★★★★

TALLMADGE, Benjamin: army officer, congressman
Born Brookhaven, New York, February 25, 1754; son of Benjamin and Susannah (Smith) Tallmadge; married Mary Floyd, March 18, 1784; second marriage to Maria Hallett, May 3, 1808; father of seven children, including Frederick Augustus; died March 7, 1835.

After graduating from Yale in 1773, Tallmadge served as superintendent of Wetherfield High School in Connecticut until 1776. That year he was appointed lieutenant adjutant of the Connecticut militia, advancing to captain later that year and to major the following year. Tallmadge fought in the battles of Brandywine, Long Island, and Monmouth, and captured Fort George, Long Island, in 1780. He also served as the officer in charge of taking custody of Major John André. Later, in 1783, he was brevetted a lieutenant colonel.

A Federalist, Tallmadge was elected to the United States Congress as a representative from Connecticut, serving during the 7th through the 14th congresses (1801–17). He was also a member of the Society of the Cincinnati. He died in Litchfield, Connecticut, and was buried in Litchfield's East Cemetery.

TRACY, Uriah: senator, congressman
Born Norwich, Connecticut, February 2, 1735; son of Eliphalet and Lucy (or Sarah) (Manning) Tracy; married Susan (or Susannah) Bull; father of five children; died July 19, 1807.

At the age of forty-three, Tracy graduated from Yale and in 1781 was admitted to the Connecticut bar. He served from 1794 to 1799 as state's attorney for Litchfield County, Connecticut.

From 1788 to 1793 Tracy was a member of the Connecticut House of Representatives, acting as speaker in 1793. He served as major general of the Connecticut militia. He was a delegate to the United States House of Representatives from 1793 to October 1796, at which time he became a member of the United States Senate and served until July 1807, acting as president pro tem in 1800. He was known as a facile politician and was respected by his Federalist colleagues.

He was the author of a brochure, *Reflections on Monroe's View of the Conduct of the Executive,* circa 1798. He died in Washington, D.C., and was buried in the Congressional Burying Ground there.

TRUMBULL, Benjamin: clergyman, historian
Born Hebron, Connecticut, December 19, 1735; son of Benjamin and Mary (Brown) Trumble; married Martha Phelps, December 4, 1760; father of seven children; died February 2, 1820.

Trumbull graduated from Yale in 1759 and the next year was licensed to preach by the Windham Association of Ministers. In 1760 he also became pastor of the Congregational Church in North Haven, Connecticut, serving in that position until 1820. During the Revolutionary War, from June to December of 1776, he was chaplain of General Wadsworth's brigade. He became captain of a company of sixty volunteers in North Haven.

Trumbull was the author of several works, including *A Plea, In Vindication of the Connecticut Title to the Conquested Lands, Lying West of New York,* 1774; *An Appeal to the Public . . . with Respect to the Unlawfulness of Divorces,* 1788; and *A Complete History of Connecticut . . . to the Year 1764,* in two volumes, 1818. He also began *A General History of the United States of America . . . 1492–1792,* but had completed only the first volume of the projected three-volume work by the time of his death in 1820.

TRUMBULL, John: poet, jurist
Born Westbury, Connecticut, April 24, 1750; son of John and Sarah (Whitman) Trumbull; married Sarah Hubbard, November 21, 1776; father of four children; died May 11, 1831.

After graduation from Yale in 1767, Trumbull took an M.A. there as a Berkeley fellow in 1770 and gave the valedictory oration, titled "An Essay on the Uses and Advantages of the Fine Arts." In 1772–73 he continued at Yale as a tutor. He studied law under John Adams and was admitted to the Connecticut bar in 1773.

Trumbull published a series of Addisonian essays in the *Boston Chronicle* in 1769 and 1770 and, under the pen name The Correspondent, published a series of thirty-eight essays in the *Connecticut Journal* from 1770 to 1773. He was the author of the poem *Epithalamium,* 1769; *The Progress of Dullness,* a satire on contemporary educational methods, 1772–73; and *M'Fingal,* a comic epic, 1784. The latter work was reprinted thirty times to 1840. In 1774 Trumbull wrote *An Elegy on the Times,* his first poem reflecting on national affairs. He was a literary leader of the Hartford Wits during the 1780s and 90s and contributed to an anthology called *The Echo,* first published in 1807 in the *American Mercury.* In 1820 he produced *The Poetical Works of John Trumbull,* in two volumes.

Trumbull served as state's attorney for Hartford County in 1789. He was a member of the Connecticut legislature from 1792 to 1800. He sat as a judge of the Connecticut

Supreme Court from 1801 to 1819, and on the Supreme Court of Errors from 1808 to 1819. He died in Detroit in 1831.

TRUMBULL, John: painter
Born Lebanon, Connecticut, June 6, 1756; son of Governor Jonathan and Faith (Robinson) Trumbull; married Sarah (Hope) Harvey, October 1, 1800; died November 10, 1843.

Trumbull graduated from Harvard in 1773 and studied painting under Benjamin West in London, England, in 1780, 1782–83, and 1784–85. During the Revolutionary War he served as adjutant to General Joseph Spencer of the 1st Connecticut Regiment. He was second aide-de-camp to General Washington in 1775 and major of a brigade that year in action at Dorchester Heights. In 1776 he became a deputy adjutant general with the rank of colonel under General Horatio Gates, serving at Crown Point and Ticonderoga and in Pennsylvania.

Trumbull began painting historical and Revolutionary War subjects while a pupil of West. Some of his first paintings include *Battle of Bunker's Hill; Death of General Montgomery in Attack of Quebec* (1786); *Declaration of Independence; The Surrender of Lord Cornwallis at Yorktown; Death of General Mercer at Battle of Princeton; Captured Hessians at Trenton;* and *Sortie Made by the Garrison of Gibraltar.* Trumbull traveled to Paris in 1787 and 1789. He painted *Washington Before the Battle of Princeton,* in 1792, and the next year became private secretary to John Jay, who was envoy extraordinary to Great Britain. From 1793 to 1804 Trumbull engaged in diplomatic and business speculation. He painted portraits of Timothy Dwight and Stephen Van Rensselaer. From 1808 to 1815 he lived in Europe.

In 1817 Congress commissioned Trumbull to paint four pictures in the Rotunda of the Capitol. These were *Surrender of General Burgoyne at Saratoga; Resignation of Washington; Surrender of Cornwallis at Yorktown;* and *Declaration of Independence.* Also in 1817 he became president of the American Academy of Fine Arts. He designed, and contributed his collection to, the Trumbull Gallery at Yale; this was the earliest art museum connected with an educational institution in America. He also planned a series of dormitory buildings for Yale in 1792. He designed the Congregational Church in Lebanon in 1804 and the Barclay Street quarters of the American Academy in 1831.

Trumbull published *Autobiography, Letters and Reminiscences of John Trumbull, 1756–1841,* in 1841. He died in 1843 in New York City and was buried under the Trumbull Gallery. In 1928 his body was reinterred at the New Yale Gallery of Fine Arts.

TRUMBULL, Jonathan: governor of Connecticut
Born Lebanon, Connecticut, October 12, 1710; son of Joseph and Hannah (Higley) Trumble; married Faith Robinson, December 9, 1735; father of six children (including John, Jonathan, and Joseph); died August 17, 1785.

After graduating from Harvard in 1727, Trumbull was licensed to preach by the Windham Association. In 1731 he entered his father's mercantile business and by the 1760s was an outstanding figure in Connecticut commerce. However, he went bankrupt in 1766.

Trumbull served as a member of the Connecticut General Assembly in 1733, and as speaker in 1739. From 1740 to 1750 and again in 1754 he was a member of the Connecticut Council. He was deputy governor and, from 1766 until 1769, chief justice of Connecticut. Trumbull sat as a judge of the Windham County Court in 1746 and on the Windham Probate Court in 1747. He was governor of Connecticut from 1769 to 1784.

An active supporter of the Revolutionary cause, Trumbull supplied the Continental Army with food, clothing, and munitions. He was in frequent contact with George Washington during the Revolutionary period and encouraged the raising of companies of Connecticut militia. Washington called him "Brother Jonathan," which was for a time the symbol of America, later to be supplanted by "Uncle Sam."

Trumbull held honorary LL.D.s from Yale and the University of Edinburgh (Scotland). He was a member of the American Academy of Arts and Sciences. He died on August 17, 1785.

TRUMBULL, Jonathan: senator, governor of Connecticut

Born Lebanon, Connecticut, March 26, 1740; son of Jonathan and Faith (Robinson) Trumbull; married Eunice Backus, March 1767; father of five children, including John; died August 7, 1809.

Trumbull graduated from Harvard in 1759 and received an M.A. in 1762. He entered politics as a selectman of Lebanon from 1770 to 1775. He represented Lebanon in the Connecticut legislature in the years 1774, 1775, 1779, 1780, and 1788, serving as speaker the latter year. From 1775 to 1778 he was paymaster for the forces of the New York department of the Continental Army. He was the first comptroller of the United States Treasury, serving in 1778 and 1779, and was secretary to George Washington from 1781 to 1783.

A Federalist, Trumbull served Connecticut in the United States House of Representatives from 1789 to 1795; he was speaker in the 1791–93 session. From 1795 to 1796 he was a United States Senator from Connecticut.

Trumbull served as deputy governor of Connecticut in 1796 and as governor from 1797 to 1809. He was a leader of the Federalist party in Connecticut. He died in 1809 and was buried in the Old Cemetery in Lebanon.

TRUMBULL, Joseph: army officer

Born Lebanon, Connecticut, March 11, 1737; son of Jonathan and Faith (Robinson) Trumbull; married Amelia Dyer, March 1777; died July 23, 1778.

From 1756, when he graduated from Harvard, until 1767, Trumbull worked in his father's merchant firm. He became a mem-

ber of the General Assembly of Connecticut in 1767 and served until 1773, when he joined the Connecticut Committee of Correspondence.

Trumbull was a member of the Continental Congress in 1774 and 1775. He was commissary general of Connecticut troops in 1775 and commissary general of the Continental Army with the rank of colonel from 1775 to 1777. In 1777 and 1778 he was a member of the Board of War.

Trumbull died in Lebanon at age forty-one and was buried in the Old Cemetery there.

★★★★★

WADSWORTH, James: Continental congressman

Born Durham, Middlesex County, Connecticut, July 8, 1730; died September 22, 1817.

A graduate of Yale in 1748, Wadsworth studied law and was admitted to the bar. He served as town clerk of Durham from 1756 to 1786 and as justice of the peace in 1762. He was appointed judge of the New Haven County Court in 1773 and presiding judge in 1778. During the Revolution he was a member of the Committee of Safety and served as a colonel and brigadier general in the Connecticut militia. He was promoted to second major general in 1777.

A delegate from Connecticut to the Continental Congress from 1783 to 1786, Wadsworth also served as a member of the Connecticut Executive Council from 1785 to 1789. He was comptroller of Connecticut in 1786–87 and a delegate to the Connecticut Convention to ratify the United States Constitution in 1788; he was, however, opposed to the Constitution and refused to take the oath of allegiance.

Wadsworth died in Durham at the age of eighty-seven and was buried in Old Cemetery there.

WADSWORTH, Jeremiah: army officer, congressman

Born Hartford, Connecticut, July 12, 1743; son of the

Reverend Daniel and Abigail (Talcott) Wadsworth; married Mehitable Russell, September 29, 1767; father of three children; died April 30, 1804.

Wadsworth, who held honorary degrees from Yale and Dartmouth, served his country during the Revolution as an army officer and afterward as a legislator. In addition, he engaged in business and agriculture.

Engaged in the merchant service from 1761 to 1771, Wadsworth served as commissary general to Colonel Joseph Trumbull of the Connecticut forces raised to serve in the Revolution in 1775. He became deputy commissary general of purchases for the Continental Army in 1777 and commissary general in 1778. At the request of General Rochambeau he also served as commissary agent to the French troops in America until the end of the war.

Wadsworth went to Paris in 1783 to submit a report of his transactions. Returning to America, he was sent by Connecticut to the Continental Congress, attending in 1787 and 1788, and also served at the Connecticut Convention to consider ratification of the United States Constitution in 1788. A Federalist, he was elected to the United States House of Representatives for the 1st–3rd congresses, from 1789 to 1795. After this he was a member of the Connecticut legislature in 1795 and a member of the Connecticut Executive Council from 1795 to 1801.

Wadsworth founded the Bank of North America in Philadelphia and the Hartford Bank in Connecticut. He was a director of the United States Bank and president of the Bank of New York. He was a promoter of the Hartford Manufacturing Company, started in 1788, and established the first insurance partnership in Connecticut in 1794.

Wadsworth introduced fine breeds of cattle from abroad and engaged in experiments to improve agriculture. He died in Hartford and was buried in the Ancient Burying Ground there.

WEBSTER, Noah: lexicographer
Born West Hartford, Connecticut, October 16, 1758; son of Noah and Mercy (Steele) Webster; married Rebecca Greenleaf, October 26, 1789; father of eight children; died May 28, 1843.

After obtaining a B.A. from Yale in 1778, Webster was admitted to the Hartford, Connecticut, bar in 1781. He taught school in Goshen, New York, prepared the first part of a speller in 1782, a grammar in 1784, and a reader in 1785.

Webster agitated for a uniform copyright law from 1782 to 1789. He became a staunch Federalist, advocating strong central government. He corresponded with Benjamin Franklin concerning spelling reform and gradually came to propagate traditional spelling.

Editor of the *American Magazine,* in New York City, 1787–88, Webster then practiced law in Hartford until 1793. He launched the daily pro-Federalist newspaper *Minerva* (which became the *Commercial Advertiser* in 1797) and also the semi-weekly *Herald* in New York City (which became the *Spectator* in 1797) during the years between 1793 and 1798. In 1803 he retired on income from his schoolbooks. He represented Hampshire County in the Massachusetts legislature in 1815 and 1819 and was a founder of Amherst College, 1819–21.

Webster was the author of numerous works, including the following: *A Grammatical Institute of the English Language,* 1782; *The American Spelling Book* (which contributed to the standardization of spelling in the United States); *An American Selection of Lessons in Reading and Speaking* (which contained patriotic pieces on American history and geography); *Sketches of American Policy* (a pamphlet expressing Federalist views), 1785; *Dissertations on the English Language,* 1789; *The Prompter* (essays), 1791; *Aristides' Letter to Hamilton,* 1800; *A Compendious Dictionary of the English Language* (his first work of lexicography), 1806; *Philosophical and Practical Grammar of the English Language* (an important contribution to lexicography), 1807; and *An American Dictionary of the English Language* (his greatest work, which recorded words on the basis of their popular usage), 1828. In addition, he wrote an *Authorized Version of the English Bible* (a revision) in 1833.

Webster died at age eighty-four in New Haven, Connecticut.

WILLIAMS, William: Continental congressman

Born Lebanon, Connecticut, April 8, 1731; son of Solomon and Mary (Porter) Williams; married Mary Trumbull, February 14, 1771; father of three children; died August 2, 1811.

Four years after graduation from Harvard in 1751, Williams participated in the Lake George operations of the French and Indian War under Ephraim Williams. He helped Governor Jonathan Trumbull compose state papers; in 1775 he again aided the state by contributing a promissory note defraying the cost of sending Connecticut troops to aid in the capture of Ticonderoga. He offered his own specie for needed army supplies in 1779 and placed his home at the disposal of officers when a French regiment quartered in Lebanon in 1780 and 1781.

Williams served Lebanon as a selectman from 1760 to 1780, as town clerk from 1752 to 1796, and as a member of the lower house of the Connecticut legislature from 1757 to 1776, and again from 1781 to 1784. He worked on committees to consider the Stamp Act, to investigate Connecticut's claim to Susquehanna lands, and to resolve the case of the Michigan Indians. He represented Connecticut at conferences of delegates from New England.

From 1776 to 1778, and in 1783 and 1784, Williams was a member of the Continental Congress. He signed the Declaration of Independence in 1776 and served on the Board of War in 1777. He was a framer of the Articles of Confederation; nearly ten years later, in 1788, he was a delegate to the Connecticut Convention to ratify the United States Constitution. He was a member of the Connecticut Governor's Council from 1784 to 1803, a judge of the Windham County Courts from 1776 to 1805, and judge of probate for the Windham district from 1775 to 1809.

Williams died at the age of eighty and was buried in Lebanon.

WOLCOTT, Oliver: governor of Connecticut, secretary of the treasury

Born Litchfield, Connecticut, January 11, 1760; son of Oliver and Laura (Collins) Wolcott; married Elizabeth Stoughton, June 1, 1785; father of seven children; died June 1, 1833.

In 1776 Wolcott served in the quatermaster's corps in charge of army stores and ordnance in Litchfield. He graduated from Yale in 1778 and attended the Litchfield Law School. Later he was given honorary LL.D.s from Yale, Princeton, and Brown. He was a commissioner to settle Connecticut claims against the United States in 1784. In 1788 and 1789 he was comptroller of public accounts, during which time he reorganized the finances of Connecticut. He was auditor of the United States Treasury from 1789 to 1791 and comptroller in 1791. He initiated a plan for creation of branch banks of the Bank of the United States.

President Washington appointed Wolcott secretary of the treasury in 1795; in this capacity Wolcott followed a Hamiltonian financial program. He remained in office under President John Adams but resigned in 1800 as a result of the Adams-Hamilton break. In 1801 he was appointed by Adams as a judge of the United States Circuit Court for the second district, but his service ended in 1802 when Congress repealed the act that created the circuit court on which he was serving.

Wolcott was a partner in a New York City trading firm from 1803 to 1805, then organized his own trading firm, relinquishing it in 1815. During this time he was elected to the board of directors of the Bank of the

United States, in 1810, and became a founder of the Bank of America, chartered by New York, in 1812. He was president of this bank until 1814, when he was removed for political reasons.

Wolcott, who supported the War of 1812 as a War Federalist, was elected governor of Connecticut on the Toleration ticket in 1817. In 1818 he presided over the Connecticut Constitutional Convention, which separated church and state, disestablished the Congregational Church, and granted religious toleration. It also created a stronger executive and independent judiciary. Wolcott favored aid to agriculture and stressed the necessity of banking regulations, public schools, and labor laws. He was defeated for reelection by the state Republican factional machine in 1827.

Wolcott died in New York City in 1833 and was buried in Litchfield.

WOOSTER, David: army officer
Born Stratford, Connecticut, March 2, 1711; mar-
ried Mary Clap, March 1746; father of four children; died May 2, 1777.

Wooster graduated from Yale in 1738. He began his military career with an appointment as a lieutenant of the Connecticut Colony in 1741. In 1742 he was appointed captain of the sloop *Defense,* which protected the coast. He served as a captain in the Connecticut militia in 1745. He was an organizer of the Hiram Lodge, one of the earliest Freemason lodges in Connecticut, in 1750. During the Seven Years' War, from 1756 to 1763, he served as a colonel in the Connecticut Regiment.

In 1757 Wooster was a member of the Connecticut Assembly from New Haven. In 1775, at the outbreak of the Revolutionary War, he was appointed by this assembly as a major general of six regiments and, later, colonel of the 1st Regiment. Also in 1775 he commanded the Continental Army before Quebec, Canada, but was recalled in 1776 by the Continental Congress on a charge of incompetence. He was acquitted of the charge and retained the rank of brigadier general but was not given a command. He died the following year.

★★★★★★★★★★★★

DELAWARE

"Few men have served the State in more capacities or with greater efficiency than Governor Bassett."

—J. T. Scharf

BASSETT, Richard: senator, governor of Delaware

Born Cecil County, Maryland, April 2, 1745; son of Michael and Judith (Thompson) Bassett; married Ann Ennals; second marriage to Miss Bruff; father of Rachel (adopted), Mary, and Ann; died September 15, 1815.

Bassett became a member of the Delaware Council of Safety in 1776. Around that time he also began approximately a decade of service on the Governor's Council. The next year he served as a captain in the Dover Light Horse in the Revolutionary War.

Bassett was a delegate to the Delaware constitutional conventions in 1776 and 1792, a member of the Delaware Senate in 1782, and a member of the state House of Representatives four years later. He represented his state in the 1787 United States Constitutional Convention and participated the same year in the Delaware Convention which ratified the United States Constitution. He went to the United States Senate as a Federalist during the years 1789–93, after which he became chief justice of the Delaware Court of Common Pleas, holding that

office from 1793 to 1799. He was a Federalist presidential elector in 1797.

Bassett was governor of Delaware from 1798 to 1801. Immediately after leaving the governorship he became a judge in the United States Circuit Court for the Third District, remaining there until 1815. He died at the age of seventy in Bohemia Manor, Delaware, and was buried at Brandywine Cemetery, Wilmington, Delaware.

BEDFORD, Gunning: governor of Delaware

Born Philadelphia, Pennsylvania, April 7, 1742; son of William Bedford; married Mary Read, 1796; died September 30, 1797.

In 1775 Bedford served in the Continental Army as a major and then as a quartermaster general. The next year he was promoted to lieutenant colonel of a Delaware regiment and then to muster-master general. In 1776 he served in the Battle of White Plains. He became a prothonotary in 1779.

Bedford was a delegate to the Delaware Congress in 1783–85 and a representative of New Castle County in the state legislature during the period from 1784 to 1786. As well as attending the Delaware convention which ratified the United States Constitution, he became a member of the state senate in 1788 and was a presidential elector the following year. He held two local offices in the county—register of wills (1788) and justice of the peace (1789). He was also a member of the Delaware Privy Council from 1783 until 1790.

Bedford served as governor of Delaware in 1796 and 1797. He was a leader in the development of the Delaware public school system. He died at the age of fifty-five.

BEDFORD, Gunning: Continental congressman, jurist

Born Philadelphia, Pennsylvania, 1747; son of Gunning and Susannah (Jacquett) Bedford; married Jane Parker; died March 30, 1812.

Bedford, who called himself "Gunning Bedford, Jr." to distinguish himself from his cousin, graduated in 1771 from the College of New Jersey (now Princeton) and was admitted to the Delaware bar the next year. During the Revolutionary War he was aide-de-camp to George Washington.

A member of the Delaware legislature and the Delaware Council, Bedford also went to the Continental Congress from his state in the years 1783–86. He became the state's attorney general in 1784. He attended the Annapolis Convention in 1786 and the Delaware Constitutional Convention, as well as the United States Constitutional Convention. At the latter he proposed equal representation of the states, short presidential terms, and a powerful legislative branch.

Bedford was elected to the Delaware Senate in 1788 and the next year was appointed by George Washington as the first judge of the United States District Court for Delaware. He was a presidential elector in the years 1789 and 1793. He also served his community as president of the trustees of the Wilmington Academy. He died in Wilmington and was buried in the first Presbyterian Churchyard there.

BENNETT, Caleb Prew: governor of Delaware

Born Chester County, Pennsylvania, November 11, 1758; son of Joseph and Elizabeth (Prew) Wiley Bennett; married Catherine Britton, April 5, 1792; died May 9, 1836.

Bennett joined the Continental Army in 1775 and rose to the rank of sergeant in 1777. During the winter of 1777–78 he served at Valley Forge. In 1778 he received a commission as a second lieutenant and served at the battles of Brandywine and Germantown. He was commissioned a first lieutenant two years later.

For twenty-six years, from 1807 to 1833, Bennett served as treasurer of New Castle County, Delaware. He became a major in the artillery of the Delaware militia in 1813 and commanded the Port of New Castle during the War of 1812. Bennett was the first Democratic governor of Delaware, holding that office from 1833 to 1836.

Bennett died in Wilmington, Delaware, and was buried in the Friends Meeting House Cemetery there.

★★★★★

CLAYTON, Joshua: physician, governor of Delaware

Born Dover, Delaware, December 20, 1744; son of John and Grace Clayton; married Rachael McCleary, 1776; died August 11, 1798.

Clayton attended the University of Pennsylvania from 1757 to 1762. At the age of thirty-two he was commissioned a major in the Bohemia Battalion of Maryland, acting as second in command. He was then commissioned a colonel and appointed to General Washington's staff.

Clayton served as an elected member of the Delaware House of Assembly in 1785. In 1786 he was state treasurer of Delaware, returning the following year to the House of Assembly. President of Delaware from 1789 to 1792, Clayton became the state's first governor and served a four-year term beginning in 1792. He represented Delaware in the United States Senate from January 19, 1789, until his death. Clayton died in Bohemia Manor, Delaware.

★★★★★

EVANS, John: Continental congressman
No record of birth or death.

Evans was a member of the Delaware Assembly from 1774 to 1776, also acting as a deputy for the Delaware Constitutional Convention in 1776. He was a member of the Continental Congress in 1776 and 1777 but did not serve owing to ill health. In 1777 he became a justice of the Delaware Supreme Court.

★★★★★

JONES, Jacob: naval officer
Born Smyrna, Delaware, March 1768; son of Jacob Jones; married Miss Sykes; second marriage to Ruth Lusby, 1821; father of six children (including Richard); died August 3, 1850.

Jones's first job in public life was clerk of the Delaware Supreme Court. Commissioned a midshipman in the United States Navy, he served on the frigate *United States* in 1799 and was promoted to lieutenant two years later. He was a second lieutenant on the ship *Philadelphia* when it ran aground and was captured off Tripoli in 1803. He assumed command of the *Wasp* in 1810; about this time he was awarded the Gold Medal by Congress.

In 1812 Jones captured the *Frolic,* a British sloop of war commanded by Captain Whingates. Soon after, he was promoted to captain and given command of the ship *Macedonian* in Stephen Decatur's squadron operating in the Mediterranean in 1813. Later he rose to commander of the Mediterranean Squadron, serving in this capacity from 1821 to 1823. From 1826 to 1829 he was navy commissioner of the Pacific Squadron. For the remainder of his life, Jones was in charge of the Philadelphia Naval Asylum.

★★★★★

KEARNEY, Drye: Continental congressman
Born Kent County, Delaware; died circa November 1, 1791.

After studying law, Kearney was admitted to the bar of New Castle County, Delaware, in 1784 and began a legal practice in Dover. During the years 1787–88 he represented his state in the Continental Congress. He died in Dover.

★★★★★

LATIMER, Henry: senator, congressman, physician
Born Newport, Delaware, April 24, 1752; died December 19, 1819.

Latimer graduated from the University of Pennsylvania in 1773 and from Edinburgh (Scotland) Medical College in 1775. He practiced medicine in Wilmington, Delaware, and during the Revolutionary War served as a surgeon.

In 1787–88 and in 1790 Latimer was a member of the Delaware House of Representatives, serving as speaker the latter year. From February 14, 1894, to February 7, 1895, he served in the United States House of Representatives (3rd Congress). He was a member of the United States Senate from February 7, 1795, to February 28, 1801.

Latimer died in Philadelphia and was buried in the Presbyterian Cemetery in Wilmington.

★★★★★

McCOMB, Eleazer: Continental congressman
No record of birth; died December 1798.

McComb, who served as a captain in the Delaware militia during the Revolution, was appointed to the Delaware Privy Council in 1779. He was sent to the Continental Congress from Delaware in 1783 and 1784.

A member of a commission to confer concerning the Chesapeake and Delaware Canal in 1786, McComb was auditor of accounts for the state of Delaware from 1787 to 1793. He moved from Dover to Wilmington, Delaware, about 1792, and there he engaged in shipping and became a director of the Bank of Delaware in 1795. He died in Wilmington.

McKINLY, John: army officer, president of Delaware
Born North Ireland, February 24, 1721; married Jane Richardson, circa 1761; died August 31, 1796.

McKinly arrived in Delaware in 1743 and served as a lieutenant in the Delaware militia in 1747 and 1748. He was commissioned a major in the New Castle County Regiment in 1756. He served as sheriff of New Castle County from 1757 to 1760 and was chief burgess of the Borough of Wilmington (Delaware) from 1759 to 1774 (with the exception of three years). He was a member of the Delaware Assembly in 1771.

Chairman of the Delaware Committee of Correspondence in 1773, McKinly served as a colonel in the New Castle County Regiment in 1775 and as a brigadier general in charge of three battalions later that year. He was elected to the first Delaware legislature and was speaker of the lower house in 1776. He served as president of the Delaware Council of Safety in 1776 and was chosen first president and commander-in-chief of Delaware in 1777.

McKinly was a founder of the first medical society in Delaware and was a trustee of the First Presbyterian Church of Wilmington in 1789. He died in Wilmington.

McLANE, Allan: army officer
Born Philadelphia, Pennsylvania, August 8, 1746; married Rebecca Wells, 1769; died May 22, 1829.

After touring Europe in 1767, McLane settled in Kent County, Delaware, in 1774. He served as an adjutant in Caesar Rodney's Volunteer Regiment in 1775 and was commissioned a captain in Colonel John Patton's Additional Continental Regiment in 1777. He was placed in command of dismounted dragoons under Major Henry Lee in 1779.

McLane was a member of the Delaware House of Representatives from 1785 to 1791. Later, during the War of 1812, he was in charge of the defenses of Wilmington. McLane died at the age of eighty-two.

MITCHELL, Nathaniel: governor of Delaware, army officer
Born Laurel, Delaware, 1753; son of James and Margaret (Dogworthy) Mitchell; married Hannah Morris; father of Theodore; died February 21, 1814.

Commissioned a captain in the Continental Army, Mitchell was transferred to Colonel Samuel Patterson's Delaware Battalion of "Flying Camp" and then to Colonel William Grayson's Additional Continental Regiment in 1777. He was promoted to major in 1777 and became a brigade major and inspector to General Peter Mühlenberg in 1779. He was captured by the British, imprisoned, then paroled in 1781.

He was a member of the Congress of Confederation from Delaware from 1786 to 1788. Treasurer of Sussex County, Delaware, for seventeen years from 1788 to 1805, Mitchell then was elected governor of Delaware, serving from 1804 to 1808. He was a member of the Delaware House of Representatives (1808–10) and of the Delaware Senate (1810–12).

Mitchell died in Laurel and was buried in Broad Creek Episcopal graveyard of Christ Church in Delaware.

★★★★★

PARKE, John: army officer, poet
Born Dover, Delaware, April 7, 1754; son of Thomas Parke; died December 11, 1789.

Parke received an A.B. degree from the College of Philadelphia (now the University of Pennsylvania) in 1771 and an A.M. degree in 1775. After finishing his formal education, Parke was appointed assistant quartermaster general of the Continental Army in Cambridge, Massachusetts, and in 1776 became a lieutenant colonel of artificers in New York City.

Parke was author of *The Lyric Works of Horace, Translated into English Verse: to Which Are Added, a Number of Original Poems, by a Native of*

America, published in 1786. He died in Kent County, Delaware.

PATTEN, John: congressman
Born Kent County, Delaware, April 26, 1746; died December 26, 1800.

Patten, who attended common schools, was a farmer by trade. He served in the Continental Army, advancing in rank from lieutenant to major and participating in all battles from Long Island to Camden during the Revolutionary War.

Patten was a member of the Continental Congress from Delaware in 1785 and 1786 and of the United States House of Representatives in the 3rd and 4th congresses, from 1793 to February 14, 1794, and from 1795 to 1797. He died in "Tynhead Court," near Dover, Delaware, and was buried in the Presbyterian Churchyard there.

PEERY, William: Continental congressman
No record of birth; died December 17, 1800.

In his early years Peery studied law and engaged in farming. He was an organizer and a commissioned captain of an independent company during the Revolutionary War. He served in the Delaware House of Representatives in 1782, 1784, 1787, 1793, and 1794.

In 1785 Peery was admitted to the bar and began practicing law in Sussex County, Delaware. He was a member of the Continental Congress from Delaware in 1785–86. He served as treasurer of Sussex County from 1785 to 1796 and was appointed a member of a commission to purchase land and build a courthouse and prison for Sussex County in 1791.

Peery died in Cool Spring, Delaware, and was buried in the Presbyterian Churchyard there.

★★★★★

READ, George: president of the Continental Congress, senator
Born North East, Maryland, September 18, 1733; son of John and Mary (Howell) Read; married Gertrude (Ross) Till, January 11, 1763; father of one daughter and four sons (including John); died September 21, 1798.

Read was admitted to the Philadelphia bar in 1753. While attorney general of the Lower Counties of Delaware, from 1763 to 1774, he protested the Stamp Act. He was a member of the Delaware Provincial Assembly from 1765 to 1777, and in 1769 he aided in obtaining the adoption of the Non-Incorporation Agreement in New Castle County, Delaware. In 1774 he helped secure relief for Boston.

From 1774 to 1777 Read served as an organizer and a member of the First and Second Continental congresses. He was a signer of the Declaration of Independence and in 1776 served as presiding officer of the Delaware Constitutional Convention. In 1776 and again from 1782 to 1788 he was a member of the Delaware Legislative Council, serving at different times as speaker and vice president. He was president of the Continental Congress in 1777–78, acceding to that position when John McKinley was imprisoned by the British.

As a member of the Delaware House of Representatives in 1779 and 1780, Read served in the assembly drafting the act authorizing Delaware congressional delegates to sign the Articles of Confederation. In 1782 he was elected a judge in the Admiralty Court. Two years later he was appointed by New York and Massachusetts as a commissioner to adjust those states' boundary dispute. In 1786 he was a representative to the Annapolis Convention and in 1787 a delegate to the United States Constitutional Convention in Philadelphia.

Read served as a Federalist member of the United States Senate from Delaware from 1789 to 1793 and as chief justice of Delaware from the end of his term as senator until his death. He died in New Castle, Delaware, and was buried in the Immanuel Churchyard there.

RIDGELY, Nicholas: legislator

Born Dover, Delaware, September 30, 1762; son of Dr. Charles Greenberry and Mary (Wynkoop) Ridgely; married Mary Brereton, May 20, 1806; died April 1, 1830.

In 1787 Ridgely was a delegate from Kent County to the Delaware Convention which ratified the United States Constitution. In 1792 he attended the convention which formed the Delaware Constitution. He was a member of the Delaware Legislative Council in 1788, 1789, and 1790. From 1791 to 1801 he was attorney general of Delaware. He was a delegate from Kent County to the Second State Constitutional Convention in 1791–92. He was elected to membership in the first Delaware House of Representatives in 1792; he was reelected in 1796, 1797, 1799, 1800, and 1801. He was chancellor of Delaware from 1802 to 1830.

Ridgely's nonpolitical activities included his serving as deputy of the second session of the convention which met in Philadelphia in 1786 to organize the Protestant Episcopal Church in the United States. Ridgely died in Dover and was buried in the Christ Churchyard there.

RODNEY, Caesar: congressman

Born Dover, Delaware, October 7, 1728; son of Caesar and Elizabeth (Crawford) Rodeney; died June 29, 1784.

From 1755 to 1758 Rodney was high sheriff of Kent County, Delaware. He also served Kent County as register of wills, recorder of deeds, clerk of the Orphans Court, clerk of peace, and justice of the peace.

Rodney was a captain in the Delaware militia in 1756. Two years later he became a judge. In 1759 he was superintendent of printing of Delaware currency. In 1769 he became a co-trustee of the Kent County Loan Office and from 1755 to 1784 was its sole trustee.

In 1769 Rodney was appointed third justice of the Supreme Court for Three Lower Counties, advancing to second justice in

1773. He was elected a Kent County delegate to the Delaware Colonial Legislature in 1758, serving again from 1761 to 1770 and from 1772 to 1776; he was speaker of that body in 1769, 1773, 1774, and 1775. In 1765 he was a representative from Kent County to the Stamp Act Congress. He was also a member of the Committee of Correspondence.

In 1768 Rodney helped draw up an address to the King objecting to the Townshend Act. He was a member of the Continental Congress from 1774 to 1776 and in 1777 and 1778. In 1774 he served as a colonel in the "upper" regiment of the Kent County militia. He later became a brigadier general of the militia and of the western battalion of Sussex County.

In 1775 Rodney was speaker of the regular session of the Delaware House of Assembly and presided over the colonial assembly at New Castle in 1776. He voted for the adoption of the Declaration of Independence in 1776 and was a signer.

Rodney was chairman of the Kent County branch of the Council of Safety in 1776. He recruited Kent County men for the Continental Army and served as brigadier general in command of the Delaware militia when the British invaded Delaware in 1777. That year he became major general of the Delaware militia and judge of admiralty.

From 1778 to 1781 Rodney served as president of Delaware, and he was Delaware's war executive until 1781. Two years later he became a member and speaker of the upper house of the Delaware legislature. He died in Dover and was buried in the Christ Episcopal Churchyard there.

RODNEY, Thomas: Continental congressman, jurist

Born Sussex County, Delaware, June 4, 1744; son of Caesar and Elizabeth (Crawford) Rodeney; married Elizabeth Fisher, April 8, 1771; father of at least three children (including Caesar Augustus); died January 2, 1811.

From 1770 to 1774 Rodney was a justice of the peace in Kent County, Delaware. In 1775 he was a member of the Colonial Assembly of Government of Three Lower Counties (New Castle, Kent, and Sussex), representing Kent County. In that year he was also a member of the Council of Safety and of the Committee of Observation, Kent County. In 1775, too, he organized and became colonel of a volunteer militia.

Rodney was a member of the Delaware Assembly to elect delegates to the Continental Congress in 1774. Four years later he became chief justice of the Kent County Court. In 1779 he was a register of wills, and he served as judge of the Delaware Admiralty Court from 1778 to 1785.

From 1781 to 1783 and again from 1785 to 1787 Rodney served as a member of the Continental Congress. He was a member of the lower house of the Delaware General Assembly in 1786 and 1787, serving as speaker the latter year. He was superintendent of the Kent County Almshouse in 1802 as well as an associate justice for the Delaware Supreme Court. In 1803 he was appointed by President Jefferson a United States judge for the Mississippi Territory, a position in which he served until his death in Natchez.

★★★★★

SYKES, James: Continental congressman, lawyer
Born 1725; died April 4, 1792.

Sykes studied law, was admitted to the bar, and established a legal practice. He served as a lieutenant in Captain Caesar Rodney's Company of the Dover militia in 1756. A member of the Council of Safety in 1776, he participated in the Delaware Constitutional Convention at New Castle in 1776 and 1790 and was a delegate to the Continental Congress from Delaware in 1777 and 1778.

Clerk of the peace from 1777 to 1792, Sykes also served as prothonotary of Kent County from 1777 to 1793. He was a member of the Delaware Council in 1780 and of the Delaware legislature which ratified the United States Constitution, in 1787.

Sykes was a presidential elector in 1792 and voted for Washington and Adams. He served as judge of the High Court of Errors and Appeals of Delaware. He died in Dover and was buried in the Christ Church burial ground.

★★★★★

TILTON, James: congressman, hospital administrator
Born Kent County, Delaware, June 1, 1745; died May 14, 1822.

Tilton received an M.B. degree from the College of Philadelphia (now the University of Pennsylvania) in 1768 and an M.D. in 1771. In 1776 he served as a surgeon in the Delaware Regiment of the Continental Army. From 1777 to 1780 he was in charge of the military hospitals in Princeton and Trenton, New Jersey, and in New Windsor, Maryland. To improve sanitary conditions in the hospitals, he built "hospital huts," each of which housed six patients. In 1780 he was promoted to senior hospital physician and surgeon. He operated the hospital in Williamsburg during the Yorktown campaign.

From 1783 to 1785 Tilton was a member of the Continental Congress and a member of the Delaware House of Representatives. He served as a government commissioner of loans in Delaware from 1785 to 1801.

Tilton was the author of *Economical Observations on Military Hospitals: and the Prevention and Cure of Diseases Incident to an Army,* published in 1813. The next year his *Regulations for the Medical Department* was published. From 1813 to 1815 he was a physician in and surgeon general of the United States Army and made a tour of inspection along the Northern frontier, instituting widespread sanitary reforms.

Tilton died near Wilmington, Delaware,

and was buried in the Wilmington and Brandywine Cemetery.

★★★★★

VAN DYKE, Nicholas: president of Delaware, Continental congressman

Born New Castle, Delaware, September 25, 1738; son of Nicholas and Lytie (Dirks) Van Dyke; married Elizabeth Nixon; second marriage to Charlotte Standly; father of at least one son (Nicholas); died February 19, 1789.

Van Dyke was admitted to the bar of the Pennsylvania Supreme Court in 1765. In addition to serving on the Delaware Provincial Committee of Correspondence, he was a member of the Delaware committee to solicit funds for the relief of the people of Boston in 1774. In 1776 he became a member of the New Castle Council of Safety and participated in formulating the rules for the Delaware Constitutional Convention. At the convention he served on the committee charged with provisioning the state's troops, assisted in preparing the declaration of rights, and wrote the preliminary draft of the Delaware Constitution.

In 1777 Van Dyke accepted an appointment as a judge in the Court of Admiralty and began a period of service in the Continental Congress which was to last until 1782. He was one of the signers of the Articles of Confederation. From 1783 to 1786 he was president of the state of Delaware. He also served on the Delaware Council in 1786. Three years later he died in New Castle County, Delaware, and was buried in Immanuel Churchyard in New Castle.

VINING, John: senator, congressman

Born Dover, Kent County, Delaware, December 23, 1758; died February 1802.

After studying law and being admitted to the bar in 1782, Vining began a legal practice in New Castle County. He represented Delaware in the Continental Congress during the years 1784 through 1786 and was a member of the Maryland House of Representatives in 1787 and 1788. He was a delegate from Delaware to the United States House of Representatives during the 1st and 2nd congresses (1789–93). In 1793, after serving for a short time in the Delaware Senate, he became a United States Senator, serving until his resignation on January 19, 1798.

Vining died in Dover and was buried in the Episcopal Cemetery.

★★★★★★★★★★★★★★

GEORGIA

"His Excellency and council, Colonel Lachlan McIntosh, and other gentlemen, with the militia, dined under the cedar trees, and cheerfully drank to the UNITED, FREE, AND INDEPENDENT States of America."
—CONNECTICUT GAZETTE AND UNIVERSAL INTELLIGENCER and PENNSYLVANIA EVENING POST, October 8, 1776

BALDWIN, Abraham: senator, university president

Born North Gilford, Connecticut, November 22, 1754; son of Michael and Lucy (Dudley) Baldwin; died March 4, 1807.

Baldwin was a 1772 Yale graduate and a licensed minister. After tutoring at Yale from 1775 until 1779, he served as chaplain to the 2nd Connecticut Brigade of the Continental Army during the years 1779–83. He was admitted to the bar in Fairfield County, Connecticut, in 1783 and to the Georgia bar a year later.

After representing Wilkes County in the Georgia House of Assembly in 1785, Baldwin was a delegate to the Continental Congress during 1785–88 and participated in the United States Constitutional Convention in 1787. He went as a Federalist from Georgia to the first five congresses of the United States House of Representatives (1789–99) and to the United States Senate during the period from 1799 to 1807. In 1801 he was elected president pro tem of the Senate, and the following year he became United States Commissioner charged with negotiating the cession of Georgia lands to the United States Government.

Baldwin was a founder of the University of Georgia in 1785 and its first president, serving from 1786 until 1800. In that year he assumed the presidency of the board of trustees and remained in this capacity until 1807. He was an original member of the Connecticut branch of the Society of the Cincinnati. Counties in Georgia and Alabama are named for him. He died in Washington, D.C., and was buried in Rock Creek Cemetery there.

BARNETT, William: congressman, physician

Born Amherst County, Virginia, March 4, 1761; died October 25, 1834.

Barnett studied medicine in Virginia, then moved with his father to Georgia. Returning to Virginia at the outbreak of the Revolutionary War, he joined the military company from Amherst County which was under the command of the Marquis de Lafayette. He was present at the surrender of Cornwallis at Yorktown.

At the end of the war Barnett returned to

Georgia and settled on the Broad River in Elbert County, where he practiced medicine. In 1780 he became county sheriff. After a period in the Georgia Senate, serving briefly as president, he represented Georgia as a States' Rights Democrat in the United States House of Representatives. His term began on October 5, 1812, when he filled a vacant seat, and lasted until 1815.

After his tenure in Congress, Barnett was appointed commissioner to establish the boundaries of the Creek Indian Reservation. He later moved to Montgomery County, Alabama, where he died at the age of seventy-three. He was buried in Smyrna Churchyard near Washington, Wilkes County, Georgia.

BROWNE, Thomas: army officer, Loyalist
No record of birth; died August 3, 1825.

After he was tarred and feathered because of his strong Loyalist views, desire for vengeance guided Browne's war career. In 1776 he began raiding patriot positions and the next year he aided the British attack on Fort McIntosh, Georgia. He formed a regiment called the King's Rangers in 1778 and became a lieutenant colonel.

Known for his sadism and brutality, Browne led numerous raids during 1778–80; he was occasionally repulsed but never defeated. He held Augusta, Georgia, irregularly during 1780–81. In 1781 he was captured with three hundred of his men; after his exchange he engaged in his last conflict in 1782.

Browne's estates in South Carolina and Georgia were confiscated after the war. He lived in the Bahamas from 1783 to 1809, when he moved to land granted him by the British government on St. Vincent in the British West Indies. He lived there until his death sixteen years later.

BROWNSON, Nathan: governor of Georgia, Continental congressman
Born Woodbury, Connecticut, May 14, 1742; died November 6, 1796.

After graduating from Yale in 1761 and studying medicine, Brownson established a medical practice in Woodbury. He moved to Liberty County, Georgia, circa 1764. Around the time of the Revolution he was a member of the Provincial Congress (1775), a military surgeon, and a Georgia delegate to the Continental Congress (1776–78).

Brownson served as a member and then as speaker of the Georgia House of Representatives (1781 and 1788) and became governor of the state in 1782. He participated in the Georgia Convention which ratified the United States Constitution in 1788 and attended the Georgia Constitutional Convention the next year. From 1789 to 1791 he was a member of the state senate, also serving as president.

Brownson died on his plantation near Riceboro, Georgia, and was buried in the Old Midway Burial Ground.

★★★★★

CARNES, Thomas Petters: congressman
Born Maryland, 1762; died May 5, 1822.

After studying law and being admitted to the bar, Carnes began practice in Milledgeville, Georgia. He was a member of the Georgia House of Representatives for several terms: 1786–87, 1789, 1797, 1807–08. He was solicitor general for the Western Circuit of Georgia, and from 1789 to 1792 was attorney general of the state of Georgia. He served as a member of the United States House of Representatives, 3rd Congress, from Georgia, from 1793 to 1795. In 1798 he was a delegate to the Georgia Constitutional Convention. That same year he became judge of the Western Circuit Court of Georgia, serving for five years. In 1806 he was a member of the commission established to settle boundary disputes between Georgia and North Carolina. He again served as judge of the Western Circuit Court from 1809 to 1810.

Carnes died on his farm in Franklin (now

Hart) County, Georgia. He was buried on his estate.

CLARK, John: governor of Georgia

Born Edgecombe County, North Carolina, February 28, 1766; son of General Elijah Clarke; married Nancy Williamson, 1787; died October 12, 1832.

At the age of twenty-one, Clark was commissioned a major in the Georgia militia. In 1792 he was commissioned a captain in the Continental Army, and in 1811 he became a major general in the Georgia militia. After the Revolution, he received a generous grant of bounty lands.

A presidential elector in 1816, Clark was governor of Georgia from 1819 to 1823. He was appointed Indian agent in Florida in 1827. He died of yellow fever at St. Andrew's Bay, Florida.

CLARKE, Elijah: army officer

Born Edgecombe County, North Carolina, 1733; married Hannah Arrington; father of at least one son (John Clark); died January 15, 1799.

Clarke started his military career when commissioned a captain in the Georgia militia in 1776; he later became a colonel and, in 1781, a brigadier general. During the Revolutionary War he served at the battles of Kettle Creek, Musgrove's Mill, and Beattie's Mill, and saw action during both sieges of Augusta, Georgia. For his distinguished military service, Clarke was given an estate in Wilkes County by the state of Georgia. Later, in 1787, he participated in a battle with Indians at Jack's Creek.

In 1793 Clarke was commissioned a major general in the French Army and became involved with the French minister Edmond Genet in a scheme to seize the Spanish lands in America. The plan failed, however, when Genet was recalled. The following year Clarke attempted to set up a state in Creek Indian territory. He established several forts, but he was forced by the Georgia militia to give up the venture.

Clarke died in Wilkes County, Georgia.

CLAY, Joseph: merchant, Continental congressman

Born Yorkshire, England, October 16, 1741; son of Ralph and Elizabeth (Habersham) Clay; married Ann Legardere, January 2, 1763; died November 15, 1804.

A rice planter and merchant, Clay was associated at various times with the Joseph Clay Company, Seth John Cuthbert and Company, and Clay, Talfair and Company; he was also a partner in William Fox and Company. A member of the Georgia Revolutionary Committee in 1774, he participated in the seizure of six hundred pounds of powder from the King's magazine in Savannah, Georgia. The following year he was a member of the Provisional Congress and two years later served as paymaster general of the Southern Department of the Continental Army. A member of the Continental Congress from 1778 to 1780, he was one of twenty-five rebel leaders who were indicted for treason by the Royalist Assembly in 1780.

Like his son Joseph, Clay was active in the affairs of the state of Georgia, serving in 1782 as state treasurer. He was a member of the board created by the Georgia Assembly to establish an institution of higher education, thus becoming a founder of the University of Georgia, the first state university chartered in America.

Clay died in Savannah, Georgia, and was buried in the Colonial Park Cemetery, Savannah.

CLAY, Joseph: jurist, clergyman

Born Savannah, Georgia, August 16, 1764; son of Joseph and Ann (Legardere) Clay; married Mary Savage, November 25, 1789; died January 11, 1811.

Six years after graduating from Princeton in 1784, Clay was admitted to the Georgia bar. He was an influential member of the Convention of 1795, which revised the Georgia Constitution. In 1796 he was appointed a United States district judge for

Georgia and in 1801 became the United States judge for the 5th Circuit Court of Georgia; however, he was legislated out of office in 1802.

Ordained to the ministry of the Baptist Church in 1804, Clay served as a member of the general committee of the Georgia Baptist Association. He left Georgia in 1807 to assume the position of pastor of the First Baptist Church of Boston.

Clay died in Boston and was buried in the Old Granary Burying Ground there.

★★★★★

DE BRAHM, William Gerard: geographer
Born 1717; no record of first marriage; second marriage to Mary (Drayton) Fenwick, February 18, 1776; father of at least one child; died 1799.

De Brahm came to America in 1751 and founded the town of Bethany, Georgia. He was surveyor of Georgia from 1754 to 1764. He planned the towns of Ebenezer and Fort George, Georgia, in 1757 and 1761, respectively, and supervised the construction of the fortifications in Charleston, South Carolina, 1755, and Savannah, Georgia, 1762. In 1757, he drew the first map of Georgia and South Carolina. From 1764 to 1770 he was surveyor general for the Southern District. In 1765 he was commissioned to mark the northern boundary line of New Jersey. He drew a map of the Atlantic Ocean in 1772.

De Brahm was the author of *The Atlantic Pilot,* 1772; *The Levelling Balance and Counter-Balance,* 1774; *De Brahm's Zonical Tables for the Twenty-Five Northern and Southern Climates,* 1774; *Time, an Apparition of Eternity,* 1791; *Apocalyptic Gnomon Points Out Eternity's Divisibility,* 1795. He died at the age of eighty-two.

★★★★★

ELBERT, Samuel: governor of Georgia
Born Prince William Parish, South Carolina, 1743; married Elizabeth Rae; father of six children; died November 1, 1788.

Elbert was commissioned a captain of a grenadier company of the Georgia militia and was a member of the Georgia Council of Safety in 1774. Two years later he was promoted to lieutenant colonel, then to colonel. In 1783 he was brevetted a brigadier general.

Elbert was governor of Georgia in 1785–86. He also held office as sheriff of Chatham County, vice president of the Georgia Society of the Cincinnati, and grand master of the Georgia Masonic Order. He died in Savannah, Georgia.

★★★★★

FEW, William: Continental congressman, senator, banker
Born Baltimore, Maryland, June 8, 1748; son of William and Mary (Wheeler) Few; married Catherine Nicholson; father of three children; died July 16, 1828.

Few was involved in a wide variety of government and private enterprises both in the state of Georgia and in New York City. He was a member of the Georgia General Assembly in 1776 and 1783 and a member of the Executive Council of Georgia in 1776. Two years later he was surveyor general of Georgia. A lieutenant colonel in the Continental Army, he was a commissioner to the Indians during the Revolutionary War.

Few was a member of the Continental Congress (1780–1782 and 1785–1788) and a representative from Georgia to the drafting sessions of the United States Constitution, which he signed in 1787. He was a member of the United States Senate, representing Georgia, from 1789 to 1793, then spent the next four years as judge of the Second United States Judicial Circuit of Georgia.

In 1799 Few moved to New York City, where he was a member of the New York General Assembly from 1802 to 1805. He was an inspector of New York prisons, an alderman of New York City, director of the Manhattan Bank from 1804 to 1814, and president of the City Bank of New York. He died in Fishkill-on-the-Hudson, New York, at the age of eighty.

★★★★★

GIBBONS, William: Continental congressman

Born Bear Bluff, South Carolina, April 8, 1726; died September 27, 1800.

Gibbons belonged to the Georgia bar. A leader in the opposition to the Crown, he was a member of the Sons of Liberty in 1774 and of the party which broke into the King's powder magazine in Savannah in 1775. In the same year he was active in the Georgia Provincial Congress and on the state Committee of Safety. From 1777 to 1781 he served on the executive council which the Georgia Provincial Congress had created. He then served several terms in the Georgia House of Representatives—in 1783, 1785–89 (acting as speaker in 1786 and 1787), and 1791–93. He was a delegate to the Continental Congress from 1784 to 1786.

Gibbons also served as an associate justice in the Chatham County (Georgia) Court. In 1789 he presided over the state constitutional convention. He was a leading rice planter in the region. He died in Savannah.

GRAHAM, John: colonial official

Born Scotland, 1718; married Frances Crooke, 1755; father of four sons; died November 1795.

In 1753 Graham came to Georgia and became a merchant in Savannah, remaining in that occupation until 1765, when he turned to planting. He joined the Georgia Governor's Council in 1763, where he stayed until 1776. In 1775 he opposed the sending of delegates to the Continental Congress. He became lieutenant governor of the colony of Georgia in 1776 but fled to England later that year. He returned in 1779.

Graham accepted an appointment in 1782 as superintendent of Indian Affairs for the Mississippi region, with headquarters in Charleston, South Carolina. The same year, when the British evacuated Charleston, he moved to Florida and then returned to England. He became a merchant in London and died in Naples, Italy, thirteen years later.

GUNN, James: senator

Born Virginia, March 13, 1753; died July 30, 1801.

After attending common schools and studying law, Gunn was admitted to the bar and began a law practice in Savannah, Georgia. He served in the Revolutionary War and was captain of the dragoons defending Savannah in 1782. After a period as colonel in the 1st Regiment of the Chatham County militia, he was promoted to brigadier general in the Georgia militia.

Gunn was elected to the Continental Congress in 1787 but did not serve. He was a member of the United States Senate from Georgia from 1789 until 1801. He died that year in Louisville, Georgia, and was buried in Old Capitol Cemetery there.

GWINNETT, Button: Continental congressman

Born Down Halherley, England, circa 1735; son of Samuel and Anne (Emes) Gwinnett; married Ann Bourne, April 19, 1757; died May 16, 1777.

In 1765 Gwinnett became a planter on St. Catherine Island off the coast of Georgia. He was justice of the peace in 1767 and 1768 and a member of the Georgia Colonial Assembly in 1769. In 1776, while attending the Continental Congress, he signed the Declaration of Independence. Later in 1776 he began a one-year term as speaker of the Georgia Assembly, during which time he played an important part in the drafting of the first Georgia Constitution.

Gwinnett became president of the state of Georgia as well as commander-in-chief of the state militia in 1777. His activities in the latter capacity were investigated after the militia made an unsuccessful expedition against the British in Florida, but he was cleared of charges of negligence. He died as a result of wounds suffered in a duel with his chief political opponent, Lachlan McIntosh, which took place near Savannah, Georgia.

★★★★★

HABERSHAM, James: merchant, planter, colonial governor

Born Beverley, England, January 1713; son of James Habersham; married Mary Bolton, December 26, 1740; father of ten children; died August 28, 1775.

Habersham, who came to Savannah, Georgia, at the age of twenty-five, organized the firm of Harris and Habersham in 1744; he raised the first cotton in the colony and advocated the introduction of slavery. He was appointed councilor and secretary of the Province of Georgia in 1754. From 1767 to 1771 he was president of the upper house of the Georgia General Assembly. He was the acting governor of Georgia from 1771 to 1773, during which time he dissolved the assembly because of its refusal to approve his choice of speaker.

Among Habersham's philanthropic activities was his establishing the Bethesda Orphanage. Unlike his sons John and Joseph, he allied himself with the Loyalists during the Revolutionary period. He died in New Brunswick, New Jersey, and was buried in Savannah, Georgia.

HABERSHAM, John: Continental congressman

Born at the estate "Beverly," near Savannah, Georgia, December 23, 1754; son of James and Mary (Bolton) Habersham; died December 17, 1799.

Habersham, after attending the College of New Jersey (now Princeton), engaged as a merchant. He was a first lieutenant and then a brigade major in the 1st Georgia Regiment of the Continental Army during the Revolutionary War; he was taken prisoner twice.

A Georgia delegate to the Continental Congress in 1785 and 1786, Habersham was appointed as Indian agent by General Washington. He was also commissioner to the Beaufort Convention to adjust the Georgia–South Carolina boundary. He was a member of the first board of trustees of the University of Georgia and the first secretary of the Georgia branch of the Society of the Cincinnati. From 1789 to 1799 he was col-

lector of customs for the Port of Savannah.

Habersham died near Savannah and was buried in Colonial Park Cemetery there.

HABERSHAM, Joseph: patriot, postmaster general, mayor

Born Savannah, Georgia, July 28, 1751; son of James and Mary (Bolton) Habersham; married Isabella Rae, May 1776; father of ten children; died November 17, 1815.

Habersham, after receiving his education at the College of New Jersey (now Princeton), was an organizer of the firm of Joseph Clay and Company at the age of twenty-two. In 1773, while a member of the Georgia Council of Safety, he raised a body of volunteers which captured Sir James Wright, the Georgia governor, and held him under guard in his own home for a month. Habersham later became colonel in the 1st Georgia Battalion of the Continental Army.

Habersham became a member of the Georgia Provincial Congress in Savannah on July 4, 1775. He was a member of the Continental Congress in 1785 and 1786. He was speaker of the Georgia General Assembly from 1785 to 1790 and also attended the Georgia Convention of 1788, which ratified the United States Constitution. He was mayor of Savannah in 1792.

Habersham held the position of postmaster general of the United States under presidents Washington, Adams, and Jefferson, serving from 1795 to 1801. From 1802 to 1815, he was president of a branch of the Bank of the United States. He died in Savannah.

HALL, Bolling: congressman

Born Dinwiddie County, Virginia, December 25, 1767; died February 25, 1836.

Hall, who fought in the Revolutionary War, moved to Hancock County, Georgia, in 1792, and later served two terms in the Georgia House of Representatives (1800–02 and 1804–06). A War Democrat, he was a member of the United States House of Representatives from 1811 to 1817.

Hall became engaged in planting near

Montgomery, Alabama, in 1808. In 1824 he was chairman of the reception committee to welcome General Lafayette. He died at the estate "Ellerslie," in Autauga (now Elmore) County, Alabama, and was buried there.

HALL, Lyman: statesman, signer of the Declaration of Independence, governor of Georgia

Born Wallingford, Connecticut, April 12, 1724; son of John and Mary (Street) Hall; married Abigail Burr, May 20, 1752; second marriage to Mary Osborn; father of one son; died October 19, 1790.

A graduate of Yale, Hall was ordained to the ministry in 1749; he was dismissed from his pulpit in 1751 but was later reinstated. For the next two years he filled various vacant pulpits, and then abandoned the ministry for the study of medicine. In 1756 he moved to Georgia as part of a South Carolina colony.

In 1775 Hall became a member of the Provincial Congress of Georgia, took part in colonizing the Midway District of Georgia, and was a delegate to the Continental Congress. He was a signer of the Declaration of Independence. As governor of Georgia in 1783, he was one of the early advocates of setting aside public land for the purposes of higher education. He died in Burke County, Georgia.

HAMMOND, Samuel: army officer, congressman

Born Richmond County, Virginia, September 21, 1757; son of Charles and Elizabeth (Steele) Hammond; married Rebecca (Elbert) Rae, 1783; second marriage to Eliza A. O'Keefe, May 25, 1807; died September 11, 1842.

At the age of seventeen Hammond served as a volunteer during Lord Dunmore's War, and the following year he was commissioned a captain in the Virginia Volunteers. In 1779 he was commissioned a captain in the Continental Army and, in 1780, a major in LeRoy Hammond's Regiment. A participant in the battles of King's Mountain, Cowpens, Eutaw, and others in South Carolina and Georgia, he was commissioned a lieutenant colonel at the end of the Revolutionary War.

After a period in the Georgia legislature, representing Chatham County, Hammond saw military service once again, against the Creek Indians in 1793. He then returned to serve Chatham County as surveyor general. He attended the 8th Congress of the United States House of Representatives, as a delegate from Georgia, from 1803 to 1805. He was a colonel and the military and civil commandant of the northern part of the District of Louisiana from 1804 to 1806. He was a judge in the Court of Pleas for the District of Louisiana in 1811 and president of the Territorial Council of Missouri in 1813. Surveyor general of South Carolina in 1827, he was the secretary of the State of Louisiana from 1831 to 1835.

Hammond died in Hamburg, South Carolina, ten days before his eighty-fifth birthday.

HOUSTOUN, John: governor of Georgia, Continental congressman

Born near Waynesboro, Georgia, August 31, 1744; son of Sir Patrick Houstoun; married Miss Bryan; died July 20, 1796.

After organizing the First Georgia Provincial Congress in 1775, Houstoun became a delegate to the Continental Congress, where he served until 1776. From 1778 to 1784 he was governor of Georgia; in 1786, chief justice of the state; and in 1787, a commissioner to settle the boundary dispute between Georgia and South Carolina. The latter year he served as justice of Chatham County, Georgia.

In 1789 and 1790 Houstoun was mayor of Savannah, Georgia and, in 1792, judge of the Superior Court of the Eastern Circuit of Georgia. He died in White Bluff, near Savannah.

HOUSTOUN, William: Continental congressman

Born Savannah, Georgia, 1755; died March 17, 1813.

Houstoun attended higher schools in England, where he studied law. He was admitted to Inner Temple in London at the age of twenty-one.

A participant in Revolutionary activities, Houstoun was a member of the Continental Congress, from Georgia, from 1784 to 1787. In 1785 he was an agent from Georgia to settle the boundary dispute with South Carolina. A delegate to the United States Constitutional Convention in Philadelphia in 1787, he declined to sign the Constitution.

Houstoun was an original trustee of the University of Georgia. He died in Savannah and was buried in St. Paul's Churchyard in New York City.

HOWLEY, Richard: colonial governor, Continental congressman
Born Liberty County, Georgia, 1740; died December 1784.

After serving in the Georgia legislature in 1779, Howley was elected by the legislature to the office of governor of Georgia in 1780. That year and the next he was also a member of the Continental Congress. In 1781 he co-authored a pamphlet titled "Observations upon the Effects of Certain Late Political Suggestions by the Delegates of Georgia." He was chief justice of Georgia in 1782. He died in Savannah, Georgia.

★★★★★

JACKSON, James: senator, governor of Georgia
Born Moreton-Hampstead, England, September 21, 1757; son of James and Mary (Webber) Jackson; married Mary Young; father of five children; died March 19, 1806.

Having come to America in 1772, Jackson participated in the first Georgia Constitutional Convention in 1777. He received a commission as lieutenant colonel in the Continental Army in 1782, was commissioned a colonel in the Chatham County (Georgia) militia in 1784, and rose to brigadier general two years later.

Jackson was a delegate to the United States House of Representatives during the 1st Congress (1789–91), was a United States Senator from 1793 to 1795, and served as governor of Georgia—a post he had declined in 1788—from 1798 to 1801. After his term as governor, Jackson returned to the United States Senate and served until his death. He was buried in the Congressional Cemetery in Washington, D.C.

JONES, George: senator, mayor
Born Savannah, Georgia, February 25, 1766; son of Noble Wymberley Jones; died November 13, 1838.

Jones, like his father a physician by profession, was imprisoned on an English ship in 1780 and 1781 during his participation in the American Revolution. As well as serving in both houses of the Georgia legislature, in 1793–94 and again in 1802–03 he was a member of the Savannah board of aldermen. In 1804 he became judge of the Eastern Judicial Circuit of Georgia and held this position until 1807.

Jones served very briefly in the United States Senate, from August 27 to November 7, 1807. During the War of 1812 he was captain of a company of Savannah reserves. From 1812 to 1814 he was mayor of Savannah; in 1814 he returned to the board of aldermen, serving for about a year.

Jones died in Savannah and was buried in Bonaventure Cemetery there.

JONES, James: congressman
Born Maryland; died January 11, 1801.

After attending an academy in Augusta, Georgia, and studying law, Jones was admitted to the Georgia bar and began a law practice in Savannah. In 1790 he became a first lieutenant in the East Company of the Chatham County Regiment of the state militia.

Jones served in the Georgia House of Representatives from 1796 to 1798 and was a delegate to the state constitutional convention in 1798. A Republican, he was elected to the United States House of Representatives during the 6th Congress (1799–1801). He died in Washington, D.C., and was buried in the Congressional Cemetery.

JONES, Noble Wymberley: physician, Continental congressman
Born near London, England, circa 1724; son of Noble Jones; married Sarah Davis; father of six children (including George); died January 9, 1805.

Jones practiced medicine in Savannah, Georgia, from 1748 to 1756. He served in Oglethorpe's regiment, rising from cadet to first lieutenant. He was a member of the Georgia Commons House of Assembly for nineteen years (1755–74) and was speaker in the years 1768–69. He participated in the Continental Congress during 1775–76 and again from 1781 to 1783.

In addition to serving on the Georgia Council of Safety and in various other provincial congresses, Jones was a member and speaker of the state assembly in 1782. In 1795 he presided over the state constitutional convention. He also was president of the Georgia Medical Society.

Jones died in Savannah and was buried in Bonaventure Cemetery there.

★★★★★

LANGWORTHY, Edward: Continental congressman
Born Savannah, Georgia, 1738; an orphan; died November 2, 1802.

In 1775 Langworthy organized the Georgia Council of Safety and served as its first secretary. From 1777 to 1779 he was a delegate from Georgia to the Continental Congress. He was a signer of the Articles of Confederation.

After moving to Maryland in 1785, Langworthy, in association with William Goddard, issued the *Maryland Journal* and the *Baltimore Advertiser* in 1785–86. For the next four years he was a teacher of the classics at the Baltimore Academy.

In 1791 Langworthy began work on the first attempted history of Georgia. He wrote *Memoirs of the Life of the Late Charles Lee* in 1792.

During the last seven years of his life he served as clerk of customs in Baltimore.

LONGSTREET, William: inventor
Born Allentown, New Jersey, October 6, 1759; son of Stoffel and Abigail (Wooley) Longstreet; married Hannah Randolph, 1783; father of at least six children; died September 11, 1814.

At an early age Longstreet was interested in mechanical instruments. He moved to Augusta, Georgia, in 1783 and began to work seriously on steam engines. Five years later he was given a patent by the Georgia legislature on a steam engine he had constructed. He invented and patented the "breast-roller" of cotton gins before 1801. He designed a portable sawmill and built a small steamboat which ran on the Savannah River in Georgia in 1806. He died in Augusta.

★★★★★

McGILLIVRAY, Alexander: Indian chief
Born 1759; son of Lachlan and Schoy (Marchand) McGillivray; children include Alexander and Elizabeth; died February 17, 1793.

Chief of the Upper Creek Indian tribe, McGillivray acted as a British agent among the Southern Indians during the Revolution. He was connected with the Loyalist trading firm of Panton, Leslie and Co., and as a result of his Loyalist activities his property was confiscated by the state of Georgia.

After 1784 McGillivray aligned himself with Spain in an attempt to separate the area west of the Alleghenies from the United States, and he made constant raids on American frontier settlements between 1786 and 1790. Appointed Spanish commissary to enforce Spain's monopoly of trade with the Creeks in 1784, he then signed the Treaty of New York with the United States (by which the Creeks were given large areas of land) in 1790. His property in Georgia was returned and he was appointed a brigadier general in the United States Army.

Two years later, McGillivray, along with Francisco Carondelet, the Spanish governor of Florida, signed a convention which repudiated the Treaty of New York and reaffirmed McGillivray's allegiance to Spain. He began making plans for a unified effort on the part of all Southern Indians to drive out the Americans, but he died in Pensacola before the plans could be completed.

McINTOSH, Lachlan: army officer, Continental congressman

Born Raits in Badenoch, Scotland, March 17, 1725; son of John Mohr and Marjory (Fraser) McIntosh; married Sarah Threadcraft; died February 20, 1806.

McIntosh arrived in America in 1736. He was a member of the Provincial Congress of Georgia from the Parish of St. Andrew in 1775 and was a colonel of a battalion of the Georgia militia in 1776. In command of the Western Department in 1778, he also commanded the 1st and 5th South Carolina regiments in the attack on Savannah, Georgia, in 1779. He was brevetted a major general in 1783.

A delegate to the Continental Congress in 1784, McIntosh never attended its sessions. He was twice appointed a commissioner to reconcile the boundary dispute between Georgia and South Carolina, and in 1785 Congress appointed him a commissioner to deal with the Southern Indians.

A charter member of the Georgia branch of the Society of the Cincinnati (1784), McIntosh died in Savannah and was buried in the Colonial Cemetery there.

MARSHALL, Daniel: clergyman

Born Windsor, Connecticut, 1706; son of Thomas and Mary (Drake) Marshall; married Hannah Drake, November 11, 1742; second marriage to Martha Stearns, June 23, 1747; father of three children; died November 2, 1784.

Marshall was converted by George Whitefield in 1744 and served as preacher to the Mohawk Indians in the upper Susquehanna River region in 1747 and 1748. He preached in the Baptist section in northern Virginia in 1748 and to the Separate Baptists, Sandy Creek Church, in Guilford County, North Carolina, in 1775. He was ordained pastor of Abbot's Creek (North Carolina) Separate Baptist Church in 1758.

Marshall became pastor of the Separate Baptist Church near the Georgia line in South Carolina about 1763 and founded the first Baptist Church in Georgia, near Kiokee Creek, in 1772. He was an organizer of the Georgia Association of Baptists in 1784, the year of his death.

MATHEWS, George: governor of Georgia, army officer

Born Augusta County, Georgia, September 10, 1739; son of John Mathews; married Miss Woods; second marriage to Mrs. Reed; third marriage to Mrs. Flowers; father of six children; died August 30, 1812.

Mathews commanded a company of Georgia volunteers against the Indians in 1757 and later served in the Battle of Point Pleasant, October 10, 1774. He was a colonel in the 9th Virginia Regiment at the battles of Brandywine and Germantown during the Revolution. He later was wounded and captured but was exchanged in 1781. He then joined General Nathanael Greene as a colonel of the 3rd Virginia Regiment. After the war he became a farmer in Oglethorpe County, Georgia, and was named a brigadier general in the Georgia Volunteers that year.

Mathews was elected governor of Georgia in 1787 and again in 1793. He served in the United States House of Representatives from Georgia during the 1st Congress, from 1789 to 1791. He was employed by the United States Government on the recommendation of William H. Crawford to persuade the Spanish governor of West Florida to turn over his province to the United States in 1810, but he failed. A brigadier general in the Georgia militia on an expedition to capture West Florida in 1811, he captured Fernandina, Florida, in 1812.

Mathews died in Augusta, Georgia, and was buried in St. Paul's Churchyard there.

MERIWETHER, David: congressman

Born Clover Field, near Charlottesville, Virginia, April 10, 1755; father of at least one child (James); died November 16, 1822.

A lieutenant during the Revolution, Meriwether served with the Virginia troops at the siege of Savannah, Georgia; after the war, in 1785, he settled in Wilkes County, Georgia. He was commissioned a brigadier general in the Georgia militia in 1797.

A member of the Georgia House of Representatives, Meriwether served as speaker from 1797 to 1800. He was elected to the United States House of Representatives as a Democrat for the 7th–9th congresses, from December 6, 1802, to 1807. He was appointed commissioner to the Creek Indians in 1804 and served as a Democratic presidential elector in 1816 and 1820. He died near Athens, Georgia, and was buried on his plantation.

MILLEDGE, John: senator, governor of Georgia

Born Savannah, Georgia, 1757; son of Captain John and Mrs. Milledge (maiden name Robe); married Martha Galphin; second marriage to Ann Lamar; father of four children; died February 9, 1818.

Milledge served with the Continental Army in the defense of Savannah, the siege of Atlanta, and the assault to retake Savannah during the Revolution. He became attorney general of Georgia in 1780 and later was a member of the Georgia General Assembly. He was elected to the United States House of Representatives from Georgia for the 3rd–5th and the 7th congresses (1793–99 and 1801–02).

Milledge was a member of a committee established to choose the site for the University of Georgia in 1800; the site chosen was outside of the state grant, so Milledge bought it for $400,000 and gave it to the University. He was governor of Georgia from 1802 to 1806; upon completion of his term, he was sent to the United States Senate, in which he served until 1809. He served as president pro tem the latter year.

Milledgeville, the capital of Georgia from 1805 to 1868, was named for him, as were streets in Athens and Augusta. There is also a Milledge Chair of Ancient Languages at the University of Georgia. He is buried in Summerville Cemetery in Augusta.

MITCHELL, David Brydie: governor of Georgia, Indian agent

Born Muthill, Perthshire, Scotland, October 22, 1766; son of John Mitchell; died April 22, 1837.

Mitchell arrived in Savannah, Georgia, in 1783 and was later (1795) elected attorney general of Georgia. He was a member of the Georgia House of Representatives in 1796 and was commissioned a major general in the Georgia militia in 1804. He served as governor of Georgia from 1809 to 1813 and again from 1815 to 1817. A liberal supporter of internal improvements, education, road building, and especially frontier defense, he also signed the first Georgia law illegalizing dueling.

Mitchell was appointed United States Indian agent to the Creek Nation in 1817 and concluded a treaty in which the Creeks ceded 1,500,000 acres of land to Georgia in 1818. His commission as agent was terminated after he was charged with smuggling African slaves into the vicinity in 1821 (the charge was upheld by President Monroe).

Mitchell died in Milledgeville, Georgia.

★★★★★

PANTON, William: trader

Born Aberdeenshire, Scotland, 1742; son of John and Barbara (Wenys) Panton; never married; died February 26, 1801.

Panton came to America circa 1770 and became a member of the merchant firm Moore and Panton in Savannah, Georgia. In 1775 he established the firm of Panton, Forbes, and Company for trade with the Creek Indians in East Florida. In 1784 he left the firm to head Panton, Leslie, and Company, a firm that held exclusive charter from

Spain for trade with the Indians in West Florida until 1801.

Through the many trading posts that he established, Panton dealt with Choctaw, Creek, Cherokee, and Chickasaw Indians. He died at sea and was buried at Great Harbours in the Berry Islands.

PIERCE, William Leigh: army officer, Continental congressman
Born Georgia, 1740; married Charlotte Fenwick circa 1783; father of two sons (including William Leigh); died December 10, 1789.

During the Revolutionary War, Pierce served in the Continental Army as aide-de-camp to General Nathanael Greene. Congress presented him with a sword for his conduct at the Battle of Eutaw Springs.

In 1783 Pierce left the army as a brevetted major and became head of the merchant house William Pierce and Company. He was a member of the Georgia House of Representatives in 1786. He served concurrently as a member of the Continental Congress and the United States Constitutional Convention of 1787, where he wrote notes on the proceedings.

Pierce was an original member and vice president of the Society of the Cincinnati and a trustee of the Chatham County Academy. He died in Savannah at the age of forty-nine.

★★★★★

TALIAFERRO, Benjamin: congressman
Born Virginia, 1750; died September 3, 1821.

Taliaferro received his preparatory education in Virginia schools. During the Revolutionary War he was a lieutenant in the Continental Army, serving in the rifle corps commanded by General Morgan. In 1780, after being promoted to captain, he was captured by the British at Charleston.

After the war, Taliaferro settled in Georgia, where he was elected to the state senate, serving for a time as its president. In 1798 he served as a delegate to the Georgia Constitutional Convention. He was elected to the United States Congress as a representative from Georgia in 1799, a position he held until his resignation in 1802. He went on to serve as a Superior Court Judge in Georgia and, later, as a trustee of Georgia University.

Taliaferro died in Wilkes County, Georgia, in 1821.

TATTNALL, Josiah: senator, governor of Georgia
Born Bonaventure (near Savannah), Georgia, 1764; died June 6, 1803.

Tattnall, who attended Eton College in England, served under General Anthony Wayne in the Continental Army in 1782. He later became colonel of a regiment of the Georgia militia, which was organized to protect the state against Indians, and in 1801 was promoted to brigadier general.

Tattnall served as a member of the Georgia House of Representatives from 1795 to 1796. Filling a vacancy, he became a United States Senator from Georgia in 1796, serving until 1799. He was elected governor of Georgia in 1801 but resigned the following year.

Tattnall died in Nassau, New Providence, British West Indies, and was buried in Bonaventure Cemetery in Savannah.

★★★★★

WALTON, George: senator, governor of Georgia
Born Farmville, Virginia, 1741; son of Robert and Sally (or Mary) (Hughes) Walton; married Dorothy Camber, 1775; father of two children; died February 2, 1804.

Admitted to the Georgia bar in 1774, Walton was a signer of the Declaration of Independence and played an active role in events leading to the Revolution and during the war itself. In 1775 he was a member of the Committee on Resolutions, the Committee of Correspondence, and Liberty Pole, a group that called for and organized the Georgia Provincial Congress. In addition he acted as secretary to committees of intelligence, helped draw up articles of association, and wrote addresses to the people and the King. He was president of the Georgia Council of Safety.

Walton was a delegate to the Continental Congress in 1776–77 and 1780–81, serving on committees on the Western lands, the treasury board, Indian affairs, and the executive committee in charge of federal affairs in Philadelphia. With George Taylor he represented the government and negotiated a treaty with the Six Nations in Easton, Pennsylvania, in 1777. Commissioned a colonel in the 1st Regiment of the Georgia militia in 1778, he was captured by the British at the siege of Savannah and exchanged the next year.

Walton was elected governor of Georgia, serving in 1779–80. In 1781 he was disqualified from holding any office in the state patriot legislature by the Loyalist Assembly; however, he was immediately appointed commissioner of Augusta, Georgia, and authorized to lay out the city of Washington (Georgia). He served another term as governor in 1789–90.

The Confederation commissioned Walton to negotiate a treaty with the Cherokee Indians in Tennessee in 1783, and he served as chief justice of Georgia from 1783 to 1789 and again in 1793. He was named commissioner to locate the boundary line between Georgia and South Carolina in 1786 and was a member of the Georgia Constitutional Convention of 1788. He served as a presidential elector in 1789 and as judge of the Superior Court of Georgia in 1790–92, 1793–95, 1799, and 1804.

Georgia sent Walton to the United States Senate in 1795, and he served there until February 20, 1796. He was a founder and trustee of Richmond Academy, a member of the committee that located Franklin College, and a trustee of the University of Georgia. He also served as a judge on the Georgia Middle Circuit from 1799 to 1804.

Walton died in College Hill, Georgia, and was buried in Augusta.

WILLIS, Francis: congressman
Born Frederick County, Virginia, January 5, 1745; died January 25, 1829.

During the Revolutionary War, Willis served as a captain and then as a colonel. In 1784 he moved to Wilkes County, Georgia, where he was elected to the United States House of Representatives, serving from 1791 to 1793. Later he moved to Maury County, Tennessee. He died at the age of eighty-four.

WOOD, Joseph: Continental congressman
Born Pennsylvania, 1712; died September 1791.

Around 1774 Wood moved to Sunbury, Georgia. He served as a major, lieutenant colonel, and colonel of the 2nd Pennsylvania Battalion (which became the 3rd Pennsylvania Regiment) during the American Revolution, on duty in Canada in 1776. After the war he returned to Georgia, engaged in planting, and became a member of the Georgia Council of Safety. He represented Georgia in the Continental Congress from 1777 to 1779. He died near Sunbury in 1791.

★★★★★

ZUBLY, John Joachim: Continental congressman, clergyman
Born St. Gall, Switzerland, August 27, 1724; son of David Zubly; married Ann Tobler, November 12, 1746; father of two children; died July 23, 1781.

Zubly was ordained to the ministry of the Presbyterian Church at the German Church in London, England, in 1744. Sixteen years later he became the first pastor of the Presbyterian Church (later the Independent Presbyterian Church) in Savannah, Georgia. In 1770 the College of New Jersey (now Princeton) awarded him an honorary A.M. degree and, in 1774, an honorary D.D.

After participating in the Georgia Provincial Congress in 1775, Zubly was a Georgia delegate to the First Continental Congress

(1775–77), where he opposed a complete break with England. Accused of having given information to Sir James Wright, the royal governor of New York, he was banished from Georgia and had half his property confiscated during the years 1777–79. He lived in South Carolina until the royal government was restored in Georgia in 1779, whereupon he returned to Savannah and resumed his ministerial duties until his death. He was buried in Colonial Park in Savannah.

Zubly wrote *The Stamp Act Repealed* (1766); *An Humble Inquiry* (1769); *Great Britain's Right to Tax Her Colonies* (1774); and *The Law of Liberty* (sermon), 1775.

★★★★★★★★★★★★★★

MARYLAND

"General Smallwood endeavored to cover the retreat, and is collecting the remains of our scattered troops, for which purpose he has established posts at Salisbury and Charlotte, and has prevailed on a considerable body, not less than one thousand volunteers, to make a stand at Charlotte."

—NEW-JERSEY JOURNAL, September 17, 1780

ALEXANDER, Robert: Continental congressman

Born Cecil County, Maryland; no record of death.

A lawyer, Alexander was a member of the Maryland Provincial Convention for three years, 1774–76. In 1775 he also served as secretary to the Baltimore Committee of Observation and as member of the Council of Safety. He represented Maryland at the Continental Congress in 1775 and 1776, but after the Declaration of Independence he fled the state, joined the British Fleet, and became a member of the Associated Loyalists of America. In 1780 he was found guilty of treason, and his property was confiscated. Two years later he sailed for London, where he died.

ARCHER, John: physician, congressman, army officer

Born Harford County, Maryland, May 5, 1741; married Catherine Harris; father of ten children; died September 28, 1810.

Archer was awarded a B.A. from Princeton in 1760, and an A.M. and a B.M. from the Philadelphia College of Medicine in 1763 and 1768 respectively. The latter was the first medical degree awarded in America.

In 1776 Archer received a commission as a major in the Continental Army; later that same year he was a member of the convention which framed the Maryland Constitution and Bill of Rights. In addition to serving as a presidential elector, he was a representative from Maryland to the United States House during the years 1801 through 1807 (7th, 8th, and 9th congresses).

Archer was a founder and executive member of the Medical and Chirurgical Faculty of Maryland in 1799; other professional accomplishments included his introduction of senega to the treatment of croup and his contributions to the Medical Repository in New York. Five of his children, including Stevenson, became physicians. He died in Harford County and was buried at Presbyterian Cemetery, Churchville, Maryland.

★★★★★

BANNEKER, Benjamin: mathematician, abolitionist

Born Ellicott's Mills, Maryland, November 9, 1731; son of Robert and Mary Banneker; died October 1806.

Banneker was educated at home and also attended an integrated neighborhood school for a time. He later inherited his father's farm.

At an early age Banneker showed unusual mechanical ability, constructing a wooden clock even though he had had no previous training. He took part in the gentlemen's game of exchanging difficult mathematical problems. In 1773 he began making astronomical calculations for almanacs, and accurately calculated an eclipse in 1789. Soon after this he sold his farm and concentrated on the study of mathematics and astronomy. Named to the Capitol Commission (the first presidential appointment granted to a Negro), Banneker assisted L'Enfant in a survey of the District of Columbia in 1790. Two years later he published an almanac. He also wrote a dissertation on bees and conducted a study of locust plague cycles. He wrote a famous letter to Jefferson on segregationist trends in America.

Banneker died in Baltimore shortly before his seventy-fifth birthday.

BARNEY, Joshua: naval officer

Born Baltimore, July 6, 1759; son of William and Frances (Holland) Barney; married Anne Bedford, March 1780; father of one child; died December 1, 1818.

Barney saw much action as a naval officer during the Revolutionary War. After being commissioned a lieutenant in the United States Navy in 1776, he was captured by the British and exchanged in 1777. He was then stationed on the ship *Virginia,* which took several British ships as prizes. He commanded several armed merchant ships between 1778 and 1780, and was again captured by the British, who imprisoned him in England. He escaped in 1781 and was given command of the armed merchantman *Hyder-*

Alley the following year. By brilliant maneuvering he captured a larger British ship, *General Monk,* and received a sword from Pennsylvania for his services in that engagement.

After declining an appointment as one of six captains of the United States Navy in 1794, Barney served as a commodore in the French Navy from 1796 to 1802. He commanded privateers during the War of 1812 and commanded a special force to defend Washington, D.C., in 1814. He fought with distinction near Bladensburg and served as a naval officer at Baltimore in 1815. He died in Pittsburgh, Pennsylvania, three years later.

BORDLEY, John Beale: agriculturist

Born Annapolis, Maryland, February 11, 1727; son of Thomas and Ariana (Frisby) Bordley; married Margaret Chew, 1750; second marriage to Mrs. Sarah Mifflin, October 8, 1776; died January 26, 1804.

After serving as prothonotary of Baltimore County, Maryland, during the years 1753–62, Bordley became a judge in the Maryland Provincial Court in 1766 and in the Court of Admiralty the following year. In 1768 he was commissioner charged with settling the Maryland-Delaware boundary dispute.

From 1770 on, Bordley engaged in agricultural experimentation with new machinery, seeds, and crop rotation on extensive lands at the mouth of the Wye River and on Pool's Island, Maryland. A founder of the Philadelphia Society for Promoting Agriculture in 1785, he also served as the society's vice president from 1785 until 1804.

Bordley wrote the following essays: "A Summary View of the Courses of Crops in the Husbandry of England and Maryland" (1784), "Money, Coins, Weights, and Measures" (1789), and "Essays and Notes on Husbandry and Rural Affairs" (1801). He died on his farm near Joppa, Maryland.

BOUCHER, Jonathan: clergyman

Born Cumberland, England, March 24, 1738; son

of James and Ann (Barnes) Boucher; married Eleanor Addison, 1773; died April 27, 1804.

Boucher attended schools at Bromfield and Wigton in England. After his ordination to the ministry of the Church of England in 1762, he was rector at St. Mary's Church, Caroline County, Virginia, until 1770. From there he moved to St. Anne's in Annapolis (1770–73) and thence to Queen Annes Parish in Prince Georges County, Maryland (1773–75).

Boucher was chaplain of the lower house of the Maryland legislature during the years 1772–75. A Loyalist, he was an advocate of the Anglican Episcopate in America and preached the doctrine of the religious obligation of subjects to obey their king. He left America and served parishes in Paddington and Epsom, in England, until his death in 1804.

Among Boucher's published works was *A View of the Causes and Consequences of the American Revolution* (1797).

BOWIE, Robert: governor of Maryland
Born Prince Georges County, Maryland, March 1750; son of Captain William and Margaret (Sprigg) Bowie; married Pricilla Mackall, 1770; died January 8, 1818.

In 1776 Bowie received a commission as a captain in the 2nd Battalion of the Maryland Flying Artillery. From 1785 until 1790 he was a member of the Maryland House of Delegates, going on to serve in the Maryland legislature from 1801 to 1803. He was elected governor of the state and held that office during the years 1803–07 and again in 1811. He also was a presidential elector (1809).

In 1810 Bowie became a director of the first state bank incorporated in Annapolis, Maryland. He died in Nottingham, Maryland, and was buried in Mattaponi Cemetery, in the county of his birth.

BOWIE, Walter: congressman
Born Mattaponi, near Nottingham, Prince Georges County, Maryland, 1748; died November 9, 1810.

Bowie attended the Reverend John Evers-field's School near Nottingham and Craddock's School near Baltimore. A farmer and large landowner, he also was interested in shipping. He attended the Maryland Constitutional Convention in 1776 and became a captain and later a major in the Prince Georges County Company during the Revolutionary War.

After a twenty-year tenure in the Maryland House of Delegates (1780–1800), Bowie, a Democrat, was a member of the state senate from 1800 to 1802. On March 24 of that year he filled a vacant seat in the United States House of Representatives, in which he remained during the 7th and 8th congresses (1802–05).

Bowie died near Collington in Prince Georges County and was buried in the family burying ground on his estate.

BOWLES, William Augustus: adventurer
Born Frederick County, Maryland, October 22, 1763; son of Thomas and Eleanor Bowles; married the daughter of a Creek Indian chief; father of many children (including Chief Bowles); died December 23, 1805.

Bowles was an ensign in the Maryland Loyalist Corps in 1778. He was dismissed in disgrace but reinstated in 1781 and put on half pay in 1783. After journeying through the southern states for a number of years, he came into contact with the former governor of Virginia, Lord Dunmore, and John Miller. These two men put him in charge of a trading company to deal with the Creek Indians.

Bowles led a number of raids in the southern United States during the latter part of the eighteenth century. In an attempt to supplant Panton, Leslie and Company, he attacked Panton's storehouse in 1790 and 1799 but was unsuccessful both times. He did manage to take Fort St. Marks but was captured soon afterward. He was taken to Spain to be imprisoned but escaped, only to be recaptured in 1803. He died in Spain two years later.

BOZMAN, John Leeds: lawyer, historian
Born Oxford Neck, Maryland, August 25, 1757;

son of John and Lucretia (Leeds) Bozman; died April 20, 1823.

Bozman, who graduated from Pennsylvania College (now the University of Pennsylvania) circa 1776, studied law under Judge Robert Greensborough and at Middle Temple in London, England. On his return to America he was admitted to the Maryland bar.

Bozman served as deputy attorney general of Maryland from 1789 until 1807 and later retired to his farm in Maryland to devote himself to writing. He is the author of *Observations on the Statute of 21 Jac. I. Church 16 in Application to Estates Tail* (1794), *An Essay on the Late Institution of American Society for Colonizing the Free People of Color of the United States* (1820), and *The History of Maryland, from Its First Settlement . . . to the Restoration,* two volumes (1837).

★★★★★

CARMICHAEL, William: diplomat, Continental congressman

Born Queen Annes County, Maryland; son of William Carmichael; married twice (second marriage to Antonia Reynon); father of one child; died February 9, 1795.

Carmichael was educated in Edinburgh, Scotland. As secretary of a commission to enlist aid from France for the colonies in 1775, he was largely responsible for Lafayette's coming to America. In 1776 he was sent to Berlin to propose treaty relations with Frederick the Great.

Carmichael was a member of the Continental Congress (representing Maryland) in 1778 and 1779. As secretary to Minister Plenipotentiary John Jay, he attempted to secure a treaty with Spain, and he was acting chargé d'affaires in that country from 1790 to 1794. He died in Madrid, Spain, and was buried there.

CARROLL, Charles: Continental congressman, lawyer

Born Annapolis, Maryland, March 22, 1723; son of Dr. Charles Carroll; died March 23, 1783.

Carroll's education began at English House, West Lisbon, Portugal. He then went to England, where he attended Eton and Cambridge before entering Middle Temple, Garden Court, to study law.

Returning to America, Carroll began his practice of law in Annapolis, Maryland, in 1746. In 1755 he filled a vacancy, caused by his father's death, in the Maryland Lower House of Assembly. He served on numerous committees in the Maryland conventions and framed many important state documents, including the Declaration of Rights adopted by the 1776 Convention of Maryland. He became a member of the Council of Safety in 1775. The following year, on November 10, he filled a vacancy in the Continental Congress, serving until February 15, 1777. At that time he became a member of the first Maryland Senate and served another term from 1781 to 1783.

Carroll died in Mt. Clare, near Baltimore.

CARROLL, Charles: Continental congressman, senator

Born Annapolis, Maryland, September 19, 1737; son of Charles and Elizabeth (Brooke) Carroll; married Mary Darnall, June 5, 1768; father of two children; died November 14, 1832.

Carroll attended College de St. Omer in French Flanders and, in 1757, Collège de Louis le Grand in Paris, France. A leading figure during the Revolutionary era, he was a member of the Annapolis Committee of Correspondence in 1774 and 1775; of the Maryland Revolutionary Convention in 1775 and 1776; and, later, of the Maryland Committee of Correspondence and the Committee of Safety. From 1776 to 1778 he attended the Continental Congress as a representative from Maryland. He signed the Declaration of Independence on August 2, 1776, and was the last surviving signer.

Carroll was a member of the Maryland Senate from 1778 to 1788 and again from 1791 to 1801. From 1789 to 1792, he represented Maryland in the United States Senate as a Federalist. In addition to his political activities, he was a member of the first board of directors of the B.&O. Railroad.

Known as Charles Carroll of Carrollton, he died in Baltimore. He was buried at Doughoregan Manor, near Ellicott City, Howard County, Maryland.

CARROLL, Daniel: congressman

Born Prince Georges County, Maryland, July 22, 1730; son of Kean and Eleanor (Darnall) Carroll; married Elizabeth Carroll (a second cousin), 1750; died May 7, 1796.

Carroll started his political career as a delegate from Maryland to the Continental Congress in 1781, where he served until 1784. Also in 1781 he signed the Articles of Confederation. He attended the Maryland Constitutional Convention in 1787 and was a Maryland delegate to the United States House of Representatives from 1789 to 1791.

In 1791 Carroll was a member of the commission to survey the District of Columbia on the banks of the Potomac River. He died in Rock Creek, Maryland.

CARROLL, John: clergyman, educator

Born Upper Marlboro, Maryland, January 8, 1735; son of Kean and Eleanor (Darnall) Carroll; died December 3, 1815.

John Carroll's career in the clergy was as distinguished as the political career of his older brother, Daniel. He was educated at Collège de St. Omer in France, graduating in 1753; six years later he was appointed to a professorship at that institute. After taking his final vows as a Jesuit, he was ordained in 1767. He returned to America in 1773 and was named prefect-apostolic by Pope Pius VI, serving from 1784 to 1785. He was named the first Roman Catholic bishop in the United States in 1789 and was consecrated the following year. In 1808 he became the first archbishop of Baltimore.

Carroll also made great contributions to education in the early days of the United States. He founded Georgetown Academy in 1789, St. Mary's College in 1792 and St. Joseph College (Emmitsburg, Maryland) in 1809. He was awarded an honorary LL.D. from St. Mary's in 1793.

Carroll died in Georgetown, Washington, D.C.

CHASE, Jeremiah Townley: Continental congressman

Born Baltimore, Maryland, May 23, 1748; died May 11, 1828.

Chase began his political activities at the age of twenty-six, when he served as a member of both the observation and the correspondence committees. Two years later, in 1776, he was a delegate to the Maryland Constitutional Convention. After moving to Annapolis, Maryland, in 1779, he became a member of the Governor's Council for two terms, 1780–84 and 1786–88. He was mayor of Annapolis in 1783 and a member of the Continental Congress, representing Maryland, during the years 1783–84. An anti-Federalist, he was a member of the convention to ratify the United States Constitution in 1788. A judge of the General Court in 1789, he served as chief justice of the Court of Appeals until his resignation in 1824.

Chase died in Annapolis and was buried in City Cemetery.

CHASE, Samuel: Continental congressman, associate justice of the United States Supreme Court

Born Somerset County, Maryland, April 17, 1741; son of the Reverend Thomas and Martha (Walker) Chase; married Ann Baldwin, May 21, 1762; second marriage to Hannah Giles, March 3, 1784; father of four children; died June 19, 1811.

Admitted to the bar at the age of twenty, Chase was a member of the Maryland Assembly from 1764 to 1784. From 1774 to 1778, in 1784, and in 1785 he was also a delegate to the Continental Congress. In 1774 he was a member of the Maryland Committee of Correspondence, and the following year he was a delegate to the Maryland Convention and served on the Maryland Council of Safety. A signer of the Declaration of Independence, Chase served on thirty congressional committees during the years 1777–78. He was chief judge of the Baltimore Criminal Court in 1788.

An opponent of the United States Constitution, Chase voted against ratification at the Maryland Constitutional Convention in 1788. In 1791 he was chief judge of the Maryland General Court. He was an associate justice of the United States Supreme Court for fifteen years, from 1796 to 1811. Owing to accusations of biased and underhanded trial conduct toward the Jeffersonians in 1799, impeachment proceedings were brought against him in 1804; he was acquitted the following year.

CHRISTIE, Gabriel: congressman
Born Perryman, Maryland, 1755; died April 1, 1808.

Christie was a member of a militia company during the Revolutionary War. He served in the Maryland House of Delegates and in 1787 was appointed by Governor William Smallwood a commissioner to "straighten and amend the post road from Havre de Grace to Baltimore town."

Christie was sent to the United States House of Representatives from Maryland during the 3rd, 4th, and 6th congresses (1793–97, 1799–1801). He was a commissioner of Havre de Grace (1800–01 and 1806) and was appointed collector of the Port of Baltimore, where he served until 1808. After his death in Baltimore, he was buried in Spesutia Churchyard, Perryman, Maryland.

CONTEE, Benjamin: Continental congressman, congressman, clergyman
Born Brookfield, near Nottingham, Prince Georges County, Maryland, 1755; died November 30, 1815.

Contee attended private schools and served as a lieutenant and a captain in the 3rd Maryland Battalion in the Revolutionary War. He was a member of the Maryland House of Delegates, 1785–87, and a member of the Continental Congress, from Maryland, 1787–88. He attended the 1st Congress of the United States House of Representatives as a delegate from Maryland, 1789–91.

After traveling to various European countries and studying theology, Contee was ordained to the ministry in the Episcopal Church in 1803 and soon afterward became pastor of the Episcopal Church in Port Tobacco, Charles County, Maryland. He was presiding judge of the Charles County Orphans Court until his death. He was buried at Bromont, his former home, near Port Tobacco.

COVINGTON, Leonard: congressman, army officer
Born Aquasco, Maryland, October 30, 1768; died August 13, 1820.

After a liberal schooling, Covington entered the United States Army as cornet of cavalry in 1792. He was commissioned lieutenant of the Dragoons by General Washington the following year and joined the army under General Wayne. He distinguished himself at Fort Recovery and at the Battle of Miami. He was promoted to captain but resigned in 1795 to become a farmer.

Covington served as a member of the Maryland House of Delegates for many years and was a member of the United States House of Representatives as a Democrat from Maryland for the 9th Congress (1805–07). He resumed his military career in 1809 with an appointment by President Jefferson to lieutenant colonel of the Light Dragoons; he rose to full colonel later that year. The following year he was put in command of Fort Adams on the Mississippi River and took possession of Baton Rouge and a portion of West Florida.

In 1813 Covington was ordered to the northern frontier, where he was appointed brigadier general by President Madison. He was mortally wounded at the Battle of Chryslers Field, and died at French Mills, New York. His remains were removed to Sackets Harbor, Jefferson County, New

York, and he was buried at Mount Covington.

CRABB, Jeremiah: congressman
Born Montgomery County, Maryland, 1760; died 1800.

Crabb was a prosperous landowner in Montgomery County. In the Revolutionary War, he served as a second lieutenant in the 1st Maryland Regiment and at the age of seventeen was promoted to first lieutenant; however, he resigned his commission because of illness resulting from the winter spent at Valley Forge. He later returned to military duty, serving as a general with General Harry Lee during the Whiskey Rebellion in Pennsylvania.

Crabb, a Democrat, was a delegate from Maryland to the United States House of Representatives, 4th Congress, 1795–96, resigning before the end of his term. He died near Rockville, Maryland, and was buried in the family burying ground near Derwood, in Montgomery County.

CRAIK, James: physician
Born Arbigland, Scotland, 1730; married Marianne Ewell, November 13, 1760; father of at least one son (George W.); died February 6, 1814.

Craik studied medicine at the University of Edinburgh in Scotland. He was commissioned a surgeon in the Virginia militia in 1754 and was chief medical officer under Colonel George Washington from 1755 to 1763. He was assistant director of the general hospitals of the Middle District of the Continental Army from 1777 to 1780. He became chief hospital physician of the Continental Army in 1780, and chief physician and surgeon in 1781, serving in the latter capacity until 1783.

In 1798 Craik acceded to two posts: director of the general hospital department of the United States Army and physician general. Along with Dr. Elisha Cullen Dick, he attended President Washington during his final illness, in 1799. He remained physician general until 1800.

Craik, owner of a large plantation, spent the remainder of his life practicing medicine in Port Tobacco, Charles County, Maryland. He died in Alexandria, Virginia, at the age of eighty-three.

CRAWFORD, John: physician
Born May 3, 1746; died May 9, 1813.

Crawford was awarded a medical degree from the University of Leyden in Holland. He set forth the theory of infection or contagion, his most useful contribution to medical science. In 1798 he helped to found the Baltimore Library; he also helped found the Society for the Promotion of Useful Knowledge and the Baltimore Dispensary. He died in Baltimore and was buried in the Presbyterian Cemetery.

CRESAP, Michael: army officer
Born Allegany County, Maryland, June 29, 1742; son of Thomas Cresap; married Mary Whitehead; died October 18, 1775.

Cresap precipitated Dunmore's War in 1774 by leading the whites in the Yellow Creek Massacre, in which several families of peaceful Indians were slaughtered. That same year he served as a captain in the Virginia militia, which defeated the Indians at Point Pleasant. The following year he was commissioned by the Maryland Assembly to recruit troops for the Continental Army. He died in New York City.

CRESAP, Thomas: pioneer
Born Skipton, England, circa 1702; married Hannah Johnson, circa 1727; father of Michael; died circa 1790.

Cresap, who arrived in Maryland in 1717, was one of the most prominent men of the Appalachian border. In 1734 he served as a captain in the Maryland militia. An Indian trader and translator, he organized the Ohio Company in 1749. Though not an active combatant, he contributed greatly to the patriot cause during the American Revolution.

★★★★★

DENT, George: congressman

Born "Windsor Castle," on the Mattawoman, Charles County, Maryland, 1756; died December 2, 1813.

Dent served in the Revolutionary War as a first lieutenant in the militia of Charles and St. Marys counties, under Captain Thomas H. Marshall, and then as a first lieutenant in the 3rd Battalion of the Flying Camp Regular Troops of Maryland, in 1776. In 1778 he was commissioned a captain in the 26th Battalion of the Maryland militia.

Dent was a member of the Maryland House of Assembly from 1782 to 1790, serving as speaker pro tem in 1788 and as speaker in 1789 and 1790. He was a justice of the Charles County Court, 1791–92, and at the same time was a member of the Maryland Senate, holding the position of president in 1792. A Democrat, Dent served in the United States House of Representatives from 1793 to 1801 (3rd through 6th congresses), acting as speaker pro tem at various times from 1797 to 1799. He was appointed by President Jefferson as United States marshal of the District Court for the Potomac District, Washington, D.C., in 1801.

In 1802 Dent moved to Georgia, where he died eleven years later, near Augusta. He was buried on his plantation near Augusta.

DIGGES, Thomas Atwood: writer

Born Maryland, circa 1741; died circa 1821.

Digges was a friend of Washington, Jefferson, Franklin, and Madison. He spent several years in Lisbon during the Revolutionary War and is generally accepted as the author of *The Adventures of Alonzo: Containing Some Striking Anecdotes of the Present Prime Minister of Portugal.* An imitation of a picaresque novel, the book is said to have been written in 1775, by "a native of Maryland and some years' resident in Lisbon."

DULANY, Daniel: lawyer

Born Annapolis, Maryland, June 28, 1722; son of Daniel and Rebecca (Smith) Dulany; married Rebecca Taskier, 1749; died March 17, 1797.

Dulany attended Eton College, Clare Hall of Cambridge University, and Middle Temple. He journeyed to America and was admitted to the Maryland bar in 1747.

Dulany became a member of the lower house of the Maryland legislature in 1751, serving until 1754. In 1757, and until 1774, he was a member of the Maryland Council. During that time (1759–61) he was commissary general of the Province of Maryland, also holding the office of secretary of the province from 1761 to 1774.

Although a Loyalist, Dulany urged representation for the colonies in Parliament. He was one of the most powerful colonial lawyers in the pre-Revolutionary period, but his property and position eventually suffered because of his politics.

Dulany is the author of a pamphlet, *Consideration on the Propriety of Imposing Taxes in the British Colonies for the Purpose of Raising a Revenue, by Act of Parliament,* published in 1765. He died in Baltimore.

DUVALL, Gabriel: associate justice of the United States Supreme Court

Born at the estate "Marietta," near Buena Vista, Prince Georges County, Maryland, December 6, 1752; son of Benjamin and Susanna (Tyler) Duvall; married Mary Bryce, July 24, 1787; second marriage to Jane Gibbon, May 5, 1795; father of one son (Edmund Bryce); died March 6, 1844.

Duvall was elected muster master and commissary of stores for Maryland in 1776. He served as a private in the Maryland militia during the battles of Brandywine and Morristown.

In 1778 Duvall was admitted to the Maryland bar. In 1783 and 1784 he served on the Maryland Governor's Council, and from 1787 to 1794 he was a member of the Maryland House of Delegates. He attended the United States House of Representatives during the 3rd and 4th congresses (November 11, 1794, to March 28, 1796). He was chief justice of the Maryland General Court from 1796 to 1802 and the first comptroller of the United States Treasury (under Thomas Jefferson) from 1802 to 1811.

From 1812 to 1835 Duvall was an associate justice of the United States Supreme Court. He dissented in the cases of *The Trustees of Dartmouth College vs. Woodward* and *Mima Queen and Child vs. Hepburn.* This last case upheld the use of hearsay evidence in proving the freedom of a slave's ancestor.

Duvall died in Prince Georges County and was buried at "Marietta."

★★★★★

EDEN, Robert; colonial governor

Born Durham, England, September 14, 1741; son of Robert and Mary (Davidson) Eden; married Caroline Calvert (sister of Lord Baltimore), 1765; father of two sons; died September 2, 1784.

Prior to the Revolutionary War, Eden was commissioned as the governor of Maryland for the English Crown (1768). During the pre-war period, he served as governor, surveyor general, and chancellor of the province.

The Continental Congress, believing Eden to be an enemy of the colonists, requested the Maryland Council of Safety to arrest him. He returned to England, where, in 1776, a baronet was created for him to reward his faithful service while in the colonies. After the war, he returned to recover his property in Annapolis, Maryland, where he died.

EDWARDS, Benjamin: congressman

Born Stafford County, Virginia, August 12, 1753; married (wife's name unknown); father of at least one son (Ninian); died November 13, 1829.

Edwards was engaged in agriculture and business in Montgomery County, Maryland. He was a member of the Maryland House of Delegates for several years as well as a delegate to the Maryland Convention which ratified the United States Constitution in 1788. Chosen to fill a vacancy, he was a member of the United States House of Representatives during the 3rd Congress, serving from January 2 to March 3, 1795.

Edwards left Maryland to live in Todd County, Kentucky. He died in Elkton, Kentucky, and was buried on his estate there.

★★★★★

FORBES, James: Continental congressman

Born near Benedict, Maryland, circa 1731; died March 25, 1780.

In 1777 Forbes served simultaneously as justice of the peace of Charles County, Maryland, tax commissioner of Charles County, and a member of the Maryland General Assembly. He was a member of the Continental Congress, representing Maryland, from 1778 to 1780. He died in Philadelphia and was buried in Christ Protestant Episcopal Churchyard.

FORREST, Uriah: congressman

Born near Leonardtown, Saint Marys County, Maryland, 1756; died July 6, 1805.

Forrest served as a first lieutenant, captain, and major in the Maryland militia during the Revolutionary War. He was wounded at the Battle of Germantown and lost a leg at the Battle of Brandywine.

At the age of thirty Forrest became a member of the Continental Congress from Maryland (1786–87). He went on to become a Federalist member of the United States House of Representatives during the 3rd Congress, from 1793 to November 8, 1794, when he resigned. He then was commissioned a major general in the Maryland militia (1795), and later became a clerk in the District of Columbia Circuit Court, serving from 1800 until his death in 1805.

Forrest died at the estate "Rosedale," near Georgetown, District of Columbia, and was buried in Oak Hill Cemetery in Washington, D.C.

★★★★★

GALE, George: congressman

Born Somerset County, Maryland, June 3, 1756; married; father of at least one son (Levin); died January 2, 1815.

Gale served in the military during the

Revolutionary War. In 1788 he was a member of the Maryland Convention which ratified the federal constitution, and the following year he began a two-year term in the United States House of Representatives (1st Congress). In 1791 President Washington appointed him superintendent of distilled liquors in the District of Maryland.

Gale died at the estate "Brookland," in Cecil County, Maryland, and was buried in the family burying ground.

GIST, Mordecai: army officer

Born Reisterstown, Maryland, March 6, 1743; son of Thomas and Susannah (Cockey) Gist; married Cecil Carnan; second marriage to Mary Sterrett, January 23, 1778; third marriage to Mrs. Mary Cattell, 1783; father of two sons (Independent and States); died August 2, 1792.

Gist, who attended common schools, engaged in mercantile pursuits circa 1770 in Baltimore. In 1774 he was a captain in a Baltimore volunteer unit; two years later he was commissioned a major and then a colonel in the 1st Maryland Battalion under General Smallwood. He served in the Battle of Germantown in 1777, received a commission as brigadier general in 1779, and was commended by Congress in 1780 for his role in the Battle of Camden the year before. During 1780 and 1781 he served in the recruiting and supply departments of the army.

GOLDSBOROUGH, Robert: Continental congressman

Born Cambridge, Maryland, December 3, 1733; son of Charles and Elizabeth (Ennalls) Goldsborough; married Sarah Yerbury, March 27, 1755; died December 22, 1788.

After graduating from Philadelphia College (now the University of Pennsylvania) in 1760, Goldsborough was admitted to Middle Temple in London and then to the English bar in 1757. Returning to America, in 1764 he became a member of the Maryland House of Delegates, followed by a term as attorney general of Maryland (1766–68).

He attended the Continental Congress in 1774–75 and in 1776 and the Maryland Convention in 1775, as well as serving on the Maryland Council of Safety in 1775.

In 1776 Goldsborough was elected to the Maryland Constitutional Convention. He also was a member of the first Maryland Senate. Although chosen as a delegate to the Maryland Convention which ratified the federal constitution in 1788, he apparently did not attend. He died in Cambridge.

GREEN, Jonas: printer, journalist

Born New London, Connecticut, circa 1712; son of Deacon Timothy Green; married Anne Catherine Hoof, April 25, 1738; father of fourteen children; died April 11, 1767.

After learning printing in New London, Green moved to Boston and worked as a printer for the firm Kneeland and Green. Circa 1735 he moved to Philadelphia and worked as a printer for both Benjamin Franklin and Andrew Bradford. Moving to Annapolis, Maryland, in 1738, he became the public printer and established the *Maryland Gazette* in 1745. He suspended the paper in December 1765 after the passage of the Stamp Act but resumed publication the following month. In 1777 the paper was suspended because he had opposed the Stamp Act, but two of his sons revived it in 1779.

Reputedly one of the best printers in the colonies, Green was known for the neatness and correctness of his work. In 1765 he printed Thomas Bacon's *Laws of Maryland*, which is considered his best work. Green's other activities included service to the city of Annapolis as an alderman and postmaster and to the church as a vestryman of St. Anne's Church. He died in Annapolis.

★★★★★

HALL, John: Continental congressman

Born near Annapolis, Maryland, November 27, 1729; died March 8, 1797.

After studying law, Hall was admitted to the Maryland bar and began his practice in Annapolis. A member of the Maryland

Council of Safety, he was a delegate to the Maryland Conference of 1775. He attended the Continental Congress as a representative from Maryland in 1775, 1777, 1780, 1783, and 1784. After that he resumed his practice of law. He died at the estate "The Vineyard" (now known as "Iglehart"), near Annapolis, Maryland, and was buried in the family burial ground at "The Vineyard."

HANSON, John: Continental congressman
Born Mulberry Grove, Charles County, Maryland, April 13, 1721; son of Samuel and Elizabeth (Story) Hanson; married Jane Contee; father of nine children (including Alexander Contee); died November 22, 1783.

Hanson, an early advocate of colonial independence, was a member of the Maryland Assembly from 1757 to 1773. In 1775, he was a member of the Maryland Convention. Active in raising troops and providing arms and ammunition for the Revolutionary Army, he also established a gun-lock factory in Frederick, Maryland.

In 1779 Hanson was a delegate to the Continental Congress. Along with Daniel Carroll, he labored successfully to persuade Virginia and other states to relinquish their claims to unsettled Western lands—an action required by Maryland before it would agree to sign the Articles of Confederation. President of the Congress of Confederation in 1781 and 1782, he is sometimes called the first President of the United States. He died in Oxon Hill, Prince Georges County, Maryland.

HARRISON, William, Jr.: Continental congressman
Born Maryland; son of William and Elizabeth (?) Harrison; no record of death.

Harrison was a member of the Continental Congress, from Maryland, from 1785 to 1787. He engaged in ship building in St. Michaels, Maryland, in 1810. In 1812 he was first lieutenant in the Independent Light Dragoons, 9th Cavalry Regiment of the Maryland militia, serving later as captain and commander of the troop. He was a justice of the court at St. Michaels in 1813.

HELMSLEY, William: Continental congressman
Born at Clover Fields Farm, near Queenstown, Maryland, 1737; died June 5, 1812.

Helmsley, a planter, was provincial treasurer of Eastern Shore, Maryland, in 1773, and surveyor of Talbot County, Maryland. A colonel in the 20th Battalion of Queen Annes County Militia in 1777, he was also justice of the peace of Queen Annes County.

From 1779 to 1781, and in 1786, 1790, and 1800, Helmsley was a member of the Maryland Senate. From 1782 to 1784 he was a member of the Continental Congress, from Maryland. He died in Queen Annes County and was buried in Clover Fields Farm Cemetery.

HENRY, John: senator, governor of Maryland
Born Dorchester County, Maryland, November 1750; son of Colonel John and Dorothy (Rider) Henry; married Margaret Campbell, March 6, 1787; father of two children; died December 16, 1798.

After his graduation from the College of New Jersey (now Princeton) in 1796, Henry was admitted to Middle Temple in London, England. He was a delegate to the Continental Congress, from Maryland, from 1778 to 1781 and from 1784 to 1787. He strongly supported the authority of George Washington and the provisioning and strengthening of the army.

From 1789 to 1797 Henry was a member of the United States Senate, representing Maryland. He served as governor of Maryland in 1797 and 1798. He died in Dorchester County, Maryland.

HINDMAN, William: senator
Born Dorchester County, Maryland, April 1, 1743; son of Jacob and Mary (Trippe) Hindman; died January 19, 1822.

A graduate of the University of Pennsylvania at the age of eighteen, Hindman studied at the Inns of Court in London, England, in 1765. He was admitted to the Maryland bar that same year.

Hindman was a member of the Maryland Senate from 1777 to 1784 and a member of the Continental Congress, from Maryland, from 1784 to 1788. He was a member of the Governor of Maryland's Executive Council from 1789 to 1792. He held a seat in the United States House of Representatives during the 2nd–5th congresses (1793–99). The following year he served in the Maryland House of Delegates, and from December 12, 1800 to 1801, he was a member of the United States Senate, from Maryland.

Hindman died in Baltimore and was buried in St. Paul's Burial Ground.

HOWARD, John Eager: army officer, senator, governor of Maryland

Born Baltimore County, Maryland, June 4, 1752; son of Cornelius and Ruth (Eager) Howard; married Peggy Chew, May 18, 1787; father of Benjamin Chew; died October 12, 1827.

At the age of twenty-four, Howard was commissioned a captain in Colonel Carvil Hall's "Flying Camp" and served at the Battle of White Plains (October 28, 1776). The following year he was commissioned a major in the 4th Maryland Regiment. He was a lieutenant colonel in the 5th Maryland Regiment at the time of the Battle of Camden on March 11, 1778. He led a charge at the critical moment in the Battle of Cowpens on January 17, 1781. For this, he received a Gold Medal and the thanks of the Continental Congress.

Howard was a delegate to the Continental Congress in 1787 and 1788, after which he held the office of the governor of Maryland from 1788 to 1791. He represented Maryland in the United States Senate from 1796 to 1803. The latter year he was commissioned a brigadier general in the United States Army. He was the Federalist candidate for the vice president of the United States in 1816. He died in Belevedere, Maryland.

★★★★★

JENIFER, Daniel: colonial statesman

Born Charles County, Maryland, 1723; son of Dr. Daniel Jenifer; died November 16, 1790.

After a period as justice of the peace of Charles County, in 1760 Jenifer was appointed a commissioner to settle a boundary dispute between Pennsylvania and Delaware. Six years later he became a member of the Provincial Court of Maryland. From 1773 to 1776 he served on the Governor's Council; in 1775 he presided over the Maryland Council of Safety. He was also president of the state senate from 1777 to 1780.

Known as "Daniel Jenifer of St. Thomas," Jenifer was a delegate to the Continental Congress in the years 1778–82. He attended the United States Constitutional Convention in Philadelphia in 1787, and was a signer of the United States Constitution. Twice he ran unsuccessfully for governor of Maryland, in 1782 and again in 1785. He died in Annapolis, Maryland.

★★★★★

KEY, Philip: congressman

Born probably near Leonardtown, St. Marys County, Maryland, 1750; died January 4, 1820.

After being educated in England, Key studied law. He engaged in farming in Maryland, was admitted to the bar, and established a legal practice. He served in the Maryland House of Delegates in the years 1773, 1779–90, and 1795–96 (during the latter term he also was speaker). In 1774 he was a member of the St. Marys County Committee of Correspondence. He represented his state in the United States House of Representatives from 1791 to 1793.

Key declined a cabinet appointment offered by President Monroe as well as the governorship of Maryland. He died in St. Marys County and was buried probably in the churchyard in Chaptico, Maryland.

KEY, Philip Barton: congressman

Born Charlestown, Cecil County, Maryland, April 12, 1757; son of Francis and Anne Arnold (Ross) Key; married Ann Plater, July 4, 1790; father of two sons and six daughters; died July 28, 1815.

In 1778 Key served as a captain in Chalmer's Regiment of Maryland Loyalists in the British Army. He went to England in 1783. After his admission to the Middle Temple, Inns of Court, in London in 1784, he returned to Maryland the next year and was admitted to the bar. From 1794 until 1799 he was a member of the Maryland House of Delegates.

Key was chief justice of the Fourth United States Circuit Court during the years 1800–02. In 1805 he served as counsel for Justice Samuel Chase in his trial before the United States Senate. He was a member of the United States House of Representatives from 1807 to 1815. He died in Georgetown, D.C., and was buried in Oak Hill Cemetery in Washington, D.C.

KILTY, William: jurist

Born London, England, 1757; son of John and Ellen (Ahern) Kilty; married Elizabeth Middleton; died October 10, 1821.

Kilty, who was educated at the College of St. Omer in France, came to America circa 1774. In April 1778 he became a surgeon's mate in the 4th Maryland Regiment; four years later he rose to surgeon.

During the period 1799–1800 Kilty was authorized by the Maryland legislature to make a compilation of the laws of Maryland. He then served as chief justice of the Circuit Court of the District of Columbia (1801–06) and as chancellor of Maryland (1806–21). He was a founder of the Society of the Cincinnati. He died in Annapolis, Maryland.

★★★★★

LEE, Thomas Sim: governor of Maryland, Continental congressman

Born Prince Georges County, Maryland, October 29, 1745; son of Thomas and Christiana (Sim) Lee; mar-
ried Mary Diggs, October 27, 1771; father of ten children; died November 9, 1819.

Lee was serving on the Maryland Provincial Council when the Revolutionary War broke out. He saw action as major of a battalion from Prince Georges County before leaving the military in 1779 to become governor of Maryland. During his three-year tenure as governor, he supported all efforts to defeat the British.

In 1783–84 Lee was a delegate to the Continental Congress. He was a member of the Maryland Convention that ratified the United States Constitution in 1788. In 1792 he served as a presidential elector; later that year he again acceded to the governorship, serving until 1794.

Lee died on his estate in Frederick County, Maryland, and was buried in the Roman Catholic Cemetery near Upper Marlboro, Maryland.

LEEDS, John: mathematician, astronomer

Born Bay Hundred, Talbot County, Maryland, May 18, 1705; son of Edward and Ruth (Ball) Leeds; married Rachel Harrison, February 14, 1726; father of three children; died March 1790.

In 1734 Leeds became justice of the peace of Talbot County. For thirty-nine years (1738 to 1777) he served as clerk of the Talbot County Court. He was a regular member of the commission from Maryland to mark off the long-disputed Maryland-Pennsylvania boundary line in 1762.

In 1766 Leeds held a variety of positions, including treasurer of the Eastern Shore district of Maryland, justice of the Provincial Court, and a naval officer of the Port of Pocomoke. In that year he also became surveyor general of Maryland, serving until circa 1775, and again from 1783 to 1790.

Leeds observed the transit of Venus, and his findings were published in 1770 in *Royal Society of London's Philosophical Transactions . . . for the Year 1769.* He died in Wade's Point, Maryland.

LLOYD, Edward: state senator

Born November 15, 1744; son of Edward and Ann (Rousby) Lloyd; married Elizabeth Tayloe, November 19, 1767; died July 8, 1796.

In 1771 Lloyd was a member of the Maryland House of Burgesses from Talbot County. Three years later he served as a member of the Committee of Correspondence for Talbot County. From 1777 to 1780 he was a member of the lower house of the Maryland legislature under the new state constitution. During that time he was also a member of the Executive Council.

Lloyd served from 1781 to 1796 as a member from Eastern Shore to the Maryland Senate. He was a Maryland delegate to the Congress of Confederation of 1783–84. He served as a delegate from Talbot County to the Maryland Convention that ratified the United States Constitution.

LLOYD, James: senator

Born at the estate "Farley," near Chestertown, Maryland, 1745; died 1820.

Lloyd studied law, was admitted to the bar, and began a legal practice. In 1776 he was commissioned a second lieutenant in the Kent County (Maryland) militia and saw action in the Revolutionary War. A Democrat from Maryland, he served in the United States Senate from December 11, 1797, to December 1, 1800, at which time he returned to the practice of law. He served as a general during the War of 1812.

Lloyd died at "Ratclift Manor," near Easton, Maryland, and was buried at "Clover," in Queen Annes County, Maryland.

★★★★★

McHENRY, James: United States Secretary of War, Continental congressman

Born Ballymena, County Antrim, Ireland, November 16, 1753; son of Daniel and Agness McHenry; married Margaret Allison Caldwell, January 8, 1784; father of at least three children (including John); died May 3, 1816.

McHenry, who arrived in Philadelphia in 1771, became a surgeon in Colonel Robert Magaw's 5th Pennsylvania Battalion in 1776 and senior surgeon with the Flying Hospital at Valley Forge in 1778. He served as secretary to George Washington from 1778 to 1780 and was a member of General Jean Lafayette's staff in 1780. He was commissioned a major in 1781.

A member of the Continental Congress from 1783 to 1786, McHenry served in the Maryland Senate from 1781 to 1786 and later from 1791 to 1796. He was a delegate from Maryland to the United States Constitutional Convention in 1787 and was named United States Secretary of War in 1796, serving until 1800.

McHenry published a Baltimore directory in 1807 and was president of the first Bible society founded in Baltimore, in 1813. Fort McHenry (Maryland) is named for him. He was the author of "A Letter to the Honourable Speaker of the House of Representatives of the United States" (a speech in defense of his actions as secretary of war), 1803. He died in Baltimore and was buried in Westminster Churchyard there.

McKIM, Alexander: congressman

Born Brandywine, Delaware, January 10, 1748; died January 18, 1832.

After moving to Baltimore, McKim became a member of the Maryland House of Delegates in 1778. He served with the Baltimore Independent Cadets and the 1st Baltimore Cavalry during the Revolution and fought under Lafayette in the Virginia campaign of 1791. A member of the Maryland Senate from 1806 to 1810, he was elected to the United States House of Representatives, as a Democrat, for the 11th–13th congresses (1809–15).

McKim engaged in the mercantile business and became justice of the Court of Quarter Sessions. He served as presiding judge of the Baltimore County Orphans Court until 1832, when he died. He was buried in Greenmount Cemetery in Baltimore.

MARTIN, Luther: Continental congress-man, state official

Born New Brunswick, New Jersey, February 9, 1744; son of Benjamin and Hannah Martin; married Maria Cresap, December 25, 1783; father of Maria and Eleanora; died July 10, 1826.

After his graduation from the College of New Jersey (now Princeton) in 1766, Martin taught school in Queenstown, Maryland, until 1769, when he moved to Somerset County to study law. He became superintendent of a grammar school in Onancock, Virginia, in 1770 and was admitted to the Virginia bar the following year.

In 1774 Martin was a member of the Annapolis Convention which drafted Maryland protests to the British, and in 1777 he published "To the Inhabitants of the Peninsula between the Delaware River and the Chesapeake to the Southward of the British Lines," a reply to an appeal by Lord William Howe.

Martin served as Maryland's first attorney general from 1778 to 1805. In 1785 he was named a delegate to the Continental Congress, representing Maryland. He was a member of the United States Constitutional Convention in Philadelphia in 1787 (where he expressed his opposition to strong central government) and a member of the Maryland Convention which ratified the Constitution in 1788.

Martin wrote and published letters in Baltimore newspapers during 1797 and 1798 defending his father-in-law, Captain Michael Cresap, who was charged with murdering the family of an Indian chief. He also wrote a pamphlet, "Modern Gratitude," which included an autobiographical sketch of his early life, in 1802.

A Federalist counsel for Judge Samuel Chase in his impeachment trial in 1804, Martin also served as a counsel in the treason trial of Aaron Burr in 1807. He was chief justice of the Court of Oyer and Terminer for the city and county of Baltimore from 1813 to 1816 and was again attorney general of Maryland from 1818 to 1822. He was involved in the case of *McCulloch vs. State of Maryland* in 1819, in which he favored states' rights.

Martin suffered a paralytic stroke in 1820, and the Maryland legislature passed an act the next year that required every lawyer in the state to pay a five-dollar annual license tax to be turned over to trustees for his use. However, the act was repealed in 1823. Martin spent the last years of his life in the home of Aaron Burr in New York City. He was buried in that city's Trinity Cemetery.

MERCER, John Francis: governor of Maryland, congressman

Born Stafford County, Virginia, May 17, 1759; son of John and Ann (Roy) Mercer; married Sophia Sprigg, 1785; father of Margaret; died August 30, 1821.

A graduate of the College of William and Mary in 1775, Mercer was commissioned a lieutenant in the 3rd Virginia Regiment of the Continental Army in 1776. He was promoted to captain in 1777, served as aide-de-camp to General Charles Lee in 1778, and resigned in 1779. Mercer studied law under Thomas Jefferson in Williamsburg, Virginia, in 1779 and 1780. He then returned to active military duty, gaining a commission as lieutenant colonel in the Virginia Cavalry (Continental Army) in 1780 and raising a corps of militia grenadiers in 1781. He served at Yorktown, witnessing the surrender of General Charles Cornwallis.

Mercer was a member of the Virginia House of Delegates in 1782 and from 1785 to 1786, and represented Virginia in the Continental Congress in 1782 and 1783. He was a delegate from Maryland to the United States Constitutional Convention in 1787 and a member of the Maryland House of Delegates in 1788–89, 1791–92, 1800–01, and 1803–06. He was elected to the United States House of Representatives for the 2nd–3rd congresses, from 1791 to April

1794. He was elected governor of Maryland in 1801, serving until 1803.

Mercer died in Philadelphia and was buried in St. Peter's Church graveyard there. His remains were later reinterred in a private cemetery, Cedar Park, in West River, Maryland.

MOLYNEUX, Robert: clergyman, educator
Born Formby, Lancashire, England, July 24, 1738; died December 9, 1808.

Molyneux, who joined the Society of Jesus in 1757, arrived in Maryland in 1771 and was appointed pastor of St. Mary's Church in Philadelphia in 1773. He served as pastor of St. Joseph's Church in Philadelphia and opened a parochial school in 1782. Vicar general of the Southern District of Maryland about 1782, Molyneux participated in the diocesan synod of 1791. He was president of Georgetown College circa 1791–96 and became American superior of the Society of Jesus in 1806. He was the author of *Sermon on the Death of Father Farmer* (one of the first Catholic publications in the United States), published in 1786.

MURRAY, Alexander: naval officer
Born Chestertown, Maryland, July 12, 1754; son of Dr. William and Ann (Smith) Murray; married Mary Miller, June 18, 1782; father of Alexander; died October 6, 1821.

Commissioned a lieutenant in the Continental Army at the outbreak of the Revolution, Murray became a captain in 1776 and participated in the battles of White Plains and Flatbush. He served aboard an American privateer for a time and was then (1781) commissioned a lieutenant in the United States Navy, later (1798) rising to captain.

Commander of the ships *Insurgent* and *Constellation* during the naval war with France in 1798, Murray commanded the *Constellation* against the Barbary pirates in the Mediterranean Sea in 1803 and commanded the ship *Adams* in 1805. He became commanding naval officer in Philadelphia in 1808 and ranking American naval officer in 1811, serving in both capacities until his death. He died in Philadelphia.

★★★★★

NEALE, Leonard: clergyman, college president
Born Port Tobacco, Maryland, October 15, 1746; son of William and Anne (Brooke) Neale; died June 18, 1819.

After attending the Jesuit College of St. Omer in Flanders, Belgium (circa 1758–62), Neale went to Bruges College in Belgium (1762–66) and then to the Society of Jesus Seminary in Ghent, Belgium (1767–77). For the next two years he was a missionary in England. He then served in British Guiana from 1779 to 1783, when he went to Maryland. During his ten-year stay at St. Thomas Manor in Maryland (1783–93), he participated in the first Diocesan Synod of Baltimore, which was held in 1791.

From St. Thomas Manor Neale went to St. Mary's Church in Philadelphia, where he was pastor from 1793 to 1799, as well as vicar of the general Philadelphia area. In 1799 he became president of Georgetown College in Maryland and served until 1806. In 1800 he became bishop coadjutor of Baltimore, a position he held until 1815, when he became archbishop. He served in this capacity until 1817.

Neale died in Maryland and was buried in Visitation Chapel at Georgetown College.

NELSON, Roger: army officer, congressman
Born Frederick County, Maryland, 1759; son of Dr. Arthur and Lucy (Waters) Nelson; married Mary Brooke Sim, 1787; second marriage to Eliza Harrison, February 2, 1797; father of eight children; died June 7, 1815.

After attending the College of William and Mary, Nelson was commissioned a lieutenant in the Maryland militia in 1780, later advancing to brigadier general. In 1785 he was admitted to the Maryland bar. He became a member of the Maryland House of Delegates in 1795 and returned in 1801 and

1802. He was a delegate from his state to the United States House of Representatives during the 8th through the 11th congresses (November 6, 1804, to May 14, 1810). He served as associate judge in the 6th Judicial Circuit of Maryland from 1810 until 1815, the year of his death. He was buried in Mount Olivet Cemetery in Frederick, Maryland.

NICHOLSON, James: naval officer

Born Chestertown, Maryland, 1737; son of Joseph and Hannah (Smith) Scott Nicholson; married Frances Wilter, April 30, 1763; father of eight children (including Hannah [Mrs. Albert Gallatin]); died September 2, 1804.

In 1775 Nicholson was in command of the *Defence*. The next year Congress appointed him as captain in the Continental Navy. In 1777 he commanded the *Virginia* and became a senior officer in the Continental Navy. Two years later he accepted command of the frigate *Trumbull*, rising in 1781 to command a fleet which included the *Nesbit*.

After the war Nicholson moved to New York City, where he became active in the Republican party. He was named commissioner of loans for New York in 1801, a position he held until his death.

★★★★★

OTTERBEIN, Philip William: clergyman

Born Dillenburg, Germany, June 3, 1726; son of Johann Daniel and Wilhelmina Henrietta (Hoerlen) Otterbein; married Susan LeRoy, April 19, 1762; died November 17, 1813.

Otterbein attended Reformed Seminary in Herborn, Germany, and was ordained a vicar of the German Reformed Church in 1749. He came to America in 1752, settling in New York.

Otterbein was pastor to several German Reformed congregations: Lancaster, Pennsylvania, 1752–58; Tulpehocken, Pennsylvania, 1758–60; Frederick, Maryland, 1760–65; York, Pennsylvania, 1765–74; Second Evangelical Reformed Church, Baltimore, Maryland, 1774–1813. In 1789 he formed the organization which was the basis of the United Brethren Church; the church's first annual conference was held near Frederick, Maryland, in 1800.

Otterbein wrote *Die Heilbringende Menschwerdung und der Herrliche Sieg Jesu Christi*, 1763. He died in Baltimore at the age of eighty-seven.

★★★★★

PACA, William: governor of Maryland, Continental congressman

Born Abingdon, Maryland, October 31, 1740; son of John and Elizabeth (Smith) Paca; married Mary Chew, May 26, 1763; second marriage to Anne Harrison, 1777; father of five children; died October 13, 1799.

After graduating from the College of Philadelphia in 1759, Paca studied law at Inner Temple, London, England. He was admitted to practice before the Mayor's Court in Philadelphia in 1761 and three years later to the Maryland Provincial Court bar. In 1768 he became a member of the Maryland Provincial Legislature and served as a member of the committee that directed construction of the state house in Annapolis. He was a Continental congressman from 1774 to 1779 and a member of the Maryland Committee of Correspondence and of the Committee of Thirteen for Foreign Affairs.

A signer of the Declaration of Independence, Paca also served in the Maryland Constitutional Convention and the first Maryland Senate. After serving in 1778 as chief judge of the Maryland General Court, he was appointed chief justice of the Court of Appeals in Admiralty and Prize Cases in 1780.

Paca served two terms as governor of Maryland from 1782 to 1785. He raised subscriptions for Washington College and was an honorary member of the Society of the Cincinnati. He died in Abingdon and was buried in the family cemetery there.

PATTERSON, William: merchant

Born Fanad, County Donegal, Ireland, November 1, 1752; son of William and Elizabeth (Peoples) Patterson; married Dorcas Spear; father of thirteen children (including Elizabeth Patterson Bonaparte); died July 7, 1835.

Patterson came to Philadelphia when he was fourteen years old. In 1775 he embarked on his first shipping venture, a three-year voyage to France and to the French and Dutch West Indies, during which time he accumulated a fortune of $60,000. He prospered as a merchant in Baltimore and was the first president of the Bank of Maryland. He helped organize the Merchant's Exchange in Baltimore in 1815. In 1827 he became an incorporator and the first director of the B.&O. Railroad, and the next year he was an incorporator of the Canton Company.

Patterson was named vice president of a meeting of Baltimore citizens that condemned the nullification ordinance of South Carolina in 1832. He died three years later at the age of eighty-two.

PEALE, James: painter

Born Chestertown, Maryland, 1749; son of Charles and Margaret (Triggs Matthews) Peale; married Mary Claypoole, 1785; father of six children; died May 24, 1831.

Peale learned the saddlery trade from his brother, Charles Willson Peale. After working with his brother from 1762 to 1770 he began to study painting.

Peale served with the Continental Army from 1776 to 1779 and was commissioned a captain in the 1st Maryland Infantry Regiment in 1778. In 1785 he moved to Philadelphia, where he began painting in earnest, concentrating on still lifes, landscapes, and historical figures. His miniatures of George Washington have brought him fame. His works include *Ramsay-Polk Family; The View of the Battle of Princeton;* and *A View of Belfield Farm near Germantown.*

PLATER, George: governor of Maryland, Continental congressman

Born at the estate "Sotterly," near Leonardtown, St. Marys County, Maryland, November 8, 1735; son of George and Rebecca Addison (Bowles) Plater; married Hannah Lee, December 5, 1762; second marriage to Elizabeth Rousby, July 19, 1764; father of six children; died February 10, 1792.

Plater graduated from William and Mary College in 1753. He served as a delegate in the lower house of the Maryland Assembly from 1758 to 1766; during this time also (1757 to 1771) he was justice of the peace of St. Marys County. He was a naval officer of the Patuxent District from 1767 to 1771; a judge of the Maryland Provincial Court from 1771 to 1773; and a member of the Maryland Executive Council in 1773 and 1774.

While a member of the Maryland Council of Safety in 1776, Plater was appointed collector to obtain money for military operations against Canada. That year he was also a member of a committee which was formed to draft a declaration of rights and organize a government for Maryland.

Plater was a representative from St. Marys County to the Annapolis Convention and, from 1778 to 1781, a member of the Continental Congress. He represented St. Marys County in the Maryland Senate after the American Revolution. In 1788 he served as president of the Maryland Convention that ratified the United States Constitution. The year after that he was a presidential elector.

During Plater's term as governor of Maryland from 1791 until his death in 1792, negotiations for the establishment of the District of Columbia (partly on Maryland land) were completed. He died in Annapolis and was buried at "Sotterly."

POTTS, Richard: senator, jurist

Born Upper Marlborough, Maryland, July 19, 1753; son of William and Sarah (Lee) Potts; married Elizabeth Hughs, April 15, 1779; second marriage to Eleanor Murdoch, December 19, 1799; father of thirteen children; died November 26, 1808.

After reading law under Judge Samuel Chase, in 1776 Potts became a member of the committee of observation of Frederick County, Maryland. During the next two years he was clerk of the Frederick County Court. In 1777 he was aide to Governor Thomas Johnson in the Maryland militia. He served as a member of the Maryland House of Delegates from 1779 to 1780 and from 1787 to 1788. In 1781 and 1782 he was a delegate to the Continental Congress. He became prosecuting attorney for Frederick, Montgomery, and Washington counties in 1784. Four years later he served at the Maryland ratifying convention in Annapolis.

From 1789 to 1791 Potts served as United States attorney for the Maryland District and, in 1791 and 1792, and from 1796 to 1801, as chief judge of the Fifth Judicial District. His term as a United States Senator lasted from 1793 to October 24, 1796. He served as judge of the Maryland Court of Appeals from 1801 to 1804.

Potts died in Frederick and was buried in Mount Olivet Cemetery in Baltimore, Maryland.

★★★★★

RAMSAY, Nathaniel: army officer, Continental congressman

Born Lancaster County, Pennsylvania, May 1, 1741; son of James and Jane (Montgomery) Ramsay; married Mary Jane Peale, 1771; second marriage to Charlotte Hall, 1792; father of three children; died October 24, 1817.

In 1767 Ramsay graduated from the College of New Jersey (now Princeton). He was a delegate to the Maryland Convention in 1775 and a signer of the Maryland Declaration of Freemen. He represented Maryland in the Continental Congress in 1775 and from 1785 to 1787.

In 1776 Ramsay was captain of Smallwood's Maryland Regiment. Later that year he was commissioned lieutenant colonel of the 3rd Maryland Regiment of the Continental Army, serving until 1781. He fought at the Battle of Monmouth in 1778 and helped check the retreat begun by General Charles Lee.

Ramsay was a United States marshal in the District of Maryland from 1790 to 1798 and naval officer at the Port of Baltimore from 1794 to 1817. He died in Baltimore and was buried at the First Presbyterian Church there.

REED, Philip: senator, congressman, army officer

Born near Chestertown, Kent County, Maryland, 1760; died November 2, 1829.

Reed completed his preparatory studies before serving in the Revolutionary Army, in which he attained the rank of captain of infantry. In 1787 he was a member of the Maryland House of Delegates. From 1791 to 1794 he served as sheriff of Kent County. He was a member of the Executive Council in 1805 but resigned in 1806. He filled a vacancy in the United States Senate on November 25, 1806, and served until 1813.

In the War of 1812, Reed served as a lieutenant colonel in the 21st Regiment of the Maryland militia. In 1814, as lieutenant colonel commandant of the 1st Regiment, he defeated the British in the Battle of Caulk's Field. He was made a brigadier general in the Maryland militia in recognition of his service.

After a contested election in Maryland, Reed became a member of the United States House of Representatives and served in the 15th and 17th congresses (1817 to 1819 and from March 19, 1822, to 1823). He died in Huntingtown, Kent County, and was buried in the cemetery of Christ Church, near Chestertown.

RIDGELY, Richard: Continental congressman

Born Queen Caroline Parish, Anne Arundel County, Maryland, August 3, 1755; died February 25, 1824.

Ridgely attended St. John's College in Annapolis, Maryland, then went on to study law. In 1776 he was an assistant clerk to the Council of Safety and later became clerk. He was admitted to the bar in 1780 and practiced law in Baltimore. He was an advocate in the Maryland Court of Chancery.

In 1785 and 1786 Ridgely was appointed a member of the Continental Congress from Maryland, but he declined to serve in the latter year. From 1786 to 1791 he was a member of the Maryland Senate. He was appointed judge of the county court in 1811 and served for thirteen years.

Ridgely died in Howard County, Maryland, and was buried on the Dorsey Hall estate, near Columbia, in Howard County.

ROGERS, John: Continental congressman
Born Annapolis, Maryland, 1723; died September 23, 1789.

Rogers had a liberal schooling, studied law, and established a legal practice after his admission to the bar. In 1774 and 1775 he was a member of the Committee of Safety, and from 1774 to 1776 he was a member of the Maryland provincial conventions. He was trustee of Lower Marlboro Academy in 1775 and a member of the Continental Congress from Maryland that year and the next. He served as a second major of battalion in Prince Georges County, Maryland.

In 1776 Rogers was a judge of the Court of Admiralty and in 1777 a member of the executive council of the Maryland government. A presidential elector in 1788, he voted for Washington and Adams. From 1778 to 1789 he served as chancellor of Maryland.

Rogers died in Upper Marlboro, Prince Georges County.

ROSS, David: Continental congressman
Born Prince Georges County, Maryland, February 2, 1755; died in 1800.

Ross studied law before his appointment by General Washington as major of Grayson's additional Continental Regiment in 1777. He resigned to manage his father's large estate after the latter's death. In 1783 he was admitted to the bar and practiced in Frederick, Maryland. He represented Maryland in the Continental Congress from 1786 to 1788. He died in Frederick County, Maryland.

RUMSEY, Benjamin: Continental congressman, jurist
Born at Bohemia Manor, Cecil County, Maryland, October 6, 1734; died March 7, 1808.

Rumsey attended Princeton. He was a member of the Maryland Convention in 1775 and later served on a committee to prepare instructions to the Maryland delegates in Congress. He also was a member of a committee to raise supplies for provincial forces.

In 1776 Rumsey was appointed a colonel in the Lower Battalion of Hartford County by the Provincial Convention. He was also a member of the Council of Safety that year. He served in the Continental Congress from 1776 to 1778 and for the next twenty-seven years was chief justice of the Maryland Court of Appeals.

Rumsey died in Joppa, in Hartford County, Maryland, and was buried in Old St. John's Cemetery.

★★★★★

SCOTT, Gustavus: lawyer, Continental congressman
Born Prince William County, Virginia, 1753; son of James and Sarah (Brown) Scott; married Margaret Caile, February 16, 1777; father of nine children; died December 25, 1800.

After gaining admission to Middle Temple in London in 1771, Scott was admitted to the English bar the following year. Having returned to America, he was a delegate to the Maryland Convention in 1775 and in 1776 was a member of the Maryland Constitutional Convention, where he drafted the first state constitution.

Scott served two terms in the Maryland House of Delegates (1780–81 and 1783–85), during which he helped draft a bill establishing a state university. In 1784 he was elected a delegate to the Continental Congress. President Washington appointed him to the board of commissioners for Washington, D.C., in 1794.

Scott died at his home "Rock Hill," in Washington, D.C., and was buried on his farm in Virginia.

SENEY, Joshua: Continental congressman
Born near Church Hill, Queen Annes County, Maryland, March 4, 1756; died October 20, 1798.

Seney, a 1773 graduate of the University of Pennsylvania at Philadelphia, studied law, was admitted to the bar, and established a legal practice; he also engaged in agriculture. He became high sheriff of Queen Annes County in 1779. After serving in the Maryland House of Delegates from 1785 to 1787, he was a member of the Continental Congress from Maryland during 1787–88.

Seney represented Maryland in the United States House of Representatives during the 1st and 2nd congresses, from 1789 until May 1, 1792, when he resigned. He then became chief justice of the 3rd Judicial District of Maryland, holding that office until 1796. In 1792 he also was a presidential elector for Washington and Adams.

Seney died near Church Hill and was buried in a private cemetery on Everett farm, between Church Hill and Sudlersville, Maryland.

SMALLWOOD, William: army officer, governor of Maryland
Born Charles County, Maryland, 1732; son of Bayne and Priscilla (Heaberd) Smallwood; died February 12, 1792.

Smallwood served in the Maryland Assembly in 1761. In 1775 he became a delegate to the Maryland Convention of that year and joined the Association of Freemen of Maryland. The following year he commanded a regiment of the state militia, served in the Battle of Long Island, and was commissioned a brigadier general in the Continental Army. During 1778 and 1779 he protected General Washington's

stores near the head of the Elk River at Wilmington, Delaware, and suppressed the Tory revolt on the Eastern Shores of Maryland.

In 1780 Smallwood was commissioned a major general. During the years 1780–83 he was sent to Maryland to obtain supplies and reinforcements; he also served as a drillmaster. He was governor of Maryland from 1785 to 1788; during his tenure he called the Maryland Convention which ratified the United States Constitution.

Smallwood died in Prince Georges County, Maryland, and was buried in Charles County, Maryland.

SMITH, Robert: cabinet officer
Born Lancaster, Pennsylvania, November 3, 1757; son of John and Mary (Buchanan) Smith; married Margaret Smith; father of eight children; died November 26, 1842.

Smith graduated from the College of New Jersey (now Princeton) in 1781 and was admitted to the Baltimore bar about three years later. A Republican, he served in the Maryland Senate from 1793 to 1795, in the Maryland House of Delegates from 1796 to 1800, and on the Baltimore City Council from 1798 to 1801.

Smith was United States Secretary of the Navy from 1802 to 1805, during which time he maintained a blockading squadron in the Mediterranean during the war against the Barbary states. He served as acting attorney general in 1805 and was Jefferson's representative in diplomatic negotiations with the British concerning the impressment of American seamen in 1808.

United States Secretary of State under Madison from 1809 to 1811, Smith resigned after being criticized by the President in 1811. He later received positions partially through the influence of his brother General Samuel Smith. He died in Baltimore.

SMITH, Samuel: senator, mayor
Born Carlisle, Pennsylvania, July 27, 1752; son of John and Mary (Buchanan) Smith; married Marga-

ret Spear, 1778; father of eight children; died April 22, 1839.

Smith, a graduate of the College of New Jersey (now Princeton), served as a captain, major, and lieutenant colonel in the Revolutionary War and organized a company of volunteers in 1775. He participated in the battles of Long Island and Monmouth and helped suppress the "Whiskey Rebellion" in 1791. He was commissioned a brigadier general in the militia in 1794.

A member of the United States House of Representatives from Maryland during the 3rd–7th and the 14th–17th congresses (1793 to 1803, and January 31, 1816, to December 17, 1822), Smith was acting secretary of the navy in 1801. He was sent to the United States Senate from Maryland from 1803 to 1815 (serving as president pro tem from 1805 to 1808) and from 1822 to 1833.

Smith was the author of non-importation legislation in 1806 and was a leader in opposing the nomination of Madison in 1808. As a major general, he headed the forces that defended Baltimore against the British during the War of 1812.

Originally a Federalist, Smith later became a Jeffersonian Republican and served as mayor of Baltimore from 1835 to 1838. He died in Baltimore at the age of eighty-six and was buried in the Old Westminster Burying Ground there.

SMITH, William: Continental congressman, congressman

Born Donegal Township, Lancaster County, Pennsylvania, April 12, 1728; died March 27, 1814.

Smith, a merchant, moved to Baltimore in 1761 and was appointed to the Committee of Correspondence in 1774. He became a member of the Committee of Observation in 1775 and was named to a committee appointed by Congress to constitute a naval board in 1777.

A member of the Continental Congress from Maryland in 1777–78, Smith served on a committee to organize the defense of Baltimore and to address and receive General Washington in 1781. A Federalist, he was a Maryland delegate to the United States House of Representatives during the 1st Congress (1789–91), then, in 1791, became the first auditor of the United States Treasury. He was a presidential elector in 1796 and a member of the Maryland Senate in 1801.

Smith died in Baltimore.

SPRIGG, Thomas: congressman

Born Prince Georges County, Maryland, 1747; died December 13, 1809.

During the Revolution, Sprigg served as an ensign in the Maryland Battalion of Flying Camp in 1776. He was the first register of wills in Washington County, Maryland, from 1777 to 1780. Sprigg was appointed lieutenant of Washington County by the governor and the Maryland Council in 1779. He was sent to the United States House of Representatives from Maryland for the 3rd and 4th congresses from 1793 to 1797. He died in Washington County.

STERETT, Samuel: congressman

Born Carlisle, Pennsylvania, 1758; died July 12, 1833.

A graduate of the University of Pennsylvania, Sterett held several local offices in Baltimore and was a member of the independent military company of Baltimore merchants in 1777. He was appointed private secretary to the president of Congress in 1782 and became a member of the Maryland Senate in 1789. An Anti-Federalist, he was a Maryland delegate to the United States House of Representatives for the 2nd Congress (1791–93).

Sterett was secretary of the Maryland Society for Promoting the Abolition of Slavery in 1791, and was a member of the Baltimore Committee of Safety in 1812. He served as a captain of an independent company at the Battle of North Point in 1814 and was wounded at the Battle of Bladensburg.

Sterett served as grand marshal at the laying of the foundation stone of the B.&O. Railroad in 1828. He died in Baltimore and was buried at Westminster Church.

STODDERT, Benjamin: secretary of the navy

Born Charles County, Maryland, 1751; son of Thomas and Sarah (Marshall) Stoddert; married Rebecca Lowndes, June 17, 1781; died December 17, 1813.

Stoddert served as a captain in the Pennsylvania Regiment in 1777 but resigned in 1779 to begin a career as a merchant in the firm of Forrest, Stoddert, and Murdock, of Georgetown, Maryland. He was an incorporator and later president of the Bank of Columbia, which was organized in 1794. Stoddert aided the governor of Maryland in the acquisition of lands at fair prices in the District of Columbia.

President John Adams appointed Stoddert the first secretary of the navy in May 1798, and he served in that position until 1801. While in office he organized a fleet of fifty ships during the war scare with France in 1798–99, drew up a bill for governing the Marine Corps, began construction of a naval hospital in Newport, Rhode Island, and started work on locating and establishing navy yards.

Stoddert died in Bladensburg, Maryland.

STONE, Michael Jenifer: congressman

Born at the estate "Equality," near Port Tobacco, Charles County, Maryland, 1747; died 1812.

Stone was elected to the Maryland House of Delegates, serving from 1781 to 1783, and was a member of the Maryland Convention to ratify the United States Constitution in 1788. He was elected to the United States House of Representatives from Maryland for the 1st Congress (1789–91). He then was appointed judge of the Maryland First Judicial District. He died in Charles County and was buried on his estate, "Equality."

STONE, Thomas: Continental congressman

Born at the estate "Poynton Manor," Charles County, Maryland, 1743; son of David and Elizabeth (Jenifer) Stone; married Margaret Brown, 1768; father of at least three children; died October 5, 1787.

Admitted to the Maryland bar in 1764, Stone served in the Continental Congress in 1775, 1779, 1784, and 1785. He was a member of the committee that framed the Articles of Confederation and was a signer of the Declaration of Independence. He was a member of the Maryland Senate from 1776 to 1787 and opposed the movement for paper currency. He served as a Maryland commissioner in the negotiations with Virginia over jurisdiction of Chesapeake Bay and participated in the Congress of Confederation in 1784 and 1785.

Because of family illness, Stone declined election to the Constitutional Convention in Philadelphia in 1787. He died that year in Alexandria, Virginia, and was buried in "Garden" Cemetery, Havre de Venture, Charles County.

STRAWBRIDGE, Robert: clergyman

Born Drumsna, Carrick-on-Shannon, County Leitram, Ireland; son of Robert Strawbridge; father of six children; died August 1781.

Strawbridge arrived in Maryland sometime between 1759 and 1766. He probably was a founder of the first Methodist society in America, a small society formed in the log cabin church at Sam's Creek, Maryland, which continued for about sixteen years. He made preaching tours in eastern Maryland and neighboring states and cooperated with Wesley's missionaries, conforming with English forms of Methodist procedure in 1769.

Strawbridge was appointed to the Baltimore Methodist circuit in 1773 but withdrew from the Methodist Conference about 1775 over the issue of the administration of sacraments by laymen. He died near Towson, Maryland, and was buried at Mount Olivet Cemetery in Baltimore.

STUART, Philip: congressman, army officer

Born near Fredericksburg, Virginia, 1760; died August 14, 1830.

Early in his life, Stuart moved to Maryland from Virginia and served in the Continental Army as a lieutenant in the 3rd Continental Dragoons. He was wounded at Eutaw Springs in 1781 and was transferred to Baylor's Dragoons the next year. He was a lieutenant in the 2nd Artillerists and Engineers from 1798 to 1800 and served in the War of 1812.

A Federalist, Stuart served Maryland in the House of Representatives, from 1811 to 1819. He died in Washington, D.C., and was buried in the Congressional Cemetery.

★★★★★

TILGHMAN, Matthew: Continental congressman

Born Queen Annes County, Maryland, February 17, 1718; son of Richard and Anna Maria (Lloyd) Tilghman; married Anna Lloyd, April 6, 1741; father of five children (including Anna Maria); died May 4, 1790.

When he was nineteen years old, Tilghman was adopted by his cousin Matthew Tilghman Ward. In 1741 he was appointed associate justice of the Talbot County (Maryland) Court, and he served as justice of the quorum from 1749 to 1769. He served in the Maryland Assembly from 1751 to 1758, from 1760 to 1761, and from 1768 to 1775, acting as speaker in 1773 and 1774. In 1768 he was a member of the committee to draft a remonstrance to the King against the Townshend Acts. In 1769 he signed the Non-Importation Agreement.

From 1774 to 1776 Tilghman presided over the Maryland conventions which formed the Association of Freemen of Maryland. He served as chairman of the Talbot County Committee of Correspondence and, in 1775, as president of the Council of Safety. Head of every Maryland delegation to the Continental Congress from 1774 to 1777, he declared in favor of independence and recommended a session of the Maryland Convention to remove the Convention's restrictions on independence. He was president of the first Maryland Constitutional Convention in Annapolis in 1776. He was a member of the Maryland Senate from 1776 to 1783, serving as president for part of his tenure.

Tilghman died in Queen Annes County, Maryland, and was buried in the family cemetery.

★★★★★

VAN HORNE, Archibald: congressman

No record of birth; died Prince Georges County, Maryland, 1817.

Van Horne was appointed an adjutant in the 14th Regiment of the Maryland militia in 1798 and received a captain's commission four years later. He began his legislative career in 1801 with his election to the Maryland House of Delegates, serving until 1803; he served again in 1805, also holding the speakership, and later in 1814–16. He represented Maryland in the United States House of Representatives during the 10th and 11th congresses (1807–11), and was a member of the state senate during 1816 and 1817, the year of his death.

★★★★★

WEEMS, Mason Locke: clergyman, book agent

Born Anne Arundel County, Maryland, October 11, 1759; son of David and Esther (Hill) Weems; married Frances Ewell, July 2, 1795; father of ten children; died May 23, 1825.

Ordained a deacon and then a priest of the Anglican Church in 1784, Weems was one of the first two candidates ordained for American service. He served as an Anglican priest in Maryland from 1784 to 1792 and then acted as a book agent for Mathew Carey from 1794 to 1825, traveling over most of the eastern and southern United States.

Weems was the author of *The Life and Mem-*

86

orable Actions of George Washington (his best known work, in which he created the story of Washington and the cherry tree), in five editions from 1800; *Life of General Francis Marion,* 1809; *God's Revenge Against Murder,* 1807; *The Drunkard's Looking Glass,* 1812; *God's Revenge Against Duelling,* 1820; and *Bad Wife's Looking Glass,* 1823. He died in Beaufort, South Carolina, and was buried at the estate "Bel Air," near Dumfries, Virginia.

WICKES, Lambert: naval officer
Born Eastern Neck Island, Maryland, 1735; son of Samuel Wickes; died October 1, 1777.

Wickes spent most of his career as a seaman involved in activity related to the Revolution. Having gone to sea, he became master of merchant ships sailing from the Philadelphia and Chesapeake Bay ports in 1769. He became part owner of a vessel in 1774 and refused to carry East India tea from London.

Given command of the armed ship *Reprisal* in 1776, Wickes carried William Bingham to Martinique. He captured four prizes, including the H.M.S. *Shark.* He transported Benjamin Franklin to France in 1776, his ship becoming the first American warship to enter European waters. He raided the English Channel, upturning five British ships in 1777. Commanding a flotilla of three ships, he took eighteen British prizes off the coast of England the same year.

Wickes drowned when his ship foundered off the Newfoundland banks on its way back to the colonies.

WILLIAMS, Otho Holland: army officer
Born Prince Georges County, Maryland, March 1747; son of Joseph and Prudence (Holland) Williams; married Mary Smith, 1786; father of four sons; died July 15, 1794.

After being appointed a first lieutenant in a Maryland company raised in 1775, Williams participated in the siege of Boston and was promoted to captain. In 1776 he was appointed a colonel in the 6th Maryland Regiment, then was commissioned a major in the Continental Army. Later that year he was wounded and taken prisoner; at first he was paroled in New York City, but then was charged with secretly communicating military information to George Washington and thrown into provost's jail. He was exchanged as a prisoner in 1778, enabling him to take part in the battles of Monmouth and Camden. In 1782 he was promoted to brigadier general.

Williams served as a naval officer of the Baltimore District from 1783 to 1789. During this time, in 1787, he founded the town of Williamsport, Maryland. He was collector of the Port of Baltimore from 1789 until 1793 and died in Miller's Town, Virginia, a year later. He was buried in Riverview Cemetery, Williamsport.

WINDER, Levin: governor of Maryland
Born Somerset County, Maryland, September 4, 1757; son of William and Esther (Gillis) Winder; married Mary Sloss; father of three children; died July 1, 1819.

Levin Winder was commissioned a first lieutenant in the Continental Army in 1776 and in the same year became a captain of the 4th Regiment of the Maryland militia. He advanced to commissions as major in 1777 and lieutenant colonel in 1781 before he retired from the military in 1783.

From 1806 to 1809 Winder, a Federalist, represented Somerset County in the Maryland House of Delegates, serving as speaker in 1809. He was governor of Maryland from 1812 to 1815. He was also a member of the Maryland Senate in 1816. He died in Baltimore.

WRIGHT, Robert: senator, governor of Maryland
Born at the estate "Marborough," near Chestertown, Queen Annes County, Maryland, November 20, 1752; son of Solomon and Mary (Tidmarsh) Wright; married Sarah DeCourcy; second marriage to Miss Ringgold; father of two children; died September 7, 1826.

After attending Washington College in

Chestertown, Wright was admitted to the Maryland bar in 1773. He served with the Maryland Minute Men against the Loyalists on the Eastern Shore of Virginia in 1776, and as a captain of the Maryland militia from 1779 to 1784. He entered Maryland politics as a member of the Maryland House of Delegates from Queen Annes County in 1776 and 1784, and from Kent County in 1786. He was a member of the Maryland Senate in 1787, governor of Maryland from 1806 until 1809, and clerk of Queen Annes County in 1810.

On the national level, as a Jeffersonian Democrat, Wright served as a United States Senator from Maryland from 1801 to 1806. He was a member of the United States House of Representatives from Maryland during the 11th–14th congresses, 1810 to 1817, and again during the 17th Congress, from 1821 to 1823. During the 14th Congress he served on the House Judiciary Committee; he was a member of the House Committee on Foreign Affairs in the latter term.

Wright presided as judge of the District Court for the lower Eastern Shore of Maryland from 1822 to 1826. He died at "Blakeford," Queen Annes County, and was buried in Cheston-on-Wye.

WRIGHT, Turbutt: Continental congressman

Born at the estate "White Marsh," near Chester Mills (now Centerville), Maryland, February 5, 1741; died 1783.

Engaged in farming, Wright was a member of the Maryland General Assembly from 1773 to 1774 and a signer of the Association of Freemen of Maryland in 1775. He sat in the Maryland Constitutional Convention in 1776 and in 1777 was appointed to the Council of Safety. He was commissioned a justice of Queen Annes County in 1779 and served as register of wills from 1779 until 1780. He represented Maryland in the 1781–82 session of the Continental Congress.

Wright's contributions to education included his subscribing to a fund for the establishment of Washington College in Chestertown. He died and was buried at "White Marsh" in 1783.

★★★★★★★★★★★★★

MASSACHUSETTS

"To-day General Gage has issued a proclamation, offering pardon in the King's name to all those, excepting Samuel Adams and John Hancock, who will forthwith lay down their arms, and return to their usual occupations. Those who do not accept the mercy he offers, and who give protection to those gentlemen, or assist them in any way, are to be treated as rebels and traitors."

PENNSYLVANIA JOURNAL, June 28, 1775

ADAMS, Abigail: first lady of the United States

Born Weymouth, Massachusetts, November 23, 1744; daughter of the Reverend William and Elizabeth (Quincy) Smith; married John Adams, October 25, 1764; mother of John Quincy (sixth President of the United States), Thomas, Charles, and Abby; died October 28, 1818.

Abigail Adams was the wife of the second President of the United States, John Adams, and the mother of the sixth President, John Quincy Adams. Her grandson Charles Francis Adams published two volumes of her letters, titled *Letters of Mrs. Adams, the Wife of John Adams* and *Familiar Letters of John Adams and His Wife During the Revolution,* which contain valuable background material on the wartime era in the United States and a look at European society of that time as well.

Contemporaries with opposing political beliefs argued that Mrs. Adams asserted undue political influence over her husband. She died of typhoid fever in her hometown, Braintree (now Quincy), Massachusetts, and was buried there.

ADAMS, Abijah: journalist

Born Boston, Massachusetts, circa 1754; married Lucy Ballard, July 11, 1790; stepfather of David C. Ballard; died May 18, 1816.

Trained as a tailor, Adams became a clerk and bookkeeper for the Boston-based *Independent Chronicle,* a Jeffersonian journal controlled by his brother Thomas, in 1799. That same year, he was indicted for libel as a result of the paper's position on the Alien and Sedition Acts and was given a short jail sentence. He advanced to co-editor (with Ebenezer Rhodes) in 1800. In 1811 he was convicted of libel owing to offensive comments on the judicial conduct of Theophilus Parsons, chief justice of the Massachusetts Supreme Court. He later received a pardon.

ADAMS, John: second President of the United States

Born Braintree (now Quincy), Massachusetts, October 30, 1735; son of John and Susanna (Boylston) Adams; married Abigail Smith, October 25, 1764; father of John Quincy (sixth President of the United

States), Thomas, Charles, and Abby; died July 4, 1826.

Graduated from Harvard in 1755, Adams was admitted to the Boston bar three years later. His opposition to the Stamp Act marked his entry into politics. In 1770 he was elected Boston's representative to the Massachusetts General Court, and he served as one of the state's delegates to the First Continental Congress in 1774. He was a member of the drafting committee for the Declaration of Independence and also was a signer of the document.

It was Adams who proposed George Washington for commander-in-chief of the Continental Army. In 1777 Adams resigned his position as chief justice of the Superior Court of Massachusetts (to which he had been appointed two years earlier) to become a member of the newly created Board of War. He was also elected commissioner to France in that year. His diplomatic accomplishments included the securing of foreign aid from the Netherlands in 1782 and the negotiation (with Jay and Jefferson) of the Treaty of Paris with Great Britain in 1783. He became the first United States minister to Great Britain, serving from 1785 to 1788.

Adams became the first vice president of the United States in 1788 and was reelected for a second term. Four years later, in 1796, he was elected the second President of the United States. During his tenure he acted as a buffer between Hamilton and Jefferson, although he inclined more toward Hamilton and the Federalists. He signed the Alien and Sedition Acts, and resisted pressure to declare war on France in 1798. One of his last acts was to appoint John Marshall chief justice of the United States Supreme Court.

Adams retired to Quincy in 1801, having been defeated for a second term by Thomas Jefferson, with whom he later conducted a memorable correspondence. He was the author of numerous published works, including *Thoughts on Government* (1776), *Defense of the Constitutions of the Government of the United States*

of America (1787), and *Novanglus and Massachusettensis* (1819). Adams died in Quincy on July 4, 1826—the fiftieth anniversary of independence and the same day of death of Adams's longtime colleague Thomas Jefferson. He was buried under the old First Congregational Church in Boston.

ADAMS, Samuel: governor of Massachusetts, Continental congressman

Born Boston, Massachusetts, September 27, 1722; married Elizabeth Wells, 1764; father of two children; died October 2, 1803.

Adams was appointed tax collector of Boston in 1756 and later drafted instructions given by the town of Boston opposing the Stamp Act of 1764. The leading spirit behind the Boston Tea Party, he also organized the Sons of Liberty with John Hancock in 1765.

Adams was elected to the Massachusetts General Court in 1765, where he served until 1774; in that year he was sent as a delegate to the Continental Congress, serving until 1782. A signer of the Declaration of Independence, he spoke in opposition to the adoption of the United States Constitution in 1788.

Adams served as lieutenant governor of Massachusetts from 1789 to 1794 and as governor from 1794 to 1797. The four-volume *Writings of Samuel Adams* was published over a four-year period, 1804–08. He was buried at the Granary Burial Ground in Boston.

ALDEN, Ichabod: army officer

Born Duxbury, Massachusetts, August 11, 1739; died November 11, 1778.

Alden was commissioned a lieutenant colonel in the Continental Army in 1775. He commanded the 25th Continental Infantry and then, in 1776, became a colonel in the 7th Massachusetts Regiment. He was killed in an attack by a raiding party of Indians, Tories, and British at Cherry Valley, New York, and was buried at Fort Schuyler, New York.

ALLAN, John: army officer

Born Edinburgh Castle, Scotland, January 3, 1747; son of William and Isabella (Maywell) Allan; married Mary Patton, October 10, 1767; father of five children; died February 7, 1805.

Allan's family settled in Nova Scotia in 1749. In Halifax he was justice of the peace, clerk of sessions, and clerk of the Supreme Court, and he engaged in agricultural and mercantile businesses. He was a member of the Nova Scotia Provincial Assembly from 1770 until 1776, when he went to Massachusetts to fight in the American Revolution.

Allan led the St. John Expedition of 1777 and became a colonel in the Massachusetts militia the same year. He was the appointed agent of the Continental Congress to the Eastern Indians from 1777 to 1783, during which time he kept the Indians from joining the British side. After the American Revolution, Allan became leader of the American sympathizers in Nova Scotia.

During the years 1784–86 Allan engaged in mercantile business in the Passamaquoddy Bay area of Maine. He died on Allan's Island.

AMES, Fisher: congressman

Born Dedham, Massachusetts, April 9, 1758; son of Nathaniel and Deborah (Fisher) Ames; married Frances Worthington, July 15, 1792; died July 4, 1808.

Ames, a 1774 Harvard graduate, was admitted to the Suffolk (Massachusetts) bar in 1781. A member of the Massachusetts Convention which ratified the United States Constitution in 1787, he also was a leader in its support. He represented the city of Dedham in the Massachusetts General Court in 1788 and was elected as a Federalist from Massachusetts to the United States House of Representatives, serving in the 1st through the 4th congresses (1789–97). His speech in support of the Jay Treaty in 1796 is said to have secured its passage.

Ames was a member of the Massachusetts

Governor's Council from 1799 to 1801; four years later he declined the presidency of Harvard College. His writings are collected in *Works of Fisher Ames* and *Speeches of Fisher Ames in Congress.* He died in Dedham and was buried in the Old First Parish Cemetery there.

ASPINWALL, William: physician

Born Brookline, Massachusetts, June 4, 1743; son of Thomas and Joanna (Gardner) Aspinwall; married Susanna Gardner, 1776; father of seven children; died April 16, 1823.

Aspinwall, a 1764 graduate of Harvard, served as a volunteer in the Battle of Lexington in 1775. A brigade surgeon in the Continental Army, he was deputy director of the army hospital at Jamaica Plain, Massachusetts, from 1776 to 1781. He established a hospital for smallpox inoculation at Brookline, his birthplace, where he practiced medicine until 1823.

In the political arena, Aspinwall served as a member of the Massachusetts General Court, the Massachusetts Senate, and the Governor's Council. He died at the age of eighty-nine.

ATTUCKS, Crispus: insurrectionist

Born circa 1723; died March 5, 1770.

Attucks is famous for his role in the incident known as the Boston Massacre. It was he who led a group of fifty or sixty men from Dock Square to State Street, where they met a small group of British soldiers under the command of Captain Preston. Attucks was killed when the British fired on the crowd.

AUCHMUTY, Robert: Loyalist

Born Boston, Massachusetts; son of Robert Auchmuty; died November 1788.

Educated by private tutors, Auchmuty began to practice law in Boston circa 1760 and became judge of vice admiralty for Massachusetts and New Hampshire in 1767. He served with John Adams as an attorney for the British Captain Preston in the Boston

Massacre case of 1770. His home in Roxbury became a well-known rendezvous for Tories in the Boston area, and he quartered British officers at his home during 1775–76.

In 1773 Auchmuty's letters to friends in England who were sympathetic to the American cause were sent by Franklin to Boston, where they were published. Three years later Auchmuty went to England and became a member of the New England Club of Loyalists. His property in Boston was confiscated in 1779. He was granted a pension by the British government near the end of the war and died soon afterward.

AUSTIN, Jonathan Loring: commonwealth official

Born Boston, Massachusetts, January 2, 1748; son of the Honorable Benjamin and Elizabeth (Waldo) Austin; married Hannah Ivers, 1781; father of James T.; died May 10, 1826.

Austin, a 1766 Harvard graduate, served as a major in the volunteer New Hampshire Regiment in 1775 and was secretary of the Massachusetts Board of War circa 1775–76. In 1777 he was sent to Paris to advise Benjamin Franklin of General Burgoyne's surrender at the Battle of Saratoga. He remained there as Franklin's private secretary until 1779.

Austin represented Boston in the Massachusetts Senate in 1801, and Cambridge elected him to the state House of Representatives for the years 1803–06. After a period as secretary to the Commonwealth of Massachusetts (1806–08), he went on to become treasurer during 1811–12. He died in Boston.

★★★★★

BACKUS, Isaac: clergyman

Born Norwich, Connecticut, January 9, 1724; son of Samuel and Elizabeth (Winslow) Backus; married Susannah Mason, November 29, 1749; died November 20, 1806.

Educated by a local clergyman, Backus was ordained to the ministry in 1748 of the Separatist (New Light) Congregational Church in Middleborough, Massachusetts. He severed his New Light connection because of a difference on the question of infant baptism and established a Baptist church in the town in 1756. He remained there until circa 1802.

Backus gained fame as an itinerant preacher, making nearly a thousand trips away from home to preach in other Baptist settlements in New England. He was agent of the Warren Association, the governing body of the Baptist Church in New England. An advocate of religious liberty in Massachusetts, he vigorously opposed the establishment of the Congregational Church in the state. He also was sent to the First Continental Congress in 1774 to speak on behalf of religious liberty in Massachusetts. In 1788 he helped organize the Baptist churches in Virginia and the following year he participated in the Massachusetts Convention which ratified the United States Constitution.

Backus wrote *A History of New England, with Particular Reference to the Denomination called Baptists,* three volumes (1777, 1784, 1796). He died at the age of eighty-two.

BACON, John: congressman, jurist

Born Canterbury, Connecticut, April 5, 1738; son of John and Ruth (Spaulding) Bacon; married Elizabeth Goldthwaite; died October 25, 1820.

Bacon graduated from Princeton in 1765 and served as pastor of the Old South (Congregationalist) Church in Boston during the years 1771–75. He served on the Committee of Correspondence, Inspection, and Safety in 1777 and participated in the Massachusetts Constitutional Convention in 1779 and 1780. In the latter year he began a series of terms in the Massachusetts House of Representatives, serving in 1780, 1783, 1784, 1786, 1789–91, and 1793. While there he removed many discriminatory provisions from the state constitution.

Bacon also was a frequent member of the Massachusetts Senate, being elected for the years 1781, 1782, 1794–96, 1798, and 1803–06. In 1806 he was president of that body. He was a Massachusetts delegate to the United States House of Representatives from 1801 to 1803 (7th Congress) and was a presidential elector the following year.

In addition, Bacon had a long judicial career. He was assistant judge of the Court of Common Pleas of Berkshire County from 1779 to 1807 and presiding judge from 1807 until 1811. In 1809 he became chief justice of the Massachusetts Supreme Court. He died at the age of eighty-two in Stockbridge, Massachusetts, and was buried in the town cemetery.

BALDWIN, Loammi: civil engineer
Born North Woburn, Massachusetts, January 21, 1745; son of James and Ruth (Richardson) Baldwin; married Mary Fowle, 1772; second marriage to Margery Fowle, 1791; father of George and Loammi; died October 20, 1807.

Baldwin was apprenticed to a cabinetmaker, then became engaged in surveying and engineering circa 1765 in Woburn, Massachusetts. Having been appointed lieutenant colonel in the 38th Infantry Regiment of the Continental Army in 1775, he served with Washington's army in the attack on Trenton, New Jersey, in 1776. The following year he was discharged owing to ill health.

In addition to representing Woburn in the Massachusetts General Court during the years 1778–79 and 1800–04, Baldwin was sheriff of Middlesex County for approximately five years, beginning in 1780. He was chief engineer for the Middlesex Canal, which connected the Charles and the Merrimac Rivers, during the ten-year period from 1793 to 1803. He discovered the strain of apple known in later years by his name and was a member of the American Academy of Arts and Sciences. He died and was buried in Woburn.

BARKER, Jeremiah: physician
Born Scituate, Massachusetts, March 31, 1752; son of Samuel and Patience (Howland) Barker; married five times; died October 4, 1835.

Barker studied medicine under Dr. Bela Lincoln. He was a ship's surgeon during the Revolutionary War, serving in a privateer and then in the Penobscot expedition. After the war he practiced medicine in Gorham, Maine. He was a member of the Massachusetts and Maine medical societies. He was the author of *Vade Mecum; A Book of Anatomy.*

BELKNAP, Jeremy: clergyman
Born Boston, Massachusetts, June 4, 1744; son of Joseph and Sarah (Byles) Belknap; married Ruth Eliot, 1767; died June 20, 1798.

Belknap, a 1762 Harvard graduate, taught school in Milton, Massachusetts, and in Greenland, New Hampshire, from 1762 until 1766. In that year he was ordained to the ministry of the Congregational Church and became pastor of a church in Dover, New Hampshire, where he remained for twenty years. From there he moved to the Federal Street Church in Boston and was pastor there from 1787 to 1798.

Belknap engaged in the writing of a history of New Hampshire in 1767. He served as chaplain to the American troops in Cambridge, Massachusetts, in 1775. In 1791 he helped found the Antiquarian Society of Boston, which became the Massachusetts Historical Society three years later, and served as secretary of this organization until 1798.

Belknap wrote *History of New Hampshire*, three volumes (1784, 1791, 1792); *The Foresters* (1787); *American Biography*, two volumes (1794, 1798); and *Dissertations on the Character, Death, and Resurrection of Jesus Christ, and the Evidence of His Gospel* (1795). He died at the age of fifty-four and was buried in Boston.

BLODGETT, Samuel: merchant, manufacturer
Born Woburn, Massachusetts, April 1, 1724; son of Caleb and Sarah (Weyman) Blodgett; married Hannah White, 1748; father of Samuel; died September 1, 1807.

After serving in the French and Indian War, Blodgett engaged in farming and then became a general merchant in Boston. Later he started manufacturing potash and pearl-ash, extending operations to other Massachusetts towns also, and then expanded into the lumber business.

Blodgett, who was the first justice in the Inferior Court of Hillsborough County, Massachusetts, was a sutler to the Continental Army during the Revolutionary War. From 1794 until 1806 he engaged in the construction of a canal from Amoskeag Falls to the Merrimac River which was completed with the help of the Massachusetts legislature. He died at the age of eighty-three in Derryfield, Massachusetts.

BLOWERS, Sampson Salter: jurist, Loyalist

Born Boston, Massachusetts, March 10, 1742; son of John and Sarah (Salter) Blowers; married Sarah Kent, 1774; died October 25, 1842.

Blowers graduated from Harvard in 1763 and studied law under Lieutenant Governor William Hutchinson. He was admitted to the Massachusetts bar in 1766 and practiced in Boston, serving in 1770 as one of the three defense attorneys in the trial of the British soldiers in the aftermath of the Boston Massacre. A supporter of the royal government, he went to England in 1774, but returned to Boston in 1778, where he was arrested because of his Loyalist stand.

After his release from prison, Blowers traveled to Nova Scotia, Canada. Upon his return to the United States in 1779, he was appointed judge of the Rhode Island Court of Vice Admiralty in Newport. Following the British evacuation of Newport later in 1779, he went to England, but returned soon afterward to become solicitor general of New York. He served in this position until 1783, when he was again forced to flee to Nova Scotia.

Blowers became attorney general of Nova Scotia in 1784 and was speaker of the Nova

Scotia House of Representatives from 1785 to 1788. He spent the next nine years as a member of the Nova Scotia Legislative Council, then began a thirty-six-year tenure as chief justice of Nova Scotia. He died in Halifax, Nova Scotia, at the age of one hundred.

BOLLAN, William: lawyer, colonial agent

Born England, 1710; married Frances Shirley, September 19, 1743; father of Frances Shirley; died May 24, 1782.

After studying law under Robert Auchmuty, Bollan practiced law in Boston circa 1732–45 and served as advocate general of Massachusetts from 1743 to 1745. He was Massachusetts agent in London from 1745 until 1762, having been sent to secure remuneration for the expenses of the Louisburg expedition. He then became London agent for the Massachusetts Council, serving from 1762 to 1769. During his tenure he opposed the attempt to alter the Massachusetts charter (1749), the order against erecting slitting mills (1750), and the act forbidding the issue of paper money (1751). In 1775, when the conflict with England was reaching its climax, he proposed conciliatory measures. He died in London seven years later.

BOURNE, Shearjashub: congressman, lawyer

Born Barnstable, Massachusetts, June 14, 1746; died March 11, 1806.

After graduating from Harvard in 1764, Bourne studied law, was admitted to the bar, and established a legal practice in Boston. He was a member of the Massachusetts House of Representatives in the years 1782–85 and 1788–90. After participating in the Massachusetts Convention which ratified the United States Constitution in 1788, he served the state in the United States House of Representatives from 1791 until 1795 (2nd–3rd congresses). He held the position of justice of the Suffolk County Court of Common Pleas during the years

1799–1806. He died in Boston at the age of fifty-nine.

BOWDOIN, James: governor of Massachusetts

Born Boston, Massachusetts, August 7, 1726; son of James and Hannah (Pordage) Bowdoin; married Elizabeth Erving, September 15, 1748; father of James; died November 6, 1790.

Bowdoin graduated from Harvard in 1745 and was later awarded an LL.D. from the University of Edinburgh. After a period in the Massachusetts General Court (1753–56) he became a member of the Massachusetts Council in 1757. He served as president of the state Provincial Congress in 1775 and participated in the state's constitutional convention four years later.

Bowdoin held the office of governor of Massachusetts from 1785 to 1787, during which time he ordered the suppression of Shays's Rebellion (1786). He attended the 1788 Massachusetts Convention which ratified the federal constitution.

Active in the area of education, Bowdoin was the first president of the American Academy of Arts and Sciences. He became a fellow of Harvard in 1779 and later was a fellow of the royal societies of London and Edinburgh. Bowdoin College is named for him. He died in Boston.

BOWDOIN, James: merchant, diplomat

Born Boston, Massachusetts, September 23, 1752; son of James and Elizabeth (Erving) Bowdoin; married Sarah Bowdoin, May 18, 1781; died October 11, 1811.

Bowdoin graduated from Harvard in 1771 and engaged in mercantile pursuits in Boston the same year, remaining in this occupation until circa 1786. From that year until 1790 he represented Dorchester in the Massachusetts General Court, also participating in the state convention which ratified the United States Constitution in 1788 (he supported ratification). He went to the Massachusetts Senate in 1794 and again in 1801 and was a member of the Governor's Council in 1796. Politically, he supported the Jeffersonians.

As minister to Spain (1804–08), Bowdoin spent most of his time abroad in Paris negotiating with Napoleon concerning the American acquisition of the Florida Territory. He wrote the pamphlet *Opinions Respecting the Commercial Intercourse between the U.S.A. and the Dominions of Britain* (1797). He bequeathed his library, his collection of European paintings, and land and cash to Bowdoin College, which was named for his father. He died in Buzzard's Bay, Massachusetts.

BRADBURY, Theophilus: congressman, jurist

Born Newbury, Massachusetts, November 13, 1739; son of Theophilus and Ann (Woodman) Bradbury; married Sarah Jones, 1762; died September 6, 1803.

A 1757 Harvard graduate, Bradbury taught school for a time in Falmouth, Massachusetts (now Maine). After being licensed in 1762 to practice law before the Maine Court of Common Pleas, he began a practice in Falmouth. The next year he was appointed collector of excise for the Maine District of Massachusetts. Two years later, in 1765, he was admitted to the bar of the Superior Court in the Maine District. He became state attorney for the district in 1777 and served until 1779, when he moved to Newburyport, Massachusetts.

Bradbury served in the Massachusetts Senate from 1791 to 1794 and represented the state as a Federalist in the United States House of Representatives from 1795 until his resignation on July 24, 1797 (4th–5th congresses). From 1797 to 1803 he held the position of judge in the Massachusetts Supreme Court. He died in Newburyport and was buried in the town cemetery.

BRIGHAM, Elijah: congressman

Born Westboro (now Northboro), Massachusetts, July 7, 1751; died February 22, 1816.

Brigham, a 1778 graduate of Dartmouth, studied law for a time before engaging in business in Westboro. He held several state offices: member of the Massachusetts House of Representatives (1791–93), member of the Massachusetts Senate (1796–98, 1801–05, 1807–10), and state councilor (1799–1800, 1806). During approximately this same period, from 1795 until 1811, he also served as a justice in the Court of Common Pleas.

A Federalist, Brigham was a Massachusetts delegate to the United States House of Representatives, 12th–14th congresses (1811–16). He died in Washington, D.C., and was buried in the Congressional Cemetery.

BROOKS, John: army officer, governor of Massachusetts
Born Medford, Massachusetts, May 1752; son of Caleb and Ruth (Albree) Brooks; married Lucy Smith, 1774; father of two children; died March 1, 1825.

Brooks was a 1773 graduate of Dr. Tufts's medical school. He served as a captain of the Reading Company of Minutemen and fought at Concord. He was commissioned a captain in the Continental Army in 1776 and later served as a lieutenant colonel in the 8th Massachusetts Regiment. In 1786 he was commissioned a major general in the Middlesex (Massachusetts) militia.

Brooks was a member of the Massachusetts General Court in 1785–86 and participated in the state convention which adopted the United States Constitution in 1788. In 1791 he became United States marshal for the Massachusetts District and a member of the state senate from Middlesex County. He then served again in the United States Army, this time as a brigadier general, from 1792 to 1796. After a period as adjutant general of the state (1812–16) he held the office of governor from 1816 to 1822.

In addition to his political and military activities, Brooks was president of the Massachusetts Medical Society and belonged to the Massachusetts Society of the Cincinnati

and the Washington Monument Society. In 1815 he also joined the board of overseers of Harvard. He was awarded three honorary degrees by Harvard: an A.M., 1787; an M.D., 1810; and an LL.D., 1817. He died in Medford.

BROWN, Benjamin: congressman, physician
Born Swansea, Massachusetts, September 23, 1756; died September 17, 1831.

Having studied medicine, Brown established a medical practice in Waldoboro, Massachusetts (now Maine). He served as surgeon on the American frigate *Boston,* which was commanded by Commodore Tucker and which conveyed John Adams to France in 1778 after his selection as American commissioner to that country. Later he was captured along with Commodore Tucker in the American warship *Thorne* at the mouth of the St. Lawrence River and was imprisoned on Prince Edward Island. He managed to escape to Boston.

Brown was a delegate to the Massachusetts House of Representatives in the years 1811–12 and again in 1819. He served one term in the United States House of Representatives, 1815–17 (14th Congress). He died in Waldoboro and was buried in the town cemetery.

BROWN, John: army officer
Born Haverhill, Massachusetts, October 19, 1744; son of Daniel and Mehitabel Brown; married Huldah Kilbourne; died October 19, 1780.

After graduating from Yale in 1771 and reading law with his brother-in-law, Oliver Arnold, in Providence, Rhode Island, Brown was admitted to the Tryon County (Rhode Island) bar. He then began a legal practice in Johnstown, New York, but moved to Pittsfield, Massachusetts, in 1773. The next year he became a member of the Pittsfield Committee of Correspondence and of the Provincial Congress. He served in the latter body until 1775.

Brown went to Montreal in 1775 to discover the strength and nature of revolutionary sentiment in Canada. Later that year he received a commission as a major in the Continental Army, serving in battles at Lake Champlain, Montreal, and Fort Chambly. He served under General Montgomery in the unsuccessful attempt to take Quebec in 1776 and was clearly insubordinate in this action. He resigned his commission the next year.

Brown published a handbill attacking Benedict Arnold. After his election in 1777 as a colonel in the Berkshire militia, he captured Fort George. Returning to Pittsfield to resume his law practice, he became a member of the Massachusetts General Court in 1778 and judge in the county Court of Common Pleas in 1779. He was ambushed and killed while leading a group of militiamen.

BROWN, Moses: merchant, philanthropist
Born Newbury, Massachusetts, October 2, 1742; son of Joseph and Abigail (Pearson) Brown; married Mary Hall, 1772; second marriage to Mary White, 1786; father of Mrs. William B. Bannister; died February 9, 1827.

Brown was apprenticed to a chaise maker in Massachusetts, then became a carriage manufacturer in that state. He later engaged in the sugar and molasses trade with the West Indies. Increasing his investments, he came to own several warehouses, distilleries, and wharves in Newburyport, Massachusetts.

Brown made many financial contributions to Andover Theological Seminary, including $10,000 to the Association Foundation in 1808, $1,000 for the library, and $25,000 to establish a professorship in ecclesiastical history in 1819. He also willed $6,000, to be kept at interest until reaching $15,000, to the people of Newburyport for the construction and support of a grammar school. He was eighty-four when he died.

BROWN, William Hill: author
Born Boston, Massachusetts, 1765; son of Gowen and Elizabeth (Hill) Brown; died September 2, 1793.

Brown contributed poetry to the *Massachusetts Magazine* in Boston during the period from 1789 to 1793 and wrote a series of patriotic essays for the *Columbia Centinel,* a Boston newspaper, in 1790. He actively participated in lobbying for the legislation which permitted the opening of theaters in Massachusetts.

Brown wrote the following plays, all of which were produced in Boston: *André,* based on the execution of Major John André; *West Point Preserved, or The Treason of Arnold;* and *Penelope.* His novels include *The Power of Sympathy, or The Triumph of Nature* (his first, written in 1789) and *Ira and Isabella, or the Natural Children.* He died in Murfreesboro, North Carolina.

BROWNE, William: governor of Bermuda, jurist
Born Salem, Massachusetts, March 5, 1737; son of Samuel and Catherine (Winthrop) Browne; married Ruth Wanton; died February 13, 1802.

Browne graduated from Harvard in 1755. He was elected to the Massachusetts Assembly in 1762 and became collector for the Port of Salem in 1764. He was dismissed from the latter post two years later for criticizing Parliament. In 1770 he became judge of the Essex County (Massachusetts) Court of Common Pleas and in 1774 he took office as a judge in the state Superior Court.

In the meantime, in 1771, Browne had been commissioned colonel in the Essex militia. He evacuated Boston with Lord Howe in 1776 and fled to England. The Massachusetts legislature permanently banished him from the state in 1778, and the state confiscated his property the following year. Later, from 1781 to 1788, he served as governor of Bermuda. He died in London.

BULFINCH, Charles: architect
Born Boston, Massachusetts, August 8, 1763; son of Thomas and Susan (Apthorp) Bulfinch; married Hannah Apthorp, November 20, 1788; father of eleven children (including the author Thomas Bulfinch); died April 15, 1844.

Bulfinch graduated from Harvard in 1781. He designed the Old Hillis Street Church in Boston in 1788, the Boston Theatre, and the Beacon Monument in 1789. He served for a long period on the board of selectmen of the City of Boston, beginning in 1791 and continuing until 1817; he was chairman of the board from 1799 on.

Bulfinch designed the Boston State House in 1800 and was architect for the India Wharf, the Cathedral of the Holy Cross, the New South Church, the Connecticut State House, and the Maine State Capitol. In 1817 he succeeded Benjamin Latrobe as architect of the Capitol Building in Washington, D.C., and continued in that position until 1830.

Bulfinch is considered one of the best of the early American architects. He died in Boston at the age of eighty.

BULLOCK, Stephen: congressman

Born Rehoboth, Massachusetts, October 10, 1735; died February 2, 1816.

Bullock, who attended common schools, was a schoolteacher by profession. A captain in the 6th Company of Colonel Thomas Carpenter's Regiment during the Revolutionary War, he served in the Battle of Rhode Island in 1778. He participated in the first Massachusetts Constitutional Convention (1780), and was a member of the state House of Representatives for terms in 1783, 1785–86, and 1795–96. A Federalist, he represented his state in the United States House of Representatives from 1797 to 1799 (5th Congress).

Bullock also was a judge in the Court of Common Pleas of Bristol County, Massachusetts, and served on the Governor's Council from 1803 to 1805. He died in the town of his birth and was buried on Burial Place Hill.

BYLES, Mather: clergyman, author

Born Boston, Massachusetts, March 26, 1707; son of Josiah (or Josias) and Elizabeth (Mather) Greenough Byles; married Mrs. Anna Gale, 1733; second marriage to Rebecca Tailer, 1747; father of nine children (including Mather); died July 5, 1788.

Byles earned an A.B. from Harvard in 1725 and an A.M. in 1728, and later received an honorary S.T.D. from the University of Aberdeen in Scotland. After his ordination to the ministry of the Congregational Church in 1732, he began a forty-four-year tenure as minister of the Hollis Street Congregational Church in Boston. A Tory during the Revolutionary War, he let British troops use his church. After the evacuation of the British, local patriots dismissed him from his post. He was tried and banished from the pulpit, but the banishment was not enforced.

Byles wrote *The Flourish of the Annual Spring* (1741), *Poems on Several Occasions* (1744), and *The Conflagration Applied to the Grand Period, or Catastrophe of Our World, When the Face of Nature Is To Be Changed by a Deluge of Fire, As Formerly It Was by That of Water, The God of Tempest and Earthquakes* (1755). He died in Boston.

★★★★★

CABOT, George: senator, businessman

Born Salem, Massachusetts, December 3, 1751; son of Joseph and Elizabeth Cabot; married Elizabeth Higginson, 1774; died April 18, 1823.

Educated at Harvard, Cabot was elected to the Massachusetts Provincial Congress in 1776. In 1788 he served in the Massachusetts Convention that adopted the United States Constitution. As United States Senator from Massachusetts from June 1791 to May 1796, he framed the Act of 1792, which granted bounties for codfishing.

Cabot became director of the Massachusetts Bank in 1784, and was president of the Boston branch of the United States Bank in 1803. He was the chief promoter of the Essex Bridge and of the Beverly Cotton Manufactory in 1788. After serving as director of the Suffolk Insurance Company, he became president of the Boston Marine Insurance Company circa 1809.

Cabot died in Boston and was buried in the Mount Auburn Cemetery in Cambridge, Massachusetts.

CARR, Francis: congressman, businessman
Born Newbury, Massachusetts, December 6, 1751; father of at least one son (James); died October 6, 1821.

Carr, who attended common schools, became engaged in a mercantile business as a young man. He was a Haverhill delegate to the Massachusetts House of Representatives from 1791 to 1795 and again from 1801 to 1803. He represented Orrington (now a part of Maine) in the House from 1806 to 1808 and served in the Massachusetts Senate from 1809 to 1811.

Carr was a Massachusetts delegate to the United States House of Representatives (filling a Democratic vacancy) from April 6, 1812, to 1813 (12th Congress). He died in Bangor, Maine, and was buried in Mount Hope Cemetery there.

CHANDLER, John: army officer, senator
Born Epping, New Hampshire, February 1, 1762; son of Captain Joseph and Lydia (Eastman) Chandler; married Mary Whittier (also spelled Whitcher), August 28, 1783; died September 25, 1841.

Chandler served in the Continental Army in 1777 and 1780, participating in the Battle of Saratoga, the turning point of the Revolutionary War. He was a member of the Massachusetts Senate in 1803, 1804, and 1819, also serving as a Massachusetts delegate to the United States House of Representatives during the 9th and 10th congresses (1805–09).

After holding office as sheriff of Kennebec County, Massachusetts (now Maine), from 1809 to 1812, Chandler was commissioned a brigadier general in the United States Army during the War of 1812. He was a delegate to the Maine Constitutional Convention in 1819, president of the Maine Senate the following year, and a member of the United States Senate from Maine from 1820 to 1829. He was director of the United States Branch Bank in Portland, Maine, in 1829 and 1830.

Chandler was a founder of Monmouth Academy and a trustee of Bowdoin College for seventeen years (1821–38). From 1829 to 1837 he was collector of customs for the District of Portland and Falmouth. He died in Augusta, Maine.

CHAUNCY, Charles: clergyman
Born Boston, Massachusetts, January 12, 1706; son of Charles and Sarah (Walley) Chauncy; married Elizabeth Hirst, February 14, 1727; second marriage to Elizabeth Townsend, January 8, 1738; third marriage to Mary Stoddard, January 15, 1760; died February 10, 1787.

Chauncy graduated from Harvard in 1721, receiving an A.M. in 1724. He became pastor of the First Church in Boston, Massachusetts, in 1727, serving for fifty-one years. A leader of religious liberals of the time, he objected to the revivalism of Jonathan Edwards on the grounds that emotions were a poor guide to religion when compared to the intellect. He opposed movements to reestablish a close connection between the church and the provincial government. Contrary to Edwards and Calvin, Chauncy believed that salvation was possible for all men.

Chauncy was the author of several works: *Sermon on Enthusiasm,* 1742; *Seasonable Thoughts on the State of Religion in New England,* 1743; *Complete View of Episcopacy,* 1771; *Salvation for All Men Illustrated and Vindicated as a Scripture Doctrine,* 1782; and *The Benevolence of the Deity,* 1784.

CHIPMAN, Ward: Loyalist
Born Marblehead, Massachusetts, July 30, 1754; son of John and Elizabeth (Brown) Chipman; married Elizabeth Hazer, October 24, 1786; father of Ward; died February 9, 1824.

Chipman received an M.A. from Harvard in 1770. Six years later he went to England, returning the following year. He served in a civilian capacity for Britain for the remainder of the Revolutionary War, finally leaving America near the end of the war.

Chipman left England for Canada in 1784 and established a residence in St. John, New Brunswick. He was a representative from St.

John to the first House Assembly of New Brunswick in 1785 and returned to that body in 1802. In 1796 he was appointed an agent to determine the St. Croix Treaty of 1783. A member of the New Brunswick Council in 1806, he was appointed a judge of the Supreme Court of New Brunswick three years later.

Chipman was an agent for the Crown to locate the northwest angle of Nova Scotia in 1816. President and commander-in-chief of New Brunswick in 1823, he advocated the separation of New Brunswick from Nova Scotia. He died in Fredericktown, New Brunswick.

CHURCH, Benjamin: physician, Loyalist
Born Newport, Rhode Island, August 24, 1734; son of Benjamin Church; married Hannah Hill, circa 1758; died 1776.

Church attended Boston Latin School, 1745–50, and graduated from Harvard in 1754. After settling in Raynham, Massachusetts, circa 1768, he practiced medicine. He published political essays supporting the colonial cause but also wrote replies advocating the Tory position. It is believed that he wrote for the Loyalist paper the *Censor,* 1773–75.

In 1774 Church served as a member of the Committee of Correspondence and as a delegate to the Massachusetts Provincial Congress; during this time he came under suspicion for his alleged dealings with Tories. In 1775, while he was serving as chief of the 1st Continental Army Hospital in Cambridge, Massachusetts, he is known to have consulted with the British general, Gage, although he claimed to have been taken prisoner. In October of that year, Church was tried by a court-martial presided over by General Washington and was found guilty of having sent a secret letter to a British officer at Newport during the preceding summer. He was paroled and left Boston for the West Indies in 1776. He died when the ship was lost at sea.

CLAPP, Asa: shipmaster, merchant, legislator
Born Mansfield, Massachusetts, March 15, 1762; son of Abiel and Bathsheba (Pratt) Clapp; married Eliza Quincy, 1787; died April 17, 1848.

Clapp was an officer on an American ship, the *Charming Sally,* during the Revolutionary War. He was then in the merchant service in the West Indian trade until 1798, when he became a merchant in Portland, Maine.

In 1811 Clapp was a member of the Council of Massachusetts. During the War of 1812 he gave financial support to the government, subscribing half of his fortune to the national loan. He was a commissioner to obtain subscriptions to the capital stock of the Bank of the United States in 1816; he himself was the largest subscriber in Maine.

In 1819 Clapp was a member of the Maine Constitutional Convention. The following year he became a member of the Maine House of Representatives, serving until 1823. He was the wealthiest man in Maine at that time. He died in Portland.

CLARK, Jonas: clergyman
Born Newton, Massachusetts, December 14, 1731; son of Thomas and Mary (Bowen) Clark; married Lucy Bowen, September 27, 1757; father of thirteen children (including Polly, Betsey, Lucy, Liddy, Patty, Sally, Thomas, Jonas, William, Peter, Bowen, and Harry); died November 15, 1805.

After graduating from Harvard, Clark was ordained to the ministry of the Congregational Church in 1755. From that year until 1805 he served as pastor of the First Parish Church in Lexington, Massachusetts. He was a close friend of and adviser to John Hancock and Samuel Adams.

Clark was the author of *The Importance of Military Skill, Measures for Defense, and a Martial Spirit in a Time of Peace,* 1768, and *The Fate of Blood Thirsty Oppressors and God's Tender Care of His Distressed People,* 1776. He died in Lexington.

CLARKE, Richard: merchant

Born Boston, Massachusetts, May 12, 1711; son of William and Hannah (Appleton) Clarke; married Elizabeth Winslow, May 3, 1733; father of six children (including Jonathan, Isaac, and Susannah Clarke Copley); died February 27, 1795.

After his graduation from Harvard in 1729, Clarke began to operate the mercantile firm of Richard Clarke and Sons in Boston. In 1773 the firm became a factor for the East India Company; that same year, the company was one of the consignees of the tea used in the Boston Tea Party.

Clarke was attacked by a mob of the Sons of Liberty in his warehouse when he and other consignees refused to resign their commissions as factors. He was forced by public pressure to sign the Non-Importation Agreement. Because of repeated mob attacks on him during the years 1773–75, Clarke went to England, where he joined the Loyalist Club of London. Some of his property was later confiscated by the United States Government. He died in London.

COBB, David: army officer, congressman, jurist

Born Attleborough, Maryland, September 14, 1748; son of Thomas and Lydia (Leonard) Cobb; died April 17, 1830.

A 1766 graduate of Harvard, Cobb was a delegate to the Massachusetts Provincial Congress in 1775. After his military service, which included commissions as a lieutenant colonel in the Massachusetts militia in 1777, a brevetted brigadier general in 1783, and a major general in 1786, he served as a judge of the Bristol County (Massachusetts) Court of Common Pleas from 1784 to 1796.

A Federalist, Cobb served briefly as speaker of the Massachusetts House of Representatives. In 1809 he became the third lieutenant governor of Massachusetts, and in 1812 he was chief justice of Hancock County and a member of the Massachusetts Board of Military Defense. He died in Taunton, Massachusetts, and was buried in Plain Cemetery there.

COFFIN, John: Loyalist

Born Boston, 1756; son of Nathaniel and Elizabeth (Barnes) Coffin; married Ann Mathews; father of Judith; died June 12, 1838.

Appointed ensign in the British Army by General Gage for his gallantry at the Battle of Bunker Hill in 1775, Coffin organized and commanded the Orange Grangers in the battles of Long Island and Germantown. He was with the New York Volunteers (Loyalists) at the battles of San Lucie and Bryars Creek (1778 and 1779), Camden (1780), and Hampton, Hobkerks Hill, and Eutaw Springs (1781). He rose to colonel in 1797, to major general in 1803, and to general in 1819. A member of the Canadian Assembly, he was chief magistrate of Kings County, New Brunswick, Canada, and a member of the Kings County Council. He died in Kings County.

COFFIN, Peleg, Jr.: congressman

Born Nantucket, Massachusetts, November 3, 1756; died March 6, 1805.

Coffin was president of the New England Marine Insurance Company. He was a member of the Massachusetts House of Representatives in 1783, 1784, and 1789, and attended the Massachusetts Senate in 1785–86, 1790–92, 1795–96, and 1802. He served Massachusetts in the United States House of Representatives in 1793–95 (3rd Congress). He was treasurer of Massachusetts from 1797 to 1802.

Coffin died in Boston and was probably buried in Friends Burial Grounds. He was reinterred in Mount Auburn Cemetery in 1833.

COOPER, Samuel: clergyman

Born Boston, Massachusetts, March 28, 1725; son of the Reverend William and Judith (Sewall) Cooper; married Judith Bulfinch; father of two daughters; died December 23, 1783.

Cooper graduated from Harvard in 1743

and became assistant pastor of the Brattle Square Church in Boston that same year; however, he was not ordained to the ministry of the Congregational Church until 1746. The following year he became pastor of the Brattle Square Church, serving in that capacity until his death. In 1767 he received his D.D. from the University of Edinburgh (Scotland).

Cooper was a leader in pre-Revolutionary agitation in Boston. He was vice president of the Massachusetts Academy of Arts and Sciences in 1780, a member of the Society for the Promotion of the Gospel, and a member of the corporation of Harvard (1767–83).

COPLEY, John Singleton: painter
Born Boston, Massachusetts, 1738; son of Richard and Mary (Singleton) Copley; married Susannah Clarke, November 16, 1769; father of four children; died September 9, 1815.

Largely self-taught and precocious as an artist, Copley was famous as a painter of historical subjects and as a pioneer of the American pastellists. He became a fellow of the Society of Artists of Great Britain in 1766, and nine years later he went to England because of his Loyalist sympathies. He was given his choice of commissions by the nobility, although he did not consider those portraits so good as his earlier work in America. He was made an associate member of the Royal Academy in 1775 and became a full member in 1783.

Copley's works include *The Boy with the Squirrel*, 1766; *The Death of Lord Chatham; The Red Cross Knight; Abraham Offering Up Isaac; Hagar and Ishmael in the Wilderness; The Death of Major Pierson; The Arrest of Five Members of the Commons by Charles the First; The Siege of Gibraltar;* and *The Resurrection.* He painted portraits of John Hancock, Samuel Adams, John Adams, John Quincy Adams, Mrs. Thomas Boylston, Lady Wentworth, Mrs. Robert Harper, Lord Cornwall, and the Earl of Mansfield. He died in London, England.

COX, Lemuel: engineer
Born Boston, Massachusetts, 1736; son of William and Thankful (Mandsley) Cox; married Susannah Hickling, 1763; died February 18, 1806.

Cox supervised the construction of the first bridge over the Charles River, between Charleston, Massachusetts, and Boston, 1785–86. An architect, he was the builder of the Essex Bridge from Salem to Beverly, Massachusetts. He also built a bridge at Waterford, Ireland, in 1793. In 1796 he received a grant of land from Massachusetts for inventing the first machine to cut card wire. He died in Charleston, Massachusetts.

CRAIGIE, Andrew: financier, apothecary
Born Boston, Massachusetts, June 18, 1743; son of Andrew and Elizabeth Craigie; married Elizabeth Shaw; died September 19, 1819.

Craigie was Continental apothecary general from 1775 to 1783, and was commissioned a lieutenant colonel in the Continental Army in 1779. In 1783 he became a member of the Society of the Cincinnati. Speculation in government certificates and supplies earned him a large fortune; he owned much real estate in Boston and Cambridge (Massachusetts), including a mansion in Cambridge which became one of the most important social centers in New England. He was director of the First United States Bank. He died in Cambridge.

CRANE, John: army officer
Born Braintree, Massachusetts, December 18, 1744; son of Abijah and Sarah (Beverly) Crane; married Mehitable Wheeler, 1767; died August 21, 1805.

Crane served with the Massachusetts militia during the French and Indian War. A member of the Sons of Liberty, he participated in the Boston Tea Party in 1773.

Crane was commissioned a captain in the Rhode Island Artillery in 1775 and later became a major. In 1777 he became a colonel in the 3rd Artillery of the Continental Army. Six years later he was brevetted a brigadier general. He served in the siege of Boston and at the battles of Saratoga and

Red Bank. For his military services he was granted an estate in Maine by the Massachusetts legislature.

Crane was a judge of the Massachusetts Court of Common Pleas from 1790 to 1805. He died in Whiting, Maine.

CUFFE, Paul: seaman, colonist

Born Cuttyhunk, Elizabeth Islands, near New Bedford, Massachusetts, January 17, 1759; son of Cuffe and Ruth (Moses) Slocum; married Alice Pequit, February 25, 1783; died September 9, 1817.

Cuffe made a large fortune as the owner and captain of several merchant ships which were completely manned by Negroes. He was active in the passage of the Massachusetts Act of 1783, which gave Negroes legal rights and privileges. In 1811 he visited Africa and four years later transported thirty-eight colonists to Sierra Leone in Africa at his own expense.

CURWEN, Samuel: Loyalist

Born Salem, Massachusetts, December 28, 1715; son of George and Mehitable (Parkman) Curwen; married Abigail Russell, May 1750; died April 9, 1802.

A 1735 graduate of Harvard, Curwen was a captain in the Massachusetts militia during the expedition against Louisbourg (1744). He was impost officer of Essex, Massachusetts, and a Massachusetts judge of admiralty.

A Loyalist, he went to England in 1775; while there, he wrote accounts of the boredom and trivia of the Loyalist life in London. When he returned to Massachusetts in 1784, he was not prosecuted for his political sympathies.

Curwen was the author of *Journal and Letters,* 1764. He died in Salem, Massachusetts, at the age of eighty-six.

CUSHING, Thomas: Continental congressman

Born Boston, Massachusetts, March 24, 1725; son of Thomas and Mary (Bromfield) Cushing; married Deborah Fletcher, 1747; died February 28, 1788.

Cushing, a graduate of Yale, was a prominent Boston merchant. He was a member of the Massachusetts General Court from 1761 to 1774, serving as speaker after 1766. In 1773 he became a member of the Boston Committee of Correspondence. The following year he was a member of the Massachusetts Committee of Safety and also of the Provincial Congress of Massachusetts.

Cushing was a member of the Continental Congress from 1774 to 1776. In 1775 he was commissary general of Massachusetts. In 1780 he was president of the New Haven–Price–Hartford Convention and also was a founder of the American Academy of Arts and Sciences. He was lieutenant governor of Massachusetts from 1780 to 1788.

Cushing held an honorary M.A. from Yale (1750) and an honorary LL.D. from Harvard (1785) and served as a fellow of Harvard from 1786 until his death. He died in Boston and was buried in the Granary Burial Ground.

CUSHING, William: associate justice of the United States Supreme Court

Born Scituate, Massachusetts, March 1, 1732; son of John and Mary (Cotton) Cushing; married Hannah Phillips, 1774; died September 13, 1810.

A 1751 graduate of Harvard, Cushing was admitted to the bar in 1755. He was judge of the Probate Court of Lincoln County, Massachusetts (now part of Maine), in 1760 and 1761. In 1772 he became a judge in the Massachusetts Superior Court, holding the position of chief justice from 1777 to 1789. He attended the first Massachusetts Constitutional Convention in 1779 and was vice president of the Massachusetts Convention which ratified the United States Constitution in 1788.

From 1789 to 1810 Cushing was an associate justice of the United States Supreme Court. A founder of the American Academy of Arts and Sciences, he was a fellow from 1780 to 1810. He held an honorary A.M.

from Yale (1753) and an honorary LL.D. from Harvard (1785). He died in Scituate, Massachusetts.

CUTLER, Manasseh: clergyman, congressman

Born Windham County, Connecticut, May 13, 1742; son of Hezekiah and Susanna (Clark) Cutler; married Mary Balch, September 7, 1766; died July 28, 1823.

A 1765 graduate of Yale, Cutler was admitted to the Massachusetts bar in 1767 and received an A.M. from Yale in 1768. Licensed to preach in 1770, he was ordained to the ministry of the Congregational Church the following year and served as pastor in Ipswich Hamlet (now Hamilton), Massachusetts, until 1823.

Cutler served as a chaplain in the Revolutionary War. An organizer of the Ohio Company, he took colonizers to the Ohio River Valley in 1786. A founder of Marietta, Ohio, in 1787, he was instrumental in drafting the Ordinance of 1787 for the administration of the Northwest Territory.

In 1795 Cutler declined the position of judge of the Supreme Court of the Ohio Territory, and later returned to Massachusetts. In 1800 he was the representative from Ipswich to the Massachusetts General Court. A Federalist, he was a Massachusetts delegate to the United States House of Representatives from 1801 to 1805 (7th and 8th congresses).

A botanist, Cutler used the Linnaean system to systematize and catalog the flora of New England. He gained membership in the American Philosophical Society in 1784; in the American Academy of Arts and Sciences in 1791; in the Philadelphia Linnaean Society in 1809; in the American Antiquarian Society in 1813; and in the New England Linnaean Society in 1815. He held an honorary LL.D. from Yale (1789). He died in Hamilton, Massachusetts, at the age of eighty-one.

★★★★★

DALTON, Tristram: senator

Born Newbury, Massachusetts, May 28, 1738; died May 30, 1817.

Dalton graduated from Harvard in 1755. He was admitted to the bar but did not practice law, choosing instead to become a businessman.

Dalton was a delegate from Massachusetts to the convention of committees of the New England Provinces in Providence, Rhode Island, in 1766. A member of the Massachusetts House of Representatives from 1782 to 1788, he served as speaker in 1784 and 1785. He was a Massachusetts delegate to the United States Senate in 1789–91 (1st Congress).

Dalton was surveyor of the Port of Boston from 1814 to 1817. He died in Boston and was buried in St. Paul's Episcopal Churchyard in Newburyport, Massachusetts.

DANA, Francis: Continental congressman, jurist

Born Charlestown, Massachusetts, June 13, 1743; son of Richard and Lydia (Trowbridge) Dana; married Elizabeth Ellery, 1773; father of Richard Henry and Martha; died April 25, 1811.

A graduate of Harvard, Dana was admitted to the bar in 1767. He was a member of the Sons of Liberty. He declined an appointment as a delegate to the Massachusetts Provincial Congress and instead traveled to Great Britain to determine for himself if reconciliation between the colonies and Britain was possible. He decided that separation was inevitable.

Dana was a member of the Massachusetts Council from 1776 to 1780. A delegate to the Continental Congress, 1776–78 and 1784–85, he served as chairman of a committee on the army in 1778. From 1780 to 1783 he was the unofficial minister to Russia and sought to secure recognition of the United States and aid in the war with Great Britain. At the close of the war, in 1783, he presented his credentials to the Russian government, seeking recognition of the United States and acceptance as American minister to Russia; however, Russia refused.

In 1787 Dana was elected to the United States Constitutional Convention but was unable to attend because of illness. He was an associate justice of the Massachusetts Supreme Court from 1785 to 1791 and was chief justice from 1791 to 1806. He died in Cambridge, Massachusetts, and was buried in Old Cambridge Cemetery.

DANA, Richard: jurist, patriot

Born Cambridge, Massachusetts, June 26, 1700; son of Daniel and Naomi (Croswell) Dana; married Lydia Trowbridge, May 31, 1737; father of four children (including Francis); died May 17, 1772.

Dana, a graduate of Harvard, was admitted to the Massachusetts bar and practiced law in Marblehead and Charlestown, Massachusetts. He later practiced in Boston, becoming a prominent member of that city's bar.

Dana was a prominent figure in the colonial cause in the years preceding the American Revolution. He served with Otis, Quincy, Hancock, Warren, and the Adamses in preparing addresses to patriots and petitions to the King and Parliament. He was a member of the Boston Sons of Liberty. He died in Boston.

DANE, Nathan: lawyer, Continental congressman

Born Ipswich, Massachusetts, December 29, 1752; son of Daniel and Abigail (Burnham) Dane; married Mrs. Mary Brown, November 1779; died February 15, 1835.

Dane attended Harvard from 1774 to 1778 and four years later was admitted to the Massachusetts bar. From 1782 to 1785 he was a member of the Massachusetts General Court, and from 1785 to 1787 he was a delegate from Massachusetts to the Continental Congress. In 1787 he was co-drafter of the administration ordinance of the Northwest Territory.

In 1793 Dane became a judge in the Massachusetts Court of Common Pleas for Essex County, and two years later he was appointed a commissioner to revise the laws of the Commonwealth of Massachusetts. In 1812 he was a presidential elector. He established the Dane Professorship of Law at Harvard and was the founder of Dane Hall there. He also founded the Massachusetts Temperance Society, the first society of its kind in America.

Dane's eight-volume *General Abridgement and Digest of American Law* was published in 1823, with a supplementary volume appearing in 1829. He died in Beverly, Massachusetts.

DAVIS, John: jurist

Born Plymouth, Massachusetts, January 25, 1761; son of Thomas and Mercy (Hedge) Davis; married Ellen Watson, 1786; died January 14, 1847.

Davis graduated from Harvard in 1781 and was admitted to the bar in 1786. He was a delegate from Plymouth to the Massachusetts Convention which ratified the United States Constitution in 1788. A member of the Massachusetts House of Representatives three times, he served in the Massachusetts Senate from Plymouth County in 1795. That same year he became comptroller of the United States Treasury.

From 1796 to 1801 Davis was United States attorney for the District of Massachusetts, and from 1801 to 1841 he was a United States judge. He was a fellow of the American Academy of Arts and Sciences and also of Harvard. He was treasurer of Harvard in 1810 and a member of the board of overseers in 1827.

Davis was awarded an honorary A.M. in 1801. He died in Boston.

DAWES, William: Revolutionary leader

Born Boston, Massachusetts, April 6, 1745; son of William and Lydia (Boone) Dawes; married Mehitable May, May 3, 1768; second marriage to Lydia Gendall, November 18, 1795; father of two children; died February 25, 1799.

On April 18, 1775, Dawes rode with Paul Revere from Lexington to Concord to spread the alarm that British troops were attempting a raid on the countryside. Dawes started by way of Brighton Bridge and the Cambridge Road. He then slipped through the British lines and met Revere at Parson Clark's in Lexington, where John Hancock and Samuel Adams were staying. With a new recruit, Samuel Prescott, Dawes and Revere set out for Concord; either Dawes or Prescott managed to elude the British and reach his destination. Dawes later joined the Continental Army as a commissary.

DEAN, Josiah: congressman

Born Raynham, Massachusetts, March 6, 1748; died October 14, 1818.

After attending common schools, Dean was employed in rolling-mill and ship-building businesses. He served Raynham as a selectman in 1781 and as town clerk in 1805. He was a presidential elector on the Jefferson ticket in 1804, and from that year until 1807 he served in the Massachusetts Senate. A Democrat, he was a delegate from New York to the United States House of Representatives in 1807–09 (10th Congress). He then served in the Massachusetts House of Representatives in 1810–11. He died in Raynham and was buried in the Pleasant Street Cemetery.

DEARBORN, Benjamin: musician

Born Portsmouth, New Hampshire, 1754; son of Dr. Benjamin Dearborn; died February 22, 1838.

Dearborn began publishing the *Freeman's Journal, or New Hampshire Gazette* in 1775. In 1779 he opened a school to instruct "young misses," and in 1791 he opened the Portsmouth Academy. The following year he moved to Boston, where he developed a new notation system for musical instruction and also a new type of printing press for songs. He composed music, including psalms and hymns. He died in Boston.

DEARBORN, Henry: army officer, congressman, secretary of war

Born North Hampton, New Hampshire, February 23, 1751; son of Simon and Sarah (Marston) Dearborn; married Mary Bartlett, 1771; second marriage to Dorcas Marble, 1780; third marriage to Mrs. Sarah Bowdoin, 1813; father of Henry Alexander Scammell Dearborn; died June 6, 1829.

Dearborn was organizer and captain of a company in the New Hampshire militia in 1772. Five years later he was commissioned a major in the 3rd New Hampshire Regiment. He was commissioned a brigadier general and then a major general in the New Hampshire militia. He served as deputy quartermaster general with the rank of colonel on General Washington's staff in 1781. He was appointed United States marshal for the District of Maryland in 1790.

Dearborn was a member of the United States House of Representatives from Massachusetts for the 3rd and 4th congresses (1793–97). He was secretary of war under President Jefferson from 1801 to 1809. President Madison appointed him collector for the Port of Boston, and he served from 1809 to 1812. Madison then appointed him senior major general in the United States Army, and he served in the War of 1812.

From 1822 to 1824 Dearborn was United States minister to Portugal. Dearborn, Michigan, is named for him. He died in Roxbury, Massachusetts, and was buried in Forest Hills Cemetery in Boston.

DE BERDT, Dennys: colonial agent

Born circa 1694; son of John De Berdt; married Martha; children include Dennis and Esther; died April 11, 1770.

In 1765 De Berdt was sent to London, England, as agent for the Massachusetts Colony and for the Colony of Delaware. While in England, he helped secure the repeal of the Stamp Act.

DELANO, Amassa: merchant

Born Duxbury, Massachusetts, February 21, 1763; son of Samuel and Abigail (Drew) Delano; married Hannah Appleton; no children; died April 21, 1823.

Delano served as a private in the Continental Army from 1776 to 1779. He engaged in shipping trade with the West Indies until 1787 and commanded ships in trade with China and other parts of the world from 1790 to 1810. He was the author of *Narrative of Voyages and Travels in the Northern and Southern Hemispheres, Comprising Three Voyages Around the World,* 1817. He died in Boston.

DERBY, Elias Hasket: ship owner, merchant

Born Salem, Massachusetts, August 16, 1739; son of Captain Richard and Mary (Hodges) Derby; married Elizabeth Crowninshield, April 23, 1761; father of seven children; died September 8, 1799.

Derby, who followed his father into the shipping business, was one of the wealthiest merchants in New England at the close of the Revolutionary War. He sent his ship, the *Light Horse,* from Salem to St. Petersburg, Russia, with a cargo of sugar in 1784; this was the first ship to display the stars and stripes to the Baltic. The following year he sent the ship *Grand Turk* to Canton, China, making it the first New England ship to sail to the Orient.

Most of Derby's fleet was built under his personal supervision. It was on his advice that the government adopted the bonded warehouse system. He built a mansion in Salem in 1797, where he died.

DERBY, Richard: ship owner, merchant

Born Salem, Massachusetts, September 16, 1712; son of Richard and Martha (Hasket) Derby; married Mary Hodges, 1735; second marriage to Mrs. Sarah (Langley) Hersey, 1771; father of John and Elias Hasket; died November 9, 1783.

Derby went to sea at an early age, and by 1736 he was the captain of the merchant sloop *Ranger.* He bought his own vessel and retired to Salem as a merchant, owning his own fleet by 1756.

Derby profited from the various European wars of the time by trading with all the belligerents. He later supported the Revolutionary cause. In an effort to get the support of the British public for the colonists after the battles of Lexington and Concord, his ship *Quero* was sent to England with dispatches stating that British soldiers had fired first.

DEXTER, Timothy: merchant

Born Malden, Massachusetts, January 22, 1747; son of Nathan and Esther (Brintnall) Dexter; married Elizabeth (Lord) Frothingham; father of Samuel and Nancy; died October 23, 1806.

Dexter worked on a farm from 1756 to 1763. He then began a six-year apprenticeship to a leather dresser in Charleston, Massachusetts, after which time he established his own leather-dressing business in Newburyport, Massachusetts, where he remained until 1791. That year he bought up depreciated certificates of indebtedness of the Revolutionary War and became a wealthy man upon the adoption of Hamilton's funding policy. He sold 42,000 warming pans as cooking utensils in Cuba and also cornered the whalebone market.

Dexter was noted for his philanthropic activities and his donation of substantial sums of money to numerous charities, but he was not without his eccentricities. He called himself "Lord" Timothy Dexter and maintained a luxurious mansion in Newburyport. He engaged a ship-carver to make more than forty life-sized statues of George Washington, Lord Nelson, Louis XIV and others, which he placed on his front grounds. He also had a statue made of himself with the inscription "I am first in the East." He subsidized a former fish peddler to write odes in his honor. Once he had a coffin placed in his front room, where he held a mock funeral over himself and beat his wife when she did not shed any tears. He offered to finance various public improvements in Newburyport on the condition that all the projects be named for him. He also had a gilded eagle placed on the roof of his house. In 1802 he wrote and had printed a pamphlet titled *A Pickle for the Knowing Ones,* which contained not a single mark of punctuation. Instead, Dexter added to the end of the pamphlet two pages containing the word "stop" repeated several times, with the notation that readers could insert them whenever they wished.

DORRELL, William: founder of a religious sect

Born Yorkshire, England, March 15, 1752; married Molla Chase, 1779; died August 23, 1846.

Dorrell, whose name was also spelled Dorrel, Dorril, Dorral, and Dorriel, came to America with the British Army under General Burgoyne in 1775, but deserted two years later. He experienced a religious revelation and began to preach. By 1794 he had a group of followers, known as Dorrellites, in northern Massachusetts who eventually discredited their sect by their unsocial behavior.

Dorrell, who espoused vegetarianism as a central part of his original doctrine, experienced numerous subsequent revelations: he claimed that each generation had a Messiah, that he was the Messiah of his generation, and that those who were resurrected from the state of sin to the spiritual life were not responsible to civil law. He also claimed that he could not be harmed by a human being, but he was beaten by Captain Ezekiel Foster until he was forced to renounce this doctrine. This incident resulted in the end of the sect.

Dorrell, desiring eternal salvation, starved himself to death because he thought his earthly body would live forever if he continued to eat. He died in Leyden, Massachusetts.

DOWNER, Eliphalet: surgeon

Born Norwich (now Franklin), Connecticut, April 3, 1744; son of Joseph and Mary (Sawyer) Downer; married Mary Gardner, 1766; died April 1806.

Downer practiced medicine in Brookline, Massachusetts, from 1766 to 1774. He served as surgeon on board the Continental privateer *Yankee* and was captured and imprisoned in England. In 1777 he escaped to France and that same year served as surgeon

on the Continental sloop *Dolphin*. He shipped on board the *Lexington* and was again captured, but again escaped. He was the surgeon general of the Continental Army on the Penobscot Expedition in 1779. He died in Brookline and was buried in the Walnut Street Cemetery.

DRAPER, Margaret Green: journalist

Born circa 1730; married Richard Draper, May 30, 1750; died 1807.

After the death of her husband in 1774, Mrs. Draper published *The Massachusetts Gazette and Weekly News-Letter* until 1776, when she left Boston with the British. She died in London, England.

DWIGHT, Thomas: congressman

Born Springfield, Massachusetts, October 29, 1758; died January 2, 1819.

Dwight graduated from Harvard in 1778, then studied law. After gaining admission to the bar, he established a legal practice in Springfield, Massachusetts. He was a member of the Massachusetts House of Representatives in 1794 and 1795 and a member of the Massachusetts Senate from 1796 to 1803.

A Federalist, Dwight was a Massachusetts delegate to the United States House of Representatives from 1803 to 1805. From 1806 to 1809 and in 1811 he was a selectman for the Town of Springfield. He was a member of the Massachusetts Governor's Council in 1808 and 1809. He died in Springfield and was buried in Peabody Cemetery.

★★★★★

EDES, Benjamin: journalist

Born Charlestown, Massachusetts, October 14, 1732; son of Peter and Esther (Hall) Edes; married Martha Starr, circa 1754; father of two children (Benjamin and Peter); died December 11, 1803.

Edes was the founder (in 1755), co-owner, editor, and publisher of the *Boston Gazette and Country Journal,* a leading New England radical paper advocating the cause of liberty. He published editorials and propaganda by Samuel and John Adams, John Hancock, and other leaders of the Revolution. A staunch patriot, he was a member of the Sons of Liberty and took part in the Boston Tea Party. He retired in 1798 after forty-three years with the newspaper and died five years later.

EMMONS, Nathanael: clergyman

Born East Haddam, Connecticut, April 20, 1746; son of Deacon Samuel and Ruth (Cone) Emmons; married Deliverance French, April 6, 1775; second marriage to Martha Williams, November 4, 1779; third marriage to Mrs. Abigail (Moore) Mill, September 28, 1831; died September 23, 1840.

Emmons, who graduated from Yale in 1767, was a zealous patriot during the American Revolution and a strong Federalist thereafter. He was pastor of the Congregational Church in Franklin, Massachusetts, for fifty-four years (1773–1827). His six-volume *Works of Nathanael Emmons, D.D.* was published in 1842, two years after his death at the age of ninety-four.

★★★★★

FISKE, John: naval officer, merchant

Born Salem, Massachusetts, April 11, 1744; son of the Reverend Samuel and Anna (Gerrish) Fiske; married Lydia Phippen, 1766; second marriage to Martha Lee Hibbert, 1783; third marriage to Sarah Gerry, 1786; father of three children; died September 28, 1797.

Fiske was a member of the Salem Committee of Safety and Correspondence in 1775, but his chief contributions to the American Revolution were made on the seas as a naval officer. He was captain of the brigantine *Tyrannicide* in 1776, and also commanded the brigantine *Massachusetts*, harassing enemy shipping off the coasts of Western Europe in 1777.

As a merchant, Fiske traded in the Mediterranean and the East and West Indies, purchasing several ships after the Revolution. A member of the Salem Marine Society in 1791, he was commissioned a major general in the Massachusetts militia in 1792. He died five years later.

FITCH, Samuel: lawyer, Loyalist

Born Lebanon, Connecticut, January 16, 1724; son of Joseph and Anne (Whiting) Fitch; married Elizabeth Lloyd, March 1753; father of four children (including William); died October 4, 1799.

Fitch, who graduated from Yale in 1742, was admitted to the Connecticut bar, then moved to Boston to establish a legal practice (1750). From 1768 to 1776 he was acting advocate of the General Court of Admiralty.

In 1776 Fitch was banished from Boston because of his Loyalist leanings; his property was later confiscated by the Act of September 1778. He settled in London, where he died in 1799. He was buried at Saint Mary's Church in Battersea, England.

FLAGG, Josiah: musician

Born Woburn, Massachusetts, May 28, 1737; son of Gershom and Martha Flagg; married Elizabeth Hawkes, April 7, 1760; died circa 1795.

Flagg established a liaison between psalmody and classical music in New England. He introduced the anthem to the English colonies in 1764. Five years later he founded and drilled a military band. During the Revolutionary War he served as a lieutenant colonel in Elliott's Regiment.

FOSTER, Dwight: senator, congressman

Born Brookfield, Massachusetts, December 7, 1757; died April 29, 1823.

After graduating from Brown University at the age of seventeen, Foster studied law, was admitted to the bar in 1778, and established a legal practice in Providence, Rhode Island. He was justice of the peace of Worcester County, Massachusetts, from 1781 until his death in 1823. He was both special justice of the Court of Common Pleas and sheriff of Worcester County in 1792. He was a member of the Massachusetts House of Representatives in 1791 and 1792 and again in 1808 and 1809.

Foster, a Federalist, was a Massachusetts delegate to the United States House of Representatives from 1793 until June 6, 1800, when he relinquished his seat to fill a vacancy in the Senate; his tenure there ended three years later. During this period (in 1799) he was also a delegate to the Massachusetts Constitutional Convention.

Foster was chief justice of the Court of Common Pleas from 1801 to 1811. He was a member of the Massachusetts Governor's Council and also held other state and local offices. He died in Brookfield and was buried in the town cemetery.

FOSTER, Hannah Webster: author
Born 1759; daughter of Grant Webster; married the Reverend John Foster, April 1785; mother of two children; died April 17, 1840.

Hannah Foster wrote two novels which enjoyed great popularity in America in the late 1700s and early 1800s. The first was *The Coquette; or, The History of Eliza Wharton . . . By a Lady of Massachusetts,* the story of an illicit love affair. It became the sensation of the time in New England after its publication in 1797; by 1837 it had gone through three editions. Her second novel, *The Boarding School; or, Lessons of a Preceptress to her Pupils,* was published in 1798.

Foster died in Montreal, Quebec, Canada, on April 17, 1840, at the age of eighty-one.

FRANKLAND, Lady Agnes Surriage: social leader
Born Marblehead, Massachusetts, April 1726; daughter of Edward and Mary (Pierce) Surriage; married Sir Charles Henry Frankland, 1755; second marriage to John Drew, 1782; died April 23, 1783.

Lady Agnes was educated by her future husband, and she became his mistress in 1746, nine years prior to their marriage. She was a leader in Boston Society during the years 1756–58, and later accompanied her husband to Lisbon and then to England. She was buried in Saint Pancras' Church in Chichester, England.

FREEMAN, James: clergyman
Born Charlestown, Massachusetts, April 22, 1759; son of Constant and Lois (Cobb) Freeman; married

Martha Curtis, July 17, 1783; father of one adopted child; died November 14, 1835.

Freeman graduated from Harvard in 1777. He was chosen reader by the vestry of King's Chapel in Boston (the first Episcopal Church in New England) in 1782 and was ordained to the ministry in the Protestant Episcopal Church five years later. He then converted to Unitarianism, and his break with the Episcopal Church and Trinitarianism resulted in the establishment of King's Chapel as the first Unitarian Church in America. Freeman served as minister there for thirty-nine years, from 1787 to 1826. During this period he received an honorary D.D. from Harvard (1811).

Freeman was recording secretary of the Historical Society from 1798 to 1812, and also a member of the American Academy of Arts and Sciences. In 1820 and 1821 he was a member of the Massachusetts Constitutional Convention. He wrote *Sermons on Particular Occasions,* published in 1812. He died in Newton, Massachusetts.

FREEMAN, Nathaniel: jurist, army officer, physician
Born Dennis, Massachusetts, March 28, 1741; son of Edmund and Martha (Otis) Freeman; married Tryphosa Colton, May 5, 1763; second marriage to Elizabeth Gifford, April 7, 1799; father of twenty children (including Frederick and Nathaniel); died September 20, 1827.

Freeman studied medicine under Dr. Cobb in Thompson, Connecticut, then studied law under his great-uncle, James Otis, Sr., in Sandwich, Massachusetts, in 1765. That year he began a thirty-nine-year medical practice in Sandwich, where he also practiced law.

Favoring the colonial cause during the American Revolution, Freeman was a member of the Sandwich Committee of Correspondence and, in 1775, a delegate from Sandwich to the Watertown Provincial Congress. He was appointed a lieutenant colonel and then a colonel in the 1st Barnstable Regiment of Massachusetts. He negotiated with the Penobscot Indians and served in an expedition against the British in Rhode Island. In 1778 he began a two-year term in the Massachusetts legislature. During that term he was employed by General George Washington on a mission to West Point. By the time of his resignation from the Massachusetts militia in 1793, Freeman was a brigadier general.

Freeman served as chief justice of the Massachusetts Court of Common Pleas and was a founder of the Sandwich Academy. In 1802 he wrote "Charge to the Grand Jury . . . at Barnstable." He died in Sandwich at the age of eighty-six.

FRENCH, Jacob: composer

Born Stoughton, Massachusetts, July 15, 1754; son of Jacob and Miriam (Downs) French; married Esther Neale, May 26, 1779; no record of death.

French taught singing in schools in Providence, Rhode Island, during 1796 and 1797. He published *The New American Melody* in 1789, *The Psalmodist's Companion* in 1793, and *The Harmony of Harmony* in 1802. He is best known for the anthem "The Heavenly Vision" and the tune "Dormant." He may have been living in Northampton, Massachusetts, at the time of his death.

FRYE, Joseph: army officer

Born Andover, Massachusetts, March 19, 1712; son of Sergeant John and Tabitha (Farman) Frye; married Mehitable Poor, March 31, 1733; died July 25, 1794.

While an ensign in Hale's 5th Massachusetts Regiment in 1744 and 1745, Frye served in the capture of Louisburg. He rose to captain during King George's War (1747–49) and was commissioned a major in 1754. He served as commanding officer of Fort Cumberland in Acadia (now Nova Scotia), Canada, in 1759 and 1760.

In 1770 Frye moved to a new settlement in Maine which was named Fryeburg seven years later in his honor. He later became a brigadier general in the Continental Army

and favored the separation of Maine from Massachusetts, serving in 1786 as a delegate to a convention which met to consider the measure.

★★★★★

GARDINER, John: lawyer

Born Boston, Massachusetts, December 11, 1737; son of Silvester and Anne (Gibbins) Gardiner; married Margaret Harries, 1764; father of John Sylvester John; died October 15, 1793.

Gardiner, who obtained an M.A. in 1755 from the University of Glasgow, Scotland, studied law at Inner Temple in London from 1758 to 1761. After his admission to the English bar in 1761, he practiced law in the Welsh circuit of England from that year until 1768. He was attorney general of the island of St. Christopher, West Indies, from 1768 until 1770, practicing law there from the latter year until 1783. In 1784 he became a naturalized United States citizen.

Gardiner practiced law in Boston from 1784 until 1786, when he moved to Pownalboro, Massachusetts. A member of the Massachusetts General Court from 1789 to 1793, he advocated repeal of the laws of primogeniture. He drowned in the wreck of the *Londoner* off Cape Ann, Massachusetts, in 1793.

GARDINER, Silvester: physician

Born South Kingstown, Rhode Island, June 29, 1708; son of William and Abigail (Remington) Gardiner; married Anne Gibbins, December 11, 1732; second marriage to Abigail Eppes, 1772; third marriage to Catherine Goldthwait, February 18, 1785; father of six children (including John); died August 8, 1786.

Gardiner established an apothecary shop in Boston in 1744 and later established similar stores in Hartford and Meriden, Connecticut. In 1753 he purchased land in Maine and founded the town of Pittston (now Gardiner). He practiced medicine in Boston and proposed the establishment of a smallpox hospital in 1761.

In 1788 Gardiner, a Loyalist, was banished from America, and his lands were confiscated. He went to Halifax, Nova Scotia, and later to England, returning to the United States in 1785. He died in Newport, Rhode Island, and was buried in Trinity Church Graveyard there.

GARDNER, Gideon: congressman
Born Nantucket, Massachusetts, May 30, 1759; died March 22, 1832.

Gardner was a successful ship master and ship owner and also engaged in mercantile activities. He attended the United States House of Representatives during the 11th Congress (1809–11) and in 1813 took a petition for tax relief from the citizens of Nantucket to Congress. He died in Nantucket and was buried in the Friends Burying Ground.

GERRY, Elbridge: vice president of the United States
Born Marblehead, Massachusetts, June 17, 1744; son of Thomas and Elizabeth (Greenleaf) Gerry; married Ann Thompson, January 12, 1786; father of three sons and four daughters; died November 23, 1814.

Gerry, a 1762 Harvard graduate, served in the Massachusetts General Assembly from 1772 to 1775. Around this time he also was a representative to the Massachusetts General Court (1772–73), a member of the Committee of Correspondence (1773), and a member of the first and second Massachusetts provincial congresses (1774–75). In addition, he was active on the first and second committees of safety and helped raise troops and supplies for the Continental Army.

A member of the Continental Congress from 1776 until 1785, Gerry signed both the Declaration of Independence and the Articles of Confederation. From 1776 to 1789 he served as president of the Treasury Board. In 1778 he attended the New Haven price-fixing convention, organized to attempt to eliminate profiteering; then, from 1780 to 1783, he himself engaged successfully in trade and profiteering. In 1786 he was a member of the Massachusetts House of Representatives, and the following year he was a delegate to the United States Constitutional Convention in Philadelphia.

An Anti-Federalist, Gerry served two terms in the United States House of Representatives, from 1789 to 1793 (1st and 2nd congresses). He accompanied Marshall and Pinckney on a diplomatic mission to France in 1797. He was governor of Massachusetts from 1810 until 1812, when he became vice president of the United States under Madison. He held this office until 1814, the year of his death. During his tenure he presented a bill changing the electoral districts of Massachusetts so as to elect more Republican state senators than warranted by actual Republican voting strength (hence the term "gerrymander").

Gerry was the author of *Observations on the New Constitution and on the Federal and State Conventions by a Columbian Patriot* (1788), which expressed anticonstitutional views. He died in Washington, D.C., and was buried in the Congressional Cemetery there.

GILL, John: journalist
Born Charlestown, Massachusetts, May 17, 1732; son of John and Elizabeth (Abbot) Gill; married Ann Kneeland, January 1756; father of several children; died August 25, 1785.

In 1755, along with Benjamin Edes, Gill began publishing the *Boston Gazette and Country Journal.* The paper became a prominent radical organ, as evidenced by the fact that the Boston Tea Party group met in its office before setting out. Gill and Edes were the official printers for the state of Massachusetts for several years until the partnership was dissolved in 1775. That year Gill was arrested because of the liberal and radical content of the paper; he was freed shortly afterward. He then published the *Continental Journal and Weekly Advertiser* from 1776 until 1785, when he disposed of the paper as a protest against the state stamp act. He was then reappointed the official state printer but died later in the year.

GOODHUE, Benjamin: senator, congressman

Born Salem, Massachusetts, September 20, 1748; son of Benjamin and Martha (Hardy) Goodhue; married Frances Richies, January 6, 1778; second marriage to Anna Willard, November 25, 1804; died July 28, 1814.

Goodhue, who graduated from Harvard in 1766, participated in the Massachusetts Constitutional Convention in 1779 and 1780. During the years 1780–82 he was both a member of the Massachusetts House of Representatives and a delegate from Salem to the Massachusetts General Court. After a period in the state senate (1786–88), he attended the 1st through the 4th congresses of the United States House of Representatives (1789–June 1796), where he was a staunch Federalist and supported the Jay Treaty.

On June 11, 1796, Goodhue became a member of the United States Senate, where he served until November 8, 1800. He died in Salem fourteen years later and was buried in Broad Street Cemetery there.

GORDON, William: clergyman, historian

Born Hertfordshire, England, 1728; married Elizabeth Fields; died October 19, 1807.

Gordon, educated for the clergy in London, England, was minister of the Independent Church in Ipswich, England, from 1752 to 1764. He then was pastor of the Old Gravel Lane Church in Southwick, England, from 1764 until 1770, when he came to America and began preaching to the Massachusetts Historical Society. In 1772 he was ordained pastor of the Third Congregational Church in Roxbury, Massachusetts. The same year, he published *Plan of a Society for Making Provision for Widows,* in which he advocated old-age pensions.

Gordon was appointed chaplain for the Massachusetts Provincial Congress in 1775. In 1777 he delivered to the Massachusetts General Court a sermon celebrating the first anniversary of American independence; the sermon subsequently was widely published. During the period 1776–86 he collected letters and other materials and interviewed generals and statesmen in order to write an objective history of the American Revolution. However, in 1786 he was forced to revise the manuscript because both Englishmen and Americans considered it too objective. The work was published in four volumes in 1788 as *The History of the Rise, Progress and Establishment of the United States of America.*

In 1789 Gordon became a pastor in Huntingdonshire, England, and remained until 1802, when he returned to Ipswich. He died there five years later.

GORE, Christopher: senator, governor of Massachusetts

Born Boston, Massachusetts, September 21, 1758; died March 1, 1827.

After graduating in 1776 from Harvard, Gore studied law, was admitted to the bar, and began a practice in Boston. He was elected to terms in the Massachusetts House of Representatives in 1788, 1789, and 1808. Around this time he also served as United States attorney for the District of Massachusetts (1789–96). After spending some time abroad as commissioner to England (1796–1803) and then as chargé d'affaires in London (1803–04), he returned to America and served in the Massachusetts Senate in 1806 and 1807.

Gore was governor of Massachusetts for a brief period in 1809. On May 5, 1813, he filled a vacancy in the United States Senate but resigned almost exactly three years later, on May 30, 1816. In that year he also was a Federalist presidential elector. His other activities included service as an overseer (1810–15) and a fellow (1812–20) of Harvard.

Gore died in Waltham, Massachusetts, and was buried in the Granary Burying Ground in Boston.

GORHAM, Nathaniel: businessman, Continental congressman

Born Charlestown, Massachusetts, May 1738; son of Nathaniel and Mary (Soley) Gorham; married Rebecca Call, 1763; father of nine children; died June 11, 1796.

Around the beginning of the Revolution Gorham was a member of the Massachusetts legislature (1771–75) and a delegate to the Massachusetts Provincial Congress (1774–75). He served on the Massachusetts Board of War from 1778 until 1781, participated in the state constitutional convention in 1779 and 1780, and went to the state senate in 1780. From 1781 to 1787 he was a delegate to the Massachusetts House of Representatives, serving as speaker in 1781, 1782, and 1785.

Gorham attended the Continental Congress in the years 1782–83 and 1785–87, serving as president in 1786. In 1785 he was an incorporator of the Charles River Bridge and accepted an appointment as judge of the Court of Common Pleas in Middlesex, Massachusetts. He attended the United States Constitutional Convention in 1787 and then the Massachusetts Convention which ratified the federal constitution the following year.

Engaging in land speculation, Gorham obtained, along with Oliver Phelps, title to six million acres of land. The strain of trying to meet his financial obligations to the state of Massachusetts led to a breakdown in his health, and he died in the town of his birth at the age of fifty-eight.

GRAY, William: merchant, state official

Born Lynn, Massachusetts, July 8, 1750; son of Abraham and Lydia (Calley) Gray; married Elizabeth Chipman, March 29, 1782; father of ten children; died November 3, 1825.

Gray, who served in the Revolutionary War, was one of the first northeastern merchants to enter into trade with Russia, India, and China. Becoming one of the leading merchants of Salem, Massachusetts, he employed about three hundred seamen annually. In 1788 he was a delegate to the Massachusetts Convention which ratified the United States Constitution. He served in the state senate from 1807 until 1809. Unlike other Salem merchants, he supported the embargo policies of Jefferson and Madison.

From 1810 until 1812 Gray was lieutenant governor of Massachusetts. He served as president of the Boston branch of the Bank of the United States from 1811 to 1816. He died in Boston.

GREATON, John: army officer

Born Roxbury, Massachusetts, March 10, 1741; son of John and Catherine (Lenton) Greaton; married Sarah Humphreys, 1760; father of several children (including Ann and Richard); died December 16, 1783.

Greaton, a trader, joined the Sons of Liberty in 1774. In that year also he was commissioned a lieutenant in the Massachusetts militia, rising to colonel the next year and serving in the 24th, 36th, and 3rd Massachusetts regiments in the Continental Army. In 1776 he was commissioned a colonel in the 24th Infantry of the Continental Army; in 1783 he became a brigadier general. He participated in an expedition to Canada. He died in Roxbury, the town of his birth.

GREEN, Francis: Loyalist, philanthropist

Born Boston, Massachusetts, August 21, 1742; son of Benjamin and Margaret (Pierce) Green; married Susannah Green, October 18, 1769; second marriage to Harriet Matthews, 1785; father of nine children (three by first marriage, six by second); died April 21, 1809.

Green served as an ensign in the French and Indian War in 1754. He was present at the battles of Louisburg (1758) and Martinique and at the capture of Havana (1762), in the meanwhile graduating from Harvard in 1760. Around the time of the Revolution he became a captain in the 3rd Company of Loyal Associated Volunteers (1775).

Green accepted an appointment as a magistrate in Halifax, Nova Scotia, in 1776 but went to New York the following year, only to have his Loyalist sympathies cause him banishment to England, where he stayed from 1778 until 1784. He then spent the years from 1784 to 1787 as sheriff of Halifax County, Nova Scotia. Settling in Massachusetts in 1797, he became the state's first joint treasurer.

Green was the first American to write on the training of deaf-mutes (he had become interested in the subject because one of his children was a deaf-mute). He published many articles and translations and wrote *The Art of Imparting Speech* (1783). He also helped establish a school for deaf-mutes in London, England. He died in Medford, Massachusetts.

GREENLEAF, Moses: army officer

Born Newburyport, Massachusetts, May 19, 1755; son of Jonathan and Mary (Presbury) Greenleaf; married Lydia Parsons, September 1776; died December 18, 1812.

After serving as a private (1775) and a second lieutenant (1775–76) in the Massachusetts militia, Greenleaf became a lieutenant in 1776 and took part in the siege of Boston. From 1777 until 1781 he served with the 11th Massachusetts Regiment under Colonel Benjamin Tupper, receiving a commission as captain in 1779.

Greenleaf was associated with his father in the ship-building business from 1781 until 1790, when he also retired from the army. He then farmed in New Gloucester, Maine, until his death.

GRIDLEY, Jeremiah: attorney general of Massachusetts

Born Boston, Massachusetts, March 10, 1702; son of Richard and Rebecca Gridley; married Abigail Lewis; father of three daughters; died September 10, 1767.

Gridley graduated from Harvard in 1725. In 1742 he helped found the Marine Society. He became a Freemason in 1748, rising to grand master for all of North America the following year and serving in that position until his death. After a period as a member of the Massachusetts General Court (1755–57), he served as attorney general of the Province of Massachusetts from 1757 to 1767. During his tenure he defended the legality of writs of assistance (which required colonists to contribute to the support of the British Army) against James Otis before the Superior Court of Judication in 1761. He died in Brookline, Massachusetts.

GRIDLEY, Richard: army officer, military engineer

Born Boston, Massachusetts, January 3, 1711; son of Richard Gridley; married Hannah Deming, February 25, 1730; father of nine children; died June 21, 1796.

Gridley served as an engineer during the siege of Louisburg in 1745. He drew plans for the battery and other fortifications at Boston Harbor in 1746 and six years later built Fort Western (in Augusta, Maine) and Fort Halifax. Commissioned a colonel in the British Army, he served under Winslow in the expedition to Crown Point in 1756, under Amherst in 1758, and under Wolfe in the Quebec expedition in 1759. The latter year he commanded the Massachusetts artillery.

In 1775 Gridley received a commission as chief engineer and was commander of artillery for the Continental Army at Cambridge, Massachusetts. The same year he was commissioned a major general, planned the defensive works of Bunker Hill on the night before the battle, and later rose to colonel. From 1777 until 1780 he was engineer general of the Eastern Department of the army. He died in Stoughton, Massachusetts.

GROUT, Jonathan: congressman

Born Lunenburg, Massachusetts (now part of Vermont), July 23, 1737; died September 8, 1807.

Grout studied law, was admitted to the bar, and began a practice in Petersham,

Massachusetts. He served in the expedition against Canada during the years 1757–60. He later saw a considerable amount of battle action during the Revolutionary War.

Grout was a delegate to the Massachusetts House of Representatives in 1781, 1784, and 1787, and to the state senate in 1788. In that year he also attended the Massachusetts Constitutional Convention. He went as a Democrat to the 1st Congress of the United States House of Representatives (1789–91).

Grout died in Dover, New Hampshire, and was buried in Pine Hill Cemetery there.

★★★★★

HALL, Samuel: printer
Born Medford, Massachusetts, November 2, 1740; son of Jonathan and Anna (Fowle) Hall; died October 30, 1807.

Hall was with the *Newport Mercury* from 1762 until 1768, at which time he founded the first printing house in Salem, Massachusetts. He published the *Essex Gazette,* which was a major agent of the colonial cause. He founded the *New England Chronicle* in 1776, the *Salem Gazette* in 1781, the *Massachusetts Gazette* in 1785, and the *Courier of Boston* in 1789. He was known for the publishing of children's books. He retired in 1805 and died in Boston two years later.

HANCOCK, John: merchant, governor of Massachusetts
Born Quincy, Massachusetts, January 12, 1736; son of the Reverend John and Mary (Hawke) Hancock; married Dorothy Quincy, August 28, 1775; died October 8, 1793.

Hancock became a partner in Thomas Hancock and Company in 1763. In 1766 he was a member of the Massachusetts General Assembly. Two years later he became involved in the opposition to the British colonial policy as a result of the celebrated *Liberty* affair; his ship and its cargo of Madeira wine were seized for failure to pay a duty, and Hancock was faced with bankruptcy if pen-

alties resulting from the suits against him were enforced.

A member of the Massachusetts General Court in 1769, Hancock was the head of the town committee of Boston the following year. He was the treasurer of Harvard in 1773, and from 1774 to 1775 he was the president of the Provincial Congress. He was exempted from General Thomas Gage's amnesty proclamation of 1775; he escaped arrest by the British troops sent to Concord to arrest him and Samuel Adams only by a warning from either William Dawes or Samuel Prescott in April 1775.

Hancock was president of the Continental Congress from 1775 to 1777. The following year he had the honor to be the first signer of the Declaration of Independence. After the war, in 1788, he served as president of the Massachusetts Convention which ratified the United States Constitution. He was buried in the Old Granary Burying Ground in Boston.

HANCOCK, Thomas: merchant
Born Cambridge Farms (now Lexington), Massachusetts, July 13, 1703; son of the Reverend John and Elizabeth (Clark) Hancock; married Lydia Henchman, November 5, 1730; died August 1, 1764.

From the age of thirteen until the age of twenty, Hancock was an apprentice to a bookseller and bookbinder. In 1723 he started his own bookstore in Massachusetts. He then engaged in a partnership which supplied a Newfoundland fishing fleet with various supplies and also owned a fleet of freighters. He became one of the wealthiest Boston merchants of his era.

From 1746 to 1758 Hancock engaged in a partnership to supply British forces in Nova Scotia; in 1749 he supplied Colonel Edward Cornwallis. These dealings gave him the opportunity to found Halifax, and, with his partner, he acted as agent for the Province of Nova Scotia in 1755. He increased his wealth through smuggling activities. He died in Massachusetts.

HARADEN, Jonathan: naval officer, privateer

Born Gloucester, Massachusetts, November 11, 1744; son of Joseph and Joanna (Emerson) Haraden; married Hannah Dearman, June 8, 1767; second marriage to Mrs. Eunice (Diman) Mason, March 11, 1782; third marriage to Mrs. Mary Scallon, October 12, 1797; died November 23, 1803.

Haraden was a lieutenant on the sloop (later brigantine) *Tyrannicide* of the Massachusetts Navy in 1776, rising to commander the next year. Together with another ship, he sailed around the British Isles and France in search of prizes. That same year he cruised in the West Indies.

In 1778 Haraden, while commander of the privateering ship *General Pickering,* engaged and captured three ships at one time. In 1780 he encountered a larger ship, the British privateer *Achilles,* and forced it to run off. He was captured with the *General Pickering* at St. Eustatius, West Indies, in 1781. After obtaining his freedom the following year, he commanded the privateer *Julius Caesar.*

Haraden died in Salem, Massachusetts.

HAWLEY, Gideon: missionary

Born Stratfield, Connecticut, November 5, 1727; son of Gideon and Hannah (Bennett) Hawley; married Lucy Fessenden, June 14, 1759; second marriage to Mrs. Elizabeth Burchard, October 7, 1778; father of five children; died October 3, 1807.

A year after his graduation from Yale in 1749, Hawley was licensed to preach by the Fairfield East Association of the Congregational Church. In 1752 he was a missionary to the Indians in Stockbridge, Massachusetts. He established a mission among the Six Nations on the Susquehanna River and acted as an interpreter from 1754 to 1756. He went on a temporary mission to the Indians at Marshpee, Massachusetts, in 1758, but the Indians petitioned to have him made their permanent minister. This request was granted by the Commissioners of the Society for Propagating the Gospels. He died in Marshpee at the age of seventy-nine.

HAWLEY, Joseph: patriot

Born Northampton, Massachusetts, October 8, 1723; son of Joseph Hawley; married Mercy Lyman, November 30, 1752; died March 10, 1788.

Hawley graduated from Yale at the age of nineteen and was admitted to the Massachusetts bar seven years later. He was largely influential in the dismissal from the church of Jonathan Edwards. From 1747 to 1788 he was a member of the board of selectmen of Northampton, often serving as chairman. He was commissioned a major in the 2nd Hampshire County Regiment of the Massachusetts militia in 1754.

Hawley was a member of the Massachusetts General Court in 1751, 1754, 1755, and 1756. In 1773 he settled a boundary dispute between Massachusetts and New York. During the years 1774 through 1776 he was the leading proponent of the Revolution in the Connecticut Valley.

Hawley favored the disestablishment of the church and, in 1780, refused to take a seat in the Massachusetts Senate because of the religious oath members of that body were required to take. He was active in maintaining law and order during the western Massachusetts riots in 1782. He died in Hampshire County, Massachusetts.

HEATH, William: army officer

Born Roxbury, Massachusetts, on March 2, 1737; son of Samuel and Elizabeth (Payson) Heath; married Sarah Lockwood, April 19, 1759; died January 24, 1814.

A member of the Massachusetts General Court in 1761, Heath joined the Ancient and Honorable Artillery Company of Boston in 1765. He was a member of the Massachusetts Provincial Congress, 1774–75. He organized the forces at Cambridge before the Battle of Bunker Hill in 1775. In 1775 he served under General Washington as a brigadier general in the Continental Army, then was commissioned a major general in 1776. Having been in charge of an unsuccessful attack on Fort Independence (New York) in

1777, he was severely reprimanded by Washington and received no more field commands from then until the close of the war, being restricted mainly to staff duty. From 1777 to 1778 he was in command of the Eastern Military District and, in 1779, of the District of the Lower Hudson.

In 1788 Heath attended the Massachusetts Convention which ratified the United States Constitution. He was a member of the Massachusetts Senate in 1791 and 1792, and was a judge of the Probate Court in Norfolk, Massachusetts, in 1792. He was elected lieutenant governor of Massachusetts but declined to serve. He died in Roxbury, Massachusetts.

HEWES, Robert: manufacturer

Born, Boston, Massachusetts, 1751; son of Ann (Frye) Hewes (father's name unknown); died July 1830.

In 1780 Hewes made an unsuccessful attempt to start a glass factory in Temple, New Hampshire. He organized the Essex Glass Works in Boston in 1787; the name was changed to the Boston Crown Glass Company in 1809. He was granted a patent on the manufacture of glass in Massachusetts for the years between 1787 and 1802. He retired in 1824.

Hewes was also part owner of a glue factory, a soap works, and a slaughterhouse; he also taught fencing to the Boston elite. He was the author of *Rules and Regulations for Sword Exercise of Cavalry,* 1802, and *On the Formation and Movements of Cavalry,* 1804. He died in Boston and was buried in the burying ground on the Boston Common.

HIGGINSON, Stephen: merchant

Born Salem, Massachusetts, November 28, 1743; son of Stephen and Elizabeth (Cabot) Higginson; married Susan Cleveland, 1764; second marriage to Elizabeth, 1789; third marriage to Sarah Perkins, 1792; died November 22, 1828.

Higginson was a privateer in the American Revolution. He held a seat in the Massachusetts legislature in 1782, and that year and the next he attended the Continental

Congress. A lieutenant colonel in the Massachusetts militia, he served in the suppression of Shays's Rebellion in 1786. From 1797 to 1801 he was the navy agent of Boston.

A leading Massachusetts Federalist, Higginson wrote the *Examination of Jay's Treaty by Cato,* 1795. He died in Boston at the age of eighty-five.

HOLTEN, Samuel: physician, congressman, jurist

Born Salem Village (now Danvers), Massachusetts, June 9, 1738; son of Samuel and Hannah (Gardner) Holten; married Mary Warner, March 30, 1758; died January 2, 1816.

Holten established a medical practice in Gloucester, Massachusetts, circa 1756, then moved his practice to Danvers in 1758. From 1768 to 1776 he was a member of the Massachusetts General Court. He attended the 1774 and 1775 Massachusetts provincial congresses, abandoning the medical profession the latter year. In 1776 Holten was a member of the Massachusetts Committee of Safety. He attended several sessions of the Continental Congress as a delegate from Massachusetts: 1778–80, 1782–83, 1784–85, 1786–87. He was a signer of the Articles of Confederation.

In 1781 Holten was an incorporator of the Massachusetts Medical Society. A member of the Massachusetts Senate in 1787, he sat in the United States House of Representatives, as a delegate from Massachusetts, during the 3rd Congress (1793–95). From 1796 to 1815 he was a judge in the Essex County (Massachusetts) Probate Court. He died in Danvers and was buried in Holten Cemetery there.

HULL, William: territorial governor, army officer

Born Derby, Connecticut, June 24, 1753; son of Joseph and Eliza (Clark) Hull; married Sarah Fuller, 1781; father of one adopted son, Isaac (a naval hero); died November 29, 1825.

Hull graduated from Yale in 1772 and was admitted to the Connecticut bar three years later. That same year he joined the Continental Army as a captain in the Derby militia, and advanced through the grades to major and then to lieutenant colonel. He served in the battles of White Plains, Trenton, Princeton, Saratoga, Monmouth, and Stony Point. He was an organizer of the Society of the Cincinnati. In 1787 he helped suppress Shays's Rebellion.

Circa 1790 Hull became a judge in the Massachusetts Court of Common Pleas. He served in the Massachusetts Senate from 1790 to 1805. The latter year he was appointed governor of the Michigan Territory by President Jefferson and held that office until 1812. In 1812 he served as a brigadier general in the United States Army during its defense of Michigan and its attack on upper Canada. He surrendered to General Isaac Brock after a futile attack on the British in upper Canada, then surrendered at Detroit without even giving battle. Because of these failures he was court-martialed and found guilty of cowardice and neglect of duty, and sentenced to death. However, he was vindicated in 1824. He died the following year in Newton, Massachusetts.

HURD, Nathaniel: silversmith, engraver
Born Boston, Massachusetts, February 13, 1730; son of Jacob and Elizabeth (Mason) Hurd; died December 17, 1777.

Trained by his father to engrave on silver and gold, Hurd experimented with engraving on copper, although he confined it mainly to bookplates. In 1762 he engraved a cartoon of two counterfeiters who were objects of public interest. His portrait was painted by John Singleton Copley, and it now hangs in the Cleveland Museum of Art.

HUTCHINSON, Thomas: colonial governor
Born Boston, Massachusetts, September 9, 1711; son of Thomas and Sarah (Foster) Hutchinson; married Margaret Sanford, May 16, 1734; father of Thomas, Elisha, William, Sarah, Margaret; died June 3, 1780.

Hutchinson graduated from Harvard at the age of sixteen, receiving an M.A. from that school in 1730 and, later, a D.C.L. from Oxford University in England. A merchant in Boston, he was chosen a selectman of the town in 1737. He served in the Massachusetts House of Representatives in 1737–38 and from 1740 to 1749, acting as speaker from 1746 to 1748. A judge of probate and justice of common pleas of Suffolk County (Massachusetts) in 1752, he was the acting governor of the Massachusetts Bay Colony from 1759 to 1771, and governor from 1771 to 1774. He was the political rival of Samuel Adams.

Hutchinson was the author of *A Letter on the Present State of the Bills of Credit,* 1736; *History of the Colony of Massachusetts Bay,* three volumes, 1764–1828; and *Strictures upon the Declaration of the Congress at Philadelphia,* 1776. He died in Brompton, England, and was buried in Croydon, England.

★★★★★

ILSLEY, Daniel: congressman
Born Falmouth, Massachusetts (now Maine), May 30, 1740; died May 10, 1813.

Ilsley was engaged in a distillery business and a shipping business. He was a member of the Committee of Correspondence and Safety and served as a major and a mustering officer in Falmouth during the Revolutionary War. A member of the Massachusetts House of Representatives in 1773 and 1774, he was also a delegate to the Massachusetts Convention which ratified the United States Constitution in 1788. A Democrat, he was a Massachusetts delegate to the United States House of Representatives during the 10th Congress (1807–09). He died in Portland, Maine, and was buried in the Eastern Cemetery there.

INGRAHAM, Joseph: sea captain
Born Boston, Massachusetts, March 1762; son of Duncan and Susannah (Blake) Ingraham; married Jane Salter, October 11, 1785; father of three sons; died 1800.

Ingraham was one of the earliest sea captains engaging in the American Northwest–

China trade. He became captain of the ship *Columbia* on a voyage to the Cape Verde Islands. On a trip to the Northwest in 1791 he discovered six islands in the Pacific. He was a lieutenant on the United States Navy brig *Pickering,* which sailed in 1799 and was never heard from again.

★★★★★

JACKSON, Jonathan: Continental congressman

Born Boston, Massachusetts, June 4, 1743; died March 5, 1810.

After graduating from Harvard in 1761, Jackson engaged in a mercantile business in Newburyport, Massachusetts. In 1775 he was elected to the Massachusetts Provincial Congress and two years later became a member of the state House of Representatives. He served in the Continental Congress in 1782.

In 1789 Jackson became a member of the Massachusetts Senate and also was appointed United States marshal for the District of Massachusetts, holding this office until 1791. From 1802 to 1806 he served as treasurer of the Commonwealth of Massachusetts, later becoming inspector and supervisor of internal revenue.

In addition to his political activities, Jackson was president of the Massachusetts State Bank and president of the corporation of Harvard. He died in Boston and was buried in the Granary Burying Ground there.

JEFFRIES, John: physician, balloonist

Born Boston, February 5, 1745; son of David and Sarah (Jaffrey) Jeffries; married Sarah Rhoads, 1770; second marriage to Hannah Hunt, September 8, 1787; father of fourteen children; died September 16, 1819.

Jeffries graduated from Harvard in 1763 and obtained an M.D. from Marischal College, University of Aberdeen, Scotland, in 1769. After serving as assistant surgeon on a British naval vessel from 1771 to 1774, he was a surgeon major with British troops during the years 1775–79 and then surgeon general of forces in Nova Scotia. In 1780 he became surgeon general of American forces at Charleston, South Carolina.

Jeffries made the first attempt to gather scientific data on free air. He made two balloon ascents, the first over London in 1784 and the second over the English Channel on January 7, 1785. This latter voyage, in which he flew from Dover to the Forest of Guines at Ardes, France, was the first aerial crossing of the English Channel. For this achievement, he was made a baron of Cinque Ports.

In 1789 Jeffries gave the first public lecture on human anatomy in New England. He was the author of *Narrative of Two Aerial Voyages* (1786). He died in Boston.

★★★★★

KENDRICK, John: navigator, trader

Born Cape Cod, Massachusetts, 1740; son of Solomon and Elizabeth (Atkins) Kendrick; married Huldah Pease, December 1767; died December 12, 1794.

Kendrick, a pioneer in the maritime fur trade, was one of the first American seamen to engage in trade with the Orient. During the Revolutionary War he commanded privateers. In 1787, commanding the expedition of the ships *Columbia* and *Washington,* he left for Northwest America. Two years later he sailed for China. In 1791 he again sailed for the Northwest coast, also visiting Japan on this trip.

Kendrick sailed again for China in 1793 and traded on the Northwest coast during the years 1793–94. In the latter year he took part in the interisland war in the Hawaiian Islands. He died in Honolulu Harbor that year.

KIMBALL, Jacob, Jr.: musician

Born Topsfield, Massachusetts, February 22, 1761; died February 6, 1826.

Kimball was a drummer in the Massachusetts militia in 1775. He graduated from Harvard in 1780, studied law, and was admitted to the bar. He taught music in various New England towns, composed hymns and psalm tunes, and compiled *The Rural Harmony* (1793) and *The Essex Harmony* (1800). He died in an almshouse in Topsfield, Massachusetts.

KINSLEY, Martin: congressman
Born Bridgewater, Massachusetts, June 2, 1754; died June 20, 1835.

Kinsley studied medicine after graduating from Harvard in 1778. During the Revolutionary War he was purveyor of supplies for the Continental Army. He served in the Massachusetts House of Representatives for terms in the years 1787–88, 1790–92, and 1795–96, also holding the office of treasurer of Hardwick, Massachusetts, from 1787 until 1792. In 1797 he moved to Hampden, Massachusetts.

From 1801 to 1804 Kinsley was a member of the Massachusetts General Court from Hampden; he held this position again in 1806. He served on the Massachusetts Executive Council in the years 1810–11, was judge of the Court of Common Pleas in 1811, and then became judge of the Probate Court. He was a member of the state senate in 1814 and of the United States House of Representatives from 1819 to 1821. He died in Roxbury, Massachusetts.

KNOWLTON, Thomas: army officer
Born West Boxford, Massachusetts, November 1740; son of William and Martha (Pinder) Knowlton; married Anna Keys, April 5, 1759; died September 16, 1776.

Knowlton served in the British Army during the Seven Years' War. From 1762 to 1775 he farmed in Ashford, Massachusetts. In 1775 he was elected captain of an Ashford Company and served in the Battle of Bunker Hill. The next year he received a commission as a major in the 20th Infantry of the Continental Army, was promoted to lieutenant colonel in Durkees's Regiment by the Continental Congress, and served in the Battle of Long Island. He was killed during the Battle of Harlem Heights, New York, in 1776.

KNOX, Henry: army officer, secretary of war
Born Boston, Massachusetts, July 25, 1750; son of William and Mary (Campbell) Knox; married Lucy Flucker, June 16, 1774; father of twelve children; died October 25, 1806.

In 1771 Knox established the London Book Store. The following year he was second in command of the Boston Grenadier Corps. He accepted a commission in 1775 as colonel in charge of artillery for the Continental Army. It was he who brought the artillery equipment from Fort Ticonderoga which aided in forcing the British out of Boston early in 1776. Also in that year he was in charge of artillery at New York City and at Long Island, became a field commander (at Trenton, New Jersey), and rose to brigadier general.

Knox started a government arsenal at Springfield, Massachusetts, in 1777, and led at the battles of Brandywine (1777), Germantown (1777), and Monmouth (1778). In 1779 he was the principal founder of the academy which eventually became the United States Military Academy. While on court-martial duty he became one of the tribunal which tried Major John André for treason and condemned him to death (1780). The next year he commanded and placed the artillery for the siege of Yorktown. He was promoted to major general the same year.

From 1782 until 1785 Knox was in command at West Point. He conceived and organized the Society of the Cincinnati in 1783 and served as its first secretary and as vice president in 1805. In 1785 the Continental Congress elected him the first United States Secretary of War, a position he held until 1794. He and Thomas Jefferson founded the United States Navy.

Knox settled in Maine in 1796 and became a brickmaker, cattle-raiser, shipbuilder, and lumber-cutter; he also was a close friend of and adviser to George Washington. He died and was buried in Thomaston, Maine.

★★★★★

LARNED, Simon: congressman

Born Thompson, Connecticut, August 3, 1753; died November 16, 1817.

Larned, who attended common schools, was sheriff of Berkshire County in the years just prior to the Revolutionary War. During the war he served as a captain in Colonel Shepard's regiment. In 1784 he became engaged in the mercantile business in Pittsfield, Massachusetts.

In 1791 Larned was a member of the Massachusetts General Court. He was Berkshire County treasurer from 1792 to 1812. During this period, from November 5, 1804, until sometime the following year, he was a delegate from Massachusetts to the United States House of Representatives.

During the War of 1812 Larned served as a colonel of the 9th Infantry of the United States Army and participated in the Battle of Plattsburg. In the latter years of his life he was president of the Berkshire Bank. He died and was buried in Pittsfield.

LEARNED, Ebenezer: army officer

Born Oxford, Massachusetts, April 18, 1728; son of Colonel Ebenezer and Deborah (Haynes) Learned; married Jerusha Baker, October 5, 1749; second marriage to Eliphal Putnam, May 23, 1800; died April 1, 1801.

During the French and Indian War, Learned served as a captain of Rangers and was a captain in a company in Colonel Ruggles's Regiment. He served as a delegate to the Massachusetts Provincial Congress in 1774 (in Concord) and in 1775 (in Cambridge).

Learned served with the Massachusetts militia at the Battle of Bunker Hill. He was commissioned a colonel in the 3rd Infantry of the Continental Army in 1776 and in 1777 was promoted to brigadier general. He was in command of a brigade at Saratoga.

In 1779 Learned represented Oxford at the Massachusetts Constitutional Convention. He was a member of the Massachusetts legislature in 1783 and chairman of the Massachusetts Constitutional Convention in 1789. He died in Oxford.

LEE, Silas: congressman

Born Concord, Massachusetts, July 3, 1760; died March 1, 1814.

Lee graduated from Harvard in 1784 and was admitted to the bar. He was a member of the Massachusetts House of Representatives in 1793, 1797, and 1798. A Federalist, he served in the United States House of Representatives from 1799 to August 20, 1801 (6th and 7th congresses).

President Jefferson appointed Lee United States attorney for the Maine District in 1802, a position he held for twelve years. In 1803 he was justice of the peace and of quorum. From 1805 to 1814 he was a probate judge, and in 1810 he served as chief judge of the Court of Common Pleas.

Lee died in Wiscasset, Maine, and was buried in Evergreen Cemetery there.

LELAND, John: clergyman

Born Grafton, Massachusetts, May 14, 1754; son of James and Lucy (Warren) Leland; married Sarah Divine, September 30, 1776; father of nine children; died January 14, 1841.

Leland was licensed as a preacher in the Baptist Church in Massachusetts in 1774. He preached in Orange County, Virginia, from 1777 to 1791. He was a leader in the movement to disestablish the Episcopal Church in Virginia and an advocate of the abolition of slavery.

From 1791 until his death Leland lived in Cheshire, Massachusetts, where he was active in preaching and Baptist missionary work. He worked for the disestablishment of the Congregational Church in Massachusetts. He was a Republican member of the Massachusetts legislature in 1811. In 1820 he wrote *Short Essays on Government.* He died in Cheshire at the age of eighty-six.

LEONARD, Daniel: Loyalist, jurist

Born Norton, Massachusetts, May 18, 1740; son of Ephraim and Judith (Perkins) Leonard; married Anna White, 1767; second marriage to Sarah Hammock, 1770; father of one son (Charles) and three daughters; died June 27, 1829.

Leonard graduated from Harvard in 1760 and circa 1767 was admitted to the Massachusetts bar. He was King's attorney for Bristol County, Massachusetts, in 1769–70. For the next four years he was a member of the Massachusetts General Court, during which time he was a leading spokesman for the royal cause. In 1774 he held the office of mandamus councilor of Massachusetts.

In 1775 Leonard entered the British lines and served as a customs commissioner. Signing his name Massachusettensis, he published seventeen articles defending royal policy in the *Massachusetts Gazette* in 1774–75. John Adams directed his *Novanglus Papers* to these articles.

Leonard left Boston with British forces in 1777 and went to England, where he was admitted to the bar. He served as chief justice of Bermuda from 1782 to 1806. He died in London and was buried there.

LEONARD, George: congressman, jurist

Born Norton, Massachusetts, July 4, 1729; died July 26, 1819.

Leonard, after graduating from Harvard in 1748, was admitted to the bar and began to practice law in Norton in 1750. About this time he became register of probate, an office he held for thirty-four years.

From 1764 to 1766 Leonard served in the Massachusetts Provincial Assembly and from 1770 to 1775 on the state's Executive Council. He was judge of probate from 1784 to 1790. He was a judge of the Massachusetts Court of Common Pleas from 1785 to 1789 and chief justice from 1798 to 1804.

Leonard was a member of the United States House of Representatives during the 1st (1789–91) and 4th (1795–97) congresses. In 1792–93 he was a member of the Massa-

chusetts Senate. He served in the Massachusetts House of Representatives in 1801–02.

Leonard died in Raynham, Massachusetts, at the age of ninety and was buried in the local cemetery in Norton.

LEONARD, George: Loyalist

Born Plymouth, Massachusetts, November 23, 1742; son of Nathaniel and Priscilla (Rogers) Leonard; married Sarah Thacher, October 14, 1765; died April 1, 1826.

In 1774–75 Leonard served as a lieutenant of the Associated Loyalists, which aided the British during the blockade of Boston. In 1776 he went with the Boston Loyalists to Halifax, Nova Scotia. He was an agent for Associated (Loyalist) Refugees in Rhode Island in 1779. A director of the Associated Loyalists from 1780 to 1782, he engaged in preying on the colonials' commerce on Long Island and on Staten Island.

From 1782 to 1784 Leonard was a land agent in Halifax. He was superintendent of trade and fisheries in Nova Scotia from 1786 to 1790. He spent the last thirty-six years of his life as a member of the Nova Scotia Governor's Council. He died in Halifax and was buried at Sussex Vale, Nova Scotia.

LINCOLN, Benjamin: army officer, secretary of war

Born Hingham, Massachusetts, January 24, 1733; son of Benjamin and Elizabeth (Thaxter) Lincoln; married Mary Cushing, January 15, 1756; father of eleven children; died May 9, 1810.

Lincoln served his hometown of Hingham as town clerk in 1757 and as justice of the peace five years later. In 1772–73 he was a member of the Massachusetts legislature. He served in the Massachusetts Provincial Congress in 1774–75, first as secretary and as member of the committee on supplies and later as president.

Lincoln was an adjutant of the 3rd Regiment (Suffolk County) of the Massachusetts militia in 1755; he was commissioned a major in 1763, a lieutenant colonel in 1772, and a brigadier general in 1776. He was a third major general in command of the Massachusetts militia near Boston in 1776. In that year also he commanded militia regiments during the reinforcement of the Continental Army in New York City.

In 1777 Lincoln was a major general in the Continental Army in command of the militia in Vermont. In command of the Southern Department of the Continental Army in 1778, he was captured with his forces at Charleston by Clinton the next year. He was United States Secretary of War in 1781 but resigned after the Treaty of Peace. In 1784 and 1786 he served as a Massachusetts commissioner to deal with the Penobscot Indians concerning land purchases.

Lincoln led the Massachusetts militia in the effort to suppress Shays's Rebellion. In 1788 he served as lieutenant governor of Massachusetts and in 1789 was collector at the Port of Boston. The latter year he was appointed a negotiator with the Creek Indians on the borders of the Southern states; in 1793 he entered into negotiations with the Indians north of the Ohio.

Lincoln, a noted essayist on Indian tribes, was a member of the American Academy of Arts and Sciences and a member of the Massachusetts Historical Society. He also held an honorary M.A. from Harvard. He died in Boston.

LINCOLN, Levi: attorney general, governor of Massachusetts
Born Hingham, Massachusetts, May 15, 1749; son of Enoch and Rachel (Fearing) Lincoln; married Martha Waldo, November 23, 1781; father of nine children (including Enoch and Levi); died April 14, 1820.

Lincoln, after his graduation from Harvard in 1772, was admitted to the bar in Worcester, Massachusetts, and began the practice of law. From 1775 to 1781 he was judge of probate in Worcester County.

From 1779 to 1781 Lincoln was a member of the first Massachusetts Constitutional Convention. He was a member of the Massachusetts General Court in 1796 and a member of the Massachusetts Senate from 1796 to 1797. In 1800–01 he was a delegate from Massachusetts to the United States House of Representatives (6th Congress).

Lincoln was United States Attorney General under Thomas Jefferson from 1801 to 1804. In 1806 and from 1810 to 1812 he served on the Massachusetts Governor's Council. He was lieutenant governor of Massachusetts in 1807–08 and governor in 1808–09. He died in Worcester and was buried in Rural Cemetery there.

LITTLE, George: naval officer
Born Marshfield, Massachusetts, April 15, 1754; son of Lemuel and Penelope (Eames) Little; married Rachel Rogers, June 24, 1779; father of at least one son (Edward Preble); died July 22, 1809.

In 1778 Little was commissioned a second lieutenant in the Massachusetts Navy and was promoted to first lieutenant a year later. Also in 1779 he served as first officer of the *Hazard,* and in 1782 he was promoted to captain in charge of the *Winthrop.* A year later he was discharged.

Returning to the service, Little was appointed a captain in the United States Navy in 1799. In command of the *Boston* in 1799–1800, he captured several prizes, including the Danish ship *Flying Fish* and the French ships *Deaux Anges* and *Berceau.* He was discharged in 1801 and died in Weymouth, Massachusetts, eight years later.

LLOYD, James: physician
Born Oyster Bay, Long Island, New York, March 24, 1728; son of Henry and Rebecca (Nelson) Lloyd; married Sarah Corwin; father of at least one child (James); died March 14, 1810.

From 1745 to 1750 Lloyd studied medicine under Dr. William Clark in Boston, and for the next two years he studied obstetrics and surgery under William Smellie and William Cheselden in London, England. He began to practice surgery in Boston in 1752.

Lloyd was the first physician to practice midwifery in America and was an early advocate of vaccination for smallpox. He was the only noted physician to remain in Boston during the American Revolution. He died in Boston.

LORING, Joshua: naval officer

Born Boston, Massachusetts, August 3, 1716; son of Joshua and Hannah (Jackson) Loring; married Mary Curtis, 1740; father of at least one son (Joshua); died October 1781.

Loring was apprenticed to a tanner, James Mears, in Roxbury, Massachusetts. He commanded the brigantine *Privateer,* which was captured by the French during the war between the French and the English in 1744. He was released from prison later in the year. In 1757 he was commissioned a captain in the British Navy, and two years later he commanded naval operations on lakes George, Ontario, and Champlain. He was severely wounded in 1760 but participated in the capture of Quebec and the conquest of Canada under General Amherst.

Loring settled in Roxbury at the conclusion of the war and was appointed a member of General Gage's council. He was under great pressure from the Americans to resign from this council and was denounced by the Massachusetts Provincial Council in 1775 as being an enemy of independence. In 1778 he was banished from Massachusetts by action of the General Court, his property was confiscated, and he left for England. He died in Highgate, England.

LORING, Joshua: Loyalist

Born Hingham, Massachusetts, November 1, 1744; son of Joshua and Mary (Curtis) Loring; married Elizabeth Lloyd, October 19, 1769; father of at least two children (Sir John Wentworth and Henry Lloyd); died August 1789.

Loring served with the British Colonial Army and was commissioned an ensign in 1761 and a lieutenant in 1765. He retired three years later and received a twenty-thousand-acre grant in New Hampshire for his military services. He became permanent high sheriff of Massachusetts in 1769.

Loring signed a protest against the Massachusetts Committee of Safety and in 1774 a document approving the course of action taken by Massachusetts Governor Thomas Hutchinson. The next year he signed a similar document to General Thomas Gage, who had replaced Hutchinson. Loring was appointed by Gage in 1775 as the sole vendermaster and auctioneer of Massachusetts. He was forced to flee from Boston with the British Army the next year, and he went to Halifax.

In 1777 Loring served as commissary of prisoners in the British Army and is reported to have been exceptionally cruel to American captives, although he sent a letter to General George Washington denying charges of cruelty. He was later banished from Massachusetts and spent the rest of his life in England. He died in Edgefield, England.

LOVELL, James: Continental congressman

Born Boston, Massachusetts, October 31, 1737; son of John and Abigail Lovell; married Mary Middleton, November 24, 1760; father of at least two children (including James); died July 14, 1814.

Lovell graduated from Harvard in 1756. From 1757 to 1775 he was a teacher at the Boston Latin School and master of North Grammar School. In 1770 he was chosen the first orator to commemorate the Boston Massacre, which had made him a staunch opponent of British measures. After the Battle of Bunker Hill in 1775, he was arrested by the British for spying and was imprisoned in Halifax, Nova Scotia, in 1776. Later that year he was exchanged and returned to Boston.

Lovell was a delegate from Massachusetts to the Continental Congress from 1776 to 1782, serving on the committee on foreign affairs in 1777. He was possibly involved in the Conway Cabal, a plot to remove George Washington as commander-in-chief of the Continental Army, in 1777. He was a receiver of Continental taxes in Boston from

1784 to 1788 and a collector of customs in Massachusetts in 1788–89. He was a naval officer for Boston and also for Charleston, South Carolina, from 1789 to 1814. He died in Windham, Maine.

LOVELL, John: educator
Born Boston, Massachusetts, April 1, 1710; son of John and Priscilla (Gardiner) Lovell; married Abigail Green, circa 1735; father of James; died 1778.

Lovell graduated from Harvard in 1728 and the following year became an usher at Boston Latin School. He wrote articles for the *Weekly Rehearsal* in Boston from 1731 to 1735. In 1734 he became master or principal of the Latin School, a position he held for forty-one years. Most of the leaders of Boston during the next fifty years, and especially during the Revolutionary period, were former pupils of Lovell. A Loyalist, he fled from Boston in 1776 and died in Halifax, Nova Scotia, soon afterward.

LOWELL, John: Continental congressman, jurist
Born Newburyport, Massachusetts, June 17, 1743; son of the Reverend John and Sarah (Champney) Lowell; married Sarah Higginson, January 3, 1767; second marriage to Susanna Cabot, May 31, 1774; third marriage to Rebecca (Russell) Tyng; father of nine children (including John, Francis Cabot, and Charles); died May 6, 1802.

Lowell, after graduating from Harvard in 1760, was admitted to the Massachusetts bar, and in 1776 was elected a delegate to the Essex County Convention. He was a representative from Newburyport to the Massachusetts Provincial Assembly in 1771, 1772, 1774, and 1776. In 1778 he was a representative from Boston to the Massachusetts General Court. He served as a delegate to the Massachusetts Constitutional Convention in 1779–80.

From 1781 to 1783 Lowell was a member of the Continental Congress. In 1782 he served as a judge to hear appeals in admiralty cases. He was a member of the corpo-

ration of Harvard from 1784 to 1802 and was elected to the board of directors in 1784. Also that year he served on a commission appointed to settle the boundary dispute between Massachusetts and New York. He was a United States judge for the Massachusetts District in 1789 and chief judge of the First Circuit in 1801.

Lowell served as president of the Massachusetts Agricultural Society and was a founder of the American Academy of Arts and Sciences. He received an honorary LL.D. from Harvard in 1792. He died in Roxbury.

LYMAN, William: congressman, diplomat
Born Northampton, Massachusetts, December 7, 1755; died September 2, 1811.

Lyman graduated from Yale in 1776. He fought in the Revolutionary War and later served as an aide to General Shepard with the rank of major during Shays's Rebellion. In 1787 he was a member of the Massachusetts House of Representatives and in 1789 was a member of the Massachusetts Senate.

A Democrat, Lyman was a Massachusetts delegate to the United States House of Representatives from 1793 to 1797 (3rd and 4th congresses). From 1796 to 1800 he was a brigadier general in the Massachusetts militia. He served as a United States consul in London, England, from 1805 to 1811.

Lyman died in Cheltenham, Gloucestershire, England, and was buried in a cathedral in Gloucester, England. A memorial monument to him was later erected in the Old Cemetery at Northampton.

★★★★★

McINTIRE, Samuel: architect
Born Salem, Massachusetts, January 1757; son of Joseph and Sarah (Ruck) McIntire; married Elizabeth Field, 1778; father of Samuel Field; died February 6, 1811.

McIntire was a designer of many colonial houses, churches, and public buildings in Old Salem, Massachusetts. His first important architectural endeavor was the design of the great house built by Jerathmeel Peirce (later, in 1801, he remodeled the great parlor of the Peirce house). Among his other designs were a house on Salem Common (built 1782–89); the Assembly House, 1782; Washington Hall, 1785; Salem Court House and the Nathan Read House, 1793; and the Theodore Lyman House in Waltham, Massachusetts, and the Derby Mansion, 1795. He also designed several other houses for members of the Derby family.

Among his finest works were the Cook and Gardner houses in 1804. McIntire's later works included hotels and business buildings of large scale (for example, the Archer [now Franklin] Building, his most extensive undertaking, in Salem, 1809–10).

McIntire was a pioneer in sculpture and furniture design and carved several bas-reliefs for gates of Boston Common. He was noted for his mantelpieces and cornices. His interiors are on exhibit in the Metropolitan Museum of Art in New York City, the Boston Museum of Fine Arts, and the Essex Institute in Salem. He died in Salem.

McNEILL, Daniel: naval officer, privateer
Born Charlestown, Massachusetts, April 5, 1748; son of William and Catherine (Morrison) McNeill; married Mary Cuthbertson, February 10, 1770; second marriage to Abigail Harvey, circa 1772; father of ten children (including Daniel); died 1833.

A commander of privateers during the Revolution, McNeill served on the ship *Hancock* in 1776, and later on the ships *America*, *Eagle*, *Ulysses*, *Wasp*, and *General Mifflin*. He was commissioned a captain in the United States Navy in 1798 and commanded the ship *Portsmouth* and later, in 1801, the frigate *Boston*. He served in the undeclared naval war against France and also in the war against the Barbary states.

McNEILL, Hector: naval officer, privateer
Born County Antrim, Ireland, October 10, 1728; son of Malcolm and Mary (Stuart) McNeill; married Mary Wilson, November 12, 1750; second marriage to Mary Watt, December 26, 1770; father of five children; died December 25, 1785.

In 1737 McNeill's family arrived in America, settling in Boston. He served in the French and Indian War and was appointed a captain in the Continental Navy in 1776. In command of the frigate *Boston,* he was a member of the privateer fleet in 1777. He was court-martialed and dismissed or suspended from the service on the charge of not coming to the rescue of a sister ship in distress. He commanded two privateers later in the Revolution and died at sea soon after the end of hostilities.

McNUTT, Alexander: colonizer
Born Londonderry, Ireland, circa 1725; son of Alexander and Jane McNutt; died circa 1811.

On arriving in America, McNutt settled near Staunton, Virginia, before 1753. He served as an officer in the militia commanded by Major Andrew Lewis in 1756. A captain in the Massachusetts militia in 1760, he was also a representative for the Boston firm of Apthorp and Hancock to attract settlers to Nova Scotia, 1758–61. He was granted 1,745,000 acres of land in Nova Scotia to promote immigration in 1765. He moved to Jamaica Plain, Massachusetts, in 1778 and during the years 1778–81 repeatedly urged the Continental Congress to draw Nova Scotia into the Revolution.

MALCOLM, Daniel: merchant, sea captain, patriot
Born Georgetown, Maine, November 29, 1725; son of Michael and Sarah Malcolm; married Ann Fudge; father of several children; died October 23, 1769.

A sea captain and the owner of several vessels, Malcolm was a leader of the Sons of Liberty and a warden of Christ Church in Boston. He was the most active antagonist of the customs authorities, and he presided at a meeting in 1768 where the merchants of Boston agreed not to import any British goods for eighteen months (the first organized merchants protest against Acts of Parliament). Malcolm led the patriots in the first clash with the British armed forces in 1768. He died in Boston and was buried in Copp's Hill Burying Ground there.

MANLEY, John: naval officer

Born Boston, Massachusetts, circa 1734; married Hannah Cheevers, February 26, 1763; second marriage to Friswith Arnold, December 14, 1791; died February 14, 1793.

Master of the ship *Little Fortesque* in 1768–69, Manley was commissioned a captain in the Continental Army in 1775 and commanded the schooner *Lee* against the British. He captured several valuable prizes and was promoted to commander of the fleet and master of the schooner *Hancock* in 1776, and also was commissioned a captain in the Continental Navy.

While commanding the frigate *Hancock,* Manley was captured and imprisoned by the British in 1777–78. After his release he sailed as a privateer in command of the ships *Marlborough* and *Cumberland* and was again captured by the British, but escaped in 1779. He was captured a third time while serving aboard the ship *Jason* and imprisoned for two years. He returned to the navy for a last successful voyage on the ship *Hague* in 1783. He was buried with military honors in Boston.

MASON, Jonathan: senator

Born Boston, Massachusetts, September 12, 1756; son of Jonathan and Miriam (Clark) Mason; married Susannah Powell, 1779; father of six children; died November 1, 1831.

Mason, a graduate of the College of New Jersey (now Princeton), read law with John Adams in the office of Josiah Quincy, then (in 1779) was admitted to the Massachusetts bar. He delivered the annual oration commemorating the Boston Massacre in 1780 and served in the Massachusetts House of Representatives from 1786 to 1796 and from 1805 to 1808.

With Harrison Gray Otis, Joseph Woodward, and Charles Ward Apthorp, Mason established a real estate syndicate in Boston and purchased the southwestern slope of Beacon Hill in 1795, turning it into a fashionable residential district.

Mason was a member of the Massachusetts Executive Council in 1797–98 and the Massachusetts Senate in 1799–1800 and 1803–04. Named to the United States Senate (Federalist) on November 14, 1800, he served there until 1803, taking part in debates on repealing the Judiciary Act of 1801. He moved to request that President Jefferson remove the Embargo at a special meeting in Boston in 1808, and the motion was carried. He was a Massachusetts delegate to the United States House of Representatives (Federalist) from 1817 to 1820 (15th and 16th congresses).

Mason was a member of the South Boston Association and a director of the Boston branch of the United States Bank. He died in Boston and was buried in Mount Auburn Cemetery in Cambridge, Massachusetts.

MATHER, Samuel: clergyman

Born Boston, Massachusetts, October 30, 1706; son of Cotton and Elizabeth (Clark) Mather; married Hannah Hutchinson, August 23, 1733; father of Hannah, Samuel, Thomas, and Increase; died June 27, 1785.

Mather received an A.B. degree from Harvard in 1723 and then became chaplain of Castle William, Boston Harbor, serving from 1724 to 1732. He was minister of the Second Congregational Church of Boston from 1732 to 1741. Dismissed by the church, he established, with a minority of his old parishioners, a new church and served as its minister until his death.

Mather was awarded several honorary degrees during his lifetime: M.A., University of Glasgow (Scotland), 1731; D.D., University of Aberdeen (Scotland), 1762; D.D., Harvard, 1773. He was the author of *Life of the Very Reverend and Learned Cotton Mather,* 1729; *Attempt to Show That America Must Be Known to the Ancients,* 1773; and *The Sacred Minister,* 1773. He died in Boston and was buried in Copp's Hill Burying Ground there.

MATIGNON, Francis Anthony: clergyman

Born Paris, France, November 10, 1753; died September 19, 1818.

Matignon was ordained a priest in the Roman Catholic Church in 1778 and served as a curate until 1782. After earning a B.D. from the Seminary of St. Sulpice, he received a Ph.D. in divinity from the Sorbonne in 1785. He was a professor of theology at the College of Navarre from 1785 to 1789.

Soon after arriving in Baltimore in 1792, Matignon moved to Boston and became a pastor, serving until his death in 1818. He was active in raising funds for Holy Trinity Church on Franklin Square in Boston. He died in Boston and was buried in St. Augustine's Cemetery there.

MATTOON, Ebenezer: congressman

Born North Amherst, Massachusetts, August 19, 1755; died September 11, 1843.

A graduate of Dartmouth in 1776, Mattoon later attained the rank of major in the Continental Army. After leaving the service he taught school and engaged in farming. A member of the Massachusetts House of Representatives in 1781 and later in 1812, Mattoon also served as a justice of the peace from 1782 to 1796. He was a presidential elector in the years 1792, 1796, 1820, and 1828.

Mattoon was a member of the Massachusetts Senate in 1795 and 1796; became a major general, 4th Division, Massachusetts militia; and served as sheriff of Hampshire County, Massachusetts, from 1796 to 1816. A Federalist, he was a Massachusetts delegate to the United States House of Representatives, from February 2, 1801, until 1803. He served as a major general in the Massachusetts militia from 1799 to 1816, then advanced to adjutant general. Although he became blind in 1818, he served

as a delegate to the Massachusetts Constitutional Convention in 1820.

Mattoon died in Amherst at the age of eighty-eight and was buried in the West Cemetery in Amherst.

MECOM, Benjamin: printer

Born Boston, December 29, 1732; son of Edward and Jane (Franklin) Mecom; died after 1776.

Manager of the *Antigua Gazette* (which was owned by Benjamin Franklin) from 1752 to 1757, Mecom had his own printing firm in Boston from 1757 to 1763. He printed editions of *The New England Primer Enlarged,* 1757, and *The New England Psalter,* 1758. He operated an unsuccessful printing office in New York from 1763 to 1765, then published the *Connecticut Gazette* from 1765 to 1768. The latter year Mecom founded the *Penny Post* in Philadelphia and published it for two years. He was last heard of when his name was mentioned in a letter from William Smith to Benjamin Franklin in 1776.

MERRILL, Daniel: clergyman

Born Rowley, Massachusetts, March 18, 1765; son of Thomas and Sarah (Friend) Merrill; married Joanna Colby, August 14, 1793; second marriage to Susanna Gale, October 14, 1794; father of thirteen children; died June 3, 1833.

Merrill served as a private in the 3rd Massachusetts Infantry during the Revolution. He graduated from Dartmouth in 1789 and studied theology under Dr. Spring in Newburyport. He was licensed to preach in 1791 and was ordained to the ministry of the Congregational Church in Sedgewick, Maine, in 1793. However, in 1805 he converted to the Baptist Church and was ordained to that church's ministry.

Merrill served as a member of the Massachusetts General Assembly circa 1813. He was a founder of Waterville (now Colby) College in 1813 and lived in Nottingham West (now Hudson), New Hampshire, from 1814 to 1821. He served as pastor of the Baptist Church in Sedgewick from 1821 to 1833. He was the author of *The Mode and*

Subjects of Baptism Examined, 1805; *Eight Letters on Open Communion,* 1805; and *Balaam Disappointed,* 1815.

MORTON, Sarah Wentworth Apthorpe: poet

Born Boston, Massachusetts, August 1759; daughter of James and Sarah (Wentworth) Apthorpe; married Perez Morton, February 24, 1781; mother of five children; died May 14, 1846.

Sarah Morton wrote under the pseudonym Philenia. A contributor to the *Massachusetts Magazine* from 1789 to 1793, she enjoyed great popularity in her time, and her style was widely copied and imitated. She may have been the author of the earliest American novel, *The Power of Sympathy.* Her works include *Quabi, or the Virtues of Nature, an Indian Tale,* published in Boston in 1790; *The African Chief* (verses), 1792; and *Beacon Hill, a Local Poem, Historical and Descriptive,* 1797. She died in Quincy, Massachusetts.

MURRAY, John: clergyman

Born Alton, England, December 10, 1741; married Eliza Neale, before 1770; second marriage to Judith (Sargent) Stevens, October 1788; died September 3, 1815.

Excommunicated by the Methodist Church after accepting the teachings of Universalism as taught by John Relly in England, Murray came to America in 1770. He was a roving preacher for four years and then settled in Gloucester, Massachusetts, in 1774. He served as chaplain for Rhode Island troops in 1775, organized the first Universalist Church in America in 1779, and was pastor of the Universalist Society of Boston in 1793.

Murray wrote *Letters and Sketches* in 1812 and an autobiography in 1813. He died in Boston and was buried in Mount Auburn Cemetery in Cambridge, Massachusetts.

MURRAY, Judith Sargent Stevens: author

Born May 1, 1751; daughter of Captain Winthrop and Judith (Sanders) Sargent; married Captain John Stevens, October 3, 1769; second marriage to the Reverend John Murray, October 6, 1788; died July 6, 1820.

From 1792 to 1794 Judith Murray contributed poems, essays, and stories to local newspapers and wrote essays under the heading "The Gleaner" for the *Massachusetts Magazine.* She edited and completed her husband's autobiography, *Letters, Sketches of Sermons and Autobiography of Reverend John Murray* (three volumes), 1812–13. Her early works were collected and published as *The Gleaner* (three volumes) in 1798. She died in Natchez, Mississippi.

★★★★★

NICHOLSON, Samuel: naval officer

Born Chestertown, Maryland, 1743; son of Joseph and Hannah Smith (Scott) Nicholson; married Mary Dowse, February 9, 1780; father of at least four children; died Charleston, Massachusetts, December 29, 1811.

Nicholson, who was commissioned a captain in the Continental Navy in 1776, secured the English cutter *Dolphin* for the United States. In 1778 he commanded the frigate *Deane.* Six years later he received a commission as a captain in the United States Navy. Nicholson superintended the construction of the frigate *Constitution* and in 1801 became the first superintendent of the Charlestown, Massachusetts, Navy Yard. In 1901 the torpedo ship *Nicholson* was named for him.

NIXON, John: army officer

Born Framingham, Massachusetts, March 1, 1727; son of Christopher and Mary (Seaver) Nixon; married Thankful Berry, February 7, 1754; second marriage to Hannah (Drury) Gleason, February 5, 1778; father of five sons and five daughters; died March 24, 1815.

In 1745 Nixon served in the expedition against Louisburg. In 1755 he was commissioned a lieutenant and then a captain in the Continental Army. Three years later he became captain of a company in Colonel Ruggles's Regiment at Half Moon, New York. He commanded a company of Minutemen at Lexington and Concord, Massachusetts, on April 19, 1775.

Nixon became a colonel in the 4th Infantry of the Continental Army in 1776 and was elected a brigadier general the same year. He resigned from military service in 1780. He died in Middlebury, Vermont, at the age of eighty-eight.

NORMAN, John: engraver, publisher
Born England, 1748; died June 8, 1817.

Very few facts are known about Norman's personal life, except that he came to America circa 1774. At intervals he printed the *Geographical Gazetteer of Massachusetts.* He published "A Map of the Present Seat of War" in 1776, and made the plates for *An Impartial History of the War in America between Great Britain and the United States* (2 volumes, 1781–82).

In 1789 Norman published the first Boston Directory and engraved a portrait of General Washington that had appeared in the *Philadelphia Almanack for the Year of Our Lord 1780.* He published *Wetherwise's Federal Almanack for the Year of Our Lord 1790.* In 1791 he began publishing *The American Pilot.* He died in Boston and was buried on Copp's Hill there.

★★★★★

O'BRIEN, Jeremiah: naval officer
Born Kittery, Maine, 1744; son of Morris and Mary (Hutchins) O'Brien; married Elizabeth Fitzpatrick; no children; died September 5, 1818.

O'Brien led a group of volunteers in the seizure of the British sloops *Unity* and *Margaretta* in 1775, which marked the first naval engagement of the American Revolution. He was then commissioned captain of both the *Unity* (renamed the *Machias Liberty*) and the *Diligent,* serving in this capacity in 1775 and 1776. These were the first ships of the Massachusetts Navy.

O'Brien was a privateer from 1777 until 1780, when he was captured by the British. He escaped the following year and resumed his privateering activities as commander of

first the *Hibernia* and later the *Tiger.* From 1811 until his death he was the customs collector for the Machias District of Maine.

OLIVER, Andrew: colonial official
Born Boston, Massachusetts, March 28, 1706; son of Daniel and Elizabeth (Belcher) Oliver; married Mary Fitch, June 20, 1728; second marriage to Mary Sanford, December 19, 1734; father of seventeen children (including Andrew); died March 3, 1774.

Oliver, a graduate of Harvard, was a delegate from Boston to the Massachusetts General Court from 1743 to 1745. With Thomas Hutchinson, he was a member of the commission that negotiated with the Six Nations in Albany, New York, in 1748. He was a member of the Provincial Council from 1746 to 1765 and secretary of the Province of Massachusetts from 1756 to 1771.

After the passage of the Stamp Act in 1765, Oliver was appointed distributor of stamps; however, after a mob attacked his home, he agreed not to carry out his duties. In 1770 he was commissioned by the King as lieutenant governor of Massachusetts and served from 1771 to 1774. He was identified, along with Hutchinson, with the Tory party. In 1768 and 1769 he wrote letters to the English governor describing the unsettled conditions in the colonies and advising remedies. These letters were obtained by Benjamin Franklin and forwarded to the popular party in Boston, causing Oliver a further loss of popularity among the colonists.

Oliver died in Boston before the beginning of the Revolution and was buried there.

OLIVER, Andrew: jurist, scientist
Born Boston, Massachusetts, November 13, 1731; son of Andrew and Mary (Fitch) Oliver; married Mary Lynde, May 28, 1752; died December 6, 1799.

Oliver graduated from Harvard. From 1761 to 1775 he was judge of the Inferior Court of Common Pleas for Essex County,

Massachusetts. He was a delegate from Salem to the Massachusetts General Court, 1762–67. He was appointed a mandamus councilor in 1774 but refused to serve.

Oliver was a founder of the American Academy of Arts and Sciences and was elected a member of the American Philosophical Society in 1773. He wrote "An Essay on Comets, in Two Parts," 1772 (reprinted 1811), and "Elegy on the Late Professor Winthrop," first published in the *Independent Chronicle,* 1779. He died in Salem.

OLIVER, Peter: Loyalist

Born Boston, Massachusetts, March 26, 1713; son of Daniel and Elizabeth (Belcher) Oliver; married Mary Clarke, July 5, 1733; father of six children; died October 1791.

Oliver graduated from Harvard at the age of seventeen and later received an honorary D.C.L. from Oxford University. He was judge of the Inferior Court of Common Pleas of Plymouth County, Massachusetts, from 1747 to 1756. He was a judge of the Superior Court in 1756 and chief justice of the court from 1771 to 1774. The latter year the grand juries of Worcester and Suffolk counties refused to serve under him because of his acceptance of an independent salary from the British Crown.

Oliver was appointed a mandamus councilor in 1774. The following year he was a signer of an address to General Gage. He left for Halifax with the British forces when they evacuated Boston in 1776, living in Birmingham, England, until his death. He was the author of *The Scripture Lexicon,* 1787.

ORR, Hugh: inventor, firearms manufacturer

Born Lochwinnoch, Renfrewshire, Scotland, January 2, 1715; son of Robert Orr; married Mary Bass, August 4, 1742; father of ten children (including Robert); died December 6, 1798.

Orr came to America in 1740, and the following year found employment as a scythemaker in East Bridgewater, Massachusetts. He became the owner of the shop circa 1745. He then became a manufacturer of firearms and in 1748 made five hundred muskets, believed to be the first such weapons manufactured in the colonies.

The inventor of the trip-hammer, Orr also invented a machine to clean flaxseed, in 1753. In 1775 he began producing muskets again and built a foundry for casting cannon in Bridgewater, Massachusetts. In 1785 he brought a mechanic from Scotland to build machines for carding and roping wool in his shop.

A member of the Massachusetts Senate in 1786, Orr obtained state grants for the encouragement of the textile industry. He brought various mechanics to the United States from Europe and introduced many new types of machinery. He died in Bridgewater.

OSGOOD, Samuel: Continental congressman

Born Andover, Massachusetts, February 3, 1748; son of Captain Peter and Sarah (Johnson) Osgood; married Martha Brandon, January 4, 1775; second marriage to Maria Bowne Franklin, May 26, 1786; died August 12, 1813.

Osgood, who graduated from Harvard in 1770, was a member of the Essex Convention of 1774, which was opposed to the more radical element of the American Revolution. In 1775 he served in the Continental Army as a major and then as a colonel and aide-de-camp to General Artemas Ward. That same year he became a member of the Massachusetts Provincial Congress. In 1779 he was a delegate to the Massachusetts Constitutional Convention, and the following year he was a delegate to the convention for the limitation of prices in Philadelphia.

From 1780 to 1784 Osgood was a member of the Continental Congress. He was appointed a director of the Bank of North America in 1781. In 1784 he was largely responsible for the commissioning of the United States Treasury and served as its first commissioner from 1785 to 1789. He was postmaster general under President Washington from 1789 to 1791.

In 1800 Osgood was speaker of the New York Assembly. In 1801 and 1802 he was superintendent of the internal revenue for the District of New York. He was naval officer for the Port of New York, 1803–13. He was an organizer and incorporator of the Society for the Establishment of a Free School for Education of Poor Children and a founder of the American Academy of Fine Arts.

Osgood died in New York City and was buried at the Brick Presbyterian Church there.

OTIS, James: lawyer, colonial legislator
Born West Barnstable, Massachusetts, February 5, 1725; son of James and Mary (Allyne) Otis; married Ruth Cunningham, 1755; father of three children; died May 23, 1783.

A graduate of Harvard, Otis was admitted to the Plymouth County (Massachusetts) bar in 1748 and established a legal practice in Boston in 1750. In 1754 he served as the King's attorney. He published *The Rudiments of Latin Prosody . . . and the Principles of Harmony in Poetic and Prosaic Composition* in 1760.

While serving as the King's advocate general of the vice admiralty court in Boston, Otis opposed the issuance of British writs of assistance. In collaboration with Oxenbridge Thacher, he put forth a natural-law argument to challenge the legality of the writs before the Massachusetts Superior Court in 1761; however, he lost the case.

Otis was an active member of the Sons of Liberty. He served in the Massachusetts General Court from 1761 to 1769 (acting as speaker in 1766) and in 1771. Along with Samuel Adams and Joseph Hawley, he directed the majority in the Court during his tenure. He also prepared a rough draft of the state papers that issued from the Court. He helped draft the Massachusetts circular letter adopted by the Court in 1768, but lapses in his sanity lessened his influence after 1769.

Otis wrote the following pamphlets, which laid a broad basis for American political theorizing on natural law: *A Vindication of the Conduct of the House of Representatives* (1762); *The Rights of the British Colonies Asserted and Proved* (1764); *Considerations on Behalf of the Colonists, In a Letter to a Noble Lord; A Vindication of the British Colonies;* and *Brief Remarks on the Defence of the Halifax Libel on the British-American Colonies.* He died in Andover, Massachusetts, after being struck by a bolt of lightning.

OTIS, Samuel Allyne: Continental congressman
Born in Barnstable, Massachusetts, on November 24, 1740; died April 22, 1814.

After his graduation from Harvard in 1759, Otis became engaged in a mercantile business in Boston. He was a member of both the Massachusetts House of Representatives and the Board of War in 1776. The following year he was a collector of clothing for the Continental Army. A member of the Massachusetts Constitutional Convention, he also served in the Massachusetts House of Representatives from 1784 to 1787, acting as speaker in 1784.

Otis was a member of the Continental Congress, representing Massachusetts, in 1787–88. From 1789 to 1814 he was secretary of the United States Senate. He died in Washington, D. C., and was buried in Congressional Cemetery there.

★★★★★

PAINE, Robert Treat: Continental congressman, jurist
Born Boston, Massachusetts, March 11, 1731; son of Thomas and Eunice (Treat) Paine; married Sally Cobb, March 15, 1770; father of eight children (including Robert Treat); died May 12, 1814.

Paine graduated from Harvard in 1749. Six years later he served as a chaplain on the Crown Point expedition during the French and Indian War. He was admitted to the Massachusetts bar in 1757, and in 1768 he was an associate prosecuting attorney in the Boston Massacre trial.

From 1773 to 1775 Paine served as a member of the Massachusetts Provincial Assembly and as speaker of that body from 1777 to 1778. He was a delegate to the Provincial Congress in 1774 and 1775 and a member of the Continental Congress from 1774 to 1778. He signed the Declaration of Independence and the "Olive Branch" petition and declaration to King George III. He was later sent with a commissioner to negotiate a treaty with the Indians of Upper New York.

The first attorney general of Massachusetts (1777 to 1790), Paine served on a committee to prepare a draft of the Massachusetts Constitution in 1778 and on the Massachusetts Governor's Council in 1779 and 1780. The latter year he was a founder of the American Academy of Arts and Sciences. From 1790 to 1804 he was a judge in the Massachusetts Supreme Court, then became a counselor for the Commonwealth of Massachusetts.

Paine died in Boston and was buried in the Old Granary Burial Ground there.

PALMER, Joseph: manufacturer, army officer
Born Higher Abbotsrow, Shaugh Prior, Devonshire, England, March 31, 1716; son of John and Joan (Pearse) Palmer; married Mary Cranch, 1745; father of three children; died December 25, 1788.

At the age of thirty Palmer came to America, and six years later he and his brother-in-law, Richard Cranch, erected a glass manufactory in Germantown (now part of Quincy), Massachusetts.

Palmer was a member of the Massachusetts Provincial Congress in 1774 and 1775 and served as a member of the Cambridge Committee of Safety. A year later he was commissioned a colonel in the 5th Suffolk Regiment of the Massachusetts militia. In 1776 he was also chosen brigadier general for Suffolk County and the next year was appointed brigadier general to command forces on a secret expedition to attack the enemy at Newport, Rhode Island. The expedition failed.

Palmer started a salt factory circa 1784 in Boston Neck, Massachusetts, and died four years later in Dorchester.

PARKER, John: army officer
Born Lexington, Massachusetts, July 13, 1729; son of Josiah and Anna (Stone) Parker; married Lydia Moore, May 25, 1755; father of seven children; died September 17, 1775.

Parker left his farm to fight at the battles of Louisburg and Quebec during the French and Indian War. He was captain of a company of Massachusetts Minutemen at the outbreak of the Revolutionary War. In April 1775 he assembled 130 men to defend the house in Lexington in which John Hancock and Samuel Adams were staying. The British attacked, and eight Americans were killed and ten wounded. Parker led a force in pursuit of the British as far as Concord, Massachusetts, but he became too ill to serve in the Battle of Bunker Hill. He died the following autumn.

PARSONS, Theophilus: jurist
Born Byfield, Massachusetts, February 24, 1750; son of the Reverend Moses and Susan (Davis) Parsons; married Elizabeth Greenleaf, January 13, 1780; father of twelve children (including Theophilus); died October 30, 1813.

Parsons graduated from Harvard at the age of nineteen and began a law practice in Falmouth, Massachusetts (now Maine), in 1774. He was a dominant member of the Essex County Convention and was opposed to the proposed Massachusetts Constitution of 1778. His report of the convention, *The Essex Result*, exposed the weakness of the executive under that constitution and outlined the main principles for government that were later adopted by the Federalists. In 1788 he was a delegate to the Massachusetts Convention that ratified the United States Constitution.

Parsons was a member of the Massachusetts legislature from 1787 to 1791 and again in 1805. He was a popular lawyer in Boston during the first six years of the nineteenth century. As chief justice of the Supreme Judicial Court of Massachusetts from 1806 to 1813, he insisted on a number of procedural reforms aimed at speeding the trial process. He formed the law of the new Commonwealth of Massachusetts, and indirectly that of other states, through his establishing of rules for applying legal precedents. These rules were derived from English law, unwritten colonial law, and generally recognized principles of business. His decisions were particularly useful in the fields of shipping and insurance.

An improved method of lunar observation developed by Parsons was adopted in Nathaniel Bowditch's *New American Practical Navigator* (1802). Parsons was a principal founder of the Boston Athenaeum and of the Social Law Library. He was a fellow of the American Academy of the Arts and Sciences and in 1806 became a fellow of Harvard College. He was granted an honorary LL.D. from Brown University in 1809. He died in Boston.

PARTRIDGE, George: congressman
Born Duxbury, Massachusetts, February 8, 1740; died July 7, 1828.

Partridge graduated from Harvard in 1762; he studied theology, then taught school in Kingston, Massachusetts.

In 1774–75 Partridge served as a delegate to the Massachusetts Provincial Congress. For the next four years and again in 1788 he was a member of the Massachusetts House of Representatives. He became sheriff of Plymouth County, Massachusetts, in 1777 and served in that capacity until 1812. He was a representative from Massachusetts to the Continental Congress from 1779 to 1782 and again from 1783 to 1785. He served Massachusetts as a member of the United States House of Representatives in 1789–90.

Partridge endowed the Partridge Seminary at Duxbury. He died in Duxbury at the age of eighty-eight and was buried in the Mayflower Cemetery there.

PATERSON, John: army officer, congressman, landowner
Born Newington Parish, Wethersfield, Connecticut, 1744; son of John and Ruth (Bird) Paterson; married Elizabeth Lee, June 2, 1766; died July 19, 1808.

After graduating from Yale in 1762 and practicing law for a time in Connecticut, Paterson moved to Lenox, Massachusetts, in 1774. That year he was elected a member of the Berkshire County Convention, which adopted a boycott against products made in England. From his work with this "Solemn League and Covenant" he became, later in the year, a representative from Lenox to the First Massachusetts Provincial Congress, returning for the second session of the congress the following year.

Paterson raised a regiment of the Massachusetts militia in 1775 and was commissioned a colonel; the next year he was commissioned a colonel in the 15th Infantry of the Continental Army and served in a rear position at the Battle of Bunker Hill. Ordered to the relief of American troops in Canada, he also accompanied the troops on retreat through Crown Point and Ticonderoga and served in the battles of Trenton and Princeton.

Commissioned a brigadier general in 1777, Paterson participated in the capture of General Burgoyne at the Battle of Saratoga and wintered with Washington at Valley Forge in 1777–78. He served in the Battle of Monmouth and was a member of the court-martial which tried Major André. He was brevetted a major general in 1783 and made a commander of the Massachusetts militia in 1787, aiding that year in the suppression of Shays's Rebellion.

In 1790 Paterson moved to Lisle (now Whitney Point), Broome County, New York, and became the owner of a land company with extensive holdings in New York State. In New York he served as a member of the State Assembly in 1792–93 and became a member of the New York Constitutional Convention from Broome County in

1801. He was appointed judge of Broome and Tioga counties in 1798 and again in 1807 and served as a member of the United States House of Representatives from 1803 to 1805 (8th Congress).

Paterson was an organizer of the Society of the Cincinnati and of the Ohio Company. He died in Lisle and was buried in Lenox Cemetery.

PEABODY, Joseph: privateersman, merchant

Born Middleton, Massachusetts, December 12, 1757; son of Francis and Margaret (Knight) Peabody; married Catherine Smith, August 28, 1791; second marriage to Elizabeth Smith, October 24, 1795; father of seven children; died January 5, 1844.

Peabody served in the Revolutionary War on the privateers *Bunker Hill* and *Pilgrim* and was captured while serving on the privateer *Fish Hawk.* He was imprisoned for a time at St. John's, Newfoundland, then exchanged.

Peabody became second officer on the letter-of-marque *Ranger* and was wounded in a skirmish with Loyalists. He purchased the schooner *Three Friends* and used the ship for trading in Europe and the West Indies for several years. In 1791 he established a merchant business in Salem, Massachusetts, which traded with the Baltic and Mediterranean countries and with the West Indies, China, and India. He amassed a great fortune and is believed to have employed six or seven thousand men at one time.

Peabody died in Salem shortly after his eighty-sixth birthday.

PEARSON, Eliphalet: educator

Born Newbury, Massachusetts, June 11, 1752; son of David and Sarah (Danforth) Pearson; married Priscilla Holyoke, July 17, 1780; second marriage to Sarah Bromfield, September 29, 1785; father of five children; died September 12, 1826.

Pearson, who graduated from Harvard in 1773, taught grammar school in Andover, Massachusetts, from 1775 to 1778. He then became the first principal of the Phillips Academy in Andover and held that position for eight years. He was a Hancock professor of Hebrew and Oriental languages at Harvard from 1786 to 1806 and served as acting president of the school in 1804.

In 1807 Pearson was a founder of the Andover Theological Seminary and was president of its board of trustees for fourteen years. He taught sacred theology there in 1808–09. From 1802 to 1821 he served as president of the board of trustees of Phillips Academy.

Pearson died in Greenland, New Hampshire.

PELHAM, Henry: artist, cartographer

Born Boston, Massachusetts, February 21, 1749; son of Peter and Mary (Singleton) Copley Pelham; married Catherine Butler; father of Peter and William; died 1806.

Pelham worked as a portraitist in miniatures in Boston until 1776, when he went to England because of his extreme Loyalist sympathies. There he worked as a civil engineer, as a cartographer, and as an artist. His paintings include "The Finding of Moses" and "Plan of Boston," both of which were done in 1777. He drowned in the River Kenmare in Ireland in 1806.

PHELPS, Oliver: congressman

Born Poquonock, Connecticut, October 21, 1749; son of Thomas and Ann (Brown) Phelps; married Mary Seymour, December 16, 1773; father of Oliver Leicester and Mary; died February 21, 1809.

Phelps engaged in a mercantile business in Granville, Massachusetts, from 1770 to 1775. His experience proved valuable in 1777, when he was appointed superintendent of the Massachusetts army supply purchases, a post he held for four years. During part of that time he also served as a member of the Massachusetts General Court (1778–80) and a member of the Massachusetts Constitutional Convention (1779–80).

In 1785 Phelps was a member of the Massachusetts Senate and in 1786 was appointed to the Governor's Council. He went heavily into debt when land speculation schemes in western Massachusetts, the lower Mississippi Valley, and the Western

Reserve failed. He was a delegate from Massachusetts to the United States House of Representatives during the 8th Congress (1803 to 1805). He died in Canandaigua, New York.

PHILLIPS, John: educator

Born Andover, Massachusetts, December 27, 1719; son of the Reverend Samuel and Hannah (White) Phillips; married Sarah (Emery) Gilman, August 4, 1743; second marriage to Mrs. Elizabeth Hale, November 3, 1767; died April 21, 1795.

At the age of fifteen Phillips received an M.A. from Harvard, graduating as salutatorian of his class. He was granted an honorary LL.D. from Dartmouth forty-two years later, in 1777. From 1771 to 1773 he was a member of the Massachusetts General Court and in 1778–79 moderator of the town meeting.

Deeply involved in education administration, in 1773 Phillips was made a trustee of Dartmouth, to which he was a contributor of liberal gifts throughout his life. He founded Phillips Academy (incorporated as Phillips Exeter Academy) in 1781 at Exeter, Massachusetts, and was the first president of its board of trustees. He was a trustee of the Phillips Andover Academy and served as president from 1791 until 1794. He died in Exeter the following year.

PHILLIPS, Samuel: legislator, educator

Born North Andover, Massachusetts, February 5, 1752; son of Samuel and Elizabeth (Barnard) Phillips; married Phoebe Foxcroft, July 6, 1773; father of two children (including John); died February 10, 1802.

Phillips graduated from Harvard at the age of nineteen. He served as a delegate to the Massachusetts Provincial Congress from 1775 to 1780 and to the Massachusetts Constitutional Convention in 1779–80. A member of the Massachusetts Senate from 1780 to 1801, he was president in 1785. In 1781 he was a justice in the Court of Common Pleas of Essex County and twenty years later served as lieutenant governor of Massachusetts.

Phillips founded Phillips Academy in Andover, Massachusetts, in 1778; he was a member of the original board of trustees of that institution and was its president in 1796. In 1793 he was awarded an honorary LL.D. by Harvard. He died in Andover and was buried at South Church there.

PHILLIPS, William: banker, state official

Born March 19, 1750; son of William and Abigail (Bromfield) Phillips; married Miriam Mason, September 13, 1774; father of seven children; died May 26, 1827.

Phillips became president of the Massachusetts Bank in 1804. He was a member of the Massachusetts General Court from 1805 to 1812, then lieutenant governor of Massachusetts for ten years. A Federalist, he was a presidential elector at large in 1816 and 1820 and a delegate to the Massachusetts Constitutional Convention in 1820. Three years later he served in the Massachusetts Senate.

In 1791 Phillips became a member of the board of trustees of Phillips Academy in Andover and in 1821 was made president. He was an original incorporator of the American Board of Foreign Missions and served in the presidencies of the American Bible Society, Massachusetts General Hospital, the American Education Society, and the Society for Propagating the Gospel.

PICKERING, Timothy: congressman, cabinet officer

Born Salem, Massachusetts, July 17, 1745; son of Timothy and Mary (Wingate) Pickering; married Rebecca White, April 5, 1776; father of ten children (including John and Timothy); died January 29, 1829.

Serving as both secretary of war and secretary of state, Pickering was deeply involved in military aspects of the emerging government of the United States. He graduated from Harvard in 1763, serving in his first public office—clerk of the Office of Register of Deeds for Essex County—that same year. He studied law and was admitted to the Massachusetts bar in 1768.

A selectman, town clerk, and assessor from 1772 to 1777, Pickering was also a representative to the Massachusetts General Court and register of deeds in Salem (1775). He was a judge in the Maritime Court of the Province of Massachusetts in 1775–76 and a judge in the Essex County Court of Common Pleas in 1775.

In 1776 Pickering was commissioned a lieutenant in the Essex County militia, elected to the Massachusetts legislature, and commissioned a colonel in the Continental Army. The next year he was appointed adjutant general by General Washington and elected to the Board of War by the Continental Congress.

From 1780 to 1783 Pickering served as a quartermaster general in the Continental Army. He moved to Philadelphia, then to Wyoming County, Pennsylvania, in 1787, where he organized Luzerne County. He represented that county at the Pennsylvania Convention that ratified the United States Constitution in 1789. He was a member of the Pennsylvania Constitutional Convention in 1789–90.

Pickering went on a mission in 1790 to the Seneca Indians in an attempt to prevent an Indian war. Four years after his appointment (by George Washington) as postmaster general of the United States in 1791, he served a brief tenure as secretary of war. While secretary of state from 1795 to 1800, he took actions in preparing for the "Quasi-War" with France in 1797–98. His support of Britain and his intrigues against John Adams resulted in his removal from office.

After reentering local politics in Massachusetts, Pickering became a member of the United States Senate from Massachusetts from 1803 to 1811, and a Federalist member of the United States House of Representatives during the 13th and 14th congresses (1813 to 1817). He bitterly opposed the War of 1812.

A scientific farmer in Massachusetts, Pickering wrote many articles and letters on farming. He was also a political writer and the author of a widely used drill manual. He died in Salem and was buried in the Broad Street Cemetery there.

PIKE, Nicolas: educator

Born Somersworth, New Hampshire, October 17, 1743; son of James and Sarah (Gilman) Pike; married Hannah Smith; second marriage to Eunice Smith, January 9, 1779; father of six children; died December 9, 1819.

Pike graduated from Harvard in 1766 and about seven years later became master of the Newburyport (Massachusetts) Grammar School, a position he held until circa 1800. He also taught in nearby private schools from 1774 to 1783. He was a justice of the peace for a time.

From 1788 until his death, Pike was a member of the American Academy of Arts and Sciences. He wrote the first popular arithmetic textbooks in America: *New and Complete System of Arithmetick, Composed for the Use of the Citizens of the United States* (1788) and *Abridgement of the New and Complete System of Arithmetick* (1793).

PITCAIRN, John: army officer

Born Dysart, Scotland, 1722; son of David and Katherine (Hamilton) Pitcairn; married Elizabeth Dalrymple; father of several children (including Robert and David); died June 1775.

Pitcairn was commissioned a captain in the Royal Marines in 1756 and promoted to major in 1771. Three years later he came to America. He was stationed in Boston and in 1775 was part of a detachment ordered to destroy rebel stores in Concord, Massachusetts. He was in command of the advance forces that fought a battle with Minutemen on Lexington Common in 1775, and he later insisted that the Americans had fired first. In that same year he was mortally wounded in the Battle of Bunker Hill. He was buried at Christ Church in Boston but was later reinterred at the Church of St. Bartholomew the Less, in London, England.

POMEROY, Seth: army officer

Born Northampton, Massachusetts, May 20, 1706;

son of Ebenezer and Sarah (King) Pomeroy; married Mary Hunt, December 14, 1732; father of nine children; died February 19, 1777.

Pomeroy was commissioned a captain in the Massachusetts militia in 1744 and a year later served as a major in the 4th Massachusetts Regiment in an expedition against the French fortress at Louisburg. In 1750 he organized an opposition group to Jonathan Edwards, pastor of Northampton Church. In 1774 he was a member of the Northampton Committee of Safety. He was also a representative to the first and second Massachusetts provincial congresses.

Pomeroy was commissioned a lieutenant colonel in the Continental Army and fought at the Battle of Lake George in 1775. Later that year he headed the West Massachusetts District of the Massachusetts militia in command of forts along the Massachusetts frontier. He served as military commander of the Province of Massachusetts and in 1775–76 raised and drilled troops in West Massachusetts. Also in 1775 Pomeroy became the first brigadier general in the Continental Army and fought at the Battle of Bunker Hill, the first major engagement of the American Revolution. He died two years later in Peekskill, New York.

PREBLE, Edward: naval officer
Born Falmouth (now Portland), Maine, August 15, 1761; son of General Jedidiah and Mehitable (Bangs) Roberts Preble; married Mary Deering, March 17, 1801; died August 25, 1807.

Until 1783 Preble served on the ship *Winthrop*, a captured, armed English brig of superior force. He was lieutenant in command of the brig *Pickering* in the West Indies in 1798. The next year he was captain of the frigate *Essex*, the first American warship to sail flag beyond the Cape of Good Hope (1800–02).

Preble protected American trade from French privateers in the East Indies. In 1803 he was commissioned commodore in command of the 3rd Squadron and was sent to the Mediterranean. The next year, during the Tripolitan War, he made an assault on Tripoli, but was unable to capture it. He made four subsequent attacks on the town, all of which were unsuccessful.

Preble built gunboats for the navy circa 1805 to 1807. He died in Portland, Maine.

PRESCOTT, Oliver: physician
Born Groton, Massachusetts, April 27, 1731; son of Benjamin and Abigail (Oliver) Prescott; married Lydia Baldwin, February 19, 1756; died November 17, 1804.

Prescott graduated from Harvard in 1750, then studied medicine under Dr. Ebenezer Robie. In 1775 he was commissioned a brigadier general in the Middlesex County (Massachusetts) militia and three years later became a major general in the Massachusetts militia.

From 1777 to 1780 Prescott served on the Massachusetts Committee of Correspondence and on the Supreme Executive Council. He was judge of probate in Middlesex from 1799 to 1804.

Prescott served as trustee and first president of the board of Groton Academy. He was an original incorporator of the Massachusetts Medical Society and a member of the New Hampshire Medical Society. He served as president of the Middlesex Medical Society and of the Western Society of Middlesex Husbandmen. In 1780 he was a fellow of the American Academy of Arts and Sciences. He received an honorary M.D. in 1791.

Prescott died in Groton, his longtime home.

PRESCOTT, Samuel: physician, patriot
Born Concord, Massachusetts, August 19, 1751; son of Dr. Abel and Abigail (Brigham) Prescott; died circa 1777.

Prescott successfully completed the midnight ride of warning on April 18, 1775, after Paul Revere was captured. He reached Concord, where his warning enabled the Minutemen to assemble and to hide most of the military stores before the British arrived.

In 1776 Prescott was in service at Fort

Ticonderoga. The next year he was captured by the British, and he died in Halifax, Nova Scotia.

PRESCOTT, William: army officer

Born Groton, Massachusetts, February 20, 1726; son of Benjamin and Abigail (Oliver) Prescott; married Abigail Hale, April 13, 1758; father of at least one child (William); died October 13, 1795.

In 1758 Prescott served as a lieutenant in the French and Indian War. He was a colonel of a regiment of Minutemen in 1775. That same year he was also in direct charge of fortifying Breed's Hill and was co-commander at the Battle of Bunker (Breed's) Hill. He was a member of the Council of War in Cambridge, Massachusetts. He served in the Long Island Campaign and at the surrender of Burgoyne in 1777. He died in Pepperell, Massachusetts.

★★★★★

QUINCEY, Josiah: lawyer, patriot

Born Boston, Massachusetts, February 23, 1744; son of Josiah and Hannah (Sturgis) Quincey; married Abigail Phillips, October 26, 1769; father of two children (including Josiah); died April 26, 1775.

Quincey earned a B.A. from Harvard in 1763 and an M.A. three years later. He wrote several strongly patriotic essays on the Non-Importation Agreement and other questions, including one titled *An Address of the Merchants, Traders and Freeholders of the Town of Boston.* He signed his articles "An Independent" or "An Old Man."

In 1770 Quincey and John Adams successfully defended the British soldiers accused of murder for their part in the Boston Massacre. Having emerged as one of the leaders of the patriot cause, Quincey went on a mission to England to argue the cause of the colonies. The mission took place in the years 1774–75, and he died at sea in the latter year.

Quincey's chief political work was *Observations of the Act of Parliament Commonly Called the Boston Port Bill with Thoughts on Civil Society and Standing Armies* (1774). He also wrote *Reports of Cases . . . in the Superior Court of Judicature of the Province of Massachusetts Bay between 1761 and 1772,* which was printed in 1865.

★★★★★

READ, Daniel: musician

Born Attleboro, Massachusetts, November 16, 1757; son of Daniel and Mary (White) Read; married Jerusha Sherman, 1785; father of four children; died December 4, 1836.

During the Revolutionary War, Read served for short periods in Sullivan's expedition to Rhode Island. He was a stockholder in the New Haven Connecticut City Bank and director of New Haven's library. He was also a member of the Governor's Guards.

Read was one of the earliest American psalmodists and hymn-tune writers. He published his first music book, *The American Singing Book,* in 1785. He was editor of *The American Musical Magazine,* the first periodical of its kind in America, for a year, circa 1786. His other works included *An Introduction to Psalmody,* 1790; the first number of *The Columbian Harmonist,* published in 1793; and *The New Haven Collection of Sacred Music,* 1818. Best known among his tunes are "Lisbon," "Sherburne," and "Windham." He died in New Haven.

READ, Nathan: congressman, iron manufacturer, inventor

Born Warren, Massachusetts, July 2, 1759; son of Reuben and Tamsin (Meacham) Read; married Elizabeth Jeffrey, October 20, 1790; died January 20, 1849.

Read graduated from Harvard in 1781 and taught school in Beverly and Salem (both in Massachusetts) for the next two years. He then spent four years as a tutor at Harvard.

In 1788 Read devised a double-acting steam engine and a year later invented a manually operated paddlewheel-propelled boat. He was granted patents on a portable multitubular boiler, an improved double-acting steam engine, and, in 1791, a chainwheel method of propelling boats. He organized the Salem Iron Factory over the years 1796 to 1807. In 1798 he patented a nail-cutting and -heading machine.

A Federalist, Read served in the United States House of Representatives from Massachusetts during the 6th and 7th congresses (1800–03). In 1803 he was appointed special justice of the Court of Common Pleas for Essex County, Massachusetts. Four years later he became chief justice of the Hancock County (Maine) Court of Common Pleas.

Read became a member of the American Academy of Arts and Sciences in 1791 and an honorary member of the Linnaean Society of New England in 1815. He died in Belfast, Maine.

REED, James: army officer
Born Woburn, Massachusetts, January 8, 1724; son of Thomas and Sarah (Sawyer) Reed; married Abigail Hinds, 1745; second marriage to Mary Farrar, 1791; father of two children; died February 13, 1807.

Reed was a captain during the French and Indian War, serving under General Abercromby in 1758. At the beginning of the Revolutionary War, he raised troops after the Battle of Lexington and accompanied the expedition of 1775 to Crown Point. Also in 1775 he was commissioned a colonel in the 3rd New Hampshire Regiment, seeing action that year at the Battle of Bunker Hill.

In 1776 Reed was commissioned a colonel in the 2nd Regiment of the Continental Army. He was in Canada when he was promoted to brigadier general by an act of Congress in August 1776; however, he retired from the military the following month. He died in Fitchburg, Massachusetts.

REED, John: clergyman, congressman
Born Framingham, Massachusetts, November 11, 1751; father of at least one son (John); died February 17, 1831.

Reed graduated from Yale in 1772 and went on to study theology. He was a chaplain in the United States Navy for two years. In 1780 he moved to West Bridgewater, Massachusetts, where he was ordained to

the ministry of the Congregational Church. He then became pastor of the First Congregational Society in West Bridgewater, serving until his death.

From 1795 to 1801 Reed was a Federalist member of the United States House of Representatives. He died in West Bridgewater and was buried in the Old Graveyard.

REVERE, Paul: silversmith, patriot
Born Boston, Massachusetts, January 1, 1735; son of Paul and Deborah (Hichborn) Revere; married Sarah Orne, August 17, 1757; second marriage to Rachel Walker, October 10, 1773; father of sixteen children; died May 10, 1818.

In 1765 Paul Revere applied silverwork techniques to copper plate. He did engravings for the *Royal American Magazine* and manufactured artificial dental devices. He participated in the Boston Tea Party. In 1774 he was an official courier for the Massachusetts Provincial Assembly to the Continental Congress.

On April 16, 1775, Revere rode to Concord, Massachusetts, to warn patriots to move military stores. Two days later he made a ride to warn the countryside that the British troops were marching and to warn John Hancock and Samuel Adams that they were in danger of being captured. He completed his mission to Lexington, Massachusetts, but was stopped by the British en route to Concord.

In 1776 Revere was a member of the Committee of Correspondence. He designed and printed the first official seal for the colonies, and he designed the Massachusetts State Seal. He directed the manufacture of gunpowder in Canton, Massachusetts, and discovered a process for rolling sheet copper. He died in Boston.

ROTCH, William: merchant
Born Nantucket, Massachusetts, December 15, 1734; son of Joseph and Love (Macy) Rotch; married Elizabeth Barney, October 31, 1754; died May 16, 1828.

Rotch joined his father as a partner in a

whale fishery in New Salem, Massachusetts, and continued in the business until 1785. He was the owner of the *Bedford,* which in 1783 became the first ship flying the American flag to enter a British port. From 1785 to 1794 he operated a whaling business in Dunkirk, France. He died in New Bedford, Massachusetts.

RUGGLES, Timothy: army officer
Born Rochester, Massachusetts, October 20, 1711; son of the Reverend Timothy and Mary (White) Ruggles; married Bathsheba Bourne, 1736; father of seven children (including Bathsheba); died August 4, 1795.

Ruggles graduated from Harvard in 1732 and four years later became a member of the Massachusetts General Court. From 1739 to 1752 and almost continuously until 1770 he served in the Massachusetts legislature; he was speaker in 1762–63. Circa 1753 he became a justice of the peace. In 1755 he was commissioned colonel of a regiment of the Massachusetts militia, and in 1758 he was commissioned a brigadier general. He took part in the invasion of Canada.

In 1757 Ruggles was appointed judge of the Court of Common Pleas of Worcester County, Massachusetts, and became chief justice in 1762, serving in that capacity for thirteen years. In 1765 he was elected president of the Stamp Act Congress; however, he refused to sign the petitions drawn up.

Ruggles became a member of the Council by the King's Mandamus in 1774. He attempted to form an association of Loyalists who would pledge not to "acknowledge or submit to authority of any congress, committee of correspondence or any other unconstitutional assemblies of men." General Howe appointed him to command three companies of volunteers to be called Loyal American Associates.

Ruggles was banished from Massachusetts and his lands were confiscated by the Act of 1778. He moved to an estate in Wilmot, Nova Scotia, Canada, in 1783, where he died twelve years later.

RUSSELL, Joseph: whaler
Born Dartmouth (now New Bedford), Massachusetts, September 27, 1719; son of Joseph and Mary (Tucker) Russell; married Judith Howland, 1744; father of eleven children; died October 16, 1804.

Russell was prominent in the development of the whaling industry in New England. By 1775 he owned ships that made whaling voyages and traded with the West Indies. He was also a pioneer in the manufacturing of spermaceti candles.

Russell supported the American Revolution, and most of his ships and buildings were burned by the British when they raided New Bedford in 1778. In the years 1791–93 his ship *Rebecca* made the first whaling voyage around Cape Horn to the Pacific hunting grounds.

★★★★★

SANDS, David: clergyman
Born Cow Neck (now Sands Point), Long Island, New York, October 15, 1745; son of Nathaniel and Mercy Sands; married Clementine Hallock, 1771; died June 4, 1818.

Sands established a mercantile business in Cornwall, New York, in 1765. In 1775 he became a minister in the Society of Friends and an itinerant preacher, traveling in New England during 1775–76, 1777–79, and again in 1795. He then preached in Europe from 1795 until 1805.

Sands established several churches in the Kennebec River region of Maine and is called the founder of Quakerism in Maine.

SAVAGE, Edward: painter, engraver
Born Princeton, Massachusetts, November 26, 1761; son of Seth and Lydia (Craige) Savage; married Sarah Seaver, October 13, 1794; father of eight children; died July 6, 1817.

In 1789 the president of Harvard commissioned Savage to paint a portrait of George Washington; the work was delivered at Cambridge, Massachusetts, in August 1790. The following year Savage received art instruction from Benjamin West in London, England. In Philadelphia in 1795, he exhibited a panorama depicting London and Westminster in a circle.

Savage joined with Daniel Bowen in opening the New York Museum in 1801. He painted *Family Group at Mount Vernon,* portraits of George and Martha Washington which are now owned by the Boston Museum of Fine Arts. He also made mezzotints of his own oil portraits of General Anthony Wayne, Dr. Benjamin Rush, and Thomas Jefferson, and plates of *Liberty* and *The Washington Family.* From 1809 until his death he was a partner in the Poignaud and Plantcotton Factory in Lancaster, Massachusetts.

SECCOMB, John: clergyman

Born Medford, Massachusetts, April 25, 1708; son of Peter and Hannah (Willis) Seccomb; married Mercy Williams, March 10, 1737; father of four children; died October 27, 1792.

Seccomb graduated from Harvard in 1728; while there he wrote poems which were published in Boston in 1731 and which continued to be popular among several generations of New Englanders. In 1733 he was ordained to the ministry of the Congregational Church in Harvard, Massachusetts, where he was pastor until 1757. As minister of the Congregational Church in Chester, Nova Scotia, in 1763, he wrote a *Christian History* describing the increase in the congregation in 1743–44, which was a part of the Great Awakening. He was an old-fashioned Calvinist. He died in Chester, Nova Scotia.

SEDGWICK, Theodore: senator, jurist

Born West Hartford, Connecticut, May 9, 1746; son of Benjamin and Ann (Thompson) Sedgwick; married Eliza Mason, 1768; second marriage to Pamela Dwight, April 17, 1774; third marriage to Penelope Russell, 1808; father of ten children (including Theodore and Catharine Maria); died January 24, 1813.

Sedgwick received a degree from Yale in 1772 (as of 1765) and was admitted to the bar of Berkshire County, Massachusetts, in 1766. In 1774 he acted as clerk of the Berkshire County Convention considering resistance to British taxation. Two years later he was military secretary to General John Thomas. He was elected to the Massachusetts legislature for terms in 1780, 1782, 1783, 1787, and 1788 (when he was speaker) and served in the Massachusetts Senate in 1784 and 1785.

In 1783 Sedgwick's defense of the Negro slave Elizabeth Freeman established the illegality of slavery in Massachusetts. A staunch Federalist, he was a member of the Continental Congress during 1785–88, was active in suppressing Shays's Rebellion in 1787, and participated in the Massachusetts Convention which ratified the United States Constitution in 1788. He went to the United States House of Representatives for terms from 1789 through June 1796 and again from 1799 to 1801, during which he was speaker (1st–4th, 6th congresses). From June 11, 1796, until 1799 he served in the United States Senate.

Sedgwick was a judge in the Supreme Court of Massachusetts from 1802 until 1813, a trustee of Williams College until 1813, and a corporate member of the American Academy of Arts and Sciences. He died in Boston and was buried in the family cemetery in Stockbridge, Massachusetts.

SELBY, William: composer

Born England, 1739; married Susannah Parker, January 7, 1792; died December 1798.

Selby was organist at King's Chapel in Boston from 1772 until 1774, when he became organist at Trinity Church in Rhode Island. In 1777 he returned to King's Chapel. Having become interested in choral singing, he founded the Musical Society of Boston in 1785 and composed much of the music performed at the Society's concerts. Among the songs he composed were *Ode in Honour of General Washington* (1786), *On Musick* (1789), *The Rural Retreat* (1789), *Ptalaemon to Pastoca* (1789), *Ode for the New Year* (1790), and *The Lovely Lass* (1790).

SEWALL, Jonathan: Loyalist

Born Boston, Massachusetts, August 17, 1728; son of Jonathan and Mary (Payne) Sewall; married Esther Quincy, January 21, 1764; father of Jonathan and Stephen; died September 26, 1796.

Sewall graduated from Harvard in 1748 and began teaching Latin school in Salem, Massachusetts, the same year. He left this position in 1756 and began the practice of law in Charlestown, Massachusetts. After a period as solicitor general of the state, in 1767 he became attorney general. He held this office until the next year, when he became judge in the Vice Admiralty Court of Halifax, Nova Scotia. He left this position in 1774 and sailed to England the following year. In 1778 he was legally banished from Massachusetts and his property was confiscated. He returned to Halifax in 1788 and died in St. John, New Brunswick, eight years later.

SEWALL, Samuel: congressman, jurist
Born Boston, Massachusetts, December 11, 1757; died June 8, 1814.

A 1776 graduate of Harvard, Sewall studied law, was admitted to the bar, and established a legal practice in Marblehead, Massachusetts. He was a member of the Massachusetts House of Representatives in 1783 and again from 1788 until 1796. On December 7 of that year he filled a vacancy in the United States House of Representatives, to which he subsequently was twice reelected. Thus he served in the 4th, 5th, and 6th congresses, until January 10, 1800, when he resigned. During his tenure the House appointed him a manager to conduct the impeachment proceedings against Senator William Blount of Tennessee (1798).

After serving as associate judge in the Massachusetts Supreme Court from 1801 until 1813, Sewall rose to chief justice, holding this office until his death. He died in Wiscasset, Maine, and was buried in the Ancient Cemetery, but was later reinterred in the family tomb in Marblehead.

SEWALL, Stephen: Hebraist
Born York, Maine, April 11, 1734; son of Nicholas and Mehitable (Storer) Sewall; married Rebecca Wigglewsorth, August 9, 1763; married a second time; father of one child; died July 23, 1804.

Sewall graduated from Harvard in 1761 and was hired as an instructor of Hebrew there the same year. He remained in this position until 1764, when he became the first Hancock professor of Hebrew and Oriental languages, a chair he held until 1784. During this period (in 1762–63) he also served as librarian. He was a Whig member of the Massachusetts General Court from Cambridge in 1777.

Sewall became an original member of the American Academy of Arts and Sciences in 1785. He wrote *An Hebrew Grammar Collected Chiefly from Those of Mr. Israel Lyons and the Reverend Richard Grey* (1763); *The Scripture Account of the Schechinah* (1794); and *The Scripture History Relating to the Overthrow of Sodom and Gomorrah* (1796).

SHAW, Samuel: army officer, diplomat
Born Boston, Massachusetts, October 2, 1754; son of Francis and Sarah (Burt) Shaw; married Hannah Phillips, August 21, 1792; died May 30, 1794.

In 1766 Shaw received a commission as a first lieutenant in the 3rd Continental Artillery. He became aide-de-camp to General Knox in 1779 and was commissioned a captain the next year. At the end of the war he assisted in arranging the disbandment of the Continental Army. He was secretary of the committee of officers which formed the Society of the Cincinnati.

Shaw held a post on the *Empress of China,* the first American vessel sent to Canton, in 1784. General Knox appointed him the first secretary of the War Department; he held this position during 1785–86. Shaw also was the first American consul in China, where he served from 1786 to 1789 and again from 1790 to 1792. He died at sea near the Cape of Good Hope.

SHAYS, Daniel: army officer, insurgent
Born Hopkinton, Massachusetts, circa 1747; son of Patrick and Margaret (Dempsey) Shay; married Abigail Gilbert, 1772; died September 29, 1825.

Shays served as an ensign in the battles of

Bunker Hill, Ticonderoga, Saratoga, and Stony Point, and was commissioned a captain in the 5th Massachusetts Regiment in 1777. In 1781 and 1782 he was a member of the Pelham (Massachusetts) Committee of Safety.

Shays was a leading figure in the insurrection in western Massachusetts known as Shays's Rebellion, which was caused by economic depression and in which the rebels demanded redress for economic grievances. The rebellion began when Shays chaired a committee which drew up resolutions that the Massachusetts Supreme Court should be allowed to sit, provided it dealt with no case involving debts or indictments of insurgents. He then led a force of one thousand insurgents from Wilbraham and attacked a federal arsenal in Springfield, Massachusetts, in January 1787. The arsenal was protected by the Massachusetts militia under General William Shepard, who defeated the rebels. They were then routed by General Lincoln at Petersham.

Shays fled to Vermont after the defeat and was condemned to death the same year. In 1788 he petitioned for and received a pardon. He retired to Sparta, New York, where he died many years later.

SHEPARD, William: army officer, congressman

Born Westfield, Massachusetts, December 1, 1737; son of John and Elizabeth (Noble) Shepard; married Sarah Dewey, January 31, 1760; father of nine children; died November 16, 1817.

During the French and Indian War, Shepard served in the Provincial Army and rose to the rank of captain. Around the time of the Revolution he was a member of the Westfield Committee of Correspondence, and as a lieutenant colonel in the Massachusetts Regiment of the Continental Army (1775) he served through the siege of Boston. The next year he became a lieutenant colonel in the 3rd Continental Infantry, rose

to colonel, and later moved to the 4th Massachusetts Infantry.

After the war Shepard served politically as a selectman in Westfield (1784–87) and as a member of the lower house of the Massachusetts legislature (1785–86). He attained the rank of brigadier general in the Massachusetts militia in 1786 and became a major general later the same year. Responsible for defending the federal arsenal and protecting the federal court at Springfield at the time of Shays's Rebellion, he repulsed Shays's attack on the arsenal (1787). From 1788 to 1790 he served on the Massachusetts Executive Council. He was a presidential elector in 1789 and a member of the Governor's Council from 1792 until 1797.

Shepard accepted appointments to treat with the Penobscot Indians in 1796 and with the Six Nations the following year. He then represented Massachusetts during the 5th through 7th congresses of the United States House of Representatives (1797–1803). He died in Westfield, Massachusetts, and was buried in the Mechanic Street Cemetery there.

SKILLIN, John: ship carver

Born 1746; son of Simeon Skillin; died January 24, 1800.

Skillin worked as a carver in Boston between the years 1767 and 1800. In 1778 he carved the figurehead for the Continental frigate *Confederacy*. After 1780 he was in partnership with his brother Simeon. He died in Boston.

SKILLIN, Simeon: ship carver

Born 1716; father of at least two sons, Simeon and John Samuel; died 1778.

Skillin became active as a ship carver in Boston circa 1738. In 1777 he accepted a commission to carve the figurehead for the brig *Hazard,* one of the first armed ships of the Revolutionary War. He died the following year.

SKILLIN, Simeon, Jr.: ship carver
Born either 1756 or 1757; son of Simeon Skillin; died 1806.

Skillin was active as a ship carver in Boston from circa 1776 to 1806, working for a part of this time in association with his brother John. He carved the first figurehead for the frigate *Constitution,* and, during the 1790s, carved a bust of Milton and four figures for the garden of Elias Hasket Derby in Salem, Massachusetts.

SKINNER, Thomson Joseph: congressman
Born Colchester, Connecticut, May 24, 1752; died January 20, 1809.

Skinner, who had a preparatory education, moved to Massachusetts as a young man. He served as a member of that state's House of Representatives in 1781 and 1785, and from 1789 to 1801. He also served in the Massachusetts Senate from 1786 to 1788, 1790 to 1797, and in 1802 and 1803. In 1788 he attended the Massachusetts Convention which ratified the federal constitution and became a judge in the Court of Common Pleas, a position he held until 1807.

In 1792 Skinner was a presidential elector for Washington and Adams. He was treasurer of the state of Massachusetts in 1806 and 1807. A Democrat, he filled a vacancy in the United States House of Representatives on January 27, 1797, and served until 1799 (4th–5th congresses). He returned for the 8th Congress in 1803 but resigned on August 10, 1804.

Skinner died in Boston.

SMITH, Hezekiah: clergyman
Born Hempstead, Long Island, New York, April 21, 1737; son of Peter and Rebecca (Nichols) Smith; married Hephzibah Kimball, June 27, 1771; father of six children; died January 24, 1805.

Smith, who graduated from Princeton in 1762, joined the Baptist Church in 1756 and was ordained to the ministry seven years later. In 1766 he became the first pastor of the Baptist Church in Haverhill, Massachusetts.

A founder of Rhode Island College (now Brown University), Smith helped raise funds during 1769 and 1770 and was one of the first fellows of that institution. He was an organizer of the Warren Association in 1767 and worked to obtain the separation of church and state in Massachusetts.

Smith served as a regimental chaplain in the Continental Army from 1775 to 1778 and as a brigade chaplain from 1778 to 1780.

SMITH, John: educator, clergyman
Born Rowley, Essex County, Massachusetts, December 21, 1752; son of Joseph and Elizabeth (Palmer) Smith; married Mary Cleaveland; second marriage to Susan Mason; father of at least two children; died April 30, 1809.

Smith graduated from Dartmouth in 1773, later (1803) obtaining a D.D. from Brown University. From 1773 to 1777 he was associate preacher of the Dartmouth College Church and from 1774 to 1778 was employed as a tutor at Moor's Charity School in Massachusetts.

In 1778 Smith became professor of classical languages at Dartmouth, in 1779 librarian, and in 1788 a trustee, holding all three of these positions until 1809. He was also pastor of the Congregational Church of West Hartford, Connecticut, from 1778 to 1809. He wrote *Hebrew Grammar* (1802), *Chaldee Grammar* (1802), and *Cicero de Oratore* (1804).

Smith died in Hanover, New Hampshire.

SMITH, Josiah: congressman
Born Pembroke, Plymouth County, Massachusetts, February 26, 1738; died April 4, 1803.

Smith, after graduating from Harvard, studied law, was admitted to the bar, and established a legal practice. He was a member of the Massachusetts House of Representatives in 1789–90 and was named to the Massachusetts Senate in 1792, serving there until 1794 and again in 1797. He became treasurer of Massachusetts in 1797 and was sent to the United States House of Representatives in 1801 (7th Congress). He died in Pembroke and was buried in Pembroke Cemetery.

SPRING, Samuel: clergyman

Born Northbridge, Massachusetts, March 10, 1747; son of Colonel John and Sarah (Read) Spring; married Hannah Hopkins, November 4, 1779; father of eleven children (including Gardiner); died March 4, 1819.

Spring graduated from the College of New Jersey (now Princeton) in 1771 and studied theology under John Witherspoon from that year until 1774. He served with the Continental Army as a chaplain during General Arnold's expedition to Canada, 1775–76. He was ordained to the ministry of the Congregational Church in 1777 and served as pastor of the North (now Central) Congregational Church in Newburyport, Massachusetts, until his death.

Known as the leader of an extreme Calvinist group, Spring was a founder of the Massachusetts Missionary Society in 1799 and edited its publication, *Massachusetts Missionary Magazine* (established in 1803). In addition, he was a founder of the Massachusetts General Association, a union of conservative-to-moderate Congregationalists with the expressed purpose of combating Unitarianism (1803). He secured an endowment for a seminary which espoused strict Hopkinsian principles, Andover Theological Seminary, in West Newbury, which opened its doors in 1808; the seminary represented both factions of Congregationalists.

A founder of the American Board of Commissioners for Foreign Missions in 1810, Spring was the author of *Christian Knowledge* and *Christian Confidence Inseparable* (sermons), 1785; *The Exemplary Pastor*, 1791; and *Two Discourses on Christ's Self-existence*, 1805. He was awarded an honorary D.D. by Williams College in 1806. He was seventy-two when he died in Newbury.

STILLMAN, Samuel: clergyman

Born Philadelphia, Pennsylvania, February 27, 1737 (old-style calendar); married Hannah Morgan, May 1759; father of fourteen children; died March 12, 1807.

Ordained to the ministry of the Baptist Church in 1759, Stillman became assistant pastor of the Second Baptist Church in Boston in 1763, then served as pastor of the First Baptist Church of Boston from 1765 until his death forty-two years later. A founder of Brown University, he was one of the school's original trustees in 1764 and was a fellow from 1765 to 1807.

Stillman was Calvinistic and evangelical in his philosophy. A compilation of his addresses was published in 1808 as *Select Sermons on Doctrinal and Practical Subjects.* Stillman held a number of honorary degrees: M.A., College of Philadelphia, 1761; M.A. *ad eundem,* Harvard, 1761; M.A., Brown University, 1769; D.D., Brown University, 1788. He died in Boston.

STODDARD, Amos: army officer, territorial governor

Born Woodbury, Connecticut, October 26, 1762; son of Anthony and Phebe (Reade) Stoddard; never married; died May 11, 1813.

Stoddard enlisted in the infantry in 1779. In 1784 he served as assistant clerk of the Supreme Court of Massachusetts and was commissioned an officer during the suppression of Shays's Rebellion in 1787. He was the author of *The Political Crisis,* written in 1791.

Admitted to the Massachusetts bar in 1793, Stoddard became a member of the Massachusetts legislature in 1797. He served with the Massachusetts militia from 1796 to 1798 and was commissioned a captain in the 2nd Regiment of Artillerists and Engineers in the United States Army in 1798. Nine years later he was commissioned a major.

Stoddard was named the first civil and military commandant of Upper Louisiana in 1803. The following year he served as the agent and commissioner of France at a ceremony marking the transfer of the Upper Louisiana Territory from Spain to France; he then assumed the government of the territory in the name of the United States. He was acting governor of the Louisiana Territory from 1804 to 1812. Stoddard defended Fort Meigs (Ohio) in the War of 1812 and died there the following year.

STRONG, Caleb: governor of Massachusetts, congressman

Born Northampton, Massachusetts, January 9, 1745; son of Caleb and Phoebe (Lyman) Strong; married Sara Hooker, November 20, 1777; father of nine children; died November 7, 1819.

Strong graduated from Harvard with highest honors at the age of nineteen. Admitted to the bar in 1772, he served as a selectman of Northampton that year and was a delegate to the Massachusetts Constitutional Convention in 1779. He was a member of the Massachusetts House of Representatives from 1776 to 1778 and of the Massachusetts Senate from 1780 to 1788.

Moving into the national government, Strong was a representative from Massachusetts to the United States Constitutional Convention in 1787. A United States Senator from Massachusetts from 1789 to June 1, 1796, he was active in framing the Judiciary Act and reported Hamilton's plan for a national bank in 1791.

As governor of Massachusetts from 1800 to 1807 and from 1812 to 1816, Strong refused to cooperate with the national government in supplying troops of the Massachusetts militia for federal use in 1812. He approved the calling of and the resultant report of the Hartford Convention in 1814.

Strong was awarded an honorary LL.D. by Harvard in 1801. He died in Northampton at the age of seventy-four and was buried in the Bridge Street Cemetery there.

STUART, Gilbert: painter

Born North Kingston (now Narragansett), Rhode Island, December 3, 1755; son of Gilbert and Elizabeth (Anthony) Stuart; married Charlotte Coates, May 10, 1786; father of twelve children (including Charles, Jane, Ann [Stuart] Stebbens, Agnes, and Emma); died July 9, 1828.

Stuart arrived in London in 1775, studying under Benjamin West there the following year. He contributed one portrait to the Royal Academy exhibition in 1777, three in 1779, two in 1781, and four in 1782. In 1785 he exhibited at the academy for the last time. He was brought to the public's attention by his "Portrait of a Gentleman Skating." He became a member of the Exhibition of Incorporated Society Artists in 1783.

Stuart lived in Dublin, Ireland, from 1787 to 1793, then returned to America, settling in New York City. He worked in Philadelphia from 1794 to 1796, where he painted George Washington from life three times. During this period he also painted a series of women's portraits.

Also a talented musician and conversationalist, Stuart lived in Boston from 1805 until his death. He often left his portraits unfinished. Best known among his works are the Gibbs-Channing portraits (in the Metropolitan Museum of Art, New York City) and portraits of John Adams, John Quincy Adams, Thomas Jefferson, James Madison, Joseph Story, and Judge Stephen Jones.

Stuart was buried in the Central Burying Grounds, Boston Common. He was elected to the Hall of Fame in 1910.

SULLIVAN, James: governor of Massachusetts, Continental congressman

Born Berwick, Massachusetts (now Maine), April 24, 1744; son of John and Margaret (Browne) Sullivan; married Mehitable Odiorne, February 22, 1768; second marriage to Martha Langdon, December 31, 1786; father of at least six children (including William); died December 10, 1808.

Sullivan served as a member of the Provincial Congress of Massachusetts and the Committee of Safety in 1774–75. On the bench of the Massachusetts General Court in 1775–76, he was also a justice of the Massachusetts Supreme Court from 1776 to 1782 and helped reorganize the state's laws in 1780.

A Massachusetts delegate to the Continental Congress in 1782, Sullivan was a member of the Massachusetts Executive Council in 1787. He was judge of probate for Suffolk County, Massachusetts, in 1788, attorney general of the state from 1790 to 1796, and an agent at the Halifax conference to settle the disputed Maine boundary in 1796. He was governor of Massachusetts (Democratic-Republican) in 1807–08.

Sullivan wrote pamphlets opposing the Federalist party and was a member of the American Academy of Arts and Sciences. A founder of the Massachusetts Historical Society, he was president for a number of years and a contributor to its early collections. He was the author of *The History of the District of Maine*, 1795, *The History of Land Titles In Massachusetts*, 1801, and *A Dissertation upon the United States of America*, 1801. He died in Boston and was buried in Central Boston Common Cemetery.

SUMNER, Increase: governor of Massachusetts, jurist
Born Roxbury, Massachusetts, November 27, 1746; son of Increase and Sarah (Sharp) Sumner; married Elizabeth Hyslop, September 30, 1779; died June 7, 1799.

Admitted to the Massachusetts bar in 1770, Sumner was a delegate to the Massachusetts General Court from 1776 to 1779 and a member of the Massachusetts Senate from 1780 to 1782. He was a member of the Massachusetts Constitutional Convention in 1779–80 and was elected to the Continental Congress in 1782, although he did not take his seat.

Sumner was appointed an associate justice of the Supreme Judicial Court of Massachusetts in 1782 and was a member of the Massachusetts Convention which ratified the United States Constitution in 1788. He was governor of Massachusetts from 1797 to 1799; his was a popular administration, and he worked to increase munitions.

Sumner died in Roxbury and was buried in the Granary Burial Ground in Boston.

SWAN, James: Revolutionary patriot, financier
Born Fifeshire, Scotland, 1754; married Hepzibah Clarke, circa 1776; father of four children; died July 31, 1830.

Swan arrived in Boston in 1765, became a member of the Sons of Liberty, and participated in the Boston Tea Party. During the Revolution he served as aide-de-camp to General Joseph Warren at the Battle of Bunker Hill and attained the rank of major and later colonel. He became secretary to the Massachusetts Board of War in 1777 and a member of the Massachusetts legislature as adjutant general of the commonwealth in 1778.

Swan went to France in 1787 and gained control of the remainder of the American debt to France. He was appointed an agent of the French Republic, and both as agent and as a broker he profited from having the American debt obligations to France accepted in payment for supplies furnished or to be furnished to the French marine. He was sent to debtor's prison in Paris in 1800 and spent the remaining thirty years of his life there.

Swan was the author of *A Dissuasion to Great Britain and the Colonies from the Slave Trade to Africa,* published in 1773.

SWAN, Timothy: composer
Born Worcester, Massachusetts, July 23, 1758; son of William and Lavina (Keyes) Swan; married Mary Gay, April 10, 1784; father of fourteen children; died July 23, 1842.

Swan was apprenticed to a Loyalist (Mr. Barnes) from 1772 to 1775, then lived with his brother in Groton, Massachusetts, from 1775 to 1782. He published the book *Select Harmony* (containing six of his compositions) in 1783, and his music soon became very popular. He published a song, "China," first sung in public in 1794. In addition, he published *The Songsters' Assistant* in 1800, *New England Harmony* in 1801, and *The Songsters' Museum* in 1803. Swan died in Northfield, Massachusetts.

★★★★★

TAGGART, Samuel: congressman and clergyman

Born Londonderry, New Hampshire, March 24, 1754; died April 25, 1825.

A student of theology, Taggart graduated from Dartmouth in 1774 and was licensed to preach in 1776. The following year he was ordained to the ministry and became pastor of the Presbyterian Church in Colrain, Massachusetts, a position he held until his resignation in 1818. In addition to his ministerial duties in Colrain, Taggart traveled as a missionary throughout western New York.

A Federalist, Taggart was elected to serve Massachusetts in the United States House of Representatives in 1803, serving until 1817. He then retired to his farm in Colrain, where he died in 1825. He was buried in Chandler Hill Cemetery.

TALLMAN, Peleg: congressman

Born Tiverton, Rhode Island, July 24, 1764; died March 12, 1840.

Tallman, who attended public schools, served in the Revolutionary War in the privateer *Trumbull*. In 1780 he lost an arm in a naval engagement and was later captured, remaining imprisoned in England and Ireland until 1783.

After his release, Tallman became a merchant in Bath, Maine (which was a part of Massachusetts until 1820). He was elected as a Democrat from Massachusetts to serve in the United States Congress in the years 1811–13. Tallman also served as a member of the Maine Senate from 1821 to 1822.

Tallman was overseer of Bowdoin College in Brunswick, Maine, from 1802 until his death in 1840. He was buried in Maple Grove Cemetery in Bath, Maine, but his body was later moved to Forest Hills Cemetery in Roxbury, Massachusetts.

THACHER, George: congressman, jurist

Born April 12, 1754; son of Peter and Anner (Lewis) Thacher; married Sarah Savage, July 21, 1784; father of ten children; died April 6, 1824.

Thacher studied law with Shearjashub Bourne at Harvard, graduating in 1776 and being admitted to the Massachusetts bar in 1778. In 1787 he served as a Massachusetts delegate to the Continental Congress. A Federalist, Thacher was elected to the United States House of Representatives from the Maine District of Massachusetts in 1789 and served until 1801. While in this office, he spoke in favor of the Sedition Act and the assumption of state debts.

A founder of the Second Church in Biddeford, Maine, Thacher was also a delegate to the Maine Constitutional Convention in 1819. From 1801 until his death in 1824, he served as associate judge of the Massachusetts Supreme Court. He was buried in the Woodlawn Cemetery in Biddeford.

THACHER, James: physician, army officer

Born Barnstable, Massachusetts, February 14, 1754; son of John and Content (Norton) Thacher; married Susannah Hayward, April 28, 1785; father of six children; died May 23, 1844.

Thacher served with the 1st Virginia Regiment from 1778 to 1779 and took part in the ill-fated Penobscot Expedition. In 1781, he acted as surgeon for a select corps of light infantry. He took part in the siege of Yorktown and the surrender of Cornwallis, and then, in 1783, retired from the army. The following year he began to practice medicine and surgery.

In 1823 Thacher published his Revolutionary War diary, titling it *A Military Journal.* A second edition was issued in 1826 and was reprinted in 1854 as *Military Journal.* His other works include *The American Medical Biography,* 1828, which was the first publication of its kind; *Observations on Hydrophobia,* 1812; and *American Modern Practice,* 1817.

A member of the American Academy of Arts and Sciences and the Massachusetts Medical Society, Thacher received an honorary M.D. from Harvard in 1810. He died in Plymouth, Massachusetts.

THACHER, Peter: clergyman

Born Milton, Massachusetts, March 21, 1752; son

of Oxenbridge and Sarah (Kent) Thacher; married Elizabeth (Haukes) Poole, October 8, 1770; father of ten children; died December 16, 1802.

A graduate of Harvard in 1769, Thacher was ordained and installed as pastor of the Congregational Church in Malden, Massachusetts, in 1770, a post he held until 1784. In 1776 he made a speech titled "An Oration Delivered at Watertown . . . To Commemorate the Bloody Massacre at Boston Perpetrated March 5, 1770." As a result of this address, Congress gave the clergyman recruiting powers for the seacoast defense of Masschusetts.

From 1776 to 1802 Thacher held the post of chaplain for the Massachusetts General Court; he is believed to have been the author of the Malden Resolutions to the Court. In 1780 he served as the Malden delegate to the Massachusetts Constitutional Convention.

In 1785 Thacher became pastor of the Brattle Street Church of Boston. A member of the American Academy of Arts and Sciences, Thacher founded the Massachusetts Historical Society in 1790. Among his written works were "A Narrative on the Battle of Bunker Hill." He died in Savannah, Georgia.

THOMAS, Isaiah: publisher

Born Boston, Massachusetts, January 30, 1750; son of Moses and Fidelity (Grant) Thomas; married Mary Dill, December 25, 1769; second marriage to Mary Fowle Thomas, May 26, 1779; third marriage to Rebecca Armstrong, August 10, 1819; father of at least two children (Mary Anne and Isaiah); died April 4, 1831.

Thomas learned printing at an early age and, at the age of sixteen, became printer of the *Halifax* (Nova Scotia, Canada) *Gazette*. He was also employed by the *South Carolina and American General Gazette* in Charleston, Massachusetts. Returning to Boston, Thomas, with Zechariah Fowle, founded the Massachusetts *Spy* in 1770. Later he became the sole owner of the paper. Driven from Boston in 1775 by the British occupation,

Thomas succeeded in publishing the *Spy* in various Massachusetts towns during the Revolutionary War, moving from town to town according to the fortunes of the war.

After the war, Thomas became one of America's leading publishers, turning out textbooks, almanacs, dictionaries, and magazines, including *Royal American Magazine*, 1774–75, and *Massachusetts Magazine*, 1789–96. An author as well, he wrote a two-volume work titled *The History of Printing in America* in 1810.

Thomas received an honorary A.M. from Dartmouth in 1814 as well as an honorary LL.D. from Allegheny College in 1818. Noted for his philanthropic activities, he was also the founder, incorporator, and first president of the American Antiquarian Society, in 1812. He also served as postmaster of Worcester, Massachusetts, from 1775 to 1801. He died in Worcester.

THOMAS, John: army officer

Born Marshfield, Massachusetts, November 9, 1724; son of John and Lydia (Waterman) Thomas; married Hannah Thomas, 1761; father of three children; died June 2, 1776.

Commissioned a lieutenant and a surgeon's mate in 1755, Thomas was empowered to enlist volunteers in the provinces. He served in Nova Scotia and in a Canadian expedition under Amherst in 1759–60. Thomas was appointed justice of the peace of Kingston, Massachusetts, by Governor Hutchinson in 1770.

In 1775 Thomas was commissioned a brigadier general by the Continental Congress. During the winter of 1775–76, he was in command at Roxbury, an important post in the American siege lines. He seized and fortified the strategic site of Dorchester, Massachusetts, in 1776, an action which forced the British to evacuate Boston.

Thomas was promoted to major general in 1776 and was ordered north. During this campaign, he summoned a council of war at Quebec, Canada; those in attendance unanimously decided to retreat to Sorel. Soon afterward Thomas contracted smallpox and died. He was buried in Chambly, Quebec.

THOMAS, Robert Bailey: editor, publisher
Born Grafton, Massachusetts, April 24, 1766; son of William and Azabah (Goodale) Thomas; married Hannah Beaman, November 17, 1803; died May 19, 1846.

A self-educated man, from 1790 to 1792 Thomas attended a mathematics school run by Osgood Carleton, an almanac maker, in Boston. In 1792 Thomas printed the first edition of *The Farmer's Almanack* and continued publishing annual editions for the next fifty-four years. Later called *The Old Farmer's Almanack*, it contained articles on a wide range of topics, including patriotic, geographic and epigrammatic material.

A memoir of Thomas's life appeared in the *Almanacks* of 1833–37 and 1839. He died in Boylston, Massachusetts, at the age of eighty.

THOMPSON, Benjamin (Count Rumford): physicist, philanthropist
Born Woburn, Massachusetts, March 26, 1753; son of Benjamin and Ruth (Simonds) Thompson; married Sarah (Walker) Rolfe, November 1772; second marriage to Madame Lavoisier (Marie Anne Pierrette), October 24, 1805; father of at least one child (Sarah); died August 21, 1814.

In 1773 Thompson was commissioned a major in the Second New Hampshire Provincial Regiment. Two years later he applied for a commission in Washington's army but was refused. He left for London the same year and was later appointed to the secretaryship of the Province of Georgia. He was elected a fellow of the Royal Society in 1779, and in 1780 he served as under secretary of state for the Northern Department. Circa 1781 Thompson was commissioned a lieutenant colonel in the British Army for service in America. In 1782 he was engaged in action near Charleston, South Carolina, and he served as commander of a regiment on Long Island until 1783. Knighted the following year, he offered his services to Bavaria, becoming a colonel of cavalry and general aide-de-camp in that country's army. Four years later he was made a major general and head of the war department of Bavaria. He was elected to the academies of Berlin, Munich, and Mannheim. In 1791 he was given the title Count Rumford by the elector of Bavaria.

Thompson returned to England in 1795 and began writing. His first volume of *Essays, Political, Economical, and Philosophical* was published in 1796. A third edition in two volumes followed in 1798, and in 1800 a three-volume fifth edition appeared. A fourth volume was added in 1802.

Thompson installed nonsmoking, highly efficient fireplaces in 150 homes in London, and in 1796 he established the Rumford prize and medal for a discovery or an improvement in the field of heating or lighting. In 1789 he became a foreign honorary member of the American Academy of Arts and Sciences; seven years later he established a $5,000 award fund for the Academy.

As head council of regency, Thompson prevented French and Austrian armies from entering the neutral city of Munich in 1796. He served as head of the department of general police of Bavaria. In 1800 the Royal Institution was incorporated as a result of a proposal by Rumford. He was elected a foreign associate of the Institute of France in 1803.

Thompson developed the calorimeter and the photometer, and he made several improvements in lamps and other forms of illumination. He died in Auteuil, near Paris, France.

THORNDIKE, Israel: shipper, state legislator
Born Beverly, Massachusetts, April 30, 1755; son of Andrew and Anne (Morgan) Thorndike; married Anna Dodge; father of twelve children; died May 8, 1832.

Thorndike, who attended public schools,

in 1776 was commissioned commander of the schooner *Warren;* later he commanded the privateer *Resource.* He became an active partner in the shipping firm Brown and Thorndike and was sole manager after Brown's retirement in 1800. He was involved in extensive trade with China and the Orient, operating from Salem, Massachusetts. He later expanded his business to Boston.

From 1788 to 1814 Thorndike served in the Massachusetts legislature. He was a member of the Massachusetts constitutional conventions of 1788 and 1820. In 1818 he donated the library of Professor Ebeling of Hamburg, Germany, to Harvard.

Thorndike died in Boston and was buried in the Mount Auburn Cemetery in Cambridge, Massachusetts.

TICKNOR, Elisha: educator, merchant

Born Lebanon, Connecticut, March 25, 1757; son of Colonel Elisha and Ruth (Knowles) Ticknor; married Elizabeth Billings, May 23, 1790; father of George; died June 22, 1821.

Ticknor graduated from Dartmouth in 1783 and was appointed master of Moor's Charity Schools in Hanover, New Hampshire. He served there until 1785, when he opened a private school in Boston. In 1788 he left the private school and was appointed principal of the South Writing School in Boston, where he served until 1794.

In 1795 Ticknor began operating a grocery. Three years later he organized the Massachusetts Mutual Fire Insurance Company. In 1805 he suggested the establishment of free primary schools for children unable to read. He was elected a selectman of Boston in 1815. In 1816 he and James Savage founded the Provident Institution for Savings, one of the first businesses of its kind in the United States.

Ticknor died in Boston.

TRACY, Nathaniel: merchant

Born Newburyport, Massachusetts, August 11, 1751; son of Captain Patrick and Helen (Gookin)

Tracy; married Mary Lee, February 28, 1775; father of eleven children; died September 20, 1796.

Tracy graduated from Harvard in 1769 and received his M.A. in 1772. He began a shipping business in 1769 and outfitted a fleet of privateers in 1775. During the following eight years he sent out 24 cruisers and captured 120 British vessels. During the American Revolution he rendered valuable service in capturing ammunition and supplies bound for the British Army. By 1783 all but one of his vessels had been captured or destroyed.

Tracy contributed large sums of money and supplies to the Continental Congress to finance the American Revolution. In 1781–82 he served as deputy to the Massachusetts General Court. He was a charter member of the American Academy of Arts and Sciences. He died in Newburyport.

TROWBRIDGE, Edmund: jurist

Born Cambridge, Massachusetts, 1709; son of Thomas and Mary (Goffe) Trowbridge; married Martha Remington, March 15, 1737 or 1738; died April 2, 1793.

Trowbridge graduated from Harvard in 1728 and began a long career as a prominent member of the Massachusetts bar. He was attorney general of Massachusetts from 1749 until 1767, when he became judge of the Superior Court. In the Boston Massacre trial of 1771 he gained a reputation for fairness. Trowbridge was also an expert in real property and the author of a tract on mortgages, one of the few known colonial studies in private law. He was a Loyalist at the outset of the American Revolution but later became, and remained, neutral. He died in Cambridge in 1793.

TUCKER, Samuel: naval officer

Born Marblehead, Massachusetts, November 1, 1747; son of Andrew and Mary (Belcher) Tucker; married Mary Gatchell, December 21, 1768; died March 10, 1833.

In 1775 Tucker commanded the ship *Young Phoenix,* and the next year he became captain of the *Franklin,* a ship that preyed on British vessels. He transferred to the *Hancock* and in 1777 was commissioned a captain in the Continental Navy. Later that year he commanded the frigate *Boston.*

In 1778 Tucker sailed for France carrying John Adams to his post as commissioner to France. From 1778 to 1780 he continued his attacks on British commerce. Later, from 1783 to 1785, he commanded several vessels trading with West Indian and European ports.

Tucker was a member of the Massachusetts legislature from 1814 to 1818 and was elected to the Maine House of Representatives for two terms. He died in Bremen, Maine, at the age of eighty-five.

TUFTS, Cotton: physician
Born Medford, Massachusetts, May 30, 1732; son of Simon and Abigail (Smith) Tufts; married Lucy Quincy, December 2, 1765; second marriage to Mrs. Susanna Warner, October 22, 1789; father of Cotton; died December 8, 1815.

After receiving an A.M. from Harvard in 1749, Tufts began practicing medicine in Weymouth, Massachusetts, in 1752 and became a leading practitioner there. Later, in 1785, he was given an honorary M.D. He proposed the establishing of the Massachusetts Medical Society in 1765, was an organizer of it in 1781, and became its president in 1787. He was also a charter member of the American Academy of Arts and Sciences.

Tufts represented Weymouth in meetings against the Stamp Act. He was a trustee of Derby Academy in Hingham, Massachusetts, a president of the Society for the Reformation of Morals, and a church deacon.

TUPPER, Benjamin: army officer, pioneer
Born Stoughton, Massachusetts, March 11, 1738; son of Thomas and Remember (Perry) Tupper; married Huldah White, November 18, 1762; father of seven children (including Rowena [Tupper] Sargent); died June 7, 1792.

In 1756 Tupper served as a sergeant in the French and Indian War. He was commissioned a lieutenant in the Western Massachusetts militia in 1774, and in 1775 he participated in the siege of Boston and the destruction of the British lighthouse on Castle Island. In 1776 he was commissioned a lieutenant colonel. He served as a colonel in the Massachusetts militia in the Battle of Long Island, the Saratoga campaign, and the Battle of Monmouth. He retired with the brevet rank of brigadier general in 1783.

Soon after leaving the service, Tupper became a member of the Massachusetts legislature. He was one of the Continental officers who signed the Newburgh Petition of 1783, which sought creation of new territory in the Northwest. He was the Massachusetts representative on a corps of state surveyors sent to the West by Congress, and in 1785 he conducted preliminary surveying.

Tupper aided the movement which led to the formation of the Ohio Company and accompanied the original settlers to Marietta, Ohio, in 1788. He served as judge of the Court of Common Pleas and Quarter Sessions, the first civil court in the Ohio Territory, from 1788 to 1792, the year of his death.

TURNER, Charles, Jr.: congressman, army officer
Born Duxbury, Massachusetts, June 20, 1760; died May 16, 1839.

Turner attended common schools in Duxbury and Scituate, Massachusetts. He was commissioned an adjutant in the Massachusetts militia in 1787, was promoted to major in 1790, and served as a lieutenant colonel commandant from 1798 to 1812.

In 1800 Turner was appointed the first postmaster of Scituate. He also held the office of justice of the peace and was a member of the Massachusetts House of Representatives in 1803, from 1805 to 1808, in 1817, in 1819, and in 1823. A War Democrat, he was sent (after a contested election) by Massachusetts to the United States House of Representatives, in which he served from June 28, 1809, to 1813 (11th and

12th congresses). He was a member of the Massachusetts Senate in 1816.

Turner was appointed steward of the Marine Hospital in Chelsea, Massachusetts, in 1820. That same year he was a delegate to the Massachusetts Constitutional Convention. He then returned to farming in Scituate, where he died. He was buried in the burial ground of the First Parish of Norwell.

★★★★★

VARNUM, Joseph Bradley: senator

Born Dracut, Massachusetts, January 29, 1750; son of Samuel and Hannah (Mitchell) Varnum; married Molly Butler, January 26, 1773; father of twelve children; died September 11, 1821.

Varnum served as a captain in the Dracut militia from 1770 to 1774 and was present at the Battle of Lexington. He then was a captain in the Dracut Minutemen from 1776 to 1787, during which time he served against Burgoyne (1777), fought in Rhode Island (1778), and served in the suppression of Shays's Rebellion (1786). Also during that period he became a member of the lower house of the Massachusetts legislature, serving from 1780 to 1785, and going on to the state senate for the years 1786–88. He returned to the senate in 1795 and again in 1817 through 1821.

Varnum participated in the Massachusetts Convention which ratified the United States Constitution in 1788. Elected to the United States House of Representatives in 1794, he was later charged with corrupt election practices. He served in the 4th through the 12th congresses (1795–1811) and was speaker during the 10th and 11th congresses. He then went to the Senate for a term in 1811–17, during which time he was the only New England supporter of the War Hawks (who favored starting the War of 1812). He was president pro tem in 1813. In 1820 he was a delegate to the Massachusetts Constitutional Convention.

Varnum belonged to the Massachusetts Peace Society (later the American Peace Society). He wrote *An Address Delivered to the Third Division of the Massachusetts Militia . . .* (1800). He died in Dracut and was buried in Varnum Cemetery there.

VAUGHAN, Benjamin: political economist

Born Jamaica, April 30, 1751; son of Samuel and Sarah (Hallowell) Vaughan; married Sarah Manning, June 30, 1781; father of three sons and four daughters; died December 8, 1835.

After being educated at Cambridge, Vaughan read law at Inner Temple in London and then studied medicine at Edinburgh. During the American Revolution he propagandized for independence for the colonies. Upon his marriage in 1781 he joined his father-in-law's merchant firm.

Vaughan was an unofficial member of the British commission which concluded the Treaty of Paris in 1782. He supported free trade and the French Revolution. In 1792 he became a member of Parliament from Calne, but he later fled to France as a consequence of an investigation of supporters of the French Revolution. In 1794 he was imprisoned in France but was soon released to Switzerland.

Vaughan came to America and settled in Hallowell, Maine, in 1796. He maintained a wide correspondence with American political figures and helped found the Maine Historical Society. A member of many literary and science societies, he possessed the largest individually owned library in New England, which was divided after his death among Harvard, Bowdoin College, and Augusta Insane Hospital.

Vaughan was the author of *Letters on the Subject of the Concert of Princes and the Dismemberment of Poland and France* (1793) and the editor of *Political, Miscellaneous and Philosophical Pieces . . . Written by Benjamin Franklin* (1779). He received honorary degrees from Harvard in 1807 and Bowdoin College in 1812.

VAUGHAN, Charles: merchant, real estate promoter

Born London, England, June 30, 1759; son of Samuel and Sarah (Hallowell) Vaughan; married Frances

Western Apthorp, 1790; father of at least four children (two sons and two daughters); died May 15, 1839.

Raised on his father's plantation in Jamaica, Vaughan moved to New England in 1785 and became a developer of town sites on the Kennebec River in Maine. He went to England to attempt to publicize his speculative ventures during 1790 and 1791. Apparently unsuccessful, he returned to the United States and was a merchant in Boston from 1791 to 1796. In 1798 he went bankrupt.

Vaughan was an incorporator of the Boston Library Society, the Massachusetts Society for Promoting Agriculture, the Massachusetts Society for the Aid of Immigrants, and Hallowell Academy. He died shortly before his eightieth birthday.

★★★★★

WADSWORTH, Peleg: army officer, congressman

Born Duxbury, Massachusetts, May 6, 1748; son of Peleg and Lusanna (Sampson) Wadsworth; married Elizabeth Bartlett, June 18, 1772; father of eleven children (including Henry, Zilpah [Wadsworth] Longfellow); died November 12, 1829.

Wadsworth had an active military career, serving in various capacities prior to and during the Revolution. A graduate of Harvard in 1769, he was named captain of a company of Minutemen in 1774 and was a member of the Committee of Correspondence of Plymouth County, Massachusetts. He served as aide-de-camp to Artemas Ward and then with Washington at Long Island, New York, in 1776.

In 1778 Wadsworth served under Sullivan in Rhode Island, then became adjutant general and, in 1779, brigadier general of the Massachusetts militia. During the years 1777–78 he was a representative from Duxbury to the Massachusetts legislature. He was second in command of an expedition to expel the British from Fort George, Castine, Maine, in 1779, and commanded the Eastern

Department of Massachusetts, with headquarters at Thomaston, Maine, in 1780. In February 1781 his dwelling was raided by a party of British, and he was taken captive and held until June of that year.

A land agent in 1784, Wadsworth was elected to the Massachusetts Senate in 1792 and became selectman of Falmouth (now Portland), Maine. A Federalist, he was a Massachusetts delegate to the United States House of Representatives from 1793 to 1807. He died at the estate "Wadsworth Hall," Hiram, Maine, and was buried in a family graveyard there.

WARD, Artemas: army officer, Continental congressman, congressman

Born Shrewsbury, Massachusetts, November 26, 1727; son of Nahum and Martha (How) Ward; married Sarah Trowbridge; father of eight children; died October 28, 1800.

After graduating from Harvard in 1748, Ward established a general store in Shrewsbury in 1750. He held various town offices, including assessor, clerk, selectman, moderator, and treasurer. He was commissioned a colonel in the 3rd Regiment of the Massachusetts militia in 1758.

A justice of the Worcester County Court of Common Pleas in 1762, Ward was named chief justice of the court in 1775. He was Shrewsbury's representative to the Massachusetts General Court for many years. A member of conventions held in Worcester County to champion colonial rights, he was also a member of the first and second Massachusetts provincial congresses.

Ward was commissioned a general and commander-in-chief of the Massachusetts militia in 1775 and directed the siege of Boston. He was named a major general, second in command of the Continental Army, by the Continental Congress in 1775. He resigned his commission the following year.

Ward was a member of the Massachusetts Executive Council from 1777 to 1780 and served in the Continental Congress in 1780 and 1781. The following year he became a member of the Massachusetts legislature and served there until 1787. A Federalist, he was elected to the United States House of Representatives in 1791 and again in 1793.

Ward's homestead is now the property of Harvard University and is maintained as a memorial. He was buried in Mountain View Cemetery in Shrewsbury.

WARREN, James: legislator

Born Plymouth, Massachusetts, September 28, 1726; son of James and Penelope (Winslow) Warren; married Mercy Otis, November 14, 1754; father of five children; died November 28, 1808.

Sheriff of Plymouth County, Massachusetts, from 1757 to 1775, Warren, a 1745 graduate of Harvard, was a member of the Massachusetts House of Representatives from 1766 to 1778, in 1780, and in 1787. He was speaker circa 1778 and in 1787.

Ward, a major general in the Provincial Militia in 1776, also served as paymaster general for the Continental Army in 1776 and on the Navy Board for the Eastern Department from 1776 to 1781. He was a member of the Massachusetts Governor's Council from 1792 to 1794 and a presidential elector from Massachusetts in 1804. He died in Plymouth.

WARREN, John: surgeon

Born Roxbury, Massachusetts, July 27, 1753; son of Joseph and Mary (Stevens) Warren; married Abigail Collins, November 4, 1777; father of seventeen children (including John Collins and Edward); died April 4, 1815.

Warren was a Harvard graduate in 1771, later (1786) receiving an honorary M.D. from that school. He was a surgeon in Colonel Pickering's Regiment in the Massachusetts militia in 1773 and took an active part in the Boston Tea Party. A senior surgeon at a hospital in Cambridge, Massachusetts, in 1775, Warren went to New York in 1776, where he served as surgeon general at a hospital on Long Island. He established a hospital for inoculation against smallpox when the disease became prevalent in 1778.

Warren engaged in a number of activities related to his work in medicine. He gave a private course of lectures on anatomy at a military hospital in Boston in 1780–81, was an organizer of the Boston Medical Society in 1780, and established the first school of medicine connected with Harvard in 1782. He became a professor of anatomy and surgery at Harvard in 1783. A pioneer in abdominal operations and amputation at the shoulder joint, he also was a prominent figure in fighting the yellow fever epidemic of 1798.

Grand Master of the Massachusetts Lodges of Free and Accepted Masons from 1783 to 1784, Warren was also a founder and president of the Massachusetts Humane Society. He was a member of the Agricultural Society and the American Academy of Arts and Sciences. He wrote *A View of the Mercurial Practice in Febrile Diseases* in 1813. He died in Boston.

WARREN, Joseph: physician, patriot

Born Roxbury, Massachusetts, June 11, 1741; son of Joseph and Mary (Stevens) Warren; married Elizabeth Hocton, September 6, 1764; father of four children; died June 17, 1775.

Warren graduated from Harvard in 1759 and studied medicine under his uncle, Dr. James Lloyd. He then established a medical practice in Boston. He became a Freemason in 1761 and was made provisional grand master in 1769. A Whig, he was active in the political clubs of his day.

After the Boston Massacre, Warren joined a committee appointed by the town meeting to direct Governor Hutchinson to remove British troops. He was a member of the Committee of Safety and one of three men chosen to draw up the report "A State of the Rights of Colonists" in 1772. A leader in organizing opposition to the Regulating Act, he drafted the "Suffolk Resolves" and made his celebrated second oration in commemoration of the Boston Massacre in 1775.

He sent William Dawes and Paul Revere to Lexington in April 1775 to inform John Hancock and Samuel Adams that they were in danger.

Warren served as president pro tem of the Massachusetts Provincial Congress, a member of the Committee of Safety, and head of a committee to organize an army in Massachusetts in 1775. Commissioned a major general in June 1775, he was shot shortly after by a British soldier in the Battle of Bunker Hill at Charlestown, Massachusetts.

WARREN, Mercy Otis: author

Born Barnstable, Massachusetts, September 25, 1728; daughter of James and Mary (Allyne) Otis; married James Warren, November 14, 1754; mother of five children; died October 19, 1814.

Mrs. Warren maintained an extensive correspondence with John Adams, James Winthrop, Thomas Jefferson, and Elbridge Gerry, among others. She was the author of two political satires, *The Adulateur,* 1773, and *The Group,* 1775. She also wrote *The Sack of Rome,* 1778; *The Ladies of Castile,* 1778; *Poems Dramatic and Miscellaneous,* 1790; *History of the Rise, Progress and Termination of the American Revolution,* in three volumes, 1805. She died in Plymouth, Massachusetts, at the age of eighty-six.

WATERHOUSE, Benjamin: physician

Born Newport, Rhode Island, March 4, 1754; son of Timothy and Hannah (Proud) Waterhouse; married Elizabeth Oliver, June 1, 1788; second marriage to Louisa Lee, September 19, 1819; father of six children; died October 2, 1846.

Apprenticed to Dr. John Halliburton, a surgeon, in 1770, Waterhouse entered the University of Edinburgh as a medical student in 1775. He graduated from the University of Leyden in 1780 and attended the medical department of Harvard in 1783. He then became a professor of theory and practice of physic in Harvard's medical department until 1812, when he was forced to resign.

Waterhouse pioneered the vaccination process in America. In 1800 he received from England vaccine for smallpox in the form of infected threads and immediately used it on his son. He vaccinated others with cowpox, with good results. Waterhouse sent vaccine to President Jefferson (who had about two hundred persons vaccinated) in 1802. He wrote a number of newspaper articles on the subject of vaccination.

Waterhouse lectured on natural history, mineralogy and botany at Rhode Island College (now Brown University) from 1784 to 1786 and at Cambridge, Massachusetts, circa 1788. He drew up plans for the Humane Society of the Commonwealth of Massachusetts in 1785. He became medical superintendent of all military outposts in New England in 1813, serving for seven years. In 1833 he edited John B. Wyeth's *Oregon* (published to deter western emigrations).

Waterhouse was the author of a number of works, including *A Synopsis of a Course of Lectures, on the Theory and Practice of Medicine,* 1786; *A Prospect of Exterminating the Small Pox* (his first report on smallpox), 1800; *Cautions to Young Persons Concerning Health . . . Shewing the Evil Tendency of the Use of Tobacco . . . with Observations on the use of Ardent and Vinous Spirits,* 1805; *The Botanist,* 1811; and *A Circular Letter, from D. Benjamin Waterhouse to the Surgeons of the Different Post,* 1817.

Waterhouse died at home in Cambridge and was buried in Mount Auburn Cemetery.

WATERS, Daniel: naval officer

Born Charlestown, Massachusetts, June 20, 1731; son of Adam and Rachel (Draper) Waters; married Agnes Smith, July 1759; second marriage to Mary (Wilcox) Mortimer, June 8, 1779; third marriage to Sarah Sigourney, July 29, 1802; father of one daughter; died March 26, 1816.

A member of the Malden (Massachusetts) Minutemen, Waters saw action against the British in 1776 and was asked by the Malden Committee of Safety to prepare the town's cannon. That year, in command of the schooner *Lee,* he captured two enemy vessels. He was commissioned a captain in the Continental Navy in 1777 and served on a West Indies cruise on the Continental sloop *General Gates* in 1779. He also commanded the Massachusetts ship *General Putnam.*

Waters's most famous exploit occurred in 1779 when, in command of the privateer *Thorn,* he defeated two enemy privateers of about equal armament but more heavily manned. He seized the *Sparlin* in 1780 and captained the privateer *Friendship* in 1781.

Waters died in Malden at the age of eighty-four.

WEBBER, Samuel: college president
Born Byfield, Massachusetts, 1759; died July 17, 1810.

A graduate of Harvard in 1784, Webber was ordained to the ministry of the Congregational Church the following year. He was a tutor at Harvard from 1787 to 1789 and Hollis professor of mathematics and natural philosophy from 1789 to 1804. He was granted an honorary S.T.D. from Harvard in 1806, acceding to the presidency of that institution the same year.

Webber was a member of the commission that attempted to settle the boundary between the United States and the British provinces. He was vice president of the American Academy of Arts and Sciences of Boston and a member of the American Philosophical Society. He was the author of *A System of Mathematics.*

WEST, Samuel: clergyman
Born Yarmouth, Massachusetts, February 21, 1731; son of Dr. Sackfield and Ruth (Jenkins) West; married Experience Howland, March 7, 1768; second marriage to Mrs. Lovisa (Hathaway) Jenne, January 1790; father of six children; died September 24, 1807.

West graduated from Harvard in 1754 and was ordained to the ministry of the Congregational Church. He was pastor at a church in Dartmouth (later New Bedford), Massachusetts, from 1761 to 1803.

A chaplain in the Continental Army during the Revolution, West was noted for deciphering a treasonable code letter for George Washington. (The letter had been written by Dr. Benjamin Church and was intended for the British admiral at Newport, Rhode Island.) He served on the committee that framed the Massachusetts Constitution and was a member of the Massachusetts Convention which considered ratification of the United States Constitution.

In a theological argument with Calvinists, West took the Arminian side. He died in Tiverton, Rhode Island.

WHEATLEY, Phillis: poet
Born Senegal, Africa, 1753; married Dr. John Peters, 1778; mother of three children; died December 5, 1784.

Phillis Wheatley was kidnapped and placed on a slave ship destined for Boston about 1761. She became the personal servant for the wife of John Wheatley, who gave her a liberal education and lent her her name. Her first verses included "To the University of Cambridge in New England," circa 1766; "To the King's Most Excellent Majesty," 1768; "On the Death of Reverend Dr. Sewell," 1769; *An Elegiac Poem on the Death of a Celebrated Devine . . . George Whitefield,* 1770; and *Poems on Various Subjects, Religious and Moral,* 1773.

Wheatley went to England in 1773 and returned to Boston later in the year. She was freed before her marriage to Dr. John Peters, a free Negro, in 1778 and died in Boston in poverty at the age of thirty. Her *Elegy Sacred to the Memory of Dr. Samuel Cooper* was published the year of her death. More of her writing was published posthumously, including *Memoir and Poems of Phillis Wheatley,* 1834, and *The Letters of Phillis Wheatley, the Negro-Slave Poet of Boston,* 1864.

WHEATON, Laban: congressman, jurist
Born Mansfield, Massachusetts, March 13, 1754; died March 23, 1846.

After attending Wrentham (Massachusetts) Academy, Wheaton graduated from Harvard in 1774. He studied theology at

Woodstock, Connecticut, and also studied law. Admitted to the bar in 1788, he established a legal practice in Milton, Massachusetts.

Wheaton was a judge of the Bristol County (Massachusetts) Court and a member of the Massachusetts House of Representatives from 1803 to 1808 and in 1825. A Federalist, he was elected to four consecutive terms in the United States House of Representatives beginning in 1809. He served as chief justice of the Bristol County Court of Common Pleas from 1810 to 1819 and as chief justice of the Court of Sessions from 1819 until his death. He was buried in Norton Cemetery in Norton, Massachusetts.

WHITTEMORE, Amos: inventor, manufacturer

Born Cambridge, Massachusetts, April 19, 1759; son of Thomas and Anna (Cutter) Whittemore; married Helen Weston, June 18, 1781; father of at least twelve children; died March 27, 1828.

After a public school education, Whittemore was apprenticed to a gunsmith. He later manufactured brushes for carding cotton and wool in 1795 and was superintendent of mechanical equipment in three factories.

In 1796 Whittemore obtained patents for a machine which cut nails, a loom for weaving duck, and a form of mechanical ship's log. The following year he patented a machine which eliminated all hand labor in making cotton and wool cards and attempted, unsuccessfully, to introduce the new machine in England in 1799 and 1800. His American patent on this machine was renewed in 1808.

In partnership with his brother, William, and Robert Williams, Whittemore manufactured card-making machines and cards himself from 1800 to 1812. He renewed his patent in 1808, but sold the patent rights and machinery to a company in New York City in 1812 and retired. He died in West Cambridge (now Arlington), Massachusetts.

WIDGERY, William: congressman

Born probably Devonshire, England, circa 1753; died July 31, 1822.

Widgery, who attended common schools, came to America with his parents and settled in Philadelphia, where he engaged in shipbuilding. He served as a lieutenant on a privateer during the Revolution. After studying law and gaining admission to the bar, he established a legal practice in Portland, Massachusetts (now Maine), about 1790. He was a member of the Massachusetts House of Representatives from 1787 to 1793 and again from 1795 to 1797. A delegate to the Massachusetts Constitutional Convention in 1788, he also served in the Massachusetts Senate in 1794 and on the Massachusetts Executive Council from 1806 to 1807.

Widgery, a Democrat, was elected to a term in the United States House of Representatives in 1811. He served as judge of the Court of Common Pleas from 1813 to 1821. He died in Portland and was buried in Eastern Cemetery.

WIGGLESWORTH, Edward: educator, theologian

Born Cambridge, Massachusetts, February 7, 1732; son of Edward and Rebecca (Coolidge) Wigglesworth; married Margaret Hill, October 1765; second marriage to Dorothy Sparhawk, January 6, 1778; third marriage to Sarah Wigglesworth, October 20, 1785; father of five children; died June 17, 1794.

A graduate of Harvard in 1749, Wigglesworth became a tutor there in 1764. He was Hollis professor of divinity in 1765 and a fellow of the college in 1779. He became acting president in 1780.

Wigglesworth was the author of *Calculations on American Population,* 1775; "The Authority of Tradition Considered" (lecture), 1778; and "The Hope of Immortality" (funeral sermon for John Winthrop), 1779. He died in Cambridge.

WILLARD, Joseph: university president

Born Biddeford, Maine, December 29, 1738; son of the Reverend Samuel and Abigail (Wright) Willard;

married Mary Sheafe, March 7, 1774; father of thirteen children (including Sidney and Joseph); died September 25, 1804.

Upon graduation from Harvard in 1765, Willard worked there as a Greek tutor from 1766 until 1772. He was ordained to the ministry of the Congregational Church in Beverly, Massachusetts, in 1772 and served as minister of the church until 1781.

In 1780 Willard was a founder of the American Academy of Arts and Sciences, serving as secretary and as vice president for many years. He was president of Harvard from 1781 to 1804, during which time he founded the Harvard Medical School. He was a member of the Royal Society in Gottingen, Germany, and of the Medical Society of London, England.

Willard died in New Bedford, Massachusetts.

WILLARD, Simon: clockmaker

Born Grafton, Massachusetts, April 3, 1753; son of Benjamin and Sarah (Brooks) Willard; married Hannah Willard (a cousin), November 29, 1776; second marriage to Mary (Bird) Leeds, January 23, 1788; father of eleven children; died August 30, 1848.

In 1765 Willard was apprenticed to a clockmaker in Grafton and surpassed his master's work the following year with his first grandfather clock. He established his own clock factory in Roxbury, Massachusetts, circa 1777–78. In 1802 he patented the Willard Patent Timepiece, or banjo clock, as it came to be known. In 1819 he patented the alarm clock. Willard retired in 1839 at the age of eighty-six and died nine years later.

WILLIAMS, Israel: Loyalist

Born Hatfield, Massachusetts, November 30, 1709; son of the Reverend William and Christian (Stoddard) Williams; married Sarah Chester, 1731; father of seven or eight children; died January 10, 1788.

Williams, who graduated from Harvard in 1727, served as a Hatfield selectman for thirty-one years (1732–63). He became second in command of the Hampshire County

Regiment of the Massachusetts militia in 1744 and was appointed a colonel in 1748. Throughout the French and Indian War he was responsible for the defense of Western Massachusetts.

Williams served later in several public capacities, including justice of the peace, clerk of the Hampshire County Court, and from 1758 to 1774, judge of the Hampshire County Court of Common Pleas. From 1733 until 1773 he was an intermittent member of the Massachusetts legislature, representing Hatfield. He served on the Massachusetts Governor's Council from 1761 to 1767. As executor of the will of Ephraim Williams he was instrumental in founding the "free school" which later became Williams College.

During the early years of the Revolution, Williams was considered a Loyalist in Western Massachusetts and was imprisoned for Loyalism in 1777. He was deprived of citizenship until 1780 and died eight years later in Hatfield.

WILLIAMS, John Foster: naval officer

Born Boston, Massachusetts, October 12, 1743; married Hannah Homer, October 6, 1774; died June 24, 1814.

Commissioned captain of the Massachusetts state sloop Republic in 1776, Williams transferred later in the year to the ship Massachusetts. He made two cruises in the Massachusetts state brig Hazard in 1778 and 1779, during which time he captured several prizes. One was the forced surrender of the British brig Active (eighteen guns) off St. Thomas, West Indies, in 1779. He was also commander of the Protector, the largest ship in the Massachusetts Navy.

Turning to peacetime pursuits, in 1792 Williams communicated to the Boston Marine Society drawings of a device that could distill fresh water from salt water. He surveyed Nantasket Harbor for the United States Government in 1803 and commanded the United States revenue cutter Massachusetts from 1790 until his death in 1814. He was buried in the Granary Burying Ground, in Boston.

WILLIAMS, Jonathan: army officer

Born Boston, Massachusetts, May 26, 1750; son of Jonathan and Grace (Harris) Williams; married Marianne Alexander, September 12, 1779; died May 16, 1815.

A grand-nephew of Benjamin Franklin, Williams joined his uncle in Paris, France, in 1776. He was sent to Nantes by the Continental Congress to inspect arms and other supplies being shipped from that port. In 1785 he engaged in various business ventures in Europe, and in 1796 he sat as associate judge of the Philadelphia Court of Common Pleas. In 1801 Thomas Jefferson appointed him inspector of fortifications and first superintendent of the United States Military Academy with the rank of major in the United States Army. Williams resigned in 1803, but in 1805 he accepted reappointment as a lieutenant colonel of engineers with complete authority over all cadets. He resigned this commission in 1812.

Williams wrote *Thermometrical Navigation* in 1799. He translated *The Elements of Fortification* (from the French) in 1801 and *Maneuvres of Horse Artillery* (from a work by Tadeusz Kosciuszko) in 1808. He was a founder of the Military Philosophical Society, which promoted military science and history, and was a member of the American Philosophical Society.

WINSLOW, John: army officer

Born Marshfield, Massachusetts, May 10, 1703; son of Isaac and Sarah (Wensley) Winslow; married Mary Little, 1725; second marriage to Bethiah (Barker) Johnson; father of Pelham and Isaac; died April 17, 1774.

Winslow was appointed a captain in a company of the Massachusetts militia by the Massachusetts Council in 1740 and served on a West Indian expedition. He entered the British Army the next year and served at Cartagena, returning to Massachusetts for reinforcements. From 1744 to 1751 he was with Phillips's Regiment of the British Infantry in Nova Scotia.

Commissioned a major general in the Massachusetts militia again, Winslow served on the Kennebec River in 1754. He built Fort Western as a trading post for the proprietors of the Plymouth Colony, and also built Fort Halifax. In 1755 he was appointed a lieutenant colonel and commandant of two New England battalions. During the capture of Crown Point in 1775 he commanded the provincial army raised in New England and New York.

From 1757 to 1758, and again from 1761 to 1765, Winslow was a member of the Massachusetts General Court from Marshfield. He was instrumental in surveying and supervising the Kennebec River development. In 1762 he served as commissioner on the St. Croix boundary. The town of Winslow (formerly Fort Halifax), in Kennebec County, Maine, was named for him in 1771. He died in Hingham, Massachusetts.

WINTHROP, James: jurist

Born Cambridge, Massachusetts, March 28, 1752; son of Professor John and Rebecca (Townsend) Winthrop; died September 26, 1821.

Upon graduating from Harvard in 1769, Winthrop took the job of librarian of Harvard, remaining with the university until 1777. During this time he served with the Continental forces at the Battle of Bunker Hill (1775) and was postmaster of Cambridge (1776). From 1772 to 1787 he was register of probate for Middlesex County, Massachusetts. In 1789 he served with the Massachusetts militia against Captain Daniel Shays's rebels. He was judge of the Court of Common Pleas in Middlesex in 1791.

Winthrop was an original member of the American Academy of Arts and Sciences and a founder of the Massachusetts Historical Society. As an overseer of Allegheny College, he bequeathed his large and valuable library to that institution. He was a surveyor for the proposed Cape Cod Canal

164

and was a promoter of the West Boston Bridge over the Middlesex Canal.

Winthrop was a frequent contributor of articles to *Literary Miscellany*. He died in Cambridge.

WINTHROP, John: astronomer

Born Boston, Massachusetts, December 19, 1714; son of Adam and Anne (Wainwright) Winthrop; married Rebecca Townesend, July 1, 1746; second marriage to Hannah (Fayerweather) Tolman, March 24, 1756; father of several children (including James); died May 3, 1779.

Winthrop, the first astronomer in America, graduated from Harvard in 1732 with an A.B. degree. He was Hollis professor of mathematics and natural philosophy at Harvard from 1738 until 1779. He conducted research in astronomy, publishing the results in the *Philosophical Transactions of the Royal Society*. Among his studies were a series of sunspot observations made in the Massachusetts Colony from April 19 to 22, 1739. He also made a study of the transit of Mercury over the sun in 1740 and again in 1743 and 1769.

Winthrop established the first laboratory of experimental physics in America at Harvard in 1746. In it he demonstrated laws of mechanics, light, heat, and the movement of celestial bodies according to the Newtonian system. In 1751 he introduced into the mathematical curriculum elements of fluxions (now known as differential and integral calculus). He reported on an earthquake which shook New England in 1755. By lecturing on the return of Halley's Comet, which had appeared in 1682, Winthrop was the first (in 1759) to predict the return of a comet. He made preparations for the transits of Venus in 1761 and 1769 and was director of the first astronomical expedition sent by Harvard, which was dispatched to St. John's, Newfoundland, for the 1761 transit.

In 1766 Winthrop was elected a fellow of the Royal Society. He became a member of the American Philosophical Society in 1769 and in the same year was a founder of the American Academy of Arts and Sciences. He was the author of *Relation of a Voyage from Boston to Newfoundland for the Observation of the Transit of Venus*, 1761, and *Two Lectures on the Parallax and Distance of the Sun*, 1769.

Winthrop was awarded an honorary LL.D. by the University of Edinburgh (Scotland) in 1771, and in 1773 he received the first honorary LL.D. given by Harvard. He died in Cambridge, Massachusetts, and was buried in King's Chapel Burying Ground in Boston.

WORTHINGTON, John: lawyer

Born Springfield, Massachusetts, November 24, 1719; son of John and Mary (Pratt) Worthington; married Hannah Hopkins, January 10, 1759; second marriage to Mary Stoddard, December 7, 1768; died April 25, 1800.

A 1740 graduate of Yale, Worthington established a legal practice in Springfield in 1744 and served as King's attorney in western Massachusetts in the 1750s. He took an active part in raising troops during the French and Indian War. Circa 1754–75 he was a colonel in the Hampshire regiments.

Worthington was active in land speculation, and in 1768 the town of Worthington, Massachusetts, was named for him. He was a political leader in Springfield, a member of the board of selectmen, and moderator of town meetings. He was Springfield's representative in the Massachusetts General Court from 1747 to 1774. He also attended the Albany Congress in 1754 and was a member of the Massachusetts Governor's Council from 1767 until 1769.

Worthington lost popularity when he opposed independence, but he later changed his views. He served on a commission to settle the Massachusetts-Connecticut boundary dispute in 1791. He died in Springfield.

★★★★★★★★★★★★★

NEW HAMPSHIRE

"We hear Colonel Ethan Allen is now on board a ship at New York; that he has been treated since his being taken a prisoner with the utmost barbarity, till lately, but the rigor of his oppressors has been a little softened . . . and we hope . . . he may again return into the bosom of his grateful country."

FREEMAN'S JOURNAL, December 3, 1776

ALLEN, Ethan: army officer

Born Litchfield, Connecticut, January 21, 1738; son of Joseph and Mary (Baker) Allen; married Mary Bronson, 1762; second marriage to Mrs. Frances Buchanan, 1784; father of eight children (including Fanny, Hannibal, Ethan, Herman, Heber, and Levi); died February 2, 1789.

Allen fought in the French and Indian War in 1757. In 1769 he moved to the New Hampshire Grants, control of which was disputed by New York and New Hampshire, and the next year he became a colonel commandant in the Green Mountain Boys, a group formed for the purpose of establishing the New Hampshire Grants as the separate province of Vermont. His activities led the governor of New York to offer a reward of twenty pounds in 1771 for his capture— an amount which had increased to one hundred pounds by 1774. The next year he, along with others, was appointed at the Westminster meeting to prepare a petition to the King on the subject of separate status for Vermont.

His activities on this behalf were interrupted by the Battle of Lexington. On instructions from the state of Connecticut, Allen captured Fort Ticonderoga in 1775; in the same year he was captured while serving in an expedition against Canada, but he was exchanged for Colonel Archibald Campbell three years later. He was brevetted a colonel in the Continental Army by General George Washington.

Allen presented the claims of Vermont to the Continental Congress in 1778, but without success. After he was promoted to major general in the Vermont militia, he corresponded with the commander of the British forces in Canada in 1780, but it is not known whether he actually wanted Vermont to become a British province or whether he was trying to use the correspondence to pressure Congress into making Vermont a separate state.

Allen wrote *An Animadversory Address to the Inhabitants of the State of Vermont* (1778); *A Narrative of Colonel Ethan Allen's Captivity* (1779), a tract which, incidentally, does not mention Benedict Arnold's aid in capturing Fort

Ticonderoga; and *Reason the Only Oracle of Man; or, A Compendious System of Natural Religion* (1784).

Allen moved to Burlington, Vermont, in 1787, where he died. He was buried with military honors in a valley near Winooski, Vermont.

ALLEN, Ira: pioneer, army officer
Born Cornwall, Connecticut, May 1, 1751; son of Joseph and Mary (Baker) Allen; married Jerusha Enos, circa 1789; father of three children (including Ira H.) died January 15, 1814.

Allen lived with his brothers Ethan, Herman, Heber, and Levi in the disputed area of the New Hampshire Grants (now Vermont) and was a member of the Green Mountain Boys. After representing Colchester in the Dorset Convention (Vermont) in 1776, he became a member of the constitutional committee of the Windsor Convention (Vermont) the next year, writing the preamble to the constitution and serving as secretary to the Council of Safety. He continued his state political activities as member of the Vermont Governor's Council in 1777 and as treasurer of Vermont in 1778.

Apparently hoping to force the Continental Congress to recognize the independence of Vermont, in 1780–81 Allen became involved in a plot with Great Britain to make the area a British province. Fourteen years later he went to England to try to secure arms for the Vermont militia, in which he was a major general, but he obtained them in France instead. While sailing home on the *Olive Branch,* he was captured by the British, who were suspicious of his motives for purchasing the weapons. The British courts found in Allen's favor, and he returned to the United States in 1801, only to be thrown into prison and to find that his land had been seized. The Vermont legislature later released him, and he was granted immunity from arrest for one year. He fled to Philadelphia, where he died.

Some of Allen's other activities included negotiating commercial treaties with Quebec and donating land valued at four thousand pounds to build the University of Vermont. He wrote *Natural and Political History of the State of Vermont* (1798), *Particulars of the Capture of the Ship* Olive Branch (1798), and various pamphlets listed in M. D. Gilman's *Bibliography of Vermont* (1897).

ATHERTON, Joshua: lawyer
Born Harvard, Massachusetts, June 20, 1737; son of Peter and Experience (Wright) Atherton; married Abigail Goss, 1765; died April 3, 1809.

After graduating from Harvard in 1762, Atherton practiced law in Litchfield, Connecticut, and then in Merriman, Massachusetts, during the years 1765–73. He became register of probate for the County of Hillsborough (Massachusetts) in 1773.

In 1777, because of his Loyalist beliefs, Atherton was arrested and held prisoner until the next year. In 1779 he took an oath of allegiance to the state of New Hampshire and later attended the New Hampshire constitutional conventions of 1784 and 1792. From membership in the New Hampshire Senate in 1792 and 1793 he went on to serve as the state's attorney general during the period 1793–1801. He died at the age of seventy-one.

★★★★★

BAKER, Remember: army officer
Born Woodbury, Connecticut, June 1737; son of Remember and Tamar (Warner) Baker; married Desire Hurlbut, April 3, 1760; father of Ozi; died August 1775.

Baker served in the French and Indian War from 1757 to circa 1760. In 1764 he settled in Arlington in what is now Vermont and became involved in the controversy between New York and New Hampshire over that territory. From 1770 to 1774 he was a member of Ethan Allen's Green Mountain Boys, who worked during this period to enforce claims to grants which the New Hampshire government had made in the territory. Baker was killed in an encounter with Indians while serving in General Schuyler's scouting expedition up Lake Champlain.

BARTLETT, Josiah: governor of New Hampshire

Born Amesbury, Massachusetts, November 21, 1729; son of Stephen and Hannah (Webster) Bartlett; married Mary Bartlett, January 15, 1754; father of twelve children; died May 19, 1795.

Bartlett studied medicine privately from 1745 until 1750, when he opened a practice in Kingston, New Hampshire. He represented Kingston in the New Hampshire Provincial Assembly during the years 1765–75 and became justice of the peace in Kingston in 1767. That same year he also became a colonel in a regiment of the New Hampshire militia. A delegate to the Continental Congress in 1775, 1776, and 1778, he was a signer of both the Declaration of Independence and the Articles of Confederation. He participated in the Constitutional Convention in Philadelphia in 1787.

From chief justice of the New Hampshire Court of Common Pleas (1779–82), Bartlett went on to become associate justice (1784–88) and then chief justice (1788–89) of the state Superior Court. Dartmouth awarded him an honorary M.D. in 1790. That year he left the bench to become president of the state of New Hampshire, holding that office until 1793, when he became the state's first governor. He served until 1794.

In 1791 Bartlett became the first president of the New Hampshire Medical Society, whose charter he had secured. He died in Kingston and was buried there.

BLANCHARD, Jonathan: Continental congressman

Born Dunstable, New Hampshire, September 18, 1738; died July 16, 1788.

Blanchard attended public schools. In 1775 he was chosen a member of the Council of Twelve and was a delegate to the Fifth Provincial Congress. The following year he served in the first New Hampshire House of Representatives. He was appointed attorney general of the state in 1777, and also served on the Committee of Safety during 1777 and 1778. He was a commissioner from New Hampshire to the price regulation convention in New Haven, Connecticut, in 1778.

Blanchard was a Continental congressman from New Hampshire in the years 1783, 1784, and 1787, and served as the first general of the state militia from 1784 to 1788. He died in Dunstable (which has since been merged with Nashua) and was buried in the Old South Burying Ground there.

BRADLEY, Stephen Row: senator

Born Wallingford (now Cheshire), Connecticut, February 20, 1754; son of Moses and Mary (Row) Bradley; married Merab Atwater; second marriage to Thankful Taylor; third marriage to Belinda Willard; father of at least one son (William Czar); died December 9, 1830.

Bradley graduated from Yale in 1775 and studied law under Tapping Reeve in Litchfield, Connecticut. He was commissioned a captain of volunteers in the Continental Army in 1776, rising to colonel before his resignation from the military at the end of the Revolutionary War.

After being admitted to the Vermont bar in 1779, Bradley became state's attorney for Cumberland County in 1782 and judge of Windham County the following year. In 1785 he was speaker of the Vermont House of Representatives, becoming an associate justice of the Vermont Superior Court three years later. He was a member of the Westminster City Council in 1798.

Bradley was a Vermont representative to the United States Senate from October 17, 1791, to 1795 and again from October 15, 1801, to 1813; he was president pro tem in 1802, 1803, and 1808. He introduced a bill to establish the national flag of fifteen stripes and fifteen stars, which was used from 1795 to 1814. This is sometimes called the Bradley flag.

Bradley died in Walpole, New Hampshire, and was buried in the Old Cemetery in Westminster, Vermont.

BUCK, Daniel: congressman, state official
Born Hebron, Connecticut, November 9, 1753; son of Thomas and Jane Buck; married Content Ashley, September 22, 1786; father of eleven children (including Daniel); died August 16, 1816.

Buck fought in the American Revolution and in 1780 became one of Vermont's earliest settlers. He was admitted to the Vermont bar in 1783 and served as prosecuting attorney of Orange County, Vermont, from that year until 1785. In 1783–84 he was also clerk of the Orange County Court.

After serving as a delegate to the Vermont Convention which ratified the United States Constitution in 1791, Buck served briefly as a member of the Vermont Council of Censors. He was speaker of the Vermont Assembly (1793–94); attorney general of Vermont (1794); a member of the United States House of Representatives (Federalist) during the 4th Congress (1795–97); and state's attorney of Windsor County, Vermont (1802–03).

Buck died in Chelsea, Vermont, and was buried in the Old Cemetery there.

BUTLER, Ezra: governor of Vermont, congressman
Born Lancaster, Massachusetts, September 24, 1763; son of Asaph and Jane (McAllister) Butler; married Thyphena Diggins; died July 12, 1838.

After fighting in the American Revolution, Butler was admitted to the Vermont bar in 1786. He was town clerk in Waterbury, Vermont, in 1790 and a member of the Vermont legislature from Waterbury in 1794–97, 1799–1804, and 1807–08. He was ordained to the ministry of the Baptist Church in 1801.

Butler was judge of the Chittenden County Court from 1803 to 1806 and chief justice of the Jefferson County Court in 1812–13 and again from 1815 to 1827. A Republican, he was a Vermont delegate to the United States House of Representatives from 1813 to 1815 (13th Congress). He at-tended the Vermont Constitutional Convention of 1822 and served as governor of the state from 1826 to 1828.

Butler died in Waterbury and was buried in the town cemetery.

★★★★★

CARLETON, Peter: congressman
Born Haverhill, Massachusetts, September 19, 1755; died April 29, 1828.

Carleton attended public schools in Massachusetts and, as a young man, became engaged in farming. He was active in the Revolutionary War effort, serving with a Massachusetts regiment.

Around 1789 Carleton moved to Landaff, New Hampshire, and the following year became a delegate to the New Hampshire Constitutional Convention. From 1803 to 1804, he was a member of the New Hampshire House of Representatives. He was a member of the New Hampshire Senate from 1800 to 1807. A Democrat, he served in the United States House of Representatives, 10th Congress, from 1807 to 1809.

Carleton died in Landaff and was buried in the City Cemetery.

CHAMBERLAIN, William: congressman, lieutenant governor of Vermont
Born Hopkinton, Massachusetts, April 27, 1755; died September 27, 1828.

Chamberlain received his education in common schools and, at the age of nineteen, moved to Loudon, New Hampshire. He served as a sergeant during the Revolutionary War, later becoming a land surveyor and farmer. In 1780 he moved to Peacham, Vermont, where he was clerk of the proprietors of the town the same year and town clerk from 1785 to 1787. He was town representative for twelve years and served as a member of the Vermont House of Representatives in 1785, 1787–96, 1805, and 1808. He was also justice of the peace from 1786 to 1796 and a delegate to the Vermont constitutional conventions of 1791 and 1814.

Chamberlain was made a brigadier general in the Vermont militia in 1794 and a major general five years later. In 1795 he was assistant judge of Orange County and from 1796 to 1803 was chief judge of Caledonia County. After serving as secretary of the board of trustees of the Caledonia County Grammar School from 1795 to 1812, he was president for the next fifteen years. He was state councilor for Vermont from 1796 to 1803 and a Federalist presidential elector in 1800.

Chamberlain was a member of the United States House of Representatives from Vermont during the 8th and 11th congresses (1803–05, 1809–11), then was lieutenant governor of Vermont from 1813 to 1815. He died in Peacham and was buried in the town cemetery.

CHIPMAN, Daniel: congressman
Born Salisbury, Connecticut, October 22, 1763; son of Samuel and Hannah (Austin) Chipman; married Elatheria Hedge, 1796; died April 23, 1850.

After graduating from Dartmouth in 1788, Chipman was admitted to the Rutland County (Vermont) bar in 1790. He was a member of the Vermont constitutional conventions of 1793, 1814, 1836, 1843, and 1850. In 1797 he was state's attorney for Addison County, Vermont. The following year he was a member of the Vermont General Assembly from Middlebury. A professor of law at Middlebury College for ten years (1806–16), he was speaker of the Vermont legislature in 1813 and 1814.

Chipman was a Vermont delegate to the United States House of Representatives from 1815 until his resignation on May 5, 1816. In 1823 he was appointed the first reporter of the Vermont Supreme Court. He died in Ripton, Vermont, and was buried in West Cemetery, Middlebury, Vermont.

CHIPMAN, Nathaniel: jurist, senator
Born Salisbury, Connecticut, November 15, 1752; son of Samuel and Hannah (Austin) Chipman; married Sarah Hill, 1781; father of nine children; died February 15, 1843.

Chipman graduated in absentia from Yale in 1777. He served as a lieutenant in the Continental Army at the battles of Valley Forge, Monmouth, and White Plains. He was admitted to the Litchfield, Connecticut, bar in 1779 and to the Rutland County, Vermont, bar later the same year. He was a member of the Vermont legislature in 1784 and a justice of the Vermont Supreme Court from 1787 to 1790, serving as chief justice the latter year and again from 1796 to 1798.

Chipman was a member of the New York–Vermont Boundary Commission in 1789 and helped negotiate the admission of Vermont into the Union. He was judge of the United States Court in the Vermont District from 1791 to 1793 and a Vermont delegate to the United States Senate for six years (1799–1805). A member of the Vermont Council of Censors in 1813, he was a professor of law at Middlebury College in Vermont for twenty-seven years (1816–43).

Chipman wrote *Sketches of the Principles of Government* in 1793. He died in Tinmouth, Vermont.

CHITTENDEN, Thomas: governor of Vermont
Born East Guilford, Connecticut, January 6, 1730; son of Ebenezer and Mary (Johnson) Chittenden; married Elizabeth Meigs, October 1750; father of ten children (including Martin, Noah, Giles, Truman, and Mary); died August 25, 1797.

In 1776 Chittenden represented Williston, Vermont, at the Dorset Convention, which considered the question of independence for Vermont. He helped draft the Vermont Constitution the following year. President of the Vermont Council of Safety, he later served as the first governor of Vermont (1778–89), returning to that office in 1790 for a seven-year tenure. A monument was erected in his memory by the state of Vermont in 1895. He died in Williston.

CILLEY, Joseph: army officer, legislator
Born Nottingham, New Hampshire, 1735; son of Captain Joseph and Alice (Rollins) Cilley; married

Sarah Longfellow, November 4, 1756; father of ten children; died August 25, 1799.

A member of the New Hampshire Provincial Congress, Cilley enlisted in the Coast Guard when the Revolutionary War broke out. He took part in the siege of Boston and the battles of Long Island, Trenton, and Princeton. He was commissioned a major in the 2nd New Hampshire Infantry in 1775 and served in the 8th Continental Infantry in 1776. He participated in the Battle of Ticonderoga in 1777 and was commissioned a colonel in the 1st New Hampshire Infantry that same year. In 1786 he was promoted to major general of the New Hampshire militia.

In 1790–91 Cilley was a member of the New Hampshire Senate; in 1792, he served in the New Hampshire House of Representatives. In 1797 he became a member of the New Hampshire Council and served for one year. He died in Nottingham.

CLAGETT, Clifton: congressman, lawyer
Born Portsmouth, New Hampshire, December 3, 1762; died January 25, 1829.

After studying law, Clagett was admitted to the New Hampshire bar and began to practice in Litchfield in 1787. He served as a member of the United States House of Representatives from New Hampshire during the 8th and the 15th–16th congresses (1803–05 and 1817–21).

In 1808 Clagett was appointed justice of peace and quorum, and from 1810 to 1812 he served as judge of probate for Hillsborough County. After moving to Amherst, New Hampshire, in 1812, he was appointed to the state Supreme Court. He served in the New Hampshire House of Representatives in 1816. From 1823 until his death he was judge of probate. He died in Amherst.

CLAGETT, Wyseman: lawyer
Born Bristol, England, August 1721; son of Wyseman Clagett; married Lettice Mitchell, 1759; died December 4, 1784.

After being admitted to the Court of King's Bench, Clagett practiced law in Antigua, West Indies, from 1748 to 1758. He moved to Portsmouth, New Hampshire, in 1758, and he was the King's attorney for New Hampshire Province from 1765 to 1769.

In 1769 he visited England, moving two years later to Litchfield, New Hampshire. He became a member of the Council and Committee of Public Safety in New Hampshire in 1776. From 1778 to 1781 he was special justice of the New Hampshire Superior Court. In 1781 he became solicitor general of New Hampshire, serving for three years. He died in Litchfield.

CLAGHORN, George: army officer, shipbuilder
Born July 6, 1748; son of Shubael and Experience (Hawes) Claghorn; married Deborah Brownell; father of four sons and four daughters; died February 3, 1824.

Claghorn, who served as a first lieutenant and, later, a captain in the 2nd Bristol Regiment, was wounded during the Battle of Bunker Hill. He was later commissioned a major, then a colonel. A ship-builder in New Bedford, New Hampshire, he launched the ship *Rebecca* in 1785 and in 1794 was the naval constructor of the U.S.S. *Constitution* ("Old Ironsides"), which was launched in 1797. He died in Seekonk, Rhode Island.

★★★★★

DINSMOOR, Robert:
Born Windham, New Hampshire, October 7, 1757; son of William and Elizabeth (Cochran) Dinsmoor; married Mary Park; second marriage to Mary Anderson; father of eleven children; died March 6, 1836.

Dinsmoor served with the New Hampshire militia at the Battle of Saratoga during the American Revolution. He was a deacon and a clerk in the Presbyterian Church in Windham. His works, compiled and arranged by Leonard Morrison, were published in 1898 as *Poems of Robert Dinsmoor, the Rustic Bard.* He died at the age of seventy-eight.

★★★★★

FISK, James: senator, congressman

Born Greenwich, Massachusetts, October 4, 1763; son of Stephen and Anna (Bradish) Fish; married Priscilla West, April 27, 1786; father of six children; died November 17, 1844.

As well as being an ordained minister, a lawyer, and a judge, Fisk was active in government circles in both Massachusetts and Vermont. He supported the doctrines of Thomas Jefferson and James Madison, the Embargo Act, and the War of 1812, thinking that Canada could be easily conquered.

In Massachusetts, Fisk served with a regiment of the militia during the Revolutionary War (1779–82), was a delegate to the General Assembly (1785), and was a member of the General Court from Greenwich (1791–96). In 1797 he was ordained to the ministry of the Universalist Church.

Fisk moved to Barre, Vermont, in 1798, and was admitted to the Vermont bar the following year. He was a member of the Vermont House of Representatives from 1800 to 1805, from 1809 to 1810, and in 1815; during this period (1802–09, 1816) he also served as judge of the Orange County Court. After serving as chairman of the committee to settle the Canada-Vermont boundary in 1804, he became a Republican member of the United States House of Representatives, serving from 1805 to 1809 and from 1811 to 1815. In 1815 and 1816 he was judge of the Vermont Superior Court, then became a member of the United States Senate, serving from November 4, 1817, to January 8, 1818.

Fisk was a collector of federal revenues for the District of Vermont from 1818 to 1826. He moved to Swanton, Vermont, in 1819, and was buried in the Church Street Cemetery there after his death in 1844.

FOLSOM, Nathaniel: Continental congressman, army officer

Born Exeter, New Hampshire, September 18, 1726; son of Jonathan and Anna Folsom; married Dorothy Smith; second marriage to Mary Sprague; died May 26, 1790.

Folsom was active in politics and in the military in the New Hampshire area. He served in the Crown Point expedition during the French and Indian War in 1755. He was a member of three sessions of the Continental Congress (1774–75, 1777–78, and 1779–80). He signed the Association and was a member of the New Hampshire Provincial Congress in 1775. At the same time he was also major general in command of the entire New Hampshire militia.

In addition to serving repeatedly in the New Hampshire legislature, Folsom was a member of the New Hampshire Committee of Safety and judge of the Court of Common Pleas. He died in Exeter.

FOSTER, Abiel: clergyman, congressman

Born Andover, Massachusetts, August 8, 1735; son of Asa and Elizabeth (Abbott) Foster; married Hannah Badger, May 15, 1761; second marriage to Mary Rodgers, October 11, 1769; died February 6, 1806.

Fourteen years after being ordained to the ministry in Canterbury, New Hampshire, in 1761, Foster began a period of service in the New Hampshire government. He was a member of the New Hampshire Provincial Congress in Exeter in 1775 and a member of the New Hampshire House of Representatives from 1779 to 1783. He spent the next two years as a delegate to the Continental Congress.

After serving as judge of the New Hampshire Court of Common Pleas from 1784 to 1788, he became a member of the United States House of Representatives, serving during the 1st Congress (1789–91) and the 4th through the 7th congresses (December 7, 1795, until 1803). He was a member of the New Hampshire Senate from 1791 to 1793, acting as president the latter year. At the same time (1791–93), he was a member of the New Hampshire Constitutional Convention.

After his death in 1806, Foster was buried in Center Cemetery in Canterbury.

FOWLE, Daniel: printer
Born Charlestown, Massachusetts, October 1715; son of John and Mary (Barrell) Fowle; married Lydia Hall, April 11, 1751; no children; died June 8, 1787.

Fowle was apprenticed to a printer in Boston before he became a partner with Gamaliel Rogers to form the printing firm of Rogers and Fowle, which operated from 1740 to 1750. During this time he published the *Boston Weekly Magazine* (1743), the *American Magazine and Historical Chronicle* (1743–46), and the *Independent Advertiser* (1748). After leaving the partnership, he was in business alone for four years.

Fowle later moved to Portsmouth, New Hampshire, where he served as state printer for thirty-one years (1756–87). He wrote two pamphlets, *A Total Eclipse of Liberty* (1755) and *An Appendix to the Total Eclipse of Liberty* (1756).

FREEMAN, Jonathan: congressman
Born Mansfield, Connecticut, March 21, 1745; died August 20, 1808.

Freeman, who was educated in public schools, left Connecticut for Hanover, New Hampshire, in 1769. There he engaged in agriculture, worked as town clerk, and served as justice of the peace before becoming executive councilor for the years 1789 to 1797. In 1787 he had begun a two-year term in the New Hampshire House of Representatives, followed by five years in the New Hampshire Senate. During the Senate term he was also a delegate to the Constitutional Convention (1791). He was a member of the New Hampshire Council and participated in the 5th and 6th congresses of the United States House of Representatives.

An overseer of Dartmouth from 1793 to 1808, Freeman also devoted over forty years to the college as treasurer. He died in Han-

over and was buried in Hanover Center Cemetery.

FROST, George: Continental congressman
Born Newcastle, New Hampshire, April 26, 1720; died June 21, 1796.

After working for a time as a businessman in Kittery Point, near Portsmouth, New Hampshire, Frost spent twenty years as a sea captain. He returned to Newcastle in 1760, moving to Durham, New Hampshire, ten years later. There he began a career in government service. He was a judge of the Stafford County Court of Common Pleas from 1773 to 1791, and was chief justice for several years. From 1777 to 1779 he was a New Hampshire delegate to the Continental Congress, and from 1781 to 1784 he was executive councilor.

After his death in Durham, he was buried in Pine Hill Cemetery in Dover, New Hampshire.

★★★★★

GILMAN, John Taylor: governor of New Hampshire
Born Exeter, New Hampshire, December 19, 1753; son of Nicholas and Ann (Taylor) Gilman; married Deborah Folsom, January 13, 1776; second marriage to Mary Folsom, July 5, 1792; third marriage to Mrs. Charlotte Hamilton, December 29, 1814; died August 31, 1828.

Gilman attended common schools in Exeter and engaged in his father's mercantile and shipbuilding trade circa 1767 to 1775. From 1775 to 1783 he was clerk to his father, the treasurer of New Hampshire, and then served as treasurer himself from 1783 until 1788 and again from 1791 to 1794. In the meantime, he also served in the New Hampshire legislature (1779–81), in the Continental Congress (1782–83), and on the federal board of commissioners which settled the Confederation's accounts with various states (1788–90).

Gilman served as a Federalist governor of New Hampshire from 1794 until 1805 and again during the years 1813–16. During his first tenure he aroused the Republican faction in the state by opposing the creation of any banks other than the chartered bank in Portsmouth (of which he was president). During his second tenure he supported the war effort in the state.

From 1794 to 1819 Gilman was a trustee of Dartmouth. In the Dartmouth controversy (1816–19) he opposed the removal of President Wheelock and remained neutral between the contending groups. He died in Portsmouth.

GILMAN, Nicholas: senator, congressman
Born Exeter, New Hampshire, August 3, 1755; son of Nicholas and Ann (Taylor) Gilman; died May 2, 1814.

Like his older brother, Gilman attended common schools in Exeter. Commissioned a captain in the New Hampshire militia in 1775, he served with the adjutant general until 1782. After his return to Exeter in 1783, he became active in politics. In 1786 he commanded the local militia during the currency troubles and became a delegate to the Congress of Confederation, continuing in the latter capacity until 1788. He was a delegate to the United States Constitutional Convention in Philadelphia in 1787.

A Federalist, Gilman was elected to the United States House of Representatives in 1789, serving until 1797. In 1804 and 1805 he served in the New Hampshire Senate. After changing his allegiance to the Republican Party, he was appointed to the United States Senate in 1805, serving until his death.

Gilman died in Philadelphia and was buried in Exeter, the town of his birth.

★★★★★

HALL, Obed: congressman
Born Raynham, Massachusetts, December 23, 1757; died April 1, 1828.

Hall moved from Massachusetts to Madbury, New Hampshire, and later to Upper Bartlett, New Hampshire. In Upper Bartlett he engaged in farming and later became an innkeeper. He was a member of the board of selectmen of Bartlett, New Hampshire, in

1791, 1798, 1800, 1802, 1810, 1814–19, and 1823. In 1801–02 he held a seat in the New Hampshire House of Representatives.

A judge in the New Hampshire Court of Common Pleas, Hall, a Democrat, attended the 12th Congress of the United States House of Representatives, 1811–13. In 1819 he was a member of the New Hampshire Senate. He died in Bartlett, and was buried in the Garland Ridge Cemetery, near Bartlett. He was reinterred in the Evergreen Cemetery in Portland, Maine.

HASWELL, Anthony: publisher
Born Portsmouth, England, April 6, 1756; son of William and Elizabeth Haswell; married Lydia Baldwin, April 23, 1778; second marriage to Betsey Rice, September 30, 1799; father of seventeen children; died May 22, 1816.

Haswell came to America at the age of thirteen. He wrote crude songs for the Massachusetts Sons of Liberty and saw action in the Revolutionary War in 1776 and 1777. He moved to Hartford, Connecticut, in 1781, then to Vermont, which he served as postmaster general in 1784.

Haswell was the publisher of various papers, magazines, books, and pamphlets, including the *Massachusetts Spy,* a newspaper, in 1777; *The New-England Almanack for 1781,* in conjunction with Elisha Babcock; *The Massachusetts Gazette, or the Springfield and Northampton Weekly Advertiser,* a weekly paper, in 1782; *Vermont Gazette, or Freemen's Depository,* a paper, 1783; and *The Monthly Miscellany, or Vermont Magazine,* in 1794. An early victim of the Sedition Act, he was tried in 1800, sentenced to two months in prison, and fined two hundred dollars.

Haswell wrote the *Memoirs of Captain Matthew Phelps* in 1802. He died in Bennington, Vermont.

HAVEN, Nathaniel Appleton: congressman
Born Portsmouth, New Hampshire, July 19, 1762; died March 13, 1831.

Haven graduated from Harvard with a medical degree in 1779. While practicing

175

medicine in Portsmouth, he was also engaged as a merchant. He served as a ship's surgeon in the Revolutionary War. A Federalist, he was a New Hampshire delegate to the United States House of Representatives from 1809 to 1811 (11th Congress). He died in Portsmouth and was buried in Proprietor's Burying Ground there.

HILL, James: army officer, ship-builder, legislator

Born Kittery, Maryland, December 20, 1734; son of Benjamin and Mary (Neal) Hill; married Sarah Coffin; second marriage to Sarah Hoyt; third marriage to Martha Wiggin; father of seventeen children; died August 22, 1811.

Hill participated in an expedition against the French at Crown Point, New York, in 1755. He was then a shipwright on the warship *Achilles,* which sailed to Jamaica and England.

In 1775 Hill served as a captain in the Continental Army under General John Sullivan. He was a signer of the "Association Test" in 1776, and the following year he was promoted to lieutenant colonel. He fought with Gates against Burgoyne and served as a brigadier general in the New Hampshire militia from 1788 to 1793.

A member of the New Hampshire Provincial Congress in 1775, Hill was a member of the first New Hampshire legislature under the new New Hampshire Constitution in 1784. He died at the age of seventy-six.

HOUGH, David: congressman

Born Norwich, Connecticut, March 13, 1753; died April 18, 1831.

Hough, who attended common schools, worked as a ship carpenter while a young man. In 1778 he moved to Lebanon, New Hampshire; in 1788–89 and 1794 he was Lebanon's delegate to the New Hampshire House of Representatives. A justice of the peace and a colonel in the New Hampshire militia, he was also a delegate to the New Hampshire Constitutional Convention. In 1798 he was commissioner of valuation.

From 1803 to 1807 Hough was a New Hampshire delegate to the United States House of Representatives. He then retired from public life and engaged in farming. He died in Lebanon, New Hampshire, and was buried in a cemetery near Lebanon.

HUNTER, William: congressman

Born Sharon, Connecticut, January 3, 1754; died November 30, 1827.

Hunter, who attended common schools, served as a sergeant and a lieutenant under General Montgomery during the Revolutionary War. He was a member of the Vermont House of Representatives in 1795 and 1807–08. From 1798 to 1801 he was register of probate, and from 1801 to 1816 he was judge of probate for the District of Windsor (Vermont). A Democratic elector in 1804, he was an assistant judge in the county court from 1805 to 1816.

Hunter was twice a member of the Vermont Council of Censors (1806 and 1820) and twice a member of the Vermont Executive Council (1810–13 and 1815). After switching to the Republican party, he served as a Vermont delegate to the United States House of Representatives during the 15th Congress (1817–19). He died in Windsor, Vermont, and was buried in Sheddsville Cemetery, West Windsor, Vermont.

★★★★★

JACKSON, Hall: surgeon

Born Hampton, New Hampshire, November 11, 1739; son of Dr. Clement and Sarah (Leavitt) Jackson; married Mrs. Molly (Dalling) Wentworth, December 1, 1765; father of two children; died September 28, 1797.

Jackson studied medicine under his father in Portsmouth, New Hampshire, and also attended lectures in the public hospitals of London. He was one of the earliest American physicians to perform the cataract-couching operation. During the smallpox epidemic of 1764 in Boston, he administered inoculations against the disease, and after his return from Boston he organized a smallpox hospital on Henzell's Island, near Portsmouth.

Jackson cared for the wounded at the Battle of Bunker Hill in 1775, recruiting a Massachusetts artillery company the same year. Also in 1775 the New Hampshire Provisional Congress awarded him a vote of thanks and a commission as chief surgeon in the New Hampshire troops of the Continental Army. He later served as surgeon in Pierce Long's regiment in the capture of Fort Ticonderoga.

Jackson was an honorary member of the Massachusetts Medical Society and a charter member of the New Hampshire Medical Society. He died at the age of fifty-seven.

★★★★★

KEYES, Elias: congressman
Born Ashford, Connecticut, April 14, 1758; died July 9, 1844.

Keyes attended common schools and then studied law. In 1785 he moved to Stockbridge, Vermont, and became active in state politics. He served many terms in the Vermont House of Representatives—1793–96, 1798–1802, 1818, 1820, and 1823–25. He also was a member of the Vermont Governor's Council from 1803 to 1813 and again from 1815 to 1817, in the meantime attending the Vermont Constitutional Convention in 1814.

Keyes held the position of assistant judge in the Windsor County (Vermont) Court from 1803 to 1814, rising to judge in 1815 and remaining in that post until 1818. He was a Republican member of the United States House of Representatives from 1821 to 1823. He died in Stockbridge at the age of eighty-six and was buried in Maplewood Cemetery there.

★★★★★

LANGDON, John: merchant, senator, governor of New Hampshire
Born Portsmouth, New Hampshire, June 26, 1741; son of John and Mary (Hall) Langdon; married Eliza-beth Sherburne, February 2, 1777; died September 18, 1819.

In 1774 Langdon aided in the seizure and removal of munitions from Portsmouth fort. For the next six years and in 1784, 1786–87, and 1803–05 he served in the New Hampshire legislature. He was a member of the Continental Congress in 1775 and in 1783–84. He was appointed an agent for Continental prizes in New Hampshire in 1776.

Langdon was president of New Hampshire in 1785. Two years later he attended the United States Constitutional Convention in Philadelphia. He represented New Hampshire in the United States Senate from 1789 to 1801, serving as president pro tem of the 1st Congress. He was governor of New Hampshire from 1805 to 1809 and from 1810 to 1811. In 1812 he declined the Democratic nomination as a candidate for vice president of the United States.

Langdon died in Portsmouth and was buried in North Cemetery there.

LANGDON, Samuel: clergyman, college president
Born Boston, Massachusetts, January 12, 1723; son of Samuel and Esther (Osgood) Langdon; married Elizabeth Brown, 1748; father of at least five children; died November 29, 1797.

At the age of seventeen Langdon received an A.M. from Harvard. In 1747, after a brief military career during which he served as captain of a New Hampshire regiment, he became an assistant to the Reverend Jabez Fitch at North Church in Portsmouth, New Hampshire. In 1747 he was ordained to the ministry of the Congregational Church and served as pastor of North Church for the next twenty-seven years.

Langdon helped prepare a map of New Hampshire in 1761. He received an honorary S.T.D. from the University of Aberdeen in Scotland in 1762 and served as president of Harvard from 1774 to 1780. In 1781 he became pastor of the Congregational

Church in Hampton Falls, New Hampshire.

In 1788 Langdon was a member of the New Hampshire Convention which ratified the United States Constitution. He was an original member of the American Academy of Arts and Sciences. He died in Hampton Falls, New Hampshire.

LIVERMORE, Samuel: Continental congressman, senator

Born Waltham, Massachusetts, May 25, 1732; son of Samuel and Hannah (Brown) Livermore; married Jane Brown; father of five children (including Edward St. Lowe, Arthur, and George Williamson); died May 18, 1803.

Livermore graduated from the College of New Jersey (now Princeton) in 1752 and was admitted to the New Hampshire bar four years later. From 1768 to 1770 he was a member of the New Hampshire General Court, and from 1769 to 1774 he was King's attorney and judge advocate of the New Hampshire Admiralty Court. He was an original grantee and chief proprietor of Holderness, New Hampshire. In 1776 he served as attorney general of New Hampshire.

Livermore represented New Hampshire in the Continental Congress from 1780 to 1782. For the next eight years he was chief justice of the New Hampshire Supreme Court. In 1785 he was a member of the Congress of the Confederation, and in 1788 he was a delegate to the New Hampshire Convention to ratify the United States Constitution.

From 1789 to 1793 Livermore was a member of the United States House of Representatives (1st and 2nd congresses). He was president of the New Hampshire Constitutional Convention in 1791 and was a member of the United States Senate from 1793 to 1801, serving as president pro tem in 1797 and 1799.

Livermore died in Holderness and was buried in the Trinity Church Cemetery there.

LONG, Pierce: Continental congressman

Born Portsmouth, New Hampshire, 1739; died April 13, 1789.

Long was engaged in the shipping business when he was elected to the New Hampshire Provincial Congress in 1775. During the Revolutionary War he served as a colonel in the 1st New Hampshire Regiment, participating in the battles at Ticonderoga and on Lake George and Lake Champlain. He was present at the surrender of General Burgoyne at Saratoga. He was later brevetted a brigadier general.

From 1784 to 1786 Long represented New Hampshire in the Continental Congress. In 1788 he was a delegate to the New Hampshire Convention that ratified the United States Constitution. President Washington appointed him customs collector for the Port of Portsmouth in 1789, but he did not take office because of ill health. Long died that year in Portsmouth and was buried in the Proprietors' Burying Ground.

LYON, Matthew: congressman, army officer

Born County Wicklow, Ireland, July 14, 1750; married Miss Hosford, 1771; second marriage to Beulah Chittenden, 1783; father of Elizabeth A. Roe; died August 1, 1822.

At the age of fifteen Lyon came to America. In 1774 he organized a company of Vermont militia and aided in the capture of Fort Ticonderoga. He served as an adjutant in Colonel Seth Warner's Regiment in Canada in 1775. In 1776 he was a second lieutenant with the Green Mountain Boys and captain and paymaster of the Vermont militia. The next year he was a guide to General Arthur St. Clair on his march to Fort Edward.

In 1777 Lyon moved to Arlington, Vermont. Except for a brief period in 1783, he was a member of the Vermont House of Representatives from 1779 to 1796. In 1783 he founded the town of Fair Haven, Vermont. He built and operated various mills, including a plant for manufacturing paper from wood pulp. In 1793 he established a printing office and published the *Farmer's Library,* which later became the *Fair Haven Gazette.*

Lyon was a Vermont delegate to the United States House of Representatives from 1797 to 1801 (5th and 6th congresses). He moved to Caldwell (now Lyon) County, Kentucky, in 1801, and represented Kentucky in the 8th through the 11th congresses (1803–11). He was a member of the Kentucky House of Representatives in 1802–03.

During the War of 1812 Lyon was a government contractor to build gunboats. In 1820 he was appointed a United States factor to the Cherokee Nation in the Arkansas Territory. He died in Spadra Bluff, Arkansas, and was buried in the town cemetery. The next year he was reinterred in the Eddyville Cemetery in Lyon County, Kentucky.

★★★★★

MORGAN, Justin: musician, horse breeder
Born West Springfield, Massachusetts, 1747; married Martha Day, 1774; father of Emily, Nancy, Justin, and Polly; died March 22, 1798.

A teacher of music and penmanship, Morgan was also a tavern keeper at various times. He moved to Randolph, Vermont, in 1788, serving as lister in 1789 and as town clerk from 1790 to 1793.

Circa 1795 Morgan received two horses in payment for a debt. One of the horses was small but extremely strong, and Morgan may have furthered this breed by a certain mating process. Known as the Morgan horse, the breed became very popular after Morgan's death, especially in the West. Cross-breeding with other horses almost killed off the original Morgan horse, but a small band was gathered to save them from extinction, and they thrive today.

Morgan was a composer of numerous tunes, including the hymn "Amanda" (the basis for a fantasy by twentieth-century composer Thomas Canning), "Montgomery" (printed in the *Antiquarian* by Leonard Marshall, 1849), and "Judgement Anthem."

MORRIS, Lewis Richard: congressman
Born Scarsdale, New York, November 2, 1760; son of Richard and Sarah (Ludlow) Morris; married Mary Dwight, 1786; second marriage to Theodora Olcott; third marriage to Ellen Hunt; died December 29, 1825.

From 1781 to 1783 Morris was secretary to Robert R. Livingston, United States secretary of foreign affairs. He was a member of the Springfield (Vermont) Meeting House Committee in 1785. He also served Springfield as tax collector in 1786–87, selectman in 1788, town treasurer from 1790 to 1794, clerk of the County Court from 1789 to 1796, and judge of that court from 1796 to 1801.

Morris was clerk of the Vermont House of Representatives in 1790 and 1791. The latter year he participated in the Bennington (Vermont) Convention to ratify the United States Constitution and was one of two commissioners sent to Congress to arrange Vermont's admission to the Union. He served as secretary to the Vermont Constitutional Convention at Windsor in 1793 and was the first United States marshal in the Vermont District, serving from 1791 to 1801.

Morris was a member of the Vermont Assembly in 1795, 1796, 1803, 1805, 1806, and 1808, serving as speaker the first two years. He was a brigadier general in the Vermont militia from 1793 until 1795, when he was promoted to major general. He retired from the military in 1817. A Federalist, he was a Vermont delegate to the United States House of Representatives from 1797 to 1803 (5th–7th congresses).

Morris died in Springfield, Vermont, and was buried in Forrest Cemetery in Charlestown, New Hampshire.

★★★★★

NILES, Nathaniel: congressman
Born South Kingston, Rhode Island, April 3, 1741;

son of Samuel and Sarah (Niles) Niles; married Nancy Lathrop, circa 1775; second marriage to Elizabeth Watson, November 22, 1787; father of nine children; died October 31, 1828.

Niles graduated from the College of New Jersey (now Princeton) in 1766 and received honorary A.M.s from Harvard in 1772 and from Dartmouth in 1791. Having invented a process for making wire, he erected mills in Norwich and Torrington, Connecticut. He served in the Connecticut legislature from 1779 to 1781. Circa 1782 he became one of the first settlers of West Fairlee, Vermont. In 1784 he became speaker of the lower house of the Vermont legislature as well as judge in the state Supreme Court, holding the latter office until 1788. During this time he also served on the Vermont Council (1785–87).

Niles, a Jefferson Democrat, attended the United States House of Representatives from October 17, 1791, until 1795 (2nd and 3rd congresses). In 1791 he was a leading member of the Vermont Convention which ratified the United States Constitution. Two years later he became a trustee of Dartmouth and held this position until 1820. In addition to serving on the Governor's Council from 1803 to 1809, he was a presidential elector in 1804 and again in 1813. In 1814 he was active in revising the fundamental laws of Vermont and was a delegate to the Vermont Constitutional Convention.

Niles also was an itinerant lay preacher and the author of "The American Hero," an ode. He died in West Fairlee, Vermont, and was buried in West Fairlee Center Cemetery.

★★★★★

OLIN, Gideon: congressman

Born East Greenwich, Rhode Island, November 2, 1743; father of at least one son (Abraham Baldwin); died January 21, 1823.

Olin, a farmer by trade, moved to Shaftsbury, Vermont, in 1776. He was a delegate to the Windsor Convention of 1777 and was a major during the Revolutionary War. He served in the Vermont House of Representatives in 1778, from 1780 to 1793, and in 1799, acting as speaker from 1788 to 1793. He was an assistant judge of the Bennington County (Vermont) Court from 1781 to 1798 and was chief judge of the court from 1807 to 1811.

Olin was a delegate to the Vermont Constitutional Convention in 1791 and a member of the Vermont Governor's Council from 1793 to 1798. A member of the Democratic party in Vermont, he served in the United States House of Representatives from 1803 to 1807 (8th and 9th congresses). After his political career ended, he resumed farming. He died in Shaftsbury and was buried in the town cemetery.

★★★★★

PAINE, Elijah: senator

Born Brooklyn, Connecticut, January 21, 1757; son of Seth and Mabel (Tyler) Paine; married Sarah Porter, June 7, 1790; father of eight children (including Charles, Martyn, and Elijah); died April 28, 1842.

Paine graduated from Harvard in 1781. In 1784 he was admitted to the Vermont bar, and during that year he founded the town of Williamstown in his home state. He bought a large farm and established a gristmill and a sawmill at nearby Northfield.

Paine served as secretary of the Vermont Constitutional Convention in 1786 and as a member of the Vermont House of Representatives from 1787 to 1790. From 1791 to 1795 he was an associate justice of the Vermont Supreme Court. He represented his state in the United States Senate from 1795 to 1801 and was a United States district judge from 1801 to 1842.

In 1815 Paine became postmaster of Williamstown. In 1825 he was a co-founder of the Bank of Montpelier. He held the position of bank president as well as that of postmaster until his death in 1842.

During his life Paine found time to develop a large flock of sheep, and in 1812 he built a woolen mill at Northfield. He was a trustee of the University of Vermont, Middlebury College, and Dartmouth. His honorary degrees include an A.B. from Dartmouth (1786), an LL.D. from Harvard (1812), and an LL.D. from the University of Vermont (1825).

Paine died in Williamstown and was buried in the Old Williamstown Cemetery.

PAINTER, Gamaliel: army officer, legislator

Born New Haven, Connecticut, May 22, 1743; son of Shubael and Elizabeth (Dunbar) Painter; married Abigail Chipman, August 20, 1767; second marriage to Victoria Ball, 1795; third marriage to Mrs. Ursula Bull, 1807; father of three children; died May 22, 1819.

Painter served as a lieutenant in Seth Warner's Additional Continental Regiment in 1776 and as a captain in Baldwin's Artillery Artificer Regiment. In 1777 he attended the Windsor Convention, which formed the Vermont Constitution.

In 1787 Painter bought part of the site of the future village of Middlebury, Vermont, where he laid out village streets, sold lots, and erected a gristmill. He served as assistant judge of Addison County in 1785–86 and again from 1787 to 1795. He was a member of the lower house of the Vermont legislature various times between 1786 and 1810. He was a Federalist and shared executive power with the governor as a member of the Vermont Governor's Council in 1813 and 1814.

Painter was a founder of Middlebury College in 1800 and served the school as a fellow until 1819. He died on his seventy-sixth birthday.

PARKER, Nahum: senator

Born Shrewsbury, Massachusetts, March 4, 1760; died November 12, 1839.

Parker served in the Continental Army during the American Revolution. He settled in Fitzwilliam, New Hampshire, in 1786, serving as a selectman from 1790 to 1794

and as clerk and town treasurer from 1792 to 1815. He was a member of the New Hampshire House of Representatives from 1794 to 1796, then served for two years on the New Hampshire Governor's Council. He then returned to the House of Representatives and served until 1807. From that year until June 1, 1810, he represented New Hampshire in the United States Senate.

In 1807 Parker became a justice in the Court of Common Pleas of Cheshire and Sullivan counties, New Hampshire, serving until 1813. For the next three years he was an associate justice on the Western Circuit. He served in the Cheshire County Court of Sessions in 1821 and in the Hillsborough County Court of Common Pleas in 1822. He was a member of the New Hampshire Senate and became its president in 1828.

Parker died in Fitzwilliam and was buried in the town cemetery.

PAYSON, Seth: clergyman

Born Walpole, Massachusetts, September 30, 1758; son of the Reverend Phillips and Kezia (Bullen) Payson; married Grata Payson, 1782; father of seven children; died February 26, 1820.

Payson graduated from Harvard in 1777 and was ordained to the ministry of the Congregational Church in 1782. From that time until his death he was a pastor in Rindge, New Hampshire. He was vice president of the New Hampshire Bible Society for several years and represented New Hampshire in the General Assembly of the Presbyterian Church in Philadelphia in 1815. He was a member of the New Hampshire Senate from 1802 to 1806. In 1802 his *Proofs of the Real Existence and General Tendency of Illuminism* was published.

PEABODY, Nathaniel: Continental congressman, army officer, physician

Born Topsfield, Massachusetts, March 12, 1742; son of Jacob and Susanna (Rogers) Peabody; married Abigail Little, March 1, 1763; died June 27, 1823.

After studying medicine privately with his father, Peabody began to practice medicine in New Hampshire in 1761. He served as justice of the peace of Rockingham County, New Hampshire, in 1771.

Peabody was commissioned a lieutenant colonel in the British Army but resigned in 1774 to enter the Continental Army. He was a leader at the capture of Fort William and Mary at New Castle, New Hampshire, one of the first engagements of the American Revolution. He was a member of the New Hampshire Committee of Safety and served as its chairman in 1776. In the years 1776–79, 1781–85, 1787–90, and 1793–96 he was a member of the New Hampshire House of Representatives, serving as speaker in 1793.

In 1777 Peabody was an adjutant general in the New Hampshire militia and a year later participated in the Rhode Island expedition. He served as a delegate from New Hampshire to the Continental Congress in 1779–80. He was a member of the New Hampshire constitutional conventions of 1781–83 and 1791–92, acting as chairman of the committee that drafted the New Hampshire Constitution in 1782–83. He was chosen to serve on the Governor's Council as a councilor from the New Hampshire House of Representatives in 1784 and as a councilor from the state senate in 1785. He also served in the senate in 1786 and from 1790 to 1793.

Peabody was an organizer of the New Hampshire Medical Society in 1791. From 1793 to 1798 he was a major general in the New Hampshire militia. He spent the last twenty years of his life in debtors' prison. He died in Exeter, New Hampshire, and was buried in the Old Cemetery there.

PEIRCE, Joseph: congressman
Born Portsmouth, New Hampshire, June 25, 1748; died September 12, 1812.

Peirce was born in Portsmouth and attended school there. He served with Colonel Pierce Long's regiment during the Revolutionary War (1775–76). He was a member of the New Hampshire House of Represen-

tatives in 1788–89, 1792–95, and 1800–01. He served as town clerk from 1789 to 1794.

Peirce was a New Hampshire delegate to the United States House of Representatives from 1801 until his resignation in 1802. He engaged in farming until his death in Alton, New Hampshire.

PICKERING, John: jurist
Born Newington, New Hampshire, September 22, 1737; son of Joshua and Mary (Smithson) Pickering; married Abigail Sheafe; died April 11, 1805.

Pickering graduated from Harvard in 1761, later (1792) receiving an honorary LL.D. from Dartmouth. In 1781, 1791, and 1792 he was a member of the New Hampshire constitutional conventions. A member of the New Hampshire legislature from Portsmouth from 1783 to 1787, he was an influential member of the New Hampshire Convention to ratify the United States Constitution in 1788. That year and again four years later he served as a presidential elector. He was also a member of the New Hampshire Senate and Council.

From 1790 to 1795 Pickering was chief justice of the Superior Court of Judicature and served for the next nine years as a judge in the United States District Court for New Hampshire. In 1804 he was impeached by the United States House of Representatives, convicted by the Senate, and removed from office.

Pickering died in Portsmouth.

PIERCE, Benjamin: governor of New Hampshire
Born Chelmford, Massachusetts, December 25, 1757; son of Benjamin and Elizabeth (Merrill) Pierce; married Elizabeth Andrews, May 24, 1787; second marriage to Anna Kendrick, February 1, 1790; father of nine children (including Franklin, fourteenth President of the United States); died April 1, 1839.

Pierce served as a private in the Massachusetts militia before becoming a lieutenant in command of a company. He was a brigade-major and was delegated to organize the Hillsborough (New Hampshire) County militia, in which he served from 1786 to 1807. In 1805 he was commissioned a brigadier general.

Pierce became a member of the New Hampshire House of Representatives in 1789 and served thirteen years. In 1791 he was a delegate to the New Hampshire Constitutional Convention. He served as a member of the Governor's Council from 1803 to 1809 and again in 1814, and as sheriff of Hillsborough County from 1809 to 1812 and from 1818 to 1827.

In 1827 and again in 1829 Pierce was elected governor of New Hampshire. He was a Democratic elector in 1832. He died in Hillsborough at the age of eighty-one.

PLUMER, William: senator, governor of New Hampshire
Born Newburyport, Massachusetts, June 25, 1759; son of Samuel and Mary (Dole) Plumer; married Sally Fowler, February 12, 1788; father of six children; died December 22, 1850.

Plumer read law under Joshua Atherton from 1784 to 1787. He was elected a selectman of Epping, New Hampshire, in 1783 and was admitted to the New Hampshire bar in 1787. A member of the New Hampshire legislature in 1785–86, 1788, 1790–91, and 1797–1800, he served as speaker in 1791 and 1797. He was a member of the New Hampshire constitutional conventions of 1791 and 1792. A Federalist, he represented New Hampshire in the United States Senate from June 17, 1802, to 1807; during this time he wrote *William Plumer's Memorandum of Proceedings of the United States Senate, 1803–07,* edited by E. S. Brown in 1923.

Circa 1808 Plumer became a Republican. He served as president of the New Hampshire Senate in 1810 and 1811 and as governor of New Hampshire from 1812 to 1813 and from 1816 to 1819. He supported the War of 1812.

Plumer recommended alterations in the charter of Dartmouth College and started the action which led to the Dartmouth College case. He was the founder and first president of the New Hampshire Historical Society; his sketches of American biography are now in the Society's possession. He died at Epping and was buried near there.

POOR, Enoch: army officer
Born Andover, Massachusetts, June 21, 1736; son of Thomas and Mary (Adams) Poor; married Martha Osgood, 1760; died September 8, 1780.

Poor fought in the French and Indian War in Nova Scotia in 1755. Twenty years later he was commissioned a colonel in the 2nd New Hampshire Regiment of foot soldiers. He took part in the battles of Trenton, Princeton, Saratoga, and Monmouth. In 1777 he was commissioned a brigadier general in the Continental Army; two years later he accompanied General John Sullivan in an expedition against the Six Nations.

Poor was twice a member of the New Hampshire Provincial Congress. He died in Paramus, New Jersey.

★★★★★

RICHARDS, Mark: congressman
Born Waterbury, Connecticut, July 15, 1760; died August 10, 1844.

Richards served during the Revolutionary War at Stony Point, Monmouth, Red Bank, and Valley Forge. He settled in Boston after the Revolution and was a merchant there until 1796, when he moved to Westminster, Vermont.

Richards served in the Vermont House of Representatives from 1801 to 1805, from 1824 to 1826, in 1828, and from 1832 to 1834. From 1806 to 1810 he was sheriff of Windham County. He was a Democratic presidential elector in 1812 and a member of the Vermont Governor's Council four years later.

From 1817 to 1821 Richards was a Democratic delegate from Vermont to the United States House of Representatives (15th and 16th congresses). In 1830–31 he was lieutenant governor of Vermont. He died in Westminster and was buried in the Bradley tomb at the Old Cemetery.

ROBINSON, Jonathan: senator, jurist
Born Hardwick, Massachusetts, August 11, 1756; died November 3, 1819.

Robinson had limited schooling, but he studied law and was admitted to the bar in 1796, establishing a legal practice in Bennington, Vermont. He served as town clerk from 1795 to 1801. He was a member of the Vermont House of Representatives from 1789 to 1802 and in 1818, and he was a judge in the Vermont Probate Court from 1795 to 1798 and from 1815 to 1819.

From 1801 to 1807 Robinson was chief justice of the Vermont Supreme Court. He filled a vacancy in the United States Senate on October 10, 1807, and served until 1815. He died in Bennington and was buried in the Old Cemetery.

ROBINSON, Moses: governor of Vermont, senator
Born Hardwick, Massachusetts, March 26, 1742; son of Samuel and Mercy (Lennard or Leonard) Robinson; married Mary Fay; second marriage to Susana Howe; father of six sons; died May 26, 1813.

In 1762 Robinson was town clerk of Bennington, Vermont. He was admitted to the Vermont bar by a special act of the legislature in 1777. He was a colonel in the Vermont militia during the Revolutionary War and head of a regiment on Mount Independence when Fort Ticonderoga was evacuated by General Edmund St. Clair in 1777.

Robinson was a member of the Vermont Council of Safety and a member of the convention in 1777 that declared the independence of Vermont. From 1778 to 1785 he was a member of the Vermont Governor's Council. He was the first chief justice of the Vermont Supreme Court from 1778 to 1781, and he served again from 1782 to 1784 and from 1785 to 1789.

In 1779 Robinson was a delegate from Vermont to the Continental Congress and given authorization to join articles of union and confederation with the United States. In 1782 he served on a commission established to agree on terms for the admission of Vermont to the Union. He was involved in the boundary dispute with New York. He served as a member of the Third Council of Censors, which supervised the organization of the constitution and the legislative and executive departments of Vermont.

Robinson was governor of Vermont in 1789 and 1790. He was a member of the Vermont Convention which ratified the United States Constitution in 1791. He became a member of the United States Senate on October 17, 1791, and served until October 17, 1796. He opposed the Jay Treaty in 1794.

In 1802 Robinson represented Bennington in the Vermont General Assembly. He died in Bennington and was buried in the Old Bennington Cemetery.

★★★★★

SEWALL, Jonathan Mitchell: lawyer, poet
Born Salem, Massachusetts, 1748; son of Mitchell and Elizabeth (Prince) Sewall; died March 29, 1808.

Sewall was admitted to the bar of Portsmouth, New Hampshire, then became register of probate for Grafton County, New Hampshire, in 1773. His poetical works include *Versification of President Washington's Excellent Farewell-Address* (1798); *Eulogy on the Late General Washington* (1800); *War and Washington* (1801), a patriotic ballad; *Miscellaneous Poems* (1801); and *Epilogue to Cato.* He died in Portsmouth, New Hampshire.

SHEAFE, James: senator, congressman
Born Portsmouth, New Hampshire, November 16, 1755; died December 5, 1829.

Sheafe engaged in business after graduating from Harvard in 1774. He served in the New Hampshire House of Representatives from 1788 to 1790 and then in the state senate in 1791, 1793, and 1799. The latter year he also was a member of the Executive Council and began a two-year term as a Federalist member of the 6th Congress of the United States House of Representatives. He then served in the United States Senate from 1801 until his resignation on June 14, 1802. In 1816 he was an unsuccessful candidate for governor of New Hampshire. He died in Portsmouth and was buried in St. John's Church Cemetery there.

SHERBURNE, John Samuel: congressman, jurist

Born Portsmouth, New Hampshire, 1757; died August 2, 1830.

In 1776 Sherburne graduated from Dartmouth, then matriculated at the law department of Harvard, graduating later in 1776. Soon afterward he was admitted to the bar and began practicing law in Portsmouth. The graduate of the law department of Harvard served during the Revolutionary War, attaining the rank of brigade major of the staff of the Continental Army and losing a leg at the Battle of Butts Hill, Rhode Island, in 1778.

From 1793 to 1797 Sherburne was a member of the United States House of Representatives from New Hampshire (3rd–4th congresses). After a period as district attorney for New Hampshire from 1801 to 1804, he became a judge in the United States District Court for New Hampshire. He held this position from 1804 until 1830, the year of his death.

SMITH, Israel: senator, governor of Vermont, congressman

Born Suffield, Connecticut, April 4, 1759; son of Daniel and Anna (Kent) Smith; married Abiah Smith between 1779 and 1789; father of two children; died December 2, 1810.

Smith graduated from Yale in 1781 and was admitted to the Vermont bar two years later. Between 1785 and 1791 he served four terms in the Vermont legislature. Around this time he also was appointed to the joint commission which adjusted boundary and title disputes between Vermont and New York (1789) and took part in the Vermont Convention which ratified the United States Constitution (1791).

A Republican, Smith served in the 2nd and 7th congresses of the United States

House of Representatives (October 17, 1791, to 1797, and 1801 to 1803). In 1797 he reentered the Vermont legislature and became chief justice of the state, holding this office until the next year. He then represented Vermont in the United States Senate from 1803 until October 1, 1807; in this year he became governor of Vermont, serving for about a year. He also was a Democratic presidential elector that year.

Smith died in Rutland, Vermont, and was buried in the West Street Cemetery there.

SMITH, Jeremiah: governor of New Hampshire, jurist

Born Peterborough, New Hampshire, November 29, 1759; son of William and Elizabeth (Morison) Smith; married Eliza Ross, March 8, 1797; second marriage to Elizabeth Hale, September 20, 1831; father of six children (including Jeremiah); died September 21, 1842.

Smith attended Harvard from 1777 to 1779 and graduated from Queen's College (now Rutgers) in 1780. Six years afterward he was admitted to the bar in Amherst, New Hampshire. After serving in the state House of Representatives from 1788 to 1791, he went to the 2nd through the 4th congresses of the United States House of Representatives (1791–97) and attended the New Hampshire Constitutional Convention (1791–92).

In 1797 Smith became United States district attorney for the New Hampshire District. He left this position in 1800 to become judge of probate of Rockingham County, New Hampshire, holding this office until 1802. He also served as a circuit judge in 1801 and 1802. The latter year he rose to chief justice of the New Hampshire Supreme Court, a position he held until 1809. He then became governor of New Hampshire, serving until the following year. In 1813 he returned to the chief justiceship, remaining on the bench until 1816.

In other activities, Smith was a presidential elector in 1808 and was associate counsel (with Daniel Webster and Jeremiah Mason)

in the Dartmouth College case. He died in Dover, New Hampshire, and was buried in the Winter Street Cemetery (also called the Old Cemetery) in Exeter, New Hampshire.

SPRAGUE, Peleg: congressman
Born Rochester, Massachusetts, December 10, 1756; died April 20, 1800.

Sprague, after attending Harvard for a time, graduated from Dartmouth in 1783. He worked briefly as a clerk in a store in Littleton, Massachusetts, then (in 1785) was admitted to the bar and established a practice in Winchedon.

After moving to Keene, New Hampshire, in 1787, Sprague served as a selectman from 1789 to 1791, solicitor of Cheshire County in 1794, and a member of the New Hampshire House of Representatives in 1797. He was named to the United States House of Representatives (filling a vacancy) on December 15, 1797, and served until 1799 (5th Congress).

Sprague died in Keene and was buried in Washington Street Cemetery there.

STARK, John: army officer
Born Londonderry, New Hampshire, August 28, 1728; son of Archibald and Eleanor (Nichols) Stark; married Elizabeth Page, August 20, 1758; died May 2, 1822.

Stark had an active military career, participating in a number of notable actions. He was a leader of exploring expeditions and served at Crown Point and Ticonderoga during the French and Indian War in 1759. A colonel at the Battle of Bunker Hill in 1775, he resigned his commission in 1777. However, he was promoted to brigadier general in the Continental Army later that year and captured Fort Edward. He was twice placed in command of the Northern Department.

Stark joined Washington at the Battle of Short Hills at Morristown, New Jersey, in 1778, and served with Gates in Rhode Island the next year. He also saw action at the Battle of Springfield in 1780 and was brevetted

a major general in 1783. He was ninety-three when he died in Manchester, New Hampshire.

STORER, Clement: senator, congressman
Born Kennebunk, Maine, September 20, 1760; died November 21, 1830.

After completing preparatory studies, Storer studied medicine in Portsmouth, New Hampshire, and in Europe, then established a medical practice in Portsmouth. During the American Revolution he advanced from captain to major general of the New Hampshire militia.

Storer served in the New Hampshire House of Representatives from 1810 to 1812 and was speaker for one year. He was a New Hampshire delegate to the United States House of Representatives from 1807 to 1809 (10th Congress). Storer filled a vacancy in the United States Senate from New Hampshire on June 27, 1817, and served until 1819. He was high sheriff of Rockingham County from 1818 to 1824. He died in Portsmouth and was buried in North Cemetery.

SULLIVAN, John: army officer, Continental congressman, governor of New Hampshire
Born Somersworth, New Hampshire, February 17, 1740; son of John and Margery (Browne) Sullivan; died January 23, 1795.

A delegate to the Continental Congress in 1774–75 and 1780–81, Sullivan was appointed brigadier general by the congress in 1775 and served at the siege of Boston. Commissioned a major general with command of Long Island in 1776, he was at Valley Forge in 1777–78 and completely routed combined Indian and Loyalist forces at Elmira, New York, in 1779.

Sullivan resigned his commission in 1779 and became a member of the New Hampshire Constitutional Convention of 1782. He served as New Hampshire's attorney general from 1782 to 1786 and was speaker of the New Hampshire Assembly in 1785 and 1788.

Governor of New Hampshire in 1786, 1787, and 1789, Sullivan suppressed the paper-money riots. He served as chairman of the New Hampshire Convention which ratified the United States Constitution in 1788. He was a United States district judge for New Hampshire from 1789 to 1795. Sullivan died in Durham, New Hampshire, at the age of fifty-four. He was buried in the Sullivan family cemetery in Durham.

★★★★★

TENNEY, Samuel: congressman, physician
Born Byfield, Massachusetts, November 27, 1748; died February 6, 1816.

After attending Dummer Academy, Tenney enrolled in Harvard University, graduating in 1772 with a degree in medicine. He taught school in Andover, Massachusetts, and later began his medical practice in Exeter, New Hampshire. During the Revolutionary War, he served as a surgeon.

In 1788 Tenney began his political career as a delegate to the New Hampshire Constitutional Convention. From 1793 to 1800 he served as the judge of probate in Rockingham County and in 1800 became a member of the United States Congress as a representative from New Hampshire, filling a vacancy. After his seven-year tenure in Congress, Tenney continued to pursue his literary, historical, and scientific studies until his death in Exeter in 1816. He was buried in Old Cemetery in Exeter.

THORNTON, Matthew: Continental congressman
Born Ireland, circa 1714; son of James and Elizabeth (Jenkins) Thornton; married Hannah Jack, 1760; father of five children; died June 24, 1803.

Thornton was about four years old when his family settled in America. A graduate of Dartmouth, he began the practice of medicine in Londonderry, New Hampshire, circa 1740. He served as a colonel of the militia under the Royal Government. During the Revolutionary War he was a colonel in the New Hampshire militia.

In 1758, 1760, and 1761 Thornton was a member of the New Hampshire Assembly from Londonderry. In 1775 he was president of the New Hampshire Provincial Congress and chairman of the Committee of Safety. The next year he was speaker of the New Hampshire General Assembly, and about that time he also served as a member of the New Hampshire Council and as president of the Constitutional Convention of New Hampshire. He was an associate justice of the Superior Court of New Hampshire from 1776 to 1782. A signer of the Declaration of Independence, he was a member of the Continental Congress from 1776 to 1778.

Thornton was a member of the New Hampshire Senate from 1784 to 1786 and of the New Hampshire General Assembly in 1783. In 1785 he served as state councilor. He was also chief justice of the New Hampshire Court of Common Pleas. He died in Newburyport, Massachusetts, and was buried in Merrimack, New Hampshire.

TICHENOR, Isaac: senator, governor of Vermont
Born Newark, New Jersey, February 8, 1754; married Elizabeth; died December 11, 1838.

After graduating from the College of New Jersey (now Princeton) in 1775, Tichenor read law in Schenectady, New York. He served with the Continental Army in 1776. From 1781 to 1785 he was a member of the Vermont legislature, serving as speaker in 1783–84. He served as the Vermont agent to the Continental Congress from 1782 to 1789.

In 1790 Tichenor was appointed a commissioner to settle the New York–Vermont boundary dispute. He was a judge in the Vermont Supreme Court from 1791 to 1796. A Federalist, he represented Vermont in the United States Senate in 1796–97 and 1815–21. He served as governor of Vermont from 1797 to 1807 and in 1808–09. He was buried in the Village Cemetery in Old Bennington, Vermont.

TYLER, Royall: playwright, jurist

Born Boston, Massachusetts, July 18, 1757; son of Royall and Mary (Steele) Tyler; married Mary Palmer, 1794; father of at least one child (the Reverend Thomas P.); died August 26, 1826.

Tyler graduated from Harvard in 1776, receiving an honorary B.A. from Yale the same year. He was commissioned a major in the Independent Company of Boston (Continental Army) and was an aide to General Sullivan in 1778. That year he was commissioned a major and participated in the attack on Newport, Rhode Island.

Tyler was admitted to the Massachusetts bar in 1780. In 1787 he joined General Benjamin Lincoln's staff and assisted in the suppression of Shays's Rebellion. He went to New York City in 1787 and saw two of his plays produced there. One, *The Contrast,* was the first comedy written by a native American and produced by a professional company (the American Company). The other, performed at the John Street Theatre, was *May Day in Town; or, New York in an Uproar.* Tyler wrote *The Georgia Spec; or, Land in the Moon,* which first played in Boston in 1797. He also wrote a farce, *The Farm House; or, The Female Duelists,* and three sacred dramas: *The Origin of the Feast of Purim, or, the Destinies of Haman and Mordecai; Joseph and His Brethren;* and *The Judgement of Solomon.*

Tyler entered into a literary partnership with Joseph Dennie under the names Colon and Spondee (Tyler was Spondee) and wrote numerous satirical verses and prose works. Their pieces appeared in *The Eagle; or, Dartmouth Centinel* and later in *The New Hampshire Journal; or, The Farmer's Weekly Museum.* Tyler also wrote a novel, *The Algerine Captive,* in 1797, and a series of letters in 1809 called *Yankey in London.*

Tyler served as state's attorney for Windham County, Vermont, from 1794 to 1801, then became an assistant judge of the Vermont Supreme Court. In 1807 he became chief justice of the court, serving until 1813. He was a trustee of the University of Ver-

mont from 1802 until 1813 and a professor of jurisprudence from 1811 to 1814. He died in Brattleboro, Vermont.

★★★★★

WALKER, Timothy: clergyman

Born Woburn, Massachusetts, July 27, 1705; son of Captain Samuel and Judith (Howard) Walker; married Sarah Burbeen, November 12, 1730; father of five children (including Sarah [Walker] Rolfe Thompson); died September 1, 1782.

Walker graduated from Harvard in 1725 and was ordained to the ministry of the Congregational Church in 1730. He served as pastor of the first parish established in Penacook (later Rumbord, now Concord), New Hampshire, from 1739 to 1782. In 1753 he traveled to England as agent for Rumford proprietors (after the Crown had made a settlement putting the township in New Hampshire, thus threatening Massachusetts pioneers with dispossession) and obtained a favorable decision from the Crown. He returned to America in 1755.

Walker was the author of *Diaries of the Reverend Timothy Walker,* edited by J. B. Walker and published in 1889. He died in Concord, New Hampshire.

WEARE, Meshech: president of New Hampshire

Born Hampton Falls, New Hampshire, January 16, 1713; son of Nathaniel and Mary (Waite) Weare; married Elizabeth Shaw, July 20, 1738; second marriage to Mehitable Wainwright, December 11, 1746; father of ten children; died January 14, 1786.

Weare graduated from Harvard in 1735 and went on to study law. He served as a member of the New Hampshire legislature from Hampton from 1745 to 1755 and intermittently from 1755 to 1775; he was speaker for three years and clerk for eight. A justice of the New Hampshire Superior Court for twenty-eight years (1747–75), he also served in the Albany Congress in 1754.

Weare was a colonel in the New Hampshire militia and, from 1776 to 1784, president of the New Hampshire Council. He served briefly as chairman of the New Hampshire Committee of Safety. He was chief justice of New Hampshire from 1776 to 1782 and president of the state in 1784–85. He died in Hampton Falls.

WENTWORTH, John: colonial governor
Born Portsmouth, New Hampshire, August 20, 1737; son of Mark Hunking and Elizabeth (Rindge) Wentworth; married Frances Wentworth Atkinson; father of one child; died April 8, 1820.

Wentworth, a graduate of Harvard in 1755, went to England as a representative of his father's business in 1763 and also negotiated on behalf of New Hampshire for repeal of the Stamp Act. He served as a captain general in the New Hampshire militia in 1766. He was surveyor general for His Majesty's Wood in America and royal governor of New Hampshire from 1766 to 1775. Instrumental in dividing New Hampshire into five counties, he granted the charter for Dartmouth College in 1769 and was a member of the original board of trustees.

A Loyalist, Wentworth sailed from Boston at the outbreak of the Revolution, later (1792–1808) serving as lieutenant governor of Nova Scotia. He was created a baronet in 1795. He died in Halifax, Nova Scotia, at the age of eighty-two.

WENTWORTH, John, Jr.: Continental congressman, lawyer
Born Salmon Falls, Strafford County, New Hampshire, July 17, 1745; died January 10, 1787.

After graduating from Harvard in 1768, Wentworth studied law and was admitted to the bar. He established a legal practice in Dover, New Hampshire, in 1771. Register of probate for Stafford County from 1773 to 1787, he was appointed to the Committee of Correspondence in 1774 and to the New Hampshire Committee of Safety in 1777, which he served as moderator from that year until 1786.

Wentworth was a member of the New Hampshire House of Representatives from 1776 to 1780 and was a delegate to the Continental Congress in 1778 and 1779. A signer of the Articles of Confederation, he served on the New Hampshire Council from 1780 to 1784 and in the New Hampshire Senate from 1784 to 1786. He died in Dover and was buried in Pine Hill Cemetery.

WHEELOCK: John: college president
Born Lebanon, Connecticut, January 28, 1754; son of Eleazar and Mary (Brinsmead) Wheelock; married Maria Suhm, 1786; father of Maria; died April 4, 1817.

Wheelock attended Yale for three years, then matriculated at Dartmouth, graduating in 1771. During the Revolution he served as a lieutenant colonel in a New York infantry company. He became president of Dartmouth in 1779 and served in that position for the remainder of his life; he received a D.D. from the school in 1789. He founded the Dartmouth Medical School (1798) and revived his father's Indian education program (1800).

During his tenure as president, Wheelock engaged in a long-running dispute with the school's trustees, beginning in 1806. The dispute came to a head in 1816 when the Democratic legislature, which sided with Wheelock, changed the name of Dartmouth College to Dartmouth University and expanded the board of trustees from twelve to twenty-one members. The twelve "college trustees" refused to accept the nine new "university trustees," with the result that each set of trustees attempted to function as the sole administration of the school. The case (with Daniel Webster representing the college) was tried by the United States Supreme Court *(Trustees of Dartmouth College vs. Woodward);* the decision, handed down a year after Wheelock's death, upheld the rights of the trustees under the original charter.

WHIPPLE, William: Continental congressman
Born Kittery, Maine, January 14, 1730; son of Wil-

liam and Mary (Cutt) Whipple; married Catherine Moffatt; no children; died November 28, 1785.

A merchant and mariner engaged in the slave trade from 1752 to 1760, Whipple later freed his own slaves. He was a member of the New Hampshire Provincial Congress in 1775 and a delegate to the Continental Congress in 1775, 1776, and 1778. He was a signer of the Declaration of Independence and served as a member of the Council of New Hampshire's Committee of Safety. During the war he served as a brigadier general in the New Hampshire militia.

Whipple was a member of the New Hampshire Assembly from 1780 to 1784 and an associate justice of the New Hampshire Superior Court from 1782 to 1785. He served as financial receiver for the state of New Hampshire from 1782 to 1784 and was a justice of the peace and quorum in 1784.

Whipple died in Portsmouth, New Hampshire, and was buried in the North Cemetery.

WHITE, Phillips: Continental congressman
Born Haverhill, Massachusetts, October 28, 1729; died June 24, 1811.

White attended Harvard and later (1755) served at Lake George during the French and Indian War. He moved to New Hampshire, where he was a member of that state's House of Representatives from 1775 to 1782, serving as speaker in 1775 and 1782. A probate judge for Rockingham County, New Hampshire, from 1776 to 1790, he was a New Hampshire delegate to the Continental Congress in 1782 and 1783 and served on the New Hampshire Council from 1792 to 1794. He died in South Hampton, New Hampshire, and was buried in the Old Cemetery there.

WINGATE, Paine: senator, clergyman
Born Amesbury, Massachusetts, May 14, 1739; son of the Reverend Paine and Mary (Balch) Wingate; married Eunice Pickering, May 23, 1765; father of five children; died March 7, 1838.

Wingate, who graduated from Harvard in 1759, was ordained to the ministry of the Congregational Church in 1763. He served as a pastor in Hampton Falls, New Hampshire, from that year until 1776, when he moved to Stratham, New Hampshire. He refused to sign the "Association Test" the same year.

Wingate then turned to politics, serving first as a delegate to the New Hampshire Constitutional Convention (1781) and then as a member of the New Hampshire legislature (1783). A member of the Continental Congress in 1787–88, he was sent the following year to the 1st Congress of the United States Senate. He left the Senate in 1793 to become a member of the United States House of Representatives, serving one term.

Wingate again served New Hampshire as a member of the state legislature in 1795 and as a judge of the New Hampshire Superior Court from 1798 to 1809. He died in Stratham shortly before his ninety-ninth birthday.

WITHERELL, James: congressman
Born Mansfield, Massachusetts, June 16, 1759; died January 9, 1838.

As a youth, Witherell served in the 11th Massachusetts Regiment during the Revolutionary War, from 1775 to 1783. He was licensed to practice medicine in 1788 and moved that year to Hampton, Vermont. The following year he moved his practice to Fair Haven, Vermont.

Witherell was a member of the Vermont House of Representatives from 1798 to 1802. He served as associate judge of Rutland County, Vermont, from 1801 to 1803, and as judge from 1803 to 1806. He was a member of the Vermont Executive Council from 1802 to 1806. A Democrat, he was a Vermont delegate to the United States House of Representatives from 1807 until May 1, 1808 (10th Congress).

Witherell sat as judge for the Michigan Territory from 1808 to 1828; he then became secretary of the territory, serving until 1830. He commanded troops at Detroit in the absence of General Gull, was taken prisoner, and exchanged. He died in Detroit and was buried in the Russell Street Cemetery, later being reinterred in Elmwood Cemetery.

WORCESTER, Noah: clergyman

Born November 25, 1758; son of Noah and Lydia (Taylor) Worcester; married Hannah Huntington, May 1789; died October 31, 1837.

Worcester served as a fifer with the Continental Army at the battles of Bunker Hill (1776) and Bennington (1777). He served as a town clerk, a justice of the peace, and, from 1782 to 1787, a member of the New Hampshire legislature. He was ordained to the ministry of the Congregational Church in Thornton, New Hampshire, in 1787.

Worcester was sent to northern New Hampshire as a missionary for the New Hampshire Missionary Society. In 1813 he became the first editor of a periodical called *Christian Disciple.* He was the author of *Bible News of the Father, Son, and Holy Spirit, in a Series of Letters,* 1810; *A Solemn Review of the Custom of War,* 1814; and *The Atoning Sacrifice, a Display of Love, Not of Wrath,* 1829.

Worcester died in Brighton, Massachusetts, and was buried in Mount Auburn Cemetery, in Cambridge.

★★★★★★★★★★★★★

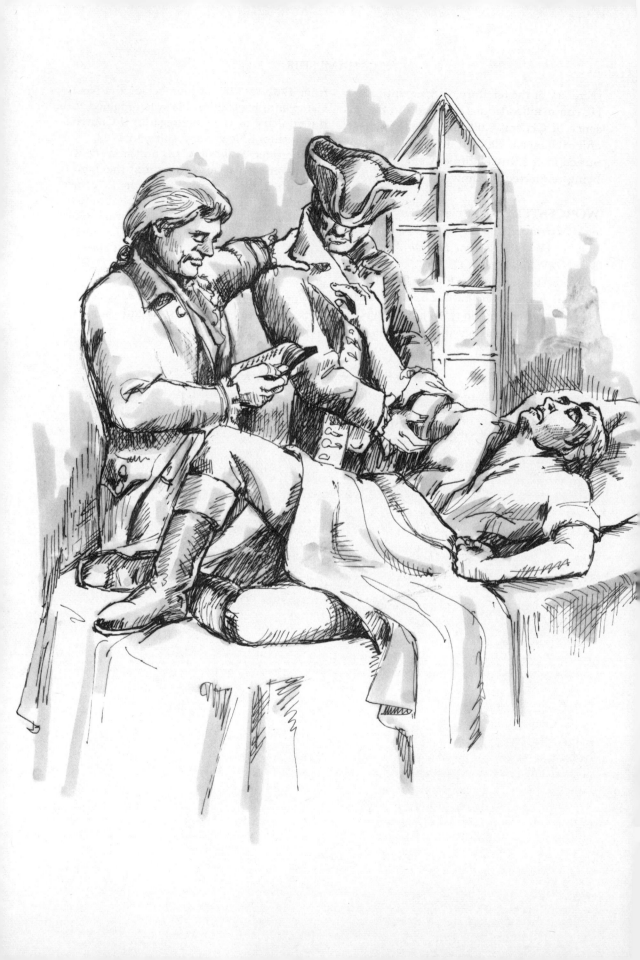

NEW JERSEY

"The rebels have hitherto been infamous for their wanton cruelties. Their brutal treatment of Governor [William] Franklin, and many other persons of distinction whom I could mention—whipping men almost to death because they will not take up arms—publicly whipping even women, whose husbands would not join the militia . . . these things . . . very ill agree with the character of humanity."
"Candidus," NEW YORK GAZETTE AND WEEKLY MERCURY, August 16, 1779

ALEXANDER, William (Lord Stirling): army officer

Born New York City, 1726; son of James Alexander; married the sister of Governor Livingston of New Jersey; died January 15, 1783.

For a time Alexander was surveyor general of New Jersey. In 1756 he attempted to establish claim to the title of 6th Earl Stirling, but the House of Lords rejected the claim in 1762. He became a member of the New Jersey Common Council and an assistant to the governor.

Alexander fought in the French and Indian War, receiving a commission as colonel in the 1st New Jersey Regiment in 1775. The following year he became brigadier general in the Continental Army, then rose to commander-in-chief at New York City. In 1777 he built forts Lee and Washington as well as Fort Stirling (which was named for him), the latter in Brooklyn Heights, New York. He headed the right wing of the Continental Army at the Battle of Long Island in 1776 and fought at the Battle of Trenton. After being promoted to major general in 1777, he led a division at the Battle of Brandywine, commanded reserves at the Battle of Germantown, and headed the left wing at the Battle of Monmouth.

Alexander served on the court of inquiry at the trial of Benedict Arnold in 1780. He was an early governor of King's College (now Columbia University). He died in Albany, New York.

★★★★★

BARBER, Francis: army officer

Born Princeton, New Jersey, 1751; married Mary Ogden; second marriage to Anne Ogden; died February 11, 1783.

After graduating from Princeton in 1767, Barber served as rector of an academy in Elizabethtown, New Jersey, circa 1769 to 1776. He became first a major and then a lieutenant colonel in the 3rd New Jersey Regiment. He took part in the Princeton campaign and fought in the battles of Brandywine and Germantown. He served as assistant inspector general to General von Steuben at Valley Forge and was wounded during the Battle of Monmouth.

In 1781 Barber was transferred to the 1st New Jersey Regiment. He quelled a mutiny of underpaid soldiers from Pennsylvania and New Jersey, thereby winning commendation from General Washington. He commanded a battalion of light infantry under Lafayette at the Battle of Green Spring. He was killed by a falling tree while the army was stationed at Newburgh, New York.

BEATTY, John: congressman

Born Neshaminy, Pennsylvania, December 19, 1749; son of the Reverend Charles and Anne (Reading) Beatty; married Mary Longstreet, March 22, 1774; second marriage to Mrs. Kitty Lalor, 1818; died April 30, 1826.

Beatty graduated from Princeton in 1769 and began the practice of medicine in Hartsville, Pennsylvania, three years later. In 1776 he received a commission as a captain in the Pennsylvania Battalion and was promoted the same year to major in the 6th Pennsylvania militia.

A member of the New Jersey legislature, Beatty attended the Continental Congress in 1784 and 1785 as well as the New Jersey Convention which ratified the federal constitution in 1787. He served in the United States House of Representatives from 1793 until 1795 (3rd Congress), when he was elected secretary of state of New Jersey. He remained in this office until 1805.

Beatty also engaged in business activities, serving as president of the Delaware Bridge Company and, from 1815 until his death, as president of the Trenton Banking Company.

BLOOMFIELD, Joseph: governor of New Jersey, congressman

Born Woodbridge, New Jersey, October 18, 1753; son of Dr. Moses and Sarah (Ogden) Bloomfield; married Mary McIlvaine, December 17, 1778; second marriage to Isabella; died October 3, 1823.

Bloomfield was admitted to the New Jersey bar in 1774. After being commissioned a captain in Colonel Elias Dayton's regiment in 1775, he was quickly promoted to major and served as judge advocate in the Northern Department of the Continental Army in 1776. Much later, in 1812, President Madison appointed him brigadier general in the United States Army.

As well as being clerk of the New Jersey Assembly and register in the state Court of Admiralty, Bloomfield served as state attorney general during the period from 1783 to 1788. He was a presidential elector in the election of 1792 and mayor of Burlington, New Jersey, from 1795 until 1800. From there he went on to the governorship of New Jersey, holding this office in the years 1801 and 1805–12. In 1811 the Bloomfield Compilation of New Jersey Laws was named in his honor. The state of New Jersey elected him to the United States House of Representatives for the 15th and 16th congresses (1817–21). He died in Burlington and was buried in the Episcopal Churchyard there.

BOUDINOT, Elias: Continental congressman

Born Philadelphia, Pennsylvania, May 2, 1740; son of Elias III and Catherine (Williams) Boudinot; married Hannah Stockton, April 21, 1762; died October 24, 1821.

In 1760 Boudinot received a license as counselor and attorney-at-law. After becoming sergeant-at-law in 1770, he was named a trustee of the College of New Jersey (now Princeton) in 1772, serving in this capacity for the remainder of his life. In 1775 he became a member of the New Jersey Committee of Safety, going on to serve as commissary general of prisoners for the Continental Army from 1776 to 1779.

Having participated in the New Jersey Provincial Congress, Boudinot was a delegate to the Continental Congress from 1777 until 1784. During that time he served as its president (1782–83), signed the peace treaty with Great Britain and the alliance treaty with France, and was secretary of the foreign affairs committee (1783–84). As well as participating in the New Jersey Convention which ratified the United States Constitution, he served in the 1st through the 3rd congresses of the United States House of Representatives (1789–95). Yale awarded him an LL.D. in 1790.

Boudinot directed the United States mint during the period from 1795 to 1805 and served as the first president of the American Bible Association from 1816 to 1821. He died in Burlington, New Jersey, at the age of eighty-one.

BOYD, Adam: congressman, jurist
Born Mendham, New Jersey, March 21, 1746; died August 15, 1835.

Boyd moved to Bergen County, New Jersey, circa 1770 and later to Hackensack, New Jersey. He was a member of the board of freeholders and justices in the years 1773, 1784, 1791, 1794, and 1798, and served as sheriff of Bergen County in 1778–81 and 1789. In other local service he was judge of the Bergen County Court of Common Pleas during 1803–05 and later for a longer period, from 1813 to 1833.

Having participated in the New Jersey House of Assembly for several terms (1782–83, 1787, and 1794–95), Boyd, a Democrat, went on to serve in the United States House of Representatives during the years 1803–05 and from March 8, 1808, until 1813 (8th and 10th–12th congresses). He died in Hackensack and was buried in the First Reformed Church Cemetery.

BRAINERD, John: missionary
Born Haddam, Connecticut, February 28, 1720; son of Hezekiah and Dorothy Hobart (Mason) Brainerd; married Experience Lyon, November 1752; second marriage to Mrs. Price; died March 18, 1781.

Brainerd, a 1746 Yale graduate, received his license to preach from the New York Presbytery in 1747. That same year the Correspondents of the Society in Scotland for the Propagation of the Faith appointed him a missionary on the western frontier, but after eight years they dismissed him for his inability to care for the Indians in that region. He was then given charge of a church in Newark, New Jersey.

Brainerd became a trustee of the College of New Jersey in 1754. He made several more unsuccessful attempts to perform missionary work, eventually settling in Deerfield, New Jersey, as pastor of a church there.

He died in Deerfield and was buried under the Presbyterian Church.

BREARLEY, David: jurist
Born Spring Grove, New Jersey, June 11, 1745; son of David and Mary (Clark) Brearley; married Elizabeth Mullen circa 1767; second marriage to Elizabeth Higbee, April 17, 1783; died August 16, 1790.

Brearley received a commission as a lieutenant colonel in the 4th New Jersey Regiment of the Continental Army in 1776 and moved to the 1st New Jersey Regiment the following year. In 1779, as well as attending the state's constitutional convention, he became chief justice of the state Supreme Court. He represented New Jersey in the United States Constitutional Convention in 1787 and chaired the New Jersey Convention which adopted the federal constitution the following year. During 1789–90 he was a federal district judge.

In other service, Brearley was vice president of the New Jersey Society of the Cincinnati and in 1786 was a delegate to the Episcopal General Convention. He died in Trenton, New Jersey.

★★★★★

CADWALADER, Lambert: army officer, congressman
Born Trenton, New Jersey, 1743; son of Dr. Thomas and Hannah (Lambert) Cadwalader; married Mary McCall, 1793; died September 13, 1823.

Cadwalader was educated at the University of Pennsylvania. At the age of thirty-three he was commissioned a lieutenant colonel in the 3rd Pennsylvania Battalion. He was a signer of the Non-Importation Agreement of 1765. In 1775 he served as a member of both the Committee of Correspondence and, like his father, Thomas, the Pennsylvania Provincial Convention. The following year he was a delegate to the Pennsylvania Constitutional Convention.

From 1784 to 1787 Cadwalader represented New Jersey in the Continental Congress. He was a member of the United States House of Representatives during the 1st Congress (1789–91) and the 3rd (1793–95). He died in Trenton, New Jersey, and was buried in the Friends Burying Ground there.

CALDWELL, James: clergyman

Born Charlotte County, Virginia, April 1734; son of John Caldwell; married Hannah Ogden, March 14, 1763; father of two children (including John E.); died November 24, 1781.

Graduated from the College of New Jersey (now Princeton) in 1759, Caldwell was ordained to the ministry by the Presbytery of New Brunswick, New Jersey, in 1761. That same year he became pastor of the First Presbyterian Church of Elizabethtown, New Jersey, and served there until 1780.

Caldwell was active in the Revolutionary War from the beginning, serving as chaplain of Dayton's New Jersey Brigade from 1776 to 1781. His church was used as a hospital by the Continental Army until it was burned by a Loyalist in 1780. In 1781 he saw action at the Battle of Springfield.

Caldwell was killed in Elizabethtown, New Jersey, by an American sentry (who was later hanged) in an argument over a package.

CHANDLER, Thomas Bradbury: clergyman

Born Woodstock, Connecticut, April 26, 1726; son of Captain William and Jemima (Bradbury) Chandler; married Jane M. Emott, 1750; father of six children; died June 17, 1790.

After graduating from Yale in 1745, Chandler went to England to attend Oxford University, where he received his M.A. He was called to service at St. John's Church in Elizabethtown, New Jersey, in 1747. Ordained to the Anglican Church in London, England, circa 1751, he became a leading advocate of American episcopacy.

Chandler was the author of *An Appeal to the Public in Behalf of the Church of England in America* (1767). He was granted D.D.s by Oxford (1766) and Columbia (1767). A Loyalist, he was attacked by the Continental Congress in 1775 in a pamphlet titled "What Think Ye of Congress Now?" Fleeing to England later that year, he did not return to America for ten years.

Chandler died in Elizabethtown and was buried at St. John's Church.

CLARK, Abraham: congressman

Born Elizabethtown, New Jersey, February 15, 1726; son of Thomas Clark; married Sarah Hatfield, 1749; father of ten children; died September 15, 1794.

Clark, a signer of the Declaration of Independence, began his public career as high sheriff of Essex County, New Jersey, and clerk of the New Jersey Colonial Assembly. In 1774 he became a member of the New Jersey Committee of Safety, and he later served as secretary of the Committee. He was a member of the New Jersey Provincial Congress which drafted the first New Jersey Constitution.

Clark was a delegate to the Continental Congress from 1779 to 1783 and in 1787–88. He was a member of the New Jersey Assembly from 1782 to 1787. A delegate to the Annapolis Convention at the age of sixty, he also served New Jersey in the United States House of Representatives during the 2nd and 3rd congresses (1791–94).

Clark died in Rahway, New Jersey, and was buried at the Rahway Presbyterian Church.

COCHRAN, John: surgeon

Born Sadsbury, Pennsylvania, September 1, 1730; son of James and Isabella Cochran; married Mrs. Gertrude Schuyler, December 4, 1760; died April 6, 1807.

Cochran was a founder of the New Jersey Medical Society, becoming its president in 1769. He was appointed physician surgeon general of the Middle Department of the Continental Army by George Washington in 1777; he was later (1785) chief physician for New York. He died in Palatine, New York.

COMBS, Moses Newell: manufacturer

Born Morris County, New Jersey, 1753; married Mary Haynes; father of thirteen children (including David and Isaac); died April 12, 1834.

Combs became a tanner and shoemaker in Newark, New Jersey, circa 1781. In 1790 he became the first to export goods manufactured in Newark. In 1806 he was treasurer of the Springfield-Newark Turnpike Company. Co-founder and director of the Newark Fire Insurance Company, from 1794 to 1818 he conducted the first night school (also one of the first free schools) in the United States for his employees and apprentices. Combs died at the age of eighty-one.

CONDICT, Silas: Continental congressman

Born Morristown, Norris County, New Jersey, March 7, 1738; died September 6, 1801.

A large landholder in Morristown and the surrounding vicinity, Condict was a member of the New Jersey Council from 1776 to 1780 and was also a member of the Committee of Safety. He served a three-year term (1781–84) in the Continental Congress as a representative from New Jersey. He was a member of the New Jersey General Assembly several times (1791–94, 1796–98, 1800), twice serving as speaker (1792–94, 1797). He died in Morristown and was buried in the First Presbyterian Church Cemetery.

CONDIT, John: surgeon, congressman

Born West Orange, New Jersey, July 8, 1755; son of Samuel and Mary (Smith) Condit; married Abigail Halsey, 1776; second marriage to Rhoda Halsey, 1785; father of eight children (including John S., Abigail Smith, Jacob A., Silas); died May 4, 1834.

In 1776 Condit was a surgeon in Colonel Van Cortlandt's battalion of Heard's brigade. He was a founder of the Orange (New Jersey) Academy in 1785 and was a member of the New Jersey legislature in 1788–89. A member of the New Jersey Council, he was a New Jersey delegate to the United States House of Representatives for the 6th, 7th, and 16th congresses (1799–1803, 1819–1820). He represented New Jersey in the United States Senate from 1803 to 1817.

Condit was an assistant collector of customs for the Port of New York and became an honorary member of the New Jersey Medical Society in 1830. He died in Orange Township, New Jersey, and was buried in the Old Graveyard in Orange.

COOPER, John: Continental congressman

Born near Woodbury, Gloucester County, New Jersey, February 5, 1729; died April 1, 1785.

Cooper, who had a liberal education, in 1774 became a member of the Gloucester County Committee of Correspondence; for the next two years he was a member of the Provincial Congress, serving on the committee that drafted the first New Jersey Constitution. He was appointed by the Provincial Congress as treasurer of the Western Division of New Jersey for 1775–76. From 1776 to 1780 and in 1784 he was a member of the New Jersey Legislative Council, representing Gloucester County.

A New Jersey delegate to the Continental Congress in 1776, Cooper served on the New Jersey Council of Safety two years later. In 1779 he was elected a judge of pleas in the Gloucester County Courts and was reelected to serve in 1784–85. He died in Woodbury, the town of his birth, and was buried in the Quaker Cemetery.

COX, James: congressman

Born Monmouth, New Jersey, June 14, 1753; died September 12, 1810.

Cox, who attended public schools, was in command of a company of militia at the battles of Germantown and Monmouth. He attained the rank of brigadier general. He was a member of the New Jersey General

Assembly from 1801 to 1807, serving as speaker from 1804 to 1807. A Democrat, he attended the United States House of Representatives during the 11th Congress (1809–10). He died in Monmouth and was buried in the Yellow Meeting House Cemetery, Upper Freehold Township, New Jersey.

CRANE, Stephen: Continental congressman

Born Elizabethtown (now Elizabeth), New Jersey, July 1709; died July 1, 1780.

Crane, who served for a time as sheriff of Essex County, New Jersey, was chosen by the Elizabethtown Associates to present a petition before the King in England in 1743. In 1750 he became a member of the town committee, later (1776) serving as chairman. He was a judge of the Court of Common Pleas during the Stamp Act controversy.

From 1766 to 1773 Crane was a member of the New Jersey General Assembly, serving as speaker in 1771. Mayor of Elizabethtown from 1772 to 1774, he then became chairman of the county committee of New Brunswick. He served New Jersey in the Continental Congress from 1774 to 1776 and was a member of the New Jersey Council in 1776, 1777, and 1779.

Crane died in Elizabethtown and was buried in the First Presbyterian Church Cemetery.

★★★★★

DAVENPORT, Franklin: senator

Born Philadelphia, Pennsylvania, September 1755; died July 27, 1832.

Davenport studied law in Burlington, New Jersey. Admitted to the bar in 1776, he began the practice of law in Gloucester City, New Jersey, and was appointed clerk of the Gloucester County Court. He was named prosecutor of pleas the following year. In 1781 he moved to Woodbury, New Jersey, and four years later was appointed first surrogate of Gloucester County.

Having enlisted as a private in Captain James Sterling's Company of the New Jersey militia, Davenport was commissioned a brigade major in 1776 and served in the battles of Trenton and Princeton. From brigade quartermaster in 1778 he advanced rapidly to assistant quartermaster of Gloucester County. He was then commissioned a colonel in the New Jersey militia and served in that capacity during the Whiskey Rebellion (1794). In 1796 he was commissioned a brigadier general in the Gloucester County militia.

Davenport was a member of the New Jersey General Assembly from 1786 to 1789. Chosen to fill a vacancy in the United States Senate from New Jersey, he served from December 5, 1798, to the end of the term. He was then elected to membership in the United States House of Representatives from New Jersey and served in the 6th Congress (1799–1801). He served as a presidential elector in the campaigns of 1792 and 1812.

In 1826, at the age of seventy-one, Davenport was appointed master in chancery. He died in Woodbury, New Jersey, and was buried in the Presbyterian Cemetery in North Woodbury.

DAYTON, Elias: army officer, Continental congressman

Born Elizabethtown (now Elizabeth), New Jersey, May 1, 1737; son of Jonathan Dayton; married Miss Rolfe; father of eight children (including Jonathan); died October 22, 1807.

At the age of nineteen Dayton was commissioned a lieutenant in the New Jersey militia; four years later he became a captain. In 1774 he was appointed to enforce the measures recommended by the Continental Congress and, in 1775, was muster master of Essex County, New Jersey. The following year he was commissioned a colonel in the 3rd Battalion of the New Jersey militia. In 1783 he was commissioned a brigadier general in the Continental Army on the recommendation of George Washington. He also served as a major general in the New Jersey militia.

Dayton represented New Jersey in the Continental Congress in 1787–88. The following year he was recorder of Elizabeth, New Jersey. In 1791–92 and 1794–96 he was a member of the New Jersey Assembly. He also served as president of the New Jersey Society of the Cincinnati. He died in Elizabethtown.

DAYTON, Jonathan: senator
Born Elizabethtown (now Elizabeth), New Jersey, October 16, 1760; son of General Elias Dayton; died October 9, 1824.

Dayton graduated from the College of New Jersey (now Princeton) in 1776. (Later, in 1798, he received an honorary LL.D. from that school.) He was commissioned a captain in the Continental Army and served at the Battle of Yorktown. He was a member of the New Jersey Assembly, in 1786–87, 1790, and 1814–15, serving as speaker in 1790. He was a delegate to the United States Constitutional Convention in 1787 and attended the Continental Congress as a representative from New Jersey from 1787 to 1789. At the end of that term he became a member of the New Jersey Council.

Dayton served in the United States House of Representatives as a delegate from New Jersey from 1791 to 1799, serving as speaker after 1795. For the next six years he served in the United States Senate. He was arrested for treason in conjunction with Aaron Burr but was never tried. The city of Dayton, Ohio, is named for him. He died in Elizabethtown, and was buried in St. John's Churchyard in Elizabethtown.

De HART, John: Continental congressman, mayor
Born Elizabethtown (now Elizabeth), New Jersey, 1728; died June 1, 1795.

De Hart studied law, was admitted to the bar, and established a legal practice. He became sergeant-at-law in 1770. In 1774 he was a signer of the Articles of Association.

From 1774 to 1775, and from February to June 1776, he was a representative from New Jersey to the Continental Congress. Also in 1776 he was a member of the committee that prepared the draft of the New Jersey Constitution, and in 1776–77 he was chief justice of the New Jersey Supreme Court. He was mayor of Elizabethtown from 1789 to 1795. He died in Elizabethtown and was buried in St. John's Churchyard.

DICK, Samuel: Continental congressman, physician
Born Nottingham, Prince Georges County, Maryland, November 14, 1740; died November 16, 1812.

After studying medicine in Scotland, Dick established a medical practice in Salem, New York, in 1770. In 1776 he served as a member of the New Jersey Provincial Congress. That same year he was a colonel in the 1st Battalion of the Salem County (New Jersey) militia. He then became an assistant surgeon in the Continental Army, serving during the Canadian campaign.

Dick was a member of the First New Jersey General Assembly. In 1778 he was appointed collector of customs of the Western District of New Jersey. In 1783–84 he represented New Jersey in the Continental Congress, and in 1787 he was a delegate to the New Jersey Convention which ratified the United States Constitution. From 1785 to 1804 he was surrogate of Salem County.

Dick died in Salem and was buried in St. John's Episcopal Churchyard.

DICKINSON, Philemon: army officer, Continental congressman
Born Croisia-dore, Talbot County, Maryland, April 5, 1739; son of Judge Samuel and Mary (Cadwalader) Dickinson; married Mary Cadwalader, July 14, 1767; second marriage to Rebecca Cadwalader; died February 4, 1809.

Dickinson graduated from the University of Pennsylvania in 1759. In 1775 he was commissioned a colonel in the Hunterdon County (New Jersey) Battalion. The same year he was commissioned a brigadier general in the New Jersey militia and the following year a major general, commander-in-chief. He defeated a Cornwallis raiding expedition by interrupting a British retreat to New York before the Battle of Monmouth in 1777.

In 1781 Dickinson was appointed commissioner of the New Jersey Loan Office. He was a member of the Continental Congress from Delaware in 1782–83 and was vice president of the New Jersey Council in 1783–84. In 1785 he was appointed a commissioner by the Continental Congress to select a site for the United States Capitol. He died near Trenton, New Jersey.

DUFFIELD, George: clergyman
Born Lancaster County, Pennsylvania, October 7, 1732; son of George and Margaret Duffield; married Elizabeth Blair, March 8, 1756; second marriage to Margaret Armstrong, March, 5, 1759; father of at least one son (George); died February 2, 1790.

Duffield graduated from the College of New Jersey (now Princeton) in 1752, and from 1754 to 1756 he was a tutor there. He was licensed to preach in 1756 and the following year became pastor of the Presbyterian Church in Carlisle, Pennsylvania, serving until 1772; meanwhile, in 1759, he had been ordained to the ministry. From 1772 to 1790 he was pastor of the Third Presbyterian Church in Philadelphia.

A captain of the local militia, Duffield was a strong patriot. He was commissioned chaplain of the Pennsylvania militia and co-chaplain of the Continental Congress. He was clerk of the Pennsylvania General Assembly and was trustee of the College of New Jersey from 1777 to 1790, the year of his death. He wrote *A Sermon Preached in the Third Presbyterian Church in the City of Philadelphia on Thursday, December 11, 1783,* which was published in 1784.

★★★★★

ELMER, Ebenezer: congressman, physician, college president
Born Cedarville, New Jersey, August 23, 1752; son of Daniel and Abigail (Lawrence) Elmer; married Hannah Seeley, 1784; father of Lucius Quintus Cincinnatus; died October 18, 1843.

Elmer served in both the Revolutionary War and the War of 1812. He rose from ensign to lieutenant in the 3rd New Jersey Regiment, serving as surgeon's mate of that regiment in 1777 and as surgeon of the 2nd New Jersey Regiment the following year. In the War of 1812 he was adjutant general of the New Jersey militia and brigadier general of the Cumberland Brigade. He was the last surviving Revolutionary officer of New Jersey.

Elmer's government positions included vice president of the State Council from 1807 to 1817 and again from 1822 to 1832; member of the New Jersey Assembly from 1789 to 1791, from 1793 to 1795, and from 1817 to 1819; the speakership of the Assembly in 1791, 1795, and 1817; and member of the United States House of Representatives from New Jersey from 1801 to 1807.

After serving as a customs collector in Bridgeton, New Jersey, in 1808, Elmer became vice president of Burlington College, serving from 1808 to 1817, and again from 1822 to 1832, a total of nineteen years. He died at the age of ninety-one in Bridgeton and was buried in the Presbyterian Cemetery there.

ELMER, Jonathan: physician, Continental congressman, senator
Born Fairfield, New Jersey, November 29, 1745; son of Daniel and Abigail (Lawrence) Elmer; married Mary Seeley, 1769; died September 3, 1817.

Elmer received an M.D. from the University of Pennsylvania in 1769. He served as a member of the New Jersey legislature and of the New Jersey Council in 1780 and 1784; a trustee of the College of New Jersey (now Princeton) from 1782 to 1795; a surrogate (a local judicial officer who has jurisdiction over the probate of wills, the settlement of estates, and the appointment and supervision of guardians) for Cumberland County; and president of the New Jersey Medical Society in 1787.

On the national level, Elmer was a delegate to the Continental Congress from 1776 to 1778, a member of the Congress of the Confederation in 1787 and 1788, and a Federalist member of the United States Senate from 1789 to 1791. He was also a member of the American Philosophical Society. He died in Burlington, New Jersey.

ERSKINE, Robert: army officer

Born Dunfermline, Scotland, September 7, 1735; son of the Reverend Ralph and Margaret (Simson) Erskine; married Elizabeth Erskine; died October 2, 1780.

Erskine attended the University of Edinburgh, Scotland, from 1748 to 1752. After an unsuccessful business venture in London, England, he invented a centrifugal hydraulic engine, which led to his election as a fellow of the Royal Society in 1771. The same year he was sent to America as a representative for British investors in the American Iron Company; however, he became a supporter of the colonists and formed a military regiment. He was commissioned a captain in the Bergen County (New Jersey) militia in 1775. He was a geographer and surveyor general for the Continental Army from 1777 until his death in 1780.

★★★★★

FAESCH, John Jacob: ironmaster

Born Basle, Switzerland, 1729; married Elizabeth Brinckerhoff; second marriage to Susan Leonard; father of four children; died May 26, 1799.

Faesch, who built and operated a blast furnace in Mount Hope, New Jersey, was a manufacturer of shot for the Continental Army during the American Revolution. Prior to the war, in 1773, he had been commissioned judge of Morris County, New Jersey. Later he served as a delegate to the New Jersey Constitutional Convention.

FELL, John: Continental congressman, jurist, merchant

Born New York City, February 5, 1721; married Susanna Moskhk; father of one child; died May 15, 1798.

Prior to the Revolutionary War, Fell was a senior partner in John Fell and Company (1759), settling near Paramus, in Bergen County, New Jersey. He was a judge in the New Jersey Court of Common Pleas from 1766 to 1774, and again from 1776 to 1786.

Fell was a leader of a meeting of Bergen County citizens for the signing of patriotic resolutions at the Hackensack Court House on June 25, 1774. He then became chairman of both the Bergen County committee which supervised the local war effort and the local Committee of Correspondence. He was a member of the First New Jersey Provincial Congress (Trenton, 1775) and a member of the Provincial Council (1776). In 1777 the Loyalist leaders captured him, but he was released the following year.

During his membership in the Continental Congress in 1778, Fell made his principal contribution as a member of the standing committee on the conducting of United States commercial affairs. He was also a member of the special foreign affairs committee (1779). He was a member of the New Jersey Council in 1782 and 1783. He died in Dutchess County, New York.

FORD, Jacob: army officer, powder maker

Born February 10, 1738; son of Jacob and Hannah (Baldwin) Ford; married Theodosia Johnes, January 27, 1767; father of six children; died January 11, 1777.

Ford became sole owner of Middle Forge in Morristown, New Jersey, in 1764. During the Revolutionary War he cast shot and shell for the guns of Washington's army, and also served as a colonel in the Morris County, New Jersey, militia in 1775, successfully defending Morristown against British raids. In 1776 he built a powder mill which supplied great quantities of powder to colonial soldiers throughout the war. He died before the end of the Revolution and was buried in the First Presbyterian Churchyard in Morristown.

FORMAN, David: army officer, jurist

Born Monmouth County, New Jersey, November 3, 1745; son of Joseph and Elizabeth (Lee) Forman; married Ann Marsh, February 28, 1767; father of eleven children; died September 12, 1797.

Forman, who was educated at the College of New Jersey (now Princeton University), suppressed a Loyalist uprising in Monmouth County, New Jersey, in 1776. The following year he was commissioned a brigadier general in the New Jersey militia, which he commanded at the Battle of Germantown. He was attached to Major General Charles Lee's staff on General Washington's order. After the war, Forman turned to a juristic career, serving for many years as a judge in the Monmouth County Court of Common Pleas.

FRANKLIN, William: colonial governor

Born Philadelphia, Pennsylvania, 1731; illegitimate son of Benjamin Franklin and Deborah Read; married Elizabeth Downes, September 4, 1762; married a second time; father of one illegitimate son (William Temple Franklin); died November 16, 1813.

William Franklin often accompanied his father, Benjamin, to Europe and also helped in his father's scientific experiments. After serving in King George's War, he became comptroller of the General Post Office and clerk of the Pennsylvania Provincial Assembly (1754–56). He was admitted to Middle Temple, London, England, and later elected to the bar. He received an honorary M.A. from Oxford University in 1762.

Franklin was the last royal governor of New Jersey, serving for fourteen years (1762–76). In 1765 he became involved in a bitter controversy with the Patriot party in New Jersey which culminated in his being captured and imprisoned as a Loyalist at the outbreak of the Revolutionary War. He became president of the Board of Associated Loyalists in New York City in 1778. His Loyalist leanings led to a break with his father, and William went to England in 1782 to settle permanently. He reconciled with his father two years later. He died in England.

FRELINGHUYSEN, Frederick: army officer, senator

Born Somerville, New Jersey, April 13, 1753; son of the Reverend John and Dinah (Van Berg) Frelinghuysen; married Gertrude Schenck; second marriage to Ann Yard; father of at least one son (Theodore); died April 13, 1804.

Frelinghuysen graduated from Princeton in 1770; four years later he was admitted to the New Jersey bar. He began a long and varied career of service to the colonial cause as a representative to the New Jersey Provincial Congress from Somerset County (1775–76). He served as a major in the Minutemen and was captain of artillery in the New Jersey militia, later advancing to aide-de-camp to General Philemon Dickinson. Frelinghuysen commanded the artillery corps at the battles of Trenton, Springfield, and Elizabethtown. He participated in the Battle of Monmouth Court House in 1778.

Frelinghuysen attended the Continental Congress from 1778 to 1783. He was a member of the New Jersey Legislative Council until 1782 and a member of the New Jersey General Assembly in 1784, 1800, and 1804. In 1787 he was a delegate to the New Jersey Convention which ratified the United States Constitution.

In 1790 Frelinghuysen was a brigadier general in the campaign against the western Indians, and four years later he served as a major general in the New Jersey militia during the Whiskey Rebellion. He was a New Jersey delegate to the United States Senate from 1793 to 1796. He was a trustee of Princeton from 1802 until his death in 1804. He died in Millstone, New Jersey, and was buried in the Old Cemetery in Weston, New Jersey.

FRENEAU, Philip Morin: journalist, poet
Born New York City, January 2, 1752; son of Pierre and Agnes (Watson) Freneau; married Eleanor Forman, 1789; died December 19, 1832.

After graduating from the College of New Jersey (now Princeton) in 1771, Freneau served on a privateer during the Revolutionary War, during which time he was captured and held in the prison-brig *Aurora.* This experience was later described in his poem "The British Prison Ship," 1781. He was an editor of and a contributor of poetry to *Freeman's Journal* in Philadelphia from 1781 until 1784, when he became master of a brig bound for Jamaica. He lived for several years in the West Indies.

In 1790 Freneau became editor of the *New York Daily Advertiser.* The following year he was translating clerk of the United States Department of State and began a three-year stay as editor of the *National Gazette,* a partisan Jefferson paper. He later became editor of the *New York Timepiece.* Called "the poet of the American Revolution," Freneau earned a reputation as the first important American lyrical poet with such poems as "The Indian Burying Ground," "The Wild Honeysuckle," and "Eutaw Springs." Other poems include "A Poem on the Rising Glory of America," 1771; "Voyage to Boston," 1774; "General Gage's Confession" and "General Gage's Soliloquy," 1775; "A Journey from Philadelphia to New York by Robert Slender," 1787; and "The Village Merchant," 1794.

Freneau became lost in a snowstorm and died of exposure near Freehold, New Jersey, two weeks before his eighty-first birthday.

★★★★★

GIBBONS, Thomas: lawyer, steamboat operator
Born Savannah, Georgia, December 15, 1757; son of Joseph and Hannah (Martin) Gibbons; died May 16, 1826.

Gibbons's life was marked by controversy. He was a Loyalist during the American Revolution, and was responsible for one of the first disputed congressional elections. He served several terms as mayor of Savannah, Georgia (1791–92, 1794–95, and 1799–1801).

Circa 1810 Gibbons purchased a summer residence in Elizabethtown, New Jersey. During the years 1817 and 1818 Gibbons operated steamboats running from Elizabethtown Point up the Raritan River to New Brunswick, where they connected with Aaron Ogden's steamers. In 1818 he broke with Ogden and ran his own ferries from Elizabethtown to New York, thus infringing on Ogden's monopoly grant. Ogden sued him in a case which eventually came to the United States Supreme Court (*Gibbons vs. Ogden,* 1824). The case, which Gibbons won, resulted in the abolition of state-chartered monopolies and the establishment of federal jurisdiction over interstate commerce. Gibbons died in New York City two years later.

GREEN, Ashbel: clergyman, university president
Born Hanover, New Jersey, July 6, 1762; son of Jacob and Elizabeth (Pierson) Green; married Elizabeth Stockton, 1785; second marriage to Christiana Anderson, 1809; third marriage to Mary McCulloh, 1815; father of Jacob; died May 19, 1848.

After participating in the Revolutionary War, Green graduated in 1782 from the College of New Jersey (now Princeton). From 1785 until 1787 he was professor of mathematics and natural philosophy there. He also served the college as a trustee for fifty-eight years (1790–1848) and as president from 1812 to 1822. During his tenure he became the first college president to introduce the study of the Bible into the curriculum.

Green was licensed to preach in 1786. From 1787 to 1793 he was assistant pastor at the Second Presbyterian Church in Philadelphia, then served as pastor from 1793 to 1812. He also was a member of the General Assembly of the Presbyterian Church

(1790–1839), chaplain to the United States Congress (1792–1800), and editor of the *Christian Advocate* (1822–34). Combining his experience in the fields of religion and education, he founded Princeton Theological Seminary and was president of the board of directors from 1812 until 1848. The University of North Carolina awarded him an honorary LL.D. in 1812.

Green wrote *Sermons on the Assembly Catechism* (1818), *Presbyterian Missions* (1820), and *Discourse Delivered in the College of New Jersey* (1822). He died in Philadelphia.

★★★★★

HARDENBERGH, Jacob Rutsen: clergyman, college president

Born Rosendale, New York, 1736; son of Colonel Johannes and Maria (DuBois) Hardenbergh; married Mrs. Dinah Van Bergh Frelinghuysen, 1756; father of several children (including John and Jacob Rutsen); died November 2, 1790.

Hardenbergh, a theology student under John Frelinghuysen, was ordained to the ministry of the Dutch Reformed Church in 1758; he was among the first of that faith to be ordained in America. As a leader of Coetus, a group which sought independence from the parent church in Holland and the establishment of a Dutch Reformed theological school in America, Hardenbergh was authorized to petition the Classis in Amsterdam for an independent American classis in 1763, but he was refused. He obtained a royal charter for the founding of Queen's College (now Rutgers University) in 1766, and was appointed to the first board of trustees in 1771. He was the first president of the school, serving from 1786 to 1790.

A reward was offered by England for Hardenbergh's capture during the Revolutionary War because of his ardent support of the patriot cause. He was a delegate to the Provincial Congress of New Jersey, which ratified the Declaration of Independence and framed the New Jersey Constitution. He was also a member of the New Jersey General Assembly. He held a D.D. (1771) and an honorary A.M. (1777) from Princeton and an S.T.D. (1789) from Columbia. He died in New Brunswick, New Jersey.

HART, John: Continental congressman

Born Stonington, Connecticut, 1711; son of Edward and Martha Hart; married Deborah Scudder, 1740; died May 11, 1779.

Hart was justice of the peace of Hunterdon County, New Jersey, in 1755. In 1761 he was a member of the 20th New Jersey Assembly, also serving in the 21st Assembly ten years later. He opposed the Stamp Act of 1765. He was a member of the First Provincial Congress of New Jersey in 1774, and from 1775 to 1776 he was a judge of the New Jersey Court of Common Pleas.

Hart was a delegate to the Continental Congress in 1776, holding the position of vice president that same year. A member of the Committee of Correspondence, he was also a signer of the Declaration of Independence. In 1776 he became a member of the first Assembly under the New Jersey Constitution, acting as speaker. He died three years later in Hopewell, New Jersey.

HELMS, William: congressman

Born Sussex County, New Jersey; died 1813.

During his military career, Helms advanced from second lieutenant to captain in the Revolutionary War and was brevetted a major in 1783. In 1791–92 he was a member of the New Jersey Assembly. A Democrat, he was a New Jersey delegate to the United States House of Representatives for the 7th through the 11th congresses (1801–11). He died in Hamilton County, Ohio.

HENDERSON, Thomas: physician, army officer, congressman

Born Freehold, New Jersey, August 15, 1743; son of John and Ann (Stevens) Henderson; married Mary Hendricks, September 23, 1767; second marriage to Rachel Burrowes, January 2, 1778; father of seven children; died December 15, 1824.

Henderson graduated from the College of New Jersey (now Princeton) in 1761. Five years later he became a member of the New Jersey Medical Society. He was a member of both the New Jersey Committee of Safety and the Freehold Committee of Observation and Inspection in 1774. A lieutenant in the local militia in New Jersey in 1775, he was a major in the Minutemen and then in the Continental Army in 1776, and also a surrogate in Monmouth County, New Jersey. In 1777 he was a lieutenant colonel in Forman's Additional Continental Regiment.

In 1777 Henderson was a member of the New Jersey Provincial Council, and from 1780 to 1784 he served in the New Jersey Assembly. Also in 1780 he became a member of the local committee of retaliation. He was a judge of common pleas in 1783 and 1799 and master of chancery in 1790. In 1793–94 and 1812–13 he was a member of the New Jersey Council, holding the office of vice president in 1794. That same year he was acting governor of New Jersey.

A Federalist, Henderson served in the United States House of Representatives during the 4th Congress (1795–97). He was also a trustee and elder in the Tennent Church in New Jersey. He died in Freehold and was buried in the Old Tennent Cemetery there.

HORNBLOWER, Josiah: engineer, jurist
Born Staffordshire, England, February 23, 1729; son of Joseph and Rebecca Hornblower; married Elizabeth Kingsland, 1755; father of twelve children; died January 21, 1809.

In 1753 Hornblower built the first steam engine constructed in America (in Belleville, New Jersey). He served in the defense of New Jersey during the French and Indian War (1755). He was commissioned a captain the following year.

In 1778 Hornblower was commissioner for tax appeals in Newark, New Jersey. In 1779 and 1780 he was a member of the New Jersey legislature, serving as speaker the lat-ter year. He sat on the New Jersey Council from 1781 to 1784 and attended the Congress of Confederation in 1785. From 1790 to 1809 he was a judge in the Essex County (New Jersey) Court of Common Pleas. He died in Newark, New Jersey.

HOUSTON, William Churchill: Continental congressman
Born South Carolina, circa 1746; son of Archibald and Margaret Houston; married Jane Smith; father of four children; died August 12, 1788.

Houston received an A.B. from the College of New Jersey (now Princeton) in 1768. From 1771 to 1783 he was a professor of mathematics and natural philosophy at that school. During this time, in 1776–77, he was also a captain in the Somerset County Foot Militia. He was a delegate from New Jersey to the Continental Congress for three terms (1775–76, 1779–82, 1784–85), holding the position of deputy secretary in 1775 and 1776. While serving as a member of the New Jersey Assembly in 1776, he was clerk pro tem and a member of the committee to settle public accounts. Two years later he attended the New Jersey Council of Safety.

Houston began a law career with his admittance to the New Jersey bar in 1781. From 1781 to 1788 he was a clerk in the New Jersey Supreme Court, and from 1782 to 1785 he was a receiver of Continental taxes in New Jersey. He was a delegate to the Annapolis (Maryland) Convention and the United States Constitutional Convention in Philadelphia; however, he did not sign the Constitution. He died in Frankford, Pennsylvania.

HOWELL, Richard: army officer, governor of New Jersey
Born Newark, Delaware, October 25, 1754; son of Ebenezer and Sarah (Bond) Howell; married Keziah Burr, November 1779; father of nine children; died April 28, 1802.

Howell was a member of the Greenwich (New Jersey) tea party while serving on the ship *Greyhound* in 1774. At the age of twenty-one he was commissioned a captain in the New Jersey militia, serving at the battles of Ticonderoga and Quebec. He was wounded in the Battle of Brandywine in 1777 and later served in the war effort as major of a brigade.

In 1779 Howell became a licensed attorney. He succeeded William C. Houston as the clerk of the New Jersey Supreme Court in 1788. During his term as governor of New Jersey (1793 to 1801), he commanded the right wing of the troop sent to put down the Whiskey Rebellion in Pennsylvania. He was also a member of the Society of the Cincinnati. He died in Burlington, New Jersey.

HUNTER, Andrew: clergyman
Born York County, New York, 1751; son of David and Martha Hunter; married Nancy Riddle, October 2, 1775; second marriage to Mary Stockton; died February 24, 1823.

Hunter graduated from the College of New Jersey (now Princeton) at the age of nineteen. After being licensed to preach by the Presbytery of Philadelphia in 1774, he made a missionary visit to Virginia. That same year he took part in the burning of the cargo of tea in Greenwich, New Jersey. In 1776 he was commissioned by the Provincial Congress of New Jersey as chaplain of Colonel Philip Van Cortlandt's battalion.

From 1786 to 1797 Hunter was in charge of the Presbyterian churches in Woodbury and Blackwood, New Jersey. Twice (1789, 1794) he was the Presbyterian Church delegate to the General Assembly. In 1788, and again in 1791, he was a trustee of the College of New Jersey, as well as professor of mathematics and astronomy from 1804 to 1808. From 1808 to 1810 he was in charge of the academy in Bordentown, New Jersey. For the last eleven years of his life he was a schoolmaster in the United States Naval Service in Washington, D.C.

★★★★★

IMLAY, James Henderson: congressman
Born Imlaystown, Monmouth County, New Jersey, November 26, 1764; died March 6, 1823.

Imlay served as a major in the Monmouth County militia during the Revolutionary War. After graduating from the College of New Jersey (now Princeton) in 1786, he studied law and worked for a while as a tutor at his alma mater. He was admitted to the New Jersey bar in 1791 and established a legal practice.

Imlay served as a member of the New Jersey Assembly for three years (1793–96), filling the position of speaker during the final year. He then was elected to the United States House of Representatives for the 5th and 6th congresses (1797–1801). In 1798 he was a manager appointed to conduct the impeachment proceedings against William Blount (a senator from Tennessee). After serving as postmaster of Allentown, New Jersey, in 1804 and 1805, he resumed his practice of law there. He died in Allentown and was buried in the Presbyterian Church Cemetery there.

★★★★★

KINSEY, James: Continental congressman, jurist
Born Philadelphia, Pennsylvania, March 22, 1731; died January 4, 1803.

After attending common schools and studying law, Kinsey was admitted to the New Jersey bar in 1753. He practiced law in the courts of Pennsylvania and New Jersey. During the pre-Revolutionary period he served in the New Jersey General Assembly (1772–75), on the Committee of Correspondence for Burlington County, New Jersey (1774–75), and in the Continental Congress (1774–75). He held the position of chief justice of the New Jersey Supreme Court from 1789 until his death fourteen years later. He died in Burlington, New Jersey, and was buried in St. Mary's Churchyard there.

KIRKPATRICK, Andrew: jurist
Born Minebrook, New Jersey, February 17, 1756; son of David and Mary (McEowen) Kirkpatrick; married Jane Bayard, November 1, 1792; father of seven children; died January 6, 1831.

Kirkpatrick graduated from the College of

New Jersey (now Princeton) in 1775 and was admitted to the New Jersey bar ten years later. In 1797 he became a member of the lower house of the New Jersey legislature. The following year he became an associate justice in the New Jersey Supreme Court, rising to chief justice in 1804 and serving until 1824.

Kirkpatrick was an original trustee of Princeton Theological Seminary and was chairman of the board of trustees from 1822 to 1831. He also served as a trustee of the College of New Jersey from 1807 until 1831, the year of his death.

KITCHELL, Aaron: senator, congressman
Born Hanover, New Jersey, July 10, 1744; died June 26, 1820.

Kitchell, who attended common schools, was a blacksmith by trade. He served many terms in the New Jersey General Assembly (1781–82, 1784, 1786–90, 1793–94, 1797, 1801–04, 1809). A Democrat, he was a member of the United States House of Representatives from 1791 to 1793; from January 29, 1795, until 1797; and again from 1799 to 1801. A few years later he became a New Jersey delegate to the United States Senate, holding that position from 1805 until March 12, 1809. In 1816 he was a Democratic presidential elector.

Kitchell died in Hanover, his birthplace, and was buried in the Presbyterian Churchyard there.

KOLLOCK, Shepard: publisher, jurist
Born Lewes, Delaware, September 1750; son of Shepard and Mary (Goddard) Kollock; married Susan Arnett, June 5, 1777; father of eight children; died July 28, 1839.

In 1777 Kollock served as a first lieutenant in the 2nd Artillery Regiment of the Continental Army. He published the *New Jersey Journal* in 1779, the *U.S. Almanac* from 1779 until 1783, and the *New York Gazetteer* from 1783 to 1786. He established the *Political Intelligencer* in 1783, changing its name to *New Jersey Journal* in 1786 and publishing it until 1818. He was the publisher of the first New York City directory. During the period 1789–91 he published *Christian's, Scholar's, and Farmer's Magazine.*

Kollock served as judge of the Court of Common Pleas of Essex County, New Jersey, from 1804 to 1839, and as postmaster of Elizabeth, New Jersey, from 1820 to 1829. Among his published works was *Poems on the Capture of General Burgoyne* (1782). He died in Philadelphia.

★★★★★

LAMBERT, John: senator, congressman
Born Lambertville, New Jersey, February 24, 1746; died February 4, 1823.

Lambert, a farmer by trade, was elected to the New Jersey General Assembly in 1780, serving until 1785. He also served briefly in the Assembly in 1788. From 1790 to 1804 he was a member of the New Jersey Council, serving as its vice president from 1801 to 1804. He was acting governor of New York in 1802–03.

A Democrat, Lambert served in the United States House of Representatives during the 9th and 10th congresses (1805–09). For the next six years he was a member of the United States Senate. He died near Lambertville and was buried in Barber's Burying Ground in Delaware Township, Hunterdon County, New Jersey.

LINN, James: congressman
Born Bedminster Township, New Jersey, 1749; died January 5, 1821.

Linn graduated from the College of New Jersey (now Princeton) in 1769. After his admission to the bar in 1772, he began practicing law in Trenton, New Jersey. He served as judge of the Somerset County Court of Common Pleas and in 1776 was a member of the New Jersey Provincial Congress.

During the Revolutionary War, Linn served as captain and, later, as first major of the Somerset County militia. During this time also (in 1777) he was a member of the New Jersey Council.

Linn was a member of the New Jersey

General Assembly in 1790–91 and served another term in the New Jersey Council from 1793 to 1797. A Democrat, he was a member of the United States House of Representatives from 1799 to 1801 (6th Congress). He was appointed by President Jefferson as supervisor of revenue in 1801 and served for eight years. From 1809 to 1820 he was secretary of state of New Jersey.

Linn died in Trenton and was buried in the Lamington Presbyterian Church Cemetery in Somerset County.

LINN, John: congressman

Born near Johnsonburg, New Jersey, December 3, 1763; died January 5, 1821.

Linn, who attended common schools in Sussex County, New Jersey, served as a private and as a sergeant during the Revolutionary War. He was a member of the New Jersey General Assembly from 1801 to 1804. He served as judge of the Court of Common Pleas for the next sixteen years. Also during this time, in 1812, he was sheriff of Sussex County.

From 1817 to 1821 Linn was a New Jersey delegate to the United States House of Representatives (15th and 16th congresses). He died in Washington, D.C., and was buried near Franklin Furnace, New Jersey, in North Hardyston Cemetery.

LIVINGSTON, William: governor of New Jersey

Born Albany, New York, November 1723; son of Philip and Catharine (Van Brugh) Livingston; married Susanna French, 1745; father of thirteen children (including Henry Brockholst, Susanna, and Sarah [Mrs. John Jay]); died July 25, 1790.

Livingston graduated from Yale in 1741 and was admitted to the New Jersey bar seven years later. In 1752 he was a counsel for the defendants in the great chancery suit between the proprietors of East Jersey and settlers.

In 1752 Livingston published the weekly paper *The Independent Reflector*. He was a member of the Essex County Committee of Correspondence in 1774, and that year and the next he represented New Jersey in the Continental Congress. He served as brigadier general in command of the New York militia in 1776 and was the first governor of New Jersey, serving from 1776 to 1790. In 1787 he was a member of the United States Constitutional Convention.

Livingston wrote a poem, "Philosophic Solitude," in 1747. "A Soliloquy" was written in 1770. He was editor of *A Digest of Laws of New York*, the first edition of which was published in 1752 and the second ten years later. He received an honorary LL.D. from Yale in 1778. He died in Elizabethtown, New Jersey.

★★★★★

MacWHORTER, Alexander: clergyman

Born New Castle County, Delaware, July 15, 1735; son of Hugh and Jane MacWhorter; married Mary Cumming, October 1759; died July 20, 1807.

MacWhorter graduated from the College of New Jersey (now Princeton) in 1757 and studied theology under the Reverend William Tennent. Licensed to preach by the Presbytery of New Brunswick in 1758, he was ordained to the ministry of the Presbyterian Church in 1759 and was pastor of a church in Newark, New Jersey, from that year until his death.

In 1775 MacWhorter was commissioned by the Continental Congress to go to North Carolina to win over Loyalists. He was present at General George Washington's council which recommended crossing the Delaware River in 1778 and served as chaplain of General Henry Knox's brigade in 1778–79. On many occasions he was forced to flee from the British because of his patriotic activities.

MacWhorter helped frame the constitution of the Presbyterian Church in the United States and was a charter trustee of the church's general assembly until 1803. He held an honorary D.D. from Yale. He was the author of *A Series of Sermons upon the*

Most Important Principles of Our Holy Religion, 1803, and *A Century Sermon,* 1807.

MOODY, James: British spy, Loyalist
Born New Jersey, 1744; father of at least three children; died April 6, 1809.

A farmer at the outbreak of the Revolution, Moody objected to the New Jersey law requiring the oath of allegiance. He enlisted in a brigade of Loyalists under the command of General Courtland Skinner in 1777 and was commissioned an ensign in 1779. Ordered arrested on sight by the New Jersey government in 1777, his property was confiscated by New Jersey in 1778.

Moody spied on the troop movements of Washington, Sullivan, and Gates before being captured at Englishtown, New Jersey, in 1780; however, he escaped soon afterward. Promoted to lieutenant in 1781, he plotted other activities, such as the capture of Continental Congress papers, but his plans were revealed by his confederates before he could carry them out.

Moody went to England in 1782, was granted a pension of 100 pounds a year, and then went to Nova Scotia in 1786, where he served as a colonel in the Nova Scotia militia from that year until his death. He was author of *Narrative* in 1783. He died in Weymouth, Nova Scotia.

MORGAN, James: congressman
Born Amboy, New Jersey, December 29, 1756; died November 11, 1822.

Morgan, who attended public schools, served as an officer in the New Jersey Regiment, Continental Army, during the Revolution. He attended the Pennsylvania General Assembly, in Philadelphia, from 1794 to 1799. A Federalist, he was a New Jersey delegate to the House of Representatives during the 12th Congress (1811–13). He later engaged in farming and was commissioned a major general in the New Jersey militia. He died in South Amboy and was buried in a private cemetery in Morgan, New Jersey.

MORRIS, Robert: judge
Born New Brunswick, New Jersey, circa 1745; son of Chief Justice Robert Hunter Morris; died June 2, 1815.

Admitted to the bar in 1770, Morris was licensed as a counselor in 1773. He served as chief justice of the New Jersey Supreme Court from 1777 to 1779 and as judge of the New Jersey District Court from 1789 to 1814. He died in New Brunswick.

MOTT, James: congressman
Born near Middletown, New Jersey, January 18, 1739; died October 18, 1823.

Mott, educated privately, was a farmer by trade. He was a captain in the 2nd Regiment of the Monmouth County (New Jersey) militia in 1775. He served in the New Jersey House of Assembly from 1776 to 1779 and was treasurer of the State of New Jersey from 1783 to 1799. A Democrat, he was a New Jersey delegate to the United States House of Representatives from 1801 to 1805 and was a Democratic presidential elector in 1808. He died near Middletown and was buried in the Middletown Baptist Churchyard.

★★★★★

NEILSON, John: army officer, Continental congressman
Born Raritan Landing, New Jersey, March 11, 1745; son of Dr. John and Joanna (Coejeman) Neilson; married Catherine Voorhees, December 31, 1768; father of eleven children (including James); died March 3, 1833.

Neilson, who attended the University of Pennsylvania, was commissioned a captain during the Revolutionary War and was made a colonel by the Pennsylvania Provincial Congress in 1775. The next year he received a commission as colonel in the 2nd Regiment of the Middlesex militia, followed by a commission as brigadier general in the New Jersey militia in 1777. He represented New Jersey in the Continental Congress in 1778–79. The latter year he was placed in command of the New Jersey militia at Elizabethtown and Newark. He then became deputy quartermaster general for New Jersey and served from 1780 to 1783.

After the war Neilson attended the New Jersey Convention which ratified the United States Constitution (1790), served as a judge in the New Jersey Court of Common Pleas (1795–98), and participated in the state assembly (1800–01). He served twenty-five years (1796–1821) as register-recorder of New Brunswick. In other service he was a trustee of Rutgers College from 1782 to 1833 and an elder of the First Presbyterian Church of New Brunswick. General Lafayette presented him with a sword in 1824. He died in New Brunswick and was buried in Van Liew Cemetery there.

★★★★★

OGDEN, Aaron: senator, governor of New Jersey

Born Elizabethtown, (now Elizabeth), New Jersey, December 3, 1756; son of Robert and Phebe (Hatfield) Ogden; married Elizabeth Chetwood, October 27, 1787; father of seven children; died April 19, 1839.

Ogden graduated from the College of New Jersey (now Princeton) in 1773 and was a teacher at Barber's Grammar School in Elizabeth until 1775. He served as a brigadier major in the 1st Regiment of the New Jersey militia from 1776 to 1783. He was admitted to the New Jersey bar in 1784. Besides commanding the New Jersey 15th Infantry from 1797 to 1800, he was also a lieutenant colonel in the 11th Infantry.

A member of the Federalist party, Ogden filled a vacancy in the United States Senate, representing New Jersey, from 1801 to 1803. In 1807 he was a member of the New York–New Jersey Boundary Commission. In 1811 he built the steamer *Sea Horse,* which ran between Elizabeth and New York City. He was governor of New Jersey in 1812 and 1813. In 1815 he applied to the New Jersey legislature for a monopoly on steamboat navigation between Elizabethtown and New York City, which was granted. He was

a litigant in the famous United States Supreme Court case *Gibbons vs. Ogden,* 1824, in which John Marshall handed down the decision stating that there could be no monopolies in interstate commerce.

Ogden was appointed collector of customs of Jersey City, New Jersey, in 1829. He died in Elizabethtown ten years later and was buried in the First Presbyterian Church Burial Ground there.

OGDEN, David: jurist

Born Newark, New Jersey, 1707; son of Josiah and Catharine (Hardenbroeck) Ogden; married Gertrude Gouverneur; father of eleven children (including Samuel, Nicholas, Sarah, and Isaac); died 1798.

Ogden graduated from Yale in 1728. From 1751 to 1774 he was a member of His Majesty's Council for the Province of New Jersey. A leading lawyer of New Jersey and New York, he was appointed to the Stamp Act Congress in 1765; however, he disagreed with its recommendations.

Ogden was an associate justice of the New Jersey Supreme Court from 1772 to 1776, but because of his Loyalist leanings, he was deprived of that position. After his property was confiscated by the rebels, he escaped to New York, where he became a member of the Board of Refugees. He went to England in 1783 but returned to America seven years later. He died in Whitestone, Long Island, New York.

OGDEN, Uzal: clergyman

Born Newark, New Jersey, 1744; son of Uzal and Elizabeth Charlotte (Thebaut) Ogden; married Mary Gouverneur, 1776; father of six children; died November 4, 1822.

Ogden was ordained to the ministry of the Episcopal Church by the Bishop of London in 1773. He preached occasionally at the Trinity Church in Newark, New Jersey, and although he was asked to become rector, he did not accept until 1788. Eleven years later he was elected the first bishop of New Jersey, but he was refused consecration by the General Convention of New Jersey. He had a reputation for doctrinal laxity and was suspended in 1805 after a dispute with his congregation. He then became a member of the New York Presbytery.

Ogden wrote a two-volume work, *Antidote to Deism,* which was published in 1795. That same year he was awarded an honorary D.D. by Princeton. He died in Newark.

★★★★★

PATERSON, William: associate justice of the United States Supreme Court, senator, governor of New Jersey
Born County Antrim, Ireland, December 24, 1745; son of Richard and Mary Paterson; married Cornelia Bell, February 9, 1779; second marriage to Euphemia White, 1785; father of three children (including Cornelia); died September 9, 1806.

Paterson graduated from the College of New Jersey (now Princeton) in 1763, then studied law under Richard Stockton. He was a founder of the Princeton literary organization known as the Well Meaning Society (now called the Cliosophic Society) and was an active member from 1765 to 1768.

Paterson was admitted to the New Jersey bar in 1768 and established a legal practice in New Bromley, returning to Princeton in 1772. He was a Somerset County delegate to the Provincial Congress in 1775 and 1776, acting as secretary the latter year. He was attorney general of the state of New Jersey from 1776 to 1783 and a member of the New Jersey Senate in 1776–77. In 1776 he was also a delegate to the New Jersey State Constitutional Convention.

In 1779 Paterson purchased a farm on the Raritan River near New Brunswick. Eight years later he served as a New Jersey delegate to the United States Constitutional Convention in Philadelphia. There he introduced the New Jersey Plan, which proposed the establishment of a unicameral legislature with equal representation for each state. The dispute between the supporters of the New Jersey and Virginia plans resulted in a compromise in which a bicameral legislature was created (the Senate, with equal representation for states, and the House of Representatives, with members chosen on the basis of population). Paterson signed the United States Constitution and advocated its adoption in New Jersey.

Paterson was a Democratic member of the United States Senate from 1789 to November 13, 1790. He was governor of New Jersey from 1790 to 1793; during his term, he revised all the pre-Revolutionary English laws still in force in the state. As an associate justice of the United States Supreme Court from 1793 to 1806, he presided over the treason trials of participants in the Whiskey Rebellion. The most notable trial was that of Matthew Lyon, who was accused of violation of the Sedition Laws of 1798. Paterson also presided at the trial of Samuel Ogden and William Smith for violation of the Neutrality Laws in giving aid to South American patriot Francisco Miranda.

The city of Paterson, New Jersey, is named in honor of William Paterson, who died in Albany, New York. He was buried in the Van Rensselaer Manor House vault near Albany.

PENNINGTON, William Sandford: governor of New Jersey
Born Newark, New Jersey, 1757; son of Samuel and Mary (Sandford) Pennington; married Phoebe Wheeler, circa 1786; second marriage to Elizabeth Pierson; died September 17, 1826.

At the age of twenty, Pennington became a sergeant in the 2nd Regiment of Artillery of the Continental Army. He was commissioned a second lieutenant, serving from 1778 to 1780, and eventually mustered out as a brevet captain.

Pennington was a member of the New Jersey Assembly in 1797, 1798, and 1799 and a member of the New Jersey Council in 1801 and 1802. He was licensed an attorney-at-law in 1803 and became clerk of Essex County. In 1804 he was elected to fill a vacancy in the New Jersey Supreme Court, in which he served as justice and recorder from 1806 to 1813. From 1813 to 1815 he was governor and chancellor of New Jersey and during the last years of his life was a judge of the United States District Court for New Jersey. He died in Newark, his birthplace and longtime home.

PETTIT, Charles: Continental congressman, businessman
Born near Amwell, Hunterdon County, New Jersey, 1736; son of John Pettit; married Sarah Reed, April 5, 1758; father of four children (including Elizabeth and Theodosia); died September 4, 1806.

Pettit received a private classical education. In 1767 he was appointed a New Jersey provincial surrogate, and from 1769 to 1778 he served as surrogate, keeper, and register of records of the Province of New Jersey. He was a clerk of the New Jersey Governor's Council and, from 1769 to 1771, clerk of the New Jersey Supreme Court. He was admitted to the New Jersey bar as an attorney in 1770 and as a counselor in 1773. He served as deputy secretary of the Province of New Jersey. In 1771, while serving as a lieutenant colonel in the New Jersey militia, he was made an aide to Governor William Franklin.

From 1776 to 1778 Pettit served as the first secretary of state of New Jersey. During the first year of that term, he was a colonel and an aide to Governor William Livingston. He served three years under General Nathanael Greene in the Continental Army as assistant quartermaster general before becoming an importer in Philadelphia.

Pettit was a member of the Pennsylvania Assembly in 1783–84 and chairman of a committee of merchants to promote national commerce. He was a member of the Continental Congress from 1785 to 1787. Recognized as a fiscal expert, he established Pennsylvania's funding system and, in 1790–91, was delegated to present Pennsylvania's Revolutionary War claims against the federal government to Congress.

Pettit served as president of the Insurance Company of North America (of which he was an original director) from 1796 to 1798 and again from 1799 to 1806. From 1791 to 1802 he was a member of the American Philosophical Society. He died in Philadelphia.

PRIME, Benjamin Youngs: physician, balladeer
Born Huntington, Long Island, New York, December 20, 1733; son of the Reverend Ebenezer and Experience (Youngs) Prime; married Mary Wheelwright Greaton, December 18, 1774; father of five children (including Ebenezer and Nathaniel Scudder); died October 31, 1791.

Prime graduated from the College of New Jersey (now Princeton) in 1751. He was a tutor at his alma mater in 1756–57, then established a medical practice in Easthampton, Long Island. He received an honorary A.M. from Yale in 1760 and an M.D. from the University of Leyden, Holland, in 1764. He upheld the American cause in the colonial conflict.

Prime was the author of *The Patriot Muse, or Poems on Some of the Principal Events of the Late War . . . by an American Gentleman* (1764). About three years after this publication he wrote "A Song for the Sons of Liberty" in New York. Just before his death in Huntington, Long Island, he wrote "Columbia's Glory or British Pride Humbled . . . a Poem on the American Revolution."

★★★★★

SCHUREMAN, James: Continental congressman, senator
Born New Brunswick, New Jersey, February 12, 1756; died January 22, 1824.

Schureman became a merchant after his graduation in 1775 from Rutgers College. During the Revolutionary War he served in the army. He began his long career in New Jersey politics with membership in the state General Assembly in 1783–85 and again in 1788. He also was a delegate to the New Jersey Provincial Congress in 1786 and a member of the Continental Congress in 1786–87. A Federalist, he was a New Jersey delegate to the 1st, 5th, and 13th congresses of the United States House of Representatives (1789–91, 1797–99, and 1813–15).

Schureman became president of New Brunswick in 1792. He represented New Jersey in the United States Senate from 1799 until his resignation on February 16, 1801. He then held the office of mayor of New Brunswick from 1801 until 1813 and again from 1821 to 1824. He also served on the New Jersey State Council in 1808 and 1810. He died in New Brunswick and was buried in the First Reformed Church Cemetery there.

SCUDDER, John Anderson: congressman, physician

Born Freehold, Monmouth County, New Jersey, March 22, 1759; died November 6, 1836.

Scudder graduated from Princeton in 1775, studied medicine, and began a practice in Monmouth County. During the Revolutionary War he served as a surgeon's mate in the 1st Regiment of Monmouth County. He was secretary of the New Jersey Medical Society in 1788–89. From 1801 to 1807 he served in the New Jersey General Assembly. A Democrat, he filled a vacancy in the United States House of Representatives on October 31, 1810, and served until 1811. He moved to Kentucky after 1810 and then to Daviess County, Indiana, in 1819. He died in Washington, Indiana, and was buried in the Old City Cemetery.

SCUDDER, Nathaniel: army officer, Continental congressman

Born Monmouth County, New Jersey, May 10, 1733; son of Jacob and Abia (Rowe) Scudder; married Isabella Anderson, March 23, 1752; father of five children; died October 16, 1781.

In 1751 Scudder graduated from the College of New Jersey (now Princeton). He was an elder in the Tennent Church near Freehold, New Jersey, and a trustee of Princeton University from 1778 until 1781.

Scudder became a member of the local Committee of Safety around the time of the Revolution and was a delegate to the First New Jersey Provincial Congress, which was held in New Brunswick in 1774. In 1776 he held the office of speaker of the New Jersey General Assembly and was a lieutenant colonel in the 1st Monmouth County Regiment of the New Jersey militia. He was commissioned a colonel five years later.

From 1777 to 1779 Scudder was a delegate to the Continental Congress. He was present at the Battle of Monmouth. His most important service was writing a letter in 1778 to John Hart, speaker of the New Jersey legislature, strongly urging that the state's delegates to the Continental Congress be empowered to ratify and sign the Articles of Confederation. He was killed while resisting an invading party of the British Army at Blacks Point, near Shrewsbury, New Jersey. He was buried in Tennent Churchyard, Monmouth Battlefield, New Jersey.

SERGEANT, Jonathan Dickinson: Continental congressman

Born Newark, New Jersey, 1746; son of Jonathan and Abigail (Dickinson) Sergeant; married Margaret Spencer, March 14, 1775; second marriage to Elizabeth Rittenhouse, December 20, 1788; father of at least eleven children (including John and Thomas); died October 8, 1793.

Sergeant graduated from the College of New Jersey (now Princeton) in 1762, attended the University of Pennsylvania the following year, and was admitted to the bar in 1767. He became a surrogate in Somerset County, New Jersey, in 1769. A member of the Sons of Liberty and active in the Stamp Act controversy, he was secretary of the first and second New Jersey provincial congresses (1774, 1775). In 1775 he also held the office of treasurer of the Province of New Jersey.

Sergeant was a delegate to the Continental Congress from New Jersey from February to June 1776 and again from November

30, 1776, until 1777. After moving to Philadelphia in 1776, he served as attorney general of Pennsylvania from 1777 to 1780. He was known for the extra-legal methods he used in prosecuting Loyalists. In 1777 he became identified with the McKean-Bryan "Constitutionalists." He also served on the Council of Safety that year.

When the Connecticut-Pennsylvania dispute was arbitrated at Trenton, New Jersey, in 1782, Sergeant represented Pennsylvania. He also acted as counsel for the state in the Wyoming land controversy. In 1788 he defended the Anti-Federalist editor Eleazar Oswald. He died in Philadelphia and was buried in Laurel Hill Cemetery there.

SINNICKSON, Thomas: congressman
Born near Salem, New Jersey, December 21, 1744; died May 15, 1817.

Sinnickson, a merchant, served as a captain in the Continental Army during the Revolutionary War. He held several local offices and was a member of the New Jersey General Assembly in 1777, 1782, 1784–85, and 1787–88. He represented his state in the 1st and 5th congresses of the United States House of Representatives (1789–91 and 1797–99) and was a Federalist presidential elector. He died in Salem and was buried in St. John's Episcopal Cemetery.

SMITH, Isaac: congressman
Born Trenton, New Jersey, 1740; died August 29, 1807.

Smith graduated from Princeton in 1755 and later studied medicine. He was a member of the Princeton faculty from 1755 to 1758. He practiced medicine in Trenton and was a colonel in the Hunterdon County militia during the years 1776–77. After that he began a long term as an associate justice in the New Jersey Supreme Court (1777–1804). He was a Federalist member of the 4th Congress of the United States House of Representatives (1795–97), and in 1797 was appointed by President Washington a commissioner to treat with the Seneca Indians.

Smith was a Democratic presidential elector in 1800. In 1805 he became the first president of the Trenton Banking Company, holding this position until 1807. He died that year in Trenton and was buried in the First Presbyterian Churchyard.

SMITH, Richard: Continental congressman, diarist
Born Burlington, New Jersey, March 22, 1735; son of Richard and Abigail (Rapier or Raper) Smith; married Elizabeth Rodman, June 5, 1762; father of five children (including Richard R.); died September 17, 1803.

Admitted to the New Jersey bar about 1760, Smith was commissioned clerk of Burlington County, New Jersey, in 1762. He was a proprietor who received a land grant of 6,900 acres (the "Otego Patent") in New York in 1768.

A delegate to the Continental Congress from 1774 to 1776, Smith kept an historically useful diary of congressional proceedings from September 12, 1775, to October 1, 1775, and from December 12, 1775, to March 30, 1776. He signed the Olive Branch petition to the King in 1775. A member of the New Jersey Council in 1776, he was treasurer of New Jersey in 1776–77. He died near Natchez, Mississippi, and was buried in the town cemetery.

SMITH, Samuel Stanhope: clergyman, college president
Born Pequea, Lancaster County, Pennsylvania, March 16, 1750; son of the Reverend Robert and Elizabeth (Blair) Smith; married Ann Witherspoon; father of nine children; died August 21, 1819.

Smith graduated from the College of New Jersey (now Princeton) in 1769. Licensed to preach by the Presbyterian Church in western Virginia in 1773, he later founded Hampden-Sydney Academy (later College) and was president there until 1779. He was a professor of moral philosophy at the College of New Jersey from 1779 until 1795, then served as president until 1812. In 1795 he called to the college the first undergraduate teacher of chemistry and natural science in the United States.

Smith was the author of works on a variety of subjects, including *Causes of the Variety of the Complexion and Figure of the Human Species,* 1788; *Oration on the Death of Washington,* 1800; *Sermons,* 1801; *Lectures on the Evidences of the Christian Religion,* 1809; *Love of Praise,* 1810; *Lectures . . . on the Subjects of Moral and Political Philosophy* (two volumes), 1812; *A Continuation of Ramsay's History of the United States;* and *The Principles of Natural and Revealed Religion.* He died in Baltimore at the age of sixty-nine.

SOUTHARD, Henry: congressman, farmer
Born Hempstead, Long Island, New York, October 7, 1747; father of Isaac and Samuel Lewis; died May 22, 1842.

Southard, who attended common schools, served as a private and later a wagon master during the Revolution. He became a farmer after the war and first assumed public office in 1787, when he began a five-year tenure as a justice of the peace. He served in the New Jersey General Assembly from 1797 to 1799 and again in 1811. A Democrat, he was sent by New Jersey to the United States House of Representatives for the 7th through the 11th congresses (1801–11) and the 14th through the 16th congresses (1815–21), retiring from public life after his last term. He died in Basking Ridge, Somerset County, New Jersey, and was buried in Basking Ridge Cemetery.

SPENCER, Elihu: clergyman
Born East Haddam, Connecticut, February 12, 1721; son of Isaac and Mary (Selden) Spencer; married Joanna Eaton, October 15, 1749 (or 1750); father of two children; died December 27, 1784.

Spencer graduated from Yale in 1746. After being ordained to the ministry of the Presbyterian Church in 1748, he served briefly as a missionary to the Oneidas. He was pastor of the Presbyterian Church in Elizabethtown, New Jersey, from 1750 to 1756 and in Jamaica, New York, from 1756 to 1758. He settled in Trenton, New Jersey, in 1764 and served as a pastor there for the last twenty years of his life.

Spencer was a trustee of the College of New Jersey (now Princeton) from 1752 to 1784 and synod delegate to the Congregational and Presbyterian Council from 1770 to 1775. The latter year he visited (with Alexander MacWhorter) the more isolated portions of the South to inform the people about the movement for independence and obtain support for the American cause. During the war (1777–81) he served as a chaplain for hospitals in the vicinity of Trenton.

Spencer was awarded an honorary D.D. by the University of Pennsylvania in 1782. He died in Trenton and was buried in a churchyard there.

STEVENS, John: continental congressman
Born Perth Amboy, New Jersey, 1715; died May 10, 1792.

Stevens was a merchant and ship owner, trading with the West Indies and Madeira. He was also a large landowner and mine owner in Hunterdon, Union, and Somerset counties in New Jersey. A member of the General Colonial Assembly in 1751, he was active in raising troops and money for the Crown Point expedition (1755) during the French and Indian War. He helped build blockhouses at Drake's Fort, Normenach, and Philipsburg. A member of the defense committee to protect New York and New Jersey against Indian attack, he was commissioner to the Indians in 1758. He was also paymaster for Colonel Schuyler's Regiment (the "Old Blues") from 1756 to 1760.

In 1765 Stevens was a member of the Committee of Four which prevented the issue of stamps under the Stamp Act in New York City. He was appointed commissioner to define the boundary line between New York and New Jersey in 1774. Vice president of the New Jersey Council from 1770 to

1782, he served as president of the Council of East Jersey Proprietors in 1783. He was a New Jersey delegate to the Continental Congress in 1783–84 and presided over the New Jersey Constitutional Convention in 1787.

Stevens died in Hoboken, New Jersey, and was buried in Frame Meeting House Cemetery in Bethlehem Township, Hunterdon County.

STEVENS, John: engineer, inventor
Born New York City, 1749; son of John and Elizabeth (Alexander) Stevens; married Rachel Cox, October 17, 1782; father of at least seven children (including John Cox, Robert Livingston, Edwin Augustus, Mary, and Harriet); died March 6, 1838.

Stevens graduated from Columbia University in 1768, then began studying law. He was appointed an attorney in New York City in 1771. He advanced from captain to colonel in the Continental Army, obtaining loans for the military during the Revolution. He was loan commissioner for Hunterdon County, New Jersey, and state treasurer from 1776 to 1779. He served as surveyor general for the Eastern Division of New Jersey in 1782–83.

Instrumental in framing the first patent laws in 1790, Stevens became a consulting engineer for the Manhattan Company (organized to furnish New York City with an adequate water supply) about 1800. He was named president of the Bergen Turnpike Company in 1802 and received a patent for a multitubular boiler the next year.

After Stevens's steamboat, "Little Juliana" (operated by twin screw propellers), was put into use on the Hudson River in 1804, he attempted to operate a regular line of steamboats on the Hudson between New York City and Albany and on other inland rivers. However, his plans were halted by lawsuits. He sent the "Phoenix," the first seagoing steamboat in the world, to Philadelphia in 1809. He then built the "Juliana" and started a regular ferry service in 1811.

Obtaining the first American railroad authorization from the New Jersey Assembly in 1815, Stevens was then authorized by the Pennsylvania legislature to build the Pennsylvania Railroad (1823). He designed and built an experimental locomotive—the first American-made steam locomotive, though never used for actual service—on his estate in Hoboken, New Jersey, in 1825. He proposed a vehicular tunnel under the Hudson as well as an elevated railroad system for New York City. He died in Hoboken.

STEWART, Charles: Continental congressman
Born Gortlea, County Donegal, Ireland, 1729. died June 24, 1800.

Stewart arrived in America in 1750 and became a farmer. He was commissioned a lieutenant colonel in the Hunterdon County, New Jersey, militia in 1771 and was active in pre-Revolutionary movements. He was commissioned colonel of a battalion of Minutemen in 1776 and appointed commissary general of issues by the Continental Congress in 1777; he was a New Jersey delegate to the Congress in 1784–85. He died in Flemington, New Jersey, and was buried in Old Stone Church in Bethlehem Township, Hunterdon County.

STOCKTON, Richard: Continental congressman
Born Princeton, New Jersey, October 1, 1730; son of John and Abigail (Phillips) Stockton; married Annis Boudinot; father of six children (including Richard and Julia [Stockton] Rush); died February 28, 1781.

Stockton graduated from the College of New Jersey (now Princeton) in 1748. Admitted to the New Jersey bar in 1754, he became a trustee of the College of New Jersey about 1765. He was a member of the New Jersey Executive Council and was named judge of the New Jersey Supreme Court in 1774.

Stockton drafted and sent to Lord Dartmouth "a plan of self-government for America, independent of Parliament, without renouncing allegiance to the Crown," in 1774. He was elected to the Continental Congress in 1776 and served on a number of committees. He was a signer of the Declaration of Independence.

Stockton visited the Northern Army with George Clymer in 1776 and was chairman of a committee to inspect the Northern Army at Ticonderoga. He was taken prisoner by the British November 30, 1776, and released on December 29. He died in Princeton before the end of the war and was buried in Quaker Cemetery there.

SYMMES, John Cleves: Continental congressman, pioneer, jurist
Born Southold, Long Island, New York, July 21, 1742; son of the Reverend Timothy and Mary (Cleves) Symmes; married Anna Tuttle; second marriage to Mrs. Mary Halsey; third marriage to Susanna Livingston; father of at least two children; died February 26, 1814.

Chairman of the Sussex County, New Jersey, Committee of Correspondence in 1774, Symmes served as a colonel in the New Jersey militia the next year. He was an associate justice of the New Jersey Supreme Court in 1777 and 1783 and served in the Continental Congress from New Jersey in 1785–86.

In 1788 Symmes received a grant of one million acres in Ohio between the Miami and Little Miami rivers ("The Miami Purchase"). He became a judge of the Northwest Territory that year and founded a settlement at North Bend (Ohio) in 1789. He also founded a colony around what is now Cincinnati, which became a significant military and trading outpost in the West. He died in Cincinnati.

★★★★★

TENNENT, William: clergyman
Born County Armagh, Ireland, June 3, 1705; son of William and Catherine (Kennedy) Tennent; married

Catherine Noble, August 23, 1738; father of at least three children; died March 8, 1777.

Sometime prior to 1730 Tennent was taken for dead and nearly buried alive as a result of an apparent cessation of his bodily activities; he later claimed to have experienced certain supernatural phenomena during this suspension. He studied theology under his brother Gilbert and was licensed to preach by the Presbyterian Church in 1731. He served as pastor of the Presbyterian Church in Freehold, New Jersey, from 1732 until his death in 1777. He was buried in the churchyard there.

THOMSON, Mark: congressman
Born Norriston Township, near Norristown, Pennsylvania, 1739; died December 14, 1803.

Thomson, a miller by profession, was justice of the peace of Sussex County, New Jersey, in 1773. He was a member of the Provincial Convention in 1774 and a member of the Provincial Congress in 1775.

Thomson was commissioned a lieutenant colonel in the 1st Regiment of the Sussex County militia in 1775. The following year he served as a lieutenant colonel in Colonel Charles Stewart's battalion of Minutemen, as colonel of the 1st Regiment of the Sussex County militia, and as colonel of the Battalion of Detached New Jersey Militia.

Thomson served in the New Jersey General Assembly in 1779 and on the state council from 1786 to 1788. In 1793 he was appointed lieutenant colonel and aide-de-camp on the staff of Governor Richard Howell of New Jersey. A Federalist, he was a delegate from New Jersey to the United States House of Representatives from 1795 to 1799 (4th and 5th congresses).

Thomson died in Marksboro, Sussex (later Warren) County, New Jersey, and was buried in the Presbyterian Church Cemetery.

TUCKER, Ebenezer: congressman
Born Tuckers Beach, New Jersey, November 15, 1758; died September 5, 1845.

Tucker attended common schools. During the Revolutionary War he served under General George Washington at the Battle of Long Island and in other engagements. Later he served as judge of the Court of Common Pleas, a justice of the Court of Quarter Sessions, and, from 1820 to 1825, judge of the Orphans Court of Burlington County.

Moving to what is now Tuckerton, New Jersey, a town named after him, Tucker became a merchant and ship-builder. He served as postmaster of Tuckerton from 1806 to 1825 and from 1831 to 1845. He sat as a New Jersey delegate to the United States House of Representatives in the 19th and 20th congresses (1825–29). He was the first collector of revenue for the Port of Tuckerton.

Tucker died at age eighty-six in Tuckerton and was buried in Old Methodist Cemetery.

★★★★★

WARD, Thomas: congressman
Born Newark, New Jersey, circa 1759; died March 4, 1842.

Ward studied law, was admitted to the bar, and established a legal practice in Newark. He advanced from captain to major during the Whiskey Insurrection in 1794. He was a sheriff of Essex County, New Jersey, in 1797, elected a judge of the Essex County Court in 1804, and reelected in 1809.

A member of the legislative council in 1808–09, Ward, a Democrat, was a New Jersey delegate to the United States House of Representatives for the 13th–14th congresses (1813–17). He served as a senior officer in the New Jersey Cavalry. He died in Newark and was buried in the First Presbyterian Churchyard there.

WILSON, Peter: educator, legislator
Born Ordiquhill, Scotland, November 23, 1746; no record of first marriage; second marriage to Catherine Duryea; father of five daughters and two sons; died August 1, 1825.

A graduate of the University of Aberdeen in Scotland, Wilson came to America in 1763. He was principal of the Hackensack Academy in New Jersey. He served as Bergen County representative to the New Jersey Assembly from 1777 to 1781 and again in 1787, and was selected in 1783 to revise and codify New Jersey laws.

Wilson was professor of Greek and Latin at Columbia from 1789 until 1792, when he became principal of Erasmus Hall Academy in Flatbush, Long Island, New York. From 1797 to 1805 he served as titular head of the academy. He taught again at Columbia from 1797 to 1820 as professor of the Greek and Latin languages and of Grecian and Roman antiquities.

In 1810 Wilson wrote *Rules of Latin Prosody for the Use of Schools,* and the following year he published *Introduction to Greek Prosody . . . with an Appendix on the Metres of Horace, Adapted to the Use of Beginners.* He was awarded an honorary M.A. by Brown University in 1786 and an honorary LL.D. by Union College in 1798. He died in New Barbadoes, New Jersey.

WITHERSPOON, John: clergyman, college president, Continental congressman
Born Gifford, Haddingtonshire, Scotland, February 5, 1723; son of the Reverend James and Anne (Walker) Witherspoon; married Elizabeth Montgomery, September 2, 1748; second marriage to Ann Dill, May 30, 1791; father of twelve children; died November 15, 1794.

At the age of sixteen, Witherspoon received an M.A. from the University of Edinburgh, Scotland, followed by a divinity degree in 1743. That year he was licensed to preach by the Haddington, Scotland, Presbytery. Ordained in 1745 to the Presbyterian ministry, he became a minister in Beith, Ayrshire, and later (1757–68) was pastor at Paisley. During this time (1764) he received an honorary D.D. from the University of St. Andrews.

Witherspoon was a prolific writer on controversial religious subjects during the years 1745 through 1768, taking a conservative position. In 1758 he was moderator of the Synod of Glasgow and Ayr. Transplanted to America, Witherspoon became president of the College of New Jersey (now Princeton) in 1768, serving until his death. He expanded the college, introducing the study of French and philosophy, and also became a leader of the Presbyterian Church in America.

In 1775 Witherspoon was a member of the Committee of Correspondence from Somerset County, and in 1776 he sat in the New Jersey Provincial Congress. He represented New Jersey in the Continental Congress from 1776 to 1782 and signed the Declaration of Independence. He was a member of the Board of War, a secret committee on the conduct of the war, in 1778. He belonged to the state council in 1780 and drafted instructions to the American peace commissioners in 1781. He was opposed to the unrestricted printing of paper money and to the issuing of bonds without provisions for their retirement.

Witherspoon was a member of the New Jersey House of Representatives in 1783 and again in 1789, serving between terms (in 1787) as a member of the New Jersey Convention to ratify the United States Constitution. He assisted in reorganization of the Presbyterian Church from 1785 until 1789 and was responsible for introducing new catechisms, credo, and order of worship. In 1789 he was moderator for the first Presbyterian National General Assembly.

Witherspoon's works include *Ecclesiastical Characteristics* (1753), an attack on humanist influences in the Presbyterian Church. His nine volumes of collected writings were published posthumously in 1815 in Edinburgh. He died near Princeton, New Jersey, and was buried in the President's Lot of the Witherspoon Street Cemetery, in Princeton.

WRIGHT, Patience Lovell: sculptor

Born Bordentown, New Jersey, 1725; married Joseph Wright, March 20, 1748; mother of three children, including Phoebe and Joseph; died March 23, 1786.

As a modeler in wax, Wright went to London, England, in 1772 and opened an exhibition room on Cockspur Street. She modeled a bas-relief of Benjamin Franklin and busts of King George III, Queen Charlotte and Lord Chatham. In an article in *London Magazine* in 1775, she was called "The Promethean Modeller." Wright is believed to have sent British military plans to Benjamin Franklin during the American Revolution. She died in London in 1786.

★★★★★★★★★★★★★

NEW YORK

"Cadwallader Colden, Esq., . . . showed an unshaken attachment to his sovereign and the constitution
. . . He had been a prisoner . . . closely confined in a common jail, or on board a sloop in the Hudson River,
for no other cause than avowing his sentiments with candor, modesty, and firmness, against independency."

NEW YORK GAZETTE AND WEEKLY MERCURY, August 17, 1778

ALSOP, John: Continental congressman
*Born New Windsor, Orange County, New York,
1724; died November 22, 1794.*

After completing his preparatory education, Alsop moved to New York City, where he became a merchant and an importer. He represented New York City in the colonial legislature and was a delegate to the Continental Congress in 1774 and 1775. The latter year he served on the Committee of One Hundred, appointed to govern New York City until the convention assembled.

Alsop was one of the incorporators of New York Hospital and served as its governor for fourteen years, beginning in 1770. He held the position of president of the New York Chamber of Commerce in 1784 and 1785. He died in Newtown, Long Island, and was buried in the Trinity Church Cemetery, New York City.

ARMSTRONG, John: army officer, secretary of war, diplomat
*Born Carlisle, Pennsylvania, November 25, 1758;
son of John and Rebecca Armstrong; married Alida
Livingston, 1789; died April 1, 1843.*

Having attended Princeton in 1775, Armstrong went off to serve in the Revolutionary War as an aide-de-camp to John Frances Mercer and Horatio Gates. In 1783 he wrote the Newburgh Letters, which threatened army action if Congress refused to pay the arrears in soldiers' salaries. When the war ended he became secretary of state and then adjutant general of Pennsylvania, further serving his state as a delegate to the Continental Congress in 1787.

Armstrong represented New York in the United States Senate during the years 1800–02 and 1803–04. From the Senate he moved to the diplomatic arena, becoming minister to France in 1804. He held this post until 1810 and is believed to have contributed to the outbreak of the French and British War in 1812. In that year he received the commission of brigadier general in command of New York City. Secretary of war in 1813–14, he is considered responsible for the failure of the Montreal and Plattsburg campaigns and the British capture of Washington, D.C., in 1814.

Armstrong died at the age of eighty-four and was buried in the cemetery in Rhinebeck, New York.

AUCHMUTY, Samuel: clergyman, Loyalist
Born Boston, Massachusetts, January 26, 1722; married Mrs. Tucker, December 1749; died March 4, 1777.

Auchmuty graduated from Harvard in 1742. He was ordained a priest in the Anglican Church in London in 1747 and became assistant to the rector at Trinity (Anglican) Church in New York City the following year. He was rector during the period 1764–77. During his rectorship, St. Paul's Chapel was built and put into use (1766).

Auchmuty was awarded S.T.D.s by Oxford in 1766 and by King's College (now Columbia) the following year. He revealed his Loyalist sympathies in pamphlets and sermons at the outbreak of the American Revolution. Soon afterward, at the age of fifty-five, he died in New York City and was buried there.

★★★★★

BARCLAY, Thomas: Loyalist, diplomat
Born New York City, October 12, 1753; son of Henry and Mary (Rutgers) Barclay; married Susanna De Lancey, October 2, 1775; died April 21, 1830.

Barclay attended Columbia, then (1777) was commissioned a major of Loyalist forces in New York. He fled to Canada at the end of the American Revolution and held office under the British government in Nova Scotia circa 1781–1811. He served as speaker of the assembly and adjutant general of the Nova Scotia militia, as well as commissary for prisoners.

In 1795 Barclay was named commissioner to carry out the terms of the Jay Treaty. Four years later he began a thirty-one-year service as consul general in New York. He was commissioner under the Fourth and Fifth Articles of the Treaty of Ghent. From 1802 to 1812 he was consul of Great Britain for the northern and eastern states in the United States. He died in New York City.

BARD, Samuel: physician, educator
Born Philadelphia, Pennsylvania, April 1, 1742; son of John and Mrs. (Valleau) Bard; married Mary Bard, 1770; father of ten children (including William); died May 24, 1821.

Graduated from King's College (now Columbia) in 1760, Bard received the M.D. from the University of Edinburgh five years later. He was professor of medicine at King's College from 1769 to 1789, also serving as dean of faculty and a trustee during his tenure. He became professor of the theory and practice of physics in 1792 and in 1811 assumed the presidency of the College of Physicians and Surgeons of New York City, serving for ten years. After the American Revolution he was personal physician to George Washington in New York. Princeton awarded him an honorary LL.D. in 1816.

In addition to his professional activities, Bard was a founder of the City Library, the Protestant Episcopal Church in Hyde Park, and the New York Dispensary. He also served as president of the Agricultural Society of Dutchess County, Hyde Park. He wrote *The Shepherd's Guide, De Viribus Opii* (1765) and *The Use of Cold in Hemorrhage* (1807). He died at the age of seventy-nine.

BAYLEY, Richard: physician
Born Fairfield, Connecticut, 1745; married Miss Charlton; died August 17, 1801.

Bayley studied medicine under John Charlton in New York City and then went to London for the years 1769–71 to study anatomy under William Hunter. During a croup epidemic in 1774 he made a study of the disease's causes and treatment which resulted in the lowering of the mortality rate by half. Having been in England again during 1775 and 1776, he served as a surgeon in the British Army under General Howe in 1776–77. In the latter year he established a practice of medicine in New York City.

Bayley, who was appointed professor of

anatomy and surgery at Columbia in 1792, was the first physician in America to amputate the arm at the shoulder joint. In 1795 he became health physician for the Port of New York. He wrote *An Account of the Epidemic Fever which Prevailed in the City of New York during Part of the Summer and Fall of 1795* (1796) and *Letters from the Health Office Submitted to the New York Common Council.*

BENSON, Egbert: congressman, jurist
Born New York City, June 21, 1746; son of Robert and Catherine (Van Borsum) Benson; died August 24, 1833.

Benson graduated from King's College (now Columbia) in 1765 and four years later was admitted to the New York bar. He held the office of attorney general of the state during the years 1771–87, and in 1777 he was a member of the first New York State Legislative Assembly. He represented New York in the Annapolis Convention in 1786 and also was a delegate from his state to the 1st and 2nd congresses of the United States House of Representatives (1789–93).

Benson served as a justice of the New York Supreme Court and then as chief judge of the 2nd United States Circuit Court, serving in the latter position from 1794 to 1802. He returned to the House of Representatives for the 13th Congress (1813–15). In other activities, he was a regent of the University of the State of New York from 1787 until 1802 and a trustee of Columbia from 1804 until 1815. He also helped found the New York Historical Society and was its first president, serving from 1805 to 1815.

Benson wrote *Vindication of the Captors of Major André* (1817). He held honorary LL.D.s from Union College (1779), Harvard (1808), and Dartmouth (1811). He died in Jamaica, New York, at the age of eighty-seven.

BLOOM, Issac: congressman
Born Jamaica, New York, circa 1716; died April 26, 1803.

Having moved to Dutchess County, New York, circa 1740, Bloom became captain of

the Minutemen of Charlotte Precinct in 1775. In 1784 he became a merchant. He served in the New York State Assembly from 1788 to 1792 and was a delegate to the New York State Convention in 1801. Around this time he also served in the state senate (1800–02). He was elected to the 8th Congress of the United States House of Representatives and began his term on March 4, 1803, but he died the next month. He was probably buried in Jamaica.

BOERUM, Simon: Continental congressman
Born New Lots (now Brooklyn), Long Island, New York, February 29, 1724; died July 11, 1775.

Having graduated from a Dutch school in Flatbush, New York, Boerum became a farmer and miller. Governor Clinton appointed him clerk of Kings County in 1750, a position in which he remained for twenty-five years. He also served as clerk of the board of supervisors until 1775, as well as participating in the Colonial Assembly from 1761 to 1775. Also in 1775 he became a deputy in the Provincial Convention and a delegate to the Continental Congress from New York. His promising public career was cut short by death at the age of fifty-one.

BROOKS, David: congressman
Born Philadelphia, 1756; died August 30, 1838.

Brooks attended public schools and studied law. In 1776 he was commissioned a lieutenant in the Pennsylvania Battalion of the Flying Camp of the Continental Army, and he was captured at Fort Washington later the same year. After his exchange four years afterward, he was appointed assistant clothier general.

Brooks was admitted to the bar, began a law practice, and settled in New York County, New York. He was a member of the New York State Assembly for terms in 1787–88, 1794–96, and 1810, and represented his state in the 5th Congress of the United States House of Representatives (1797–99). Around this time, from 1795 until 1807, he also held the position of judge of Dutchess County. After his term in Congress he was appointed commissioner to negotiate a treaty with the Seneca Indians. Holding local office once again, he was clerk of Dutchess County in the years 1807–09, 1810–11, and 1813–15. Later he accepted an appointment as an officer in the United States Customs Service.

Brooks was an original member of the Society of the Cincinnati. He died in Poughkeepsie, New York, and was probably buried in Old Rural Cemetery.

BUCHANAN, Thomas: merchant

Born Glasgow, Scotland, December 24, 1744; son of George and Jean (Lowden) Buchanan; married Almy Townsend, March 17, 1766; father of at least one son (George); died November 10, 1815.

Buchanan, who attended the University of Glasgow, came to New York City in 1763 and entered into a partnership lasting from 1763 to 1772 with his relative Walter Buchanan in the shipping firm of W. J. T. Buchanan. In 1766 he signed the original Non-Importation Agreement and in 1775 became a member of the local Committee of One Hundred.

Shifting toward the Loyalist side, Buchanan signed a pledge to General Howe in 1776. The history of his activities in the New York City Chamber of Commerce also reflects somewhat his political views: he was elected to it in 1768, served as vice president from 1780 to 1783; and was elected president in 1783 but declined to serve for fear of being too closely associated with the rebels. Throughout the American Revolution he continued in foreign trade without antagonizing either the patriot or the Loyalist side.

Buchanan belonged to the First Presbyterian Church in New York City and was a director of the United Insurance Company. He died in New York City at the age of seventy.

BURR, Aaron: vice president of the United States, senator

Born Newark, New Jersey, February 6, 1756; son of Aaron and Esther (Edwards) Burr; married Mrs. Theodosia Prevost, July 1782; second marriage to Mrs. Stephen Jumel, 1833; father of Theodosia; died September 14, 1836.

Burr graduated in 1772 from the College of New Jersey (now Princeton). After receiving a commission as a lieutenant colonel in the Continental Army in 1777, he served in the battles of Long Island and Monmouth, remaining in the service until 1779. He was admitted to the New York bar in 1782 and began a practice in New York City the following year.

Rising politically, Burr served as attorney general of New York State from 1789 until 1791, when he was elected to a six-year term in the United States Senate. In 1797 he became a member of the New York State Assembly. In the election of 1800 he tied with Thomas Jefferson for the Presidency; on the thirty-sixth ballot in the House of Representatives, Jefferson was elected President and Burr vice president. This tie between the two Republicans resulted in the Twelfth Amendment.

Burr mortally wounded his political enemy Alexander Hamilton in a duel in Weehawken, New Jersey, in 1804. His term as vice president having ended in 1805, he formulated a conspiracy to seize the Southwest Territory from Spanish America in order to set up a new republic. In 1807 he was arrested, was tried for treason before Chief Justice Marshall of the United States Circuit Court in Virginia on May 22, 1807, and was acquitted on September 1. Later that year he journeyed abroad and attempted to interest France and England in his schemes. Failing, however, he returned home in 1812 and resumed his law practice in New York City. He died on Staten Island and was buried in Princeton, New Jersey.

BUTLER, John: army officer

Born New London, Connecticut, 1728; son of Walter and Deborah Butler; married Catharine; father of at least three children (including Walter); died May 1796.

Butler served as a captain in the New York militia in the expedition against Crown Point (1755) and commanded the Indian forces in the Niagara expedition of 1759 and the Montreal expedition of 1775–80. A Loyalist during the American Revolution, he was commissioned a major in the British Army in 1777 and then lieutenant colonel in 1780. He led a mixed force of Indians and Loyalists, known as Butler's Rangers, in the campaigns of the Mohawk and Wyoming valleys, served at the battles of Oriskany and Forty Fort, and led the forces which perpetrated the Wyoming Massacre in 1778. Two years later he fled to Canada, and the state of New York confiscated his property. Settling in Niagara, Canada, he became loyal commissioner of Indian Affairs, serving from 1780 until 1796, the year of his death.

BUTLER, Walter N.: Loyalist

Born Johnstown, New York; son of Lieutenant Colonel John and Catherine Butler; died October 30, 1781.

After studying law in Albany, New York, Butler fled to Canada with his father and other Loyalist leaders from western New York in 1776. A member of General Barry S. Leger's expedition down the Mohawk Valley in 1777, he was later captured by Continental soldiers but escaped. He was a leader of Loyalists and Indians in the Cherry Valley Massacre, in which over forty people were murdered, on November 11, 1778. During a Loyalist raid on the Mohawk Valley three years later, he was mortally wounded.

★★★★★

CHEESMAN, Forman: ship-builder

Born December 11, 1763; son of Thomas and Elizabeth (Forman) Cheesman; married Ann Cummings, February 16, 1786; died October 10, 1821.

The owner of a large shipyard in New York City, Cheesman was influential in the growth of the shipbuilding industry there, helping to make New York a successful competitor with Philadelphia in that field. He was the builder of many ships, including the *Brizanza,* the *Draper,* the *Ontario,* the *Silenus,* the *Triton,* and the *Illinois.* His most famous ship was the frigate the *President,* which he built in 1800.

CLARKSON, Matthew: army officer, philanthropist

Born New York City, October 17, 1758; son of David and Elizabeth (French) Clarkson; married Mary Rutherfurd, May 24, 1785; second marriage to Sarah Cornell, February 14, 1792; died April 25, 1825.

Clarkson participated in the Battle of Long Island as a volunteer and aide-de-camp to Benedict Arnold, 1778–79. In 1779 he was attached to the staff of General Benjamin Lincoln and served with him until the end of the Revolutionary War. He took part in the siege of Savannah, Georgia, and in the defense of Charleston, South Carolina; he was also present at the surrender of Yorktown in 1781. After serving as assistant to Secretary of War Benjamin Lincoln, Clarkson was commissioned a brigadier general and then a major general in the New York State militia.

A regent of the State University of New York, Clarkson served in the New York State Assembly from 1789 to 1790. In 1791–92 he was a United States marshal. He became a member of the New York State Senate, serving from 1794 to 1796, and was one of the commissioners appointed by the New York State legislature to build a new prison in 1796. He was president of New York Hospital in 1799 and president of the Bank of New York from 1804 to 1825.

A Federalist candidate for the United States Senate in 1802, Clarkson was defeated by DeWitt Clinton. For the remainder of his life he continued to support numerous societies and movements for public improvement. He died in New York City.

CLINTON, George: vice president of the United States, governor of New York

Born Little Britain, Orange County, New York, July 26, 1739; son of Charles and Elizabeth (Denniston)

Clinton; married Cornelia Tappan, February 7, 1770; father of six children; died April 20, 1812.

Clinton began his political career as a delegate to the New York Provincial Assembly in 1768. In 1775 and 1776 he was a delegate to the Continental Congress. Commissioned a brigadier general in the Continental Army in 1777, he became the first governor of New York that same year and served for eighteen years; he served another term from 1801 to 1804. President of the New York State Convention to ratify the United States Constitution, he was a leader of the faction opposing ratification. As a result of his opposition, Madison, Hamilton, and Jay began writing the Federalist papers in an attempt to destroy his influence.

Clinton was vice president under Jefferson and Madison, 1805–13. He died in Washington, D. C., and was buried in the Congressional Cemetery there.

CLINTON, James: army officer
Born Orange County, New York, August 9, 1733; son of Colonel Charles and Elizabeth (Denniston) Clinton; married Mary DeWitt, 1764; second marriage to Mrs. Mary Gray; father of DeWitt; died December 22, 1812.

At the age of twenty-three Clinton was commissioned a captain in the New York militia and nine years later was promoted to lieutenant colonel. In May 1775 he was elected deputy of the Provincial Congress of New York and that same year was commissioned a colonel in the New York State militia. The following year he was commissioned a brigadier general in the Continental Army.

In 1780 Clinton was placed in command of the Northern Department, Albany, New York. Five years later he was appointed New York State commissioner to adjust the boundary line between Pennsylvania and New York. He served as a member of the New York State Convention which ratified the United States Constitution, an assembly presided over by his younger brother George. He died in Orange County and was buried in Little Britain.

COLDEN, Cadwallader: Loyalist, colonial governor, scientist
Born Ireland, February 17, 1688; son of the Reverend Alexander Colden; married Alice Christie, November 11, 1715; father of Jane, Elizabeth, and David; died September 28, 1776.

Colden received an A.B. from the University of Edinburgh, Scotland, in 1705. Five years later he came to America, settling in New York in 1718. In 1720 he served as surveyor general of New York, and the following year he was appointed to the New York Governor's Council. From 1761 to 1776 he served as lieutenant governor of the colony of New York. He supported the British in the Revolutionary War.

A noted botanist of his day, Colden was a master of the Linnaean system of plant classification. He signed the original charters for the Marine Society of New York and the New York Chamber of Commerce. He was the first advocate of a cooling regimen in the treatment of fevers, and he proposed a cure for cancer.

Colden was the author of the *History of the Five Indian Nations Depending upon New York,* 1727; *An Explication of the First Causes of Action in Matter, and of the Cause of Gravitation,* 1745; *Principles of Action in Matter,* 1752. He died in Long Island, New York, just after the outbreak of the Revolutionary War.

COLEMAN, William: journalist
Born Boston, Massachusetts, February 14, 1766; married Carrie M. Page; father of two sons; died July 14, 1829.

Coleman was a member of the Massachusetts House of Representatives in 1795–96. In 1797 he went into partnership in a law firm with Aaron Burr in New York City. From 1800 to 1829 he was the editor and owner of the *Evening Post,* a leading Federalist journal. He died in New York City.

COLLES, Christopher: engineer

Born Ireland, May 3, 1739; son of Richard and Henrietta (Taylor) Colles; married Anne Keough, January 14, 1764; died October 4, 1816.

Colles came to America in 1765. At the age of thirty-three he lectured on pneumatics in Philadelphia and on inland navigation in New York City the following year. He devised a plan, which was never used, for replacing New York City's well and spring water system with a system of reservoirs and pipes. From 1775 to 1777, he was an instructor of artillery in the Continental Army.

Colles designed one of the first American steam engines, suggested a system of canals and river improvements to connect the Great Lakes with the Hudson River, and planned and surveyed the roads between New York City and Philadelphia. He was a manufacturer of small household utensils in New York City in 1796, and also traded in Indian goods and furs. He built and operated a semaphoric telegraph at Castle Clinton, New York, during the War of 1812. He was later employed in the customs service in New York City. He was superintendent of the American Academy of Fine Arts.

Colles was the author of several works, including *Syllabus of Lectures on Natural Philosophy*, 1773; *A Survey of the Roads of the United States of America*, 1789; *Proposals of a Design for Inland Communication of a New Construction*, 1808; and *Description of the Universal Telegraph*, 1813. He died in New York City.

CONNOLLY, John: clergyman

Born Slane County, Ireland, 1750; died February 6, 1825.

Connolly, who was ordained into the priesthood of the Roman Catholic Church in 1775, served for a time as director of the Casanate Library. In 1814 he became the bishop of the Diocese of New York; this diocese embraced all of New York State and half of New Jersey. He established an orphan asylum and introduced the Sisters of Charity. He died at the age of seventy-five.

COOPER, Myles: clergyman, college president

Born England, 1737; son of William and Elizabeth Cooper; died May 20, 1785.

Cooper received a B.A. from Queen's College, Oxford University, England, in 1756, and an M.A. from that school in 1760. He was ordained to the ministry of the Anglican Church in 1761 and came to America the following year. He became a professor of moral philosophy and a fellow at King's College (now Columbia), New York, in 1762, and served as president from 1763 to 1775. In 1768 his alma mater awarded him an LL.D. He eventually fled to England because his Loyalist sentiments endangered his life.

Cooper wrote *Poems on Several Occasions*, 1761, and *The American Querist*, 1774. He died in Edinburgh, Scotland.

COOPER, William: jurist

Born Philadelphia, Pennsylvania, December 2, 1754; son of James and Hanna (Hibbs) Cooper; married Elizabeth Fenimore, December 12, 1775; father of James Fenimore Cooper; died December 22, 1809.

The founder of Cooperstown, New York, Cooper erected a seminary and was the first judge of the Otsego County Court of Common Pleas in 1791. He was a delegate from New York to the United States House of Representatives for the 4th and 6th congresses (1795–97 and 1799–1801). He died in Albany, New York, and was buried in Cooperstown.

CRUGER, Henry: merchant, state legislator

Born New York City, December 3, 1739; son of Henry and Elizabeth (Harris) Cruger; married Peach Blair; second marriage to Elizabeth Blair; third marriage to Caroline Smith, 1799; died April 24, 1827.

Cruger was a merchant in Bristol, England, and a member of the English House of Commons twice (1774–80 and 1784–90).

He was mayor of Bristol in 1781. An advocate of reconciliation with the American colonies, he came to the United States in 1790 and took over the New York City branch of his business. In 1792 he was a member of the New York State Senate. He died at the age of eighty-seven.

CRUGER, John: colonial legislator, mayor
Born New York City, July 18, 1710; son of John and Maria (Cuyler) Cruger; died December 27, 1791.

An alderman of New York City in 1754 and 1755, the latter year Cruger became mayor of the city and served until 1765. During that time, and until 1768, he was a member of the General Assembly. In 1765 he was a delegate to the Stamp Act Congress. That same year, as author of the "Declaration of the Rights and Grievances of the Colonists in America," he was sent as a representative to England.

An organizer of the New York City Chamber of Commerce in 1768, Cruger served as the first president of that organization in 1769. He represented New York City in the last Colonial Assembly from 1769 to 1775, serving as speaker by unanimous consent. He died in Bristol, New York, at the age of eighty-one.

★★★★★

DELAFIELD, John: merchant
Born England, March 27, 1749; son of John and Martha (Dell) Delafield; married Ann Hallett; father of eleven children (including John); died July 3, 1824.

When Delafield came to the United States in 1783, he brought with him the first copy of a provisional peace treaty between England and the United States to reach America. He soon became one of the richest traders in New York City, also attaining the position of director of the Mutual Assurance Company of New York in 1787.

After retiring from the mercantile business in 1798, Delafield became president of the United Insurance Company but lost much of his fortune when the vessels he had underwritten were destroyed during the War of 1812. He died at the age of seventy-five.

De LANCEY, James: merchant, horse-racer
Born New York City, 1732; son of James and Anne (Heathcote) De Lancey; married Margaret Allen, 1771; father of several children; died 1800.

De Lancey attended Cambridge and later became a captain in the British Army. He served in the Lake George and Niagara campaigns, 1758 and 1759, respectively. In 1760 he inherited his father's mercantile and real estate interests in New York City and brought to America the first thoroughbred racehorses. He owned the largest stable of running horses in the colonies.

De Lancey was boss of a faction that controlled the New York Provincial Assembly in its last years. In 1775 he went to England; four years later his property was confiscated by New York State. In 1783 he was vice president of the board of agents to secure restitution for losses suffered by the Loyalists.

De LANCEY, James: Loyalist
Born Westchester, New York, 1746; son of Peter and Elizabeth (Colden) De Lancey; married Martha Tippetts; father of ten children; died May 2, 1804.

From 1776 to 1783 De Lancey was the commander of De Lancey's Horse, a Loyalist raiding cavalry troop stationed outside New York City. In 1779 he was proscribed by the New York Act of Attainder and three years later fled to Nova Scotia, Canada. A member of the Nova Scotia Assembly, he was appointed to the Nova Scotia Council in 1799. He died five years later.

De LANCEY, Oliver: colonial legislator, army officer
Born New York City, September 16, 1718; son of Stephen and Anne (Van Cortlandt) De Lancey; married Phila Franks; father of four children; died October 25, 1785.

De Lancey served as alderman for the Out Ward from 1754 to 1757. He was a member of the New York City delegation to the New

York Assembly in 1759–60 and a member of the New York Provincial Council from 1760 to 1776.

De Lancey raised the New York City Regiment for an expedition against Crown Point in 1758. He was receiver general in 1763 and ten years later served as colonel-in-chief of the Southern Military District. A Loyalist, he was commissioned a brigadier general in the British Army, thus making him the highest ranking American Loyalist. He became a symbol of the Loyalists during the American Revolution, raising three battalions of troops which carried his name.

De Lancey went to England in 1783 and died in the town of Beverley two years later.

DENNING, William: congressman

Born probably St. John's, Newfoundland, April 1740; died October 30, 1819.

As a youth Denning moved to New York City where he later became a businessman. In 1775 he was a member of the Committee of One Hundred, and from 1775 to 1777 he was a deputy of the New York Provincial Congress. In 1776 and 1777 he attended a convention of state representatives. A member of the New York State Assembly, 1784–87, he was a New York State senator from 1798 to 1808. In 1799 he was a member of the Council of Appointment.

In 1809 and 1810 Denning was a member of the United States House of Representatives. He died in New York City and was buried in St. Paul's Churchyard.

DeWITT, Charles: Continental congressman

Born Kingston, New York, 1727; died August 27, 1787.

A colonel in the militia, DeWitt was a member of the Colonial Assembly from 1768 to 1776, acting as a delegate to the Provisional Convention in 1775. A member of the Provisional Congress which approved the Declaration of Independence (1775–77), he was a member of the Constitutional Committee in 1776 and of the Committee of Safety in 1777. In 1784 he represented New York in the Continental Congress.

For several years DeWitt was the editor of the *Ulster Sentinel.* He was a member of the New York State Assembly in 1781 and again in 1785–86. He was also a member of the committee which drafted the New York Constitution. He died in Kingston, New York, and was buried in the Dutch Reformed Cemetery, Hurley, New York.

DeWITT, Simeon: university chancellor, state official

Born Wawarsing, New York, December 25, 1756; son of Dr. Andries and Jannetje (Vernooy) DeWitt; married Elizabeth Lynott, October 12, 1789; second marriage to Jane Varick Hardenberg; third marriage to Susan Linn, October 29, 1810; father of six children; died December 3, 1834.

DeWitt received a B.A. from Queen's College (now Rutgers) in 1776. He left college to join the New York militia, serving as assistant geographer of the Continental Army from 1778 to 1780 and chief geographer in 1780–81. He was surveyor general of the State of New York for fifty years (1784–1834). He was a commissioner to settle the New York–Pennsylvania boundary dispute in 1786–87. He received an M.A. from Queen's College in 1788.

A surveyor of various canal routes for New York, DeWitt published a map of New York State in 1802. He was a regent and then, from 1798 to 1829, vice chancellor of the University of the State of New York, serving as chancellor from 1829 to 1834. He was a founder of the New York Society for the Promotion of Agriculture, Arts, and Manufactures, which later became a part of the Albany Institute; he was also vice president of the Albany Institute for many years. He was a member of the American Philosophical Society.

DeWitt wrote *The Elements of Perspective* (a collection of writings) in 1813 and was a contributor of scientific papers to various journals. He died in Ithaca, New York.

DUANE, James: jurist, mayor

Born New York City, February 6, 1733; son of Anthony and Althea (Kettetas) Duane; married Mary Livingston, October 21, 1759; father of ten children; died February 1, 1797.

Duane was admitted to the New York bar in 1754. In 1774 he became a member of the Committee of Correspondence and also a delegate to the Continental Congress, serving in the latter capacity for ten years. He was a member of the New York Provincial Convention in 1775, 1776, and 1777. He helped draft the Articles of Confederation. He was a member of the New York Committee of Sixty to carry out the Association and also of the subsequent Committee of One Hundred. As a member of the Poughkeepsie Convention of 1788, he advocated the ratification of the United States Constitution.

In 1784 Duane became the first mayor of New York City. From 1782 to 1785 and in 1789–90, he was a member of the New York Senate. He was the first judge of the District of New York (1789–94). He died in Schenectady, New York, and was buried beneath Christ Church, Duanesburg, New York.

DUER, William: Continental congressman

Born Devonshire, England, March 18, 1747; son of John and Frances (Frye) Duer; married Catherine Alexander, 1779; father of William Alexander and John; died May 7, 1799.

Duer was educated at Eton College and commissioned an ensign in the British Army. He was aide-de-camp to Lord Clive in 1762 and accompanied him to India in 1764. In 1768 he traveled to America, where he became a cotton manufacturer in New York and New Jersey prior to the American Revolution. He was a delegate to the New York Provincial Congress in 1775 and a colonel and deputy adjutant general in the New York militia. The following year he was a delegate to the New York Constitutional Convention, serving on the drafting committee. That same year he was a member of the New York Committee of Public Safety.

From 1777 to 1779 Duer was a delegate from New York to the Continental Congress. A member of the Board of War, he was the first judge of common pleas in Charlotte (now Washington) County, New York, serving from 1777 to 1786. He was a signer of the Articles of Confederation.

Duer was instrumental in causing the failure of the Conway Cabal's plan to remove Washington from command. He was chairman of the commission for conspiracies, which was established by Congress in 1780. A founder of the Bank of New York in 1784, he was secretary of the Board of Treasury under the Articles of Confederation of New York in 1786. That same year he was also a member of the New York Assembly and assistant secretary of the United States. He served as assistant secretary of the United States Department of Treasury in its founding year, 1789.

Duer became involved in land and other speculations and was imprisoned for debt in 1792. He died in prison in New York City and was buried in Jamaica, Long Island, New York.

★★★★★

EDDY, Thomas: reformer

Born Philadelphia, Pennsylvania, September 5, 1758; son of James and Mary (Darragh) Eddy; married Hannah Hartshorne, March 20, 1782; died September 16, 1827.

Eddy was active in a broad range of humanitarian enterprises. A bill for the establishment of a penitentiary system in New York State was drawn up by him (with General Philip Schuyler) in 1796. For thirty-one years (1796–1827) he was on the board of governors of New York Hospital. During that time he helped establish the Bloomingdale Asylum for the Insane, a free school for poor children in New York City, the House of Refuge, the New York Savings Bank, and the New York Bible Society. Another one of

Eddy's notable undertakings was his helping DeWitt Clinton carry through the Erie Canal project. In 1801 he wrote *Account of the State Prison or Penitentiary House in the City of New York.* He died in New York City.

EDWARDS, Talmadge: glove manufacturer
Born England, 1747; married Mary Sherman, 1780; father of eight children (including John); died June 4, 1821.

Edwards came to America at the age of twenty-three and later took part in the American Revolution. The father of the glove and mitten industry in America, he first sold gloves in wholesale lots in Albany, New York, in 1810. He made several innovations in the glove-manufacturing process, including an improvement in the process of tanning glove leather and the origination of the "oiltan" method of preparing buckskin. He died in Johnstown, New York.

★★★★★

FISH, Nicholas: army officer, public official
Born New York City, August 28, 1758; son of Jonathan and Elizabeth (Sackett) Fish; married Elizabeth Stuyvesant, April 30, 1803; father of several children (including Hamilton); died June 20, 1833.

Fish attended the College of New Jersey (now Princeton). During the Revolutionary War he was commissioned a major in General Scott's Brigade and the 2nd New York Regiment of the Continental Army (1776). Second in command during the Yorktown campaign, he also served in the battles of Long Island, Bemis Heights, and Monmouth. He was commissioned a lieutenant colonel at war's end.

Fish was a Federalist leader in early New York politics and a close friend of Alexander Hamilton. He was adjutant general of New York State in 1784, later acting as an alderman of New York City for eleven years (1806–17). He was president of the New York Society of the Cincinnati and chairman of the board of trustees of Columbia University. He died in his birthplace and longtime home, New York City.

FISH, Preserved: merchant
Born Portsmouth, Rhode Island, July 3, 1766; son of Preserved Fish; married three times; died July 23, 1846.

Fish went to sea as a merchantman and whaler when he was still a boy; at the age of twenty-one he was captain of his own ship. Twenty-eight years later (1815) he founded the New York firm of Fish and Grinell, which became a leading firm in shipping circles. In 1817 he became a broker with the New York Exchange Board (the nucleus of the New York Stock Exchange). He was president of the Tradesman's Bank in 1838. Originally a Quaker, he later became an Episcopalian. He died in New York City at the age of eighty.

FITCH, Asa: congressman, physician
Born Groton, Connecticut, November 10, 1765; died August 24, 1843.

Fitch served as a sergeant in Captain Livingston's Company during the Revolutionary War. He then practiced medicine in Duanesburg and Salem, New York. He was president of the Washington County Medical Society for twenty years (1806–26). He was a justice of the peace (1799–1810) and a county judge (1810–21), as well as a New York delegate to the United States House of Representatives (Federalist) during the 12th Congress (1811–13). After his death in Salem, New York, in 1843, he was buried in Evergreen Cemetery.

FLOYD, William: congressman
Born Brookhaven, New York, December 17, 1734; son of Nicoll and Tabetha (Smith) Floyd; married Isabella Jones; second marriage to Joanna Strong; died August 4, 1821.

Floyd was a major general in the Suffolk County Regiment of the New York militia. He attended the Continental Congress from 1774 to 1777 and again from 1778 to 1783. Two years later he became a deputy of the

New York Provincial Convention. He was the first New York delegate to sign the Declaration of Independence.

Floyd was a member of the United States House of Representatives from New York during the 1st Congress (1789–91). He was a member of the New York State Senate in 1777 and 1778, from 1783 to 1788, and in 1808, and served as a delegate to the New York Constitutional Convention in 1801. After his death in 1821, Floyd was buried in the Presbyterian Church Cemetery in Westerville, New York.

★★★★★

GANO, John: clergyman
Born Hopewell, New Jersey, July 22, 1727; son of Daniel and Sarah (Britton) Gano; married Sarah Stites, 1755; second marriage to Mrs. T. Bryant, 1790; father of Stephen and John; died August 10, 1804.

After attending Princeton, Gano was ordained pastor of the Baptist Church in Morristown, New Jersey, in 1754. Eight years later he became pastor of and helped reorganize the Baptist Church in New York City. He was a founder of Rhode Island College (now Brown University) and a chaplain in the Continental Army. In other educational service, he was a regent of the University of the State of New York in 1784 and a trustee of King's College (now Columbia) in 1787. He also preached in Kentucky and North Carolina.

GANSEVOORT, Leonard: Continental congressman, jurist
Born July 1751; son of Harmen and Magdalena (Douw) Gansevoort; married Hester Cuyler; died August 26, 1810.

In contrast to his older brother Peter, a distinguished army officer, Leonard Gansevoort never served in the military; however, he did contribute to the war effort in a number of nonmilitary capacities. He was a member of the Albany (New York) Committee of Correspondence and served as its treasurer until 1775. He attended the second and third provincial congresses of New York in 1775 and 1776 as well as the Convention of Representatives of the State of New York (serving as president pro tem) in 1777. He held the local offices of clerk of Albany County (1777) and city recorder (1780).

Gansevoort was a delegate to the New York State Assembly in 1778 and again in 1787. He participated in the Continental Congress in 1787–88 and in the state senate during the years 1791–93 and 1796–1802. In 1794 he was appointed colonel of light cavalry and became judge of Albany County, holding the latter position for three years. He then served as judge in the Court of Probates from 1799 until 1810, the year of his death. He died in Albany.

GANSEVOORT, Peter: army officer
Born Albany, New York, July 1749; son of Harmen and Magdalena (Douw) Gansevoort; married Catherina Van Schaick, January 12, 1778; died July 2, 1812.

In 1775 Gansevoort served with General Montgomery in the expedition against Quebec. That same year he was commissioned a major in the 2nd New York Regiment, rising rapidly to lieutenant colonel and then to colonel in the 3rd New York Regiment, both in 1776. In 1777 he commanded Fort George, defended Fort Stanwix for twenty days against a British and Indian force led by Sergeant Leger, commanded Fort Schuyler in Rome, New York, and was put in temporary command of Albany. In 1779 he was with Sullivan in the expedition against the Indian allies of the British, and the following year he was put in command at Saratoga, New York.

Gansevoort received a commission as a brigadier general in the New York militia in 1781 and accompanied General Washington on his tour of the northern battlefields in 1783. He advanced to major general in 1793. In 1802 he became military agent for the Northern Department of the United States

Army and in 1809 was commissioned a brigadier general.

Gansevoort served as a director of the New York State Bank from 1803 to 1812, as United States commissioner of Indian affairs, and as a regent of the University of the State of New York from 1808 to 1812. He died in Albany, the town of his birth.

GARRETTSON, Freeborn: clergyman

Born Maryland, August 15, 1752; son of John and Sarah (Hanson) Garrettson; married Catharine Livingston, June 30, 1793; died September 26, 1827.

Garrettson inherited his father's plantation in Maryland in 1773. Two years later he became a Methodist and freed his slaves. He also became an itinerant preacher, visiting towns in Maryland, Virginia, Pennsylvania, and New York during the period 1776 to 1784. In the latter year he attended the conference in Baltimore which organized the Methodist Church of the United States; also that year, he was ordained to the Methodist ministry. After a period as a missionary in Nova Scotia (1785–87), he became a traveling preacher, working primarily in New York (1787–1827).

Garrettson wrote *The Experience and Travels of Mr. Freeborn Garrettson* (1791) and *A Dialogue Between Do-Justice and Professing Christian* (1820). He was also a founder of the Missionary and Bible Society.

GELSTON, David: Continental congressman

Born Bridgehampton, New York, July 4, 1744; died August 21, 1828.

A signer of the Articles of Association in 1775, Gelston was a delegate to the second, third and fourth provincial congresses of New York (1775–77). In 1777 he participated in the New York Constitutional Convention as well as becoming a member of the state assembly, where he served until 1785 and where he was speaker in 1784–85. In 1780 he had accepted an appointment as commissioner of specie.

Gelston was a delegate to the Continental Congress in 1789. He served on the council of appointment in 1792–93 and in the New York Senate for terms in 1791–94, 1798, and 1802. Around this time he also was canal commissioner (1792) and surrogate of New York County (1787–1801). He was collector for the Port of New York from 1801 to 1820 and also engaged in business in New York City during this time.

Gelston died in New York City and was buried in the First Presbyterian Church Cemetery there.

GILBERT, Ezekiel: congressman, lawyer

Born Middletown, Connecticut, March 24, 1756; died July 17, 1841.

Gilbert graduated from Yale in 1778 and studied law. After his admission to the bar he began a law practice in Hudson, New York. He was elected to the New York State Assembly for terms in 1789–90 and later in 1800–01, and was a New York delegate to the United States House of Representatives during the 3rd and the 4th congresses (1793–97). From 1813 to 1815 he served as clerk of Columbia County. He died in Hudson at the age of eighty-five.

GLEN, Henry: congressman

Born Schenectady, New York, July 13, 1739; died January 6, 1814.

Glen held the position of clerk of Schenectady County for many years (1767–1809). After participating in the first, second, and third provincial congresses (1774–76), he served as a deputy quartermaster general in the Revolutionary War. He was a member of the New York State Assembly in 1786–87 and again in 1810, and he was elected to the 3rd through the 6th congresses of the United States House of Representatives (1793–1801). He died in Schenectady.

GORDON, James: congressman

Born County Antrim, Ireland, October 31, 1739; died January 17, 1810.

Gordon, who attended local schools in

Ireland, came to America in 1758 and settled in Schenectady, New York, where he worked as an Indian trader. During the Revolutionary War, in which he served as a lieutenant colonel in the Albany County (New York) Militia Regiment, he was captured and imprisoned for a time in Canada.

Gordon was elected to several terms in the New York State Assembly (1777–80, 1786, 1790). Circa 1790 he moved to Ballston Spa, New York. A Federalist, he served in the 2nd and 3rd congresses of the United States House of Representatives (1791–95) and was a member of the New York Senate from 1797 to 1804. He also served as a trustee of Union College in Schenectady from 1795 to 1809.

Gordon died in Ballston Spa and was buried in Briggs Cemetery.

GRAHAM, Isabella Marshall: philanthropist

Born Lanark, Scotland, July 29, 1742; daughter of John and Janet (Hamilton) Marshall; married Dr. John Graham, 1765; mother of four children; died July 27, 1814.

In 1789 Graham came to America and established a school for young women in New York City. Eight years later she became director of the Society for the Relief of Poor Widows with Small Children, the earliest organization of its kind in America, and in 1806 she presided over the organizational meeting of the Orphan Asylum Society. She was elected president of the board of directors of the Magdalen Society in 1811 and was active in organizing the Society for the Promotion of Industry Among the Poor in 1814. She died that year in New York City.

GREENLEAF, Thomas: printer, journalist

Born Newburyport, Massachusetts, 1755; son of Joseph and Abigail (Payne) Greenleaf; married Ritsana (or Anna) Quakenbos, October 31, 1791; father of four children; died September 14, 1798.

Greenleaf learned the printing trade in the shop of Isaiah Thomas in Boston. After moving to New York City in 1785, he be-

came manager of Eliazer Oswald's *New York Journal or the Weekly Register.* In 1787 he became the paper's owner. For a time in 1787 and 1788 the paper was a daily under the title *New-York Journal and Daily Patriotic Register,* but it reverted to weekly publication in 1788. Two years later it was published semiweekly under the title *New-York Journal and Patriotic Register.* Finally, from 1795 until 1798, the name was *Greenleaf's New Daily Advertiser,* and Greenleaf was manager. He supported Aaron Burr's party against the Federalists and often printed attacks on George Washington.

GREENWOOD, John: dentist

Born Boston, Massachusetts, May 17, 1760; son of Isaac and Mary (I'ans) Greenwood; married Elizabeth Weaver, March 22, 1788; died November 16, 1819.

Greenwood served as a rifleman and scout during the Revolutionary War. Although he had been apprenticed as a cabinetmaker before the war, he became a dentist in New York City in 1785. He is credited with originating the foot-power drill, the springs which held plates of false teeth in position, and the use of porcelain in the manufacture of false teeth. George Washington was one of his patients and found him the most satisfactory of his numerous dentists.

GRIM, David: tavern keeper, artist

Born Zweibrucken, Bavaria, Germany, August 25, 1737; son of Philip Grim; no record of first marriage; second marriage to Mary Barwick, December 24, 1781; father of eight children (including Elizabeth, Catherine, and Philip); died March 26, 1826.

Grim's family came to New York City in 1739. When he was nineteen he spent several months cruising about the West Indies aboard the *King of Prussia.* During the period 1767 to 1789 he was innkeeper at the Sign of the Three Tuns on Chapel Street in New York City, an establishment popular among German patriots. He joined the German Society of the City of New York in 1784 and was president from then until 1802 (succeeding Baron von Steuben). In 1789 he became a merchant.

Grim is most remembered for the pen-and-ink sketches he made during the last years of his life depicting New York City as he remembered it during his boyhood. Among the sketches are "Plan and Elevation of the City Hall" and "A Plan of the City and Environs of New York as They Were in the Years 1742–43 and 1744."

GROS, John Daniel: clergyman, educator, philosopher
Born Webenheim, Bavarian Palatinate, Germany, 1738; son of Lorenz Gross; died May 25, 1812.

Gros studied at the University of Marburg in 1759 and at the University of Heidelberg in 1761. Later he received an honorary S.T.D. from Columbia.

Arriving in America in 1764, Gros founded a church in Allentown, Pennsylvania. Later he was pastor of the German Reformed Church in New York City. He became a member of Coetus, which successfully freed itself from the control of the Dutch Synods. In the field of education, he was a professor at Columbia for eleven years, teaching German and geography from 1784 to 1789 and moral philosophy from 1789 to 1795. He was a regent of the University of the State of New York from 1784 to 1787 and a trustee of Columbia from 1787 to 1792.

Gros wrote *Natural Principles of Rectitude* (1795). He died in Canajoharie, New York.

★★★★★

HALSEY, Silas: congressman
Born Southampton, Long Island, New York, October 5, 1743; died November 19, 1832.

After attending public schools, Halsey studied medicine in Elizabethtown (now Elizabeth), New Jersey. He practiced medicine in Southampton from 1764 to 1776. He was under sheriff of Suffolk County from 1784 to 1787 and sheriff from 1787 to 1792. He moved to Lodi, New York, in 1793, where he practiced medicine and operated a gristmill. He was supervisor of the town of Ovid, New York, from 1794 to 1804.

A delegate from Onondaga County to the New York Assembly in 1797–98, Halsey represented Cayuga County in 1800–01. He was clerk of Seneca County, New York, twice: from 1804 to 1813 and in 1815. A Democrat, he served in the 9th Congress of the United States House of Representatives (1805–07). He was a member of the New York Senate in 1808–09.

Halsey died in Lodi at the age of eighty-nine and was buried in Old Halsey Cemetery in South Lodi.

HAMILTON, Alexander: secretary of the treasury
Born Nevis, British West Indies, January 11, 1757; son of James and Rachel (Faucette) Hamilton; married Elizabeth Schuyler, 1780; father of eight children (including James Alexander, Philip, and John C.); died July 12, 1804.

Hamilton, after working as a clerk for a time, came to America at the age of fifteen. From 1773 to 1776 he attended King's College (now Columbia), during which time he wrote pamphlets and newspaper articles defending the colonists' position against the British. In 1776 he was appointed captain of artillery in the Continental Army. From 1777 to 1781 he was secretary and aide-de-camp to General Washington; he served in the battles of Long Island and Yorktown.

In 1781 Hamilton was admitted to the New York bar and began a distinguished legal career. Twice serving as a delegate from New York to the Continental Congress (1782–83, 1787–88), he was known as a developer and exponent of the theory of a strong central government. A member of the 1786 Annapolis Convention and the 1787 New York legislature, Hamilton was largely responsible for sending a New York delegation, including himself and two anti-constitution Clinton Democrats, Robert Yates and John Lansing, to the United States Constitutional Convention in Philadelphia in 1787. Although he played only a minor role in drafting the Constitution, he signed it for the State of New York in 1787, and wrote, with John Jay and James Madison, a series of articles for the *Federalist* papers favoring the adoption of the Constitution. He attended the New York Convention which ratified the Constitution and was highly influential in securing the ratification.

Hamilton was appointed the first secretary of the treasury by Washington in 1789, serving until 1795. He identified with the Federalist party and became probably its main spokesman. As secretary of the treasury, he based his financial program on paying the domestic debt, founding the Bank of the United States, assuming state debts, raising excise taxes, and imposing protective tariffs. He presented his plan to Congress in a series of reports in 1790, the final one being the famous report on manufactures, and defended his plan largely through the implied-powers argument of the Constitution. Although he met strong opposition, all the measures were adopted except the imposition of protective tariffs; the assumption of the state debts came about only because Jefferson agreed to swing the votes for it in return for Hamilton's support on locating a national capital in the South. The adoption of the excise taxes was the main cause of the Whiskey Rebellion in Pennsylvania in 1794. Hamilton clashed with Jefferson both personally and in such matters as basic theory of government and foreign policy; this conflict led to a two-party system of government that exists in America yet today.

Hamilton resigned from his cabinet post in 1795, although he continued to attempt to advise Washington, writing part of Washington's Farewell Address in 1796. In 1798 he was appointed inspector general of the United States Army in anticipation of war with France; however, John Adams managed to avert war, thus causing a serious break in the Federalist party ranks between those members who desired war with the French and those who favored the use of diplomacy. Hamilton put his influence on Jefferson's side during the tie for the Presidency that developed between Jefferson and Aaron Burr in 1800, swinging many Federalist votes in the House of Representatives to Jefferson. This marked the start of the enmity between Burr and Hamilton.

From 1795 to 1804 Hamilton practiced law in New York City. He was a founder of the *New York Evening Post* (1801) and the Bank of New York. His influence in preventing Burr's election as governor of New York in 1804 led Burr to challenge him to a duel, to take place at Weehawken Heights, New Jersey, on July 11, 1804. Hamilton was mortally wounded and died in New York City the following day. He was buried in Trinity Churchyard in New York City.

HAMMON, Jupiter: poet
Born circa 1720; died circa 1800.

Hammon was an African slave owned by Henry Lloyd of Lloyd's Neck, Long Island, New York. In 1763, after Lloyd's death, Hammon was inherited by his son Joseph and then, during the Revolutionary War, by John Lloyd, Jr., Joseph's grandson. Hammon wrote *An Evening Thought on Salvation by Christ, with Penentential Cries; Composed by Jupiter Hammon, a Negro Belonging to Mr. Lloyd, of Queen's Village, on Long Island, the 25th of December, 1760,* printed in New York in 1761; *An Essay on the Ten Virgins,* 1779; *A Winter Piece,* Hartford, 1782; and *An Address to the Negroes of the State of New York,* 1787.

HARING, John: Continental congressman
Born Tappan, New York, September 28, 1739; died April 1, 1809.

Haring attended school in New York City, where he studied law. He was admitted to the bar and practiced in New York City and in Rockland County, New York. He was a member of the Continental Congress in 1774, 1775, and 1785–88. In 1774 and 1775, and from 1778 to 1788, he was a judge in Orange County, New York. A member of the New York provincial congresses, 1775–77, he served as president pro tem for the second and third congresses.

In 1781–82 Haring was a member of the New York State Senate, and in 1784 he served on the New York State Board of Regents. A member of the New York Convention which considered the United States Constitution in 1788, he voted to reject the document. He was a member of the New York Assembly in 1806. He died in Blauveltville, New York, and was buried in Tappan Church Cemetery.

HARPUR, Robert: educator, colonial official

Born Ballybay, Ireland, January 25, 1731; son of Andrew and Elizabeth (Creighton) Harpur; married Elizabeth Crygier, September 29, 1773; second marriage to Myra Lackey, April 1789; father of five children; no record of death.

After his education at the University of Glasgow, Harpur came to America in 1761. He was a professor of mathematics and natural philosophy at King's College (now Columbia) in New York City from 1761 to 1767. He was the school's first librarian, serving from 1762 to 1767. From 1776 to 1777, he was a member of the third and fourth provincial congresses.

From 1777 to 1784 Harpur was a member of the New York Assembly. In 1784 he was secretary of the regents of the University of the State of New York, and from 1787 to 1795 he was a member and clerk of the board of trustees. He also served on the New York Council of Safety. In 1795 he was deputy secretary of the State of New York. Secretary of the New York Land Board, he was interested in the possibilities of the American frontier. In 1795 he founded the village of Harpursville, New York.

HARTWIG, Johann Christoph: clergyman

Born Thuringen, Germany, January 6, 1714; died July 17, 1796.

Hartwig was ordained to the ministry of the Lutheran Church in London in 1745. The following year he came to America, where he served as pastor of the Lutheran Church in Rhinebeck, New York, until 1748. He maintained close relations with the Livingstons and the Van Rensselaers of New York and was a confidant of Henry Melchior Mühlenberg. He was known for his extreme asceticism and pietism.

Hartwig held many brief pastorates, including Waldeboro, Maine; Winchester, Virginia; Reading, Pennsylvania; New York City; and Frederick, Maryland. He spent much of his life as a wandering preacher. He provided in his will for the founding of an Indian school, which resulted in the establishment of Hartwicke College, Otsego County, New York. He died in Clermont, New York.

HASBROUCK, Josiah: congressman

Born New Paltz, New York, March 5, 1755; died March 19, 1821.

Before becoming a second lieutenant in the 3rd Regiment of the Ulster County (New York) militia in 1780, Hasbrouck operated a general merchandising business. He was supervisor of New Paltz, 1784–86, 1793, 1794, 1799–1805. He was a member of the New York Assembly in 1796, 1797, 1802, and 1806. He served New York in the United States House of Representatives during the 8th and 15th congresses (from April 28, 1803, to 1805, and from 1817 to 1819). He died near Plattekill, New York, and was buried in the family burial ground. He was later reinterred in the New Paltz Rural Cemetery.

HATHORN, John: congressman

Born Wilmington, Delaware, January 9, 1749; died February 19, 1825.

Hathorn, a surveyor and schoolteacher, was a captain in the New York Colonial Militia. He was appointed a colonel in the 4th Orange County (New York) Regiment in 1776 and served throughout the Revolutionary War. In 1786 he was commissioned a brigadier general in the Orange County militia, and in 1793 he became a major general in the New York State militia.

Hathorn served several terms in the New York Assembly (1778, 1780, 1782–85, 1795, 1805), acting as speaker in 1783–84. He was a member of the New York State Senate from 1786 to 1790 and from 1799 to 1803. In 1787 and 1789 he was a member of the council of appointment. In December 1788 he was elected to the Continental Congress, but there were no further sessions held. A Federalist, he was a New York delegate to the United States House of Representatives for the 1st and 4th congresses (1789–91, 1795–97).

Hathorn died in Warwick, New York, and was buried in the cemetery on the family estate; he was later reinterred in Warwick Cemetery.

HAVENS, Jonathan Nicoll: congressman
Born Shelter Island, New York, June 18, 1757; died October 25, 1799.

Havens, who graduated from Yale at the age of twenty, was a member of the New York State Assembly from 1786 to 1795. He served as town clerk from 1783 to 1787. In 1788 he was a member of the New York Convention which ratified the United States Constitution. In 1795 he was chairman of the committee for the establishing of public schools in New York, and also a justice of the peace in Suffolk County, New York. A Democrat, he was a New York delegate to the United States House of Representatives from 1795 to 1799. He died on Shelter Island and was buried in the South Burial Ground of the Presbyterian Church there.

HAZARD, Ebenezer: government official
Born Philadelphia, Pennsylvania, January 15, 1744; son of Samuel and Catherine (Clarkson) Hazard; married Abigail Arthur, September 11, 1783; father of Samuel; died June 13, 1817.

Hazard graduated from the College of New Jersey (now Princeton) in 1762, receiv-

ing his A.M. in 1765. He was a partner in the publishing firm of Noel and Hazard in New York City from 1769 to 1775. He was authorized by the New York Committee of Safety to reorganize the local postal service in 1775, and the same year he was commissioned the first postmaster of New York City by the Continental Congress. He was appointed surveyor general of the United States Post Office, serving from 1776 to 1782, and as United States postmaster general from 1782 to 1789.

Hazard was the first secretary of the Insurance Company of North America. He was manager of the Schuylkill Bridge Company and also of the Delaware and Schuylkill Canal Company. He was trustee of the Presbyterian General Assembly, curator of the American Philosophical Society, and a corresponding member of the Massachusetts Historical Society. He was a pioneer collector and publisher of original historical records and was responsible for the publication of *Belknap's History of New Hampshire,* 1784. He was the editor of *Historical Collections* (two volumes), 1792–94. He died in Philadelphia.

HAZEN, Moses: army officer
Born Haverhill, Massachusetts, June 1, 1733; son of Moses and Abigail (White) Hazen; married Charlotte de la Saussaye, December 1770; died February 3, 1803.

Hazen served in the French and Indian War as well as other colonial wars. He was a lieutenant in the expeditions against Crown Point, New York, in 1756, and against Louisburg, the French stronghold on Cape Breton Island, Nova Scotia, Canada, in 1758. After participating in General James Wolfe's expedition against Quebec, Canada, in 1759, he settled in Quebec.

In 1776, at the outbreak of the Revolutionary War, Hazen's property was seized by the British because of their suspicions concerning his loyalty to the colonies. He then joined the colonial side in earnest and formed the 2nd Canadian Regiment (also known as Hazen's Own) in 1776, serving as colonel. He took part in the battles of Brandywine and Germantown with the Continental Army under Washington. He began construction of a military road to the Canadian border in 1779 and was commissioned a brigadier general two years later. He died in Troy, New York.

HECK, Barbara Ruckle: religious leader

Born County Limerick, Ireland, 1734; daughter of Sebastian Ruckle; married Paul Heck before 1760; died August 17, 1804.

Mrs. Heck, who came to New York in 1760, was responsible for beginning the Wesleyan movement in America in 1766. This resulted two years later in the erection of the first Wesleyan chapel in America. She helped to found a Wesleyan Society in Washington County, New York, in 1770. She is called the mother of Methodism in America.

A Loyalist, Mrs. Heck was forced to move to Canada at the outbreak of the Revolutionary War. She died in Augusta, Canada.

HERKIMER, Nicholas: army officer

Born in what is now Herkimer, New York, 1728; son of Johan Jost and Katharine Herkimer; married Lany Tygert; second marriage to Myra Tygert; died August 16, 1777.

A lieutenant in the New York militia during the French and Indian War, Herkimer was the commander of Fort Herkimer in 1758. He was also chairman of the Committee of Safety of Tryon County in the Mohawk Valley in New York. In 1776, as a result of the threat posed by the large Loyalist following in the Mohawk Valley, he became brigadier general of the New York militia in charge of defense against Indian and Tory attacks.

In 1777 Herkimer was placed in charge of the relief expedition to Fort Stanwix, which was being besieged by the British at the time. During this operation he was ambushed by Tories and Indians at Oriskany

and forced to retreat, receiving mortal wounds in the course of the battle. Although it appeared to be a British victory, its adverse effect on the larger British strategy of General Burgoyne greatly benefited the overall American cause.

HICKS, Elias: clergyman

Born Hempstead Township, Long Island, New York, March 19, 1748; son of John and Martha (Smith) Hicks; married Jemima Seaman, 1771; father of eleven children; died February 27, 1830.

At the age of fifteen, Hicks became a carpenter's apprentice in New York City. Circa 1775 he became a Quaker minister and preached in almost every state and in Canada. He was an opponent of slavery, and from 1818 until his death he was recognized as a champion of liberal views. He was inclined toward extreme Quietism and emphasized an inward aspect of religion, views which led to a division in the Quaker Church in 1827–28. His branch became known as "Hicksite," as opposed to the "Orthodox" branch.

Hicks was the author of several works, including *Observations on Slavery,* 1811; *Elias Hicks's Journal of His Life and Labors,* 1828; and *The Letters of Eilas Hicks,* 1834. He died in Jericho, New York.

HOBART, John Sloss: senator, jurist

Born Fairfield, Connecticut, May 6, 1738; son of the Reverend Noah and Ellen (Sloss) Hobart; married Mary Grinnell, 1764; died February 4, 1805.

Hobart graduated from Yale at the age of twenty-one. In 1765 he was a member of both the New York Stamp Act Congress and the Sons of Liberty. He was on the Committee of Correspondence in 1774, and the following year he was a deputy to the New York Provincial Convention. From 1775 to 1777 he sat in the New York Provincial Congress, and from 1777 to 1798 he was a justice in the New York Supreme Court.

Hobart was a delegate to the Poughkeepsie Convention which ratified the United

States Constitution in 1788. In 1793 he received an honorary LL.D. from Yale. From January 11 to May 5, 1798, he sat in the United States Senate as a representative from New York. From 1798 until his death in 1805 he was United States district judge for New York.

HOLT, John: publisher
Born Williamsburg, Virginia, 1721; married Elizabeth Hunter, 1749; died January 30, 1784.

At the age of thirty-four Holt founded the *Connecticut Gazette,* which was the first newspaper printed in Connecticut. He was a junior partner in James Parker and Company and published the *New York Gazette* and the *Weekly Post-Boy* in 1760. He published a journal intermittently and under several names from 1763 to 1783. In 1775 he published the *Virginia Gazette or the Norfolk Intelligencer.* He died in New York City and was buried in St. Paul's Churchyard there.

HUMPHREY, Reuben: congressman
Born West Simsbury, Connecticut, September 2, 1757; died August 10, 1832.

Humphrey entered the military as a private during the Revolutionary War, eventually advancing to captain. For five years he was the keeper of Newgate State Prison in Simsbury, Connecticut. In 1801 he moved to New York and settled near Marcellus. He was the first judge of Onondaga County, serving from 1804 to 1807. He attended the 10th Congress (1807–09) of the United States House of Representatives as a delegate from New York. He was a member of the New York Senate from 1811 to 1815, then retired from politics to engage in farming. He died near Marcellus, New York, and was buried in the Old City Cemetery in Marcellus.

★★★★★

JAY, Sir James: physician
Born New York City, October 27, 1732; son of Peter and Mary (Van Cortlandt) Jay; died October 1815.

After obtaining an M.D. from the University of Edinburgh (Scotland) in 1753, Jay established a medical practice in New York City. In 1762 he went to England to raise funds for King's College (now Columbia); King George III knighted him during his stay. During the early years of the American Revolution, he sent military information to the colonies from England. In 1778 he returned to America and became a member of the New York Senate, serving for four years.

In 1782, after undergoing an apparent change of loyalties, Jay made an attempt to reunite England and America; failing, he journeyed to England. He practiced medicine there for a number of years but later returned to America.

Jay served as a trustee of the College of Physicians and Surgeons in Springfield, New Jersey, from 1807 to 1811. He wrote *A Letter to Governors of the College of New York* (1771) and *Reflections and Observations on the Gout* (1772). He died in Springfield.

JAY, John: chief justice of the United States Supreme Court, governor of New York, Continental congressman
Born New York City, December 12, 1745; son of Peter and Mary (Van Cortlandt) Jay; married Sarah Livingston, April 28, 1774; father of seven children (including Peter Augustus and William); died May 17, 1829.

Jay graduated from King's College (now Columbia) in 1764 and four years later was admitted to the New York City bar. In 1769 he became secretary to the royal commission settling the boundary dispute between New York and New Jersey. From 1774 to 1779 he was a delegate to the Continental Congress, serving as president the last two years. In 1776 he attended the New York Provincial Congress, where he helped draft a state constitution; the same year he became chief justice of the state, holding this office until 1778. About this time he also was commissioned a colonel in the New York militia.

Jay accepted an appointment as minister plenipotentiary to Spain in 1779. Benjamin Franklin called him to Paris in 1782 as joint commissioner for negotiating peace with Great Britain. Two years later he became United States Secretary for Foreign Affairs; during his tenure he tried to settle commercial disputes with Morocco and Prussia. Along with James Madison and Alexander Hamilton he wrote the *Federalist* papers in 1787 and 1788, which were primarily intended to persuade New York to adopt the United States Constitution. He left the office of foreign secretary in 1789 and in that year became the first chief justice of the United States. During his six-year tenure on the bench, he wrote the *Chisholm vs. Georgia* decision, which resulted in the Eleventh Amendment to the Constitution, and also formulated the Jay Treaty with Great Britain (1794), which settled outstanding disputes on matters such as debts, boundaries, and navigation rights on the Mississippi River.

From 1795 to 1801 Jay was governor of New York. He was elected president of the Westchester Bible Society in 1818 and of the American Bible Society in 1821. He died in Bedford, New York, at the age of eighty-three.

JEMISON, Mary: colonist

Born 1743; daughter of Thomas and Jane (Erwin) Jemison; married Sheninjee, circa 1761; second marriage to Hiokatoo, circa 1766; mother of eight children; died September 19, 1833.

Jemison, who was born on the Atlantic Ocean while her parents were voyaging from Belfast to Philadelphia, was captured in 1758 by Shawnee Indians at the junction of Sharps Run and Conewago Creek in Pennsylvania. Two Seneca tribeswomen adopted her and gave her the name Dehgewanus. She married the Delaware warrior Sheninjee, by whom she had two children. In 1763 she went to Little Beard's Town (now Geneseo, New York), where she turned down an opportunity to return to her people. She had six children by her second marriage.

In 1817 Jemison, known as "the White Woman of the Genesee," became a naturalized citizen. She died at the age of ninety and was buried in Letchworth Park, New York.

JOHNSON, Guy: Loyalist, superintendent of Indian affairs

Born Ireland, 1740; married Mary Johnson; died March 5, 1788.

Johnson served in the military throughout the French and Indian War. After a period as secretary to Sir William Johnson, he became a lieutenant in an independent New York company. Commander of a company of rangers under General Amherst in 1759–60, he later was commissioned a colonel and then an adjutant general in the New York militia. In 1762 he became deputy for the Six Nations and the Neighboring Indians and served occasionally as secretary to the superintendent.

Johnson was a delegate to the New York Assembly from 1773 to 1775; also during this time he became superintendent of the Northern Department of Indians (1774). At the beginning of the American Revolution he tried to organize the Indians against the colonists, and from 1778 to 1782 he led Indian riots, as well as commanding Fort Niagara from 1780 to 1782. He left the superintendency in 1782 and returned to England the next year. He died in London.

JOHNSON, Sir John: Loyalist, superintendent of Indian affairs

Born Johnstown, New York, November 5, 1742; son of Sir William and Catharine (Weisenberg) Johnson; married Mary Watts, June 30, 1773; father of Sir Adam Gordon; died January 4, 1830.

Johnson was commissioned a captain in a company of the North Carolina militia in 1760 and later became a colonel in a regiment of horse. In 1765 he was knighted in England and in 1774 was created a baronet.

The latter year he received a commission as a major general in the New York militia. During the Revolutionary War he was commissioned a lieutenant colonel and served at the Battle of Oriskany in 1777.

In 1782 Johnson was named superintendent general of the Six Nations of Indians in Quebec province, an appointment that was renewed in 1791. In 1783 he made his home in Canada and was given a tract of land to compensate for seizure of his American lands by New York. He became a member of the Quebec Provincial Council and was commissioned a colonel in the British Army. He died in Montreal at the age of eighty-seven.

JONES, Samuel: lawyer

Born Fort Hill, Long Island, New York, July 26, 1734; son of William and Phoebe (Jackson) Jones; married Eleanor Turk, 1765; second marriage to Cornelia Haring (also spelled Herring), 1768; father of two children; died November 25, 1819.

Jones was a member of the New York Committee of One Hundred. In 1777 he was directed to collect and reduce to a form proper for legislative enactment all statutes of Great Britain that were continued in force under the New York Constitution of 1777. He represented Queens County in the state assembly from 1786 to 1790 and in 1788 participated in the state convention ratifying the United States Constitution.

From 1789 to 1796 Jones was recorder of New York City. He also served in the state senate from 1791 to 1797, during which time he drafted a law that established and provided for the regulation of the office of comptroller; he held that office himself from 1797 to 1800. He died in West Neck, Long Island.

JONES, Thomas: jurist

Born Fort Neck, South Oyster Bay, Long Island, New York, April 30, 1731; son of David and Anna (Willet) Jones; married Anne De Lancey, December 9, 1762; father of Anne De Lancey (adopted); died July 25, 1792.

Jones graduated from Yale in 1750 and was admitted to the New York bar in 1755. Two years later he became clerk of the Court of Common Pleas of Queens County, New York. During this time he also served as attorney for and then member of the board of governors of King's College (now Columbia).

From 1769 to 1773 Jones was recorder of New York City, moving from there to justice of the New York Supreme Court, a position he held until 1776. Imprisoned during the American Revolution for his Loyalist sympathies, he went to England in 1781.

Jones was the author of *History of New York During the Revolutionary War.* He died in Hoddesdon, Hertfordshire, England.

★★★★★

KING, Rufus: Continental congressman, senator

Born Scarboro, Maine, March 24, 1755; son of Captain Richard and Isabella (Bragdon) King; married Mary Alsop, March 30, 1786; father of John Alsop, Charles, and James Gare; died April 29, 1827.

King graduated from Harvard in 1777, then became an aide to General Sullivan in his expedition to Rhode Island. After serving in the Massachusetts House of Representatives (1782), he became the Newburyport delegate to the Massachusetts General Court, serving in 1783, 1784, and 1785. He represented his state in the Continental Congress from 1784 to 1787 and attended the United States Constitutional Convention in Philadelphia in 1787. He also participated in the state ratification convention.

King served in the New York Assembly in the years 1789–90 and in the United States Senate from 1789 to 1796 and again from 1813 to 1825. In 1791 he was named director of the United States Bank. Branching out into international diplomacy, he became minister to Great Britain in 1796 and held that post until 1803. He returned briefly to this position during 1825–26. In 1804 he was an unsuccessful Federalist candidate for vice president.

While serving in the United States Senate, King wrote the Navigation Act (1818). He opposed the admission of Missouri as a slave state and voted against the Missouri Compromise in 1820. He proposed buying freedom for the slaves with proceeds from the sale of public lands. In 1821 he attended the New York Constitutional Convention.

King died in Jamaica, Long Island, New York, and was buried at Gracie Church there.

KIRKLAND, Samuel: missionary

Born Norwich, Connecticut, December 1, 1741; son of the Reverend Daniel and Mary (Perkins) Kirtland; married Jerusha Bingham, September 19, 1769; father of John Thornton; died February 28, 1808.

In 1765 Kirkland obtained an A.B. in absentia from the College of New Jersey (now Princeton). He had been living with the Seneca Indians since 1764 and remained until 1766. In the latter year he was ordained a minister in the Congregational Church in Lebanon, Connecticut, and began a forty-year career working with the Oneida Indians, establishing a church and teaching habits of industry.

In 1770 Kirkland placed himself under the charge of the Boston Commissioners of the Honorable Society in Scotland for Propagating Christian Knowledge. During 1774–75 he was instrumental in preventing Lord Dunmore's War from becoming a general Indian uprising; in 1775 he obtained a general declaration of neutrality from the Six Nations. He rebuilt the church in 1784 and four years later was granted 4,000 acres of land by the Indians and New York State in recognition of his services.

In 1792 and 1793 Kirkland brought together a council of the Six Nations and persuaded it to send a large delegation of chiefs to Philadelphia to negotiate with the United States Government; this work resulted in continued friendly relations between the Six Nations and the United States. In 1793 he founded Hamilton Oneida Academy for Indians, which later became Hamilton College.

Kirkland died in Clinton, New York, and was buried in Hamilton College Cemetery.

★★★★★

LAMB, John: Revolutionary patriot, army officer

Born New York City, January 1, 1735; son of Anthony Lamb; married Catherine Jandine, November 13, 1755; died May 31, 1800.

Lamb joined the Sons of Liberty in 1765; ten years later (July 1775) he was commissioned captain of an artillery company. During the Revolutionary War he served as a major in command of the Northern Department of the Continental Army. In 1777 he was taken prisoner by the British, exchanged, then appointed colonel of the 2nd Continental Artillery. He commanded the artillery at the United States Military Academy in 1779–80.

In 1781 Lamb participated in the siege and battle of Yorktown. Two years later he was brevetted a brigadier general. In 1784 he was appointed collector of customs of the Port of New York. He was a member of the New York legislature and an original member of the Society of the Cincinnati.

LANSING, John: Continental congressman, jurist

Born Albany, New York, January 30, 1754; son of Gerrit Jacob and Jannetje (Waters) Lansing; died circa 1829.

Lansing studied law under Robert Yates in Albany and under James Duane in New York City. In 1775 he was admitted to the New York bar. He was secretary to General Schuyler in 1776, 1777, and 1789. From 1780 to 1786 he was a member of the New York State Assembly. In 1784 and 1785 he served in the Continental Congress, and in 1787 he was a delegate from New York to the United States Constitutional Convention. The next year he served as a delegate to the New York Convention to ratify the federal constitution.

In 1790 Lansing was a member of the commission to fix the boundary between New York and Vermont. For the next eight years he was an associate justice of the New York Supreme Court and from 1798 to 1801 served as chief justice. He was chancellor of New York from 1801 to 1814. In 1804 he declined a unanimous nomination for the New York governorship.

Lansing served as a regent of the University of the State of New York from 1817 to 1829 and as a presidential elector in 1824. He mysteriously disappeared in New York City on December 12, 1829.

LAURANCE, John: senator, army officer, jurist
Born Falmouth, England, 1750; married Elizabeth Macdougall, 1774 or 1775; second marriage to Elizabeth Lawrence, June 30, 1791; died November 11, 1810.

Laurance came to America when he was seventeen years old, settling in New York City. He was admitted to the New York bar in 1772. In 1775 and 1776 he served as a second lieutenant in the New York Regiment, Continental Army. He was aide-de-camp to General Washington in 1776. He served as judge advocate general on the staff of the commander-in-chief of the Continental Army presiding at the trial of Major John André from 1777 to 1782.

In 1784 Laurance was elected vestryman of Trinity Church and a trustee of Columbia. He was a delegate to the Congress of Confederation from 1785 to 1787 and a member of the New York State Senate from 1788 to 1790. He was a delegate from New York to the United States House of Representatives from 1789 to 1793 (1st and 2nd congresses).

In 1794 Laurance became a director of the Bank of the United States and a judge of the United States District Court, serving in the latter position until 1796. He was a member of the United States Senate from November 8, 1796, to August 1800. He died in New York City and was buried in the First Presbyterian Churchyard on Fifth Avenue.

LEE, Ann: religious leader
Born Manchester, England, February 29, 1736; daughter of John Lee (or Lees); married Abraham Standerin, January 5, 1762; mother of four children; died September 8, 1784.

Lee joined the Shaker society in England in 1758; twenty-two years later she came to be recognized as leader of the sect. In 1774 she came to America and two years later settled in the village of Watervliet, near Albany, New York, where she founded a Shaker community.

Mother Ann, as she was called by her followers, was believed to be the second appearance of Christ. Her group, known as The Millennial Church, was persecuted because of its pacifist doctrines. In 1780 Mother Ann and other church leaders were arrested for treason as a result of their refusal to take the oath of allegiance.

Lee conducted a religious tour of New England in 1781, preaching the second coming of Christ and the need for frugality and integrity. She died and was buried in Watervliet.

LEWIS, Francis: Continental congressman
Born Llandaff, Wales, March 21, 1713; son of the Reverend Francis and Amy (Pettingal) Lewis; married Elizabeth Annesley, June 15, 1745; father of Francis Lewis and Morgan; died December 30, 1802.

Lewis came to America in 1738. An aide to General Mercer in the French and Indian War, he was captured at Fort Oswego in 1757. In 1765 he attended the Stamp Act Congress. He was a member of the Sons of Liberty, a delegate to the New York Provincial Convention (in 1774), and a member of the Committee of Fifty-one and Sixty. He served in the Continental Congress from 1775 to 1779.

In 1776 Lewis was instrumental in drawing up a new government for New York. From 1779 to 1781 he was a member of the Board of Admiralty and served on the marine, secret, and commercial committees. He died in New York City.

LEWIS, Morgan: governor of New York, army officer

Born New York City, October 16, 1754; son of Francis and Elizabeth (Annesley) Lewis; married Gertrude Livingston, May 11, 1779; died April 7, 1844.

In 1773 Lewis graduated from the College of New Jersey (now Princeton). In 1776 he was commissioned a major in the 2nd Regiment of the New York militia, later gaining a promotion to colonel and then to deputy quartermaster general. He was chief of staff at the battles of Ticonderoga and Saratoga.

After the war Lewis was admitted to the New York City bar and began a distinguished political career. He was a member of the New York Assembly in 1789–90 and in 1792. He held the office of attorney general of New York in 1791–92. He was a justice of the Supreme Court of New York from 1792 to 1801, serving as chief justice in 1801. From 1804 to 1807 he was governor of New York. He was also a member of the New York Senate and a member of the Council of Appointment.

Lewis resumed his military career at the start of the War of 1812; he was commissioned a brigadier general and then a quartermaster general in the United States Army. He was a major general serving on the Niagara frontier in 1813.

In 1821 Lewis was grand master of the Freemasons of the United States. He served as president of the New York Historical Society from 1832 to 1836, and from 1839 to 1844 he was president general of the Society of the Cincinnati. He was a founder of New York University.

Lewis died in New York City at the age of eighty-nine.

L'HOMMEDIEU, Ezra: state senator, agriculturist

Born Southold, Long Island, New York, August 30, 1734; son of Benjamin and Martha (Borune) L'Hommedieu; married Charity Floyd, 1765; second marriage to Mary Havens, 1803; died September 27, 1811.

After graduating from Yale in 1754, L'Hommedieu was admitted to the bar. From 1774 to 1777 he served as a member of the New York Provincial congresses and was a framer of the Constitution of 1777. He was a member of the New York Assembly from 1777 to 1783 and a delegate from New York to the Continental Congress from 1779 to 1783 and in 1787–88.

A member of the New York State Senate from 1784 to 1809, L'Hommedieu served on the Council of Appointment in 1784 and in 1799. From 1784 to 1809 he was clerk of Suffolk County. He was noted as the principal author of the University of the State of New York as reconstituted in 1787 and acted as a regent from 1784 to 1811. In 1801 he was a member of the Interpretative Constitutional Convention.

L'Hommedieu wrote numerous papers on agriculture for the Transactions of the New York Society for the Promotion of Agriculture, Arts, and Manufactures, of which he was vice president for many years. He died in Southold.

LIVINGSTON, Henry Brockholst: associate justice of the United States Supreme Court

Born New York City, November 25, 1757; son of William and Susanna (French) Livingston; married Catherine Keteltas; second marriage to Ann Ludlow; third marriage to Catherine (Seaman) Kortright; died March 18, 1823.

Livingston graduated from Princeton at the age of seventeen. Commissioned a captain in the Continental Army in 1776, he was promoted to major the same year and to lieutenant colonel the next, serving as an aide in the siege of Ticonderoga and the Battle of Saratoga. He left the service circa 1778.

Livingston served as private secretary to John Jay, United States minister to Spain, from 1779 to 1782. After studying law with Peter Yates in Albany, New York, from 1782 to 1783, he was admitted to the New York bar. From 1802 to 1807 he was a judge in the New York State Supreme Court. He was an associate justice of the United States Supreme Court from 1806 to 1823.

Livingston was a trustee of the New York Society Library and a member of the New York Historical Society, serving as vice president in 1805. In 1810 he received an honorary LL.D. from Harvard. He died in Washington, D.C.

LIVINGSTON, James: state legislator, army officer

Born Montreal, Quebec, Canada, March 27, 1747; son of John and Catryna (Ten Broeck) Livingston; married Elizabeth Simpson, 1771; father of nine children (including Elizabeth and Margaret); died November 29, 1832.

Livingston raised and commanded a regiment of Canadian refugees in the Continental Army in 1775. The next year he was commissioned a colonel by the Continental Congress. From 1784 to 1787 he was a member of the first board of regents of the University of the State of New York. In 1786–87 and from 1789 to 1791 he was a representative from Montgomery County to the New York Assembly. He died in Saratoga County, New York.

LIVINGSTON, John Henry: clergyman, college president

Born near Poughkeepsie, New York, May 30, 1746; son of Henry and Susanna (Conklin) Livingston; married Sarah Livingston, November 26, 1775; father of one child; died January 20, 1825.

Livingston graduated from Yale in 1762. In 1769 he was licensed to preach by Classis of Amsterdam and was ordained a year later, also graduating from the University of Utrecht that year. From 1770 to 1810 he was pastor of the Dutch Reformed Church in New York City. He was professor of theology at the General Synod of the Dutch Reformed Church from 1784 to 1825, thus establishing the first theological seminary in the United States.

Livingston was largely responsible for resolving the conflict over sovereignty between American and Dutch factions in the Reformed Church. He was president of Queen's College (now Rutgers University) from 1810 to 1825. His works include *Oratio Inauguralis de Veritate Religionis Christianae,* 1785; *The Glory of the Redeemer,* 1799; *A Funeral Service, or Meditations Adapted to Funeral Addresses,* 1812; *A Dissertation on the Marriage of a Man with His Sister-in-Law,* 1816. He died in New Brunswick, New Jersey.

LIVINGSTON, Peter Van Brugh: merchant

Born Albany, New York, October 1710; son of Philip and Catharine (Van Brugh) Livingston; married Mary Alexander, November 14, 1739; second marriage to Elizabeth Ricketts, 1767; died December 28, 1792.

Livingston graduated from Yale in 1731 and became a merchant in New York City. He supplied military expeditions and financed privateering ventures during the French and Indian War. From 1748 to 1761 he served as a trustee of the College of New Jersey (now Princeton). He signed the Non-Importation Agreement prompted by the Sugar Act of 1764.

Livingston was a member of the New York Committee of Fifty-one, which was organized to choose delegates to the First Continental Congress in 1774. He was a member of the Committee of Sixty and the Committee of One Hundred, which acted successively as provisional governments of New York in 1775. He was presiding officer of the New York Provincial Congress in 1775.

Livingston died in Elizabethtown, New Jersey.

LIVINGSTON, Philip: Continental congressman

Born Albany, New York, January 15, 1716; son of Philip and Catharine (Van Brugh) Livingston; mar-

ried Christina Ten Broeck, April 14, 1740; died June 12, 1778.

Livingston received an A.B. from Yale in 1737; nine years later he established a professorship of divinity at that school. In 1754 he was an organizer of the New York Society Library and for the next nine years served as an alderman of the East Ward in New York City. In 1756–57 he was president of the St. Andrews Society in New York City. In 1758 he served in the New York Assembly. He was a member of the New York House of Representatives from 1763 to 1769, serving as speaker in 1768.

Livingston was a delegate to the Stamp Act Congress in 1765 and an organizer of the New York Chamber of Commerce in 1768. In 1771 he was a member of the First board of governors of New York Hospital. Three years later he served with his brother Peter on the Committee of Fifty-one, which named New York delegates to the First Continental Congress. From 1774 to 1778 he himself was a member of the Continental Congress.

In 1775 Livingston, again with his older brother, served on the Committee of Sixty to enforce the terms of Congress and on the Committee of One Hundred to carry on provincial affairs until the meeting of the First Provincial Congress. In 1776 he was a member of the Board of Treasury of the Continental Congress; he was also a signer of the Declaration of Independence. The next year he was a member of the New York State Senate.

Livingston was a framer of the New York Constitution and a founder of King's College (now Columbia). He died in New York City and was buried in Prospect Hill Cemetery in York, Pennsylvania.

LIVINGSTON, Robert R.: jurist

Born New York City, August 1718; son of Robert and Margaret (Howarden) Livingston; married Margaret Beekman, December 19, 1742; father of nine children (including Robert R. and Edward); died December 9, 1775.

From 1758 to 1768 Livingston represented Dutchess County in the New York Assembly. From 1759 to 1763 he was a judge in the New York Admiralty Court and for the next five years a judge in the state Supreme Court. He was chairman of the New York Committee of Correspondence in 1765. A delegate to the Stamp Act Congress, he drafted an address of congress to King George III in 1765.

LIVINGSTON, Robert R.: Continental congressman, diplomat

Born New York City, November 27, 1746; son of Judge Robert R. and Margaret (Beekman) Livingston; married Mary Stevens, September 9, 1770; father of two children; died February 26, 1813.

Livingston graduated from King's College (now Columbia) in 1765 and was admitted to the bar five years later. He served as recorder of New York City from 1773 to 1775. In 1775 he became a member of the New York Provincial Convention and, later in the year, a delegate to the Continental Congress. As a congressman from 1775 to 1779, from 1779 to 1781, and again in 1784–85, he served on the committee appointed to draft the Declaration of Independence and on the committees on financial affairs, supplies, legal organization, foreign affairs, and military problems.

In 1777 Livingston was a delegate to the New York State Constitutional Convention. He established the New York Court of Appeals, drafting commissions for its judges and preparing their instructions, and was a member of the commission to govern New York after the British evacuation. From 1777 to 1801 he served as chancellor of New York and from 1781 to 1783 as United States secretary for foreign affairs.

Livingston administered the oath of office to General Washington as the first President of the United States in 1789. As United States minister to France in 1801, he worked to secure the treaty between the United States and France resulting in the Louisiana Purchase two years later.

Livingston, who received an honorary LL.D. from the University of the State of New York in 1792, also was noted for his many nonpolitical activities. He was president of the Society for the Promotion of the Useful Arts from 1791 to 1813; founder and first president of the American Academy of Fine Arts; and a trustee of the New York Society Library. In 1811 he became a member of the first New York Canal Commission. A friend, patron, and partner of Robert Fulton, he was granted a monopoly with Fulton on steam navigation by New York State.

Livingston died in Clermont, New York, and was buried on the estate "Clermont," near there.

LIVINGSTON, Walter: Continental congressman
Born November 27, 1740; son of Philip Livingston; father of at least one son, Henry Walter; died May 14, 1797.

In 1775 Livingston was a delegate to the New York Provincial Convention and a member of the first New York Provincial Congress. He was judge of Albany County, New York, in 1774–75. He was a commissary of stores and provisions for the Department of New York in 1775–76 and at the same time deputy commissary of the general Northern Department of the Continental Army.

Livingston served in the New York Assembly from 1777 to 1779, acting as speaker in 1778. In 1784 he was a member of the New York and Massachusetts Boundary Commission. In that same year he became a member of the board of regents of the University of the State of New York and served for three years. He was also a member of the Continental Congress in 1784 and 1785. In 1785 he was appointed commissioner of the United States Treasury. He died in New York City.

LOW, Isaac: Continental congressman
Born Raritan Landing, New Jersey, April 13, 1735;

son of Cornelius, Jr., and Johanna (Gouverneur) Low; married Margarita Cuyler, July 17, 1760; father of Isaac; died July 25, 1791.

In 1765 Low was a delegate from New York to the Stamp Act Congress. Three years later he served as head of a committee of inspection to enforce a non-importation agreement. He was chairman of the Committee of Fifty-one and a drafter of proposals for a general congress to deal with non-importation.

Low represented New York in the First Continental Congress in 1774–75. In 1775 he became a member of the Provincial Congress. In that year he was also a founder of the New York Chamber of Commerce, serving as its president until 1783. He was accused of treason and arrested in 1776, and his property was confiscated by American authorities three years later. He moved to England in 1783 and died at Cowes, Isle of Wight.

LOW, Nicholas: merchant
Born near New Brunswick, New Jersey, March 30, 1739; son of Cornelius, Jr., and Johanna (Gouverneur) Low; married Alice Fleming; father of three children; died November 15, 1826.

Low was clerk to merchant Hayman Levy in New York City. During the American Revolution he founded the merchant firm of Low and Wallace in New York City, and in 1785 he became a director of the Bank of New York. Two years later he served in the New York State Assembly. He was a member of the New York State Convention to ratify the United States Constitution in 1788.

Low had large land holdings in upper New York and in New York City. He helped develop the town of Ballston by building a hotel and a cotton factory there. The New York town of Lowville is named after him. He died in New York City.

LUDLOW, Daniel: merchant, banker
Born New York City, August 2, 1750; son of Gabriel and Elizabeth (Crommelin) Ludlow; married

Arabella Duncan, October 4, 1773; second marriage to Mrs. Van Horne; died September 26, 1814.

From 1770 to 1782 Ludlow was associated with the New York City importing business that his father had founded. From 1782 to 1790 he ran an importing firm with a partner, Edward Gould. He was a partner with his nephew in Daniel Ludlow and Company, mercantile traders, from 1790 to 1808.

Ludlow was a founder of the Manhattan Company, a subsidiary of the Bank of Manhattan Company, in 1799, serving as its president until 1808. He was a navy agent after 1801 and was a director of the Harlem Bridge Company. When his banking firm failed in 1808, Ludlow moved to Skaneateles, New York, where he died six years later.

LUDLOW, Gabriel George: Loyalist
Born New York City, April 16, 1736; son of Gabriel and Frances (Duncan) Ludlow; married Ann Ver Planck, September 3, 1760; died February 12, 1808.

Ludlow served as governor of King's College (now Columbia) in New York City. He was a colonel in the New York militia and justice of the peace of Queens County, New York. He commanded the 3rd Battalion of De Lancey's Long Island Brigade of Loyal Americans in the Revolutionary War and was commissioned a colonel at the close of the war.

From 1784 to 1808 Ludlow served on the first Council of New Brunswick. He was a member of the first City Council of St. John, New Brunswick, and served as the town's first mayor from 1785 to 1795. He was the first judge of the Vice Admiralty Court, serving from 1787 to 1803. He administered government as president of His Majesty's Council and commander-in-chief of the Province of New Brunswick from 1803 to 1808. He died in Carleton, New Brunswick.

LUDLOW, George Duncan: jurist
Born 1734; son of Gabriel and Frances (Duncan) Ludlow; married Frances Duncan Ludlow (a cousin), April 22, 1758; father of three children; died November 13, 1808.

Ludlow studied law before 1768 and practiced as an apothecary. From 1768 to 1778 he served on the New York Governor's Council. He was a judge in the New York Supreme Court from 1769 to 1778 and superintendent of police for Long Island in 1778.

A Loyalist supporter during the American Revolution, Ludlow lost all of his property to confiscation activities of the Revolutionaries in 1779 and sailed for England four years later. From 1784 to 1808 he was chief justice of the Province of New Brunswick. He died in Fredericton, New Brunswick.

★★★★★

McCOMB, John: architect
Born Princeton, New Jersey; son of James McComb; married; father of at least two sons (Isaac and John, Jr.); died 1811.

Credited with building the old Brick Church in 1767, McComb also designed the North Dutch Church in 1769 and New York Hospital in 1773, all in New York City. He served with the Continental Army during the Revolution and later (1793) resumed his practice of architecture. He was appointed city surveyor of New York City in 1794.

McCORD, Andrew: congressman
Born in what is now Stony Ford, New York, circa 1754; died 1808.

McCord attended Newburgh (New York) Academy and was later a delegate to the convention to choose deputies to the 2nd New York Provincial Congress at New Paltz in 1775. He was commissioned a quartermaster in the Ulster County (New York) militia in 1787 and served as a captain until 1798.

A member of the New York Assembly in 1795–96, 1798, 1800, 1802, and 1807 (serving as speaker the latter year), McCord was elected to the United States House of Representatives for the 8th Congress (1803–05). After his term in Congress ended, he engaged in farming. He died in his birthplace, Stony Ford, and was buried near there in a family cemetery.

McDOUGALL, Alexander: Continental congressman, army officer

Born Islay, Inner Hebrides, Scotland, July or August, 1732; son of Ronald and Elizabeth McDougall; married Hannah Bostwick, 1767; father of three children (including Elizabeth); died June 9, 1786.

McDougall, who arrived in America in 1738, commanded the privateers *Tyger* and *Barrington* from 1756 to 1783. He was the author of a written attack addressed "to the Betrayed Inhabitants of the City and Colony of New York" and signed "A Son of Liberty," 1769. He was arrested for his rebel activities and imprisoned in 1770–71. Later (1774–75) he was a member of the New York Committee of Fifty-one.

A colonel in the 1st Regiment of the New York militia in 1775, McDougall was commissioned a brigadier general in the Continental Army in 1776 and a major general in 1777. He served in the battles of Chatterton's Hill, Germantown, and White Plains. Commanding officer on the Highlands of the Hudson, he took command of West Point after the discovery of Benedict Arnold's treason in 1780. He was arrested and court-martialed for insubordination in 1782.

Elected to represent New York in the Continental Congress in 1781–82 and 1784–85, McDougall served in the New York Senate from 1783 to 1786. He was an organizer and first president of the Bank of New York and president of the New York Society of the Cincinnati. He died in New York City and was buried in a family vault at the First Presbyterian Church, in New York.

MIDDLETON, Peter: physician

Born England; married Susannah Nichols, November 1766; father of Susannah Margaret; died January 9, 1781.

Middleton, who received an M.D. from the University of St. Andrews (Scotland) in 1752, undertook one of the first recorded human dissections in America (with Dr. John Bard). He served as surgeon general on the Crown Point expedition during the French and Indian War. A founder of the St. Andrew's Society of New York, he was president from 1767 to 1770.

Middleton was a professor of physiology and pathology at King's College (now Columbia) Medical School from 1767 to 1770, then served as a professor of materia medica there from 1770 to 1773. He was named governor of the college in 1773 and served on the staff of the New York Hospital in 1774. He was author of *A Medical Discourse; or an Historical Inquiry into the Ancient and Present State of Medicine.*

MITCHELL, Isaac: editor

Born near Albany, New York, circa 1759; died November 26, 1812.

Mitchell was editor of *American Farmer and Dutchess County Advertiser* in Poughkeepsie, New York, from 1799 to 1801. The latter year he became editor of the *Guardian* of Poughkeepsie, taking over the paper's ownership the following year and renaming it *Political Barometer.* He was editor of the *Republican Crisis* in Albany from 1806 until 1812, when he became owner of the *Republican Herald* in Poughkeepsie and also began publishing the *Northern Politician.* He was the author of *The Asylum, or Alonzo and Melissa;* completely plagiarized by Daniel Jackson, Jr., in 1811, it was reprinted by Jackson in 1824 and became a best-seller.

MOFFITT, Hosea: congressman

Born Stephentown, New York, November 17, 1757; died August 31, 1825.

Moffitt advanced from ensign to lieutenant in the 4th Regiment of the Albany County (New York) militia during the Revolution. He was a justice of the peace in 1791, town clerk in 1791 and 1797, and a member of the New York Assembly in 1794–95 and 1801. Appointed a brigadier general in the New York militia in 1806, he was supervisor of the town of Stephentown from 1806 to 1809 and served as sheriff of Rensselaer County, New York, in 1810–11.

A Federalist, Moffitt was a New York delegate to the United States House of Representatives for the 13th–14th congresses (1813–17). He was a member of the board of managers of the Rensselaer County Bible Society in 1815. He died in Stephentown and was buried in the Old Presbyterian Cemetery there.

MONTGOMERY, Richard: army officer
Born Swords, Ireland, December 2, 1738; son of Thomas and Mary Montgomery; married Janet Livingston, July 24, 1773; died December 31, 1775.

Educated at St. Andrews and Trinity College in Dublin, Ireland, Montgomery was an ensign in the 17th Infantry of the British Army at the siege of Louisburg in 1757. He was commissioned a captain in 1762.

Montgomery was a member of the New York Provincial Congress from Dutchess County in 1775. He served as a brigadier general in command of Schuyler's expeditions in Quebec and Montreal in 1775 and captured Fort Chambly and Fort St. Johns as well as Montreal. He was killed during the siege of Quebec and was buried at St. Paul's Church in New York City.

MOORE, Benjamin: bishop, college president
Born Newton, Long Island, New York, October 5, 1748; son of Samuel and Sarah (Fish) Moore; married Charity Clarke, April 20, 1778; father of Clement Clarke; died February 27, 1816.

Moore, who graduated at the head of his class at King's College (now Columbia) in 1768, received his deacon's and priest's orders from the Bishop of London in 1774. He served as president pro tem of King's College from 1775 to 1784. He was professor of rhetoric and logic at Columbia from 1784 to 1786 and served as president from 1801 to 1811. He was rector of Trinity Church in New York City in 1800 and became Protestant Episcopal bishop of New York. He died in Greenwich, near New York City.

MORRIS, Gouverneur: senator, diplomat, Continental congressman
Born Morrisania, New York, January 31, 1752; son of Lewis and Sarah (Gouverneur) Morris; married Anne Carey Randolph, December 25, 1809; father of one child; died November 6, 1816.

Morris, a graduate of King's College (now Columbia), studied law under William Smith, was admitted to the New York bar in 1771, and served as a member of the New York Provincial Congress from Westchester County from 1775 to 1777. He maintained a conservative position between the radicals (who favored a "reign of terror" against the Loyalists) and the staunch Loyalists (who wished to remain united with England). He was a member of the New York State Constitutional Convention in July 1776 and drafted (with John Jay and Robert R. Livingston) the final document; he secured the provision for an elected governor rather than an executive board. A member of a committee to organize the new government of New York State, Morris was also a member of the first New York Council of Safety. He represented New York in the Continental Congress in 1777–78 and drafted instructions to Benjamin Franklin, the first United States minister to France. He was not reelected to the Congress because of his refusal to support Governor George Clinton and New York's claims to Vermont.

In 1779 Morris transferred his residence and his law practice to Philadelphia, Pennsylvania. He contributed essays on finance (signed "An American") to the *Pennsylvania Packet,* February to April 1780. He was assistant superintendent of finance under Robert Morris from 1781 to 1785 and served as a delegate from Pennsylvania to the United States Constitutional Convention in Philadelphia in 1787, where he favored a strong centralized government controlled by the rich and well-born, a president elected for life, and a senate appointed for life by the president. He was noted for his cynical contempt for democracy.

Morris went to France as the agent of Robert Morris in 1789 and assisted in the opening of the tobacco trade on better terms for America and in the selling of American lands. He participated in a plot to rescue Louis XVI from the Tuileries and was appointed minister to France by President George Washington, serving from 1792 to 1794, thus being the only foreign minister to remain in Paris during the Reign of Terror. He then traveled throughout Europe from 1794 to 1798.

A New York delegate to the United States Senate from April 3, 1800, to 1803, Morris supported Jefferson's Louisiana Purchase. He retired to Morrisania in 1803. He denounced Jefferson's Embargo Acts during the War of 1812, and approved the Hartford Convention. He died in Morrisania and was buried in St. Anne's Episcopal Churchyard, Bronx, New York.

MORRIS, Lewis: Continental congressman
Born Morrisania, New York, April 8, 1726; son of Lewis and Tryntje (Staats) Morris; married Mary Walton, September 24, 1749; father of ten children; died January 22, 1798.

Morris, who received an A.B. from Yale in 1746, became the third and last lord of the manor of Morrisania in 1762. He was a member of the New York Provincial Assembly in 1769 and chairman of the delegation to the New York Provincial Convention in New York City in 1775. He attended the Continental Congress from 1775 to 1777, where he was a member of the committee of ways and means to supply the army and the committee on Indian affairs.

Morris was a brigadier general in command of the militia of Westchester County, New York, and a member of the 4th Provincial Congress at White Plains in 1776. He signed the Declaration of Independence, July 20, 1776. He served as a judge in Westchester County, 1777–78; a member of the board of regents of the University of the State of New York, 1784–98; a member of

the New York Senate, 1777–81 and 1784–88; and a member of the Council of Appointment, 1786. He died at Morrisania and was buried in St. Anne's Episcopal Churchyard, Bronx, New York.

MORRIS, Roger: army officer
Born Netherby, England, January 28, 1727; son of Roger and Mary (Jackson) Morris; married Mary Philipse, January 1758; father of four children; died September 13, 1794.

Morris was a captain in the 48th Regiment of the British Army and served in the Braddock campaign in the French and Indian War. Promoted to major in 1757, he saw action at the battles of Quebec and Montreal and in 1760 was made lieutenant colonel of the 47th Regiment. He retired from the British Army in 1764 and served as a member of the New York Council from 1765 to 1776.

Morris, a leading Loyalist, suffered the confiscation of his property (more than 51,000 acres in New York State) in the years preceding the Revolution. He then left America to settle in Yorkshire, England. He died in York at the age of sixty-seven and was buried in St. Savioursgate Churchyard there.

MUMFORD, Gurdon Saltonstall: congressman
Born New London, Connecticut, January 29, 1764; died April 30, 1831.

Mumford, who attended common schools, served as private secretary to Benjamin Franklin in Paris and then returned to America in 1785, settling in New York City. He became associated with his brothers in a commission business in 1791.

A Federalist, Mumford was a New York delegate to the United States House of Representatives for the 9th–11th congresses (1805–11). He served as a presidential elector in 1812. He was elected a director of the Bank of New York in 1812, opened a broker's office on Wall Street in New York City in 1813, and was a founder of the New York

Exchange. He died in New York City and is buried in the Old Collegiate Dutch Church Cemetery there.

MUNRO, Henry: clergyman

Born Scotland, 1730; son of Robert and Anne Munro; no record of first marriage; second marriage to Miss Stockton; third marriage to Eve Jay, March 31, 1766; father of one child; died May 30, 1801.

Munro was educated in Scotland, receiving B.A. and M.A. degrees from St. Andrews University. He studied divinity at the University of Edinburgh, Scotland. He was ordained to the ministry of the Church of Scotland in 1757 and became chaplain of the 77th Regiment of Highlanders, which came to America that year. He accompanied the regiment on expeditions against Fort Duquesne in 1758, forts Ticonderoga and Crown Point in 1759, and Montreal in 1760.

Munro went to New York in 1762, then journeyed to England in 1764, where he became a member of the Church of England and was ordained to the ministry of the Anglican Church in 1765. He returned to America that year as a missionary to Philipsburgh, New York, and was appointed rector of St. Peter's Church in Albany, New York, in 1768. He was an active missionary on the New York Frontier from 1768 to 1776, being awarded during this time (in 1773) an honorary M.A. from King's College (now Columbia).

Munro supported the British position during the Revolution and consequently was imprisoned at Albany in 1776. However, he escaped to Canada, where he served as chaplain to British forces before returning to England in 1778. He lived in Scotland from 1783 until his death in Edinburgh in 1801.

MURRAY, John: merchant, philanthropist

Born Lancaster, Pennsylvania, 1737; son of John Murray; married Hannah Lindley, December 1766; died October 11, 1808.

Murray, a Quaker, was a member of the New York City Chamber of Commerce from 1779 to 1806, serving as president after 1798. He was director of the Bank of New York in 1789, director of an insurance company, and a member of a commission to build one of the state prisons in New York City in 1796. A director of the Humane Society, he was a founder of a society for the free education of poor children. He died in New York City.

MURRAY, Robert: merchant

Born Scotland, 1721; son of John Murray; married Mary Lindley, 1744; father of at least one child; died July 22, 1786.

Arriving in America with his father in 1732, Murray began operating a flour mill in Dauphin County, Pennsylvania, sometime before 1750. He engaged in general trade in North Carolina from 1750 to 1753, operating in New York from 1753 to 1767 and then in England from 1767 to 1775. He supported the British during the Revolution. He returned to America in 1775 and continued his trading activities until his death in 1786.

★★★★★

NORTH, William: senator, army officer

Born Fort Frederic, Pemaquid, Maine, 1755; son of John and Elizabeth (Pitson) North; married Mary Duane, October 14, 1787; father of six children; died January 3, 1836.

Having moved to Boston in 1763 after his father's death, North became a second lieutenant in Colonel Thomas Craft's train of artillery in 1776. Three years later he was appointed aide-de-camp to Baron von Steuben; their military relationship grew into a close friendship, and North later wrote a biographical sketch of von Steuben. After the war North served as an inspector of the army with the rank of major.

In 1794 North served on the commission which was to strengthen the defenses of the State of New York. He was speaker of the New York Assembly in 1795, 1796, and 1810. He was a Federalist member of the United States Senate from May 5 to August 17, 1798, during which time he voted for the

253

Alien and Sedition Acts. Commissioned a brigadier general, he then served as adjutant general of the provisional army from 1798 to 1800. In 1810 he became a member of the commission which was to report on the possibility of a canal between lakes Erie and Ontario and the Hudson River.

North died in Duanesburg, New York, and was buried at the Christ Episcopal Church there.

★★★★★

OGDEN, Samuel: manufacturer
Born Newark, New Jersey, December 9, 1746; son of David and Gertrude (Gouverneur) Ogden; married Euphemia Ogden, February 5, 1775; father of twelve children (including David); died December 1, 1810.

Ogden manufactured ammunition during the American Revolution. In Boonton, New Jersey, after the war, he was a manufacturer of nails and other iron products. He invested in land in upper New York State and founded the town of Ogdensburg, New York.

★★★★★

PASCALIS-OUVRIERE, Felix: physician
Born southern France, circa 1750; died July 29, 1833.

Pascalis-Ouvriere, known after 1801 as Felix Pascalis, studied medicine at Montpellier University, where he received his M.D. He came to America in 1793 and settled in Philadelphia, where he was named vice president of the Chemical Society of Philadelphia in 1801. From 1813 to 1820 he was a member of the editorial staff of the New York City Medical Repository. He was a founder of the New York branch of the Linnaean Society of Paris and president for one term.

Pascalis-Ouvriere was the author of several medical works, including *The Medico-Chymical Dissertations on the Causes of the Epidemic Called Yellow Fever, and on the Best Antimonial Preparations for the Use of Medicine, by a Physician, Practitioner in Philadelphia,* 1796; *An Account of the Contagious Epidemic Yellow Fever, Which Pre-*

vailed in Philadelphia in the Summer and Autumn of 1797, 1798; and *An Exposition of the Dangers of Internment in Cities,* 1823. He died in New York City.

PAINE, Ephraim: Continental congressman
Born Canterbury, Connecticut, August 19, 1730; died August 10, 1785.

Paine studied medicine, then established a practice in Amenia, New York. He was a delegate to the New York Provincial Congress in 1775 and a county judge from 1778 to 1781. In 1780 he became a member of the Council of Appointment. From 1782 to 1783 he served as supervisor of Amenia and from 1779 to 1784 as a member of the New York State Senate.

Paine served as a member of the Continental Congress in 1784 and died the following year. He was buried at the Red Meeting House Cemetery, near Amenia.

PALMER, Beriah: congressman
Born Bristol County, Massachusetts, 1740; died May 20, 1812.

Palmer attended common schools, then studied law in Cornwall, New York. He was admitted to the New York bar and established a legal practice, also engaging in surveying and farming near Burnt Hills, New York.

In 1774 Palmer moved to Ballston Spa, New York. He served with the 12th Regiment of the New York militia during the American Revolution. He served as assessor in 1779 and the next year became commissioner of roads of the Ballston District, a position he held again in 1783–84. He became postmaster the latter year.

In 1791 Palmer was appointed judge of the Court of Common Pleas and moderator of the first board of supervisors of Saratoga County. Again in 1799 he served as a member of the Albany County Committee of Safety and supervisor of Saratoga County, having first served in 1790–91.

Palmer was a member of the New York State Assembly from 1792 to 1795 and a delegate to the New York Constitutional Convention in 1801. From 1803 to 1805 he served as a member of the United States House of Representatives, 8th Congress. Three years later he became surrogate of Saratoga County and served until 1812.

Palmer died in Ballston Spa and was buried in the Village Cemetery there.

PELL, Philip: Continental congressman
Born Pelham Manor, New York, July 7, 1753; died May 1, 1811.

Pell graduated from King's College (now Columbia) in 1770, studied law, and was admitted to the New York bar. He practiced in New York City and Westchester County.

Pell served as a lieutenant in the New York Volunteers in 1776 and the next year became a deputy judge advocate in the Continental Army. He was a member of the New York State Assembly from 1779 to 1781 and again from 1784 to 1786. He was a judge advocate general in the United States Army from 1781 to 1783 and a member of the staff of General Washington during the evacuation of New York City in 1783. From 1784 to 1787 he was a regent of the University of the State of New York. For the next three years he served as surrogate of Westchester County.

In 1788–89 Pell represented New York in the Continental Congress. He died at Pelham Manor and was buried in St. Paul's Churchyard in Eastchester (now Bronx).

PINTARD, John: merchant, legislator
Born New York City, May 18, 1759; son of John and Mary (Cannon) Pintard; married Eliza Brashear, November 12, 1784; father of two children; died June 21, 1844.

In 1776 Pintard received an A.B. from the College of New Jersey (now Princeton). After graduation, Pintard served alternately in a number of capacities, including deputy to the commissioner of prisoners in New York, a book auctioneer for and editor of the *Daily Advertiser,* and secretary of the New York

Fire Insurance Company (which he later served as president).

Known as the father of historical societies in America, Pintard was an organizer of the Massachusetts Historical Society in 1789. He organized a historical museum under the auspices of the Tammany Society in 1791 and served as first sagamore and later as grand sachem. In 1804 he was an organizer of the New York Historical Society, serving as its secretary for several years and as clerk of the corporation from its founding until 1810.

Pintard was a New York City alderman in 1788–89 and a member of the New York State legislature the next year. He was a New York City inspector from 1804 to 1810.

He was instrumental in reviving the New York City Chamber of Commerce and served as its secretary from 1817 to 1827. In 1819 he organized the first savings bank in New York City and served as its president from 1828 to 1841.

Pintard was a founder of the General Theological Seminary and secretary and vice president of the American Bible Society. In 1822 he was awarded an honorary LL.D. by Allegheny College. He died in New York City.

PINTARD, Lewis: merchant
Born New York City, October 12, 1732; son of John and Catherine (Carré) Pintard; married Susan Stockton; father of several children; died March 25, 1818.

At the age of fifteen Pintard inherited his father's New York City–based shipping and commission business. During the British occupation of New York City in the Revolutionary War, he acted as commissary for American prisoners in New York. He was also responsible for administering relief funds provided by the Continental Congress.

After the war Pintard became the chief American importer of Madeira wines and a major exporter of flaxseed. He later engaged in the sugar and molasses trade with the

West Indies. In 1797 he was a school commissioner in New Rochelle, New York. He died in Princeton, New Jersey.

PINTO, Isaac: merchant, translator
Born Portugal, June 23, 1720; never married; died January 17, 1791.

Pinto became wealthy in the import-export business in New York City. From 1760 to 1762 he was a wholesale wine merchant in Charlestown (now Charleston), South Carolina. In 1790–91 he taught Spanish privately in New York City. He translated into English *The Form of Prayer for a General Thanksgiving for the Reducing of Canada* (1760); *Evening Service of Rosh Hashanah and Kippur* (1761), the first Jewish prayer book printed in America; and *Prayers for Shabbath, Rosh-Hashanah, and Kippur* (1766). He died in New York City and was buried in the Spanish and Portuguese Burial Ground there.

PLATT, Zephaniah: Continental congressman, lawyer
Born Huntingdon, Long Island, New York, May 26, 1735; father of at least one son (Jonas); died September 12, 1807.

Platt received a thorough English education and studied law. He was admitted to the bar and began the practice of law in Poughkeepsie, New York. He served in the Provincial Congress from 1775 until 1777, when he became a member of the Council of Safety. For the next six years he was a delegate to the New York Senate, and from 1784 to 1786 he was a member of the Continental Congress. In 1778 and again in 1781 he served on the Council of Appointment.

From 1781 to 1795 Platt served as judge of Dutchess County. In 1784 he founded the town of Plattsburg. He was a delegate to the New York Constitutional Convention in 1788, a regent of the state university from 1791 to 1807, and a projector of the Erie Canal. He died in Plattsburg and was buried in Riverside Cemetery.

PRINCE, William: horticulturist
Born Flushing, Long Island, New York, circa 1725; son of Robert and Mary (Burgess) Prince; married Anne Thorne; father of thirteen children (including William and Benjamin); died 1802.

A pioneer American horticulturist, William Prince was one of the first to sell budded or grafted stock and to attempt to breed new varieties. He established Prince's Nursery and developed Prince's Gage plum. He raised fruits, trees, and shrubs. Thousands of his cherry trees were used for making barrel hoops during the Revolutionary War. He died in Flushing, the town of his birth.

PROVOOST, Samuel: clergyman
Born New York City, March 9, 1743; son of John and Eve (Rutgers) Provoost; married Maria Bousfield, June 8, 1766; father of four children; died September 6, 1815.

Provoost graduated from King's College (now Columbia) in 1758. He was a fellow-commoner at St. Peter's College, Cambridge University, in England in 1761. He was ordained a deacon in the Protestant Episcopal Church in 1766 and ordained a priest ten years later.

Circa 1771 Provoost became assistant minister of Trinity Church in New York City. In 1784 he accepted an invitation to officiate at St. Paul's and St. George's chapels in the Trinity Parish in New York. In that year he was also appointed a regent of the University of the State of New York.

Provoost served as chaplain of the Continental Congress in 1785 and was elected the first bishop of New York City the next year. He received an honorary D.D. from the University of Pennsylvania in 1786 and was consecrated by the Archbishop of Canterbury the following year. In 1788 he officiated at the confirmation service at St. Peter's Church, Perth Amboy, the first such service held in New Jersey.

Provoost conducted the service at St. Paul's Chapel following Washington's inauguration in 1789. He was chaplain of the

United States Senate that year. He served as chairman of the committee that drafted the constitution of his church and was responsible for necessary changes in the prayer book following the establishment of the Church as an American entity. He presided over the Episcopal General Convention in 1801.

Provoost died in New York City and was buried in the Trinity Churchyard there.

★★★★★

RAMAGE, John: painter

Born probably Dublin, Ireland, circa 1748; married Maria Victoria Ball, March 8, 1776; second marriage to Mrs. Taylor, circa 1777; third marriage to Catharine Collins, January 29, 1787; died October 24, 1802.

Ramage attended school at the Dublin Society of Art circa 1763. In 1775 he was a goldsmith and a painter of miniatures in Boston. The next year he was commissioned a second lieutenant in the Loyal Irish Volunteers.

From 1777 to 1794 Ramage was a leading painter of miniatures in New York City; in 1789 he painted a miniature of Washington. Because of debts he had contracted in New York, he moved to Montreal, Canada, where he died in 1802. He was buried in the Christ Church Cemetery in Montreal.

RANDALL, Robert Richard: privateer, merchant, philanthropist

Born New Jersey, 1750; son of Thomas and Gertrude (Crooke) Randall; died June 1801.

Randall became a member of the Marine Society in New York in 1771. He was a privateer for the Continental Army in the Revolutionary War, then, in 1781, became a partner with his father in the firm of Randall, Son and Stewart. He was a member of the New York Chamber of Commerce in 1788.

Following the war, the Randall family bought several pieces of land in various parts of New York City. That property was willed to Robert by his father, and he in turn willed most of his fortune to a trust fund to provide care for aged, decrepit, worn-out seamen at an asylum and hospital to be called Sailors' Snug Harbor.

Randall died in New York City.

RED JACKET (Sagoyewatha): Indian chief

Born Seneca County, New York, 1758; married twice; died January 20, 1830.

Red Jacket was chief of the Seneca Indians. At the Indian council at the mouth of the Detroit River in 1786, he advocated war; however, he later tried to make peace with the United States, partly out of a desire to avoid being used as a foil of British diplomacy. In Washington, D.C., in 1801, he protested against the actions of the Pennsylvania frontiersmen. In 1821 he tried to preserve the right of the Iroquois to maintain separate customs and jurisdiction.

Red Jacket is best known for his resistance to white civilization, although he sanctioned moves toward bringing white culture to the Iroquois in 1792. By 1805 he had come to oppose all changes in Indian language, creed, and blood. He spoke out against the establishment of missions, and at the height of his power he tried to drive all white men from reservations. In 1821 he obtained a law for protecting the reservations; three years later he insisted on strict enforcement of the law, including the removal of missionaries. He was deposed as chief circa 1827.

Red Jacket died in the Seneca Village in New York and was buried in a Christian cemetery at the reservation's mission in Buffalo, New York.

RIKER, SAMUEL: congressman

Born Newtown, Long Island, New York, April 8, 1743; died May 19, 1823.

Riker, who attended common schools, was a member of the Newtown Committee of Correspondence in 1774 and a lieutenant of Light Horse in the Revolutionary War. He was supervisor of Suffolk County in 1783 and a member of the New York State Assembly the following year. On November 5, 1804, until 1805 he filled a vacancy in the United States House of Representatives; two years later he was elected to serve in the 10th Congress. He died in Newtown and was buried in the Dutch Reformed Cemetery.

RIVINGTON, James: bookseller, journalist
Born London, England, 1724; son of Charles and Eleanor (Pease) Rivington; married Elizabeth Minshull, September 14, 1752; second marriage to Elizabeth Van Horne, March 1769; father of four children; died July 4, 1802.

Rivington, in partnership with James Fletcher, published *Smollett's History of England.* He came to America in 1760 and opened a bookstore on Market Street in Philadelphia. He also opened a bookstore on Hanover Square in New York, later (1768) moving the store to Wall Street. He became a partner with Samuel Brown in a merchandising and bookselling firm in 1761 and in a picture gallery in 1763. In 1762 he extended his chain of stores to Boston. In 1766 he was proprietor of the Maryland Lottery in Annapolis. He published the poetical works of Charles Churchill. In 1769 he became a freeman of New York City.

In 1773 Rivington began publishing a newspaper called *Rivington's New York Gazetteer,* which served as a forum for open discussion of issues of the day. Two years after he began publication, the Sons of Liberty from Connecticut, having found this "open policy" offensive, ruined his printing plant. He went to London in 1776, returning about a year later to settle in New York as the King's printer. In 1777 he began publishing a newspaper with a Loyalist viewpoint. In 1783 he suspended publication of this paper to establish with other New York newspapers a mutual daily gazette, the first daily newspaper in America.

Rivington was put into debtors' prison in 1797 and died in New York City five years later.

ROBERTSON, James: printer, journalist
Born Scotland, 1740; married Amy; died circa 1812.

James Robertson and his brother Alexander published the New York *Chronicle* in 1769. James began a printery in 1771 and issued *The Albany Gazette,* the first newspaper printed in New York province outside New York City. He formed a partnership in 1773 with John Trumbull of Norwich, Connecticut. For three years they were general printers and publishers of the *Norwich Packet and the Connecticut, Massachusetts, New Hampshire, and Rhode Island Weekly Advertiser,* a Royalist paper.

In 1777–78 Robertson published the *Royal American Gazette.* He opened a printing office and established the *Royal Pennsylvania Gazette* in Philadelphia in 1778. In that year he also opened a new printing business at 857 Hanover Square in New York City. In 1780 he began the *Royal South Carolina Gazette* in Charleston, South Carolina, and was its sole proprietor and publisher until 1782. He moved to Nova Scotia and for the next four years published the *Royal American Gazette.*

ROBINSON, Beverley: Loyalist
Born Middlesex County, Virginia, January 11, 1722 (old style); son of John and Catherine (Beverley) Robinson; married Susanna Philipse, July 7, 1748; father of seven children; died April 9, 1792.

Robinson raised a company for an intended expedition against Canada and was ordered with it to New York in 1746. Later, during the Revolution, he raised the Loyal American Regiment and became colonel; he also was colonel and director of the Loyal Guides and Pioneers. Constantly on various boards and committees during the war, he furnished information as to terrain, roads, and disposition of people, directed spies and messengers, and was active in cases of defection from the American side. In 1779 he was banished from New York State and his property was confiscated. He moved to England and died in the town of Thornbury. He was buried at St. James Church in Bath, England.

RODGERS, John: clergyman, university official
Born Boston, Massachusetts, August 5, 1727; son of

Thomas and Elizabeth (Baxter) Rodgers; married Elizabeth Bayard, September 19, 1752; second marriage to Mary (Antrobus) Grant, August 15, 1764; father of five children; died May 7, 1811.

Rodgers was licensed to preach in 1747 by the Presbytery of New Castle, Delaware, and two years later was ordained to the ministry of the Presbyterian Church. For the next sixteen years he served as pastor at Saint Georges in New Castle County, Delaware.

In 1765 Rodgers became a pastor in New York City and served there until 1810. In 1768 he received an honorary D.D. from the University of Edinburgh, Scotland. During the first twenty years or so of his New York pastorate, he was a trustee of the College of New Jersey (now Princeton). In 1776 he was a chaplain in General Heath's brigade. He served as chaplain of the New York Council of Safety and of the first New York State legislature. He was a member of the committee to revise the standards of the Presbyterian Church in 1788 and moderator of the first General Assembly in Philadelphia in 1789.

Rodgers served as vice chancellor of the University of the State of New York from 1784 until his death in New York City in 1811.

ROLLINSON, William: engraver

Born Dudley, Worcester, England, April 15, 1762; son of Robert and Mary (Hill) Rollinson; married Mary Johnson, May 10, 1782; father of one child; died September 21, 1842.

Rollinson, who emigrated to America in 1789, became an engraver in New York City, where he made silver ornaments and engraved portraits, bookplates, maps, and certificates. He made a portrait of George Washington in 1790 and one of Alexander Hamilton in 1804.

While working as a banknote engraver, Rollinson developed a method of ruling lines by machine to prevent counterfeiting. He was a Mason and a member of the Society of Mechanics and Tradesmen. He served

as a lieutenant of artillery in the New York militia.

ROMAYNE, Nicholas: physician

Born New York City, September 1756; son of John and Julia (McCarty) Romeyn; married Susan Van Dam; died July 21, 1817.

Romayne entered the Medical School of King's College (now Columbia) in 1774. Six years later he received an M.D. from the University of Edinburgh, Scotland. He was an original member of the board of regents of the University of the State of New York and served from 1784 to 1787. From 1785 to 1787 he was a professor of the practice of physic at the Columbia Medical School. He was an original trustee of Columbia and served from 1787 to 1793. After 1787 he instructed private classes.

Romayne was a licentiate of the Royal College of Physicians of London and a fellow of the Royal College of Physicians of Edinburgh. He speculated in Western land, was implicated in the Blount Conspiracy of 1797, and left the United States briefly.

In 1806 Romayne became the first president of the Medical Society of the City and County of New York. A founder of the College of Physicians and Surgeons, he served as its president. This school became the Columbia College of Physicians and Surgeons in 1807, and he served as a trustee from that time. He was a professor of the institutes of medicine in 1808 and a lecturer in anatomy in 1807–08. His "Address Delivered at the Commencement of the Lectures" was published in 1808. At Queen's (now Rutgers) College he was a professor of institutes of medicine and forensic medicine from 1812 to 1816. He died in New York City.

RUTGERS, Henry: army officer, philanthropist

Born New York City, October 7, 1745; son of Hendrick and Catharine (dePeyster) Rutgers; died February 17, 1830.

Rutgers graduated from King's College (now Columbia) in 1766. He supported the

Sons of Liberty and served as a captain in the 1st Regiment of the New York militia in the Battle of White Plains (1776). He resigned command of the regiment in 1795.

Rutgers served in the New York Assembly in 1784 and in 1800. He raised a fund of $28,000 for construction of the first Great Wigwam of Tammany Hall in New York City in 1811. He gave land for the second free school established for the city's poor, and from 1828 to 1830 he was president of the Free School Society.

Rutgers served as a regent of the University of the State of New York from 1802 to 1826 and as a trustee of Princeton from 1804 to 1817. He was a benefactor of Queen's College and from 1816 to 1821 was a trustee of that institution. In 1825 the name was changed to Rutgers College in his honor.

Rutgers was president of the board of corporation of the Dutch Reformed Church, and he gave land to Rutgers Street Presbyterian Church, which opened in 1798. He died in New York City.

★★★★★

SAGE, Ebenezer: congressman, physician
Born Chatham (now Portland), Connecticut, August 16, 1755; died January 20, 1834.

Sage graduated from Yale in 1778, studied medicine, and established a practice in Easthampton, Long Island, in 1784. Circa 1801 he moved to Sag Harbor, Suffolk County, New York, and practiced medicine there. A Democrat, he was elected to the 11th, 12th, and 13th congresses of the United States House of Representatives (1809–15) and later was a delegate to the New York State Constitutional Convention (1821). He died in Sag Harbor and was buried in the Old Burying Ground; he was later reinterred in Oakland Cemetery.

SAILLY, Peter: congressman
Born Lorraine, France, April 20, 1754; died March 16, 1826.

Sailly came to America in 1783 and settled in Plattsburg, New York, where he became a merchant, fur trader, potash manufacturer, and lumber shipper. After a period as an associate justice in the Court of Common Pleas (1788–96) he served as commissioner of highways and school commissioner during 1797–98. He then rose to supervisor of schools for the year 1799–1800.

Sailly subsequently served as a member of the New York State Assembly in 1803, as judge of Clinton County from 1804 to 1806, and as a Democratic member of the United States House of Representatives from 1805 to 1807 (9th Congress). He then became collector of customs at Plattsburg in 1807, holding this position until the year of his death. He was buried in Riverside Cemetery.

SAMMONS, Thomas: congressman, farmer
Born Shamenkop, Ulster County, New York, October 1, 1762; died November 20, 1838.

Sammons attended rural schools, served as an officer in the Revolutionary War, then became a farmer. He was a delegate to the New York State Constitutional Convention in 1801 and a member of the Council of Appointment. He served in the New York State militia as a lieutenant, captain, and finally major. In 1803 he began a series of terms in the United States House of Representatives as a Democrat, going to the 8th, 9th, 11th, and 12th congresses (1803–07, 1809–13). He died at the Sammons homestead near Johnstown, in Montgomery County, New York, and was buried on the homestead in Simeon Sammons Cemetery.

SANDS, Comfort: merchant, patriot
Born Cow Neck (now Sands Point), Long Island, New York, February 26, 1748; son of John and Elizabeth (Cornell) Sands; married Sarah Dodge, June 3, 1769; second marriage to Cornelia Lott, December 5, 1797; father of eighteen children (including Robert Charles); died September 22, 1834.

Opening a store in Peck Slip, New York,

in 1769, Sands became a merchant in West Indian trade and remained so involved until 1776. He participated in non-importation agreements, was a member of several New York provincial congresses and state assemblies and of the New York Committee of Public Safety (the latter in 1776), and attended the New York State Constitutional Convention in 1777. He was auditor general of New York Province and then of New York State from 1776 until 1782. In 1778 he served on the commission which regulated the price of labor and commodities for the army in New Haven, Connecticut.

After the war, in 1784, Sands became a founder and director of the Bank of New York, the first bank of the city. From 1794 to 1798 he was president of the New York City Chamber of Commerce. He declared bankruptcy in 1801 and died thirty-three years later in Hoboken, New Jersey.

SANDS, Joshua: congressman
Born Cow Neck (now Sands Point), Long Island, New York, October 12, 1757; died September 13, 1835.

After serving as a captain during the Revolutionary War, Sands became a merchant. He was a member of the New York State Senate from 1792 to 1799, also serving as collector of customs of the Port of New York in 1797. He was a New York delegate to the United States House of Representatives during the 8th and 19th congresses (1803–05, 1825–27). In 1824 he became president of the board of trustees of the Village of Brooklyn. He died in Brooklyn, was buried in St. Paul's Church Cemetery in Eastchester, New York, and in 1852 was reinterred in Greenwood Cemetery in Brooklyn.

SAYRE, Stephen: banker, diplomatic agent
Born Southampton, Long Island, New York, June 12, 1736; son of John and Hannah (Howell) Sayre; married Elizabeth Noel, February 18, 1775; second marriage to Elizabeth Dorone, 1790; died September 27, 1818.

Sayre went to England after graduating from the College of New Jersey (now Princeton) in 1757. In 1770 he became an organizer of the banking house of Stephen Sayre and Barth-Coote-Purdon in London. He promoted the cause of the colonies in England, nonetheless became sheriff of London in 1773, and signed the petition from Americans in London protesting the closing of the Port of Boston (1774). Arrested in 1775 for his political activities, he was charged with plotting to seize the King and overthrow the government but was released because of lack of evidence.

In 1777 Sayre served as secretary to Arthur Lee on a diplomatic mission to Berlin for the United States and made an unofficial visit to Copenhagen to propose commercial relations with the United States. Two years later he posed as a United States agent in Stockholm but accomplished nothing. From 1779 until 1783 he engaged in private financial ventures in Russia, and in 1793 he bought an estate in New Jersey. He died in Brandon, Middlesex County, Virginia, at the age of eighty-two.

SCHOONMAKER, Cornelius Corneliusen: congressman
Born Shawangunk (now Wallkill), Ulster County, New York, June 1745; died spring 1796.

Schoonmaker was a surveyor and a farmer. During the Revolutionary War he was a member of the Committees of Vigilance and Safety. In addition to attending the New York State Convention which ratified the federal constitution in 1788, he served in the New York State Assembly from 1777 to 1790 and again in 1795. He also represented New York in the 2nd Congress of the United States House of Representatives (1791–93). He died in Shawangunk and was buried in the Old Shawangunk Churchyard at Bruynswick there.

SCHUYLER, Margarita: colonial hostess
Born 1701; daughter of Johannes and Elizabeth (Staats) Schuyler; married Philip Schuyler, December 29, 1720; died August 1782.

Schuyler settled with her husband on the Hudson River north of Albany, New York. Their home became a meeting place for the provincial aristocracy and British officers and tradesmen, and she functioned as an unofficial political and military adviser to English officials. She was a Loyalist during the American Revolution.

SCHUYLER, Philip John: Continental congressman, senator, army officer
Born Albany, New York, November 20, 1733; son of Johannes and Cornelia (Van Cortlandt) Schuyler; married Catherine Van Rensselaer, September 17, 1755; father of eight children (including Elizabeth, wife of Alexander Hamilton); died November 18, 1804.

In 1755 Schuyler was commissioned to raise and command a company in General William Johnson's expedition against Crown Point. In the spring of the next year he was a member of the forces under Colonel John Bradstreet who carried provisions to Oswego and cleared the Oneida portage of French raiders. He became a deputy commissary with the rank of major in the British Army under Lord George Howe in 1758. While he was stationed at Albany in the campaigns of 1759–60 he collected and forwarded provisions to Amherst's forces.

In 1763 Schuyler inherited his father's estate, thereby becoming a large landholder in the Mohawk Valley and along the Hudson River. Inheriting additional land from his uncle, he developed water power for his sawmills and gristmills, built the first water-driven flaxmill in New York, and owned a fleet of one schooner and three sloops engaged in trade on the Hudson River.

In 1764 Schuyler served on the boundary commission delegated to settle the dispute between New York and Massachusetts. He served in the New York Assembly in 1768 and in the Continental Congress in 1775 and again from 1778 to 1781. One of four major generals under Washington at the beginning of the Revolutionary War, he was assigned command of the Northern Department and organized the expedition against Canada in 1775–76. He supported New York's claims to the New Hampshire Grants (later Vermont). Congress reprimanded him in 1777 and relieved him of his command but reinstated him later the same year. When Fort Ticonderoga was lost in 1777, he was superseded by General Horatio Gates (by order of Congress) and was charged with incompetence, but a court-martial acquitted him in 1778.

In 1779 Schuyler resigned from the service but remained on the Congressional Board of Commissioners for Indian Affairs. In 1780 he chaired a committee at headquarters which was authorized to assist General Washington in reorganizing the staff departments of the army. He was elected to the New York State Senate for terms in 1780–84, 1786–90, and 1792–97, and served in the United States Senate as a Federalist in 1789–91 and again in 1797–98.

In other service, Schuyler was a member of the New York Board of Regents. He also promoted a plan for establishing Union College in Schenectady and subscribed 100 pounds to its endowment. He died in Albany and was buried in the Albany Rural Cemetery.

SCOTT, John Morin: Continental congressman
Born New York City, 1730; son of John and Marian (Morin) Scott; married Helena Rutgers, 1752; father of four children; died September 14, 1784.

Scott, a 1746 Yale graduate, was admitted to the New York bar in 1752. A Whig, he wrote articles in behalf of the Whig Presbyterian cause which appeared in the *Independent Reflector* in New York City in 1752–53 and in the "Watch Tower" column of the *New York Mercury* during 1754–55. In 1754 he proposed a bill establishing King's College (now Columbia) on nonsectarian principles.

Scott wrote an essay against the Stamp Act, signing it "Freeman." From 1756 to 1761 he was an alderman of New York City. Around the time of the Revolution he served on the New York General Committee (1775), was a leader of the radical party in New York provincial congresses (1775–77), and helped lead the democratic forces at the New York Constitutional Convention (1777). In 1776 he served as a brigadier general in the Continental Army at the Battle of Long Island and in 1777 was appointed to the state Council of Safety. He was one of the first members of the Sons of Liberty.

From 1777 until 1782 Scott served in the New York Senate. He held the office of secretary of state of New York from 1778 to 1784 and was a member of the Continental Congress from 1779 to 1783. He also was a delegate from New York in the settlement of the boundary dispute with Vermont. He was a member of the New York branch of the Society of the Cincinnati. He died in New York City and was buried in Trinity Church there.

SEARS, Isaac: patriot, privateer
Born West Brewster, Massachusetts, July 1, 1730; son of Joshua and Mary (Thacher) Sears; married Sarah Drake; father of eleven children; died October 28, 1786.

Sears, who had commanded a sloop trading between New York City and Boston in 1752, was a privateer during the French and Indian War. After the passage of the Stamp Act he became a leader in colonial resistance to the Crown; from 1765 to 1776 he led the general populace and instigated demonstrations and mob violence. He led the Sons of Liberty in destroying the cargo of a tea ship in New York City as well as serving on several Revolutionary committees.

After the battles of Lexington and Concord Sears led the patriots in their seizure of British arms and took command of New York City. In addition to recruiting for the Continental Army in Connecticut in 1776,

he was commissioned to capture British supplies for the colonial forces. He promoted privateering in Boston from 1777 to 1783.

After the war Sears returned to his merchandise business in New York City. He was elected to the New York State Assembly in 1784 and again in 1786. In other service, he was a trustee and a vestryman of Trinity Church in New York City during the years 1784–86 and held the office of vice president of the New York State Chamber of Commerce in 1784.

In 1786 Sears sailed to China on a business venture, contracted fever, and died in Canton. He was buried on French Island in Canton Harbor.

SEIXAS, Gershom Mendes: clergyman
Born New York City, January 15, 1746; son of Isaac Mendez and Rachel (Levy) Seixas; married Elkaly Cohen, September 6, 1775; second marriage to Hannah Manuel, November 1, 1789; father of fifteen children; died July 2, 1816.

The strictly orthodox Seixas was chosen rabbi for the Shearith Israel Congregation, a Spanish and Portuguese synagogue in New York City, in 1768. He was chief professor of Hebrew language, literature, and laws for the New York City Jewish community and a leading spokesman for American Jewry. The first rabbi to preach sermons in English in an American synagogue, he also was a Revolutionary patriot.

Seixas protested a Pennsylvania law which held that eligibility for an Assembly seat depended on recognition of the divine origin of the New Testament. He founded one of New York City's earliest charitable organizations, Hebra Hased Va-Amet. From 1784 to 1815 he served as a regent and then a trustee of Columbia University.

In 1789 Seixas published the sermon *Religious Discourse, Delivered in the Synagogue . . . The 26th November 1789, Agreeable to the Proclamation of the President . . . to be Observed as a Day of Public Thanksgiving;* and in 1798 he published another sermon, *A Discourse Delivered . . . on the Ninth of May 1798, Observed as a Day of Humiliation*. He died in 1816 in New York City and was buried in the New Bowery Cemetery of the Shearith Israel Congregation.

SILVESTER, Peter: congressman, lawyer
Born Shelter Island, Long Island, New York, 1734; died October 15, 1808.

After studying law, Silvester was admitted to the bar and began a legal practice in Albany, New York, in 1763. In 1772 he became a member of the Albany Common Council. Around the time of the Revolution he served on the Committee of Safety (1774) and in the 1st and 2nd provincial congresses (1775, 1776).

After moving to Kinderhook, New York, Silvester was appointed a judge in the Court of Common Pleas of Columbia County in 1786. The following year he became a regent of the University of the State of New York, holding that position until 1808. He served in the 1st and 2nd congresses of the United States House of Representatives (1789–93), in the New York State Assembly (1788, 1803–06), and in the New York Senate (1796–1800). He died in Kinderhook and was buried in the Old Van Schaack Cemetery (over which the Reformed Dutch Church was built in 1814).

SKANIADARIIO (Handsome Lake): Indian religious leader
Born village of Ganawaugus, west side of the Genesee River, 1735; died August 10, 1815.

Following a severe illness in 1796, Skaniadariio, who was also known to his people as Ganiodaiio, declared he had been informed by the Creator of certain precepts which were to constitute a new religion, Gaiwiio. From 1800 until his death he gave the Iroquois this new faith, which was based on abstention from witchcraft, drunkenness, and infidelity. The religion survived among the Iroquois for several generations, weakening the older tribal religion. Skaniadariio died in Onondaga, New York.

SMITH, John: senator, congressman
Born Mastic, Long Island, New York, February 12, 1752; died August 12, 1816.

Smith, who completed preparatory studies, was a longtime member of the New York State Assembly (1784–99) and attended the New York State Convention which ratified the federal constitution (1788). He filled a vacancy in the House of Representatives on February 6, 1800 (6th Congress), and was reelected to the 7th and 8th congresses. On February 23, 1804, he resigned his seat to fill a vacancy in the Senate; he was reelected and stayed until 1813. From that year until 1815 he served as United States marshal for the District of New York. He also was a major general in the New York State militia. He died in Mastic and was buried in Smiths Point, New York.

SMITH, Melancton: merchant, lawyer, Continental congressman
Born Jamaica, Long Island, New York, May 7, 1744; son of Samuel and Elizabeth (Bayles) Smith; father of at least one son (Melancton); died July 29, 1798.

Sheriff of Dutchess County, New York, in 1774, 1777, and 1779, Smith was a delegate from Dutchess County to the 1st New York Provincial Congress in 1775. He organized and was a captain in the 1st Company of Rangers of the Dutchess County Minutemen and, in 1777, was a member of a commission for "inquiring into, detecting, and defeating all conspiracies . . . against the liberties of America."

Smith was appointed to a commission to settle disputes between the army and contractors at West Point, New York, in 1782. He moved to New York City in 1785, where he embarked on extensive mercantile enterprises as well as a law practice.

Smith was a delegate to the Continental Congress from 1785 to 1788 and was an Anti-Federalist delegate to the Poughkeepsie Convention of 1788 to consider the ratification of the United States Constitution. He became a member of the New York State Assembly in 1791 and served as a circuit court judge in 1792. He died in New York City and was buried in the Jamaica Cemetery.

SMITH, William: jurist, historian, Loyalist
Born New York City, June 25, 1728; son of William and Mary (Het) Smith; married Janet Livingston, November 3, 1752; father of eleven children (including William); died December 3, 1793.

Smith graduated from Yale in 1745 and was admitted to the New York bar in 1750. He published (with William Livingston) the first digest of colony statutes in force at the time, *Laws of New York from 1691 to 1751, Inclusive, 1752.* His *Laws of New York . . . 1752–1762* was published in 1762. His chief contribution was *History of the Province of New York, from the First Discovery to the Year MDCC XXXII,* which was published in London in 1757 and reissued in 1814.

Smith acceded to the chief justiceship of the Province of New York in 1763 and was appointed chief justice of New York State in 1779, although he never actually served. He went to England when New York City was evacuated in 1783 and later settled in Canada, where he served as chief justice from 1789 until his death in 1793.

SMITH, William Stephens: army officer, congressman
Born Long Island, New York, November 8, 1755; son of John and Margaret (Stephens) Smith; married Abigail Amelia Adams, June 12, 1786; father of three children; died June 10, 1816.

Smith graduated from the College of New Jersey (now Princeton) in 1774. A major and aide-de-camp to General Sullivan in 1776, he participated in the Battle of White Plains. He was a lieutenant colonel in William R. Lee's regiment, fighting at the battles of Monmouth and Newport in 1778, and served as an inspector and adjutant to a corps of light infantry under General Lafayette in 1780–81. He participated in twenty-two engagements during the Revolution.

Serving as an aide to General Washington in 1781, Smith was charged with the supervision of the evacuation of New York City by the British in accordance with the treaty of peace that year. He then held a number of diplomatic posts, serving as secretary of the legation in London, England, from 1785 to 1788, visiting Prussia about 1786 to study the political organization effected by Frederick the Great, and undertaking a diplomatic mission to Spain and Portugal the following year.

Returning to the United States, Smith was federal marshal, supervisor of the revenue, and surveyor for the Port of New York from 1789 to 1800 and commanded the 12th Infantry in 1798. He was a New York delegate to the United States House of Representatives (Federalist) for the 13th Congress (1813–15). He presented his credentials of election to the 14th Congress but did not qualify, and Westel Willoughby, Jr., successfully contested his election in December 1815.

A founder of the Society of the Cincinnati in New York, Smith served as president from 1795 to 1797. He was sixty when he died in Lebanon, New York.

STANFORD, John: clergyman
Born Wandsworth, Surrey, England, October 20, 1754; son of William and Mary Stanford; married Sarah Ten Eyck, June 26, 1790; father of at least four children; died January 14, 1834.

Stanford arrived in the United States in 1786 and served as pastor of the First Baptist Church in Providence, Rhode Island, in 1788–89. Moving to New York, he founded a church, school, and residence on Fair (now Fulton) Street in New York City in 1795 and was pastor of the church until 1798. He served as a preacher in Baptist churches in New York, New Jersey, Pennsylvania, and Connecticut. He urged city officials to separate young offenders from hardened criminals and was responsible for founding the House of Refuge in 1825. He was the author of *The Aged Christian's Cabinet* (1829).

SWART, Peter: congressman, lawyer
Born Schoharie, New York, July 5, 1752; died November 3, 1829.

After admission to the bar, Swart established a legal practice in Schoharie. He served as judge of the Schoharie County Court of Common Pleas in 1795 and was a member of the New York State Assembly in 1798–99.

Elected to the United States House of Representatives for the 10th Congress (1807–09), Swart then returned to New York, where he served as sheriff of Schoharie County in 1810 and 1813. He was a delegate to the New York Senate from 1817 to 1820, then resumed his law practice in Schoharie. He died there and was buried in the Old Stone Fort Cemetery.

★★★★★

TALBOT, Silas: naval officer, congressman
Born Dighton, Bristol County, Massachusetts, January 11, 1751; son of Benjamin and Rebecca (Allen) Talbot; married Miss Richmond, 1772; second marriage to Miss Morris; third marriage to Mrs. Pintard; father of at least four children; died June 30, 1813.

A merchant in Providence, Rhode Island, Talbot was appointed captain of the Rhode Island Regiment in 1775. Soon afterward he was commissioned a captain in the newly formed Continental Navy. He later attained the ranks of major and lieutenant colonel before being captured by the British in 1779, remaining a prisoner until 1781.

Talbot began his political career in 1792, serving as a member of the New York Assembly (1792–93) and then as a New York representative to Congress (1793–95). Commissioned a captain in the United States Navy in 1794, Talbot became superintendent of the construction of the frigate *President* in New York City. He later went on to become commander of the naval station in

Santo Domingo and cruised the waters of the West Indies in the command ship *Constitution*.

Talbot died in New York City and was buried in Trinity Churchyard.

TEN BROECK, Abraham: army officer, jurist
Born Albany, New York, May 13, 1734; son of Dirck and Grietja (Cuyler) Ten Broeck; married Elizabeth Van Rensselaer, November 1, 1763; father of five children; died January 19, 1810.

Ten Broeck served as a member of the New York Colonial Assembly from 1761 to 1765, and from 1775 to 1777 he was a deputy of the New York Provincial Congress. The latter year he was a delegate to the New York Constitutional Convention. A brigadier general in the New York militia during the American Revolution, he had a key role in the Battle of Bemis Heights, which resulted in the forced retreat of General Burgoyne in 1777.

Resigning his commission in 1781, Ten Broeck became the first judge of the Court of Common Pleas of Albany County, New York, remaining in that position for thirteen years. His political career included his serving as Albany's mayor from 1779 to 1783 and from 1796 to 1799; in 1780 he was elected to the New York State Senate and served until 1783. He was also president and director of the Albany Bank. He died in Albany.

THOMAS, David: army officer, congressman
Born Pelham, Massachusetts, June 11, 1762; son of David and Elizabeth (Harper) Thomas; married Jeannette Turner, 1784; died November 27, 1831.

Thomas took part in the expeditions of the Massachusetts militia for the relief of Rhode Island in 1777. He reentered the Massachusetts militia in 1781 and served with the 3rd and the 5th regiments. He later served in the New York militia and attained the rank of major general in command of the 3rd Division.

An Anti-Federalist, Thomas was a member of the New York Assembly in 1793, 1798, and 1799, and was elected to the United States House of Representatives in 1801, serving until 1808. After his terms in Congress, he served as treasurer of the State of New York from 1808 to 1810 and as agent for the Bank of America in 1811. He died in Providence, Rhode Island.

THOMPKINS, Caleb: congressman
Born near Scarsdale, New York, December 22, 1759; died January 1, 1846.

From 1804 to 1806 Thompkins served as a member of the New York State Assembly. He was a judge in both the Court of Common Pleas and the Westchester County Court from 1807 to 1811 and from 1820 to 1824. He was a delegate from New York to the United States House of Representatives from 1817 to 1821 (15th and 16th congresses). He died in Scarsdale and was buried in the First Presbyterian Church Cemetery in White Plains, New York.

THOMPSON, Joel: congressman, lawyer
Born Stanford, New York, October 3, 1760; died February 8, 1843.

Thompson served in the Continental Army in 1779 and 1780. After the war, he was admitted to the bar and began practicing law in Duanesburg and Sherburne, New York. He was a member of the New York State Assembly in 1798 and served again in 1803–04. From 1799 to 1807 he was assistant justice of the Chenango County Court of Common Pleas, and for the next seven years he served as judge of Chenango County.

A Federalist, Thompson was a delegate from New York to the United States House of Representatives from 1813 to 1815 (13th Congress). After his term in Congress, he resumed his law practice in Sherburne. He died in Brooklyn and was buried in Greenwood Cemetery.

THOMPSON, John: congressman, jurist
Born Litchfield, Connecticut, March 20, 1749; died 1823.

Thompson attended common schools. In 1788 he was appointed a justice in Stillwater Township, New York. He served as a member of the New York State Assembly in 1788 and 1789. A Democrat, he served in the United States House of Representatives from 1799 to 1801 (6th Congress) and from 1807 to 1811 (10th and 11th congresses). In 1801 he served as a delegate to the New York Constitutional Convention.

Appointed by the governor as the first judge of Saratoga County, New York, in 1791, Thompson served in that capacity for eighteen years. He died in Stillwater, New York, and was buried there.

TILLOTSON, Thomas: state official, physician
Born Maryland, 1750; died May 5, 1832.

Tillotson was a practicing physician in Maryland at the time of the outbreak of the Revolutionary War. He was commissioned a first lieutenant in the Maryland militia in 1776. Four years later he was appointed by Congress as surgeon general of the Northern Department of the Continental Army, a position he held for the remainder of the war.

Circa 1784 Tillotson moved to New York and resumed his medical practice. From 1788 to 1790 he was a member to the New York State Assembly from Red Hook, Dutchess County. In 1791 he was a member of the council of appointment. He served in the New York Senate from 1791 to 1799. He was elected to the United States House of Representatives in 1801; however, he did not qualify for or take the seat, and he resigned on August 10, 1801. From 1801 to 1806, and in 1807 and 1808, he was secretary of the State of New York.

Tillotson died in Rhinebeck, New York, and was buried in the vault at the rear of the Rhinebeck Reformed Dutch Church.

TREDWELL, Thomas: congressman, lawyer
Born Smithtown, Long Island, New York, February 6, 1743; died December 30, 1831.

Tredwell graduated from Princeton in 1764 and studied law. He was admitted to the New York bar and established a legal practice in Plattsburg, New York. In 1774–75 he was a delegate to the Provincial Congress of New York. He was a delegate to the New York constitutional conventions of 1776, 1777, and 1801. From 1777 to 1783 he served in the New York State Assembly. He was a judge in the Court of Probate from 1778 to 1787 and served in the New York State Senate from 1786 to 1789 and again from 1803 to 1807. From 1787 to 1791 he was surrogate of Suffolk County.

In 1788 Tredwell was a delegate to the state convention which ratified the United States Constitution. He filled a vacancy in the United States House of Representatives and served from May 1791 to 1795 in the 2nd and 3rd congresses. He was surrogate of Clinton County, New York, from 1807 until his death. He died in Plattsburg and was buried in a private burial ground in Beekmantown, near Plattsburg.

TROUP, Robert: army officer
Born New York City, 1757; probably the son of Robert and Elinor (Bisset) Troup; died January 14, 1832.

Troup, after graduating from King's College (now Columbia), studied law circa 1780–83. During the American Revolution he served as a lieutenant in the Continental Army and as aide-de-camp to Brigadier General Timothy Woodhull. He was promoted to lieutenant colonel in 1777. He was on the staff of General Horatio Gates and was present at the Battle of Stillwater and at the surrender of Burgoyne in 1777. In 1778 he was secretary of the Board of War.

Troup served for a time in the New York State Assembly. In 1787–88 he supported the adoption of the United States Constitution. He was involved in land speculation in western New York from 1794 to 1832 and was a judge in the United States District Court of New York in 1796. He also gave financial aid to the founding of Hobart College and, from 1801 to 1831, was an agent for the Pulteney estate. He died in New York City.

TUCKEY, William: organist, choirmaster, composer
Born Somersetshire, England, 1708; married; father of several children; died September 14, 1781.

From 1753 to 1756 Tuckey served as parish clerk of Trinity Church in New York City. In 1755 he offered a "Concert of Vocal and Instrumental Musick," which was the first in a long series of concerts, culminating in the 1770 performance of the overture and sixteen numbers from Handel's *Messiah,* the first American rendering of that work. Tuckey composed "Anthem Taken Out of the 97th Psalm," later called "Liverpool"; it is his only extant work. He died in Philadelphia and was buried in Christ Church Burial Grounds there.

★★★★★

VAN CORTLANDT, Philip: congressman, army officer
Born New York City, August 21, 1749; son of Pierre and Joanna (Livingston) Van Cortlandt; never married; died November 1, 1831.

Van Cortlandt graduated from King's College (now Columbia) in 1768. In 1775 he was a member of the Provincial Convention at the Exchange in New York City as well as serving as a Westchester County representative in the First New York Provincial Congress. The same year he became a lieutenant colonel in the 4th New York Regiment, then rose to colonel in the 2nd New York Regiment at Valley Forge. He participated in the court-martial which heard charges preferred by the Pennsylvania authorities against Benedict Arnold in 1778. Three years later he was ordered to join the Continental forces in time to take an active part in the campaign against Cornwallis which culminated in the latter's surrender. He distinguished himself at the Battle of

Yorktown under General Lafayette and was brevetted a brigadier general in 1783.

After the Revolution, in 1788, Van Cortlandt attended the Poughkeepsie Convention, at which he voted for ratification of the United States Constitution. In addition to service as supervisor, school commissioner, and road master of the town of Cortlandt, New York, he was a delegate to the New York State Assembly in 1788 and 1790 and to the state senate from 1791 to 1793. He served eight consecutive terms in the United States House of Representatives (1793–1809).

In 1831, when General Lafayette toured the United States, Van Cortlandt accompanied him. He also was a charter member of the Society of the Cincinnati. He died in Croton, New York, at the age of eighty-two and was buried in Hillside Cemetery in Peekskill, New York.

VAN CORTLANDT, Pierre: state official

Born New York City, January 10, 1721; son of Philip and Catharine (DePeyster) Van Cortlandt; married Joanna Livingston, May 28, 1748; father of several children, (including Philip); died May 1, 1814.

During the French and Indian War, Van Cortlandt served in the provincial militia. In 1768 he was elected to the New York Assembly. In 1775, at the outbreak of the Revolutionary War, he became a colonel in the 3rd Regiment of the Westchester militia. In addition to attending the 2nd, 3rd, and 4th New York provincial congresses, in 1776 he became a leader in the Committee of Safety and the following year became president of the Council of Safety. He presided over the first New York Constitutional Convention and was the first lieutenant governor of the state, serving from 1777 to 1795.

Van Cortlandt was a member of the board of regents of the University of the State of New York from 1784 until 1795. He donated land to and subscribed to the building fund for the local Methodist meeting house. He died at his estate in Croton, New York, and was buried in the family cemetery there.

VAN DER KEMP, Francis Adrian: political writer

Born Kampen, Overyssel, Netherlands, May 4, 1752; son of John and Anna (Leyclekker) van der Kemp; married Reinira Engelberta Johanna Vos, May 20, 1782; father of three children; died September 7, 1829.

Van der Kemp studied at Groningen University from 1770 to 1773 and then attended Baptist Seminary in Amsterdam. After his admission as a candidate for the ministry in 1775, he was installed as pastor of a church in Leyden the following year. During the period from 1776 to 1787 he wrote many political works (often anonymously) which got him into trouble with the Dutch authorities. He was interested in and supported the American Revolution.

Van der Kemp came to America after being banished from the Netherlands in 1787. He experimented with agriculture near Kingston, New York, and helped organize the Society of Agriculture and Natural History, also serving the community as justice of the peace. He translated twenty-four manuscript volumes of Dutch colonial records. He died in Olden Barneveld (now Barnevelde), New York.

VAN GAASBECK, Peter: congressman, merchant

Born Ulster County, New York, September 27, 1754; died Kingston, New York, 1797.

Van Gaasbeck, who attended grammar schools, became a merchant in Kingston, New York, as a young man. He served as a captain and then as a major in the Ulster County militia during the Revolutionary War. An Anti-Federalist, he was a New York delegate to the 3rd Congress of the United States House of Representatives (1793–95). He died in 1797 and was buried in the First Reformed Dutch Churchyard.

VAN RENSSELAER, Jeremiah: congressman

Born New York, August 27, 1738; father of at least one son (Solomon Van Vechten); died February 19, 1810.

Van Rensselaer, a 1758 Princeton graduate, was active on the Committee of Safety of Albany, New York. He represented his state in the United States House of Representatives during the 1st Congress (1789–91). Around that time he also became a member of the New York State Assembly (1789) and a member of the first board of directors of the Bank of Albany (1791). Seven years later he became president of the bank and served until 1806.

Van Rensselaer was a Democratic presidential elector in 1800. The next year he began a four-year term as lieutenant governor of New York. In 1804 he became curator of the Evangelical Lutheran Seminary in Albany. He died in Albany and was buried in the Dutch Reformed Cemetery.

VAN SCHAACK, Peter: Revolutionary leader, lawyer

Born Kinderhook, New York, March 1747; son of Cornelius and Lydia (Van Dyck) Van Schaack; married Elizabeth Cruger, 1765; father of ten children; died September 17, 1832.

Van Schaak graduated from King's College (now Columbia) in 1766. He was admitted to the New York bar three years later and in 1773 was appointed to revise the statutes of the Colony of New York. The following year he was active both on the New York Committee of Fifty-one, which corresponded with other colonies, and on the New York Committee of Sixty, which enforced the non-importation of manufactured goods from Great Britain. In 1775 he became a member of the New York Committee of One Hundred as well as a member of the Committee of Safety.

Despite these activities, in 1776 Van Schaack chose not to take up arms against Great Britain and the following year refused to pledge allegiance to the State of New York. On parole until 1778, he was banished from the colonies in that year and went to England. His citizenship having been restored in 1784, he returned to Kinderhook in 1785 and was readmitted to the New York bar.

Van Schaak wrote *Conductor Generalis*, published in 1786. From that year until his death he practiced law in Kinderhook and taught privately.

VAN SCHAICK, Gosen: army officer

Born Albany, New York, September 16, 1736; son of Sybrant and Alida (Roseboom) Van Schaick; married Maria Ten Broeck, November 15, 1770; father of six children; died July 4, 1789.

During the French and Indian War, Van Schaick served as a captain in the New York militia and was active in the campaign against Fort Frontenac in 1758. He received a commission as a lieutenant colonel in the 2nd Regiment of the New York Provincials in 1760 and served in the 1st New York Regiment from 1760 to 1762. Later, in 1776, he received a commission as a colonel in the 1st New York Regiment of the Continental Army. He served in the battles of Ticonderoga and Monmouth and in 1779 led an expedition against the Onondaga Indians. Four years later he was brevetted a brigadier general and retired soon afterward. He died in Albany.

VARDILL, John: clergyman, spy

Born New York City, 1749; son of Thomas and Hannah (Tiebout) Vardill; married; father of one child; died January 16, 1811.

Vardill graduated from King's College (now Columbia) in 1766 and received an M.A. in 1769. He was assistant professor of anatomy at King's College from 1766 until 1773, when he was appointed professor of natural law and a fellow of the college. He wrote articles opposing the Non-Importation Agreement.

In 1774, while in London, Vardill was ordained a deacon and priest in the Church of England and was awarded an honorary M.A. by Oxford. Also that year he was elected assistant minister of Trinity Church in New York City and Regius professor of divinity at King's College; however, he never returned to America. He spent the years from 1775 to 1781 spying on Americans and American sympathizers in England, the high point of which seems to be his theft of the entire correspondence between the American commissioners and the French Court in the period from March to October of 1777. The correspondence verified British suspicions that France would intervene on the side of the Americans.

VARICK, James: clergyman

Born Newburgh, New York, circa 1750; married; father of three sons and four daughters; died 1828.

In 1796 Varick helped establish separate services for fellow Negro members of the Methodist Episcopal Church of New York City. Three years later, along with his congregation, he organized the African Methodist Episcopal Zion Church. The church dedicated its own meeting house in 1800. In 1820, after the church declared its independence from the Methodist Episcopal Church, he became preacher along with Abraham Thompson. He then served as district chairman of the conference that was held in connection with churches of Philadelphia, New Haven, and Long Island. He was elected an elder in 1822 and that same year became a bishop, holding this office until the year of his death.

VARICK, Richard: army officer, mayor

Born New Jersey, March 25, 1753; son of Johannes and Jane (Dey) Varick; married Cornelia Hoffman Roosevelt, May 8, 1786; no children; died July 30, 1831.

In 1775 Varick became a captain in the 1st New York Regiment and military secretary to General Philip John Schuyler. Later he was promoted to lieutenant colonel and then to deputy muster master general in the Northern Department of the Continental Army. He became an aide to Benedict Arnold at West Point in 1780. The next year

General Washington appointed him recording secretary responsible for the arrangement, classification, and copying of all correspondence and records of the Continental Army. He held this position until 1783.

Varick served as recorder of New York City from 1784 to 1786. In the latter year he and Samuel Jones were placed in charge of the codifying of New York statutes. He subsequently held two more state offices: speaker of the state assembly, 1787–88, and attorney general, 1788–89. In 1790 he was elected mayor of New York City, an office he held for eleven years.

Varick served as president of the Society of the Cincinnati from 1806 to 1831. In 1817 he was an appraiser for the Erie Canal. He helped found the American Bible Society and was president in 1828 and 1831. He died at the age of seventy-eight.

★★★★★

WALKER, Benjamin: congressman

Born London, England, 1753; died January 13, 1818.

Walker attended the Blue-Coat School in England and later came to America, settling in New York City. During the Revolution he served as aide-de-camp to General von Steuben and also was a member of Washington's staff.

Naval officer of customs for the Port of New York from 1791 to 1798, Walker in the meantime (1797) had moved to Fort Schuyler (now Utica), New York. He was agent for the landed estate of the Earl of Bath. He was elected to the United States House of Representatives as a Democrat from New York for the 7th Congress (1801–03). He died in Utica and was buried in the Old Village Burying Ground there. His remains were reinterred in Forest Hill Cemetery in 1875.

WATSON, Elkanah: businessman, agriculturist

Born Plymouth, Massachusetts, January 22, 1758; son of Elkanah and Patience (Marston) Watson; married Rachel Smith, March 3, 1789; father of five children; died December 5, 1842.

Watson had a varied business career which began when he was employed by the Brown family, merchants in Rhode Island, in 1773. He went to South Carolina to invest funds for his employers in 1777 and became a partner (with M. Cossoul) in a merchant firm two years later. He embarked for France to carry money and dispatches to Benjamin Franklin in 1779 and, while in Europe, made a special study of inland waterways in Holland.

Watson organized the Bank of Albany (New York) and promoted two canal companies and also a stage line from Albany to Schenectady. He lobbied successfully for a charter which authorized a company to build a canal around Niagara Falls. He secured a charter for the New York State Bank and staged a cattle show which preceded incorporation of the Berkshire Agricultural Society (which sponsored the first county fair in the United States in 1810).

Watson wrote *A Tour of Holland,* 1790; *History of Agricultural Societies on the Modern Berkshire System,* 1820; *History of the Rise and Progress, and Existing Condition of the Western Canals in the State of New York,* 1820; *Men and Times of the Revolution, or Memoirs of Elkanah Watson,* published posthumously in 1856. He died in Port Kent, Essex County, New York.

WATSON, James: senator

Born Woodbury, Connecticut, April 6, 1750; died May 15, 1806.

After graduating from Yale in 1776, Watson studied law. He was commissioned a lieutenant in the Connecticut Regiment in 1776 and a captain in 1777. After admission to the bar, he practiced law and was appointed purchasing commissary for the Connecticut Line by the Assembly in 1780.

Moving to New York City in 1786, Watson engaged in mercantile activities and was a member of the New York Assembly in 1791 and 1794–96; he served as speaker in 1794. A regent of New York University from 1795 to 1806, he attended the New York State Senate from 1796 to 1798.

Watson, a Democrat, filled a vacant New York seat in the United States Senate from August 17, 1798, to March 19, 1800, when he resigned. President Adams appointed him naval officer of New York City. He was a member of the Society of the Cincinnati and an organizer and the first president of the New England Society in New York City (1805–06). He died in New York City.

WATTS, John: congressman

Born New York City, August 27, 1749; died September 3, 1836;

The last man to serve as recorder of New York under the Crown, Watts, who had studied law, was a member of the New York State Assembly from 1791 to 1793. He was a member of a commission to build Newgate Prison in New York City from 1796 to 1799. He was sent by New York to the United States House of Representatives for the 3rd Congress (1793–95). He served as judge of Westchester County from 1802 to 1807 and established and endowed the Leake and Watts Orphan House. He died in New York City and was buried in a vault in Trinity Churchyard there.

WESTON, William: civil engineer

Born near Oxford, England, circa 1752; died August 29, 1833.

In 1790 Weston engineered a stone bridge across the Trent River at Gainsborough, England, and also a turnpike road. He arrived in the United States early in 1793 and contracted with the Schuylkill and Susquehanna Navigation Company, of Pennsylvania, to engineer its canal, devoting two years to the project. He then examined and reported on locks under construction at the Great Falls of the Potomac in 1795.

Engineer for the Western Island Lock Navigation Company of New York in 1796–97, Weston was a pioneer in the design and construction of locks and canals. He sought sources of future water for New York City in 1799. He designed piers for the permanent bridge across the Schuylkill River in Philadelphia and also a deep coffer dam in connection with the bridge. He returned to England in 1800.

Weston was the author of *An Historical Account of the Rise, Progress and Present State of the Canal Navigation in Pennsylvania,* 1795. He died in London.

WHARTON, Charles Henry: clergyman
Born St. Marys County, Maryland, June 5, 1748; son of Jesse and Anne (Bradford) Wharton; married Mary Weems, June 2, 1798; second marriage to Ann Kinsly; no children; died July 23, 1833.

Wharton attended the Jesuit College, St. Omer, France, from 1760 to 1762. He was ordained a Jesuit priest in 1772 and served as chaplain to Roman Catholics in Worcester, England, from 1773 to 1777. However, he left the Roman Catholic Church in 1783 and came to America, where he became rector of Immanuel (Episcopal) Church in New Castle, Delaware, in 1785.

Deputy to the first general convention called to prepare a constitution for the Episcopal Church in 1785, Wharton served as rector of the Swedish Church in Wilmington, Delaware, in 1791–92, and of St. Mary's Church, Burlington, New Jersey, from 1798 until his death. He was president of Columbia College in New York for a short time in 1801 and edited the *Quarterly Theological Magazine and Religious Repository* from 1813 to 1817. He was elected to the American Philosophical Society in 1786.

Wharton was the author of *A Letter to the Roman Catholics of the City of Worcester from the Late Chaplain of the Society . . . Stating the Motives which Induced Him To Relinquish Their Communion, and Become a Member of the Protestant Church,* 1784, and *A Short and Candid Inquiry into the Proof of Christ's Divinity in which Dr. Priestly's History of Opinions Concerning Christ Is Occasionally Considered,* 1791.

WHITE, Henry: merchant, Loyalist
Born Maryland, March 28, 1732; married Eva Van Cortlandt, May 13, 1761; died December 23, 1786.

White developed large mercantile holdings in New York City during the years between 1758 and 1769. He was a member of the New York City Council from 1769 to 1776, served as governor of King's College (now Columbia), and was a founder of the Marine Society of New York.

White joined with other New York merchants in opposing the Stamp Act and the Townshend Act in 1766. A founder and president of the New York City Chamber of Commerce (1772–73), he was a consignee of the East India Company in 1773. He went to England in 1775 and returned when the British occupied New York City in 1776. However, his property in New York City was confiscated under the Act of Attainder in 1779, and he returned to London later that year, remaining there for the last seven years of his life.

WICKES, Eliphalet: congressman
Born Huntington, Long Island, New York, April 1, 1769; died June 7, 1850.

Employed as an express rider during the Revolution, Wickes was present at the storming of Stony Point in 1779 and carried news to General Gates at Providence, Rhode Island. He later studied law, was admitted to the New York bar, and established a legal practice in Jamaica, Long Island.

Wickes was elected to the United States House of Representatives from New York for the 9th Congress (1805–07). He was the first postmaster of Jamaica, serving from 1797 to 1835, except for a brief period in 1806–07. He was master in chancery for a time. He died in Troy, New York, and was buried in Oakwood Cemetery there.

WILLETT, Marinus: army officer, mayor
Born Jamaica, Long Island, New York, July 31, 1740; son of Edward and Aletta (Clowes) Willett; married Mary Dearsee, April 2, 1760; second mar-

riage to Mrs. Susannah Vardill, October 3, 1793; third marriage to Margaret Bancker, circa 1799; father of at least five children; died August 22, 1830.

Willett, who attended King's College (now Columbia), was a wealthy merchant in New York City. An early supporter of the American Revolution, he was a leader of the Sons of Liberty. He was a second lieutenant in Oliver De Lancey's New York Regiment and helped to seize arms from the New York City arsenal in 1775. He served as a first lieutenant in the 1st New York Regiment in 1775–76 and as a lieutenant colonel in the 3rd New York Regiment in 1776. In 1777 he was voted a sword by Congress after his courageous defense of Fort Stanwix. Finally, he joined General Washington's army in 1778.

As a politician, Willett served as sheriff of the city and county of New York from 1784 until 1788 and again from 1792 to 1796. Between terms, he concluded the Creek Indian treaty in 1790. He was mayor of New York City from 1807 to 1811. He died in Cedar Grove, New York, at the age of ninety.

WILLIAMS, John: congressman

Born Barnstable, England, September 1752; died July 22, 1806.

As a young man, John Williams served one year as surgeon's mate on an English man of war, having studied medicine and surgery at St. Thomas Hospital in London. He came to America in 1773 and settled in New Perth (now Salem), New York, where he practiced medicine. He eventually became a wealthy landowner.

Williams was a member of the New York Provincial Congress from 1775 to 1777, also receiving an appointment as a surgeon in the New York State militia in 1775. He was made a colonel in the Charlotte County (New York) Regiment in 1776, followed ten years later by a commission as brigadier general. He sat in the New York State Senate in 1777–78 and in the New York State Assembly in 1781–82. In 1784 he was ap-

pointed a member of the first board of regents of New York University.

Williams became a delegate to the New York Convention to ratify the United States Constitution in 1788 and a member of the Council of Appointment the next year. He served New York in the United States House of Representatives from 1795 to 1799 (4th and 5th congresses). He also served as a judge of the County Court.

Williams promoted and directed a company organized to build the Erie Canal. He died in Salem and was buried there.

WILLIAMSON, Charles: land promoter

Born Bulgray, Scotland, July 12, 1757; son of Alexander and Christian (Robertson) Williamson; married Abigail Newell, 1782; father of four children; died September 4, 1808.

In 1775 Williamson was commissioned an ensign in the 25th Regiment of Foot but was captured by the Continental Navy en route to America. He became a land promoter and representative of a British syndicate of speculators in western New York in 1791. Hoping to encourage immigration to this area, he built a hotel in Geneva, New York, laid out turnpikes, built bridges, and provided post riders. He became an American citizen circa 1792 and served in the New York Assembly from 1796 to 1800. In 1803 he returned to England, resumed British citizenship, and advised the British government on American Affairs. He died in Havana, Cuba, in 1808.

WILSON, Nathan: congressman

Born near Greenwich, Massachusetts, December 23, 1759; died July 25, 1834.

Wilson attended school in Greenwich but later moved to New Perth (now Salem), New York, where he engaged in farming. He enlisted as a private in the 16th Regiment of the Albany County (New York) militia, and in 1791 was appointed adjutant of the Washington County Regiment of the New York militia.

Wilson served his community first as

town collector in 1801 and 1802 and then as sheriff of Washington County from 1802 until 1806. A Democrat, he was a New York delegate to the United States House of Representatives during the 10th Congress (June 3, 1808, to 1809). He served as a justice of the peace from 1808 to 1816. He died near Salem and was buried in the Evergreen Cemetery.

WILSON, Samuel: meat packer

Born Menotomy (now Arlington), Massachusetts, September 13, 1766; son of Edward and Lucy (Francis) Wilson; married Betsey Mann, January 3, 1797; father of four children; died July 31, 1854.

At age fourteen, Wilson enlisted as a service boy in the Continental Army. He moved to Troy, New York, in 1789 and engaged at various times in brickmaking, farming, distilling, and operating a general store. With his brother Ebenezer he started a meat-packing company and was a meat inspector for the United States Army during the War of 1812. Wilson, whose nickname was "Uncle Sam," came to be identified with the meat eaten by soldiers encamped near Troy, and the use of the name "Uncle Sam" as a personification of the federal government quickly spread among soldiers stationed throughout upstate New York. The term eventually became the popular characterization of the United States, replacing Brother Jonathan in cartoons and plays as the symbol of America.

Wilson died in Troy in 1854 and was buried in Oakwood Cemetery there.

WISNER, Henry: Continental congressman

Born Goshen, New York, circa 1720; son of Hendrick and Mary (Shaw) Wisner; married Sarah (or Mary) Norton, circa 1739; second marriage to Sarah Waters, April 1769; father of five children; died March 4, 1790.

After beginning his career as an assistant justice of the New York Court of Common Pleas, Wisner served as an Orange County representative to the New York Colonial Assembly from 1759 to 1769. He sat in the First and Second Continental congresses (1774–77) and signed the Non-Importation Agreement. As a member of the New York Provincial Congress from 1775 to 1777, he served on a committee which drafted the New York State Constitution. Wisner was also a member of the New York State Senate from 1777 to 1782.

During the American Revolution, Wisner operated a powdermill in Ulster County, New York, later building two other powder-mills in Orange County. He assisted the Continental Army by supplying powder and improving roads. He helped plan the first chain of defenses on the Hudson River in 1776 and two years later served as a member of a committee of eight appointed by the New York Provincial Convention to confer with General Putnam concerning new defenses on the Hudson. This resulted in the West Point fortifications.

Wisner established an academy at Goshen, New York, in 1784. He was also a member of the first board of regents of the State University of New York from 1784 to 1787. As a member of the New York Constitutional Convention in 1788, he voted against adoption of the United States Constitution because he was distrustful of delegating so much power to the federal government. He died in 1790 and was buried in Old Wallkill Cemetery in Phillipsburg, New York.

WOODHULL, Nathaniel: colonial legislator, army officer

Born Mastic, Long Island, New York, December 30, 1722; son of Nathaniel and Sarah (Smith) Woodhull; married Ruth Floyd, 1761; father of one child; died September 20, 1776.

Woodhull was commissioned a major in the New York Regiment in 1758 and became a colonel in the 3rd Regiment of New York Provincials two years later. From 1768 to 1775 he was a member of the New York Colonial Assembly. He represented Suffolk County in a convention which chose the

New York delegates to the First Continental Congress.

In 1775 Woodhull was appointed a brigadier general and also became president of the New York Provincial Congress, of which he was a representative from Suffolk County. After the British landings in 1776 he was assigned to remove supplies from Long Island but was captured by the British near Jamaica, New York. He received ill treatment from his captors and died soon afterward, in New Utrecht, Long Island. He was buried in Mastic.

WRIGHT, Joseph: portrait painter

Born Bordentown, New Jersey, July 16, 1756; son of Joseph and Patience (Lovell) Wright; married Miss Vandervoort, 1787; father of three children; died 1793.

Wright settled in London at age sixteen and studied painting with John Trumbull under Benjamin West. By 1780 he had exhibited at the Royal Academy. In 1782 he painted a portrait of the Prince of Wales and later of George IV. In the same year he painted portraits of fashionable ladies in Paris under the patronage of Benjamin Franklin and then sailed for America.

Wright painted General and Mrs. George Washington in Philadelphia in 1783 and did another Washington portrait the following year. He established himself in New York in 1787. In 1792 Washington appointed him the first draftsman and die-sinker for the United States Mint; the first United States coins and medals are attributed to him. He also made dies for the George Washington medal (awarded by Congress to Major Henry Lee), which was fashioned after the Houdon bust.

Wright also painted portraits of Madison and his family, and his 1786 portrait of John Jay now hangs in the collections of the New York Historical Society. He died in Philadelphia at the age of thirty-seven.

★★★★★

YATES, Abraham: Continental congressman

Born Albany, New York, August 1724; son of Christoffel and Catelynte (Winne) Yates; married Antje De Ridder; father of four children; died June 30, 1796.

Yates, also known as Abraham Yates, Jr., served for many years on the Albany Common Council—from 1754 to 1773. During that time he also was sheriff of Albany County (1755–59). From 1774 to 1776 he was an associator, member, and chairman of the Albany Committee of Correspondence, and he participated in all New York provincial congresses and conventions from 1775 to 1777, serving as president pro tem in 1775 and 1776. He chaired the convention committee which drafted the first New York State Constitution and was a member of the Council of Appointment in 1777. He also was active on the first and second New York Councils of Safety, in 1777 and 1778.

Yates served in the New York State Senate from 1778 to 1790, also holding the office of receiver of Albany in 1778 and 1779. An ardent Anti-Federalist, during the 1780s he wrote frequently (under the names Rough Hewer and Rough Hewer, Jr.) in defense of the sovereignty of his state and in opposition to congressional aggrandizement. He served in the Continental Congress in 1787–88 and was a presidential elector in 1792.

Yates was the first postmaster of Albany, in 1783, and mayor of that city from 1790 to 1796. He died in Albany and was buried in Albany Rural Cemetery.

YATES, Peter Waldron: Continental congressman

Born Albany, New York, August 23, 1747; died March 9, 1826.

After studying law and being admitted to the New York bar, Yates established a legal practice in Albany. He was a member of the Committee of Correspondence in 1775 but declined to serve a second term. In 1784 he became a regent of the University of the State of New York. In that year he also began a term in the state assembly which lasted until 1785. After participating in the Continental Congress during the years 1785–87, he resumed his law practice. He died in Caughnawaga, New York.

YATES, Robert: jurist

Born Schenectady, New York, January 27, 1738; son of Joseph and Maria (Dunbar) Yates; married Jannetje Van Ness, March 5, 1765; father of six children (including John Van Ness); died September 9, 1801.

After studying law with William Livingston, Yates was admitted to the New York bar in 1760. From 1771 to 1775 he was a member of the board of aldermen of New York City. A radical Whig member of the Albany Committee of Safety, he also participated in four New York provincial congresses and conventions as an Albany County representative during the years 1775–78. He was assigned to a secret committee which was to obstruct the channel of the Hudson River in 1776–77 and also served on the Committee of Thirteen which drafted the first New York State Constitution.

From 1777 to 1790 Yates was a justice of the New York Supreme Court, rising to chief justice in 1790 and holding that position until 1798. He was appointed a member of the commission that settled the New York–Vermont boundary dispute in 1780 and the New York–Massachusetts boundary dispute in 1786. A leader of the Anti-Federalists circa 1780–85, he was appointed to represent New York in the United States Constitutional Convention in Philadelphia in 1787. He attacked the constitution in a series of letters (signed Brutus and, later, Sydney) which appeared in the *New York Journal* during 1787 and 1788. In 1800 he was chosen commissioner for settling land titles in Onondaga County, New York.

Yates's collected papers were published as *Political Papers Addressed to the Advocates for a Congressional Revue* (1786) and *Secret Proceedings and Debates of the Convention Assembled . . . for the Purpose of Forming the Constitution of the United States* (1821).

YOUNG, Thomas: physician

Born New Windsor, New York, March 2, 1732; son of John and Mary (Crawford) Young; married Mary Winegar; father of six children; died June 24, 1777.

In 1753 Young began the study of medicine in Amenia, New York, where he was especially successful in treating smallpox. In 1764 he moved to Albany, New York. When the Stamp Act was passed he actively opposed its operation. After moving to Boston in 1766, he delivered the first of the annual orations in commemoration of the Boston Massacre (1771) and became a member of the Boston Committee of Correspondence, second in activity only to Samuel Adams. In 1774 he moved to Philadelphia to avoid a British plot to kidnap him. There he became secretary of the Whig Society.

In 1776, along with a small group of leaders including Benjamin Franklin, Young helped frame the Pennsylvania Constitution. He supported the movement to make the New Hampshire Grants territory into the state of Vermont (he suggested this name) and tried to influence the United States Congress in the cause of Vermont statehood, for which activity Congress voted censure.

Young was co-author with Ethan Allen of *Reason, The Only Oracle of Man, or A Compendious System of Natural Religion* (1784). He died of a fever contracted while practicing as senior surgeon in a Continental hospital in Philadelphia.

★★★★★★★★★★★★★★

NORTH CAROLINA

"The Virginia forces, under Colonel Howe, abandoned Norfolk this morning, after removing the poor inhabitants, with such effects as they could carry with them, and demolishing the intrenchments, which Lord Dunmore threw up a little before he fled on board the fleet . . ."

CONSTITUTIONAL GAZETTE, February 28, 1776

ALEXANDER, Abraham: legislator
Born 1717; died April 23, 1786.

In 1762 Alexander became justice of the peace of Mecklenburg County, North Carolina. Four years later he served on the commission that established the town of Charlotte. A delegate to the North Carolina Assembly during 1769–70, he also served on the Mecklenburg County Committee of Safety. He was an elder in the Presbyterian Church as well as serving (in 1777) as a trustee of Queen's Museum and Liberty Hall Museum.

ANDERSON, Joseph: senator, jurist
Born near Philadelphia, Pennsylvania, November 5, 1757; son of William and Elizabeth (Inslee) Anderson; married Only Patience Outlaw, 1797; father of seven children; died April 17, 1837.

In 1776 Anderson was commissioned a second lieutenant in the United States Army, rising to captain in 1777 and major in 1783. After the war he was admitted to the bar and, in 1791, was appointed United States judge of the territory south of the

Ohio River, in which capacity he served until 1796. He represented Tennessee in the United States Senate during the years 1797–1815 and became the first comptroller of the United States Treasury in 1815, serving for twenty-one years.

Anderson was a trustee of Blount College and of Washington College (Tennessee), and was a charter member of the Delaware chapter of the Society of the Cincinnati. Anderson County, Tennessee, was named for him. He died in Washington, D.C., and was buried in the Congressional Cemetery there.

ASHE, John: colonial legislator, army officer
Born Grovely, North Carolina, 1720; son of John Baptista and Elizabeth (Swann) Ashe; married Rebecca Moore; died October 24, 1781.

Ashe was speaker of the North Carolina Colonial Assembly from 1762 to 1765. He served on the North Carolina Committee of Correspondence and Committee of Safety as well as in the state's Provincial Congress. He was commissioned a colonel in the North

Carolina militia in 1775, and promoted to brigadier general three years later. His defeat at Briar Creek by General Prevost in 1779 gave control of Georgia to the British and made communication possible between Georgia, the Carolinas, and the Indians. The same year a military tribunal censured him for cowardice. Ashe County and Asheville (North Carolina) were named for him. He died in Sampson County, North Carolina.

ASHE, John Baptista: congressman
Born Rocky Point, North Carolina, 1748; son of Samuel and Mary (Porter) Ashe; married Eliza Montfort; father of at least one son (Samuel); died November 27, 1802.

Ashe was a commanding captain in the Continental Army in 1776 and later a lieutenant colonel. He served in the North Carolina House of Commons from 1784 to 1786, becoming speaker the latter year. After a year (1787–88) in the Continental Congress, he was elected to the North Carolina Senate in 1789.

Ashe participated in the North Carolina Convention which ratified the United States Constitution. A Federalist, he was elected to the United States House of Representatives for the 1st and 2nd congresses (1789–93). He was elected governor of North Carolina in 1802 but died before his inauguration. He was buried in Churchyard Cemetery in Halifax, North Carolina.

ASHE, Samuel: governor of North Carolina
Born near Beaufort, North Carolina, 1725; son of John Baptista Ashe; married Mary Porter; second marriage to Elizabeth Merrick; father of two children (including Samuel); died February 3, 1813.

Ashe was president of the North Carolina Council of Safety during the years 1774 to 1776, also attending the state's constitutional convention the latter year. He presided as chief justice of the first North Carolina Supreme Court that same year and continued in this position for nearly two decades—until 1795. From there he went on to the governorship of North Carolina, serving until 1798. His youngest son Samuel became a Federalist and campaigned in the early 1800s against the Republicans, who were led by the elder Ashe.

Ashe also served his state as president of the board of trustees of the University of North Carolina. He died in Rocky Point, North Carolina.

★★★★★

BLOODWORTH, Timothy: senator, Continental congressman
Born New Hanover County, North Carolina, 1736; died August 24, 1814.

Bloodworth became a member of the New Hanover Committee of Safety in 1775. From serving in the North Carolina legislature during 1779–84 he went on to represent his state in the Continental Congress from 1784 until 1787. He opposed the adoption of the United States Constitution. In 1795 he began a six-year term in the United States Senate, after which he was collector of customs for the Port of Wilmington (1807–14). He died in Washington, D.C.

BLOUNT, Thomas: congressman
Born Edgecome County, North Carolina, May 10, 1759; son of Jacob and Barbara (Gray) Blount; married Jacky Sullivan Sumner; died February 7, 1812.

Having enlisted in the 5th North Carolina Regiment of the Continental Army in 1776, Blount was captured by the British the next year and imprisoned in England until 1781. He participated in the North Carolina Convention which ratified the United States Constitution and served in the North Carolina legislature from 1789 to 1793.

A merchant in Tarboro, North Carolina, Blount was a Democratic representative in the United States House of Representatives from North Carolina for several terms— 1793–99, 1805–09, and 1811–12 (3rd–5th, 9th–10th, and 12th congresses). He died in Washington, D.C., and was buried in the Congressional Cemetery.

BLOUNT, William: senator

Born Bertie County, North Carolina, March 26, 1749; son of Jacob and Barbara (Gray) Blount; married Mary Grainger, February 12, 1778; father of two children; died March 21, 1800.

Blount was paymaster of the North Carolina militia in 1777. Three years later he began a four-year stay as a member of the North Carolina House of Commons. In 1788 he began a two-year term in the North Carolina Senate. He was a delegate to the Continental Congress in 1786–87, and a member of the United States Constitutional Convention and a signer of the Constitution in 1787. Two years later he attended the North Carolina Convention which ratified the Constitution.

President George Washington appointed Blount governor of the territory south of the Ohio River (Tennessee), a position he filled from 1790 to 1795. He was superintendent of Indian affairs from 1790 until 1796, when he·became chairman of the first Tennessee Constitutional Convention. He was the first member of the United States Senate from Tennessee, serving from August 2, 1796, until July 8, 1797, when he was expelled for plotting with the British to attack Spanish Florida and Louisiana. The following year he was elected to the Tennessee legislature, later becoming president of the Tennessee Senate. Blount County, Tennessee, was named for him. He died in Knoxville, Tennessee, and was buried in the First Presbyterian Church Cemetery there.

BURGES, Dempsey: congressman

Born Shiloh, Camden County, North Carolina, 1751; died January 13, 1800.

In 1775 and 1776 Burges was a member of the Provincial Congress. He served as a major in the Pasquotank Minutemen and later as a lieutenant colonel in Gregory's Continental Regiment during the Revolutionary War. He was a delegate from North Carolina to the United States House of Representatives from 1795 to 1799 (4th–5th congresses). He died in the county of his birth and was buried in the Shiloh Baptist Churchyard.

BURKE, Thomas: governor of North Carolina

Born County Galway, Ireland, 1747; son of Ulrick and Letitia (Ould) Burke; married Mary Freeman, 1770; father of Mary; died December 2, 1783.

Burke was educated at Dublin University in Ireland. In 1772 he received his license to practice law from the Superior Court of Orange County, North Carolina. He attended North Carolina provincial congresses in 1775 and 1776, serving on thirteen congressional committees the latter year. He represented his state in the Continental Congress during 1776–78.

Burke was governor of North Carolina in 1781 and 1782 and was so successful in organizing the state's military forces that in 1781 the Tories made a raid on Hillsboro for the express purpose of capturing him. He escaped in 1782 and died the following year, in Hillsboro. Burke County, North Carolina, is named after him.

BURTON, Robert: Continental congressman

Born near Chase City, Mecklenburg County, Virginia, October 20, 1747; died May 31, 1825.

Burton, educated in private schools, became a planter in Granville County, North Carolina, in 1775. During the Revolutionary War he served as a quartermaster general. After a period on the Governor's Council in 1783 and 1784, he represented his state at the Continental Congress in 1787–88. In 1801 he was appointed to the commission charged with establishing the boundary line between North Carolina, South Carolina, and Georgia. He died in Granville (now Vance) County, North Carolina, at the age of seventy-seven and was buried at his estate, "Montpelier," in Williamsboro (now Henderson), North Carolina.

★★★★★

CALDWELL, David: clergyman

Born Lancaster County, Pennsylvania, March 22, 1725; son of Andrew and Ann (Stewart) Caldwell; married Rachel Craighead, 1766; died August 25, 1824.

Caldwell graduated from the College of New Jersey (now Princeton) in 1761. He was licensed to preach by the New Brunswick, New Jersey, Presbytery in 1763 and was ordained to the ministry in 1765 by the Presbyterian Church of Trenton, New Jersey. In 1768 he became a pastor in the Province of North Carolina, where he preached, practiced medicine, and conducted a classical school.

Active in the war effort, Caldwell tried, unsuccessfully, to prevent the Battle of Alamance in 1771. Because of his activities, General Charles Cornwallis offered a reward of two hundred pounds for his capture, forcing him into hiding for a while. The British also plundered his home.

In 1776 Caldwell served as a member of the North Carolina Constitutional Convention. He was also a delegate to the North Carolina Convention to ratify the United States Constitution. He died in North Carolina at the age of ninety-nine.

CARTER, John: colonial legislator

Born Virginia, 1737; married Elizabeth Taylor, 1758; father of Landon; died 1781.

John Carter was one of the first settlers of the community of Watauga, North Carolina, where he became the chairman of the Watauga Court. A member of the North Carolina Provincial Congress in 1776, he served in the North Carolina Senate from the Washington District in 1777 and 1781. He was also a public entry-taker.

CARTER, Landon: pioneer, public official

Born Virginia, January 29, 1760; son of John and Elizabeth (Taylor) Carter; married Elizabeth Maclin, 1784; died June 5, 1800.

Carter served in the Revolutionary War from 1780 until 1783, also serving as a captain in John Sevier's expedition against the Cherokee Indians in 1780. He was appointed major in the North Carolina militia by the state legislature in 1788 and was made a lieutenant colonel, commander of the Southwest Territory militia, Washington District, two years later. He then served as a colonel during the Indian campaign in 1792 and 1793.

A member of the North Carolina House of Commons in 1784 and 1789 (elected from Washington County), Carter served as secretary of the state of Franklin from 1784 to 1789. In 1784 he also attended the Jonesborough Convention. The speaker of the first senate of Franklin, he advocated its entry as a state.

After serving as treasurer of the Washington District government of the Southwest Territory, Carter was elected by the first Tennessee legislature as treasurer for the districts of Washington and Hamilton in 1796. He was a trustee and incorporator of Martin Academy and a trustee of Greenville College. Carter County, Tennessee, was named for him; Elizabethton, Tennessee, was named for his wife. He died at the age of forty.

CASWELL, Richard: army officer, governor of North Carolina, Continental congressman

Born Cecil County, Maryland, August 3, 1729; died November 10, 1789.

Caswell, a surveyor in Raleigh, North Carolina, entered public life as deputy surveyor of North Carolina and clerk of Orange County, North Carolina.

He was a member of the North Carolina Assembly from 1754 to 1771 and was speaker for the last two years. He presided over the North Carolina Provincial Congress during the American Revolution and over the North Carolina Constitutional Convention in 1776. From 1774 to 1776 he was North Carolina's delegate to the Continental Congress.

During the war he served as a colonel in

the North Carolina Partisan Rangers, Continental Army, from 1776 to 1777. He later became a major general in the North Carolina militia.

Caswell was elected the first governor of North Carolina in 1776 and served a four-year term. He was comptroller general of the state in 1782 and acceded to the governorship again in 1785, serving until 1787. He was president of the North Carolina Senate from 1782 to 1784 and again in 1789. In 1789 he presided over the North Carolina Convention to ratify the United States Constitution.

Caswell died in Fayetteville, North Carolina, and was buried in the family cemetery in Lenoir County, North Carolina.

CHAVIS, John: clergyman, educator
Born West Indies, 1763; died 1838.

Chavis was sent to the College of New Jersey (now Princeton) and Washington Academy (now a part of Washington and Lee University) as an experiment to see whether a Negro was capable of learning in the same way as a white man; the experiment was successful. Licensed to preach in the Presbyterian Church in 1801, he was a minister to both white people and slaves in North Carolina from 1809 to 1832. He was also a private tutor to the children of the wealthy white people in the region. He was the author of *The Extent of the Atonement*, 1832.

CLEVELAND, Benjamin: army officer, legislator
Born Prince William County, Virginia, March 26, 1738; son of John and Martha (Coffee) Cleveland; married Mary Graves; died October 1806.

A justice in the Wilkes County Court, North Carolina, Cleveland was elected to the North Carolina House of Commons in 1778. Two years later he was elected to the North Carolina Senate. A captain in the 2nd Regiment of the North Carolina militia during the Revolutionary War, he was a hero in the Battle of King's Mountain, which led to the defeat of the English in the South.

Cleveland died in Tugalo Valley, South Carolina.

COCKE, William: army officer, senator
Born Amelia County, Virginia, 1748; son of Abraham Cocke; married Sarah Maclin; second marriage to Mrs. Kissiah Sims; died August 22, 1828.

Cocke fought in the Revolutionary War and was a member of the Virginia Assembly in 1777. The following year he was a member of the North Carolina legislature. He was a leader of the attempt to establish a separate state of Franklin from 1784 to 1788; during those four years he was a brigadier general in the militia of the state of Franklin.

In 1796 Cocke became a member of the Tennessee Constitutional Convention, serving also in the United States Senate that year and the next, and from 1799 to 1805. He was appointed judge of the first Tennessee Circuit Court in 1809 but was impeached and removed from office in 1812. He then fought in wars against the Seminole and Creek Indians until 1815. He was an Indian agent for the Chickasaw Nation during 1814 and 1815, and became a member of the Mississippi legislature in 1822.

Cocke was a founder of the University of Tennessee. He died in Columbus, Mississippi, and was buried there.

CUMMING, William: Continental congressman
Born Edenton, North Carolina; no record of death.

After completing his education, Cumming was admitted to the bar and practiced law. In 1776 he was a member of the North Carolina Provincial Congress. He was a member of the North Carolina House of Commons for several years (1781, 1783, 1784, 1788). From 1784 to 1786 he served in the Continental Congress. In 1790 he was nominated to a justiceship.

★★★★★

DAVIDSON, William Lee: army officer
Born Lancaster, Pennsylvania, 1746; son of George

Davidson; married Mary Brevard; died February 1, 1781.

Davidson was commissioned a major in the 4th North Carolina Regiment in 1776. After joining Washington's army in New Jersey that same year, he participated in the battles of Brandywine, Germantown, and Monmouth. In 1777 he was commissioned a lieutenant colonel, and in 1780 he was the brigadier general in command of the Salisbury (North Carolina) District. The following year he was dispatched by General Greene to interrupt the passage of Cornwallis across the Catawba. He was killed in action at Cowan's Ford, Mecklenburg County, North Carolina.

DAVIE, William Richardson: officer, governor of North Carolina

Born Egremont, Cumberlandshire, England, June 20, 1756; son of Archibald Davie; married Sarah Jones, 1782; father of six children; died November 29, 1820.

Davie, who graduated from Princeton in 1776 with highest honors, helped raise a cavalry troop near Salisbury, North Carolina, in 1777–78. He was commissioned a lieutenant, then a captain, and then a major. In 1780 he was licensed to practice law and also became commissary general under General Nathanael Greene in the Carolina campaign. The following year he was appointed commissary general of the North Carolina Board of War.

In 1782 Davie worked as a lawyer, riding the North Carolina circuits. He was a member of the North Carolina legislature from 1786 to 1798, and governor of North Carolina from 1793 to 1799. He was influential in obtaining state laws, in sending representatives to Annapolis and Philadelphia constitutional conventions, and in ceding Tennessee to the Union and fixing the state boundaries. In 1798 he was chairman of the boundary commissions.

Davie again served in the military by commanding North Carolina troops in 1797. In 1798–99 he was a brigadier general in an undeclared naval war with France, and he served as peace commissioner to that country in 1799. Under a presidential appointment, he negotiated the Tuscarora treaty of 1802.

Davie was the first president of the South Carolina Agricultural Society and a founder of the University of North Carolina. He died near Waxhaw Church, South Carolina.

DICKSON, Joseph: planter, congressman

Born Chester County, Pennsylvania, April 1745; died April 14, 1825.

Dickson, educated in Rowan County, North Carolina, was a tobacco and cotton planter by trade. A member of the Rowan County Committee of Safety in 1775, he was commissioned a captain in the Continental Army later that year. He served under Colonel McDowell and, in 1780, was a major of the "Lincoln County Men" at the Battle of King's Mountain. He was promoted to colonel for his bravery in opposing Lord Cornwallis's invasion of North Carolina in 1781. Before the end of the Revolutionary War, he was commissioned a brigadier general.

In 1781 Dickson was clerk of the Lincoln County Court. He served in the North Carolina Senate from 1788 to 1795. He was a commissioner to establish the University of North Carolina at Chapel Hill. From 1799 to 1801 he attended the 6th Congress of the United States House of Representatives as a delegate from North Carolina. He helped in the election of Thomas Jefferson over Aaron Burr.

In 1803 Dickson moved to Tennessee and became a planter in Davidson (now Rutherford) County. He was a member of the Tennessee House of Representatives from 1807 to 1811, serving as speaker from 1809 to 1811. He died in Rutherford County and was buried on his plantation northeast of Murfreesboro, Tennessee.

DOAK, Samuel: clergyman, college president

Born Augusta County, Virginia, August 1749; son

of Samuel and Jane (Mitchaell) Doak; married Esther H. Montgomery; second marriage to Margaretta H. McEwan; father of four children (including John W. and Samuel W.); died December 12, 1830.

After graduating from the College of New Jersey (now Princeton) in 1775, Doak was a teacher and tutor at various academies. After being licensed to preach by the Presbytery of Hanover, he became a frontier preacher. He founded the Salem Church in Little Limestone, Tennessee, and also churches in Concord, New Providence, and Carter's Valley, Tennessee.

Doak was a member of the convention which formed the state of Franklin, later to become a part of Tennessee. He founded a log-cabin school on his farm, which was incorporated as Martin Academy in 1783; later, in 1795, this became Washington College, the first seat of higher learning west of the Alleghenies. Doak served as president of the school from 1795 until 1818, when he started Tusculum Academy (now Tusculum College) in Bethel, Tennessee.

★★★★★

FANNING, David: Loyalist
Born Amelia County, Virginia, circa 1755; son of David Fanning; married, April 1782; died March 14, 1825.

David Fanning was one of three persons who were excluded from pardon by the general amnesty act at the end of the Revolutionary War. He had become a Loyalist in 1775, when he began marauding expeditions against the Whigs. Commissioned a colonel in the militia in 1781, he captured the official of a judicial court (or court-martial) sitting at Pittsboro, North Carolina, in July of that year and captured Governor Burke in Hillsboro, North Carolina, in September. After the Revolutionary War, Fanning settled in New Brunswick, where he became a member of the provincial parliament, serving from 1791 to 1801.

FANNING, Edmund: colonial official, army officer
Born Long Island, New York, April 24, 1739; son

of James and Hannah (Smith) Fanning; married Phoebe Burns, November 30, 1785; father of four children; died February 28, 1818.

Before the Revolutionary War, Fanning was very active in government in North Carolina. He graduated from Yale in 1757 and was admitted to the North Carolina bar in 1762. Four years later he was appointed judge of the superior court for Salisbury District. He became private secretary to Governor Tryon of New York in 1771, serving as a surrogate in New York City the same year. In 1774 he was surveyor general of the Province of New York. He then returned to North Carolina, where he was a colonel in the militia, a register of deeds, and a member of the North Carolina Assembly in 1776 and 1778.

Fanning led a distinguished career in the British Army, beginning with his raising and commanding of a corps known as the Associated Refugees, or the King's American Regiment of Foot, in 1777. As a result of his Loyalist position, his property was confiscated by North Carolina in 1779; he subsequently moved to Nova Scotia, where he became councilor and lieutenant governor (1783). He was also lieutenant governor of Prince Edward Island in 1786. He rose to colonel in the British Army in 1782, to major general the following year, to lieutenant general in 1790, and to general in 1808. He died in London, England.

FORNEY, Peter: congressman
Born near Lincolnton, North Carolina, April 21, 1756; married; father of at least one son (Daniel Munroe); died February 1, 1834.

Forney served as a captain during the Revolutionary War. He was a Democratic presidential elector five times (1804, 1808, 1816, 1824, 1828) and a Democratic member of the United States House of Representatives from North Carolina during the 13th Congress (1813–15).

In private life, Forney was successfully engaged in an iron manufacturing business. He died at the estate "Mount Welcome," in

Lincoln County, North Carolina, and was buried in a private burying ground there.

FRANKLIN, Jesse: senator, governor of North Carolina

Born Orange County, Virginia, March 24, 1760; son of Bernard and Mary (Cleveland) Franklin; married Meeky Perkins; died August 21, 1823.

During the American Revolution, Franklin served as a captain and an adjutant in the North Carolina Regiment. He entered politics as a member of the North Carolina House of Commons in 1784, returning in 1793, 1794, 1797, and 1798. He was a delegate to the United States House of Representatives from 1795 to 1797 and to the United States Senate from 1799 to 1805 and again from 1807 to 1813. During this same period, he was a member of the North Carolina Senate (1805–06) and a trustee of the University of North Carolina (1805).

Franklin was a United States Commissioner appointed to deal with the Chickasaw and the Cherokee Indians in 1816. Four years later he was elected governor of North Carolina, serving in 1820 and 1821. He died in Surry County, North Carolina, and was buried in the National Park at Guilford Battleground, near Greensboro.

★★★★★

GALES, Joseph: journalist, reformer, mayor

Born Eckington, England, February 4, 1761; son of Thomas Gales; married Winifred Marshall, May 4, 1784; father of three children (including Weston Raleigh and Joseph); died August 24, 1841.

In 1787 Gales founded the *Sheffield Register.* He sold copies of Thomas Paine's *Rights of Man* and befriended the author as well. An active supporter of England's Constitutional Society, he also advocated the abolition of slavery, universal manhood suffrage, and the abolition of imprisonment as punishment for debt. In 1794 he left England and fled to Altona, Schleswig-Holstein, Germany. The following year he came to Philadelphia.

In his new job as reporter for the *American Daily Advertiser,* Gales made the first verbatim report of proceedings in the United States Congress. He then became owner and editor of the *Independent Gazetteer* in North Carolina, going on to found the *Raleigh Register,* a weekly paper, in 1799. He served as mayor of Raleigh for nineteen years and as state printer. In 1834 he compiled the first two volumes of the *Annals of Congress.*

Gales served as secretary of the Peace Society in Washington, D.C., and was secretary and treasurer of the American Colonization Society until 1839. He died in Raleigh, North Carolina, at the age of eighty.

GILLESPIE, James: congressman

Born Kenansville, North Carolina; died January 11, 1805.

Gillespie attended the North Carolina Constitutional Convention in 1776. From 1779 to 1783 he was a member of the North Carolina House of Commons, followed by a period as state senator (1784–86). He was elected to several terms in the United States House of Representatives, serving from 1793 to 1799 and from 1803 to 1805 (3rd, 4th, 5th, and 8th congresses). He died in Washington, D.C., and was buried in the Congressional Cemetery.

GRAHAM, Joseph: army officer

Born Chester County, Pennsylvania, October 13, 1759; son of James and Mary (McConnell) Graham; married Isabella Davidson, 1787; died November 12, 1836.

Educated at Queen's Museum in Charlotte, South Carolina, Graham joined the Continental Army as an enlisted man in 1778 and later became captain of a company of mounted infantry. In 1780 he commanded the reserve forces during the defense of Charlotte; the following year he organized a company of dragoons and rose to the rank of major.

Graham attended the North Carolina conventions which ratified the federal constitution in 1788 and the Bill of Rights in 1789. He served in the state senate from 1788 until 1794 and then on the Council of State in the years 1814–15. He was an original trustee of the University of North Carolina. A series of letters and articles which he started writing in 1820 for Archibald D. Murphy provide a valuable record of revolutionary times in North Carolina. He died in Lincoln County, North Carolina.

GROVE, William Barry: congressman
Born Fayetteville, North Carolina, January 15, 1764; died March 30, 1818.

Grove, a lawyer, served in the North Carolina House of Commons in 1786, 1788, and 1789. Also in 1788 he was a delegate to the North Carolina Convention to ratify the United States Constitution, where he voted against postponement. The following year he was a delegate to the convention which did ratify the federal constitution.

Grove was a trustee of the University of North Carolina and was president of the Fayetteville branch of the Bank of the United States. A Federalist, he was elected to six consecutive terms in the United States House of Representatives (the 2nd through the 7th congresses) in the years 1791–1803. In 1802 he ran unsuccessfully for reelection.

Grove died in Fayetteville and was buried in Grove Creek Cemetery there.

★★★★★

HALL, James: clergyman
Born Carlisle, Pennsylvania, August 22, 1744; son of James and Prudence (Roddy) Hall; died July 25, 1826.

Hall graduated with distinction from Princeton in 1774, and the following year he was licensed to preach by the Presbytery of Orange. He was commander and chaplain of a self-organized company of cavalry on an expedition into South Carolina during the Revolution. He was the organizer and moderator of the General Assembly of the Presbyterian Church in 1803, and later (1812) moderator of the Synod of the Carolinas. An organizer of the American Bible Society and of the North Carolina Bible Society (also serving as its first president), he established the first Protestant mission of the lower Mississippi Valley at Natchez in 1800; this was the first in a series of missionary efforts in the lower valley of the Mississippi.

Hall was an early patron of the University of North Carolina and one of the chief promoters of the Princeton Theological Seminary. He was the author of *Narrative of a Most Extraordinary Work of Religion in North Carolina* and *Report of a Missionary Tour through the Mississippi and the Southwestern County.* He died in Bethany, North Carolina, and was buried there.

HARNETT, Cornelius: patriot, Continental congressman
Born Chowan County, North Carolina, April 20, 1723; son of Cornelius and Mary (Holt) Harnett; married Mary Harnett; died April 28, 1781.

From 1754 to 1775 Harnett was a member of the North Carolina General Assembly, serving as a representative from Wilmington. He was the chairman of the Cape Fear (North Carolina) Sons of Liberty, 1765–66, and a leader of the opposition to the Stamp Act; he was known as the "Sam Adams of North Carolina."

Harnett was president of the North Carolina Provincial Congress in 1776. The same year he was a member of the committee which drafted the first North Carolina state constitution and was the author of the clause forbidding an established church and guaranteeing religious freedom. He was a member of the Continental Congress from 1777 to 1780, during which time he signed the Articles of Confederation. He died while a British prisoner on parole in Wilmington.

HAWKINS, Benjamin: senator
Born Granville (now Warren) County, North Carolina, August 15, 1754; son of Philemon and Delia (Martin) Hawkins; died June 6, 1816.

Hawkins attended Princeton from 1773 until 1776, when he began a two-year service as French interpreter for George Washington. He was a member of the North Carolina House of Commons in 1778–79 and 1784. In 1780 he was chosen by the North Carolina legislature to procure arms and munitions to defend the state.

A member of the Continental Congress from 1781 to 1784 and in 1786–87, Hawkins was appointed by the congress to negotiate treaties with the Creek and Cherokee Indians in 1785. In 1789 he was a delegate to the North Carolina Convention to ratify the United States Constitution. From 1789 to 1795 he was a member of the United States Senate, representing North Carolina. He acted as Indian agent for all tribes south of the Ohio River from 1796 to 1816.

Hawkins died in Crawford County, Georgia, and was buried on a plantation near Roberta, Georgia.

HAWKS, John: architect
Born Dragley, Lincolnshire, England, 1731; married Mary Fisher, 1770; father of one child; died February 16, 1790.

Hawks came to North Carolina in 1764, having been commissioned by the English Court to construct a mansion for the colonial governor of North Carolina; the mansion, begun in 1767, was completed in 1770. From 1770 to 1773 he was commissioner of finance for Governor Tryon of the Colony of North Carolina. From 1773 to 1784 he was both clerk of the upper house of the North Carolina General Assembly and justice of the peace of Craven County, North Carolina. From 1784 to 1790 he served as the first auditor of North Carolina. He died in New Bern, North Carolina.

HENDERSON, Richard: colonizer
Born Hanover County, Virginia, April 20, 1735; son of Samuel and Elizabeth (Williams) Henderson; married Elizabeth Keeling, December 28, 1763; father of several children (including Archibald and Leonard); died January 30, 1785.

Henderson grew up in North Carolina, his family having moved there when he was seven, and was admitted to the North Carolina bar. He was associate justice of the North Carolina Superior Court in 1768. He had become acquainted with Daniel Boone and had organized Richard Henderson and Company in 1764. He organized the Louisa Company (later renamed the Transylvania Company) with the intention of establishing a proprietary colony in the West (1774) and bought land from the Cherokee Indians between the Kentucky and Cumberland rivers. The Revolutionary War made it impossible for him to secure the recognition of his colony from England, and he was also opposed by Virginia and North Carolina.

In 1779–80 Henderson was a North Carolina commissioner working with the Virginia commissioners to survey the boundary between the two states. He promoted and carried out the colonization of what is now western Tennessee, establishing a settlement at the site of the present-day city of Nashville in 1779–80. He was elected to the North Carolina legislature in 1781 and was a member of the North Carolina Council of State the following year. He died in Hillsborough, North Carolina.

HEWES, Joseph: Continental congressman
Born Kingston, New Jersey, January 23, 1730; son of Aaron and Providence (Worth) Hewes; died November 10, 1779.

Hewes was the founder of a mercantile and shipping business in Edenton, North Carolina, in 1763. From 1766 to 1775 he was the borough representative in the North Carolina Colonial Assembly, serving as a member of the Committee of Correspondence in 1773. He was a delegate to all five North Carolina provincial congresses and a signer of the Declaration of Independence.

A member of the Continental Congress from 1774 to 1777 and in 1779, Hewes served on a secret committee, a committee on claims, and a committee to prepare a plan of confederation; he was chairman of the committee of marine, which directed United

States naval affairs in 1776–77. He appointed John Paul Jones as a naval officer and provided him with a ship. In 1776 he aided Washington in the planning of military operations. He was a borough member of the North Carolina House of Commons in 1778. He died during a session of the Continental Congress in Philadelphia and was buried in that city.

HILL, Whitmel: Continental congressman

Born Bertie County, North Carolina, February 12, 1743; died September 26, 1797.

Hill graduated from the University of Pennsylvania at the age of seventeen and was connected with early Revolutionary activities. He served to the rank of colonel during the Revolutionary War. He became a delegate to the Assembly of Freemen in Hillsboro, North Carolina, in 1775 and was a member of the North Carolina Congress and a delegate to the North Carolina Constitutional Convention the following year. In 1777 he was a member of the North Carolina House of Commons, and from 1778 to 1781 he served in the Continental Congress. During this time, from 1778 to 1780, he held a seat in the North Carolina Senate, returning for another term in 1784–85.

Hill died in Hills Ferry, near Hamilton, North Carolina, and was buried in the family cemetery on his estate. He was reinterred in Trinity Cemetery, near Scotland Neck, North Carolina, in 1887.

HOGUN, James: army officer

Born Ireland; married Ruth Norfleet; father of one child; died January 4, 1781.

Hogun came to North Carolina in 1751. In 1775–76 he was a delegate from Halifax County to the North Carolina provincial congresses; in 1776 he was elected first major of the Halifax militia. He was assigned to command the North Carolina Brigade of the Continental Army under General Washington and fought at the battles of Brandywine and Germantown.

In 1779 Hogun was assigned by Washington to command Philadelphia, and the following year he was in charge of a brigade for the defense of Charleston, South Carolina. The brigade was captured soon afterward by the British, and Hogun was offered a pardon, but he elected to stay with the men of his brigade. He died as a result of the strain of imprisonment at Haddrell's Point, South Carolina.

HOLLAND, James: congressman

Born Anson County, North Carolina, 1754; died May 19, 1823.

Holland served as a major in the North Carolina militia and also in the Continental Army during the entire course of the Revolutionary War (1775–83). During that time (1777–78) he was also sheriff of Tryon County, North Carolina. From 1782 to 1785 he was justice of the peace of Rutherford County. Active in state politics, he served as a member of the North Carolina Senate in 1783 and 1797, and in the North Carolina House of Commons in 1786 and 1789. He was a delegate to the Second North Carolina Constitutional Convention, which adopted the United States Constitution in 1789.

Holland was a member of the first board of trustees of the University of North Carolina from 1789 to 1795. In 1793 he was admitted to the North Carolina bar and began his practice of law in Rutherfordton. An Anti-Federalist, he held a North Carolina seat in the United States House of Representatives for the 4th Congress and the 7th–11th congresses (1795–97 and 1801–11). He then engaged in farming near Columbia, Tennessee, where he served as justice of the peace from 1812 to 1818. He died on his estate in Maury County, Tennessee, and was buried in the Holland Family (now Watson) Cemetery near Columbia.

HOOPER, William: Continental congressman

Born Boston, Massachusetts, June 17, 1742; son of the Reverend William and Marie (Dennie) Hooper;

married Anne Clark, 1767; father of William, Thomas, and Elizabeth; died October 14, 1790.

Hooper graduated from Harvard at the age of eighteen and four years later was admitted to the Massachusetts bar. He was deputy attorney general of North Carolina and sat in the North Carolina General Assembly in 1773. From 1774 to 1777 he was a delegate to the Continental Congress. In 1776 he was the speaker of both the Hillsboro and the Halifax (North Carolina) conventions. On August 2, 1776, he signed the Declaration of Independence.

From 1772 to 1782, and again in 1784, Hooper was a borough member of the North Carolina House of Commons. He was one of the United States commissioners who decided the territorial rights controversy between New York and New Jersey (1786). He died in Hillsboro, North Carolina, and was buried in the Guilford Battle Ground in North Carolina.

HOWE, Robert: army officer

Born Bladen County, North Carolina, 1732; son of Job and Sarah (Yeamons) Howe; married Sarah Grange; died December 14, 1786.

Howe was justice of the peace of Bladen County in 1756 and of Brunswick County, North Carolina, in 1764. From 1764 to 1775 he was a member of the North Carolina Assembly. In 1766–67 and from 1769 to 1773 he was in command of Fort Johnston, after which he was commissioned a colonel of artillery. In 1772–73 he was a member of the North Carolina Assembly, and in 1774 he was a delegate to the Colonial Congress in New Bern, North Carolina.

A member of the North Carolina Committee of Correspondence, Howe was commissioned a colonel in the 2nd North Carolina Regiment in 1775. With General Woodford at Norfolk, Virginia, he drove Lord Dunmore out of that part of Virginia. In 1776 he was commissioned a brigadier general in the Continental Army, commanding the Southern Department; he was com-

missioned a major general the following year. He commanded Savannah in 1778 and later West Point and New York.

Howe was elected to the North Carolina House of Commons in 1786, but he died (in Brunswick County) before taking his seat.

HUSBANDS, Hermon: insurrectionist

Born Cecil County, Maryland, October 3, 1724; son of William and Mary Husbands; no record of first marriage; second marriage to Mary Pugh, July 3, 1762; third marriage to Amy (Emmy) Allen, 1766; died 1795.

Husbands, a member of the Society of Friends, was connected with the Regulators, a group of people from the back-country of North Carolina who were protesting official corruption and extortion. He was arrested for inciting a riot in 1768, but a popular uprising in his support led the authorities to release him on bail; he was subsequently acquitted. In 1769 he became a member of the North Carolina Assembly, but he was expelled for writing a "false, seditious, and libelous" letter to the press in 1770. The following year he was freed when a grand jury failed to indict him.

Husbands was forced to flee from North Carolina because of his association with the Regulators, who had been defeated by the government forces at the Battle of Alamance in 1771. After settling in Pennsylvania, he became a leader in the Whiskey Rebellion and served on the Committee of Safety in 1794. He was captured, tried, and condemned to death but was later pardoned.

★★★★★

IREDELL, James: associate justice of the United States Supreme Court

Born Lewes, England, October 5, 1751; son of Francis and Margaret (McCulloh) Iredell; married Hannah Johnston, July 18, 1773; died October 20, 1799.

After serving as comptroller of customs in Edenton, North Carolina, in 1768, Iredell was collector of customs for the Port of North Carolina from 1774 to 1776. The following year he became judge of the Superior Court of North Carolina, becoming attorney general of the state in 1779. He was a member of the North Carolina Council of State in 1787.

Iredell wrote "An Answer to Mr. Mason's Objections to the New Constitution" in support of the United States Constitution. He was floor leader at the North Carolina Convention and a major force in the adoption of the Constitution in North Carolina. As associate justice of the United States Supreme Court from 1790 until his death, he wrote the dissenting opinion in the case of *Chisholm vs. Georgia* and was responsible for the majority report in the case of *Calder vs. Bull.* He died in Edenton.

★★★★★

JACKSON, Andrew: seventh President of the United States
Born Waxhaw, South Carolina, March 15, 1767; son of Andrew and Elizabeth (Hutchinson) Jackson; married Rachel (Donelson) Robards, 1791 (remarried December 1794); father of Andrew, Jr. (adopted); died June 8, 1845.

While a young man, Jackson served in the American Revolution in the Battle of Hanging Rock. He was captured by the British and imprisoned at Camden, South Carolina. Later, in 1787, having studied law in Salisbury, North Carolina, he was admitted to the North Carolina bar. The following year he moved to Nashville, Tennessee.

In 1791 Jackson accepted an appointment as prosecuting attorney for the South West Territory under Governor William Blount; later that year he became judge advocate in the Davidson County militia. In 1796 he was a delegate to the Tennessee Constitutional Convention. After serving for a short while in the United States House of Representatives, on March 4, 1797, he became a member of the United States Senate, serving there for nearly a year. From 1798 to 1804 he held the position of judge in the Tennessee Supreme Court.

During this time—in 1802—Jackson was elected a major general in the state militia. He defeated the Creek Indians at Horseshoe Bend, Alabama, in March 1814 and was appointed a major general in the United States Army two months later. At the Battle of New Orleans on January 8, 1815—three weeks after the signing of the Treaty of Ghent—Jackson and the American forces defeated the British soundly; as a result of this victory, Jackson became a major hero of the War of 1812. In 1818, sent to punish Seminole Indians who were raiding on the Florida border, but, misinterpreting his orders, he crossed the border into Florida, captured Pensacola (which belonged to Spain), and hanged two British gunrunners who had been inciting the Seminoles. The incident placed the United States in danger of war with Spain and Great Britain and brought criticism on Jackson. John Quincy Adams was the only member of President Monroe's cabinet to defend Jackson, placing the blame on Spain. Jackson, rather than being chastised, instead was appointed the first governor of the Florida Territory, which Spain had ceded in 1820. He was appointed on March 10, 1821, but resigned on July 18 of the same year.

Jackson, having been elected to another Senate term in 1823, became the Democratic presidential nominee in 1824, running against Henry Clay, John Quincy Adams, and William Crawford. As no candidate received a majority in the electoral college, the election went to the House of Representatives, where Jackson lost when Clay threw his support to Adams. Four years later, however, Jackson defeated Adams and became the seventh President of the United States, serving from March 4, 1829, to March 3, 1837.

Jackson's cabinet split as a result of the Peggy O'Neill incident, which involved the wife of Secretary of War John Eaton and was brought about primarily by political differences between Secretary of State Martin Van Buren and Vice President John C. Calhoun. Supporters of the latter were surprised by the strength of Jackson's defense of the Union during the nullification crisis in 1832. It was at this time that Jackson made his famous statement: "Our Federal Union! It must and shall be preserved." He became further alienated from Calhoun when William Crawford revealed Calhoun's attempt to censure Jackson for his conduct in the 1818 Seminole campaign, and he chose Van Buren to succeed Calhoun as his vice president the next term. Earlier, in 1830, Jackson had given a political rebuff to Clay when he vetoed a bill calling for the construction of a road from Maysville to Lexington, Kentucky, on the grounds that it was a matter of local concern. Then, in 1832, he vetoed a bill —which Clay had supported—rechartering the Bank of the United States, thus making the Bank question a leading issue in the election of that year.

For the election, Jackson replaced the Democratic Party's caucus system of nominating with the national nominating convention, a method that he introduced ostensibly to better reflect the will of the people but which in fact was intended primarily to effect Van Buren's nomination for the vice presidency. He defeated Clay in the election, winning by a margin greater than that of his victory over Adams in 1828.

In 1833, when South Carolina decided to prohibit the collection of duties within the state, Jackson retaliated by initiating the Force Bill of 1833 and threatened to use force if necessary to execute the law. The Compromise Tariff of 1833 eased this crisis. Jackson then supported the states' rights position of Georgia in that state's removal of the Cherokee Indians. He also removed funds from the Bank of the United States and placed them in "pet" state banks. He removed Secretary of Treasury McLane for refusing to make this transfer of funds, replacing him with James Duane, who also refused. Finally Jackson appointed Roger B.

Taney, who made the transfer. Jackson rewarded Taney's loyalty by appointing him to the United States Supreme Court in 1836.

Jackson, credited with being the father of the spoils system, raised the power of the executive branch to a new high through his use of patronage and the veto and through his refusal to implement Supreme Court decisions. After his presidency, he supported Van Buren for President in 1836 and 1840 and James K. Polk in 1844. He also spoke in favor of the annexation of Texas.

Jackson died on June 8, 1845, at the age of seventy-eight. He was buried at his home, "The Hermitage," near Nashville, Tennessee.

JOHNSTON, Samuel: Continental congressman, senator, governor of North Carolina

Born Dundee, Scotland, December 15, 1733; son of Samuel and Helen (Scrymoure) Johnston; married Frances Cathcart; died August 18, 1816.

Johnston, who came to America from Scotland in 1736, served as provincial treasurer of the northern division of North Carolina and, in 1760, was a member of the North Carolina Assembly. He became a member of the Committee of Correspondence in 1773 and was a delegate to the first through the fourth North Carolina provincial congresses, serving as president of the third and fourth congresses.

During the Revolutionary War, Johnston was deputy naval officer of the Port of Edenton, North Carolina, as well as moderator of the Revolutionary Convention in 1775 and colonial treasurer of North Carolina the same year. He was also member at large of the North Carolina Provincial Council of Safety, district paymaster of troops, and member of the commission charged with codifying the laws then in force.

Besides participating in the North Carolina Senate in 1779, 1783, and 1784, Johnston represented his state in the Continental

Congress during the years 1780–82, declining to serve as president of the Congress. In 1785 he accepted an appointment to the commission settling the Massachusetts–New York boundary dispute. He was governor of North Carolina from 1787 to 1789. During this time he also presided over the North Carolina Convention which refused to adopt the federal constitution in 1788 and then the convention which did ratify in 1789. He was elected as a Federalist to the United States Senate.

Johnston was the first trustee of the University of North Carolina, serving for twelve years in this capacity. From 1800 to 1803 he was judge of the Superior Court of North Carolina. He died near Edenton and was buried in Johnston Burial Ground.

JONES, Allen: Continental congressman
Born Halifax County, North Carolina, December 24, 1739; son of Robert (also known as Robin) and Sarah (Cobb) Jones; married Mary Haynes, January 21, 1762; second marriage to Rebecca Edwards, September 3, 1768; died November 14, 1807.

Jones, who was educated at Eton College in England, entered public life as clerk of the Superior Court for Halifax District and as a member of the North Carolina House of Commons from Northampton County. In 1771 he assisted in the suppression of the "Regulators" and in 1775 became a member of the Committee of Safety for Halifax District.

During 1774–76 Jones represented Northampton in five North Carolina provincial congresses, serving on committees charged with the provision of military defense, the establishment of temporary forms of civil government, the authorization of North Carolina congressmen to concur with those of other colonies in declaring independence, and the framing of the state constitution of 1776. Also in 1776 he was commissioned a brigadier general in the North Carolina militia for the Halifax District.

From 1777 to 1779 Jones served in the state senate, acting as speaker the latter two years. He participated in the Continental Congress in 1779 and 1780 and became a member of the council extraordinary charged with the conduct of the war in 1781. After serving in the North Carolina Council of State in 1782, he again represented Northampton County in the state senate in 1783, 1784, and 1787. He died in Northampton County.

JONES, Willie: Continental congressman, legislator
Born Northampton County, North Carolina, circa 1741; son of Robert (also known as Robin) and Sarah (Cobb) Jones; married Mary Montfort, June 27, 1776; died June 18, 1801.

Jones, who attended Eton for several years, was aide to Governor Tryon of North Carolina in the Alamance campaign against the Regulators. Before the Revolution he chaired the Halifax Committee of Safety and represented Halifax County in five North Carolina provincial congresses. During the fourth congress he was elected superintendent of Indian affairs for the southern colonies. During the fifth congress, as a member of the committee which was delegated to draft the North Carolina Constitution, he greatly influenced the decisions regarding the document's form and character and is credited with writing it as well.

In 1777 Jones became a member of the North Carolina House of Commons from the borough of Halifax, and in 1779 and 1780 he represented Halifax County there. He participated in the Continental Congress during 1780–81, about the same time as the tenure of his older brother Allen. He served on the Council of State in 1781 and 1787 and was elected to the state senate for terms in 1782, 1784, and 1788. He attended the state ratification convention of 1788, where he opposed adoption of the United States Constitution.

Jones sat on the first board of trustees of the University of North Carolina and on the commission which located the state capital and provided for the building of a statehouse. He died in Raleigh, North Carolina.

★★★★★

LOCKE, Matthew: congressman

Born in the North of Ireland, 1730; son of John and Elizabeth Locke; married Mary Brandon, 1749; second marriage to Mrs. Elizabeth Gostelowe; died September 7, 1801.

Locke settled near the present city of Salisbury, North Carolina, circa 1752. He served as a justice of the peace and as a vestryman. He was a member of the North Carolina House of Commons in 1770–71, 1773–75, 1777–81, 1783–84, and 1789–92. He was an agent and a member of the Rowan Committee of Safety from 1774 to 1776. He represented North Carolina in the third through the fifth provincial congresses in 1775–76.

Locke served as paymaster, as brigadier general, and circa 1776–81 as auditor of Salisbury District. He was a member of the North Carolina Senate in 1781–82 and 1784 and a trustee of Salisbury Academy in 1784. From 1793 to 1799 he was a North Carolina delegate to the United States House of Representatives. He died in Salisbury and was buried in the Thyatira Churchyard there.

★★★★★

McDOWELL, Charles: army officer

Born Winchester, Virginia, 1743; son of Joseph and Margaret (O'Neal or O'Neil) McDowell; married Grace (or Grizel) (Greenlee) Bowman, circa 1780; died March 31, 1815.

After serving as a captain in a militia regiment in a backwater region of the South, McDowell was commissioned a lieutenant colonel in 1776 and commanded a rear guard of the Continental Army. He helped to bring about the first American victory in the South after Gates's defeat and then served as a brigadier general in command of an expedition against the Cherokee Indians in 1782.

A member of the North Carolina Senate in 1778 and from 1782 to 1788, McDowell served as a commissioner for settling the boundary between Tennessee and North Carolina in 1797. He died in Burke County, North Carolina.

McDOWELL, Joseph: congressman, army officer

Born Winchester, Virginia, February 15, 1756; son of Joseph and Margaret (O'Neal or O'Neil) McDowell; married Margaret Moffett; father of eight children (including Joseph Jefferson); died February 5, 1801.

McDowell, who was involved in numerous actions during his military career, served with his brother Charles McDowell's regiment in the North Carolina militia during the Revolution and took part in the Rutherford expedition against the Cherokee Indians in 1776. He also participated in a number of battles against the Loyalists in North Carolina, including Ramsour's Mill, 1780. Promoted to major in McDowell's regiment, he was in command at the Battle of King's Mountain in 1780 and commanded a detachment of riflemen from Burke County, North Carolina, in the Battle of Cowpens, 1781. He attacked the Cherokee Indians that year and commanded the regiment during his brother's expedition against the Cherokees in 1782.

McDowell served in the North Carolina House of Commons from 1785 to 1788 and in the North Carolina Senate from 1791 to 1795. He was a delegate to the North Carolina conventions to ratify the United States Constitution in 1788 and 1789. He was a North Carolina delegate to the United States House of Representatives for the 5th Congress (1797–99). He died in 1801 and was buried at "Quaker Meadows," near Morgantown, North Carolina.

McDOWELL, Joseph: congressman

Born at the estate "Pleasant Gardens," near Morgantown, North Carolina, February 25, 1758; died March 7, 1799.

McDowell was commissioned a major during the Revolution, participating in the Battle of King's Mountain, and then became a general in the North Carolina militia. He was admitted to the North Carolina bar in 1791, having attended schools in Winchester, Virginia, and studied law. He then practiced in Burke (now McDowell), Rowan, and Rutherford counties from 1785 to 1792.

McDowell was elected a North Carolina delegate to the United States House of Representatives for the 3rd Congress (1793–95) and then resumed his law practice. He also engaged in farming and served as a member of the commission which was to settle the boundary between North Carolina and Tennessee in 1796. He died at "Pleasant Gardens" and was buried on Round Hill there.

McMINN, Joseph: governor of Tennessee
Born Marlborough Township, Pennsylvania, June 22, 1758; son of Robert and Sarah (Harlan) McMinn; married Hannah Cooper, May 9, 1795; second marriage to Nancy Williams, January 5, 1812; died November 17, 1824.

McMinn attended the Tennessee Territorial Legislature in 1794, the Tennessee Constitutional Convention in 1796, and the Tennessee legislature from 1796 to 1804, serving as speaker of the latter body three times. He was governor of Tennessee from 1815 to 1821, then served as agent to the Cherokee Indians in 1823–24, during which time he negotiated a treaty by which the Cherokees ceded vast tracts in eastern Tennessee. McMinn County and the town of McMinnville (both in Tennessee) are named for him. He died in Cherokee Agency, Tennessee.

MACON, Nathaniel: congressman, senator
Born Edgecomb (later Bute, now Warren) County, North Carolina, December 17, 1758; son of Gideon and Priscilla (Jones) Macon; married Hannah Plummer, October 9, 1783; father of three children; died June 29, 1837.

During the Revolutionary War, Macon served in the New Jersey militia but left the army in 1777 to return to North Carolina to study law. He fought as a private in the Battle of Camden in 1780.

Macon held a number of legislative positions in North Carolina and in the federal government after 1780, including member, North Carolina Senate, 1780–82 and 1784–85; member, North Carolina House of Commons, 1790; and Republican member, United States House of Representatives, 2nd–14th congresses, 1791–1815. He was speaker of the House from 1801 to 1807.

Macon supported continuation of the treaty with France and the Louisiana Purchase (1803). He urged President Jefferson to purchase Florida as well. He opposed the Jay Treaty and the Alien and Sedition Acts. As chairman of the foreign relations committee in 1809, he opposed Macon's Bill No. 2 (named for him, as was Bill No. 1, although he was not the author of either), which gave the President the power to suspend relations with either France or Great Britain because of interference with American commerce. He favored the War of 1812 but opposed conscription.

Macon, a Republican, was a North Carolina delegate to the United States Senate from December 13, 1815, to November 14, 1828, and was president pro tem after 1826. He participated in the Missouri debate, opposed compromise, and defended slavery. Macon County, North Carolina, was named for him in 1828. In 1832 he opposed nullification. He served as president of the North Carolina Constitutional Convention in 1835 but declined to vote for the amended constitution.

Macon died in Warren County, North Carolina, and was buried at his home in Bucks Creek, North Carolina.

MARTIN, Alexander: senator, governor of North Carolina
Born New Haven County, New Jersey, 1740; son of

Hugh and Jane Martin; never married; died November 2, 1807.

Martin received an A.B. from the College of New Jersey (now Princeton) in 1756. He then moved to Salisbury, North Carolina, where he became a merchant and a justice of the peace in 1764. He was deputy King's attorney in 1766 and a judge in 1774–75. Admitted to the North Carolina bar in 1772, he was a member of the North Carolina House of Commons in 1773–74 and the second and third provincial congresses in 1775.

Martin was commissioned a lieutenant colonel in the 2nd North Carolina Regiment, Continental Army, in 1775 and became a colonel the following year. He participated in the defense of Charleston, South Carolina, and served under Washington in the battles of Brandywine and Germantown. Arrested for cowardly behavior after the latter engagement, he was acquitted by a court-martial. He resigned his commission in 1777.

A member of the North Carolina Senate from 1778 to 1782, in 1785, in 1787–88, and in 1804–05, Martin served as speaker from 1778 to 1782, in 1785, and in 1805. He was a member of the North Carolina Board of War and then, in 1780–81, of the North Carolina Council Extraordinary. He was acting governor of North Carolina in 1781–82 and governor from 1782 to 1784 and from 1789 to 1792. He advocated clemency for Tories; favored increased power for the Continental Congress; encouraged education and the growth of agriculture, commerce, and manufacturing; and proposed using convict labor for making internal improvements.

Martin represented his state in the Continental Congress in 1786 and was a member of the North Carolina Convention which ratified the United States Constitution in 1787. A trustee of the University of North Carolina from 1790 to 1807, he was president of the board in 1792–93.

A Republican, Martin was a delegate to the United States Senate from 1793 to 1799; he was not reelected because he had voted for the Alien and Sedition Acts. He died at his estate "Danbury," near Crawford (now Danbury), North Carolina, and was buried there.

MEBANE, Alexander: congressman
Born Hawfields, North Carolina, November 26, 1744; died July 5, 1795.

Mebane, who attended common schools, was a delegate to the North Carolina Provincial Congress in 1776 and was justice of the peace that year and sheriff of Orange County in 1777. Auditor of the Hillsboro (North Carolina) District in 1783–84, he was a member of the Hillsboro Convention in 1788 and the Fayetteville Convention in 1789. He was a member of the North Carolina House of Commons from 1787 to 1792 and was elected to a term in the United States House of Representatives in 1793. He died in Hawfields.

MENEWA: Indian chief
Born circa 1766; died 1835.

A scourge of the Tennessee frontier, Menewa was called Hothlepoya, "the crazy war hunter," in his younger days. Known as Menewa (meaning "the great warrior") during the uprising of Tecumseh, second chief of the Oakfuskee Creek Indians in Alabama, he was against ceding tribal lands to the white man. He was defeated by Andrew Jackson at the Battle of Horseshoe Bend in 1814.

Menewa later adapted to the ways of the white man and became a trader. He was a member of a delegation sent to Washington to protest the treaty signed by William McIntosh in 1826. When some of the Creeks joined the Seminole Indians during the Seminole War in 1835, Menewa fought on the side of the white man with the promise that he could remain on his native land until his death. However, the promise was later broken, and he was sent with the rest of his tribe to the Oklahoma reservation, where he died soon afterward.

MOORE, Alfred: army officer, associate justice of the United States Supreme Court

Born New Hanover County, North Carolina, May 21, 1755; son of Judge Maurice and Anne (Grange) Moore; married Susanna Eagles, September 1, 1775; died October 15, 1810.

Licensed to practice law in 1775, Moore was a captain in the 1st North Carolina Regiment, Continental Army, until 1777. He became a colonel in the Brunswick County Regiment of the North Carolina militia and participated in the Battle of Guilford Court House in Wilmington, Delaware.

Moore, a Federalist, was elected to represent Brunswick County in the North Carolina Senate in 1782 and also served as attorney general of the state from that year until 1791. A trustee of the state university from 1789 to 1807, he was a member of the North Carolina House of Commons in 1792. He was elected judge of the North Carolina Superior Court in 1798 and appointed an associate justice of the United States Supreme Court in 1799. He died in Bladen County, North Carolina.

MOORE, James: army officer

Born New Hanover County, North Carolina, 1737; son of Maurice and Mary (Porter) Moore; married Ann Ivie; father of four children; died April 1777.

After serving as a captain during the French and Indian War, Moore was a member of the North Carolina Provincial House of Commons from 1764 to 1771 and in 1773. He was the leader of a Cape Fear mob which marched to Brunswick to prevent enforcement of the Stamp Act in North Carolina in 1766. He served as a colonel in the artillery in 1768 and in 1771.

Moore became a member of the North Carolina Assembly in 1773. He was the first to sign a circular letter from the committee which called the First Revolutionary Provincial Congress in 1774. A delegate from New Hanover County to the Third Provincial Congress, held in Hillsboro, North Carolina, in 1775, he was commissioned a colonel in the 1st North Carolina Continental Regiment later that year and was appointed a brigadier general in command of the North Carolina militia in 1776. He died in Wilmington, Delaware, the following year.

MOORE, Maurice: jurist

Born New Hanover County, North Carolina, 1735; son of Maurice and Mary (Porter) Moore; married Anne Grange; father of Alfred; died April 1777.

Moore became an associate judge of the North Carolina courts in 1758 and served as a member of the North Carolina House of Commons from 1757 to 1760, in 1762, from 1764 to 1771, and in 1773–74. He was a member of the Governor's Council in 1760–61 and again from 1768 to 1773. He was an associate judge of the Province of North Carolina until 1765.

Moore was a colonel in Governor Tryon's first armed expedition against the Regulators. He sat as judge at the Hillsboro (North Carolina) trial of 1768 and at a special court in Hillsboro that sentenced twelve Regulators to death on treason charges in 1771. Moore later became more lenient toward the members of the movement and served on a committee which tried to induce Regulators to support the patriotic cause in 1775. He was a Brunswick delegate to the North Carolina provincial congresses. He died in Wilmington, North Carolina.

★★★★★

NASH, Abner: governor of North Carolina, Continental congressman

Born Templeton Manor, Prince Edward County, Virginia, August 8, 1740; son of John and Ann (Owen) Nash; married Justina (Davis) Dobbs; second marriage to Mary Whiting Jones, 1774; died December 2, 1786.

Nash was a member of the Virginia House of Burgesses in the years 1761 and 1762. He then began a long series of terms in the North Carolina House of Commons, serving in 1764, 1765, 1770–71, 1777 (when he was speaker), 1778, 1782, 1784, and 1785. In

1768 he became a brigade major in the North Carolina militia. During the years 1774 to 1776 he participated in five North Carolina provincial congresses as well as serving on the state provincial council in 1775 and 1776 (he was agent of the council the latter year also).

After a time as speaker of the North Carolina Senate in 1779–80, Nash served as governor of the state during 1780 and 1781. He then attended Continental congresses every year during the period from 1782 to 1786. The latter year he was elected to the Annapolis Convention but did not attend. He died that year in New York City and was buried at the estate "Pembroke," near New Bern, North Carolina.

NASH, Francis: army officer
Born Templeton Manor, Prince Edward County, Virginia, 1742; son of John and Ann (Owen) Nash; married Sarah Moore; father of at least two children; died October 7, 1777.

After serving as justice of the peace and clerk in the North Carolina Court of Pleas and Quarter Sessions in 1763, Nash went to the House of Commons in 1764 and again in 1765, 1771, and 1773–75. In 1771 he served as a captain in the British Army and fought against the Regulators in the Battle of Alamance. Apparently switching allegiances, he became a member of the North Carolina Provincial Congress in 1775. That same year, Nash, who had served as a colonel in the North Carolina militia, became a lieutenant colonel and then a colonel in the 1st North Carolina Regiment of the Continental Army. Two years later he rose to brigadier general, led a brigade at Germantown, Pennsylvania, and was mortally wounded during the action there.

Nash County, North Carolina, and Nashville, Tennessee, are named in his honor.

★★★★★

OUTACITY: Indian chief
Born probably in Tennessee; died circa 1777.

A Cherokee Indian, Outacity, who was also known as Ostenaco and Mankiller, flourished during the period 1756 to 1777. He took an active part in the uprising led by Oconostota in 1757. In 1762 he visited England under the guidance of Henry Timberlake and had an audience with King George III; Timberlake arranged this in order to increase his reputation of having influence over the Indians. Outacity fought on the side of Great Britain during the American Revolution.

★★★★★

PENN, John: Continental congressman
Born near Port Royal, Caroline County, Virginia, May 17, 1741; son of Moses and Catherine (Taylor) Penn; married Susannah Lyme, July 28, 1763; father of three children; died September 14, 1788.

Penn read law privately and was licensed to practice in Bowling Green, Virginia, in 1762. In 1774 he moved to Granville County, North Carolina, and became a member of that state's provincial congress the following year. He served as a member of the Continental Congress from 1775 to 1780, signed the Declaration of Independence in 1776, and was on the North Carolina Board of War in 1780. He was a representative from North Carolina to ratify the Articles of Confederation and in 1784 was appointed North Carolina receiver of taxes for the Confederation. He died near Williamsburg, North Carolina, and was buried at the Guilford Battle Ground at Greensboro.

PERSON, Thomas: state legislator
Born probably Brunswick County, Virginia, January 19, 1733; son of William and Ann Person; married Johanna Thomas, 1760; died November 16, 1800.

In 1756 and again in 1776 Person served as a justice of the peace; in 1762 he was a sheriff. A member of the North Carolina Assembly in 1764, he became head of the Granville delegation in all North Carolina provincial congresses from 1774. He was a member of the committee which proposed the Halifax Resolution of April 12, 1776, instructing delegates to the Continental Congress to vote for a declaration of independence. He also served for a time on the North Carolina Council.

Person was a member of the committee which drafted a bill of rights for North Carolina and a member of the committee which drew up the North Carolina Constitution of 1776. That year he was also a general in the North Carolina militia and a member of the North Carolina Council of Safety. He then served as a member of the North Carolina Council of State.

Person was elected to the Continental Congress in 1784 but did not serve. He was a member of the North Carolina House of Commons from 1777 to 1786, from 1788 to 1791, from 1793 to 1795, and in 1797. In 1787 and 1791 he was a member of the North Carolina Senate. He served as chief commissioner to settle North Carolina accounts with the United States in 1787. A delegate to the Fayetteville (North Carolina) Convention in 1789, he opposed ratification of the United States Constitution.

Person was appointed a charter trustee of North Carolina State University in 1789 and was a generous benefactor until 1795. He died in Franklin County, North Carolina, and was buried at Personton.

POLK, Thomas: army officer, Continental congressman

Born Cumberland County, Pennsylvania, circa 1732; son of William and Margaret (Taylor) Polk; married Susan Spratt, 1755; father of nine children (including William); died January 26, 1794.

Polk led his troops in the War of Sugar Creek in 1760. Eight years later he served as a commissioner of Charlotte, North Carolina; also that year he became the first treasurer of that city. He served in the North Carolina House of Commons from 1766 to 1771 and again from 1773 to 1774. As a captain of the North Carolina militia from 1758 to 1771, he fought against the Regulators.

In 1772 Polk was a member of the survey-ing team that ran the North Carolina–South Carolina boundary line. In 1775 he was a member of the Mecklenburg Committee, a delegate to the North Carolina Provincial Congress, and a colonel in the North Carolina militia. In 1776 he was commissioned a colonel in the 4th North Carolina Continental Regiment, and later served in the battles of Brandywine and Valley Forge. He was commissary general of provisions in North Carolina in 1780, then became commissary of purchases for the Continental Army. In 1781 he was commissioned a colonel commandant.

Polk served as councilor of North Carolina in 1783–84 and as a delegate to the Continental Congress in 1786. His interest in higher education led him to become a promoter of Queen's College in Charlotte, which he served as a trustee in 1771; he was also a trustee of Liberty Academy in 1777 and of Salisbury Academy in 1784. He died in Charlotte.

POLK, William: army officer

Born Charlotte, North Carolina, July 9, 1758; son of Thomas and Susan (Spratt) Polk; married Grizelda Gilchrist, October 15, 1789; second marriage to Sarah Hawkins, January 1, 1801; father of fourteen children; died January 14, 1834.

Polk studied at Queen's College before becoming a major in the 9th Regiment of the North Carolina militia in 1776. He served in the battles of Brandywine, Germantown, Camden, and Guilford Court House. Circa 1782 he was a lieutenant colonel commandant with the 4th South Carolina Cavalry. In 1783 he was a surveyor general in the North Carolina Land Office.

After serving brief tenures in the North Carolina House of Commons (1785–86, 1787, and 1790), Polk became supervisor of internal revenue for North Carolina and served in that capacity until 1808. He was president of the North Carolina State Bank from 1811 to 1819 and president of the Neuse River Navigation Company.

A trustee of the University of North Carolina for forty-four years (1790 to 1834), Polk served as president of the board of trustees from 1802 to 1805. He was grand master of the Masons for North Carolina and Tennessee from 1799 to 1802. He managed Jackson's campaigns in North Carolina in 1824 and in 1828. Counties in both Tennessee and North Carolina are named after him. He died in Raleigh, North Carolina.

★★★★★

REED, John: miner
Born Hesse-Cassel, Germany, January 6, 1757; married Sarah Kisor; father of eight children; died March 28, 1845.

Reed served as a mercenary for the British during the American Revolution. In 1784 he became a farmer in Cabarrus County, North Carolina. He discovered gold on his property in 1802 and began mining operations the next year; during his lifetime the mine produced over $10 million worth of gold. As a result of his discovery, gold mining became second only to agriculture in economic importance in North Carolina. He later bought a large plantation in Cabarrus County, where he died at the age of eighty-eight.

RHEA, John: congressman
Born County Donegal, Ireland, 1753; son of Joseph and Elizabeth (McIlwaine) Rhea; died May 27, 1832.

Rhea came to the United States in 1769 and graduated from Princeton in 1780. From 1785 to 1790 he was a member of the North Carolina House of Commons. He was a member of the North Carolina Convention for ratification of the United States Constitution. He was an incorporator or trustee of Washington College, of Greenville (now Tusculum) College, and of Blount College (now the University of Tennessee).

In 1796 Rhea served as a delegate to the first Tennessee Constitutional Convention. In that year he became a member of the Tennessee legislature and served again the next year. A Democrat, he was a Tennessee delegate to the United States House of Representatives from 1803 to 1815 (8th–13th congress) and from 1817 to 1823 (15th–17th congresses).

Rhea was a United States commissioner in 1816 and signed a treaty with the Choctaw Indians. Rhea County, Tennessee, is named for him. He died in Blountville, Tennessee.

ROANE, Archibald: governor of Tennessee
Born Derry Township, Tennessee, circa 1759; son of Andrew and Margaret (Walker) Roane; married Anne Campbell; died January 4, 1819.

In 1787 Roane, along with Andrew Jackson and others, signed a petition requesting North Carolina to grant independence to people of the western part of the state. A year later he was granted permission to practice law before the court of Washington County, North Carolina (now part of eastern Tennessee).

Roane became attorney general of the Tennessee district of Hamilton in 1790, and in 1796 he became a member of the Tennessee Constitutional Convention. He served as a judge of the Tennessee Supreme Court of Errors and Appeals. From 1801 to 1803 he was governor of Tennessee. A circuit judge from 1811 until 1815, he then served as a judge of the Tennessee Supreme Court until his death.

ROBERTSON, James: pioneer
Born Brunswick County, Virginia, June 28, 1742; son of John and Mary (Gower) Robertson; married Charlotte Reeves, October 20, 1768; father of eleven children; died September 1, 1814.

In 1769 Robertson crossed the Blue Ridge Mountains with Daniel Boone. He became a member of the court created by the Watauga Association in North Carolina. He participated in Lord Dunmore's War at Battle Point Pleasant in 1774. He served as an agent to the Cherokee Indians for North Carolina and Virginia and, holding the rank of captain, in 1777 he conducted the defense of Watauga Fort against the Cherokees.

Robertson was appointed agent by the North Carolina Assembly of 1778 to reside permanently among the Cherokees. He resigned a year later to explore the Cumberland Valley. In 1780 he led a group of settlers to the present site of Nashville, Tennessee, and adopted the Cumberland Compact as a basis of government. He served as presiding officer of the court established at the settlement. A colonel in the regional militia, in 1781 he made an alliance with the Chickasaw Indians.

In 1785 Robertson became a trustee of the University of Nashville. In the same year he served as a county representative in the North Carolina Assembly. Two years later he led the Coldwater Expedition against the Indians.

As brigadier general of the territorial government southwest of Ohio, he aided Blount in negotiating the Holston Treaty of 1791. In 1796 he was a Davidson County representative in the Tennessee Constitutional Convention. He served in the Tennessee Senate in 1798.

Robertson was a Tennessee delegate to the first treaty of Tellico between the United States and the Cherokee Nation in 1798. He died in Chickasaw Bluffs, Tennessee, and was buried in the Old City Cemetery at Nashville.

ROCHESTER, Nathaniel: merchant
Born Westmoreland County, Virginia, February 21, 1752; son of John and Hester (Thrift) Rochester; married Sophia Beatty, 1788; father of nine children; died May 17, 1831.

In 1775 Rochester was a member of the Revolutionary Committee of Safety for Orange County, North Carolina. He attended two North Carolina provincial conventions, in 1775 and 1776. He was commissioned a major in the North Carolina militia and in 1776 advanced to lieutenant colonel. He was deputy commissary of general stores and clothing. The next year he was appointed a commissioner to establish and superintend an arms manufactory in Hillsboro, South Carolina. In 1777 he also served in the South Carolina Assembly.

Rochester went into business with Colonel Thomas Host in Hillsboro, then (in 1778) in Hagerstown, Maryland. He served a term in the Maryland legislature. In 1807 he was president of the Hagerstown Bank. He was a founder of Monroe County, New York, and served as county clerk in 1821. He was a founder of the city of Rochester, New York, and organized a bank there in 1824. He died in Rochester seven years later.

★★★★★

SEVIER, John: governor of Tennessee, congressman, army officer
Born near New Market, Virginia, September 23, 1745; son of Valentine and Joanna (Goade) Sevier; married Sarah Hawkins, 1761; second marriage to Catherine Sherill, August 14, 1780; died September 24, 1815.

During the years 1773–74 Sevier served in Lord Dunmore's War as a captain in the Virginia colonial militia under George Washington. He was a commissioner in the Watauga Association in Knoxville, North Carolina (now Tennessee), and in 1776 became a member of the Knoxville Committee of Safety. After being elected a representative to the North Carolina Provincial Congress, he was appointed a lieutenant colonel in the North Carolina militia. Among his military accomplishments were leading 240 men to victory over the British at the Battle of King's Mountain on October 7, 1780, and making three raids against Indians during 1781–82.

Together with William Blount, Sevier established a settlement at Muscle Shoals, Alabama, circa 1783. He was elected governor of the state of Franklin and served from 1785 until 1788, when the regime collapsed following a battle with the Tipton faction. The following year he was elected to the North Carolina Senate. He voted for ratification of the United States Constitution at the North Carolina Convention called for that purpose. In 1791 he was commissioned a brigadier general in the state militia.

Sevier represented North Carolina in the 1st Congress of the United States House of Representatives, from 1789 until September 24, 1791. During the 1790s he was an active land speculator in the West. He served as a trustee of Washington College in Tennessee and of Blount College (now the University of Tennessee). He was the first governor of Tennessee (1796–1801) and was reelected in 1803, serving until 1809. After a period in the Tennessee Senate (1809–11) he was a Tennessee delegate to the United States House of Representatives from 1811 to 1815 (12th and 13th congresses). In 1815 he accepted an appointment to the commission surveying the boundary of the Creek Cession.

Sevier died in Alabama and was buried in Knoxville, Tennessee.

SHARPE, William: Continental congressman

Born near Rock Church, Cecil County, Maryland, December 13, 1742; died July 1, 1818.

After studying law, Sharpe was admitted to the bar and established a legal practice in Mecklenburg County, North Carolina, in 1763. He also became a surveyor. He moved to Rowan (now Iredell) County, North Carolina, and in 1775 became a member of the Provincial Congress. In 1776 he was a delegate to the North Carolina Constitutional Convention in Halifax and served as an aide to General Rutherford in his Indian campaign. The following year Governor Caswell appointed him a commissioner to treat with Indians.

Sharpe participated in the Continental Congress during the years 1779–82 and was a member of the North Carolina House of Representatives in 1781–82. He died near Statesville, North Carolina, and was buried in Snow Creek Graveyard.

SHELBY, Evan: army officer, state senator

Born Tregaron, Cardiganshire, Wales, 1719; son of Evan and Catherine (Davies) Shelby; married Laetitia Cox, 1744; second marriage to Isabella Elliott, 1787; father of at least one son (Isaac); died December 4, 1794.

Shelby came to America circa 1734 and settled in Hagerstown, Maryland. He laid out part of the road from Fort Frederick to Fort Cumberland in General Braddock's campaign of 1755. After being commissioned captain of a company of rangers and a captain in the Pennsylvania militia as well, he served under General John Forbes in the capture of Fort Duquesne in 1758.

In 1762 Shelby became manager of the Potomac Company for Maryland. Moving to Virginia in 1773, he became a landowner in Fincastle County and commanded the county's company of the Virginia militia in Lord Dunmore's War in 1774. Having been commissioned a major in the Virginia militia in 1776, he led an expedition of two thousand men against Chickamauga Indian towns on the lower Tennessee River in 1779.

Shelby served in the North Carolina Senate in 1781. During the years 1786–87 he was a brigadier general in the Washington District (North Carolina) militia. In 1787 he acted as a commissioner for North Carolina in the negotiations for a temporary truce with Colonel John Sevier and refused the position of governor of the state of Franklin. In that year he also resigned as brigadier general.

Shelby died in Bristol in Sullivan County, Tennessee, and was buried in East Hill Cemetery in Bristol.

SITGREAVES, John: Continental congressman

Born England, 1757; died March 4, 1802.

Sitgreaves attended Eton College and then came to America, where he studied law. After his admission to the bar he began a practice in New Bern, North Carolina.

During the Revolutionary War he rose to the rank of lieutenant and later became a military aide to General Caswell. He was appointed commissioner in charge of confiscated property.

During 1778–79 Sitgreaves was clerk of the North Carolina Senate. He attended the Continental Congress in 1784–85 and the North Carolina House of Commons in 1784 and again from 1786 to 1789, serving as speaker in 1787–88. He then held the office of United States district judge for North Carolina from 1789 until 1802. He died in Halifax, North Carolina, and was buried in the City Cemetery in Raleigh, North Carolina.

SMITH, Daniel: senator
Born Stafford County, Virginia, October 28, 1748; son of Henry and Sarah (Crosby) Smith; married Sarah Michie, June 20, 1773; father of two children; died June 6, 1818.

Smith attended the College of William and Mary. He held local offices as a deputy surveyor in 1773 and justice of the peace in 1776. In 1777 he aided in the organization of Washington County, Virginia, and became a major in the county militia. Two years later he worked on the surveying crew which extended the boundary between Virginia and North Carolina, thus establishing the disputed Walker's Line. After serving as high sheriff of Augusta County (1780) and rising to colonel in the militia (1781), he moved in 1783 to the Cumberland Settlements, which are now part of Tennessee. The following year he was director for the laying out of the town of Nashville.

In 1785 Smith became a trustee of Davidson Academy. His military rank rose further in 1788 when he became a brigadier general of the Mero District (North Carolina) militia. The following year he attended the North Carolina Convention which ratified the federal constitution. He was named secretary of the territory south of the Ohio River in 1790.

Smith made the first map of Tennessee, which was published in 1794. He was a member of the Tennessee Constitutional Convention in 1796 and represented the state in the United States Senate in 1798–99 and again from 1805 to 1809. He was the author of *A Short Description of the Tennessee Government* (1793). He died at the estate "Rock Castle," in Sumner County, Tennessee.

SPAIGHT, Richard Dobbs, Jr.: governor of North Carolina, congressman
Born New Bern, North Carolina, 1796; son of Richard Dobbs Spaight; died May 2, 1850.

Spaight attended New Bern Academy, then graduated from the University of North Carolina in 1815. He studied law, was admitted to the bar in 1818, and established a legal practice in New Bern. He attended various legislative bodies, including the North Carolina House of Commons (1819–22); the United States House of Representatives (1823–25); and the North Carolina Senate (1825–26). He was governor of North Carolina from 1835 to 1837, also serving as a delegate to the North Carolina Democratic Convention in 1835. In the latter years of his life he worked as a farmer. He died in New Bern and was buried in a family sepulcher in Clermont, North Carolina.

STEARNS, Shubal: clergyman
Born Boston, Massachusetts, January 28, 1706; son of Shubal and Rebecca (Lairabee or Lariby) Stearns; married Sarah Johnson, March 27, 1727; died November 20, 1771.

Influenced by the "Great Awakening" of 1745, Stearns attached himself to the New Lights (Separatists) and became a preacher among them. Ordained to the ministry of the Baptist Church by the Reverend Wait Palmer in 1751, he preached in the New England area from 1751 to 1753. With several other married couples, he moved first to Opequon Creek (in 1753), then to Cacapon, Virginia, and finally to Sandy Creek, North Carolina, where he served as pastor of the

Baptist Church from 1755 until his death. As a preaching evangelist, he greatly influenced the growth of the Baptist faith in the Carolinas, Georgia, and Virginia and paved the way for the union of Regular and Separatist Baptists, producing a blend of Calvinistic orthodoxy and evangelistic fervor.

STOKES, Montfort: senator, governor of North Carolina

Born Lunenberg County, Virginia, March 12, 1762; son of David and Sarah (Montfort) Stokes; married Mary Irwin; second marriage to Rachel Montgomery; father of at least one son (Montfort S.); died November 4, 1842.

Stokes enlisted in the Continental Navy in 1776 and was later captured and imprisoned for a time by the British. He served as a clerk in the North Carolina Senate from 1786 to 1791 and as a clerk of the Superior Court of Rowan County, North Carolina, in 1790. For thirty-three years (1805–38) he was a trustee of the University of North Carolina.

He was a presidential elector a number of times—1804, 1812, 1824, and 1828. After serving in the War of 1812 as a major general in the North Carolina militia, he became a North Carolina delegate to the United States Senate, holding that post from December 4, 1816, until 1823. He was president of the North Carolina Constitutional Convention, which was held in Raleigh in 1823, and a member of the North Carolina Senate from 1826 to 1829 and the North Carolina House of Commons in 1829–30. He served as governor of North Carolina from 1830 to 1832.

During the last ten years of his life, Stokes was involved in Indian affairs on the western frontier. In 1832 he became a commissioner to investigate conditions in the present state of Oklahoma. He was a sub-agent for the Cherokee, Seneca, and Shawnee Indians in Arkansas in 1836 and an agent from 1837 to 1841. He died at Fort Gibson, Arkansas, and was buried with military honors in the Fort Gibson Cemetery.

SUMNER, Jethro: army officer

Born Nansemond County, Virginia, circa 1733; son of Jethro and Margaret (Sullivan) Sumner; married Mary Hurst, circa 1764; father of Jacky Sullivan (Sumner) Blount; died between March 15 and 19, 1785.

During the French and Indian War, Sumner served as a lieutenant in the Virginia militia (1755 to 1761) and commanded Fort Bedford. He was justice of the peace of Warren County, North Carolina, in 1768 and sheriff from 1772 to 1777. He was Warren County's representative in the North Carolina Revolutionary Provisional Congress in 1775, which later elected him major of Minutemen.

Sumner was commissioned a colonel in the 3rd Battalion of the North Carolina Regiment of the Continental Army in 1776, later rising to brigadier general. In 1779 he led a brigade to South Carolina, where he participated in the Battle of Stone Ferry. He also recruited while in North Carolina and assisted in defending North Carolina against the Cornwallis invasion of 1780. He was in charge of the North Carolina militia from 1781 to 1783. He died in Warren County two years later.

SWAN, John: Continental congressman

Born Pasquotank County, North Carolina, 1760; died 1793.

Swan attended the College of William and Mary circa 1780. A farmer in North Carolina, he was appointed to fill a vacancy in the Continental Congress in 1788. He urged that North Carolina adopt the proposed Constitution. He died at the age of thirty-three and was buried on his plantation, "The Elms," in Pasquotank County.

★★★★★

TATHAM, William: civil engineer, geographer

Born Hutton-in-the-Forest, Cumberland, England,

April 13, 1752; son of the Reverend Sandford and Miss (Marsden) Tatham; never married; died February 22, 1819.

As clerk of the Watauga Association, Tatham drafted a petition for the inhabitants on western waters for incorporation into the government of North Carolina in 1776. Four years later he was involved with Colonel John Todd in preparing the *History of the Western Country*. Around 1783 he attained the position of clerk of the Virginia Council of State and the next year was admitted to the North Carolina bar. In 1787 he was a delegate to the North Carolina General Assembly and became a lieutenant colonel in the state militia about the same time.

Tatham journeyed to London, England, about 1796 and became a contributor to various publications concerning engineering and agriculture. He was the construction superintendent of Wapping Docks on the Thames in 1801. Returning to the United States in 1805, he spent the next five years surveying the coast from Cape Fear to Cape Hatteras. A draftsman and geographer for the United States Department of State from circa 1810 to circa 1815, he was the first to define the functions of a national library for the United States.

Tatham was also known as an author, his works including *Memorial on the Civil and Military Government of the Tennessee Colony* (1790), *Remarks on Inland Canals* (1798), and *The Political Economy of Inland Navigation, Irrigation, and Drainage* (1799). He died in Richmond, Virginia.

TATOM, Absalom: congressman
Born North Carolina, 1742; died December 20, 1802.

Tatom served as a sergeant in the Greenville (North Carolina) militia in 1763. He was commissioned a first lieutenant in the 1st North Carolina Continental Regiment in 1775. The following year he was promoted to captain but resigned from the Continental Army shortly thereafter. Two years later, Tatom enlisted as assistant quartermaster and keeper of the North Carolina arsenal service at Hillsborough. That same year (1778) he became a contractor for the city. In 1779 he became major of detachment in the North Carolina Light Horse and also served as clerk of the Randolph County Court.

In 1781 Tatom served as district auditor of Hillsborough and the following year was appointed by Congress a commissioner to survey lands granted to Continental soldiers in the western territory (which lands later became Tennessee). Also in 1782, he served as private secretary to Governor Thomas Burke and as state tobacco agent.

The Continental Congress elected Tatom to serve as surveyor of North Carolina in 1785. That same year he became commissioner to sign North Carolina's paper money. A delegate to the Constitutional Convention in 1788, he was elected a Republican representative from North Carolina to Congress in 1795; however, he resigned the following year. He went on to serve in the North Carolina House of Commons from 1797 until his death in 1802. He died in Raleigh, North Carolina, and was buried in Old City Cemetery.

THOMAS, Philemon: congressman
Born Orange County, Virginia, February 9, 1763; died November 18, 1847.

Thomas, educated in common schools, was a veteran of the Revolutionary War by his nineteenth birthday. After the war, he moved to Mason County, Kentucky, and served as a delegate to the convention which framed the Kentucky Constitution. He served as a member of the Kentucky House of Representatives from 1796 to 1799; in 1800 he was elected to the Kentucky Senate, serving until 1803. Three years later he moved to Louisiana, where he also became a member of that state's House of Representatives.

A leader of an uprising against Spanish authorities who controlled Mississippi and

Louisiana, Thomas was the commander of the forces which captured the Spanish fort at Baton Rouge in 1810. He served in the War of 1812 and became a major general in the Louisiana militia in 1814. A Democrat, he was elected to the United States Congress as a representative from Louisiana in 1831, serving for four years.

Thomas died in Baton Rouge and was buried in the Old American Graveyard. Later his body was reinterred in Baton Rouge's National Cemetery.

TURNER, James: senator, governor
Born Southampton County, Virginia, December 20, 1766; father of at least one son (Daniel); died January 15, 1824.

Turner, who attended common schools, became engaged in planting in Warren County, North Carolina, as a young man. He served as a private in the North Carolina Volunteers during the Revolutionary War. He was a member of the North Carolina House of Commons from 1797 to 1800 and served as a member of the North Carolina Senate in 1801–02.

Turner, a Democrat, was governor of North Carolina from 1802 to 1805. He was a North Carolina delegate to the United States Senate from 1805 until November 21, 1816, when he resigned. He died on the plantation "Bloomsbury," near Warrenton, North Carolina, and was buried in the Bloomsbury Cemetery.

★★★★★

WADDELL, Hugh: army officer
Born Lisburn, County Down, Ireland, 1734; son of Hugh and Isabella (Brown) Waddell; married Mary Haynes, 1762; father of three children; died April 9, 1773.

Waddell served as a lieutenant in the regiment of James Innes, which helped drive the French from Ohio in 1754. He then became clerk of the Governor's Council of North Carolina, serving until 1755. Later that year he was placed on frontier duty in western Carolina. While serving as Virginia commis-

sioner, he negotiated an offensive-defensive alliance with the Cherokee and Catawba tribes in 1756.

Waddell was a major in command of three companies which were dispatched to aid John Forbes's expedition against Fort Duquesne in 1758. The following year, after being promoted to colonel, he commanded two companies and was given authority to summon the militia of the frontier counties and to cooperate with South Carolina or Virginia. He defended Fort Dobb against Indian attack in 1760.

Waddell served as justice of the peace of Rowan and Bladen counties, North Carolina, and represented the former in the North Carolina Assembly from 1757 to 1760 and the latter in 1762, 1766–67, and 1771. He was a leader of the colonists in opposition to General William Tryon's attempt to enforce the Stamp Act in 1765 and took part in the suppression of the Regulator movement in North Carolina in 1771. He died in Bladen County.

WALKER, Felix: congressman
Born Hampshire County, Virginia (now West Virginia), July 19, 1753; died 1828.

Walker attended country schools near Columbia, South Carolina, and in Burke County, North Carolina, and later (1769) became a merchant in Charleston, South Carolina. He also engaged in farming. Along with Daniel Boone and others, he founded Boonesboro, Kentucky, in 1775.

Clerk of the Court of Washington District (now primarily in Tennessee) in 1775–76 and of the Washington County Court in 1777–78, Walker also served in the Revolution and in the Indian wars. He was a lieutenant with Captain Richardson's company in a rifle regiment from Mecklenburg County and became a captain of light dragoons on Nolachucky River.

Following his military service, Walker once again became a court clerk, serving in the Rutherford County (North Carolina)

Court from 1779 to 1787. He was a member of the North Carolina House of Commons in 1792, from 1799 to 1802, and in 1806. He then resumed farming, also engaging in trading and in land speculation in Haywood County, North Carolina.

Walker was elected to the United States House of Representatives as a Democrat from North Carolina for the 15th–17th congresses (1817–23). Following his service in Congress, he settled in Mississippi and again turned to farming and trading. He died in Clinton, Mississippi, and was probably buried in a private cemetery.

WEAKLEY, Robert: congressman
Born Halifax County, Virginia, July 20, 1764; died February 4, 1845.

Weakley attended schools in Princeton, New Jersey, then served with the Continental Army until the end of the Revolution. After the war he turned to agriculture in a section of North Carolina which later became Tennessee. A member of the North Carolina Convention that ratified the United States Constitution, he served in the first Tennessee House of Representatives in 1796. He was a Tennessee delegate to the United States House of Representatives for the 11th Congress (1809–11).

Weakley was appointed United States commissioner to treat with the Chickasaw Indians in 1819 and served as a member of the Tennessee Constitutional Convention in 1834. He died near Nashville, Tennessee, and was buried in a family vault at "Lockland," his estate in what is now suburban Nashville.

WHITE, James: army officer, pioneer, legislator
Born Rowan County, North Carolina, 1747; son of Moses and Mary (McConnell) White; married Mary Lawson, April 14, 1770; father of seven children (including Hugh Lawson); died August 14, 1821.

After serving as a captain in the North Carolina militia from 1779 to 1781, White began to explore along the French Broad and Holston rivers in 1783. He settled at the present site of Knoxville, Tennessee, in 1786.

White was elected to the North Carolina House of Commons from Hawkins County in 1789, became a justice of the peace and a major in the North Carolina militia in 1790, and was a delegate to the Tennessee Constitutional Convention in 1796. Also in 1796 he was elected a Knox County delegate to the Tennessee Senate, and in 1801 and 1803 he served as presiding officer of that body.

White was the donor of the site for Blount College (now the University of Tennessee) and became a trustee in 1794. He was commissioned a brigadier general in the Tennessee militia about 1798. He died in Knoxville and was buried near the First Presbyterian Church there.

WHITE, Thomas: Continental congressman
Born Philadelphia, Pennsylvania, June 16, 1749; father of at least one son (Edward Douglass); died October 1809.

White studied at the Jesuit College, St. Omer, France, then returned to America to study medicine at the University of Pennsylvania. He also studied law for a time. After moving to Davidson County, North Carolina, he became a member of the North Carolina Assembly in 1785 and was sent by the state to the Continental Congress the following year, serving until 1788. Superintendent of Indian affairs for the Southern District in 1786, he was also a member (representing Davidson County) of the First Territorial Legislature, held in 1794.

White was a delegate to the United States Congress from the territory south of the Ohio River (now part of Tennessee) from 1794 to 1796. He moved to Louisiana in 1799 and was appointed judge of the Attakapas (Louisiana) District in 1804, later serving as judge of St. Martin Parish. He died in Attakapas.

WILLIAMS, Benjamin: congressman, governor of North Carolina

Born near Smithfield, North Carolina, January 1, 1751; died July 20, 1814.

Williams, who attended country schools, became engaged in farming as a young man. He was a member of the North Carolina Provincial Congress in 1774–75. At the outbreak of the Revolutionary War he was commissioned a second lieutenant in the Continental Army, rising to captain in 1776. For his gallantry at Guilford Court House in 1781, he was promoted to colonel.

Williams served in the North Carolina House of Commons in 1779, 1785, and 1789, and in the North Carolina Senate in 1781, 1784, 1786 and 1788. He was a North Carolina delegate to the 3rd Congress of the United States House of Representatives (1793–95). From 1799 to 1802, and again in 1807–08, he was governor of North Carolina.

Williams died in Moore County, North Carolina, and was buried near Carbonton.

WILLIAMS, John: Continental congressman

Born Hanover County, Virginia, March 14, 1731; died October 10, 1799.

After studying law, Williams was admitted to the North Carolina bar and established a legal practice in Williamsboro. He was a founder of the University of North Carolina. He began a long career in North Carolina politics in 1768 with his appointment as deputy attorney general. He was a delegate to the North Carolina Provincial Congress in 1775 and was a member and speaker of the North Carolina House of Commons in 1777–78. During 1778 and 1789 he was a North Carolina delegate to the Continental Congress. He was a judge in the North Carolina Supreme Court for the last twenty years of his life. He was buried in the family cemetery in Montpelier.

WILLIAMSON, Hugh: congressman, scientist

Born West Nottingham, Pennsylvania, December 5,

1735; son of John W. and Mary (Davison) Williamson; married Maria Apthorpe, January 1789; father of two sons; died May 22, 1819.

After graduating from the College of Philadelphia (now the University of Pennsylvania) in 1757, Williamson studied medicine in Edinburgh, London, and Utrecht. He took an M.D. degree at Utrecht in 1764 and an honorary degree at the University of Leyden, then became a professor of mathematics at the College of Philadelphia. He became a member of the American Philosophical Society in 1768. He was commissioned to study the orbits of Venus and Mercury in 1769 and later published "An Essay on Comets."

Williamson was the first to carry news of the Boston Tea Party to England. In 1775 he wrote an anonymous letter to Lord Mansfield called "The Plea of the Colonies." After returning to America in 1776, he began a mercantile business in Charleston, South Carolina, and later moved to Edenton, North Carolina, where he traded with the French West Indies. He became physician to North Carolina Governor Caswell and was sent to New Bern to inoculate the troops against smallpox. He also served as surgeon general of the North Carolina troops and served at the battle of Camden.

Williamson was a member of the Continental Congress from 1782 to 1785 and from 1787 to 1789, also serving in the North Carolina House of Commons in 1782 and 1785. He attended the Annapolis Convention in 1786. As a delegate to the United States Constitutional Convention in 1787, he worked for ratification by publishing "Remarks on the New Plan of Government" in a North Carolina newspaper. In 1789 he became a delegate to the Fayetteville Convention, after serving the previous year as an agent to settle North Carolina accounts with the federal government. He sat in the 1st and 2nd congresses of the United States House of Representatives as a delegate from North Carolina (1789–93).

Williamson was a prominent member of

several cultural and historical societies, including the Holland Society of Science, the Society of Arts and Science of Utrecht, the New York Historical Society, and the Literary and Philosophical Society of New York, of which he was also a founder. He was an original trustee of the University of North Carolina and a trustee of the College of Physicians and Surgeons at the State University of New York.

Williamson's "Letters of Sylvius," in which he opposed paper currency and advocated the excise tax rather than the land or poll tax, was published anonymously; the letters later appeared in *Historical Papers Published by the Trinity College Historical Society.* Other writings include "Of the Fascination of Serpents"; "Conjectures Respecting the Native Climate of Pestilence"; "Observations on Navigable Canals"; *Observations on the Climate in Different Parts of America,* published in 1811; and a two-volume work, *The History of North Carolina,* published in 1812.

WINCHESTER, James: army officer
Born Carroll County, Maryland, February 6, 1752; son of William and Lydia (Richards) Winchester; married Susan Black, 1803; father of fourteen children (including Marcus); died July 26, 1826.

During the American Revolution, Winchester served with the Maryland Battalion of Flying Camp. He was wounded and captured at Staten Island in 1777 and exchanged the next year. In 1780 he was again captured in Charleston, South Carolina, but released soon afterward. He was promoted to captain and served at Yorktown in 1781.

In 1785 Winchester moved to Middle Tennessee. He became a member of the North Carolina Convention to ratify the United States Constitution in 1788. In 1796 he was speaker of the Tennessee Senate. Having advanced from captain to colonel to brigadier general, he was commissioned a brigadier general of the United States Army in command of the Army of the Northwest during the War of 1812. He served as a commissioner to run the Chickasaw Boundary Line between Tennessee and Mississippi in 1819, and he was a founder of the city of Memphis.

Winchester died in 1826 and was buried at "Cragfont," near Memphis.

WINSTON, Joseph: congressman
Born Louisa County, Virginia, June 17, 1746; son of Samuel Winston; father of three children; died April 21, 1815.

As a member of the Hillsboro (North Carolina) Convention in 1775, Winston took steps to organize a provincial government. Later that year he was commissioned a major in the North Carolina militia. The following year he took part in an expedition against Scotch Loyalists assembled at Cross Creek and fought against the Cherokee Indians as a ranger of Surry County, North Carolina. He served at the Battle of King's Mountain in 1780. During the Revolution he also was a member of the North Carolina House of Commons (1777) and a commissioner to treat with the Cherokees.

Winston served in the North Carolina Senate in 1790, 1791, 1802, 1807 and 1812. He was a member of the United States House of Representatives during the 3rd, 8th, and 9th congresses (1793–95 and 1803–07). A presidential elector in 1800, he voted for Jefferson and Burr.

From 1807 to 1813 Winston was a trustee of the University of North Carolina. He was ultimately promoted to the rank of lieutenant colonel of the Stokes County (North Carolina) militia. The city of Winston (now Winston-Salem), North Carolina, was named for him. He died in Germantown, North Carolina, and was buried at the Guilford Battle Ground, near Greensboro.

★★★★★★★★★★★★★

PENNSYLVANIA

"Yesterday afternoon General Washington with his suite, attended by the several New York militia companies, a troop of gentlemen of the Philadelphia lighthorse, commanded by Captain Markoe, and a number of the inhabitants of New York, set out for the provincial camp at Cambridge, near Boston. Last night he rested at King's Bridge, and this morning proceeded on his journey."

PENNSYLVANIA JOURNAL, July 5, 1775

ALLEN, Andrew: Continental congressman, Loyalist
Born Philadelphia, Pennsylvania, June 1740; son of William and Margaret (Hamilton) Allen; married Sally Coxe, April 21, 1768; died March 7, 1825.

Allen graduated from the University of Pennsylvania in 1759 and was admitted to practice before the Pennsylvania Supreme Court in 1765. Four years later he became attorney general of the Province of Pennsylvania. He served as recorder of the city of Philadelphia in 1774 and as a member of the Pennsylvania Committee of Safety the following year. He was elected a delegate to the Continental Congress from Pennsylvania for the years 1776–77. However, he later renounced loyalty to Congress, took oaths of allegiance to the King, and went to England, where he died.

ALLISON, Richard: army medical officer
Born near Goshen, Orange County, New York, 1757; died March 22, 1816.

Allison was a surgeon's mate in the 5th Pennsylvania Regiment, Continental Army,

for five years—from 1778 to 1783. He was then transferred to the 1st Pennsylvania Regiment, where he served as a surgeon's mate until his promotion to regimental surgeon in 1788. He saw duty in campaigns under General Josiah Harmar and General Arthur St. Clair.

Allison traveled to Europe in 1788 and, after his return, was appointed surgeon to the Legion of the United States in 1792, receiving an honorable discharge when the Legion dissolved four years later. In 1796 he established a medical practice in Cincinnati. He died in that city and was buried in Wesleyan Cemetery, Cumminsville, Ohio.

ANDERSON, Isaac: congressman
Born near Valley Forge, Pennsylvania, November 23, 1760; died October 27, 1838.

During the Revolutionary War, Anderson carried dispatches between General Washington's Valley Forge headquarters and Congress, which was in session at York, Pennsylvania. He also served with the Continental Army, becoming an ensign in the

5th Battalion, Chester County militia, and later (1779) receiving a commission as a first lieutenant in the 5th Battalion, 6th Company.

After the war, Anderson became justice of the peace for Charlestown Township, Pennsylvania. In 1801 he was elected to the Pennsylvania House of Representatives. Two years later he was elected as a Jefferson Democrat to the United States House of Representatives, where he served during the 8th and 9th congresses (1803–07). He was a Democratic presidential elector in 1816.

Anderson was also a farmer and a sawmill operator. He died at "Anderson Place," Charlestown Township, Pennsylvania, and was buried in his family's burying ground near Valley Forge.

ARMSTRONG, John: army officer, Continental congressman

Born County Fermanagh, Ireland, October 13, 1717; son of James Armstrong; married Rebecca Lyon; father of John and James; died March 9, 1795.

Armstrong, a surveyor, laid out the town of Carlisle, Pennsylvania. After being commissioned a captain in the Pennsylvania militia in 1756, he quickly advanced to the rank of lieutenant colonel later the same year. He fought in the French and Indian War and earned the title "Hero of Kittanning" when he led a successful night attack on the Delaware Indians at Kittanning.

Armstrong received a commission as brigadier general in the Continental Army in 1776 and became a major general the following year. During the years 1778–80 and 1787–88 he was a member of the Continental Congress. He died in Carlisle at the age of seventy-seven and was buried in the Old Carlisle Cemetery.

ARMSTRONG, John: army officer, explorer

Born New Jersey, April 20, 1755; son of Thomas and Jane (Hamilton) Armstrong; married a daughter of Judge William Goforth; father of William Goforth; died February 4, 1816.

Armstrong served as an officer in the Pennsylvania militia from 1777 to 1784 and in the Continental Army from 1784 to 1793. During the latter period he was commandant of two forts: Fort Pitt in 1785–86 and Fort Hamilton after 1791. Between command posts he explored an area from the Wabash River to Lake Erie (1790) and took part in General Josiah Harmar's unsuccessful expedition against Indians in what is now Indiana and in Arthur St. Clair's expedition—also unsuccessful—against the same Indians (1790 and 1791).

Armstrong later returned to this area to become treasurer of the Northwest Territory. In 1796 he founded Armstrong's Station on the Ohio River, where he died twenty years later.

ATLEE, Samuel John: Continental congressman, army officer

Born Trenton, New Jersey, 1739; died November 25, 1786.

Atlee's military career began during the French and Indian War with his appointment as commander of a company of provincial service from Lancaster County, Pennsylvania. He was commissioned an ensign in Colonel William Clapham's Augusta Regiment in 1756 and promoted to lieutenant the following year. He served in the Forbes campaign and in a battle near Fort Duquesne in 1758 and was commissioned a captain the following year. In 1776, after being appointed colonel in the Pennsylvania Musketry Battalion, he was captured by the British at the Battle of Long Island. He was exchanged in 1778.

After his release, Atlee, who had studied law, left the military to enter the public arena. He served as a delegate from Pennsylvania to the Continental Congress from 1778 to 1782 and was a member of the state's General Assembly in 1782, 1785, and 1786. In further public service, he was elected supreme executive councilor for Lancaster County in 1783 and the next year was appointed to the board of commissioners dealing with the Indians living on unpurchased lands in Pennsylvania. He was a charter member of the Society of the Cincinnati. He died in Philadelphia and was buried in Christ Churchyard.

★★★★★

BACHE, Richard: businessman, postmaster general

Born Settle, England, September 12, 1737; son of William and Mary (Blyckenden) Bache; married Sarah Franklin, October 3, 1767; died July 29, 1811.

Bache came to New York City with his brother Theophylact in 1765. The following year he moved to Philadelphia, where he made the acquaintance of Benjamin Franklin, whose only daughter he subsequently married. With his brother he went into business as an underwriter of marine insurance risks.

At the beginning of the Revolutionary War Bache was president of the Republican Society of Philadelphia and was also active on the Pennsylvania Committee of Correspondence and Board of War. Franklin appointed him secretary, comptroller, and registrar general of Pennsylvania during 1775–76. In the latter year he went on to succeed Franklin as postmaster general of the American colonies under the Articles of Confederation, remaining in this position until 1782. He died at the age of seventy-three in Berks County, Pennsylvania.

BAILEY, Francis: printer, journalist

Born Lancaster County, Pennsylvania, circa 1735; son of Robert and Margaret (McDill) Bailey; married; father of at least one son (Robert); died 1815.

Bailey was publisher of the *Lancaster Almanac* during the years 1771 to 1796. After 1772 he owned a printing shop in Lancaster which published many foreign materials, chiefly German-language works, as well as the fourth edition of Thomas Paine's *Common Sense* (1776). He became coroner of Lancaster County in 1777 and served as a brigade major in the Pennsylvania militia at Valley Forge the next year.

Bailey published the *United States Magazine* in Philadelphia in 1778–79. In 1781 he was chosen the official printer for the Continental Congress and for the state of Pennsylvania. That same year he became editor of *Freeman's Journal, or the North American Intelligencer,* a weekly which opened its columns to all political factions and whose contributors included Philip Freneau, James Wilson, and George Osborne.

In 1797 Bailey established a printing office in Sadsbury, Pennsylvania, meanwhile continuing as state printer. Gradually he turned his business over to his son. He died in Octoraro, near Philadelphia.

BARRY, John: naval officer

Born County Wexford, Ireland, 1745; son of John and Catherine Barry; married Mary Burns; second marriage to Sarah Austin, July 7, 1777; died September 13, 1803.

Barry commanded the United States Navy ship *Lexington* in 1776, then was promoted to captain and given command of the *Effingham* the following year. As commander of the *Raleigh,* he captured many British ships between 1778 and 1781. While in command of the *Alliance,* he captured the British ships *Atalanta* and *Trepassy* in 1781. Two years later he retired from the Navy.

In 1794 Barry was appointed senior captain in command of the ship *United States* during the Algerine conflict, and four years later he was given command of United States naval forces in the West Indies. He commanded the American naval station at Guadeloupe in 1800 and 1801.

BAYARD, John Bubenheim: merchant, Continental congressman

Born Cecil County, Maryland, August 11, 1738; son of James and Mary (Ashton) Bayard; married Margaret Hodge; second marriage to Mrs. Mary Hodgden; third marriage to Johannah White, 1787; died January 7, 1807.

Bayard, who received his education from Nottingham Institution, became a member of the Philadelphia mercantile firm of John Rhea in 1756 and remained with the company until his death. He signed the Non-Importation Agreement of 1765 and went on to further involvement in politics as a member of the Pennsylvania Provincial Congress in July, 1774. Two years later he served on the Philadelphia Council of Safety. During the years 1776–77 he participated in the battles of Brandywine, Germantown, and Princeton, also rising during this time to major in the 2nd Battalion of Philadelphia Associators (who were volunteers with the Continental Army). Later in 1777 he was promoted to colonel.

Bayard was speaker of the Pennsylvania Assembly in 1777–78 as well as a member of the Board of War. He became a member of the Supreme Executive Council of Pennsylvania in 1781 and represented his state at the Continental Congress during the period from 1785 to 1787. He was elected mayor of New Brunswick, New Jersey, in 1790. He died at the age of sixty-eight and was buried in the First Presbyterian Churchyard in New Brunswick.

BELL, Robert: publisher
Born Glasgow, Scotland, circa 1732; married circa 1766; father of two children; died September 23, 1784.

An apprentice bookbinder, Bell came to America in 1766. Four years later he was established as a bookseller and auctioneer. He published an edition of *The History of the Reign of Charles the Fifth, Emperor of Germany* (Robertson) in 1770, Blackstone's *Commentaries* in 1771, and the first edition of *Common Sense* (Thomas Paine) in 1776. Bell opposed restrictions on selling books by auction passed by the Pennsylvania Assembly in 1784 and wrote the pamphlet *Bell's Address to Every Free Man* to defend his views. Bell died in Richmond, Virginia, where he was buried.

BIDDLE, Clement: army officer, merchant
Born Philadelphia, Pennsylvania, May 10, 1740; son of John and Sarah (Owen) Biddle; married Mary Richardson; second marriage to Rebekah Cornell; father of thirteen children (including Clement Cornell); died July 14, 1814.

In 1765 Biddle signed the Philadelphia Non-Importation Agreement. Six years later he became a partner in his father's shipping house. The Second Continental Congress having appointed him quartermaster general with the rank of colonel for the militias of Pennsylvania and New Jersey in 1776, he participated in the battles of Trenton, Princeton, Brandywine, and Portsmouth. In 1776 he also was aide-de-camp to General Nathanael Greene, and the following year he became commissary general of forage. In 1781 he became quartermaster general (colonel) in the Pennsylvania militia.

Having served in 1788 as a justice in the Pennsylvania Court of Common Pleas, the next year he was appointed a United States marshal by President Washington. During the 1780s and 1790s he was General Washington's factor (purchasing agent and seller of produce for Mount Vernon). He died in Philadelphia at the age of seventy-four.

BIDDLE, Edward: Continental congressman
Born Philadelphia, Pennsylvania, 1738; died September 5, 1779.

Biddle entered the provincial army as an ensign in 1754. He was later promoted to lieutenant and then to captain, serving until his resignation in 1763.

After being admitted to the bar, Biddle practiced law in Reading, Pennsylvania. From 1767 to 1775 and again in 1778 he was a member of the Pennsylvania Assembly, holding the office of speaker in 1774. The following year he participated in the Provincial Convention in Philadelphia. He was also active as a Continental congressman in 1774–76, 1778, and 1779, the year of his death. He was buried in St. Paul's Church-yard in Baltimore.

BIDDLE, Nicholas: naval officer

Born Philadelphia, Pennsylvania, September 10, 1750; son of William and Mary (Scull) Biddle; died March 7, 1778.

In 1775 the Continental Congress gave Biddle the rank of lieutenant and command of the privateer *Franklin;* later the same year he was commissioned a captain and given command of the *Andrea Doria.* After capturing numerous ships in the North Atlantic during 1775 and 1776, he assumed command of the ship *Randolph,* which was assigned to the West Indies in 1776. There he captured more ships, including the British vessel *Triton* in 1777. He was killed in the explosion of the *Randolph* during an engagement with the British ship *Yarmouth* near Charleston, South Carolina.

BINGHAM, Anne Willing: society leader

Born Philadelphia, Pennsylvania, August 1, 1764; daughter of Thomas and Anne (McCall) Willing; married William Bingham, October 26, 1780; died May 11, 1801.

During the years 1783–88 Mrs. Bingham traveled in various European capitals, including London, the Hague, and Paris, where she was presented to Louis XVI. She dominated Philadelphia society in the 1790s. Known for her Federalist preferences and for her aristocratic manners and tastes, she copied her home in Philadelphia, "Mansion House," from the home of the Duke of Manchester. She died at the age of thirty-six and was buried in Philadelphia.

BINGHAM, William: banker, senator

Born Philadelphia, Pennsylvania, March 8, 1752; son of William and Mary (Stamper) Bingham; married Anne Willing, October 26, 1780; father of two children; died February 7, 1804.

Bingham graduated from the University of Pennsylvania in 1768. Two years later he was appointed British consul at St. Pierre, Martinique. In 1781 he was a founder and director of the Pennsylvania Bank (which was chartered later in the year as the Bank of North America). He represented Pennsylvania at the Continental Congress from 1786 to 1789, going on to serve in the Pennsylvania Assembly from 1790 until 1795. He then served in the United States Senate until 1801.

In other activities, Bingham founded the city of Binghamton, New York; was the first president of the Philadelphia and Lancaster Turnpike Corporation; served as vice president of the Society for Political Inquiries; and was a trustee of the University of Pennsylvania. He wrote *A Letter from an American on the Subject of the Restraining Proclamation* (1784) and *Description of Certain Tracts of Land in the District of Maine* (1793). He died in Bath, England, and was buried in the Paris Church there.

BOEHM, Martin: clergyman

Born Lancaster County, Pennsylvania, November 30, 1725; son of Jacob Boehm; married Eve Steiner, 1753; father of Henry; died March 23, 1812.

Chosen a Mennonite preacher in 1756, three years later Boehm became a bishop in the Mennonite Church. He was later excluded from the Mennonite communion because of his liberalism and his unorthodox point of view. In 1800 he founded (with William Otterbein) the Church of United Brethren in Christ and was chosen bishop (again with Otterbein) at its first annual conference the same year. Two years later he also became affiliated with the Methodist Church. He died at the age of eighty-six.

BOND, Thomas: physician

Born Calvert County, Maryland, 1712; son of Richard and Elizabeth (Chew) Bond; married Sarah Roberts; father of seven children; died March 26, 1784.

Having studied medicine under Dr. Alexander Hamilton in Annapolis, Maryland, and in Paris, Bond began his practice in Philadelphia circa 1734. In 1752 he helped found the Pennsylvania Hospital in Philadelphia, which is now the oldest hospital in the United States. In 1766 he delivered the first course in clinical lectures in the country. He wrote the following: "An Account of Worm Bred in the Liver," "A Letter to Doctor Fothergill on the Use of Peruvian Bark in Scofula," and "Essay on the Utility of Clinical Lectures."

In addition to his professional activities, Dr. Bond was a member of the original board of trustees of the College of Philadelphia (now the University of Pennsylvania); a founder of the American Philosophical Society (1768); a member of the Philadelphia Committee of Safety (1776); and president of the Humane Society of Philadelphia (1780).

BOUDE, Thomas: congressman, lumber executive

Born Lancaster, Pennsylvania, May 17, 1752; died October 24, 1822.

Boude, who attended private schools, served as a lieutenant under General Anthony Wayne in the 2nd, 4th, and 5th Pennsylvania battalions during the period from 1776 to 1783. He was promoted to captain and then brevetted a major. He helped organize the Society of the Cincinnati.

After the war Boude established a lumber business in Columbia, Pennsylvania. He was a member of the Pennsylvania House of Representatives from 1794 to 1796, later representing his state as a Federalist in the 7th Congress of the United States House of Representatives (1801–03). He died at the age of seventy and was buried in the Brick Graveyard of Mt. Bethel Cemetery.

BOWEN, Daniel: artist, showman

Born circa 1760; died February 29, 1856.

Bowen, who modeled wax portraits of Franklin and Washington, was one of the first museum proprietors in America. He advertised a museum and waxworks in New York City in 1789 and 1794, in Philadelphia in 1790 and 1793–94, and in Boston in 1791. He opened the Columbian Museum in Boston in 1795 and was its proprietor until it burned twelve years later. He also exhibited a panorama of New Haven in Philadelphia in 1818. He died in Philadelphia.

BRACKENRIDGE, Hugh Henry: jurist, author

Born Campbeltown, Scotland, 1748; no record of first marriage; second marriage to Sabina Wolfe, 1792; father of at least one son (Henry Marie); died June 25, 1816.

Brackenridge came to York County, Pennsylvania, in 1753 and ten years later— at the age of fifteen—took charge of an academy in Maryland. He graduated from Princeton in 1771 (receiving an M.S. in 1774) and studied law under Samuel Chase in Annapolis, Maryland.

In 1771 Brackenridge collaborated with Philip Freneau on the poem *The Rising Glory of America.* After his move in 1781 to Pittsburgh, in 1786 he helped found the *Pittsburgh Gazette,* the first newspaper in the city, and established the Pittsburgh Academy a year later. His was the first bookstore in Pittsburgh also (1789).

During the years 1793–94 Brackenridge was a member of the state assembly and took part in the Whiskey Rebellion; he was later exonerated by Alexander Hamilton. In 1799 he became editor of the *United States Magazine* in Philadelphia and assumed the office of justice of the Pennsylvania Supreme Court, in which capacity he served until 1816. He wrote two plays: *The Battle of Bunker Hill* (1776) and *The Death of General Montgomery* (1777), which was performed by Harvard students. He also wrote *Modern Chivalry* (1792–1815), *The Standard of Liberty* (1804), and *Law Miscellanies* (1814).

BRADFORD, Thomas: publisher

Born May 4, 1745; son of William and Rachel (Budd) Bradford; married Mary Fisher, 1768; father of six children (including Samuel, William, and Thomas); died May 7, 1838.

Bradford attended the University of Pennsylvania. In 1762 he began working under his father on the *Pennsylvania Journal and Weekly Advertiser* and became a full partner four years later. He took an active part in the resistance to the Stamp Act, and in 1777 the British temporarily suspended the operation of his press while they were occupying Philadelphia. During the Revolutionary War he advanced from captain in the Pennsylvania militia to lieutenant colonel in the Continental Army.

In 1797 Bradford started a paper called the *Merchant's Daily Advertiser* which specialized in business news, and the following year changed the name to the *True American* and added a literary supplement. He was a charter member of the American Philosophical Society. He died at the age of ninety-three.

BRADFORD, William: printer, patriot
Born New York City, January 19, 1722; son of William and Sytji (Santvoort) Bradford; married Rachel Budd, August 15, 1742; father of six children (including Thomas and William); died September 25, 1791.

In 1742 Bradford founded the *Weekly Advertiser or Pennsylvania Journal,* which during its fifty-one years of publication was the most widely circulated American newspaper of its time, successfully rivaling Benjamin Franklin's *Pennsylvania Gazette.* Its editorial commentaries significantly influenced and directed pre-Revolutionary public opinion, the dedicated Bradford actively supporting the colonial cause. He opposed the Stamp Act of 1765, signed the Non-Importation Resolutions of 1765, and joined the Sons of Liberty. He originated and used the journalistic slogan "Unite or Die" in 1774–75.

In 1775 Bradford was printer for the First Continental Congress. He also served in the Pennsylvania militia during 1776–78 and became chairman of the Pennsylvania Navy Board in 1778. He died in Philadelphia and was buried in Trinity Churchyard in New York City.

BRADFORD, William: attorney general, jurist
Born Philadelphia, Pennsylvania, September 14, 1755; son of William and Rachel (Budd) Bradford; married Susan Vergereau Boudinot; died August 23, 1795.

Bradford earned the A.B. from Princeton in 1772 and the A.M. in 1775 and studied law under Edward Shippen. He served in the Continental Army during the years 1776 to 1779, rising from private to colonel and seeing action at Valley Forge, White Plains, Fredericksborough, and Raritan. After his admission to the Pennsylvania bar he practiced law in Yorktown, Pennsylvania.

Bradford held the office of attorney general of Pennsylvania from 1780 until 1791, when he began a three-year tenure in the state Supreme Court. He then became the second attorney general of the United States under President Washington, serving in 1794 and 1795. He was on intimate terms with the Washington circle (the so-called Republican Court). He also was indirectly responsible for the Pennsylvania Senate's removal of capital punishment (except for first-degree murder) from the statute books. He died at the age of thirty-nine and was buried in St. Mary's Churchyard in Burlington, New Jersey.

BRODHEAD, Daniel: army officer
Born Albany, New York, September 17, 1736; son of Daniel II and Hester (Wyngart) Brodhead; married Elizabeth Dupui; second marriage to Rebecca Mifflin; died November 15, 1809.

Brought up on large family holdings in Bucks County, Pennsylvania, Brodhead became deputy surveyor general in Reading in 1773. He raised a company of riflemen to join George Washington in battle, was promoted to lieutenant colonel after the Battle of Long Island in 1776, and rose to colonel the next year. Having been given command of a regiment at Pittsburgh in 1779, he raided and terrorized the Delaware Indians from then until 1781.

Brodhead, a strong military disciplinarian, was involved in a number of disputes with officers and civilians in Pittsburgh; as a result he was tried by court-martial but acquitted. General Washington later brevetted him a brigadier general. He also served for a time as surveyor general of Pennsylvania. He died at the age of seventy-three.

BROWN, Robert: congressman
Born Weaversville, Pennsylvania, December 25, 1744; died February 26, 1823.

Brown attended common schools and was apprenticed to a blacksmith. Commissioned a first lieutenant in the Pennsylvania Flying Camp at the beginning of the Revolutionary War, he was captured in 1776 at the surrender of Fort Washington. After imprisonment on the prison ship *Judith* and later in the old New York City Hall, he was paroled on board ship in 1777.

From 1783 to 1787 Brown, a Democrat, was a member of the Pennsylvania Senate. He also served several terms in the United States House of Representatives, beginning when he filled a vacant seat on December 4, 1798, and lasting until 1815 (5th–13th congresses). He died near the town of his birth and was buried in the East Allen Presbyterian Churchyard.

BRYAN, George: colonial official, jurist
Born Dublin, Ireland, August 11, 1731; son of Samuel and Sarah (Dennis) Bryan; married Elizabeth Smith, April 21, 1757; died January 27, 1791.

In 1752 Bryan came to America and began a three-year partnership in a mercantile firm with James Wallace. In 1762 he became commissioner of Philadelphia Harbor. Two years later he and Thomas Willing defeated Benjamin Franklin and Joseph Galloway for seats in the Pennsylvania Assembly. The same year he became a judge in the Pennsylvania Orphans' Court and the state Court of Common Pleas. He was a delegate to the Stamp Act Congress in 1765.

In 1776 Bryan became a naval officer at the Port of Philadelphia and a member of the Supreme Executive Council of Pennsylvania. He was acting president of the state from 1777 to 1779. In the latter year he

also served on the Pennsylvania-Virginia boundary line commission and in the Pennsylvania Assembly, where it is believed he drafted the law abolishing slavery in that state.

For eleven years (1780–91), Bryan held the position of judge in the Supreme Court of Pennsylvania. He became a member of the Pennsylvania Council of Censors in 1784. He also was a trustee of the University of Pennsylvania. He died in Philadelphia.

BUCHER, John Conrad: soldier, clergyman
Born Neunkirch, Switzerland, June 10, 1730; son of Hans Jacob and Anna Dorothea (Burgauer) Bucher; married Mary Magdalena Hoke, February 26, 1760; father of six children; died August 15, 1780.

Bucher attended the University of Marburg in Germany from 1752 to 1755, then came to the United States. Commissioned an ensign in the 1st Battalion of the Pennsylvania militia in 1758, he commanded the garrison at Carlisle, Pennsylvania, during 1759 and 1760. In the latter year he was promoted rapidly, rising to lieutenant in the 2nd Pennsylvania Battalion and then to adjutant and captain.

In 1763 Bucher began preaching. Four years later he was ordained to the ministry by the German Reformed Church and subsequently made occasional missionary trips to the West. He was the first minister to preach in the German language beyond the Allegheny Mountains. He was chaplain to the so-called German Regiment under Baron Von Arnt from 1775 to 1777. He died in Annville, Pennsylvania, and was buried in Lebanon, Pennsylvania.

BUTLER, Richard: army officer, Indian agent
Born St. Bridget's, Dublin, Ireland, April 1, 1743; son of Thomas and Eleanor (Parker) Butler; married Mary Smith; died November 4, 1791.

Having become an Indian agent in 1775, Butler received a commission as a major in the 8th Pennsylvania Regiment the following year. In 1777 he served as a lieutenant colonel with Morgan's Rifles. In 1783 he was brevetted a brigadier general and became Indian commissioner under the Articles of Confederation. Three years later he was chosen superintendent of Indian affairs for the Northern District.

Butler also was a member of the Pennsylvania Senate and held the position of judge in the Court of Common Pleas. He presided over the Court of Inquiry investigating General Josiah Harmar in 1790 and the next year became a major general in the United States Army, second in command to General Arthur St. Clair. He died during St. Clair's expedition against the Ohio Indians.

★★★★★

CADWALADER, John: army officer
Born Philadelphia, Pennsylvania, January 1742; son of Dr. Thomas and Hannah (Lambert) Cadwalader; married Elizabeth Lloyd, October 1768; second marriage to Williamina Bond, January 30, 1779; died February 10, 1786.

Cadwalader was educated at the University of Pennsylvania. In 1776 he was commissioned a colonel of a Philadelphia battalion; later that year he rose to brigadier general in the Pennsylvania militia. He participated in the battles of Trenton, Brandywine, Princeton, and Germantown. He is perhaps most famous for challenging and wounding General Conway (of the Conway Cabal, a plot to undermine the authority of George Washington) in a duel during the winter of 1777–78. Cadwalader died in Shrewsbury, Kent County, Maryland, and was buried at Shrewsbury Church.

CADWALADER, Thomas: surgeon
Born Philadelphia, 1708; son of John and Martha (Jones) Cadwalader; married Hannah Lambert, 1738; died November 14, 1799.

Thomas Cadwalader was one of the most noted physicians in eighteenth-century America. He performed the earliest recorded autopsies in the colonies, beginning in 1742. In 1751 he subscribed to the founding of the Pennsylvania Hospital.

Cadwalader did not limit himself to medicine. From 1751 to 1774 he served as a member of the Common Council of Philadelphia and from 1755 to 1776 as a member of the Provincial Council of Pennsylvania. Like his son Lambert, he was a signer of the Non-Importation Agreement of 1765.

Cadwalader's interests extended to many areas. Together with Benjamin Franklin, he helped found the Philadelphia Library in 1731. In 1751, at the age of forty-three, he was a trustee of the University of Pennsylvania. He was also a member of the American Philosophical Society.

Cadwalader died in Trenton, New Jersey.

CARR, Thomas Matthew: clergyman
Born Galway, Ireland, 1750; died September 29, 1820.

Carr studied theology in Toulouse, France. After being ordained an Augustinian priest in the Roman Catholic Church, he was chosen to establish an Augustinian house in the United States in 1795. Arriving in America in 1796, he was assigned by Bishop John Carroll to St. Mary's in Philadelphia. He also directed the activities of the missions in Wilmington, Delaware; New Castle, Delaware; Trenton, New Jersey; Burlington, New Jersey; and South Jersey, New Jersey.

Carr became an associate of George Washington toward the end of the latter's life. Washington was a contributor to St. Augustine's in Philadelphia, which was completed in 1802 and which Carr served as rector for eighteen years. When Washington died, in 1799, Carr delivered a memorial address at St. Mary's.

CATHCART, James Leander: diplomat
Born County Westmeath, Ireland, June 1, 1767; son of Malcolm and (Miss Humphreys) Cathcart; married Jane Bancker, June 5, 1798; father of twelve children; died October 6, 1843.

While serving as a seaman on the schooner *Maria* of Boston, Cathcart was captured in 1785 and sold into slavery in

Algiers. While a prisoner, he served as clerk of the Marine in 1787 and 1788, and also clerk for Bagnio Gallera and clerk to the prime minister. In 1792 he became chief Christian secretary to the Dey and Regency of Algiers. He sailed for Philadelphia in 1796, eleven years after his capture, carrying a letter from the Dey to President Washington.

Appointed U.S. consul at Tripoli in 1797, he was a special diplomatic agent accompanying William Eaton to Tunis. He was appointed consul at Tunis in 1803. He was also consul at Madeira, Portugal, from 1807 until 1815 and consul at Cadiz, Spain, from 1815 until 1817.

CHAPMAN, John: congressman
Born Wrightstown Township, Bucks County, Pennsylvania, October 18, 1740; died January 27, 1800.

Chapman presumably studied medicine, as he called himself a practitioner of physic. In 1779 he was commissioned a justice of the peace and a judge of the Court of Common Pleas of Bucks County. He then settled in Upper Makefield, Pennsylvania, in a house which prior to 1776 had been the headquarters of Colonel Alexander Hamilton while General Washington's army was camped on the west bank of the Delaware River, just before the Battle of Trenton.

From 1787 to 1796 Chapman was a member of the Pennsylvania Assembly. A Federalist, he served Pennsylvania in the United States House of Representatives during the 5th Congress (1797–99). He died in Upper Makefield, Pennsylvania, and was buried in the Friends Burying Ground in Wrightstown, Pennsylvania.

CHEW, Benjamin: jurist
Born West River, Maryland, November 29, 1722; son of Dr. Samuel Chew; married Mary Thomas; second marriage to Elizabeth Oswald; father of at least one daughter (Peggy); died January 20, 1810.

Admitted to the Philadelphia bar in 1754, Chew served as city recorder of Philadelphia

from that year until 1775. He was attorney general of Pennsylvania from 1755 to 1769, and register general of Pennsylvania from 1765 to 1777. A member of the Pennsylvania Executive Council in 1775–76, he also served as chief justice of the Pennsylvania Supreme Court from 1774 to circa 1776. He was a judge and president of the High Court of Errors and Appeals of Pennsylvania, 1791–1808. He died in Germantown, Pennsylvania.

CIST, Charles: publisher, printer
Born St. Petersburg, Russia; son of Charles Jacob and Anna (Thomasson) Thiel; married Mary Weiss, June 7, 1781; father of Charles and Jacob; died December 1, 1805.

In 1769, after graduating from the University of Halle (Germany), Charles Thiel came to America, changed his name to Cist, and settled in Philadelphia. A translator for Henry Miller, he became a partner in the printing firm of Styner and Cist in 1775. He printed *The American Crisis* by Thomas Paine in 1776 and *Pharmacopoeia Simpliciorium* by William Brown in 1778.

In 1786 Cist published the *American Herald* and *Columbus Magazine.* He organized the Lehigh Coal Company in 1792 and then became the public printer in Washington, D.C., during John Adams's administration. He died in Bethlehem, Pennsylvania, and was buried in the Moravian Cemetery.

CLARKSON, Matthew: Continental congressman, mayor
Born New York City, April 1733; died October 5, 1800.

After moving from New York City to Philadelphia, Clarkson served on the benches of the Court of Common Pleas, the Quarter Sessions of Peace, and the Philadelphia Orphans' Court, 1771–72. Although appointed a Pennsylvania delegate to the Continental Congress in 1785, he may not have served. In 1789 he became a member of the board of aldermen of Philadelphia; three years later he became mayor of that city, serving until 1796. He died in Philadelphia and was buried in Christ Church Burying Grounds.

CLINGAN, William: Continental congressman

Born probably near Wagontown, West Colen Township, Chester County, Pennsylvania; died May 9, 1790.

A member of the Continental Congress from Pennsylvania, 1777–79, Clingan was one of the first signers of the Articles of Confederation, in 1778. He was president of the county courts of Pennsylvania from 1780 to 1786. Throughout this time—from 1757 to 1786—he was justice of the peace of Chester County, Pennsylvania. He was buried in the Upper Octorara Burial Grounds in Chester County.

CLYMER, George: merchant, Continental congressman

Born Philadelphia, March 16, 1739; son of Christopher and Deborah (Fitzwater) Clymer; married Elizabeth Meredith, 1756; father of one child; died January 23, 1813.

Clymer, the founder of the shipping firm of Merediths and Clymer in Philadelphia, played an active role in the struggle for American independence. A member of the Pennsylvania Committee of Safety, he was also a delegate from Pennsylvania to the Continental Congress from 1776 to 1778 and from 1780 to 1783. He served on the boards of war and treasury.

Clymer was a signer of both the Declaration of Independence (on July 20, 1776) and the United States Constitution (in 1788). He was also a member of the Pennsylvania Convention which ratified the Constitution. He later served in the 1st Congress of the United States House of Representatives.

Clymer was the first president of the Philadelphia Bank and the Academy of Fine Arts; from 1805 to 1813 he was vice president of the Philadelphia Agricultural Society. He died in Morrisville, Bucks County, Pennsylvania, and was buried in Friends Graveyard, Trenton, New Jersey.

CLYMER, George E.: inventor

Born Bucks County, Pennsylvania, 1754; married Margaret Backhouse; father of three daughters; died August 27, 1834.

Clymer invented the Columbian, an improved printing press which was the first outstanding American invention in the printing field. For this he was awarded a gold medal for invention from the King of the Netherlands. He died in London, England.

COATES, Samuel: merchant, philanthropist

Born Philadelphia, August 24, 1748; son of Samuel and Mary (Langdate) Coates; married Lydia Saunders, 1775; second marriage to Amy Hornor, 1791; died June 4, 1830.

Coates established his own mercantile business at age nineteen, entering into a partnership in the firm Reynell and Coates three years later. In 1785 he left the company to found his own firm, which he headed until his death.

Coates was the manager of the Pennsylvania Hospital from 1785 to 1826 and served as president of the board of directors in 1812. From 1786 to 1823 he helped to organize and sustain the Overseers of Public Schools, which managed the Quaker schools of Philadelphia.

Coates was a director of the First Bank of the United States from 1800 to 1812. He died in Philadelphia.

COBBETT, William: journalist

Born Farnham, Surrey, England, March 9, 1763; son of George and Ann (Vincent) Cobbett; married Ann Reid; died June 18, 1835.

After coming to the United States as a political refugee from England in 1792, Cobbett settled in Philadelphia and became an English teacher. He became involved in political disputes and was one of the founders of party journalism in America; he defended the Federalist viewpoint and engaged in pamphlet "wars" with the Republicans. His writings were sarcastic and vicious, including personal attacks on many famous men. He wrote under the pseudonym Peter Porcupine, publishing *Porcupine's Gazette and Daily Advertiser,* 1797–98. After attacking Dr. Benjamin Rush for his extensive and nearly disastrous practice of bleeding patients during the yellow fever epidemic of 1797, Cobbett was sued for libel by Rush and lost the case. For the next two years he published the *Rush-Light* in New York City. In 1800 he was allowed to return to England, but he was again forced to flee to the United States seventeen years later. He settled on a farm in Long Island, New York, but two years later, in 1819, he returned to England to stay.

Cobbett wrote several works, including *Observations on the Emigration of Dr. Joseph Priestly,* 1794; *A Bone to Gnaw for the Democrats,* 1795; *A Little Plain English Addressed to the People of the United States,* 1795; *The Life and Adventures of Peter Porcupine,* 1796; *A Journal of a Year's Residence in the United States,* part one, 1818; parts two and three, 1819.

CONRAD, Frederick: congressman

Born Worcester Township, Montgomery County, Pennsylvania, 1759; died August 3, 1827.

Conrad, who attended common schools, was elected to the Pennsylvania Assembly three times—1798, 1800, and 1802. In 1804 and 1805 he was paymaster of the 51st Regiment of the Pennsylvania militia. A Federalist, he was a delegate from Pennsylvania to the United States House of Representatives for the 8th–9th congresses (1803–07).

In 1807 Conrad was appointed justice of the peace. He was appointed prothonotary and clerk of courts in 1821 and was reappointed three years later. He became a farmer while living near Center Point, Pennsylvania, and later moved to Norristown, Pennsylvania. He died in Norristown and was buried in Wentz's Reformed Church Cemetery, near Center Point.

CONYNGHAM, Gustavus: naval officer

Born County Donegal, Ireland, 1744; son of Gustavus Conyngham; married Ann Hockley, 1773; died November 27, 1819.

Conyngham, who came to America in 1763, was commissioned captain of the ship *Surprise* in the Continental Navy in 1777 and captured the ships *Joseph* and *Prince of Orange* that same year. He then took command of the ship *Revenge* and arrived at Philadelphia in 1779 with sixty prizes. He was captured by the British and shipped to England, but he escaped. Recaptured in 1780, he was exchanged the following year.

After the war, Conyngham became a merchant in Philadelphia and was a member of the Philadelphia Common Council during the War of 1812. He died at the age of seventy-five and was buried in St. Peter's Churchyard in Philadelphia.

COOMBE, Thomas: clergyman

Born Philadelphia, November 1, 1747; died August 15, 1822.

Coombe went to England in 1768 and was ordained to the ministry of the Church of England the following year. He returned to America in 1772 to serve as assistant minister to the congregations of Christ Church and St. Peter's until 1778. He was friendly toward the cause of the colonies, but his ordination oath made it impossible for him to approve of the Declaration of Independence. In 1778 he moved to New York City and the following year went to England. He was chaplain to the Earl of Carlisle and later chaplain in ordinary to King George III. He was prebendary of Canterbury for eight years (1800–08). From 1808 until his death fourteen years later, he was the rector of three united London parishes.

Coombe was the author of *The Harmony between the Old and New Testaments Respecting the Messiah,* 1774; *Influences of Christianity on the Condition of the World,* 1790 (both of these being sermons); *The Peasant of Auburn; or The Emigrant* (poem), 1783.

CORBIN, Margaret: heroine
Born in what is now Franklin County, Pennsylvania, November 12, 1751; daughter of Robert Cochran; married John Corbin, 1772; died January 16, 1800.

Margaret Corbin accompanied her husband when he marched to war with the 1st Company of the Pennsylvania Artillery of the Continental Army in 1776. She took her husband's place when he was killed while defending a cannon against the Hessians in the Battle of Fort Washington; she fought until she was severely wounded and was captured, but she was not held prisoner. She then went to Philadelphia, where she was granted a lifetime pension by the Continental Congress for her bravery. She died in Westchester County, New York, at the age of forty-eight.

COXE, Tench: political economist, Continental congressman
Born Philadelphia, Pennsylvania, May 22, 1755; son of William and Mary (Francis) Coxe; married Catherine McCall; second marriage to Rebecca Coxe; died July 16, 1824.

Coxe attended the College of Philadelphia (now the University of Pennsylvania). He was a delegate to the Annapolis Convention in 1786 and a member of the Continental Congress in 1787–88. He was assistant secretary of the treasury of the United States, 1789–92; United States commissioner of revenue, 1792–97; and United States purveyor of public supplies, 1803–12.

Coxe was president of the Pennsylvania Society for the Encouragement of Manufactures and Useful Arts and one of the first to urge the cultivation of cotton as a staple in the South. He was also active in the promotion of cotton manufacture. He was the author of *An Examination of the Constitution of the United States*, 1788, and *View of the United States*, 1794. He died in Philadelphia and was buried in Christ Church Burying Ground there.

CRAGHAN, George: Indian trader, agent
Born near Dublin, Ireland; father of several children (including Susannah); died August 31, 1782.

Craghan came to America in 1741 and established an Indian trading post in Carlisle, Pennsylvania, later establishing posts in the Upper Ohio region. He was an agent for Pennsylvania in negotiations with the Indians and, from 1756 to 1772, deputy superintendent of Indian affairs. He was present at the capture of Fort Duquesne in 1758 and of Detroit in 1760.

In 1765 Craghan opened the Illinois country to English settlers by concluding a peace treaty with Pontiac. He owned much land in New York, Pennsylvania, Indiana, Illinois, and Ohio. He was a member of the Indiana Land Company and the Grand Ohio Company. He was a member of the Committee of Correspondence in Pittsburgh in 1775. He died in Passyunk, Pennsylvania.

CROUCH, Edward: congressman
Born Walnut Hill, near Highspire, Lancaster (now Dauphin) County, Pennsylvania, November 9, 1764; died February 2, 1827.

Crouch, who attended common schools, fought in the Revolutionary War. Later, in 1794, he commanded a company in the Whiskey Insurrection.

After the Revolution, Crouch became a merchant in Walnut Hill and was a member of the Pennsylvania House of Representatives from 1804 to 1806. A presidential elector on the Democratic ticket in 1812, he was an associate judge of Dauphin County the following year. Serving Pennsylvania, he was a member of the United States House of Representatives during the 13th Congress (October 12, 1813, to 1815). He died in Walnut Hill and was buried in Paxtang Cemetery.

★★★★★

DALE, Richard: naval officer
Born in Norfolk County, Virginia, on November 6, 1756; son of Winfield and Ann (Sutherland) Dale; married Dorothea Grathorne, September 15, 1791; father of Richard and John M.; died February 26, 1826.

Dale served with British Navy from 1776

to 1777, when he joined the colonial cause. He served as 1st lieutenant on the *Bon Homme Richard* under John Paul Jones in the battle with the *Serapis* in 1779. He was commissioned a lieutenant in 1781 and served in the Merchant Marines from 1783 to 1794. He was commissioned a captain in the United States Navy in 1794. He commanded a squadron in the Mediterranean during the hostilities with Tripoli, 1801–02. He died in Philadelphia.

DALLAS, Alexander James: secretary of the treasury

Born on the island of Jamaica, British West Indies, June 21, 1759; son of Robert and Sarah (Cormack) Dallas; married Arabella Smith, September 4, 1780; father of George Mifflin; died January 16, 1817.

Dallas came to the United States and was naturalized in 1783. He was admitted to the Pennsylvania bar in 1785 and was appointed a master in chancery and the counselor of the Supreme Court of Pennsylvania. Two years later he became editor of *Columbian* magazine. In 1791, he was the secretary of the Commonwealth of Pennsylvania. From 1801 to 1814 he was United States district attorney of the Eastern District of Pennsylvania.

As secretary of the treasury from 1814 to 1816, Dallas secured a bill (in 1816) establishing the Second Bank of the United States. His government finance policies pulled the country out of the depression after the War of 1812 by restoring public credit and advocating national banks and a protective tariff.

Dallas wrote *Features of Mr. Jay's Treaty*, 1795; *Laws of the Commonwealth of Pennsylvania*, four volumes, 1793–1801; *Reports of Cases Ruled and Adjudged in the Several Courts of the U. S. and Pennsylvania*, four volumes, 1790–1807; *Treasury Reports: An Exposition of the Causes and Character of the War*, 1815. He was also editor of the *First Reports of the U. S. Supreme Court*. He died in Trenton, New Jersey.

DAWKINS, Henry: engraver

Born probably in England; married Priscilla Wood, *October 2, 1757; father of seven children; no record of death.*

Dawkins came to New York City in 1753. The earliest example of his work in America is a bookplate for John Burnet of New York, dated 1754. In 1757 he was assistant engraver to James Turner of Philadelphia, and the following year he started his own business. While residing in Philadelphia, he became a member of the Grand Lodge of the Masons and was elected junior warden in 1764. In 1776 he was arrested in New York City on suspicion of counterfeiting Continental and Provincial currency; four years later he was convicted of the charge and fined $1,500.

DECATUR, Stephen: naval officer

Born Newport, Rhode Island, 1752; son of Stephen and Priscilla (Hill) Decatur; married Ann Pine, December 20, 1774; father of Ann, James, John, and Stephen; died November 14, 1808.

Master of the sloop *Peggy* in 1774, Decatur became a privateer when the Revolutionary War broke out. He was commander and part owner of the merchant ships *Ariel* and *Pennsylvania* from 1782 to 1798. In 1798 he was commissioned a captain in the United States Navy. He commanded the *Delaware* as the senior officer of the squadron operating off northern Cuba during the hostilities with the French, 1798–99. He commanded the *Philadelphia* as the head of the Guadeloupe Squadron in 1800 and 1801.

After his discharge from the navy in 1801, Decatur established a gunpowder works in Millsdale, Pennsylvania. He died in Millsdale and is buried in St. Peter's Churchyard in Philadelphia.

DE HAAS, John Philip: army officer

Born Holland, 1735; son of John Nicholas De Haas; married Eleanor Bingham; died June 3, 1786.

De Haas's family came to America in 1737. At the age of twenty-two he was commissioned an ensign in the Provincial Battalion of Pennsylvania, during the French and Indian War. In 1758 he took part in the expedition against Fort Duquesne. From

1765 to 1779 he was magistrate of Lancaster County, Pennsylvania.

In 1776 De Haas was appointed a colonel in the 1st Pennsylvania Battalion of the Continental Army and participated in the Canadian campaign under General Benedict Arnold. He was commissioned a brigadier general in 1777, but he resigned later that year. In 1778 he organized the local militia for a campaign against the Indians in the Wyoming Valley but was relieved of his command by General Arnold.

De Haas died in Philadelphia.

DENNING, William: cannon maker
Born 1736; died December 19, 1830.

Denning, who served as an artificer in the Continental Army during the Revolutionary War, is said to have made the first successful attempt at manufacturing wrought-iron cannons. He made two small cannons in Middlesex, Pennsylvania; one of these, used in the Battle of Brandywine, was captured by the British and placed in the Tower of London, where it stands to this day. He declined an offer made by the British to show them how to make cannons. He died in Mifflin Township, Pennsylvania, at the age of ninety-four.

DENNY, Ebenezer: army officer, mayor
Born Carlisle, Pennsylvania, March 11, 1761; son of William and Agnes (Parker) Denny; married Nancy Wilkins, July 1, 1793; father of three sons (Harmer, William, and St. Clair) and two daughters; died July 21, 1822.

At the age of fifteen Denny was commissioned an ensign in the 1st Pennsylvania Regiment and fought near Williamsburg, Virginia. He also served with the advance units at the siege of York. He was an aide-de-camp under St. Clair in the Carolinas and then was adjutant to Harmer. In 1794 he was commissioned a captain and put in command of the Le Boeuf expedition.

Denny's political career began in 1777, when he became a member of the first Pennsylvania Constitutional Convention, representing Bedford County. In 1803, and again in 1808, he was treasurer of Allegheny County, Pennsylvania. In 1816 he became the first mayor of Pittsburgh. He was also the director of the Pittsburgh branch of the Bank of the United States and the Bank of Pittsburgh.

DICKINSON, John: Continental congressman
Born Talbot County, Maryland, November 8, 1732; son of Samuel and Mary (Cadwalader) Dickinson; married Mary Norris, July 19, 1770; died February 14, 1808.

Dickinson studied law in Philadelphia, then attended Middle Temple in London, England, from 1753 until 1757, when he returned to Philadelphia and was admitted to the bar. He was awarded an LL.D. from the College of New Jersey (now Princeton) in 1768. A member of the Assembly of Lower Counties (Delaware) in 1760, he later became speaker. He was a representative from Philadelphia in the Pennsylvania legislature from 1762 to 1764 and from 1770 to 1776. He printed a pamphlet entitled "The Late Regulations Respecting the British Colonies on the Continent of America Considered" in 1765. That same year he was a delegate to the Stamp Act Congress, representing Pennsylvania.

In 1774 Dickinson was chairman of the Committee of Correspondence, and from 1774 to 1776 and from 1779 to 1781 he was a member of the Continental Congress. In 1775 he was chairman of a committee of safety and defense. An advocate of conciliation with England, he voted against the Declaration of Independence in the belief that a peaceful settlement was still possible; however, when war came, he was a staunch supporter of the Revolutionary effort. He was a colonel in the 1st Battalion, raised in Philadelphia.

Dickinson was president of the Supreme Council of Delaware in 1781 and president of the Supreme Council of Pennsylvania from 1782 to 1785. A delegate from Delaware to the United States Constitutional

Convention in 1787, he is noted for publishing a series of letters signed "Fabius" in which he urged adoption of the Constitution. He also wrote *Letters from a Farmer in Pennsylvania to the Inhabitants of the British Colonies* (1768), which urged non-importation instead of violence. He died in Wilmington, Delaware.

DOD, Thaddeus: clergyman, educator
Born Newark, New Jersey, March 18, 1741; son of Stephen and Deborah (Brown) Dod; married Phebe Baldwin, circa 1773; died May 20, 1793.

Dod graduated from the College of New Jersey (now Princeton) in 1773 and was licensed to preach as a Presbyterian minister two years later. In 1777 he was ordained to the ministry in the Presbytery of New York and preached on the western frontier. He founded a church in Ten Mile, Pennsylvania, in 1779 and began to teach school in 1782.

In 1789 Dod received a charter to organize the Washington Academy and served as principal that year and the next. He also organized a school in Canonsburg, Pennsylvania. The two schools later became Washington College and Jefferson College; soon afterward they merged to become Washington and Jefferson College. He died in Ten Mile.

DUCHÉ, Jacob: clergyman
Born Philadelphia, Pennsylvania, January 31, 1737 (or 1738); son of Colonel Jacob and Mary (Spence) Duché; married Elizabeth Hopkinson, June 19, 1759; father of at least one son (Thomas Spence); died January 3, 1798.

Duché graduated from the College of Philadelphia in 1757 and later attended Cambridge University. He was ordained a deacon in 1759 and was ordained to the ministry in the Anglican Church in England in 1762. He was a teacher of oratory. After serving as assistant rector of the united parishes of Christ Church and St. Peter's in Philadelphia, he became rector and served from 1775 to 1777. He was chaplain of the Continental Congress during that same period.

Duché was imprisoned when the British took Philadelphia, but he later became a strong Loyalist and moved to England in 1777. He was the secretary and the chaplain of the Orphan Asylum, St. George's Fields, Lambeth Parish, England. In 1792 he was allowed to return to America.

Duché wrote *The Life and Death of the Righteous,* 1760; *Pennsylvania, A Poem,* 1756; *The Duty of Standing Fast in Our Spiritual and Temporal Liberties,* 1775; and *Discourses on Various Subjects,* 1779. He died in Philadelphia.

Du COUDRAY, Philippe Charles Jean Tronson: army officer
Born Rheims, France, September 8, 1738; died September 11, 1777.

An army engineer and adjutant general of artillery, Du Coudray volunteered for service in the American Revolution. He was promised the rank of major general by Benjamin Franklin, but was named inspector general instead; this was a compromise to allay the jealousy of the colonial leaders. Placed in charge of the fortifications along the Delaware River, he drowned near Philadelphia after four months of service.

DUNCAN, James: army officer
Born Philadelphia, Pennsylvania, 1756; died June 24, 1844.

Duncan, who attended Princeton, served as the first prothonotary of Adams County, Pennsylvania. He was commissioned a lieutenant in Colonel Hazen's Regiment in 1776 and was promoted to captain in 1778. He was elected to the United States House of Representatives, as a delegate from Pennsylvania, for the 17th Congress, but he resigned before Congress assembled. He died in Mercer County, Pennsylvania.

DUNLAP, John: printer
Born Strabane, Ireland, 1747; married Mrs. Elizabeth (Hayes) Ellison, February 4, 1773; died November 27, 1812.

Dunlap came to Philadelphia at the age of ten and was apprenticed to his uncle William Dunlap as a printer; in 1766 he took over the shop. In 1771 he founded *The Pennsylvania Packet,* a weekly journal which in 1784 became the first daily newspaper in America. He founded the 1st Troop of the Philadelphia City Cavalry in 1774. He was promoted to first lieutenant in 1781 and to captain in 1794.

Dunlap is famous as the printer of the Declaration of Independence and also of the United States Constitution, which he published in *The Pennsylvania Packet and Daily Advertiser.* In 1778 he was printer for the Continental Congress. He was a member of the Philadelphia Common Council from 1789 to 1792. He was a major in charge of the Pennsylvania Cavalry during the suppression of the Whiskey Rebellion in 1794. He died at the age of sixty-five and was buried at Christ Church in Philadelphia.

DuPONCEAU, Pierre Etienne: lawyer, author

Born on the Isle de Rhe, France, June 3, 1760; married Anne Perry, May 21, 1788; died April 2, 1844.

DuPonceau, who was known as Peter Stephen DuPonceau in the United States, was appointed a captain in the Continental Army on February 18, 1788, and shortly afterward became aide-de-camp to the newly appointed Major General von Steuben at Valley Forge. From October 22, 1781, to June 4, 1783, he was Livingston's under secretary. He was admitted as an attorney in the Court of Common Pleas in Philadelphia on June 24, 1785, and in 1786 became an attorney in the Supreme Court.

In 1810 DuPonceau translated from Bynkershoek's original Latin *A Treatise on the Law of War . . . Being the First Book of his Quaestiones Juris Publici,* with notes. He was internationally recognized for his contributions to philology, including his work on the North American Indian languages. He received an honorary LL.D. from Harvard in 1820 and founded the Law Academy of Philadelphia the following year. He was elected president of the American Philosophical Society in 1828 and was a member of the Academy of Arts and Sciences.

DuPonceau was the author of *A Dissertation on the Nature and Extent of the Jurisdiction of the Courts of the United States,* 1824; *A Brief View of the Constitution of the United States,* 1834; *English Phonology,* 1817; and *A Discourse on the Early History of Pennsylvania,* 1817. He died in Philadelphia.

Du SIMITIÈRE, Pierre Eugène: artist

Born Geneva, Switzerland, circa 1736; died October 1784.

Du Simitière spent ten years in the West Indies as a portrait painter. He arrived in New York City in 1765, then moved to Burlington, New Jersey, and finally settled in Philadelphia in 1766. He was elected a member of the American Philosophical Society because of his studies in natural history, later (1776–81) serving as its curator. He was America's first good portraitist and painted many of the leaders of the Revolution. He died in Philadelphia and was buried in St. Peter's Cemetery.

★★★★★

EDWARDS, Morgan: clergyman

Born Trevethin Parish, Monmouthshire, England, April 28, 1722; no record of first marriage; second marriage to Mrs. Singleton; died January 28, 1795.

Born in England, Edwards dedicated his life to the Baptist ministry, beginning his preaching at the age of sixteen while attending Baptist College, Bristol, England. During his stay as pastor of a church in Cork, Ireland (1750–59), he became an ordained minister. From 1761 to 1771 he was pastor of the Baptist Church in Philadelphia, Pennsylvania. He then moved to Newark, Delaware, where he lectured and helped plan a proposed twelve-volume history of Baptists in America.

EGE, George: congressman

Born near Womelsdorf, Berks County, Pennsylvania, March 9, 1748; died December 14, 1829.

Ege's political activities included membership in the Pennsylvania House of Representatives, beginning in 1783, and service in the United States House of Representatives, in which he filled a vacancy during the 4th and 5th congresses (December 8, 1796–October 1797). He was an associate judge in Berks County from 1791 to 1818.

Ege, who was involved in land and iron enterprises, was the builder and operator of Schuylkill County Forge, near Port Clinton, Pennsylvania. He died in Charming Forge, Berks County, Pennsylvania, and was buried in Zion's Church Cemetery in Womelsdorf.

ELLICOTT, Andrew: surveyor, mathematician

Born Bucks County, Pennsylvania, January 24, 1754; son of Joseph and Judith (Bleaker) Ellicott; married Sarah Brown, 1775; father of nine children; died August 28, 1820.

Ellicott founded Ellicott City, Maryland, in 1774, at the age of twenty. Among his surveying works were the completion of the Mason-Dixon Line in West Pennsylvania in 1784; his contributions while a member of the Pennsylvania commissions for running western (1785) and northern (1786) state boundaries; a survey of the islands in the Ohio and Allegheny Rivers in 1788; the publication of the first map of the territory of Columbia (now Washington, D.C.); the drawing up of the Ellicott Plan (a survey of Washington, D.C.); the reformulation of L'Enfant's plans of Washington, D.C., under the direction of Thomas Jefferson; the laying out of plans for the town of Presqu' Isle (Erie), Pennsylvania, in 1794; and the survey of the frontier between Florida and the United States in 1796.

Ellicott served as a major during the American Revolution and published the *U.S. Almanack* after 1782. In 1813 he became a professor of mathematics at the United States Military Academy at West Point, New York, where he died on August 28, 1820.

ETTWEIN, John: clergyman

Born Freudenstadt, Würtemberg, June 29, 1721; married Johanna Maria Kymbel, 1746; died January 2, 1802.

Ettwein was a young shoemaker who became a convert to the Moravian Church and moved to Marienborn, where he became a missionary and a deacon, ordained at the age of twenty-five. In 1754 he came to America, where he was a missionary to the Middle States until 1763. He rose to the position of head of Moravian conversions in North Carolina, serving from 1763 until 1766, at which time he became assistant to Bishop N. Seidel in Bethlehem, Pennsylvania.

Although he was arrested as a Loyalist, Ettwein later became a Moravian representative to the Continental Congress and the Pennsylvania Assembly and was chaplain of the Continental Army hospital in Bethlehem in 1776 and 1777. He revived the Society of United Brethren for Propagating the Gospel among the Heathen, acting as president in 1787. For seventeen years (1784–1801) he was a bishop of the Moravian Church in North America. He died in Bethlehem, Pennsylvania.

EVANS, Oliver: inventor, steam-engine builder

Born New Castle County, Delaware, 1755; son of Charles Evans; married Miss Tomlinson, 1780; father of two children; died April 5, 1819.

Evans made important contributions to agriculture and industry. He perfected a machine for wool manufacture that could produce 1,500 cards of wool per minute. After completing a series of improvements in flour-mill machinery operated by water power in 1785, he petitioned legislatures in Pennsylvania and Maryland for exclusive rights to use his "improvements in flour mills and steam carriages" in those states; permission was wholly granted in Maryland, granted with restrictions in Pennsylvania.

Subsequent to becoming involved in the engine-building business in 1803, Evans established the Mars Iron Works in 1807, designed and constructed the Philadelphia water works in 1817, and became the first steam-engine builder in America. Fifty of his engines were in use throughout the Atlantic coast states by the time of his death in 1819.

Evans was the author of *The Young Mill-Wright and Miller's Guide*, 1795, and *The Abortion of the Young Engineer's Guide*, 1805.

EWING, James: army officer, legislator
Born Lancaster County, Pennsylvania, August 3, 1736; son of Thomas and Susanna (Howard) Ewing; married Patience Wright; died March 1, 1806.

Ewing was a lieutenant in the Pennsylvania militia during the French and Indian War. He was a member of the Pennsylvania General Assembly from 1771 to 1775 and was appointed a brigadier general in the Pennsylvania militia in 1776. He served as vice president of Pennsylvania from 1782 to 1784 and was a member of the Pennsylvania Senate from 1795 to 1799. He was a trustee of Dickinson College from 1783 until his death in 1806, in Hellam, Pennsylvania.

EWING, John: clergyman, university provost
Born East Nottingham, Maryland, July 22, 1732; son of Alexander Ewing; married Hannah Sergeant, circa 1758; died September 8, 1802.

Ewing graduated from the College of New Jersey (now Princeton) in 1754. After tutoring at his alma mater for two years, he taught philosophy at the College of Philadelphia in 1758 and 1759. He was ordained a minister in the Presbyterian Church in 1758 and became pastor of the First Presbyterian Church in Philadelphia the following year.

For twenty-three years (1779–1802) Ew-

ing served the State University of Pennsylvania (which merged with the College of Philadelphia to form the University of Pennsylvania in 1791) as provost and professor of natural philosophy. He was vice president of the American Philosophical Society and served on several boundary commissions. He was the author of papers which were collected and published posthumously in 1809 as *A Plain Elementary and Practical System of Natural Experimental Philosophy*.

★★★★★

FARMER, Ferdinand: missionary
Born Swabia, Germany, October 13, 1720; died August 17, 1786.

Farmer, whose original surname was Steinmeyer, was a Roman Catholic priest who studied under the followers of Loyola in Landsberg, Germany, in 1743. He came to America and was placed in charge of a mission in Lancaster, Pennsylvania, serving from 1752 until 1758, when he took charge of the German parish of Saint Joseph in Philadelphia. The first Roman Catholic congregation in New York was organized by him in 1775; this was the nucleus of the present-day St. Peter's.

Farmer refused to accept the position of chaplain in a company of Loyalist Roman Catholic volunteers that the British hoped to form in 1778. He served as a charter trustee of the University of the State of Pennsylvania. An astronomer and a mathematician, he was a member of the American Philosophical Society. He died in Philadelphia.

FENNO, John: editor
Born Boston, Massachusetts, August 23, 1751; son of Ephraim and Mary (Chapman) Fenno; married Mary Curtiss, May 8, 1777; father of John Ward; died September 14, 1798.

Fenno, after serving for a time as secretary to General Artemas Ward, went to New York in 1789, where he founded the *Gazette of the United States* later in the year; the paper's purpose, according to Fenno, was to express "favorable sentiments of the federal Constitution and the Administration." He established the *Gazette* in Philadelphia on April 14, 1790, and the paper was soon adopted by Federalists as a semi-official party journal, with Alexander Hamilton and other prominent Federalists contributing articles. The *Gazette* carried on a bitter disputation throughout the 1790s with Benjamin Bache's *Aurora* and Philip Freneau's *National Gazette.*

Fenno died in Philadelphia during the yellow fever epidemic of 1798; his son continued publication of the *Gazette* until 1800.

FINDLEY, William: congressman
Born Northern Ireland, circa 1741; died April 4, 1821.

Findley was a member of the Pennsylvania Council of Censors (1783), the Pennsylvania Assembly (1785–86), and the Pennsylvania Supreme Executive Council (1789–90). After serving as a delegate to the Pennsylvania Constitutional Convention in 1790, he spent twenty-two years in the United States House of Representatives, from 1791 to 1799 and again from 1803 to 1817.

Findley was involved in the Whiskey Insurrection of 1794, later writing *History of the Insurrection in the Four Western Counties of Pennsylvania* (1796).

He died near Greensburg, Pennsylvania, and was buried in the Unity Meeting House Cemetery near Latrobe, Pennsylvania.

FITCH, John: metal craftsman, inventor, steamboat developer
Born Windsor, Connecticut, January 21, 1743; son of Joseph and Sarah (Shaler) Fitch; married Lucy Roberts, December 29, 1767; father of one child; died July 2, 1798.

Fitch established a brass shop in East Windsor, Connecticut, in 1764. During the Revolutionary War he was in charge of the Trenton Gun Factory. He spent five years (1780–85) surveying lands along the Ohio Valley and in the Northwest Territory; in 1782 he organized a company to ac-

quire and exploit lands in the latter region.

Fitch successfully launched and operated his first steamboat in 1787. The following year he launched a sixty-foot steam-paddle-propelled boat, which was used to carry passengers from Philadelphia, Pennsylvania, to Burlington, New Jersey. Although he received American and French patents for his steamboat in 1791, he lost his financial backing because of his failure to give sufficient attention to construction and operating costs. He had already perfected and constructed four steamboats.

Fitch died in Bardstown, Kentucky.

FITZSIMMONS, Thomas: Continental congressman, congressman, businessman
Born County Tubber, Wicklow, Ireland, 1741; married Catharine Meade, November 23, 1761; died August 26, 1811.

Fitzsimmons, whose last name was also spelled Fitzsimons, was a member of the Continental Congress in 1782 and 1783, a member of the Pennsylvania House of Representatives in 1786 and 1787, and a delegate to the United States Constitutional Convention in 1787. He was also a member of the United States House of Representatives during the 1st and 3rd congresses (1789–95).

Outside of his congressional activities, Fitzsimmons was president of the Philadelphia Chamber of Commerce, a trustee of the University of Pennsylvania, and founder and director of the Bank of North America (1781). He died in Philadelphia and was buried in Saint Mary's Roman Catholic Churchyard there.

FORREST, Thomas: congressman
Born Philadelphia, Pennsylvania, 1747; died March 20, 1825.

Forrest was commissioned a captain in Colonel Thomas Proctor's Pennsylvania Artillery in 1776, was promoted to major in 1777, and became a lieutenant colonel in 1778. Three years later he resigned his commission. He was a member of the

United States House of Representatives from Pennsylvania during the 16th and 17th congresses (from 1819 to 1821 and from October 8, 1822, to 1823). He died in Germantown (now a part of Philadelphia).

FOXALL, Henry: foundry owner

Born Monmouthshire, England, May 24, 1758; married Ann Howard; married a second time; died December 11, 1823.

Foxall became superintendent of an important iron works in Dublin, Ireland, in 1794, also serving as a lay minister for a time. In 1797 he arrived in Philadelphia, where he formed a partnership with Robert Morris, Jr., which they called the Eagle Fire Works. While owner of the Columbian Foundry in Georgetown, D.C., during the years 1800 to 1815, he donated land and funds for the Foundry Chapel in Washington, D.C. (1814). He died in Mandsworth, England.

FRANKLIN, Benjamin: statesman

Born Boston, Massachusetts, January 17, 1706; son of Josiah and Abiah (Folger) Franklin; took Deborah Read as common law wife, September 1, 1730, later married her; father of two legitimate children (Francis Folger and Sarah); father of two illegitimate children (including William); died April 17, 1790.

Although Franklin was a self-educated man, he was swamped with honorary degrees as he gained fame. Both Harvard and Yale bestowed honorary M.A. degrees on him in 1753, with the College of William and Mary following suit three years later. He was granted an honorary LL.D. from St. Andrews College in 1759 and an honorary D.C.L. from Oxford University, England, in 1762.

While still in his teens, Franklin was a contributor of articles to the *New England Courant*, a Boston newspaper published and printed by his brother James, to whom he was apprenticed. From 1730 to 1750 he was the owner of the *Pennsylvania Gazette*. In 1731 he established a circulation library in Philadelphia. From 1732 to 1757 he wrote and published *Poor Richard's Almanac*, one of the first American literary productions to attain international renown, largely because of its common-sense philosophical aphorisms.

Franklin served twenty-eight years in the Pennsylvania Assembly, first as clerk (1736–51) and then as a representative from Philadelphia (1751–64). He was deputy postmaster of Philadelphia from 1737 to 1753, and aided the British in the French and Indian War.

Among Franklin's many inventions were the Pennsylvania Fireplace (now known as the Franklin Stove), Fergusson's Clock (both circa 1744), and bifocals. In 1752 he performed his famous kite experiment to test the theory of the identity of lightning and electricity.

Franklin was a founder of the American Philosophical Society in 1743 and of the Philadelphia City Hospital in 1751. The latter year he also founded the Academy for the Education of Youth, which was incorporated in 1753. It later became the College of Philadelphia and is now the University of Pennsylvania.

In 1753 Franklin began a twenty-one-year tenure as joint deputy postmaster general of the American colonies. The following year he was Pennsylvania's representative at the Albany, New York, Congress of 1754. There he submitted his "Plan of Union," which was adopted by Congress but vetoed by the colonial legislatures; this plan would later prove to be a great influence on the drafters of the Articles of Confederation and the United States Constitution.

Franklin was in England from 1757 to 1762 as a political agent for the Pennsylvania Assembly, in which capacity he presented a case against the Penn family for refusing to support defense expenditures. He returned to England in 1766 to obtain the recall of the Pennsylvania Charter. That same year he was questioned before the House of Commons during debates on the repeal of the Stamp Act. He was a colonial agent of Georgia in 1768, of New Jersey in 1769, and of Massachusetts in 1770. He aided William Pitt in fruitless conciliation efforts in England.

Franklin became a member of the Second Continental Congress in 1775; he sketched a plan of union for the colonies, organized a post office, and became the first postmaster general. In 1776 he was a member of the committee which drafted the Declaration of Independence and was a signer of the document.

In foreign affairs, Franklin was a delegate of a mission to persuade Canada to join the American cause and was commissioner to negotiate a treaty with France in 1776. He was the only American with whom French Prime Minister Vergennes would deal. He signed the final commerce and defense alliance treaties in 1778 and was appointed minister to France the same year. Three years later he was appointed a commissioner to negotiate a peace treaty with Great Britain. He assumed responsibility for preliminary talks, and the peace treaty was signed in 1783.

In 1785 he returned to Philadelphia, where he served as president of the Pennsylvania Executive Council for two years. He was a member of the United States Constitutional. Convention in 1787 and was largely responsible for the representation compromise incorporated into the Constitution. His last public act was the signing of a memorial to Congress for the abolition of slavery.

Franklin was author of *Edict by the King of Prussia* and *Rules by Which a Great Empire May be Reduced to a Small One,* both satires, in the early 1770s. In 1775 he wrote *Observations on the Increase of Mankind, of the Peopling of Countries.* He began but left unfinished an *Autobiography,* which nevertheless was later published. He also wrote essays, signing some of the earliest "Silence Dogood." He died in Philadelphia and was buried in Christ Church Burial Ground there.

FRAZER, Persifor: army officer, jurist
Born Newton Township, Pennsylvania, August 9, 1736; son of John and Mary (Smith) Frazer; married Mary Taylor, October 2, 1766; died April 24, 1792.

Frazer took over the Sarum Iron Works in 1766. Nine years later he became a delegate to the Pennsylvania Provincial Council and a member of the Pennsylvania Committee of Safety. In 1776 he was appointed captain and then major in the Pennsylvania militia, later becoming a lieutenant colonel in the 5th Pennsylvania militia. In 1782 he was commissioned a brigadier general in the Pennsylvania militia.

Frazer was treasurer of Chester County, Pennsylvania, in 1781, and a member of the Pennsylvania General Assembly that year and the next. After serving as commissioner to Wyoming Valley in 1785, he became a justice of the Pennsylvania Court of Common Pleas (1786–92) and register of wills (1786).

FRIES, John: insurgent
Born Montgomery County, Pennsylvania, 1750; son of Simon Fries; married Margaret Brunner, 1770; died February 1818.

Early in his life Fries was a cooper's apprentice and an itinerant auctioneer. He moved to Bucks County, Pennsylvania, in 1775 and served as captain of a company of the Pennsylvania militia during the American Revolution and the Whiskey Insurrection.

Fries was largely responsible for the Pennsylvania opposition to a direct federal property tax levied in anticipation of a war with France in 1798, and he promised to raise a regiment of seven hundred men to oppose the collection of the tax. He was tried for treason and twice sentenced to death, but he was pardoned by President John Adams against the advice of his cabinet in 1799. Fries died nineteen years later in Bucks County, Pennsylvania.

FURGUSON, Elizabeth Graeme: poet
Born Philadelphia, February 3, 1737; daughter of

Dr. Thomas and Ann (Diggs) Graeme; married Henry Hugh Furguson, April 21, 1772; died February 23, 1801.

As a young woman, Miss Graeme was engaged to William Franklin, son of Benjamin Franklin, from 1754 to 1757. After translating *Télémaque (Fénelon)* into English, she went to London, England, for health reasons in 1764. After her mother's death she became mistress of her father's Philadelphia home, which she turned into a gathering place for Philadelphia's writers. During the Revolutionary War she became an unknowing tool of the English (through her Loyalist husband) by carrying a letter to General George Washington which urged his surrender. She died in Philadelphia and was buried at Christ Church there.

★★★★★

GALLOWAY, Joseph: Continental congressman, Loyalist

Born West River, Maryland, 1731; son of Peter Bines and Elizabeth (Rigbie) Galloway; married Grace Growden, October 18, 1753; died August 29, 1803.

Galloway, who held an LL.D. from Princeton, served in the Pennsylvania Assembly from 1756 to 1763 and again from 1765 to 1776, serving as speaker from 1766 to 1775. From 1769 to 1775 he was vice president of the American Philosophical Society. In 1774 he was a delegate to the First Continental Congress. He is famous for originating the Galloway Plan, which proposed creation of a British Empire based on constitutional principles; however, his plan was rejected in favor of independence.

Galloway chose the Loyalist side during the American Revolution, joining the British Army under General Howe in 1776. In 1777 he became civil administrator of the Port of Philadelphia, and the following year he went to England as a spokesman for American Loyalists. He wrote *Historical and Political Reflections on the Rise and Progress of the American Rebellion* (1780); *Cool Thoughts on the Consequences to Great Britain of American Independence* (1780); and *The Claim of the American Loyalists Reviewed and Maintained upon Incontrovertible Principles of Law and Justice* (1788). He died in Watford, Hertfordshire, England.

GARDNER, Joseph: Continental congressman, physician

Born Chester County, Pennsylvania, 1752; died 1794.

Gardner studied medicine and then entered into practice. In 1776 he raised a company of volunteers for the military and commanded the 4th Battalion of the Chester County militia. In addition to membership on the Committee of Safety in 1776–77, he served in the Pennsylvania Assembly from 1776 to 1778 and on the Supreme Executive Council the following year. After participating in the Continental Congress (1784–85), he resumed his medical practice in Philadelphia. He moved to Elkton, Maryland, in 1792, two years before his death.

GIBSON, George: army officer

Born Lancaster, Pennsylvania, October 1747; son of George and Elizabeth (deVinez) Gibson; married Anne West, 1772; father of John Banister; died December 14, 1791.

Gibson organized and commanded a company of frontiersmen for service in the West in 1775. The following year he negotiated a purchase of powder from the Spanish at New Orleans for the use of Virginia and Continental troops. He served as a colonel in 1777–78, then was placed in charge of an American prison camp in York, Pennsylvania, in 1779. Twelve years later he joined Major General Arthur St. Clair's expedition as a lieutenant colonel in command of the 2nd Regiment. He was mortally wounded in a battle against the Miami Indians on the Wabash River and died at Fort Jefferson, Ohio.

GIBSON, John: army officer, territorial official

Born Lancaster, Pennsylvania, May 23, 1740; son of George and Elizabeth (deVinez) Gibson; married

Ann; second marriage possibly to an Indian; died April 16, 1822.

Gibson took part in the Forbes expedition, which won Fort Duquesne from the French in 1758. He was an Indian trader at Fort Duquesne from 1758 until 1763, when he was captured by Indians during Pontiac's uprising.

In 1774 Gibson took part in Lord Dunmore's War. The following year he aided in the negotiations which resulted in the Treaty of Pittsburgh; that year also he became western agent for Virginia. In addition to serving on the Western Pennsylvania Committee of Correspondence, he was active in securing peace with the Indians. He served as a lieutenant colonel in the Continental Army in 1776 and then as a colonel from 1777 to 1781. In that year he became judge of the Court of Common Pleas and a major general of the militia in Allegheny County, Pennsylvania.

In 1789 Gibson was delegated by the state of Pennsylvania to help negotiate the purchase of the Erie Triangle from the Iroquois Confederacy. In 1790 he participated in the Pennsylvania Constitutional Convention. From 1800 until 1816 he was an organizer of the Indiana Territorial Government, also serving as secretary of the Indiana Territory and as acting governor during the War of 1812. He spoke various Indian dialects fluently. He died in Braddock's Field, Pennsylvania, at the age of eighty-one.

GIRARD, Stephen: financier, philanthropist
Born Bordeaux, France, May 20, 1750; son of Pierre and Odette (Lafargue) Girard; married Mary Lum, 1777; no children; died December 26, 1831.

Girard's first voyage was as captain of a French merchant ship sailing to Port-au-Prince in 1774. The following year he was employed as a captain by a New York City shipping firm. In 1776 he settled in Philadelphia and engaged in a mercantile business, later coming to own a merchant fleet based in Philadelphia.

During the yellow fever epidemic of 1793 Girard spent two months supervising an improvised hospital. A supporter of the Bank of the United States, he established credit in the United States and abroad, and when the Bank expired in 1811 he purchased the building and opened the Bank of Stephen Girard. He also played a key role in helping the government through the financial crisis during the War of 1812 and was instrumental in founding the Second Bank of the United States in 1816. He served as government director of this bank in 1816 and 1817.

Girard bequeathed large sums to the city of Philadelphia and the state of Pennsylvania for public improvements, contributing approximately $6 million to Philadelphia for the education of orphan boys. This gift resulted in Girard College, which opened in 1848. He died and was buried in Philadelphia.

GLONINGER, John: congressman, jurist
Born Lancaster County, Pennsylvania, September 19, 1758; died January 22, 1836.

Gloninger, who attended common schools, served as a subaltern officer with the Associators during the Revolutionary War. Later he commanded a militia battalion. Upon the organization of Dauphin County in 1785, the supreme executive council appointed him a lieutenant. In 1790, in addition to serving in the Pennsylvania House of Representatives and as a justice of the peace in Dauphin County, he began a term in the state senate which lasted until 1792.

Gloninger was commissioned associate judge of Dauphin County in 1791 and in 1813 was commissioned associate judge of Lebanon County. A Democrat, he went to the 13th Congress of the United States House of Representatives on March 4, 1813, but resigned on August 2 of that year. He then was reappointed associate judge of Lebanon County.

Gloninger died in Lebanon, Pennsylvania,

and was buried in the First Reformed Churchyard.

GOSTELOWE, Jonathan: cabinetmaker

Born Passyank (now a part of Philadelphia), Pennsylvania, 1744; son of George and Lydia Gostelowe; married Mary Duffield, June 16, 1768; second marriage to Elizabeth Towers, April 19, 1789; died February 3, 1795.

Gostelowe, a maker of mahogany and walnut cabinets, also made clock cases for Edward Duffield, whose daughter he married. In 1776 he served as a major of artillery in the Continental Army, later becoming chief commissary of the military stores in Philadelphia. He was captain of a company in the 3rd Battalion of the Pennsylvania militia in 1783 and 1784 and was a lieutenant of artillery in 1787. In 1789 he was elected chairman of the Gentleman Cabinet and Chair Makers of Philadelphia. He died in Philadelphia and was buried in Christ Church Graveyard.

GRAESSL, Lawrence: clergyman

Born Ruemannsfelden, Germany, August 18, 1753; son of Lorenz Graessl; died circa October 12, 1793.

After his ordination as a Roman Catholic priest, Graessl engaged in tutoring and in parochial duties in Munich, Germany. Urged to come to Philadelphia by Father Ferdinand Farmer, he arrived in that city in 1787 and was appointed assistant at St. Mary's Church. The next year he became curate.

Graessl served as a missionary throughout Pennsylvania, Delaware, and New Jersey, and represented Philadelphia at the First Provincial Synod in Baltimore in 1791. Bishop Carroll recommended Graessl as his successor, but the appointment did not come through until after the latter's death. He died during the yellow fever epidemic in Philadelphia in 1793 and was buried in St. Joseph's Church there.

GRATZ, Bernard: merchant

Born Langensdorf, Upper Silesia, 1738; son of Soloman Gratz; married Richea Myers, December 10, 1760; father of two children (including Rachel); died April 20, 1801.

Gratz came to Philadelphia in 1754 and was employed by David Franks in a fur trading operation until 1758, when he formed a partnership with Benjamin M. Clava. The next year he began to conduct the business by himself. With his brother Michael, he became a partner in the firm of B. & M. Gratz. In 1765 he signed the non-importation resolutions, which were a protest by the merchants of Philadelphia against the Stamp Act.

Gratz was the first recorded president of the Mickveh Israel Congregation and laid the cornerstone of the first synagogue in Philadelphia in 1782. Throughout his life he fought for the rights of Jewish people in Pennsylvania. He died in Baltimore, Maryland.

GRATZ, Michael: merchant

Born Langensdorf, Upper Silesia, 1740; son of Soloman Gratz; married Miriam Simon, June 20, 1769; father of twelve children (including Rebecca); died September 8, 1811.

Gratz emigrated to London, England, where he became an apprentice in the counting house of his cousin Solomon Henry; he entered the firm in 1756. Two years later he came to Philadelphia, was employed by David Franks, and later entered into partnership with his brother Bernard. The firm, B. & M. Gratz, secured great tracts of land in Virginia, Western Pennsylvania, Ohio, Indiana, and Illinois through the influence of Michael's father-in-law. Michael also operated a steamboat line from Pittsburgh. During the American Revolution he moved to Virginia, where he continued his business until 1798. After his death he was buried in Old Cemetery on Spruce Street in Philadelphia.

GRAYDON, Alexander: author

Born Bristol, Pennsylvania, April 10, 1752; son of Alexander and Rachel (Marks) Graydon; married Miss Wood, 1778; second marriage to Theodosia Pettit, December 16, 1799; died May 2, 1818.

Graydon was forced by his father to study law but was more interested in poetry and metaphysics. At the outbreak of the American Revolution he joined the volunteers in Philadelphia and was shocked by the punishment of Loyalists. In 1776 he was commissioned a captain, saw action under General Philip Schuyler at Lake George, and covered George Washington's retreat from Long Island to New York. The following year he was taken prisoner at the Battle of Harlem Heights but was paroled and returned to Philadelphia later the same year.

In 1785 Graydon moved to Harrisburg, Pennsylvania. He participated in the Pennsylvania Convention which ratified the United States Constitution in 1789. As well as contributing many articles to John Fenno's *Gazette,* he wrote one of the most valuable historical sources of the period, *Memoirs of a Life, Chiefly Passed in Pennsylvania within the Last Sixty Years; with Occasional Remarks upon the General Occurrences, Character, and Spirit of the Eventful Period* (1811).

GREGG, Andrew: senator
Born Carlisle, Pennsylvania, June 10, 1755; son of Andrew and Jane (Scott) Gregg; married Martha Potter, January 29, 1787; died May 20, 1835.

Gregg was a tutor at the College of Philadelphia (now the University of Pennsylvania) from 1779 until 1783. A Republican, he was elected to the 2nd through the 9th congresses of the United States House of Representatives (1791–1807). Switching to the Constitutionalist party, he was appointed to a term (1809–13) in the United States Senate, serving as president pro tem in the years 1809–10.

After a period as president of the Centre Bank in Bellefonte, Pennsylvania (1814–20), Gregg served as secretary of the Commonwealth of Pennsylvania from 1820 until 1823. He died in Bellefonte at the age of seventy-nine and was buried in Union Cemetery there.

GREW, Theophilus: mathematician
No record of birth; married Elizabeth Cusins, 1735; second marriage to Frances Bowen, 1739; third marriage to Rebecca Richards, 1747; died 1759.

Grew published widely circulated almanacs during the years 1732–57 in New York City, Philadelphia, Annapolis, and Williamsburg (Virginia). He also was employed as headmaster of the Kent County (Maryland) Public School from 1740 to 1742, then conducted a private school in Philadelphia for the study of mathematics from 1742 to 1750. In the latter year he was a consultant for the state of Pennsylvania in a survey determining the Pennsylvania-Maryland boundary. Also in 1750 he was appointed the first professor of mathematics at the College and Academy of Philadelphia. He died in Philadelphia nine years later.

GRIFFIN, Isaac: congressman
Born Kent County, Delaware, February 27, 1756; died October 12, 1827.

Griffin attended public schools and then engaged in agriculture in Fayette County, Pennsylvania. During the Revolutionary War he was commissioned a captain. He accepted an appointment as justice of the peace in 1794. A Democrat, on February 16, 1813, he filled a vacancy in the United States House of Representatives (13th Congress); he was subsequently elected to the 14th Congress and served until 1817. He died on his estate in Nicholson Township, Pennsylvania, and was buried in Nicholson Township.

★★★★★

HALL, David: printer
Born Edinburgh, Scotland, 1714; married Mary Lacock, January 7, 1748; died December 23, 1772.

After learning the printing trade in London, England, Hall came to Philadelphia as a journeyman in the office of Benjamin Franklin in 1743. Five years later he and Franklin entered into a partnership. In 1766 he became the sole owner of the firm, although he later took in a partner. He died in

Philadelphia and was buried in the Christ Church Graveyard there.

HAMILTON, James: lawyer, mayor, colonial government official

Born Assomac County, Virginia, circa 1710; son of Andrew and Ann (Brown) Preeson Hamilton; died August 14, 1783.

Hamilton was a prothonotary of the Pennsylvania Supreme Court in 1733, then served from 1734 to 1739 as a member of the Pennsylvania Assembly. He was mayor of Philadelphia in 1745. He was the first subscriber to The Philadelphia Contributionship for the Insurance of Houses from Loss by Fire, the first insurance company in America. He served in the Pennsylvania Provincial Council in 1734 and from 1745 to 1747.

Lieutenant governor of Pennsylvania from 1748 to 1754 and from 1759 to 1763, Hamilton served as acting governor of the state in 1771 and again in 1773. In those same two years he was also president of the Pennsylvania Council. During his service as lieutenant governor, he disputed constantly with the Assembly concerning such matters as defense and Indian affairs.

Hamilton did not favor the patriot cause during the Revolutionary War, but he was not an avowed Loyalist. However, he was arrested in 1777 and imprisoned for nearly a year. He died in New York City.

HAND, Edward: physician, army officer, Continental congressman

Born King's County, Ireland, December 31, 1744; son of John Hand; married Catharine Ewing, March 13, 1775; died September 3, 1802.

Hand was educated at Trinity College and served as a surgeon's mate in the British Navy before coming to Philadelphia in 1767. He was lieutenant colonel of a brigade under General William Thompson of the Continental Army in 1775, and took part in the siege of Boston and the battles of Long Island, Trenton, and Princeton. He was a member of the Lancaster County Associa- tors, a group of colonial riflemen, in 1776. The following year he was commissioned a brigadier general. He became a brevet major general in the Pennsylvania militia in 1783.

In 1784–85 Hand was a member of the Continental Congress, representing Pennsylvania, and in 1785–86 he served in the Pennsylvania Assembly. A presidential elector in 1789, he was also a member of the Pennsylvania Constitutional Convention until 1790. He was a major general of the provisional United States Army in 1798, and from 1791 to 1801 he was federal inspector of revenue. He died at "Rockford," in Lancaster, Pennsylvania.

HARMAR, Josiah: army officer

Born Philadelphia, Pennsylvania, November 10, 1753; married Sarah Jenkins, October 19, 1784; died August 20, 1813.

Harmar served as a major in the 3rd Pennsylvania Regiment in 1776, and the following year he became a lieutenant colonel in the 6th Pennsylvania Regiment. He served in the Continental Army under Washington from 1778 to 1780 and in Greene's division in the South in 1781–82. He was commissioned a colonel in 1783.

After the war Harmar became Indian agent for the Northwest Territory; in 1785 he took part in the Treaty of Fort McIntosh. Two years later he was commissioned a brigadier general. In 1790 he commanded an expedition against the Miami Indians which was not entirely successful. A court of inquiry was held, but it did not find against him.

Harmar was adjutant general of Pennsylvania from 1793 to 1799. He died in Philadelphia.

HARRIS, John: trader

Born Harris Ferry, Pennsylvania, 1726; son of John and Esther (Say) Harris; married Elizabeth McClure; died July 29, 1791.

In 1748 Harris became proprietor of an Indian trading post. He was a leader in protecting the frontier settlements in Pennsylvania from Indian attack. He built a stockade at his trading post at Paxtang on the Susquehanna during the French and Indian War and maintained close relations with the Indian tribes of the Six Nations.

Harris established the town of Harrisburg, Pennsylvania, which soon afterward became the county seat of Dauphin County, Pennsylvania, and later became the state capital. He died in Harrisburg and was buried there.

HARTLEY, Thomas: congressman

Born Colebrookdale Township, Pennsylvania, September 7, 1748; son of George Hartley; married Catherine Holtzinger; died December 21, 1800.

Hartley was admitted to the Pennsylvania bar at the age of twenty-one, and later (1791) became the first Pennsylvania lawyer to be admitted to the United States Supreme Court bar. He was a deputy to the Pennsylvania provincial conferences in Philadelphia in 1774 and 1775. In 1776 he was elected lieutenant colonel of the 6th Battalion of the Pennsylvania Regiment of the Continental Army and commanded a Pennsylvania brigade in 1777.

From 1783 to 1784 Hartley was a member of the Pennsylvania Council of Censors. A Federalist, he was a delegate from Pennsylvania to the United States House of Representatives from 1789 until his death eleven years later, in York, Pennsylvania. He was buried in St. John's Churchyard in York.

HAZELWOOD, John: naval officer

Born England, circa 1726; married Mary Edgar, August 10, 1753; second marriage to Esther Fleeson; died March 1, 1800.

After coming to Pennsylvania, Hazelwood was put in command of various merchant ships. He was appointed to the Pennsylvania Committee of Safety in charge of the construction of warships, floating batteries, and fire rafts in 1775. In 1776 he was superintendent of a fleet of rafts. He was a commodore in the Pennsylvania Navy in 1777, rising to full command of the navy

later that same year. He successfully defended the fleet against the British in the Port of Philadelphia.

In 1780 Hazelwood was commander of purchases for the Continental Army in Philadelphia and receiver of provisions for the Pennsylvania militia. In 1785 he was port warden of Philadelphia. He was owner or part owner of vessels engaged in foreign trade and a founder of the St. George Society in Philadelphia. He died in that city.

HELMUTH, Justus Henry Christian: clergyman

Born Helmstedt, Germany, May 16, 1745; son of Johann Christoph and Justina Helmuth; married Maria Barbara Keppele; father of five children; died February 5, 1825.

Helmuth, who attended the University of Halle in Germany, emigrated to America in 1769 to become pastor of the Lutheran Church in Lancaster, Pennsylvania. Ten years later he moved to Philadelphia, where he became co-pastor of St. Michael's and Zion's in Philadelphia, a position he held for forty-one years. In 1812 he founded the *Evangelisches Magazin,* the first Lutheran church paper in the United States. He was the author of *Empfindungen des Herzens in einigen Liedern,* 1781; *Denkmal der Liebe und Achtung, Welches seiner Hochwürden dem Herrn D. Heinrich Melchior Mühlenberg . . . ist Gesetzet Worden,* 1788; and *Etliche Kirchenlieder,* 1809. He died at the age of seventy-nine.

HENDEL, John William: clergyman

Born Durkheim, Germany, November 20, 1740; son of Johann Jacob and Anna Sybilla (Otten) Hendel; married Elizabeth Le Roy, 1766; father of William; died September 19, 1798.

Hendel was a student at the University of Heidelberg in Germany from 1759 to 1762. He was sent to Pennsylvania by the Synods of Holland in 1764. He held several pastorates: Lancaster, Pennsylvania, 1765–69, 1782–94; Tulpehocken, Pennsylvania, 1769–82; Philadelphia, 1794–98. He was president of Coetus in 1768, 1779, 1789, and

1791, and vice president of Franklin College from 1787 to 1794. He was a leader in the movement that resulted in the separation from the Dutch Synods and the organization of the Synod of the United States in 1793. He died in Philadelphia during the 1798 yellow fever epidemic and was buried in Franklin Square.

HENRY, William: gunsmith, Continental congressman, inventor

Born West Cain Township, Pennsylvania, May 19, 1729; son of John and Elizabeth (DeVinne) Henry; married Ann Wood, January 1755; father of seven children (including William and Joseph); died December 15, 1786.

At the age of fifteen, Henry went to Lancaster, Pennsylvania, and was apprenticed to a gunsmith. He formed a partnership with Joseph Simon for the making of firearms, and they became the principal armorers of the colonial troops during the French and Indian War.

In 1761 Henry went on a business trip to England and learned from James Watt about his steam engine. He came to be the pioneer of steam propulsion in America and gave advice and assistance to Robert Fulton and Benjamin West in their youth. In 1762–63 he built the first sternwheel steamboat. He is also credited with the invention of a screw auger and the perfection of a steam-heating system.

Henry had a long political career, beginning in 1758 with his appointment as a justice of the peace. He was assistant burgess of Lancaster from 1765 to 1775, a delegate to the Pennsylvania Assembly in 1776, and a member of the Pennsylvania Council of Safety in 1777. From 1777 to 1786 he was treasurer of Lancaster County. In 1784 he was elected by the Assembly to the Continental Congress. From 1775 to 1781 he was assistant commissary general and disbursing officer of the United States Government for the District of Lancaster. He died in Lancaster.

HIESTER, Daniel: congressman

Born Upper Salford Township, Pennsylvania, June 25, 1747; son of Daniel and Catharine (Schuler) Hiester; married Rosanna Hager, 1770; died March 7, 1804.

At the age of twenty-seven Hiester became the manager of his father's farm and tannery and also his father-in-law's estate. From 1778 to 1781 he was a member of the Pennsylvania Assembly. He was commissioned a colonel and brigadier general in the Pennsylvania militia in 1782, and served in the Revolutionary War. From 1784 to 1786 he was a member of the Supreme Council of Pennsylvania, and the following year he was commissioner for Connecticut land claims. He served Pennsylvania in the United States House of Representatives during the 1st–4th congresses (1789–96); he served Maryland during the 7th and 8th congresses (1801–04). He died in Washington, D.C., and was buried in Zion Reformed Graveyard, Hagerstown, Maryland.

HIESTER, John: congressman

Born Goshenhoppen, Pennsylvania, April 9, 1745; died October 15, 1821.

Hiester, who attended common schools, was engaged in the lumbering business in Berne Township, Pennsylvania. He served as a captain in the Pennsylvania militia during the Revolutionary War. He served Pennsylvania in the United States House of Representatives during the 10th Congress (1807–09). He died in Goshenhoppen and was buried in the Union Church Cemetery in Parker Ford, Pennsylvania.

HIESTER, Joseph: governor of Pennsylvania

Born Berks County, Pennsylvania, November 18, 1752; son of John and Mary (Epler) Hiester; married Elizabeth Whitman, 1771; died June 10, 1832.

Hiester was a delegate to the Provincial Conference in Philadelphia in 1776. That same year he served as a colonel in the Continental Army and commanded a company in Colonel Henry Haller's battalion in the

Battle of Long Island. The following year he was promoted to lieutenant colonel.

From 1780 to 1790 Hiester was a member of the Pennsylvania Assembly, and for the next four years he was a Pennsylvania Senator. In 1792 and in 1796, he was a presidential elector. He served as a Pennsylvania delegate to the United States House of Representatives during the 5th–8th congresses (1797–1805) and the 14th–16th congresses (1815–December 1820). From 1820 to 1825 he was governor of Pennsylvania.

Hiester died at the age of seventy-nine and was buried in the Charles Evans Cemetery in Reading, Pennsylvania.

HILLEGAS, Michael: merchant, treasurer of the United States

Born Philadelphia, Pennsylvania, April 22, 1729; son of Michael and Margaret Hillegas; married Henrietta Boude, May 10, 1753; father of ten children; died September 29, 1804.

From 1765 to 1775 Hillegas was a member of the Provincial Assembly of Pennsylvania. In 1776 he served as treasurer of the Province of Pennsylvania and treasurer of the Continental Congress. He contributed a large part of his fortune to the support of the American Revolution. From 1777 to 1789 he was the treasurer of the United States. One of the first subscribers to the Bank of North America, he formed the Lehigh Coal Mining Company. From 1793 to 1804 he was an alderman of Philadelphia. He was also a member of the American Philosophical Society. He died in Philadelphia.

HOGE, John: congressman

Born near Hogestown, Pennsylvania, September 10, 1760; died August 4, 1824.

Hoge served in the Revolutionary War as an ensign in the 9th Pennsylvania Regiment. At the age of twenty-two, with his brother William, he founded the town of Washington, Pennsylvania. In 1790 he was a delegate to the Pennsylvania Constitutional Convention, and from 1790 to 1795 he served in the Pennsylvania Senate. A Democrat, he

served Pennsylvania in the United States House of Representatives from November 2, 1804, until the end of the congressional term. He died in Meadow Lands, near Washington, Pennsylvania, and was buried in City Cemetery in Washington.

HOLLENBACK, Matthias: merchant, jurist

Born Lancaster (now Lebanon) County, Pennsylvania, February 17, 1752; son of John and Eleanor (Jones) Hollenback; married; father of three daughters and one son (George Matson); died February 18, 1829.

At the age of seventeen, Hollenback went to Wyoming Valley, Pennsylvania. He was commissioned an ensign in the 24th Regiment of the Connecticut militia in 1775, and was appointed an ensign in Captain Durkee's Company of Wyoming Minutemen the following year. He served in the battles of Millstone, Brandywine, and Germantown. After establishing trading posts and acquiring land, he became one of the largest landowners in the Susquehanna Valley. In 1787 he was commanding justice of the peace and a justice in the Court of Common Pleas. For the last thirty-eight years of his life he was an associate judge of the Pennsylvania Supreme Court.

HOPKINSON, Francis: Continental congressman

Born Philadelphia, Pennsylvania, October 2, 1737; son of Thomas and Mary (Johnson) Hopkinson; married Ann Borden, September 1, 1768; father of Joseph; died May 9, 1791.

Hopkinson began the study of the harpsichord at the age of seventeen and gave his first public performance at the age of twenty. He later set poems and psalms to music, and in 1759 he became the first native American to compose secular songs. In 1757 he was awarded the first diploma (an A.B.) granted by the College of Philadelphia, receiving an A.M. from that school three years later and an honorary degree from the College of New Jersey (now Princeton) in 1763.

In 1775 Hopkinson was admitted to both the Pennsylvania and the New Jersey bars, and he practiced in Philadelphia and Bordentown, New Jersey. He was appointed collector of customs for the Port of Salem, New Jersey, in 1763, and for the Port of New Castle, Delaware, in 1772. He was a member of the New Jersey Governor's Council in 1774, and from 1774 to 1776 he served in the New Jersey Provincial Congress. A member of the Continental Congress in 1776, he was a signer of the Declaration of Independence.

From 1776 to 1778 Hopkinson was a member of the Continental Navy Board. He was treasurer of the Continental Loan Office from 1778 to 1781 and served as judge of the admiralty for Pennsylvania in 1779, 1780, and 1787. He attended the 1787 Pennsylvania Convention which ratified the United States Constitution. From 1789 to 1791 he was a judge in the United States District Court for Eastern Pennsylvania. In 1789 he was secretary for the convention which organized the Protestant Episcopal Church.

Hopkinson also served the fledgling nation as a graphic designer. In 1770 he was a member of the committee that designed the seal of the American Philosophical Society. In 1776 he was one of the designers of the Great Seal of New Jersey, and the following year he designed the American Flag. In 1782 he prepared a seal for the University of the State of Pennsylvania.

Hopkinson was the author of several works: "A Prophecy" (an essay which predicted that America would declare independence); "Letter to Lord Howe," 1777; "A Letter Written by a Foreigner," 1777; "An Answer to General Burgoyne's Proclamation," 1777; and "Letter to Joseph Galloway," 1778. The latter year he also wrote "The Battle of the Kegs," which was his most effective and popular verse. In 1757–58 he was a contributor of poetry and essays to *America Magazine*; in 1775–76, he contributed to *Pennsylvania Magazine*. He was the composer of *Seven Songs,* the first book of music published by an American composer, in 1788.

Hopkinson died in Philadelphia and was buried in the Christ Church Burial Ground there.

HOSETTER, Jacob: congressman
Born near York, Pennsylvania, May 9, 1754; died June 29, 1831.

Hosetter was a pioneer in the manufacture of the tall eight-day clock. From 1797 to 1802 he was a member of the Pennsylvania General Assembly. A Democrat, he was a Pennsylvania delegate to the 15th–16th congresses of the United States House of Representatives, serving from November 16, 1818, to 1821. He died in Columbiana, Ohio.

HUMPHREYS, Charles: Continental congressman
Born Haverford, Pennsylvania, September 19, 1714; died March 11, 1786.

A Quaker, Humphreys was engaged in milling for much of his life. He served in the Pennsylvania Provincial Congress from 1764 to 1774 and in the Continental Congress, representing Pennsylvania, from 1774 to 1776. He died in Haverford and was buried in the Old Haverford Meeting House Cemetery.

HUMPHREYS, James: printer
Born Philadelphia, Pennsylvania, January 15, 1748; son of James and Susanna (Assheton) Humphreys; married Mary Yorke; died February 2, 1810.

Humphreys attended the College of Philadelphia in 1763–64, engaging in the study of medicine. After an apprenticeship to the printer William Bradford, he began his own printing house in 1770. Three years later he published Wettenhall's *Greek Grammar,* the first Greek text published in the colonies. He founded *The Pennsylvania Ledger,* which he published in 1775–76 and again in 1777–78. He then moved to the Loyalist colony at Shelburne, Nova Scotia, Canada, where he established the *Nova Scotia Packet* and engaged as a merchant from 1780 to 1797. He then returned to Philadelphia as a printer. He died in Philadelphia and was buried in the Christ Church Burial Ground there.

HUMPHREYS, Joshua: ship-builder

Born Haverford, Pennsylvania, June 17, 1751; son of Joshua and Sara (Williams) Humphreys; married Mary Davids; father of eleven children; died January 12, 1838.

Humphreys began his career as an apprentice to a ship carpenter in Philadelphia. He later became the owner of a shipyard and built many ships for the Continental Navy. One of his suggestions led to America's decision to build super-frigates of the Constitution class. He was appointed naval constructor to the new United States Government, serving from 1794 to 1801. He built government docks and wharfs in 1806. He died at the age of eighty-seven.

HUNT, Isaac: writer, clergyman

Born Bridgetown, Barbados, West Indies, circa 1742; son of Isaac Hunt; married Mary Shewell, June 17, 1767; father of one son; died 1809.

Hunt graduated from the Philadelphia Academy in 1763, later (1771) receiving an M.A. In 1764 he published *A Letter from a Gentleman in Transilvania* under the pseudonym Isaac Bickerstaff. The following year he published a series of satires, including "The Substance of the Exercise Had This Morning in Scurrility Hall."

Circa 1768 Hunt was admitted to the Pennsylvania bar. An opponent of colonial independence, in 1775 he escaped to England, where he was ordained to the ministry of the Anglican Church. While in England he wrote *The Political Family,* 1775, and *Rights of Englishmen: An Antidote to the Poison now Vending by . . . Thomas Paine,* 1779.

HUTCHINSON, James: physician, educator

Born Wakefield Township, Pennsylvania, January 29, 1752; son of Randall and Catherine (Rickey)
Hutchinson; married Lydia Biddle; second marriage to Sidney Evans Howell; died September 5, 1793.

Hutchinson studied medicine under Dr. John Fothergill in London, England, returning to America in 1777 to join the Continental Army as a surgeon. He later became surgeon general of Pennsylvania, serving from 1778 to 1784. He was a member of the Philadelphia Committee of Safety in 1788. From 1779 to 1781 he was a trustee of the University of Pennsylvania, later serving as a professor of chemistry, 1791 to 1793. He was an incorporator of the College of Physicians in Philadelphia and a member of the American Philosophical Society. He died at the age of forty-one.

★★★★★

INGERSOLL, Jared: jurist

Born New Haven, Connecticut, October 27, 1749; son of Jared and Hannah (Whiting) Ingersoll; married Elizabeth Pettit, December 6, 1781; father of Charles Jared and Joseph Reed; died October 31, 1822.

Ingersoll graduated from Yale in 1766 and was admitted to the Philadelphia bar in 1773. He was also admitted to the Middle Temple in London, England, the latter year. He was a member of the Continental Congress in 1780, a delegate to the Federal Convention of 1787, and a member of the Philadelphia Common Council in 1789. He was admitted to the United States Supreme Court bar in 1791.

As attorney general of Pennsylvania from 1790 to 1799, he pleaded *Chisholm vs. Georgia* (1792) and *Hylton vs. the United States* (1796) before the Supreme Court; the latter case was the first to involve the constitutionality of an act of Congress. He was city solicitor for Philadelphia from 1798 to 1801 and also United States district attorney for Pennsylvania in 1800–01.

Ingersoll was nominated for vice president of the United States by the Pennsylvania Federalists in 1811. Later that year he again acceded to the office of attorney general of Pennsylvania, serving until 1817. He was presiding judge of the District Court for the city and county of Philadelphia during 1821 and 1822. He died in Philadelphia.

IRVINE, James: army officer

Born Philadelphia, Pennsylvania, August 4, 1735; son of George and Mary (Rush) Irvine; died April 28, 1819.

Irvine was commissioned an ensign in the 1st Battalion of the Pennsylvania Provincial Regiment in 1760, rising to captain in 1763 and to lieutenant colonel in 1775. The latter year he was also a delegate to the Provincial Conference in Philadelphia. The following year he was commissioned a colonel in charge of the 9th Pennsylvania Regiment. As a commissioned brigadier general of the Pennsylvania militia in 1777, he was given command of the 2nd Brigade. He commanded the right flank of the American line at the Battle of Germantown. From 1782 to 1793 he was a major general in the Pennsylvania militia.

Irvine, a Constitutionalist, was a member of the Supreme Executive Council of Pennsylvania from 1782 to 1785, serving as vice president the latter two years of his term. He was a member of the Pennsylvania Assembly in 1785 and 1786. He was later a member of the Pennsylvania Senate (1795–99). He died in Philadelphia.

IRVINE, William: army officer, congressman

Born Enniskillen, Ulster Province, Ireland, November 3, 1741; married Anne Calender; children include Calender, Colonel William N., and Captain Armstrong; died July 29, 1804.

Irvine was educated at Trinity College, Dublin, Ireland. After serving as a surgeon on a British ship of war during the Seven Years' War, he journeyed to America (1763). He was a member of the Pennsylvania Provincial Convention in Philadelphia in 1774. Two years later he was commissioned a colonel in the 6th (and later in the 7th) Pennsylvania Regiment, participating in the Bat-

tle of Three Rivers that year. In 1779 he was commissioned a brigadier general in the Continental Army. The following year he participated in Lord Stirling's expedition against Staten Island and also in the unsuccessful attack at Bull's Ferry with General Wayne.

A delegate from Pennsylvania to the Continental Congress from 1786 to 1788, he also attended the Pennsylvania Constitutional Convention of 1790. He was a member of the United States House of Representatives during the 3rd Congress (December 2, 1793 to 1795). From 1801 to 1804 he was president of the Pennsylvania branch of the Society of the Cincinnati. He died in Philadelphia.

★★★★★

JACKSON, David: physician, Continental congressman

Born Oxford, Pennsylvania, circa 1747; son of Samuel Jackson; married Jane (Mather) Jackson, 1768; second marriage to Susanna Kemper; father of nine children (including David and Samuel); died September 17, 1801.

Jackson earned a B.M. from the College of Philadelphia in 1768 and soon after began to practice medicine in Philadelphia. The Continental Congress appointed him to manage the lottery for the army in 1776 and 1777. In 1779 he served briefly as a surgeon and quartermaster general in the Pennsylvania militia and then joined the medical staff of the Philadelphia General Hospital, remaining until 1780. In 1785 he served as a Philadelphia delegate to the Continental Congress.

In 1789 Jackson became a trustee of the University of the State of Pennsylvania (which merged with the College of Philadelphia in 1791 to become the University of Pennsylvania), serving in that position until 1801. He joined the American Philosophical Society in 1792 and helped organize the first Democratic Society in America the following year. In 1801 he was elected an alderman of the city of Philadelphia and served in that office until his death later in the year.

JACKSON, William: army officer, secretary to the President of the United States

Born Cumberland, England, May 9, 1759; married Elizabeth Willing, November 11, 1795; died December 18, 1828.

In 1778 Jackson served as a lieutenant in the expedition against St. Augustine, Florida. He later rose to the rank of major and served as an aide to General Benjamin Lincoln. From 1782 to 1784 he was assistant secretary of war. He was secretary of the United States Constitutional Convention in Philadelphia in 1787 and was admitted to the Pennsylvania bar the following year.

From 1789 to 1791 Jackson served as secretary to President George Washington. Later he was appointed surveyor of customs at Philadelphia, which office he held from 1796 to 1801. From 1800 to 1828 he was secretary of the Society of the Cincinnati. In 1801 he founded the *Political and Commerce Register*, serving as its editor for sixteen years.

Jackson died in Philadelphia and was buried in Christ Church Cemetery there.

JACOBS, Israel: congressman

Born near Perkiomen Creek, Pennsylvania, June 9, 1726; died circa December 1796.

Jacobs, who attended public schools, engaged in farming and the mercantile business. A member of the Pennsylvania Colonial Assembly from 1770 to 1774, he was one of the first to advocate the union of the colonies. During the American Revolution he was delegated to distribute aid to the families of poor soldiers. He served in the United States House of Representatives during the 2nd Congress (1791–93). He died in Providence Township, Pennsylvania; it is believed that he was buried in the graveyard of the Friends Meeting House there.

JENNINGS, John: army officer, jurist

Born probably Philadelphia, Pennsylvania, circa 1738; probably the son of Solomon Jennings; died January 14, 1802.

Jennings was sheriff of Northampton County, Pennsylvania, at various times during the period 1761–78. He achieved prominence in the Pennamite War by ejecting Connecticut settlers from the Wyoming Valley. In 1783 he became a private in the 3rd Regiment of the Continental Army and the following year was elected quartermaster of the 1st Company, 2nd Battalion, of the Northampton County militia.

After moving to Philadelphia, Jennings became secretary (or clerk) of the Mutual Assurance Company. In 1791 he became clerk to the commissioners of bankrupts in Philadelphia. Three years later he was chosen deputy United States marshal for the District of Pennsylvania. In 1796, as well as being elected an alderman, he became an associate justice in the Mayor's Court in Philadelphia, a position he held until his death in 1802.

JONES, David: clergyman

Born New Castle County, Delaware, May 12, 1736; son of Morgan and Eleanor (Evans) Jones; married Anne Stillwell, February 22, 1762; died February 5, 1820.

Jones, after attending Hopewell Academy in New Jersey circa 1757–58, was licensed to preach by the Baptist Church in New Jersey in 1761. He was ordained to the Baptist ministry in 1766 and from that year until 1775 served as pastor of a church in Freehold, New Jersey. In 1775 Jones moved to Great Valley Baptist Church in Chester County, Pennsylvania, where he served until 1786. He then became pastor of the Southampton Baptist Church in Bucks County, Pennsylvania, but returned to the Great Valley Church in 1792, remaining there until his death.

During his first stay in Chester County, Jones was an outspoken colonial patriot and served as chaplain of Anthony Wayne's division of Pennsylvania troops from 1776 to

1783. He was also a chaplain to Pennsylvania servicemen during the War of 1812.

Jones wrote *A Journal of Two Visits Made to . . . Indians on the Ohio River* (1774) and *The Doctrine of Laying on the Hands Examined and Vindicated* (1786). He died in Chester County and was buried in the cemetery of the church he had long served, the Great Valley Church.

JONES, John: physician

Born Jamaica, Long Island, New York, 1729; son of Dr. Evan and Mary (Stephenson) Jones; died June 23, 1791.

Jones, a 1751 graduate of the University of Rheims (France), was professor of surgery and obstetrics at King's College (now Columbia) from 1767 to 1776. In 1771 he cofounded (with Dr. S. Bard) the New York Hospital and was an attending physician there. He was an organizer of the Medical Department of the Continental Army. In 1780 he became an attending physician at the Pennsylvania Hospital and in 1790 attended President Washington in Philadelphia.

In 1787 Jones became the first vice president of the College of Physicians of Philadelphia and later served as president of the Humane Society. He wrote the first surgical textbook to appear in the American colonies, *Plain, Concise, Practical Remarks on the Treatment of Wounds and Fractures, Designed for the Use of Young Military Surgeons of America* (1775) and translated Van Swieten's *Diseases Incident to Armies.* He died in Philadelphia.

JONES, William: secretary of the navy, congressman

Born Philadelphia, Pennsylvania, 1760; died September 16, 1831.

During the Revolutionary War, Jones served with the Continental Army, participating in the battles of Trenton (1776) and Princeton (1777). After serving as a third lieutenant on the ship *St. James,* in 1781 he was commissioned a first lieutenant in the United States Navy.

Jones was a delegate from Pennsylvania to the United States House of Representatives during the 7th Congress (1801–03). During the years 1813–14 he was secretary of the navy under President Madison. He also served as president of the Bank of the United States from 1816 to 1819 and as collector of customs of Philadelphia from 1827 to 1829. He died in Bethlehem, Pennsylvania, and was buried in St. Peter's Churchyard in Philadelphia.

★★★★★

KINNERSLEY, Ebenezer: educator, electrical experimenter

Born Gloucester, England, November 30, 1711; son of William Kinnersley; married Sarah Duffield, 1739; father of two children; died July 4, 1778.

Kinnersley's family came to America in 1714. In 1743 he was ordained to the ministry of the Baptist Church. He was associated with Benjamin Franklin, Edward Duffield, Philip Synge, and Thomas Hopkins in experiments with electrical fire. His rediscovery of Dr. DuFaye's two contrary electricities of glass and sulphur led to the verification of the positive-negative theory of electricity. He delivered the first recorded experimental lectures on electricity in Faneuil Hall in Boston in 1751.

Kinnersley was elected chief master of the College of Philadelphia in 1753 and served the school as professor of English and oratory from 1755 to 1773. In 1755 he demonstrated that heat could be produced by electricity and invented the electrical air thermometer. Two years later the College of Philadelphia awarded him an honorary M.A. He was a member of the American Philosophical Society. He died in Philadelphia.

KLINE, George: editor, publisher

Born Germany, circa 1757; married Rebecca Weiss; father of eleven children; died November 12, 1800.

Kline worked as a printer in Philadelphia, having come to America at an early age. In 1785 he moved to Carlisle, Pennsylvania, where he started the Federalist weekly *The Carlisle Gazette and the Western Repository of Knowledge,* which approached the news from the frontiersman's point of view. The paper was published until 1817 and was then absorbed by the *Carlisle Spirit of the Times.* He also published Isaac Watt's *Scripture History* (1797) and John Brown's *Westminster Assembly of Divines.* He died in Carlisle.

KUHN, Adam: physician, botanist

Born Germantown, Pennsylvania, November 17, 1741; son of Adam Simon and Anna (Schrack) Kuhn; married Elizabeth Hartman, 1780; father of two children; died July 5, 1817.

Kuhn received an M.D. from the University of Edinburgh in 1767 and became professor of materia medica and botany at the College of Philadelphia (now the University of Pennsylvania) the next year, thus making him the first professor of botany in the American colonies. He remained with the school until 1789, also serving as physician at the Pennsylvania Hospital from 1775 to 1798 and as a consulting physician at the Philadelphia Dispensary in 1786.

In 1787 Kuhn helped found the College of Physicians of Philadelphia, later (1808) becoming president. In 1789 he became professor of the theory and practice of medicine at the University of the State of Pennsylvania. Later, from 1792 to 1797, he was professor of the practice of physics there. He was a member of the American Philosophical Society. The herb *Kuhnia eupatorioides* is named after him. He died in Philadelphia.

KUNZE, John Christopher: clergyman, educator

Born Artern, Saxony, August 5, 1744; married Margaretta Henrietta Mühlenberg, July 23, 1771; father of five children; died July 24, 1807.

Kunze graduated from the University of Leipzig in Germany circa 1767, then taught school in Germany until 1770, when he was called to Philadelphia as co-adjutator to Henry Melchior Mühlenberg. He was ordained to the ministry of the Lutheran Church the same year, and he eventually became the second leading American Lutheran of his time. His primary interest was in teaching English to all Lutheran ministers, because he foresaw that English would become the language of the church.

In 1773 Kunze started a pretheological school in Philadelphia which was closed at the beginning of the American Revolution. In 1779 he attempted unsuccessfully to establish a German Institute at the University of Pennsylvania. After a period as chief pastor of Philadelphia (1779–84), he served as pastor of Christ Church in New York City (1784–1807).

Taking up educational activities again, Kunze was professor of Oriental languages at Columbia from 1784 to 1787 and again from 1792 to 1799. He also was professor of theology from 1797 until his death. He wrote *Rudiments of the Shorter Catechism of Luther* (1785) and *A Hymn and Prayer Book for the Use of Such Churches As Use the English Language* (1795).

★★★★★

LACEY, John: army officer, public official

Born Buckingham, Pennsylvania, February 4, 1755; son of John and Jane (Chapman) Lacey; married Anastasia Reynolds, January 18, 1781; father of four children; died February 17, 1814.

In 1776 Lacey was commissioned captain of a volunteer company; later he organized a company in Bucks County, Pennsylvania. He served with the 4th Pennsylvania Regiment in the Canadian campaign of 1776. The next year he was commissioned lieutenant colonel of the Bucks County militia, gaining a promotion to brigadier general in 1778. During the war he also served as a sub-lieutenant and as a commissioner of confiscated estates for Bucks County.

Lacey was also active in politics during the war era. He represented Bucks County in the Pennsylvania Assembly in 1778, was a member of the Provincial Council of Pennsylvania from 1779 to 1781, and served on the Pennsylvania Supreme Executive Council from 1779 to 1782.

Lacey was appointed a justice of the peace in 1801. He also served as a member of the New Jersey Assembly. He died in New Mills, New Jersey.

LEAMING, Thomas: army officer

Born Cape May County, New Jersey, September 1, 1748; son of Thomas and Elizabeth (Leaming) Leaming; married Rebecca Fisher, August 19, 1779; father of at least two sons (Thomas Fisher and Jeromiah Fisher); died October 29, 1797.

Leaming read law under John Dickinson and was later admitted to the Philadelphia bar. In 1776 he organized a militia in Cape May County; that year he was also a member of the New Jersey Provincial Assembly. He fought at Princeton, Trenton, Germantown, and Brandywine. In 1777 he founded the firm of Bunner, Murray and Company. Another company, Thomas Leaming and Company, sponsored privateers and captured more than fifty ships.

After the war Leaming returned to law practice in Philadelphia, where he died during the yellow fever epidemic of 1797. He was buried in the Christ Church Burial Grounds.

LEIPER, Thomas: merchant

Born Lanark, Scotland, December 15, 1745; son of Thomas and Helen (Hamilton) Leiper; married Elizabeth Gray, November 3, 1778; died July 6, 1825.

Leiper came to America in 1763, settling in Maryland and then moving to Philadelphia in 1765. Circa 1770 he established a tobacco and snuff factory in Delaware County, Pennsylvania. He was a leader in opposition to the British in 1773–74. He was a member of the first troop of the Philadelphia City Cavalry and participated in the battles of Trenton, Princeton, Brandywine, and Germantown.

In 1780 Leiper began operation of a stone quarry near his factory. He was a prominent Anti-Federalist in Pennsylvania in the 1790s. He served as president of the Phila-delphia Common Council from 1801 to 1805, from 1808 to 1810, and from 1812 to 1814. He co-founded the Franklin Institute in Philadelphia in 1823 and served as a director of the Bank of the United States in 1825. He died in Delaware County.

LEWIS, William: lawyer

Born Edgemont, Pennsylvania, January 22, 1752; son of Josiah and Martha (Allen) Lewis; married Rosanna Lort; second marriage to Frances Durdin; father of three children; died August 16, 1819.

Lewis studied law under Nicholas Wain and was admitted to the Pennsylvania bar in 1773, gaining admission again after the new state constitution was adopted in 1776. In 1787 and 1789 he was a member of the Pennsylvania legislature. He was also a member of the Pennsylvania Constitutional Convention.

In 1789 Lewis served as United States attorney of the District of Pennsylvania and in 1791–92 as a judge of the United States District Court for the Eastern District of Pennsylvania. In 1794 he was counsel for petitioners against the election of Albert Gallatin to the United States Senate. A successful trial lawyer, he defended John Fries, leader of the Northampton Insurgents, in 1799.

Lewis died in Philadelphia.

LOGAN, George: senator

Born Germantown, Pennsylvania, September 9, 1753; son of William and Hannah (Emlen) Logan; married Deborah Norris, September 6, 1781; father of three children; died April 9, 1821.

Logan, a 1779 graduate of the University of Edinburgh, was a member of the Pennsylvania Assembly from 1785 to 1788. He became a member of the American Philosophical Society in 1793 and later was a founder of the Philadelphia Society for the Promotion of Agriculture. In 1798 he went on a successful unofficial mission to France and secured removal of the French embargo on American shipping; this incident led Congress to pass the Logan Act of 1799,

347

making it unlawful for any private citizen to intervene in any dispute with a foreign government.

From 1801 to 1807 Logan was a Pennsylvania delegate to the United States Senate. In direct defiance of Congress, he went to England in 1810 in an unsuccessful attempt to prevent war. He died in Stanton, Pennsylvania, and was buried in the Logan Graveyard in Philadelphia.

LOWER, Christian: congressman

Born Tulpehocken Township, Berks County, Pennsylvania, January 7, 1740; died December 19, 1806.

Lower entered the blacksmith's trade as a young man, later becoming proprietor of an iron foundry. In 1775 he was a colonel of associated battalions and in 1780 became a sub-lieutenant; during this period (from 1777 to 1779) he also served in a political capacity as commissioner of Berks County.

In 1783 Lower became a member of the Pennsylvania House of Representatives and held his seat until 1785; he served again in 1793–94 and in 1796. He was a member of the Pennsylvania Senate from 1797 to 1804. A Democrat, he was a member of the 9th Congress of the United States House of Representatives (1805–06). He died in Tulpehocken Township and was buried in the Tulpehocken Church Burial Ground.

LUDWICK, Christopher: baker

Born Glessen, Hesse (formerly Hesse-Darmstadt), Germany, October 17, 1720; married Mrs. Catharine England, 1755; second marriage to Mrs. Sophia Binder, 1798; died June 17, 1801.

From 1737 to 1740 Ludwick fought in the German Army against the Turks, and in 1741 he fought in the Prussian Army. Later that year he went to London and became a baker on an East India ship, on which he served until 1745. During the next seven years he sailed with an English ship to West Indian and European ports.

Ludwick started his own bakery in Philadelphia circa 1754. An active supporter of the Revolutionary War, he was appointed by Congress as superintendent and director of bakers in the Continental Army and served from 1777 to 1783. He bequeathed his fortune to various churches in Philadelphia and set up a fund providing for free education for poor children. He died in Philadelphia and was buried at the Trinity Lutheran Church in Germantown.

LYLE, Aaron: congressman

Born Mount Bethel, Pennsylvania, November 17, 1759; died September 24, 1825.

Lyle, who attended common schools, was a farmer by trade. He served in the Revolutionary War. He was a member of the Pennsylvania House of Representatives from 1797 to 1801 and a member of the Pennsylvania Senate from 1802 to 1804. He served as a commissioner of Washington County, Pennsylvania, from 1806 to 1809.

A Democrat, Lyle served Pennsylvania in the United States House of Representatives during the 11th through the 14th congresses (1809–17). From 1802 to 1822 he was a trustee of Jefferson (later Washington and Jefferson) College. He died in Cross Creek, Pennsylvania, and was buried in the Old Cemetery there.

★★★★★

McCAULEY, Mary Ludwig Hays (Molly Pitcher): Revolutionary heroine

Born Trenton, New Jersey, October 13, 1754; daughter of John George Ludwig Hass; married John Caspar Hays, July 24, 1769; second marriage to George McCauley, after 1789; died January 22, 1832.

McCauley received her nickname Molly Pitcher because of her efforts on the field at the Battle of Monmouth (June 28, 1778), where she carried water in a pitcher back and forth from a well to the exhausted and wounded soldiers. She then took her first husband's place when he was overcome by heat, serving at a cannon for the remainder of the battle. Later, in 1822, she was granted financial relief by an act of the Pennsylvania legislature as recognition for her wartime service.

McCLENACHAN, Blair: congressman
Born Ireland; died May 8, 1812.

McClenachan settled in Philadelphia after arriving in the United States and engaged in a mercantile business, in banking, and in shipping. A founder and member of the 1st Troop of the Philadelphia Cavalry during the Revolution, he contributed considerable amounts of money to aid the American forces and donated money and credit to the Continental Congress in 1780.

McClenachan was a member of the Pennsylvania House of Representatives from 1790 to 1795 and was elected a Pennsylvania delegate to the United States House of Representatives for the 5th Congress (1797–99). He died in Philadelphia and was buried in St. Paul's Cemetery there.

McCLENE, James: Continental congressman
Born New London, Pennsylvania, October 11, 1730; died March 13, 1806.

McClene moved to Antrim Township, Cumberland (now Franklin) County, Pennsylvania, in 1754. He was a delegate to the Pennsylvania constitutional conventions of 1776 and 1789–90 and a member of the Pennsylvania House of Representatives in 1776–77, 1790, 1791, 1793, and 1794. A member of the Pennsylvania Supreme Executive Council in 1778–79, he attended the Continental Congress in 1779–80. He died in Antrim Township.

McDOWELL, John: college president
Born Peters Township, Cumberland (now Franklin) County, Pennsylvania, February 11, 1751; son of William and Mary (Maxwell) McDowell; died December 22, 1820.

A graduate of the College of Philadelphia in 1771, McDowell served as a tutor there from 1771 to 1782. During that period (1777) he joined Captain Samuel Patton's Company and was later (1782) admitted to the Pennsylvania bar. He served as president of St. John's College from 1790 to 1806 and was a member of that school's board of visitors and board of governors from 1810 to 1818. A professor of natural philosophy at the University of Pennsylvania, he also served as provost of the school from 1806 to 1810.

McKEAN, Thomas: governor of Pennsylvania, Continental congressman
Born New London Township, Pennsylvania, March 30, 1735; son of William and Letitia (Finney) McKean; married Mary Borden, July 21, 1763; second marriage to Sarah Armitage, September 3, 1774; father of eleven children (including Joseph); died June 24, 1817.

Deputy prothonotary and register for probate of wills for New Castle County, Delaware, in 1752, McKean was admitted to the Delaware bar in 1755. He practiced law in New Castle and later in Philadelphia, serving as deputy attorney general for Sussex County, Delaware, from 1756 to 1758.

After studying law at Middle Temple in London, England, in 1758, McKean returned to Delaware to become a member of the House of Assembly, serving from 1762 to 1775 (speaker, 1772). He was trustee for the loan office of New Castle County from 1764 to 1776. In 1765 he was appointed sole notary for the lower counties of Delaware, justice of the peace, judge of the Court of Common Pleas and Quarter Sessions, and judge of the Orphans Court for New Castle County. He was appointed collector for the Port of New Castle in 1771.

McKean was an active supporter of the colonial cause from the beginning, participating in the Stamp Act Congress of 1765. He represented Delaware in the Continental Congress from 1774 to 1783, serving as president in 1781. He signed the Declaration of Independence circa 1777. (He was the first to challenge the popular impression that the Declaration had been signed July 4, 1776; it was later proved that no one had signed on that date.)

A member of the Delaware Constitutional Convention of 1776, McKean served in the Delaware House of Representatives in 1776–77 (speaker, 1777). He was president of Delaware briefly in 1777, then was named chief justice of Pennsylvania, a post he held until 1799. He was a member of the Pennsylvania Convention that ratified the United States Constitution in 1787.

A member of the Pennsylvania Constitutional Convention in 1789–90, McKean was elected governor of Pennsylvania in 1799 and served until 1808. He introduced the political "spoils system" on a large scale in Pennsylvania. He died in Philadelphia and was buried in Laurel Hill Cemetery there.

MacKENZIE, William: bibliophile

Born Philadelphia, Pennsylvania, July 30, 1758; probably son of Kenneth and Mary (Thomas) MacKenzie; never married; died July 23, 1828.

At an early age MacKenzie entered the Philadelphia counting house of John Ross, where he learned about mercantile and shipping affairs. An inheritance provided sufficient income for him to devote the rest of his life to scholarship and the collection of books. He acquired more than seven thousand volumes, which were later distributed among various libraries in the Philadelphia area.

MACLAY, Samuel: congressman, senator

Born Lurgan Township, Pennsylvania, June 17, 1741; son of Charles and Eleanor (Query) Maclay; married Elizabeth Plunket, November 10, 1773; father of six sons and three daughters; died October 5, 1811.

Maclay was a justice of the Pennsylvania Court of Quarter Sessions in 1775 and a member of the Pennsylvania Committee of Correspondence. He was a delegate to the convention of Associators at Lancaster in 1776 and later (1791) became a member of the lower house of the Pennsylvania legislature.

Maclay, a Republican, was a Pennsylvania delegate to the 4th Congress of the United States House of Representatives (1795–97). He returned to the lower house of the Pennsylvania legislature in 1797, then served in the Pennsylvania Senate from 1798 to 1802; he was speaker of the latter body in 1801–02. He was appointed to the United States Senate in 1803 and served until 1809.

Maclay was the author of the *Journal of Samuel Maclay,* which was published in 1790. He died in Burralo Valley, Pennsylvania.

MACLAY, William: senator

Born New Garden Township, Pennsylvania, July 27, 1734; son of Charles and Eleanor (Query) Maclay; married Mary McClure Harris, April 11, 1769; father of nine children; died April 16, 1804.

Maclay was a lieutenant with General John Forbes's expedition to Fort Duquesne in 1758. He was admitted to the York County, Pennsylvania, bar in 1760 and worked as a surveyor for the William Penn family. In 1763–64 he was a member of Colonel Henry Bouquet's expedition against the Indians. He became treasurer and clerk of the Northumberland County (Pennsylvania) Court in 1772 and laid out the town of Sunbury that year. He served as a commissar for the Continental Army during the Revolutionary War. He was a delegate to the Pennsylvania legislature from 1781 to 1785, in 1795, and once again in 1803. He was a member of the Supreme Executive Council in 1786.

In 1783 Maclay was named to a commission to study the navigation of the Susquehanna and in 1784–85 to a commission to deal with the Indians for the purchase of land. In 1788 he became a judge of the Pennsylvania Court of Common Pleas and also was named a deputy surveyor. He accepted an appointment as an associate judge in Dauphin County, Pennsylvania, in 1801, and served in that capacity for two years.

Maclay served in the 1st Congress of the

United States Senate (1789–91); during those years he kept a journal, later published as *Sketches of Debates in the First Senate of the United States, 1789–90–91,* which was the only continuous report of the private debates of that period. His personal notes reveal that he was possibly the first Jeffersonian Democrat.

Maclay was buried in Old Paxtong Churchyard in Harrisburg.

MARKOE, Abraham: planter

Born St. Croix, West Indies, July 2, 1727; son of Pierre and Elizabeth (Farrell) Markoe; married Elizabeth Kenny, 1751; second marriage to Elizabeth Baynton, December 16, 1773; father of Abraham and Peter; died August 28, 1806.

The son of a wealthy West Indian merchant and planter, Markoe came to Philadelphia in 1770. He was the founder and captain (1774–76) of the Philadelphia Light Horse, the first volunteer military association in America. He built a huge mansion in Philadelphia and lived there on the income provided by his West Indian plantation. He died in Philadelphia and was buried in Christ Church Graveyard there.

MARKOE, Peter: poet, dramatist

Born Santa Cruz, West Indies, circa 1752; son of Abraham and Elizabeth (Kenny) Markoe; died January 30, 1792.

Markoe was admitted to the bar at Lincoln's Inn, England, in 1775. He then journeyed to Philadelphia, where he served as a captain in the Philadelphia militia in 1775–76. He was a landowner in Northumberland County, Pennsylvania, until 1785.

Markoe's poems include "The Algerine Spy in Pennsylvania," 1787; *Miscellaneous Poems,* 1787; "The Storm, a Poem," 1788; and "The Times," 1788. He also wrote a play, *The Patriot Chief,* in 1784. He died in Philadelphia and was buried in Christ Church Graveyard there.

MARSHALL, Christopher: pharmacist

Born Dublin, Ireland, November 6, 1709; no record of first marriage; second marriage to Abigail, 1782; died May 4, 1797.

After coming to America in 1727, Marshall became a pharmacist in Philadelphia. He supported the colonial cause and was active in the enforcement of non-importation agreements and in the obtaining of supplies for military forces in 1774 and 1775. During the latter year he was a delegate to the Provincial Congress in Philadelphia. From 1777 to 1780 he was a member of the Committee of Safety in Lancaster, Pennsylvania.

Marshall kept a diary which has become an important historical source for the Revolutionary period, portions of which were published as *Extracts from the Diary of Christopher Marshall* in 1877. He died in Philadelphia and was buried there.

MARSHALL, Humphrey: botanist

Born Chester County, Pennsylvania, October 10, 1722; son of Abraham and Mary (Hunt) Marshall; married Sarah Pennock, September 16, 1748; second marriage to Margaret Minshall, January 10, 1788; died November 5, 1801.

Marshall engaged in farming in Chester County, Pennsylvania, after 1748 and built the first conservatory for plants in the area circa 1768. He constructed a hot house and botanical garden with a collection of foreign and domestic plants at his home in Marshallton, Pennsylvania. He corresponded with Dr. John Fothergill and Peter Collinson in England. He was a member of the American Philosophical Society and wrote *Arbustrum Americanum, the American Grove,* a list of native forest trees and shrubs, in 1785. He died in Marshallton.

MATLACK, Timothy: Continental congressman

Born Haddonfield, New Jersey, circa 1733; son of Timothy and Martha (Burr) Matlack; married Ellen Yarnall, October 5, 1758; second marriage to Elizabeth Claypoole, August 17, 1797; father of five children; died April 14, 1829.

Assistant to Charles Thomson, secretary

of the Continental Congress, in 1775, Matlack was in addition a member of the Provincial Conference at Carpenter's Hall in Philadelphia that year. He joined the Philadelphia Associators in 1775, commanded a battalion during the Revolution, and served in the Battle of Princeton in 1776. A participant in the Pennsylvania Constitutional Convention in 1776, he was also a member of the Pennsylvania Committee of Safety. He was keeper of the Great Seal of Pennsylvania in 1777 and served as secretary of the Pennsylvania Supreme Executive Council from 1777 to 1782. A trustee of the University of Pennsylvania in 1779, he was a Pennsylvania delegate to the Continental Congress in 1780 and 1781.

Matlack was a member of the American Philosophical Society from 1780 to 1829. An original director of the Bank of North America in 1781, he was also a founder of the Society of Free Quakers that year. He was a commissioner to inspect navigable waters of Pennsylvania and was assigned to the Delaware River in 1789. He was master of rolls of Pennsylvania from 1800 to 1809, an alderman of Philadelphia from 1813 to 1818, and treasurer of the United States District Court in Philadelphia in 1817.

Matlack died in Holmesburg, Pennsylvania, and was buried in the Free Quaker Burial Ground in Philadelphia. His remains were reinterred at Matson's Ford, opposite Valley Forge, Pennsylvania, in 1905.

MEADE, George: merchant

Born Philadelphia, Pennsylvania, February 27, 1741; son of Robert and Mary (Stretch) Meade; married Henrietta Constantia Worsam, May 5, 1768; father of ten children; died November 9, 1808.

Founder of the firm Garrett and George Meade of Philadelphia, Meade signed the Non-Importation Resolutions in 1765. He served with the 3rd Philadelphia Battalion in 1775–76 and later was a member of the Public Defense Association. He served on the Philadelphia Common Council from 1789 to 1791 and was chairman of the board of management of prisons in 1792. He died in Philadelphia.

MEASON, Isaac: iron manufacturer

Born Virginia, 1742; married Catharine Harrison, April 28, 1778; father of four children; died January 23, 1818.

Meason moved to Pennsylvania before 1771 and purchased a tract of land which he named Mount Pleasant. He served under General Anthony Wayne in the Continental Army in 1776 and became a member of the Pennsylvania Assembly in 1779. He was a member of the Supreme Executive Council of Pennsylvania in 1783.

Influential in developing the manufacture of rolling bar iron in America, Meason founded Union Furnace, the first successful iron works west of the Alleghenies, in 1791 and became a partner in Meason, Dillon and Company in 1793. He financed a mill for Thomas C. Lewis in 1816, two years before his death.

MELSHEIMER, Friedrich Valentin: clergyman

Born Negenborn, Germany, September 25, 1749; son of Joachim Sebastian and Clara Margaretha Melsheimer; married Mary Agnes Man, January 18, 1779; died June 30, 1814.

Melsheimer, who attended the University of Helmstedt, in 1776 was appointed chaplain to a dragoon regiment of Brunswick auxiliaries hired by the British Crown for service in the American colonies. He was wounded and captured at the Battle of Bennington the next year. Remaining in America, he served as pastor of five small Lutheran churches in Dauphin County, Pennsylvania, from 1779 to 1783. He served as a pastor in Manheim, Pennsylvania, from 1784 to 1786. Professor of Greek, Latin, and German at Franklin College in 1786–87, he worked to keep the college in existence (1787–89). He was pastor of St. Matthew's in Hanover, Pennsylvania, from 1789 to 1814. He was the author of *Catalogue of Insects of Pennsylvania,* 1806.

MEREDITH, Samuel: treasurer of the United States

Born Philadelphia, Pennsylvania, 1741; son of Reese and Martha (Carpenter) Meredith; married Margaret Cadwalader, May 19, 1772; father of seven children; died February 10, 1817.

Meredith signed the Non-Importation Resolutions in Philadelphia in 1765 and was a member of the Provincial Convention in 1775. He served as a major and a lieutenant colonel in the 3rd Battalion of Associators (known as the Silk Stocking Company) in the battles of Trenton and Princeton. Promoted to brigadier general in the Pennsylvania militia for gallantry at the battles of Brandywine and Germantown in 1777, he resigned from the army the following year.

Meredith was a member of the Pennsylvania Colonial Assembly in 1778–79 and from 1781 to 1783 and a member of the Congress of Confederation from 1786 to 1788. Surveyor of the Port of Philadelphia in 1789, he was named treasurer of the United States in 1789 and held that post for twelve years. He died at "Belmont," in Mount Pleasant, Pennsylvania.

MIFFLIN, Thomas: army officer, governor of Pennsylvania

Born Philadelphia, Pennsylvania, January 21, 1745; son of John and Elizabeth (Bagnell) Mifflin; married Sarah Morris, March 4, 1767; died January 20, 1800.

Mifflin, who graduated from the College of Philadelphia (now the University of Pennsylvania) in 1760, spent the years 1764–65 in Europe. He became a merchant in partnership with his brother, George, in 1765. An opponent of the Stamp Act, he participated in the Pennsylvania Provincial Assembly from 1772 to 1776, in 1778–79, and from 1782 to 1784, serving as president in 1783–84.

Mifflin represented Pennsylvania in the Continental Congress from 1774 to 1776. Commissioned a major in the Continental Army in 1775, he was chief aide-de-camp to George Washington in 1775 and quartermaster general from 1775 to 1778, serving concurrently as brigadier general in 1776 and as major general from 1777 to 1779. A member of the Board of War in 1777–78, Mifflin was involved in a cabal to oust Washington as commander-in-chief in 1777.

Mifflin served as a trustee of the College of Philadelphia from 1778 to 1791 and was a member of a special board of the Continental Congress seeking ways of reducing expenses in 1780. A member of the United States Constitutional Convention in 1787, he served as president of the Pennsylvania Supreme Executive Council from 1788 to 1790. He was president of the Pennsylvania Constitutional Convention, 1789–90, and was elected governor of Pennsylvania in 1790, serving until 1799. He favored war with England and an alliance with France in 1793 and helped suppress the Whiskey Rebellion in 1794.

Mifflin was a member of the American Philosophical Society from 1765 to 1799. He died in Lancaster, Pennsylvania, and was buried in the Lutheran Graveyard there.

MITCHELL, Samuel Augustus: geographer, publisher

Born Bristol, Connecticut, March 20, 1792; son of William and Mary (Alton) Mitchell; married Rhoda Ann Fuller, August 1815; died December 18, 1868.

An outstanding figure in the development of American geography, Mitchell prepared textbooks, maps, and geographic manuals, including *Mitchell's Geographic Reader,* 1840. He published *A New American Atlas* in 1831 and *Mitchell's Traveller's Guide Through The United States* in 1832. He produced a successful series of school geography books and began a series of Tourist's Pocket Maps of different states in 1834. He published *A New Universal Atlas* in 1847 and *Map of the United States and Territories* in 1861. He died in his longtime hometown, Philadelphia.

MONTGOMERY, Joseph: Continental congressman

Born Paxtang, Pennsylvania, September 23, 1733; died October 14, 1794.

A graduate of the College of New Jersey (now Princeton) in 1755, Montgomery went on to study theology. He was licensed to preach by the Presbytery of Philadelphia in 1759 and was ordained to the ministry of the Presbyterian Church in 1761, serving as a pastor from 1761 to 1777.

Montgomery was a delegate to the Pennsylvania General Assembly from 1780 to 1782 and was a Pennsylvania delegate to the Continental Congress in 1783–84. He became recorder of deeds and register of wills in Dauphin County, Pennsylvania, in 1785 and a justice of the Court of Common Pleas in 1786, serving in all three positions until his death. He died in Harrisburg, Pennsylvania, and was buried in the Lutheran Church Cemetery there.

MONTGOMERY, William: congressman

Born Londonderry Township, Chester County, Pennsylvania, August 3, 1736; died May 1, 1816.

Montgomery served as a colonel in the 4th Battalion of the Chester County (Pennsylvania) militia during the Revolution; his regiment came to be known as Flying Camp following the Battle of Long Island. He was a delegate to the Pennsylvania provincial conventions of 1775 and 1776 and was elected a Northumberland County delegate to the Pennsylvania Assembly in 1779, being reelected several times. He was sent to Wyoming, Pennsylvania, to settle boundary disputes in 1783.

Appointed presiding judge for Northumberland and Luzerne counties in 1785, Montgomery was also a justice of the peace for Northumberland County in 1791. He was elected to serve Pennsylvania in the United States House of Representatives for the 3rd Congress (1793–95). He was a major general in the Pennsylvania militia from 1793 to 1816. He was associate judge of Northumberland County from 1801 to 1813; first postmaster of Danville, Pennsylvania, from 1801 to 1803; and a Democratic presidential elector in 1808. He died in Danville at the age of seventy-nine.

MOORE, William: jurist

Born Philadelphia, Pennsylvania, May 6, 1699; son of John and Rebecca (Axtell) Moore; married Williamina Wemyss, circa 1722; father of twelve children; died May 30, 1783.

A 1719 graduate of Oxford, Moore served as a colonel in a regiment of the Chester County (Pennsylvania) militia during the French and Indian War. He was a member of the Provincial Assembly from 1733 to 1740, a justice of the peace for forty-two years (1741–83), and presiding judge of the Chester County Court during most of the period from 1750 to 1776.

In 1755 Moore became involved in a controversy with the Quaker-dominated Assembly when he helped draft and submit to that body a petition demanding protection for Pennsylvania frontier settlements, which were being subjected to repeated Indian attacks. Moore's enemies managed to have twenty-eight petitions presented to the Assembly in 1757 urging his removal as presiding judge, but Moore denied the jurisdiction of the Assembly. He was then arrested for libel against the Assembly and imprisoned in Philadelphia in 1758. He was released three months later and exonerated by the governor and council.

Moore died at Moore Hall in Chester County and was buried in the Radnor (Pennsylvania) Churchyard.

MOORE, William: patriot, jurist

Born Philadelphia, Pennsylvania, circa 1735; son of Robert Moore; married Susan Lloyd, December 13, 1757; father of three children (including Elizabeth Moore de Barbe Marbois); died July 24, 1793.

Moore was a member of the Pennsylvania Council of Safety in 1776 and a member of the Board of War in 1777. He served on the Supreme Executive Council from 1779 to 1782, serving as vice president for two years and president for one. He was judge of the Pennsylvania High Court of Errors and Appeals from 1781 to 1784. He served in the Pennsylvania Assembly in 1784 and was a trustee of the University of the State of Pennsylvania from 1784 to 1789. He was a director of the Bank of Pennsylvania and an influential member of the St. Tammany Society.

MORGAN, John: physician

Born Philadelphia, Pennsylvania, June 10, 1735; son of Evan and Joanna (Biles) Morgan; married Mary Hopkinson, September 4, 1765; died October 15, 1789.

Morgan graduated from the College of Philadelphia (now the University of Pennsylvania) in 1757 and received his M.D. degree from the University of Edinburgh in Scotland in 1763. He was admitted to the Academie Royal de Chirurgie de Paris in 1764. He later became a member of the Royal Society of London and of the Belles-Lettres Society of Rome. He was also a licentiate of the Royal College of Physicians in London and Edinburgh.

Morgan established a medical school in connection with the University of Pennsylvania in 1765 and was appointed a professor of theory and practice of physic. He was director general of hospitals in the Continental Army and physician-in-chief in 1775. He became director of hospitals east of the Hudson River in 1776–77. He was also a physician at the Pennsylvania Hospital.

Morgan was a member of the American Philosophical Society. The Philadelphia College of Physicians (organized in 1787) was an outgrowth of a suggestion of his. He was the author of an oration, *A Discourse Upon the Institution of Medical Schools in America* (1765). He published *Four Dissertations on the Reciprocal Advantages of a Perpetual Union between Great Britain and Her American Colonies* (which won him a gold medal) in 1766. He also wrote *A Recommendation of Inoculation, According to Baron Pimsdale's Method,* 1776.

Morgan died in Philadelphia.

MORRIS, Cadwalader: merchant, congressman

Born Philadelphia, Pennsylvania, February 19, 1741; son of Samuel and Hannah (Cadwalader) Morris; married Ann Strettell, April 8, 1779; father of five children; died January 25, 1795.

Morris served as a member of the 1st Troop of the Philadelphia City Cavalry during the Revolution. He was a founder and inspector of the Bank of Pennsylvania in 1780, a founder (in 1781) and director (until 1787) of the Bank of North America, and a Pennsylvania delegate to the Continental Congress in 1783–84. He was a member of the Democratic Society of Philadelphia. He operated an iron furnace and engaged in mercantile pursuits. He died in Philadelphia.

MORRIS, Elizabeth: actress

Born England, circa 1753; married Owen Morris; died April 17, 1826.

Elizabeth Morris's first definitely known stage appearance was at the Southwark Theatre in Philadelphia in 1772. She performed with the American Company in Charleston, South Carolina, in 1773 and made her New York City debut later that year. She participated in the first theatrical season in Boston in 1792 (in violation of the law, resulting in her arrest). Known throughout her career as Mrs. Owen Morris, she was associated primarily with the Chestnut Street Theatre in Philadelphia from 1794 to 1810. She was regarded as the greatest attraction on the American stage after the American Revolution, particularly in high comedy roles.

MORRIS, Robert: Continental congressman, financier

Born Liverpool, England, January 21, 1734; son of Robert Morris; married Mary White, 1773; father of seven children; died May 8, 1806.

Morris arrived in Maryland about 1747 and was later educated by a private tutor in Philadelphia. He became a member of the firm Willing, Morris and Company, shipping merchants in Philadelphia, in 1754. He signed the Non-Importation Agreement of 1765 and was warden of the Port of Philadelphia in 1766. He was a member of the Pennsylvania Council of Safety in 1775. A secret committee of the Continental Congress contracted with his company for the importation of arms and ammunition in 1775. Morris participated in the last Pennsylvania Assembly held under the colonial charter (1775).

A member of the Committee of Correspondence, Morris was a delegate to the Continental Congress in 1774 and 1775 and was a member of a secret committee formed to procure munitions. In addition, he was a member of a committee of secret correspondence which drew up instructions for Silas Deane, envoy to France, in 1776. Morris signed the Declaration of Independence in August 1776. He was elected to the first Pennsylvania Assembly under the new constitution, serving in 1776–77. A member of the Committee of Secret Correspondence (later the Committee of Foreign Affairs, then the Committee of Commerce) in 1777, he signed the Articles of Confederation in 1781.

In 1778–79 Morris was accused in the press of fraudulent commercial ventures with Silas Deane, but he was cleared of all charges. Authorized to fit out and employ ships of the United States in 1781, he assumed the task of buying supplies for the armies. He reorganized civil administration and paid off money owed Continental soldiers by securing loans from France in 1781 and from the Netherlands in 1783–84.

Morris was a member of the General Assembly of Pennsylvania for the special purpose of defending the Bank of North America, 1785–86. In 1785 he entered into a contract with the French Farmers-General which gave him a monopoly of the American tobacco trade with France. He was a member of the Annapolis Convention in 1786 and was elected to serve Pennsylvania in the United States Senate (Federalist) in 1789. He attended the United States Constitutional Convention in 1787.

Morris's fortunes collapsed in 1798 as a result of unsuccessful land speculations in New York and elsewhere. He was arrested and spent more than three years in debtors' prison. He died in near poverty in Philadelphia and was buried at Christ Church there.

MORTON, John: Continental congressman
Born Ridley, Pennsylvania, circa 1724; son of John and Mary (Archer) Morton; married Anne Justice, 1754; father of eight children; died April 1777.

A surveyor of land in Delaware County, Pennsylvania, before 1757, Morton was a justice of the peace there from 1757 to 1767. He was a member of the Pennsylvania General Assembly from 1756 to 1766 and from 1769 to 1775, serving as speaker from 1771 to 1775. He attended the Stamp Act Congress in 1765 and began a four-year term as high sheriff of Delaware County the following year. He was a judge of the Delaware County Court of Common Pleas from 1770 to 1774 and an associate judge of the Supreme Court of Appeals of Pennsylvania in 1774.

A Pennsylvania delegate to the Continental Congress from 1774 to 1777, Morton cast the deciding vote for the Declaration of Independence, which he also signed. He died in Ridley Park, in Delaware County, and was buried in St. Paul's Churchyard in Chester, Pennsylvania.

MOYLAN, Stephen: army officer
Born Cork, Ireland, 1734; son of John Moylan; married Mary Van Horn, September 12, 1778; died April 13, 1811.

Moylan, who arrived in Philadelphia in 1768, was an organizer of the Friendly Sons of St. Patrick in 1771 and was president that year and in 1796. He became army muster master general in 1775, quartermaster general in 1776, and a recruiter for the 1st Pennsylvania Regiment of Cavalry in 1776. After being commissioned a colonel, he served at Valley Forge in 1777–78; later, in 1783, he was brevetted a brigadier general. He served as United States commissioner of loans in Philadelphia in 1793. He died in that city.

MUHLENBERG, Frederick Augustus Conrad: clergyman, congressman

Born Trappe, Pennsylvania, January 1, 1750; son of Henry Melchior and Anna Maria (Weiser) Mühlenberg; married Catherine Schaefer, October 15, 1771; father of seven children (including William Augustus); died June 4, 1801.

Muhlenberg, who attended the University of Halle (Germany), was ordained a minister of the Lutheran Church by the Ministerium of Pennsylvania in 1770. He went on to serve as pastor in the towns of Stouchsburg and Lebanon, Pennsylvania, from 1770 to 1774; of Christ Church in New York City from 1774 to 1776; and of churches in Hanover, Oley, and New Goshenhoppen, Pennsylvania, from 1776 to 1779.

Muhlenberg was a member of the Continental Congress in 1779–80 and a member of the Pennsylvania House of Representatives from 1780 to 1783, serving as speaker for part of his term. President of the Pennsylvania Council of Censors in 1783–84, he served as a justice of the peace in 1784 and register of wills and recorder of deeds for Montgomery County, Pennsylvania, in 1784. A delegate to the Pennsylvania Convention to ratify the United States Constitution in 1787, he was elected to serve Pennsylvania in the 1st through the 4th congresses of the United States House of Representatives (1789–97); he was the first speaker of the house and also served as speaker of the 3rd Congress.

Muhlenberg was receiver general of the Pennsylvania land office in 1800–01. He later became a partner in the firms Muhlenberg and Wegmann, importers, and Muhlenberg and Lawersweiler, sugar refiners, both in Philadelphia. He died in Lancaster, Pennsylvania, and was buried in Woodward Hill Cemetery there.

MÜHLENBERG, Gotthilf Henry Ernest: clergyman, college president

Born Trappe, Pennsylvania, November 17, 1753; son of Henry Melchior and Anna Maria (Weiser) Mühlenberg; married Mary Hall, July 26, 1774; died May 23, 1815.

Mühlenberg attended the University of Halle in Germany before arriving in the United States. He was ordained to the ministry of the Lutheran Church in 1770 and served as a pastor in Philadelphia from 1774 to 1779 and in Lancaster, Pennsylvania, from 1779 to 1815. He received an honorary M.A. from the University of Pennsylvania in 1780 and a D.D. from the College of New Jersey (now Princeton) in 1787. At various times he was secretary or president of the Ministerium of Pennsylvania.

Mühlenberg served as the first president of Franklin College in 1787. He studied botany independently and contributed descriptions of over one hundred species and varieties of flora. He was the author of *Index Flora Lancastriense* and co-author of an English-German and German-English dictionary in two volumes in 1812. He died and was buried in Lancaster.

MÜHLENBERG, Henry Melchior: clergyman

Born Einbeck, Hanover, September 6, 1711; son of Nicolaus Melchior and Anna Marie (Kleinschmid) Mühlenberg; married Anna Maria Weiser, April 22, 1745; father of six sons and five daughters; died October 7, 1787.

Recognized as the virtual founder of the Lutheran Church in America, Mühlenberg attended the University of Gottingen from 1735 to 1738 and was then appointed a teacher in Waisenhaus at Halle. He came to Philadelphia in 1742 to prevent the union of the Lutherans of the United Congregations (Philadelphia, New Providence, and New Hanover) with other German Protestants in Pennsylvania. He organized the first Lutheran Synod in America in 1748 and visited Lutheran congregations throughout New

England. He was buried in New Providence, New Jersey.

MUHLENBERG, John Peter Gabriel: congressman

Born Trappe, Pennsylvania, October 12, 1746; son of Henry Melchior and Anna Maria (Weiser) Mühlenberg; married Anna Barbara Meyer, November 6, 1770; father of six children; died October 1, 1807.

Muhlenberg attended the University of Halle in Germany from 1763 to 1766. Returning to Pennsylvania, he was ordained a pastor by the Ministerium of the Lutheran Church in 1768 and served as a pastor at Bedminster, New Germantown, Pennsylvania, from 1769 to 1771 and in Woodstock, Virginia, from 1771 to 1776. In 1772 he served briefly as a priest of the Episcopal Church in London, England.

A member of the Virginia House of Burgesses in 1774, Muhlenberg was also chairman of the Committee of Safety for Dunmore County, Virginia, that year. He served as a colonel in the 8th Virginia Regiment of the Continental Army in 1776, gaining promotions to brigadier general in 1777 and to brevet major general in 1783. He then returned to Pennsylvania, where he became a member of the Supreme Executive Council in 1784, served as vice president of Pennsylvania from 1785 to 1787, and participated in the Pennsylvania Constitutional Convention in 1790.

Muhlenberg was elected a Pennsylvania delegate to the United States House of Representatives for the 1st, 3rd, and 6th congresses (1789–91, 1793–95, and 1799–1801). He was appointed to the United States Senate in 1801 but resigned before taking his seat. A supervisor of revenue for Pennsylvania in 1801, he served as collector of customs for Philadelphia from 1802 to 1807. He was president of the German Society of Pennsylvania in 1788 and from 1801 to 1807.

Muhlenberg died in Philadelphia and was buried in Augustus Lutheran Church Cemetery, in Trappe.

MURRAY, Lindley: grammarian

Born Swatara Creek, Dauphin County, Pennsylvania, June 7, 1745; son of Robert and Mary (Lindley) Murray; married Hannah Dobson, June 22, 1767; died January 16, 1826.

Murray attended the Friends Seminary in New York City, was admitted to the New York City bar, then became a merchant in 1779. He retired in 1783 to serve as a minister in the Society of Friends. A prolific author, he wrote the following: *English Grammar*, 1795; *English Exercises*, 1797; *A Key to the Exercises*, 1797; and *An English Grammar*, 1818. He also wrote several religious tracts, including *The Power of Religion on the Mind in Retirement, Sickness and Death*, 1787; *Selections from Bishop Home's Commentaries on the Psalms*, 1812; *Biographical Sketch of Henry Tuke*, 1815; *Compendium of Religious Faith and Practice*, 1815; and *On the Duty and Benefit of Daily Perusal of the Scriptures*, 1817. He died in Holdgate, York, Pennsylvania.

★★★★★

NESBITT, John Maxwell: merchant

Born Loughbrickland, County Down, Ireland, 1730; son of Jonathan Nesbitt; died January 22, 1802.

Nesbitt, who arrived in America in 1747, became a partner in the firm Conyngham and Nesbitt in Philadelphia in 1756. He was a member of the Committee of Correspondence in 1774, paymaster of the Pennsylvania State Navy in 1775, and treasurer of the state Council of Safety in 1776. The latter year he was also a member of the 1st Troop of the Philadelphia City Cavalry.

After becoming inspector of the Pennsylvania Bank in 1780, Nesbitt served as director of the Bank of North America from 1781 to 1792. He then became the first president of the Insurance Company of North America, on whose organizing committee he had served, and held this position from 1792 to 1796. In other political service he was a warden of the Port of Philadelphia in 1788 and an alderman in 1790.

Nesbitt was an original member of the Friendly Sons of St. Patrick, serving as vice president from 1771 to 1773 and as president in 1773–74 and again from 1782 until 1796. He died six years later in Philadelphia.

NEVILLE, John: army officer

Born Occoquan River, Virginia, July 26, 1731; son of George and Ann (Burroughs) Neville; married Winifred Oldham, August 24, 1754; father of Colonel Presley Neville; died July 29, 1803.

In 1755 Neville served under George Washington in General Braddock's expedition against Fort Duquesne. For a time he was sheriff of Winchester, Virginia, and commander of Fort Pitt. In 1776 he received a commission as lieutenant colonel in the Continental Army, rising to colonel the next year; he served in the battles of Trenton, Germantown, Princeton, and Monmouth. In 1783 he was brevetted a brigadier general.

Neville was a member of the Supreme Executive Council of Pennsylvania and participated in the state convention which ratified the federal constitution as well as in the Pennsylvania Constitutional Convention of 1789–90. From 1792 to 1795 he was an inspector in the survey for the collection of the whiskey tax in Western Pennsylvania and in 1794 was involved in the Whiskey Rebellion. Two years later he became a federal agent for the sale of public lands northwest of Ohio. He died at the age of seventy-two on Montour's Island, Pennsylvania.

NICHOLSON, John: state official

Born Wales; father of at least eight children; died December 5, 1800.

Nicholson, who came to America sometime before the Revolution, was a commissioner of accounts in Pennsylvania in 1781 and 1782, when the commission was abolished. The same year he became comptroller general of Pennsylvania and in 1785 became receiver of general taxes. Having been ap-

pointed in 1787 escheator general to liquidate the estates of persons tainted by treason, he was impeached by the Pennsylvania House of Representatives for redeeming certain of his own state certificates instead of funding them into federal certificates. Although the Senate acquitted him, he resigned in 1794.

Nicholson was also engaged in business ventures. In 1780 he became a partner in the firm Morris and Nicholson. He was a promoter of the Pennsylvania Population Company in 1794 and of the Territorial Company the following year. In 1795 he also helped found the North American Land Company. After being sent to debtors' prison he became editor of *The Supporter or Daily Repast.*

NICOLA, Lewis: patriot

Born France, 1717; died August 9, 1807.

Nicola came to Philadelphia from Dublin, Ireland, circa 1766. He edited the *American Magazine or General Repository,* engaged in a wholesale mercantile business, and was proprietor of the circulating library in Philadelphia. In 1768 he was elected to membership in one of Philadelphia's two scientific societies, later negotiating the merger by which the American Philosophical Society was formed. He served as curator of the society for many years.

In 1774 Nicola became a justice in Northampton County, Pennsylvania. In 1776 he was appointed a barrack master in Philadelphia and became town major, commanding the Home Guards until 1782. He became a colonel in the Invalid Regiment in 1777, rising to commandant eleven years later. Meanwhile, in 1783, he was brevetted a brigadier general. He was a proponent of crowning George Washington King of America.

Nicola published three military manuals during the Revolutionary War, including *A Treatise of Military Exercise* in 1776. He died in Alexandria, Virginia.

NISBET, Charles: clergyman, college president

Born Haddington, Scotland, January 21, 1736; son of William Nisbet; married Anne Tweedie, 1766; father of four children; died January 18, 1804.

Nisbet graduated from the University of Edinburgh in 1754 and from the Theological Course six years later. He was licensed to preach by the Presbytery of Edinburgh in 1760 and was ordained and became a pastor at Montrose, Scotland, in 1764. In 1783 he received a D.D. from the College of New Jersey (now Princeton).

Arriving in America in 1785, Nisbet soon afterward took office as the first president of Dickinson College, in Carlisle, Pennsylvania, serving until 1804. He also was co-pastor of the Presbyterian Church in Carlisle. He died in Carlisle and was buried in the Old Graveyard there.

NIXON, John: army officer, financier

Born Philadelphia, Pennsylvania, 1733; son of Richard and Sarah (Bowles) Nixon; married Elizabeth Davis, October 1765; father of four daughters and one son; died December 31, 1808.

In 1756 Nixon became a lieutenant in the Dock Ward Company, a Home Guard organization. Ten years later he was appointed a warden of the Delaware River Port. He was a signer of Pennsylvania paper money in 1767. In 1774 he became a member of the first Committee of Correspondence as well as a deputy to the General Conference of the Province of Pennsylvania. The following year he was a delegate to the Pennsylvania Provincial Convention, an organizer and lieutenant colonel in the 3rd Battalion of Associators, and a member of the state Committee of Safety, also serving as president pro tem of the latter.

Nixon commanded the defenses of the Delaware River at Fort Island in 1776 and served in the Philadelphia City Guard. In addition to his membership on the Continental Navy Board, in 1777 he led the Philadelphia Guard in the defense of Perth Amboy, New Jersey, and at the Battle of Princeton. The following year he served on the committee to settle and adjust the accounts of the Pennsylvania Committee and Council of Safety.

Nixon was an organizer and a director of the Bank of Pennsylvania, which was formed in 1780 to aid in financing the operations of the Continental Army. He became a director of the Bank of North America in 1784 and served as its president in 1792. He was an alderman of Philadelphia (1789–96), a member of the board of managers of Pennsylvania Hospital (1768–72), and a trustee of the College of Philadelphia (1789–91). He died in Philadelphia and was buried in St. Peter's Churchyard there.

NOAILLES, Louis Marie (Vicomte de Noailles): army officer

Born Paris, France, April 17, 1756; son of Philippe, duc de Mouchy; married Louise de Noailles (a cousin), September 19, 1773; father of at least two children; died January 5, 1804.

Noailles served with the French Army during the American Revolution. He was a colonel in the Royal-Soissonais Regiment at the Battles of Savannah and Yorktown and represented the French Army at the surrender negotiations. A member of the Estates-General, he was a leader in the nobles' renunciation of their ancient privileges in 1789. He fled France three years later and became a partner in Bingham and Company, a banking firm in Philadelphia, in 1793. He also speculated in Pennsylvania lands.

Noailles served as a military officer in the French West Indies during the Napoleonic Wars. He died of wounds received in a naval battle off Havana, Cuba.

★★★★★

O'BRIEN, Richard: mariner, diplomat

Born Maine, 1758; son of William and Rebecca (Crane) O'Bryen; married Elizabeth Robeson, March 25, 1799; died February 14, 1824.

O'Brien was an American privateer during the Revolutionary War, serving as master of the brig *Dauphin* circa 1781. After being captured by Algerine pirates, he became interested in Algiers-American relations. He was appointed to conclude the peace treaty with Tripoli in 1797 and was consul general to Algiers from that year until 1803.

In 1808 O'Brien served briefly as a member of the Pennsylvania legislature. He died in Washington, D.C.

ODELL, Jonathan: clergyman, Loyalist

Born Newark, New Jersey, September 25, 1737; son of John and Temperance (Dickinson) Odell; married Anne DeCou, May 6, 1772; father of three children (including William Franklin); died November 25, 1818.

Odell graduated from the College of New Jersey (now Princeton) in 1759 and went on to study medicine. He was ordained a deacon of the Church of England in 1766 and became a priest the following year. He was minister of St. Anne's (Anglican) Church in Burlington, New Jersey, from 1767 to 1776.

Odell chose to remain loyal to England at the outbreak of the American Revolution and became chaplain of a regiment of Pennsylvania Loyalists. He wrote bitterly satirical verses opposing the American cause and became an influential Loyalist publisher. He wrote essays and verses which were published in such papers as Rivington's *Gazette*. In 1783 he was assistant secretary to the commander-in-chief of the British forces in North America.

Odell journeyed to England in 1783, and the following year he settled in New Brunswick, Canada. From 1784 to 1818 he was clerk of the province and a member of the New Brunswick Executive Council. His poetry was published in *The Loyal Verses of Joseph Stansbury and Jonathan Odell* (1860). He died in Fredericton, New Brunswick.

O'HARA, James: army officer, manufacturer

Born Ireland, 1752; son of John O'Hara; married Mary Carson, circa 1782; father of six children; died December 16, 1819.

O'Hara, who was educated at the Seminary of St. Sulpice in Paris, France, came to America in 1772, settling in Philadelphia. Circa 1774 he became a government agent among the Indians. At the outbreak of the Revolutionary War he became a captain in the army; later (circa 1780) he served as a commissary at the general hospital and was stationed at Carlisle, Pennsylvania. From 1780 to 1783 he was assistant quartermaster for General Nathanael Greene. He was appointed a quartermaster in the United States Army by President Washington in 1792. From 1796 to 1802 he was a government contractor.

Circa 1800 O'Hara was a co-founder, with Major Isaac Craig, of the first glassworks in Pittsburgh; this was the first plant of its kind to use coal for fuel, and its first successful product was bottles. He later entered into a partnership with John Henry Hopkins in an iron works in Ligionier, Pennsylvania. A pioneer in exporting cotton to Liverpool, England, he built vessels for that purpose. He was director and president of the Pittsburgh branch of the Bank of Pennsylvania.

O'Hara was buried in the First Presbyterian Church in Pittsburgh and later reinterred in the Allegheny Cemetery in that city.

OTTO, Bodo: surgeon

Born Hanover, Germany, 1711; son of Christopher and Maris (Nienecken) Otto; married Elizabeth Sanchen, 1736; second marriage to Catharina Dahncken, 1742; third marriage to Maria Paris, 1766; father of at least three children (including John Conrad); died June 12, 1787.

A member of the College of Surgeons in Luneburg, Germany, Otto became chief surgeon for the district of Schartzfels, Germany, in 1749, emigrating to America six years later. In 1776 he was a delegate to the Pennsylvania Provincial Congress and was appointed senior surgeon for the middle division of the Continental Hospitals. He was ordered by the Continental Congress to establish a military hospital for the treatment of smallpox in Trenton, New Jersey, in 1777. In the spring of the following year he was in charge of the hospitals in Yellow Springs, Pennsylvania. He was selected for the hospital department in 1780.

Otto was a member of the American Philosophical Society. He died in Reading, Pennsylvania, and was buried in the Trinity Lutheran Churchyard there.

★★★★★

PAINE, Thomas: political writer
Born Thetford, Norfolk, England, January 29, 1737; son of Joseph and Frances (Cocke) Paine; married Mary Lambert, September 27, 1759; second marriage to Elizabeth Ollive, March 26, 1771; died June 8, 1809.

An excise officer in England, Paine was chosen to be an agent for excisemen to agitate for higher pay in 1772. Two years later he met Benjamin Franklin in England and left for Philadelphia. The following year he edited and contributed to Robert Aitken's *Pennsylvania Magazine*.

On January 10, 1776, Paine's pamphlet *Common Sense* urged an immediate declaration of independence. Four years later he expanded this idea in *Common Sense in Public Good.* He supported the colonial cause and edited twelve issues of *Crisis* from 1776 to 1783. His other publications included *Dissertations on Government, the Affairs of the Bank and Paper Money,* 1786; *Rights of Man,* in two parts, the first appearing in 1791 and the second in 1792; *Age of Reason,* first part in 1794 and second part in 1796; *Dissertation on the First Principles of Government,* 1795; and *Letter to George Washington,* 1796.

Paine returned to England in 1787, where he defended measures taken in revolutionary France and urged the English to overthrow the monarchy and establish a republic. He was popular with English radicals but was suppressed by William Pitt, then outlawed and tried for treason.

In 1792 Paine went to France as a French citizen and was elected to the National Convention. A year later he was deprived of his French citizenship, arrested, and imprisoned when Robespierre came to power. He was released from prison at the request of the American minister, James Monroe, and his seat in the National Convention was restored in 1795.

Although Paine's writings after his release from prison had undermined his reputation in America, he returned to the United States in 1802. In the United States he had been a pioneer in the movement for abolition of Negro slavery and had served as secretary to the committee on foreign affairs in the Continental Congress from 1777 to 1779.

Paine died in New York City and was buried near New Rochelle. His remains were taken to England for burial in 1819 but were later lost.

PARRISH, Anne: philanthropist
Born Philadelphia, Pennsylvania, October 17, 1760; daughter of Isaac and Sarah (Mitchell) Parrish; died December 26, 1800.

Feeling a concern for the poor of Philadelphia, Anne Parrish founded the Home of Industry (an organization for the employment of poor women) in 1795 and Aimwell School (for girls in needy circumstances) in 1796. She died in Philadelphia at the age of forty.

PATTERSON, Robert: educator
Born Hillsborough, County Down, Ireland, May 30, 1743; son of Robert Patterson; married Amy Ewing, May 9, 1774; father of eight children (including Robert M.); died July 22, 1824.

Patterson came to the United States at the age of twenty-five and from 1772 to 1775 was principal of an academy at Wilmington, Delaware. He left teaching to serve as a brigade major during the Revolutionary War.

From 1779 to 1814 Patterson taught mathematics at the University of Pennsylvania and acted as vice provost there from

1810 to 1813. He was a member of the Select Council of Philadelphia and was its president in 1799. President Jefferson appointed Patterson director of the Philadelphia mint in 1805.

In 1783 Patterson was elected to the American Philosophical Society and served as its president from 1819 to 1824. He wrote *Lectures on Select Subjects in Mechanics* (two volumes), published in 1806; *Newtonian System of Philosophy*, published in 1808; and *A Treatise of Practical Arithmetic*, published in 1818. In 1819 he received an honorary LL.D. from the University of Pennsylvania. He died in Philadelphia.

PEALE, Charles Willson: painter

Born Queen Annes County, Maryland, April 15, 1741; son of Charles and Margaret (Triggs Matthews) Peale; married Rachel Bruner, January 12, 1762; second marriage to Elizabeth DePeyster, 1791; third marriage to Hannah Moore, 1805; father of twelve children (including Raphael, Rembrandt, Titian, Rubens, Franklin, Titian Ramsay); died February 22, 1827.

Peale was apprenticed at the age of thirteen to a saddler, Nathan Walters. After seven years of apprenticeship he turned to portrait painting. He gained recognition that prompted a group of men to send him to England in 1766 to study under the American portrait painter Benjamin West.

In 1769 Peale returned to Annapolis, Maryland, then in 1776 moved to Philadelphia. He was active in recruiting for the Continental Army during the Revolutionary War. He was commissioned a captain in the 4th Battalion after serving in the battles of Trenton and Princeton in 1777. He was a member of the Pennsylvania General Assembly in 1779–80.

For ten years Peale painted miniature portraits. He established the Philadelphia Museum and was largely responsible for the establishment of the Pennsylvania Academy of Fine Arts in 1805. He painted George Washington's portrait in 1772 and went on to paint approximately sixty portraits of him.

Peale was an author as well as a painter. In 1797 he wrote *An Essay on Building Wooden Bridges*. His *Introduction to a Course of Lectures on Natural History* was published in 1800, followed three years later by *An Epistle to a Friend on the Means of Preserving Health*. Peale died in Philadelphia and was buried in St. Peter's Churchyard there.

PEMBERTON, Israel: merchant, philanthropist

Born Philadelphia, Pennsylvania, May 21, 1715; son of Israel and Rachel (Read) Pemberton; married Sarah Kirkbride, April 6, 1737; second marriage to Mary Stanbury, December 21, 1747; died April 22, 1779.

Pemberton made a fortune in his father's mercantile business in Philadelphia. He was a member of the Pennsylvania Assembly from 1750 to 1756 and again in 1766. He was manager of the Pennsylvania Hospital in Philadelphia from 1751 to 1779 and contributed large sums of money for its support.

A Quaker, Pemberton was a member of the Friendly Association for Regaining and Preserving Peace with the Indians by Pacific Measures. He was also a member of the American Philosophical Society from 1768 to 1779. He signed the Non-Importation Agreement of 1765. Because of his faith, he refused to take an oath of allegiance to Pennsylvania during the Revolution and was imprisoned by the Pennsylvania legislature in 1777–78. He died the following year.

PEMBERTON, James: merchant, philanthropist

Born Philadelphia, Pennsylvania, September 6, 1723; son of Israel and Rachel (Read) Pemberton; married Hannah Lloyd, October 15, 1751; second marriage to Sarah Smith, March 22, 1768; third marriage to Phoebe Lewis Morton, July 12, 1775; died February 9, 1809.

Pemberton made his fortune in a Philadelphia mercantile business with his father and his older brother Israel. He was a member of the Meeting for Sufferings, the executive body of the Society of Friends, for fifty-two years (1756 to 1808). He was a member and financial supporter of the Friendly Association for Regaining and Preserving Peace with the Indians by Pacific Measures and a founder of and contributor to the Society for Relief of Free Negroes in 1775, the name of which was changed in 1787 to the Pennsylvania Society for Promoting the Abolition of Slavery. Pemberton then served as vice president of this organization until 1790 and as president for the next thirteen years. He was a member of the board of managers of the Pennsylvania Hospital in Philadelphia from 1751 to 1772, serving as secretary of the board the final thirteen years of his tenure.

From 1750 to 1756 and again from 1765 to 1769 Pemberton was a delegate to the Pennsylvania Assembly. He signed the Non-Importation Agreement of 1765. Refusing to support the violence of the Revolution, he was imprisoned by the Pennsylvania legislature in 1777–78. He died at the age of eighty-five.

PEMBERTON, John: clergyman

Born Philadelphia, Pennsylvania, December 7, 1727; son of Israel and Rachel (Read) Pemberton; married Hannah Zane, May 8, 1766; died January 31, 1795.

A Quaker preacher, John Pemberton served as a missionary in Pennsylvania, New Jersey, Delaware, and Virginia. He made preaching tours of England, Scotland, and Ireland from 1750 to 1753 and again from 1781 to 1786. In 1794–95 his preaching tours included Holland and Germany.

Pemberton was a member of the Friendly Association for Regaining and Preserving Peace with the Indians by Pacific Measures. Along with his brothers Israel and James he was imprisoned in 1777–78 by the Pennsylvania legislature because of his refusal to sign an oath of allegiance. He was opposed to violence in the American Revolution. He died in Prymont, Westphalia (now part of Germany).

PENN, John: colonial official

Born London, England, July 14, 1729; son of Richard and Hannah (Lardner) Penn; married Miss Cox; second marriage to Ann Allen, May 31, 1766; died February 9, 1795.

Penn attended the University of Geneva from 1747 to 1751. From 1752 to 1755 he was a member of the Pennsylvania Provincial Council and in 1754 was a commissioner of Indian rights in Albany, New York.

Commissioned by the proprietors of Pennsylvania as lieutenant governor of that colony, Penn served from 1763 to 1777, except for. the brief period from 1771 to 1773 when his brother Richard held the office. Proprietary rule was abolished while Penn was in office, and he had boundary, frontier, and Indian troubles throughout his tenure. He died in Bucks County, Pennsylvania, and was buried at Christ Church in Philadelphia.

PENN, Richard: colonial official

Born England, 1735; son of Richard and Hannah (Lardner) Penn; married Mary Masters, May 21, 1772; father of five children (including William and Richard); died May 27, 1811.

Penn was educated at St. Johns College, Cambridge University, England. He came to America in 1763 and eight years later became lieutenant governor of Pennsylvania. In 1773 he was superseded by his brother John.

Penn returned to England in 1775, entrusted by the Continental Congress with the last conciliation offer to King George III. While in England he was a delegate to Parliament four times—from 1784 to 1790 for Appleby, in 1790 and again in 1806 for Haslemere, and from 1796 to 1802 for Lancaster. He died in Richmond, Surrey, England.

PENNINGTON, Edward: Continental congressman, merchant

Born Bucks County, Pennsylvania, December 15, 1726; son of Isaac and Ann (Biles) Pennington; married Sarah Shoemaker, November 26, 1754; died September 30, 1796.

Pennington was a Philadelphia merchant and banker. In 1761 he became a member of the Pennsylvania Assembly and also a judge of the Pennsylvania Court of Common Pleas, serving in the latter capacity until circa 1774. Also in 1761 he became trustee of the Pennsylvania Statehouse and Grounds. From 1773 to 1779 he was manager of the Pennsylvania Hospital in Philadelphia. In 1774 he served as president of the Philadelphia Committee of Correspondence and as a member of the Continental Congress.

In 1777 Pennington was arrested and exiled to Virginia because of his Quaker beliefs and his opposition to revolution. He later returned to Pennsylvania and in 1790 became a member of the Philadelphia City Council. He was a member of the American Philosophical Society from 1768 to 1796 and treasurer for the Society for the Cultivation of Silk. He died in Philadelphia.

PETERS, Richard: Continental congressman, jurist, agriculturist

Born Philadelphia, Pennsylvania, June 22, 1743; son of William and Mary (Breintnall) Peters; married Sarah Robinson, August 1776; father of six children; died August 22, 1828.

Peters graduated from the College of Philadelphia (now the University of Pennsylvania) in 1761, studied law, and was admitted to the bar in 1763. Five years later he was made a commissioner to the Indian Conference at Fort Stanwix. He served as register of admiralty in Philadelphia from 1771 to 1776.

Commissioned a captain in the Pennsylvania militia in 1775, Peters served as secretary of the War Board of the Continental Congress from 1776 to 1781; he represented Pennsylvania in the Congress in 1782–83.

From 1787 to 1790 he was a member of the Pennsylvania Assembly, serving as speaker from 1788 to the end of the term. He was a trustee of the University of Pennsylvania from 1788 to 1791. In 1791–92 he was speaker of the Pennsylvania Senate and for the next thirty-six years was judge of the United States District Court for Pennsylvania.

Peters was the first president of the Philadelphia Society for the Promotion of Agriculture. He published several volumes and more than one hundred papers on agriculture. A specialist in maritime law, he published *Admiralty Decisions in the District Court of the United States for the Pennsylvania District, 1780–1807.* He died in Philadelphia and was buried in St. Peter's Churchyard there.

PHILSON, Robert: congressman, army officer

Born County Tyrone, Ireland, 1759; died June 25, 1831.

In 1785 Philson came to the United States and settled in Berlin, Pennsylvania. He engaged in agriculture and held various local offices, including associate judge of Somerset County for twenty years. In 1800 he was commissioned a brigadier general in the 2nd Brigade, 10th Division, of the Pennsylvania militia, and during the War of 1812 he served as a brigadier general in the 2nd Brigade, 12th Division, of the Pennsylvania Volunteers.

From 1819 to 1821 Philson was a member of the United States House of Representatives (16th Congress). He died in Berlin and was buried in the Reformed Church Cemetery.

PILMORE, Joseph: clergyman

Born Tadmouth, Yorkshire, England, November 11, 1739; married Mary (Benezet) Wood, 1790; father of one child; died July 24, 1825.

While living in England, Pilmore was a lay assistant of John Wesley. He served as a lay missionary in America from 1769 to 1774 and in England from 1774 to 1784. He returned to the United States in 1784 and a year later was ordained a deacon and priest in the Protestant Episcopal Church.

For eight years Pilmore served as rector of the United Parish of Trinity, All Saints', St. Thomas's, in Philadelphia. He was a delegate to the General Convention in 1789 and rector of Christ Church in New York City from 1793 to 1804. The remaining years of his life were spent in Philadelphia, where he served as rector of St. Paul's Church. He died at the age of eighty-five.

PINE, Robert Edge: painter
Born London, England, 1730; son of John Pine; father of two children; died November 19, 1788.

Pine was a portrait artist in London, where he was a member of the Society for the Encouragement of the Arts at the Royal Academy. In 1784 he came to the United States, settling in Philadelphia.

Pine's subjects included David Garrick, King George II, John Wilkes, Robert Morris, and Benjamin Franklin. In 1785 he painted Francis Hopkinson and George Washington and his family. Other paintings include *The Surrender of Calais*, 1760, *Canute Rebuking his Courtiers*, 1763, and *The Congress Voting Independence*. Pine died in Philadelphia.

POOR, John: educator
Born Plaistow, New Hampshire, July 8, 1752; son of Daniel and Anna (Merrill) Poore; married Sarah Folsom, November 2, 1777; second marriage to Jane Neely, January 7, 1789; father of ten children (including Charles M. Poore); died December 5, 1829.

In 1777, two years after graduating from Harvard, Poor became head of the Young Ladies' Academy in Philadelphia, a position he held until 1809. In 1792 he was largely responsible for obtaining a state charter for the school, the first encouragement of this kind to be given to girls' education in the United States. He conducted a school for young ladies in New Hope, Pennsylvania, from 1815 until his death fourteen years later, in York Haven, Pennsylvania.

POTTER, James: army officer
Born County Tyrone, Ireland, 1729; son of John Potter; married Elizabeth Cathcart; second marriage to Mary (Patterson) Chambers; father of seven children; died November 1789.

Potter, who came to America in 1741, served as a captain under General Armstrong in the successful Kittanning campaign in 1755. In 1763–64 he served as a major and as a lieutenant colonel in the fight against the French and the Indians.

Potter was charged with the task of inducing settlers in western Pennsylvania to withdraw from Indian lands under the Treaty of 1768. In 1776 he was a colonel in a battalion of Associators and also served as a member of the Constitutional Convention in Philadelphia. In 1777 he was commissioned a brigadier general and fought at Trenton, Princeton, Brandywine, and Germantown.

In 1780–81 Potter, a member of the Constitutionalist party, served on the Supreme Executive Council of Pennsylvania, holding the office of vice president in 1781. In 1782 he received a commission as a major general in the Pennsylvania militia. Two years later he became a member of the Council of Censors.

Potter served briefly as deputy surveyor for Pennsylvania in Northumberland County and in 1785 served as a commissioner of rivers and streams. From 1785 to 1789 he was employed by a land-speculation company as a superintendent of development of land schemes in Penn's Valley. He died in Centre Point, Pennsylvania.

POTTS, Jonathan: physician
Born Colebrookdale, Berks County, Pennsylvania, April 11, 1745; son of John and Ruth (Savage) Potts; married Grace Richardson, May 5, 1767; father of five sons and two daughters; died October 1781.

Potts received an M.B. from the College of Philadelphia (now the University of Pennsylvania) Medical School in 1768, and earned his M.D. from there three years later.

He then began to practice medicine in Reading, Pennsylvania.

Potts was a delegate to the provincial meeting of deputies in Philadelphia and a member of the Provincial Congress there the next year. He served as deputy director general of hospitals of the Northern Department of the Continental Army in 1777 and as deputy director general of the Middle Department in 1778.

Potts died in Reading at the age of thirty-six.

PORTER, Andrew: army officer, surveyor
Born Montgomery County, Pennsylvania, September 24, 1743; son of Robert Porter; married Elizabeth McDowell, March 10, 1767; second marriage to Elizabeth Parker, May 20, 1777; father of thirteen children; died November 16, 1813.

From 1767 to 1776 Porter was in charge of an English and mathematics school in Philadelphia. He was then commissioned a captain of marines and fought at Trenton, Princeton, Brandywine, and Germantown. In 1779 he joined Sullivan's expedition against the Indians of central New York. In 1781 he supervised the manufacture of ammunition in Philadelphia for the siege of Yorktown. A year later he served as a lieutenant colonel and then as a colonel in the 4th (Pennsylvania) Artillery.

Porter was commissary for the commission that surveyed the southwestern boundary of Pennsylvania in 1784, and he assisted in determining the western termination of the Mason-Dixon Line. From 1785 to 1787 he was a commissioner charged with running the western and northern boundaries of Pennsylvania.

In 1800 Porter was commissioned a brigadier general in the Pennsylvania militia and later became a major general. He was surveyor general of Pennsylvania from 1809 to 1813. He died in Harrisburg, Pennsylvania.

PRATT, Matthew: portrait painter
Born Philadelphia, Pennsylvania, September 23, 1734; son of Henry and Rebecca (Claypoole) Pratt;
married Elizabeth Moore, December 11, 1756; died January 9, 1805.

Pratt studied under the artist Benjamin West in England in 1764. Four years later he opened a portrait-painting shop in Philadelphia, his clientele eventually coming to include such prominent families as the Penns, the Dickinsons, and the Willings. He resorted to sign painting for taverns and shops circa 1775 to 1781; one of his signs, *The Representation of the Constitution,* contains portraits of thirty-eight members of the Constitutional Convention.

Pratt's best known work, *The American School,* is at the Metropolitan Museum of Art in New York City. The Pennsylvania Academy of Fine Arts in Philadelphia owns his portrait of Benjamin West and wife. He also painted Benjamin Franklin. Pratt was buried in Christ Church Cemetery in Philadelphia.

PRESTON, Jonas: physician
Born Chester, Pennsylvania, January 25, 1764; son of Jonas and Mary (Yarnall) Preston; married Orpah Reese, 1794; second marriage to Jane Thomas, August 19, 1812; died April 4, 1836.

Preston practiced medicine after graduating from the University of Pennsylvania in 1784. He served as a member of the Pennsylvania House of Representatives from 1794 to 1800 and of the Pennsylvania Senate from 1808 to 1811. He was a director of the Bank of Pennsylvania and of the Schuylkill Navigation Company.

PROUD, Robert: educator
Born at the estate "Low Foxton," Yorkshire, England, May 10, 1728; son of William and Ann Proud; died July 5, 1813.

In 1759 Proud came to Philadelphia, where he operated a school for boys for eleven years. He was master of Friends Public School from 1761 to 1770 and from 1780 to 1790. He wrote a two-volume work, *The History of Pennsylvania, in North America, from the Original Institution and Settlement of that Province . . . in 1681, till after the Year 1770,* which was published in 1797–98. He died in Philadelphia at the age of eighty-five.

PUGH, John: congressman
Born Bucks County, Pennsylvania, June 2, 1761; died July 13, 1842.

Pugh, who attended common schools, rose from private to captain in the Continental Army during the Revolutionary War. After the war he engaged in farming and mercantile activities and served as justice of the peace.

Pugh, a Democrat, was a member of the Pennsylvania House of Representatives from 1800 to 1804 and was a Pennsylvania delegate to the United States House of Representatives during the 9th and 10th congresses (1805 to 1809). For the next eleven years he registered wills and recorded deeds in Bucks County. He died in Doylestown, Pennsylvania, and was buried in the Presbyterian Churchyard.

★★★★★

RAWLE, William: lawyer
Born Philadelphia, Pennsylvania, April 28, 1759; son of Francis and Rebecca (Warner) Rawle; married Sarah Coates Burge, November 13, 1783; father of twelve children (including William); died April 12, 1856.

Rawle studied law at Middle Temple in London, England, in 1781 and 1782 and was admitted to the Philadelphia bar in 1783. In 1786 he became a member of the American Philosophical Society, and in 1789 he served as a member of the Pennsylvania Legislative Assembly. He was also a member of the Society of Political Inquiries.

He served as United States attorney for Pennsylvania from 1791 to 1799; in 1794 and in 1799 he prosecuted the authors of the Whiskey Rebellion.

Rawle became an honorary member of the Maryland Society for Promoting the Abolition of Slavery in 1792 and served as its president from 1818 to 1836. He was a trustee of the University of Pennsylvania from 1795 to 1835.

In 1805 Rawle became a member of the Philadelphia Society for Promoting Agriculture and was a founder of the Pennsylvania Academy of Fine Arts. Two years later he was made an honorary member of the Linnaean Society. He was director of the Library Company of Philadelphia and, in 1820, founder of the Society for the Promotion of Legal Knowledge and Forensic Elegance. Two years later he served as chancellor of the Society of Associated Members of the Bar.

Rawle was the first president of the Historical Society of Pennsylvania, which was founded in 1825. He was a member of the commission to revise, collate, and digest the statutes of Pennsylvania and wrote *View of the Constitution of the United States* in 1825. He died in Philadelphia shortly before his ninety-seventh birthday.

REA, John: congressman
Born Rea's Mansion, near Chambersburg, Pennsylvania, January 27, 1755; died February 26, 1829.

After completing preparatory studies, Rea served as a lieutenant and as a captain with the Cumberland County (Pennsylvania) militia during the Revolutionary War. In 1784 he was commissioned the first coroner of Franklin County, Pennsylvania. He served in the Pennsylvania House of Representatives in 1785, 1786, 1789–90, 1792–93, and 1801–02. In 1793 and 1794 he was Franklin County auditor.

A Democrat, Rea filled a vacancy in the United States House of Representatives in 1803. He went on to serve until 1811 and took office again on May 11, 1813, serving until 1815. During the War of 1812 he served as major general of the 11th Division of Militia. In 1823 and 1824 he was a member of the Pennsylvania Senate. He died in Chambersburg and was buried in the Rocky Spring Churchyard near there.

READ, Thomas: naval officer
Born New Castle County, Delaware, 1740; son of John and Mary (Howell) Read; married Mary Peele, circa 1782; died October 26, 1788.

During the American Revolution, Read served as commodore of the Delaware River defense flotilla. He became second in command in the Pennsylvania State Navy in 1775, serving as commander of the brig *Montgomery*. He later resigned to assume a captaincy in the Continental Navy.

In February 1779 Read was ordered to protect Chesapeake Bay and in September was appointed to duty on the frigate *Bowbon*. He made a voyage to China on the frigate *Alliance* via the new route east of the Dutch Indies and through the Solomon Islands. On this trip he discovered two islands which were thought to be Ponape and another of the Carolines; the islands were renamed Morris and Alliance.

Read died in Fieldsboro, New Jersey.

REDMAN, John: physician

Born Philadelphia, Pennsylvania, February 27, 1722; son of Joseph and Sarah Redman; married Mary Sobers; father of at least three children; died March 19, 1808.

Redman received an M.D. from the University of Leyden on July 15, 1748. In 1759 he wrote *A Defense of Inoculation,* which advocated direct inoculation for smallpox. He strenuously advocated saline purgatives as opposed to emetics and bleeding in the yellow fever epidemics in Philadelphia in 1762 and 1793.

In 1786 Redman was a founder of the College of Physicians in Philadelphia, also serving as its first president until 1804. He educated young physicians, including John Morgan, Benjamin Rush, and Caspar Wistar. For twenty-nine years—from 1751 to 1780—he was a consulting physician in the Pennsylvania Hospital. He was a trustee of the College of New Jersey (now Princeton) and of the College of Philadelphia. He was an elder in the Presbyterian Church and, in 1751, a member of the Philadelphia Common Council. He was also a member of the American Philosophical Society.

Redman died in Philadelphia at the age of eighty-six.

REED, Joseph: army officer, Continental congressman

Born Trenton, New Jersey, August 27, 1741; son of Andrew and Theodosia (Bowes) Reed; married Ester de Berdt, May 22, 1770; died March 5, 1785.

Reed received a B.A. from the College of New Jersey (now Princeton) in 1757, then studied at Middle Temple in London, England, for two years. He was admitted to the New Jersey bar in 1763.

In 1767 Reed was appointed deputy secretary of the colony of New Jersey. He was appointed to the Philadelphia Committee of Correspondence in 1774 and the following year served as president of the Second New Jersey Provincial Congress. In 1775 he was also appointed lieutenant colonel of the Pennsylvania Associated Militia, and he became a military secretary to General Washington. Also in 1775 he served as a member of the Pennsylvania Committee of Safety, a member of the Continental Congress from Pennsylvania, and an adjutant general in the Continental Army with the rank of colonel. He served again in the Continental Congress in 1777–78. He participated in the Long Island campaign and in 1777 was promoted to brigadier general. He served at the battles of Brandywine, Germantown, Monmouth, and Portsmouth.

Reed became president of the Supreme Executive Council of Pennsylvania in 1778 and served for three years. He was responsible for the abolition of slavery in Pennsylvania. He was the prosecutor in the Benedict Arnold trial. From 1782 until his death in 1785 he served as a trustee of the University of Pennsylvania, of which he was also a founder.

Reed died in Philadelphia and was buried in the Arch Street Presbyterian Church Cemetery there.

REID, James Randolph: Continental congressman

Born Philadelphia, Pennsylvania, August 11, 1718; no record of death.

Reid studied law and was admitted or readmitted to the bar in 1781. He served as a Pennsylvania delegate to the Continental Congress from 1787 to 1789.

RHOADS, Samuel: Continental congressman, mayor
Born Philadelphia, Pennsylvania, 1711; died April 7, 1784.

Rhoads, who had limited schooling, worked as a carpenter and builder. In 1741 he was a member of the Philadelphia City Council. He attended the Pennsylvania Provincial Assembly from 1761 to 1764 and from 1771 to 1774. He served as commissioner to the conference of Western Indians and Six Nations in Lancaster, Pennsylvania, in 1761.

Rhoads became mayor of Philadelphia in 1774, leaving office later that year to represent Pennsylvania in the Continental Congress. From 1751 to 1781 he was on the board of managers of the Pennsylvania Hospital, of which he was also a founder. He also served on the board of directors of the Philadelphia Library. He died in Philadelphia.

RICHARD, Matthias: congressman
Born near Pottstown, New Hanover Township, Montgomery County, Pennsylvania, February 26, 1758; died August 4, 1830.

Richard completed his preparatory studies under private tutoring. He served in the ranks of Colonel Daniel Udree's 2nd Battalion in the Berks County (Pennsylvania) militia during the Revolutionary War. He participated in the battles of Brandywine and Germantown. In 1780 he served as a major in the 4th Battalion of the Philadelphia County militia.

Richard was appointed a justice of the peace in 1788 and held this office for forty years. He was judge of the Berks County Court from 1791 to 1797 and a customs inspector in 1801–02. He served in the 10th and 11th congresses (1807–11) of the United States House of Representatives. In 1813 he was appointed collector of revenue in the Pennsylvania Ninth District. Ten years later he became clerk of the Berks County Orphans Court.

After serving as an associate judge in the Berks County Courts, Richard became a merchant in Reading, Pennsylvania. He died there and was buried in Charles Evans Cemetery.

RICHARDS, John: congressman, merchant
Born New Hanover, Philadelphia County, Pennsylvania, April 18, 1753; died November 13, 1822.

Richards, who was educated by private tutors, served as a magistrate during the Revolutionary War. From 1777 to 1822 he was a justice of the peace in Philadelphia County. He was a judge of the Montgomery County Court of Common Pleas in 1784 and a member of the United States Constitutional Convention in 1787. He served his state in the United States House of Representatives from 1795 to 1797.

Richards worked as an ironmaster, a merchant, and a farmer. He was a member of the Pennsylvania Senate from 1801 to 1807. He died in New Hanover and was buried in the Faulkner Swamp Lutheran Church Cemetery.

RICHARDSON, Joseph: silversmith
Born Philadelphia, Pennsylvania, September 28, 1711; son of Francis and Elizabeth (Growdon) Richardson; married Hannah Worrell, August 24, 1741; second marriage to Mary Allen; father of six children (including Joseph and Nathaniel); died December 3, 1784.

Richardson inherited his father's silversmith shop in Philadelphia in 1829 and eventually became one of that city's leading silversmiths. In 1756 he helped organize the Friendly Association for Regaining and Preserving Peace with the Indians in Philadelphia. He presented silver jewelry to the Indian leaders. From 1756 to 1770 he was a member of the board of the Pennsylvania Hospital in Philadelphia.

RITTENHOUSE, David: inventor, astronomer, mathematician

Born Paper Mill Run, near Germantown, Pennsylvania, April 8, 1732; son of Matthias and Elizabeth (Williams) Rittenhouse; married Eleanor Colston, February 20, 1766; second marriage to Hannah Jacobs, 1772; father of three children; died June 26, 1796.

In 1763–64 Rittenhouse conducted a boundary survey for William Penn to settle a dispute with Lord Baltimore. In 1767 he designed his orrery, which could represent motions of bodies of the solar system and illustrate solar and lunar eclipses and other phenomena for a period of five thousand years, either forward or back. He conducted experiments on the compressibility of water and invented the metallic thermometer.

In 1768 Rittenhouse presented calculations to the American Philosophical Society on the transit of Venus that was to occur the following year. In 1770 he published an article, "Easy Method of Deducing the True Time of the Sun's Passing the Meridian." He is said to have made the first telescope in America, and his invention in 1785 of the collimating telescope introduced spider threads in the eyepiece.

In 1775 Rittenhouse was an engineer with the Council of Safety; he became vice president of the council the next year and president the year after that. He held membership in the Pennsylvania General Assembly and in the Pennsylvania Constitutional Convention in 1776. He was trustee of a loan fund involving Pennsylvania's loan to the Continental Congress. He served as a member of the Board of War created by the Continental Congress and as treasurer of the state of Pennsylvania.

Rittenhouse measured grating intervals and deviations of several orders of spectra. He experimented with magnetism and electricity, measured the barometric effect on a pendulum clock rate and expansion of wood by heat, and constructed a compensating pendulum and a wooden hygrometer. In 1792 he solved the mathematical problem of finding the sum of the several powers of the sines. He published *Method of Raising the Common Logarithm of any Number* in 1795 and *To Determine the True Place of a Planet, in an Elliptical Orbit* in 1796.

Rittenhouse engaged in boundary surveys involving Pennsylvania, Delaware, Maryland, Virginia, New York, New Jersey, and Massachusetts. He also conducted canal and river surveys. He served on committees to test specimens of flint glass and to inspect the first steam engine in the United States. He supervised the casting of cannon and the manufacture of saltpeter.

Rittenhouse was a professor of astronomy at the University of Pennsylvania, also serving as a trustee for a time. He was a member of a commission to organize the United States Bank. He was appointed first director of the United States mint by George Washington in 1792 and served three years. From 1791 to 1796 he was curator, librarian, secretary, vice president, and president of the American Philosophical Society. He was a foreign member of the Royal Society of London, England. He died in Philadelphia.

ROBERDEAU, Daniel: Continental congressman

Born St. Christopher, British West Indies, 1727; son of Isaac and Mary (Cunyngham) Roberdeau; married Mary Bostwick, October 3, 1761; second marriage to Jane Milligan, December 2, 1778; father of at least nine children (including Isaac); died January 5, 1795.

Before the American Revolution, Roberdeau was a successful merchant engaged largely in West Indian trade. He served as a warden of Philadelphia and from 1756 to 1761 was a member of the Pennsylvania Provincial Assembly. He was a manager of the Pennsylvania Hospital from 1756 to 1758 and from 1766 to 1776. He served on the Pennsylvania Committee of Safety and in 1776 was chairman of a Philadelphia mass meeting. He helped to unite the city with back-country groups, thus facilitating the drafting of the new state constitution.

Roberdeau served as a colonel in the 2nd Battalion of the Pennsylvania militia in 1775 and as a brigadier general the next year. In 1778 he offered in Congress to build a lead mine at his own expense in western Pennsylvania; he later built Fort Roberdeau to protect the mine. A delegate to the Continental Congress from 1777 to 1779, he served on the foreign affairs committee.

Roberdeau died at Winchester, Virginia.

ROBERTS, Job: agriculturist

Born Whitpain, Pennsylvania, March 23, 1756; son of John and Jane (Hunk) Roberts; married Mary Naylor, May 22, 1781; second marriage to Sarah Williams Thomas, October 12, 1820; father of at least two children; died August 20, 1851.

In 1785 Roberts began investigating possible ways to improve farming techniques of the day; in 1804 he published the results of his experiments as *The Pennsylvania Farmer*. He experimented with fertilizers; with the use of lime, plaster, and various barnyard manures; and with the deep plowing of land. He built an improved harrow and in 1792 devised a new roller.

In 1797 Roberts attached a water wheel to a dairy churn to make it possible to churn 150 pounds of butter a week. In 1815 he invented a machine for planting corn; also, through the technique of soaking corn before planting, he advanced the growing season of that grain. He introduced Merino sheep into Pennsylvania and was interested in the cultivation of mulberry for silk culture. He substituted green fodder for grazing for his cattle.

In 1791 Roberts was appointed a justice of the peace. Known as Squire Job Roberts, he died in Whitpain at the age of ninety-five.

RODMAN, William: congressman

Born Bensalem Township, near Bristol, Pennsylvania, October 7, 1757; died July 27, 1824.

After completing his preparatory studies, Rodman served as a private and later as a brigade quartermaster during the Revolutionary War. He commanded a company during the Whiskey Insurrection in 1794.

From 1791 to 1800 Rodman held the post of justice of the peace. He was a member of the Pennsylvania Senate from 1804 to 1808 and a presidential elector in 1809. A Democrat, he served as a delegate from Pennsylvania in the 12th Congress of the United States House of Representatives (1811–13).

Rodman died in Flushing, near Bristol, and was buried in the Episcopal Cemetery, later known as St. James Burying Ground.

ROSS, Betsy: seamstress

Born Philadelphia, Pennsylvania, January 1, 1752; daughter of Samuel and Rebecca (James) Griscom; married John Ross, November 4, 1773; second marriage to Joseph Ashburn, June 15, 1777; third marriage to John Claypoole, May 8, 1783; mother of at least seven children; died January 30, 1836.

Betsy Ross, who operated an upholsterer's shop in Philadelphia, is credited with making the first Stars and Stripes at the request of George Washington, Robert Morris, and George Ross. This credit is based on family tradition first made public by her grandson William Canby in a paper presented before the Pennsylvania Historical Society in 1870. On May 29, 1777, the Pennsylvania State Navy Board ordered payment for "Making ships' colours, etc."; other documentary evidence has not been found. The Stars and Stripes was adopted as the national flag by resolution of the Continental Congress on June 14, 1777.

Betsy Ross Ashburn Claypoole died in Philadelphia and was buried in Mount Moriah Cemetery there.

ROSS, George: Continental congressman, jurist

Born Newcastle, Delaware, May 10, 1730; son of the Reverend George and Catherine (Van Gezel) Ross; married Anne Lawler, August 17, 1751; father of three children; died July 14, 1779.

In 1750 Ross was admitted to the Pennsylvania bar. He served as prosecutor for the

Crown in Cumberland County, Pennsylvania, for twelve years. From 1774 to 1777 he was a member of the Pennsylvania Provincial Congress. He served in the Pennsylvania Assembly and on the Pennsylvania Committee of Safety in 1775.

In 1776 Ross assisted in negotiating a treaty to pacify the Indians of northwest Pennsylvania. He was vice president of the Pennsylvania Constitutional Convention in 1776 and aided in drafting the declaration of rights. A member of the Continental Congress in 1776–77, he signed the Declaration of Independence. He was commissioned judge of the Pennsylvania Admiralty Court in 1779.

Ross died in Lancaster, Pennsylvania, and was buried in Christ Churchyard in Philadelphia.

RUSH, Benjamin: physician, Continental congressman, humanitarian

Born Philadelphia, Pennsylvania, January 4, 1746; son of John Harvey and Susanna (Hall) Rush; married Julia Stockton, January 11, 1776; father of thirteen children (including James and Richard); died April 19, 1813.

Rush graduated from the College of New Jersey (now Princeton) in 1760, then studied medicine under Dr. John Redman until 1766. He attended the first lectures of Dr. William Shippen and Dr. John Morgan in the College of Philadelphia. In 1768 he received his M.D. from the University of Edinburgh, Scotland.

Returning to Philadelphia in 1769, Rush established a medical practice and for the next twenty-two years taught chemistry at the College of Philadelphia; in 1789 he also taught theory and practice at that school. In 1770 he published the first American text on chemistry, *A Syllabus of a Course of Lectures on Chemistry* (reissued in 1773). In 1772 he published anonymously *Sermons to Gentlemen upon Temperance and Exercise,* one of the first American works on personal hygiene. The next year he published "An Address to the In-

habitants of the British Settlements in America, upon Slave-Keeping." He was the first American to write on cholera infantum and the first to recognize focal infection of the teeth.

Rush continued writing throughout most of his life. His works include *Medical Inquiries and Observations,* initial volume in 1789; *An Account of the Bilious Remitting Yellow Fever, as It Appeared in the Essays, Literary, Moral and Philosophical,* 1798; and *Medical Inquiries and Observations upon the Diseases of the Mind,* 1812.

Rush was a member of the American Philosophical Society. In 1774 he was an organizer of the Pennsylvania Society for Promoting the Abolition of Slavery and served as president in 1803. He was elected to the Pennsylvania Provincial Convention in 1776 and was a member of the Continental Congress in 1776–77. He was a signer of the Declaration of Independence.

Rush was appointed surgeon general of the armies of the Middle Department of the Continental Army in 1777. He became a lecturer at the University of the State of Pennsylvania in 1780. From 1783 to 1813 he was a member of the staff at Pennsylvania Hospital.

In 1786 Rush established the first free dispensary in America. He is recognized as the "instaurator" of the American temperance movement. He persuaded the Presbyterians to found Dickinson College in 1783 and served as a trustee. In 1787 he attended the Pennsylvania Convention which ratified the United States Constitution; he and James Wilson led a successful fight for its adoption and also inaugurated a campaign that secured a more liberal and effective constitution for Pennsylvania in 1789.

President John Adams appointed Rush treasurer of the United States Mint, and he served from 1797 to 1813. He became professor of the Institutes of Medicine and Clinical Practice at the University of Pennsylvania in 1792; he was professor of theory and practice there in 1796. He was a founder of the Philadelphia College of Physicians in 1787.

Rush is considered a pioneer worker in experimental physiology in the United States. He greatly contributed to the establishment of Philadelphia as the center of American medical training during the first half of the nineteenth century. He died in Philadelphia and was buried in Christ Church Graveyard there.

RUSH, Jacob: jurist

Born Philadelphia, Pennsylvania, December 1746; died January 5, 1820.

Rush graduated from Princeton in 1765 and received an LL.D. in 1804. From 1784 to 1806 he was judge of the Court of Errors and Appeals. In 1806 he was president of the City Court of Common Pleas. He wrote *Charges on Moral and Religious Subjects* in 1803 and *Christian Baptism* in 1819. He died in Philadelphia.

RUSH, William: sculptor

Born Philadelphia, Pennsylvania, July 4, 1756; son of Joseph and Rebecca (Lincoln) Rush; married Martha Wallace, December 14, 1780; died January 17, 1833.

Rush, the first native American sculptor, was especially renowned for the figureheads that he carved to adorn prows of ships. He carved "America" for the frigate *America*, "Nature" for the *Constellation*, "Genius of the United States" for the *United States*, "Indian Trader" for the *William Penn*, and "River God" for the *Ganges*. He also produced a life-size statue of George Washington that was originally intended as a figurehead for a ship to be named the *Washington*; the statue is now on display in Independence Hall in Philadelphia.

The "Spirit of the Schuylkill" is Rush's most notable work. The first public-fountain figure erected in the United States, the original wood carving was placed in Center Square (now Penn Square) to commemorate the founding of the Philadelphia water system.

Rush did a life-size group in the work "Liberty Crowning the Bust of Washington." In 1805 he co-founded the Pennsylvania Academy of Fine Arts, the first organization of its kind in the United States. He was a director of the academy from then until his death.

★★★★★

ST. CLAIR, Arthur: president of the Continental Congress, army officer, territorial governor

Born Thurso, Aithness County, Scotland, April 3, 1737; son of William and Elizabeth (Balfour) St. Clair; married Phoebe Bayard, May 15, 1760; father of seven children; died August 31, 1818.

Commissioned an ensign in the British Army in 1757, St. Clair served with General Jeffrey Amherst at the capture of Louisburg, Canada, the next year. He resigned from the army in 1762 with the rank of lieutenant and bought an estate in Ligonier Valley in western Pennsylvania soon afterward, becoming the largest resident property owner in Pennsylvania west of the mountains. The governor of Pennsylvania appointed him colonial agent in this frontier area in 1771, and he also served as a justice of the Westmoreland County Court in 1773 and as a member of the Westmoreland County Committee of Safety.

St. Clair participated in a number of actions during the Revolution. He was sent as a colonel to take part in the retreat of the Continental Army from Canada in 1775. Commissioned a brigadier general, he served with Washington in the battles of Trenton and Princeton in 1776–77. He then rose to major general and was ordered to the defense of Fort Ticonderoga in 1777, later evacuating his post. He was exonerated by a court-martial in 1778.

A member of the Pennsylvania Council of Censors in 1783, St. Clair was a delegate from Pennsylvania to the Continental Congress from 1785 to 1787 and was president of the Congress in 1787.

St. Clair took an active part in Northwest Territory affairs. He was named the first governor of the territory, serving from 1787 to 1802. A major general commanding army troops, he was defeated by Indians near Fort Wayne in 1791. He was ordered to erect a chain of military posts from Fort Washington, near the mouth of the Miami River, to the rapids of the Maumee River; however, the work was poorly planned and executed. He resigned his commission in 1792.

A Federalist, St. Clair opposed statehood for the Northwest Territory as premature and sought to gerrymander the area into smaller territories so as to postpone statehood indefinitely. He denounced the Ohio Enabling Act of Congress as a nullity at the Ohio Constitutional Convention of 1802.

St. Clair died at his home, "Hermitage," near Ligonier, Pennsylvania.

SALOMON, Haym: merchant, banker, Revolutionary financier
Born Lissa, Poland, circa 1740; married Rachel Franks, January 22, 1777; died January 6, 1785.

Salomon fled Poland in 1772, arriving in New York about a year later, where he opened a brokerage and commission merchant's business. In 1776 the British arrested him as a spy, imprisoned him, and used him as an interpreter. He tried to induce Hessian mercenaries employed by the British near New York City to resign or desert. Having resumed business as a merchant, he continued to act as an undercover desertion agent among Hessians. In 1778 he was arrested again on the charge of being an accomplice in a plot to burn the King's fleet and destroy British warehouses around New York. He was confined to prison and condemned to death but bribed his jailer and escaped to American lines.

Later in 1778 Salomon opened an office in Philadelphia as a dealer in bills of exchange and other securities. In addition to becoming a leading broker in Philadelphia, he was a subscriber to and a major depositor in the Bank of North America. He also held the position of paymaster for the French forces in America. His large contributions to maintain the credit of the bankrupt American government earned him the title "The Financier of the Revolution." He died in debt, holding over $650,000 of United States debts which were unpayable owing to his financial situation.

SAVERY, William: cabinetmaker
Born 1721; married Mary Peters, April 19, 1746; father of eleven children (including William); died May 1787.

Savery was assessor of central wards in Philadelphia in 1754 and agent and collector of taxes for the Guardians of the Poor in Philadelphia in 1767. The work of this prosperous cabinetmaker was responsible for earning Philadelphia furniture of the colonial period the reputation as the most elaborate and ornate of any American furniture. He was influenced by Thomas Chippendale and Robert Manwaring of England. Several pieces of his furniture are now in the Metropolitan Museum of Art in New York City.

SAY, Benjamin: physician, congressman
Born Philadelphia, Pennsylvania, August 28, 1755; son of Thomas and Rebekah (Atkinson) Budd Say; married Ann Bonsall, October 1, 1776; second marriage to Miriam Moore, December 22, 1795; father of seven children (including Thomas); died April 23, 1813.

Say, who earned an M.D. from the University of Pennsylvania in 1780, conducted an apothecary shop in connection with his medical practice. A founder and junior fellow of the College of Physicians in Philadelphia, he signed the college constitution at its adoption in 1787 and served as the school's treasurer from 1791 until 1809.

In 1799 Say was an incorporator of the Pennsylvania Humane Society, which he also served as first president. The same year he attended the state senate, serving there until 1801. From November 16, 1808, to June 1809 (10th Congress) he was a Pennsylvania delegate to the United States House of Representatives. He also belonged to the Pennsylvania Prison Society.

Say wrote *A Short Compilation of the Extraordinary Life and Writings of Thomas Say* (1796) and *An Annual Oration Pronounced before the Humane Society of Philadelphia* (1799). He died in Philadelphia.

SCHLATTER, Michael: clergyman, school administrator

Born St. Gall, Switzerland, July 14, 1716; son of Paulus and Magdalena (Zallikofer) Schlatter; married Maria Schleidorm; father of nine children; died October 31, 1790.

Schlatter was ordained to the ministry of the German Reformed Church in 1739. From 1746 until 1751 he was a missionary in Pennsylvania, Maryland, Virginia, and New Jersey, founding forty-six congregations which he organized into sixteen pastoral charges. In 1754 he became superintendent of schools in Pennsylvania. He was chosen chaplain to the British Army in 1756, to the Royal American Regiment in 1757, and to the 2nd Pennsylvania Battalion in 1764. In the meantime, in 1759, he had become pastor of the Reformed churches in Philadelphia.

In 1777 Schlatter was taken prisoner by the British at the capture of Germantown, and his property was confiscated. He died in Philadelphia and was buried in Reformed Cemetery (now a part of Franklin Square).

SCOTT, Thomas: congressman, lawyer

Born Chester County, Pennsylvania, 1739; died March 2, 1796.

Scott attended rural schools, then went on to study law. He moved to Westmoreland County in 1770 and became justice of the peace three years later. He was a member of the first Pennsylvania Assembly (1776) and returned to it in 1791. In 1777 he became a member of the Supreme Council.

From 1781 until 1789 Scott served as prothonotary of Washington County, accepting a commission as justice of the county in

1786. He participated in the Pennsylvania Convention which ratified the United States Constitution in 1787 and was elected to the 1st and 3rd congresses of the United States House of Representatives (1789–91, 1793–95). He died in Washington, Pennsylvania, and was buried in the Old Graveyard; he was later reinterred in Washington Cemetery.

SEARLE, James: merchant, Continental congressman

Born New York City, 1733; son of John and Catherine (Pintard) Searle; married Ann (or Nancy) Smith, 1762; second marriage to Isabella West, 1785; father of several children; died August 7, 1797.

Between 1746 and 1762 Searle was an employee and then a member of his brother's firm, John Searle and Company, in Madeira, Spain. From 1762 until 1787 he was company agent in Philadelphia. He signed the Non-Importation Agreement of 1765 and participated in all later mercantile protests against Great Britain. In 1775 he accepted a commission as a lieutenant colonel in the Pennsylvania militia, becoming manager of the United States lottery the following year and holding that position until 1778. In that year he became a member of the United States Naval Board and of the Continental Congress, serving in the latter body until 1780 and sitting on many committees.

Searle was a trustee of the University of Pennsylvania from 1778 until 1781. During the years 1780–82 he was unsuccessful in his attempts as a commissioner to France and Holland to negotiate a loan for the state of Pennsylvania. He was appointed agent for a Madeira firm with salary and commissions in 1787, at a time when his own firm was on the brink of bankruptcy. He died in Philadelphia and was buried in St. Peter's Churchyard there.

SHIPPEN, Edward: jurist

Born Philadelphia, Pennsylvania, February 16, 1729; son of Edward and Sarah (Plumley) Shippen; married Margaret Francis, November 29, 1753; fa-

ther of nine children (including Margaret [Shippen] Arnold); died April 15, 1806.

In 1750 Shippen became a member of both the English bar and the bar of the Pennsylvania Supreme Court. He became judge of the Court of Vice Admiralty in 1752 and held this position until 1776. He served locally as a member of the Common Council of Philadelphia in 1755–56, serving as clerk of the council in 1758. The latter year he also became clerk of the City Court. From circa 1762 until 1778 he held the position of prothonotary of the Pennsylvania Supreme Court; he was the author of the earliest published law reports of this court.

A member of the Pennsylvania Provincial Council from 1770 to 1775, Shippen was a moderate Loyalist during the American Revolution. After the war he became president of the Court of Common Pleas of Philadelphia County and judge of the High Court of Errors and Appeals, serving in both capacities from 1784 to 1791. In 1785–86 he was also a justice of the peace and president of the Pennsylvania Court of Quarter Sessions of Peace, Oyer, and Terminer. He was an associate justice of the Pennsylvania Supreme Court from 1791 until 1799, when he rose to chief justice. In 1804 the Democrat-controlled Pennsylvania Assembly impeached Shippen (who was a Federalist), but the Senate acquitted him the next year. He died soon afterward in Philadelphia.

SHIPPEN, William: Continental congressman, physician
Born Philadelphia, Pennsylvania, October 1, 1712; died November 4, 1801.

After studying medicine, Shippen established a medical practice in Philadelphia. In 1749 he helped found and became a trustee of the Public Academy; in the same year he also helped found the College of Philadelphia (now the University of Pennsylvania), of which he was a trustee from 1749 until 1779. In 1765 he became a founder of the College of New Jersey (now Princeton),

serving as a trustee of that school from then until 1796.

Shippen was a member of the American Philosophical Society and served as its vice president for many years, beginning in 1768. He represented Pennsylvania at the Continental Congress during the period 1778–80. He died in Germantown, Pennsylvania, and was buried in the First Presbyterian Church Cemetery in Philadelphia.

SHIPPEN, William: physician, educator
Born Philadelphia, Pennsylvania, October 21, 1736; son of William and Susannah (Harrison) Shippen; married Alice Lee, 1760; father of one child; died July 11, 1808.

Shippen graduated from Princeton in 1754 and earned an M.D. from the University of Edinburgh in 1761. The next year, in Philadelphia, he was a pioneer in the establishing of courses in midwifery and in anatomy using dissection. He became professor of anatomy and surgery at the medical school of the College of Philadelphia in 1765.

In 1776 Shippen became chief physician and director general of the Continental Army hospital in New Jersey, rising to chief of the medical department of the Continental Army the following year. Also in 1777 he submitted to the Continental Congress a plan for reorganizing the army medical department which was adopted later in the year.

After serving as a physician at the Pennsylvania Hospital in 1778–79, Shippen became professor of anatomy at the University of the State of Pennsylvania in 1779. In 1791 he moved to the University of Pennsylvania in Philadelphia, where he was professor of anatomy, surgery, and midwifery. He was a founder of the College of Physicians of Philadelphia and held the office of president from 1805 until 1808, the year of his death.

SLAYMAKER, Amos: congressman, businessman
Born London Lands, Lancaster County, Pennsylvania, March 11, 1755; died June 12, 1837.

Slaymaker was a farmer, a builder, and a promoter. He operated a hotel on the Lancaster and Philadelphia pike and also was proprietor of a stage line which ran over the pike. During the Revolutionary War he served as an ensign in the company of Captain John Slaymaker and was a member of the association formed for the suppression of Tory activities in Lancaster County.

After a period as justice of the peace of Salisbury Township, Slaymaker was county commissioner of Lancaster County from 1806 to 1810. In 1810–11 he was a member of the Pennsylvania Senate. He filled a vacancy in the United States House of Representatives on October 11, 1814, and served until 1815 (13th Congress). He died in Salisbury, Pennsylvania.

SMILIE, John: congressman
Born Ireland, 1741; died December 30, 1812.

Smilie, who attended public schools, came to America and settled in Pennsylvania in 1760. He served in the military during the Revolutionary War. He moved to Fayette, Pennsylvania, in 1780 and served in the state House of Representatives from 1784 to 1786. In 1790 he attended the Pennsylvania Constitutional Convention and became a member of the state senate, from which he resigned three years later.

A Democrat, Smilie was elected to serve Pennsylvania in the 3rd and the 6th through the 12th congresses of the United States House of Representatives (1793–95, 1799–1812). In 1796 he was a Democratic presidential elector. He died in Washington, D.C., and was buried in the Congressional Cemetery.

SMITH, James: pioneer, army officer, author
Born Conococheague settlement, Franklin County, Pennsylvania, 1737; married Anne Wilson, May 1763; second marriage to Margaret (Rodgers) Irvin, 1785; father of seven children; died 1813.

A frontier leader, Smith settled in Franklin County, Pennsylvania, in 1760. In 1763,

and again in 1765 and 1769, he led the "Black Boys," whose purpose was to defend frontier settlements; during the 1760s he also served in the militia to defend the Pennsylvania frontier from Indians. He was a lieutenant in Bouquet's 1764 expedition against the Ohio Indians.

Smith was a member of the board of commissioners of Bedford County (Pennsylvania) in 1771; from that year until 1777 he was active in the government of Westmoreland County (Pennsylvania), serving on its board of commissioners in 1773. In 1788 he moved to Kentucky, where he attended the state constitutional convention in 1792 and served in the General Assembly.

Smith wrote *An Account of the Remarkable Occurrences in the Life and Travels of Colonel James Smith, During his Captivity with the Indians in the Years 1755–59* (1799) and a pamphlet about the Shakers which was published in 1810. He died in Washington County, Kentucky.

SMITH, Jonathan Bayard: Continental congressman
Born Philadelphia, Pennsylvania, February 21, 1742; son of Samuel Smith; married Susannah Bayard; father of at least one son (Samuel Harrison); died June 16, 1812.

Smith graduated from Princeton in 1760. Quite active around the time of the Revolution, he was a member of the Pennsylvania Provincial Conference in 1774, returning to serve as secretary of the conference in 1776. In the meantime, in 1775, he was secretary of the Pennsylvania Provincial Convention. In 1776 he helped overthrow the old provincial government. He was secretary of the Committee of Safety from 1775 to 1777.

A lieutenant colonel of a battalion of Associators, Smith served in the Brandywine campaign in 1777. He attended the Continental Congress in 1777–78 and was a member of the Board of War in 1778. Locally he held office as prothonotary of the Court of Common Pleas for the City and County of Philadelphia from 1777 to 1779 and as a justice in 1778. Circa 1794 he was auditor general of Pennsylvania. He also served as a trustee of the University of Pennsylvania and of Princeton from 1779 to 1808 and belonged to the American Philosophical Society. He died in Philadelphia.

SMITH, Robert: architect, patriot

Born probably Glasgow, Scotland, 1722; father of three children; died February 11, 1777.

After arriving in the United States, Smith became a member of the Carpenters Company in Philadelphia. He built Nassau Hall at the College of New Jersey (now Princeton) in 1754, the progenitor of a school of American architecture, and designed St. Peter's Church in Philadelphia in 1758. He became a member of the American Philosophical Society in 1768. While serving on the Pennsylvania Committee of Correspondence in 1774, he originated a plan to block the Delaware River. During his lifetime he was recognized as Philadelphia's most eminent architect.

SMITH, Thomas: Continental congressman

Born near Cruden, Aberdeenshire, Scotland, 1745; died March 31, 1809.

Smith, who attended the University of Edinburgh, studied law in Scotland and came to America in 1769, settling in Bedford, Pennsylvania, where he served as a deputy surveyor. He was admitted to the bar and practiced law in 1772. A deputy register of wills and prothonotary in 1773, he became a justice of the peace the following year.

In 1775 Smith became a member of the Committee of Correspondence and served as deputy colonel of the militia in the Revolutionary Army. He was a delegate to the Pennsylvania Constitutional Convention in 1776, a member of the Pennsylvania House of Representatives from 1776 to 1780, and a Pennsylvania delegate to the Continental Congress from 1780 to 1782.

Smith served as a judge of the Court of Common Pleas in 1791 and as a justice of the Pennsylvania Supreme Court from 1794 to 1809. He died in Philadelphia and was buried in Christ Churchyard.

SMITH, William: clergyman, educator

Born Aberdeen, Scotland, September 17, 1727; son of Thomas and Elizabeth (Duncan) Smith; married Rebecca Moore, June 3, 1758; father of five children (including Rebecca); died May 14, 1803.

Smith, who was awarded an A.M. by the University of Aberdeen in 1747, sailed for New York in 1751 and was ordained a priest of the Anglican Church on December 23, 1753. He was a teacher of rhetoric and logic at the College, Academy and Charitable School of Philadelphia in 1754 and provost from 1754 to 1779 and again from 1789 to 1791.

Smith was charged with seditious libel in 1758 but was exonerated. He served as rector of Trinity Church in Oxford, Pennsylvania, from 1766 to 1777. He became a member of the American Philosophical Society in 1768. In 1779 he founded Kent School (chartered as Washington College in 1782) and served as rector of Chester Parish, Kent County, Maryland, during that year. He was the author of *Plain Truth, Addressed to the Inhabitants of America,* which expressed Loyalist views.

Smith held honorary D.D.s from the University of Aberdeen (1759), Oxford (1759), and the University of Dublin (1763). He was also a Mason. He died in Philadelphia.

SNYDER, Simon: governor of Pennsylvania

Born Lancaster, Pennsylvania, November 5, 1759; son of Anthony and Maria Knippenburg (Kraemer) Snyder; married Elizabeth Michael; second marriage to Catherine Antes, June 12, 1796; third marriage to Mrs. Mary Slough Scott, October 16, 1814; died November 9, 1819.

A justice of the peace of Selin's Grove, Pennsylvania, about 1786, Snyder was later judge of the Court of Common Pleas for Northumberland County, Pennsylvania. He was a member of the Pennsylvania Constitutional Convention of 1789–90 and served in the Pennsylvania legislature from 1797 to 1807. He held the post of speaker for three terms.

Snyder was elected governor of Pennsylvania in 1808 and served until 1817; he was the first representative of the German farming class to be elected to that office. He was a strong states' rights Republican and opposed judicial and financial power in the state government. After he left the governorship he became a member of the Pennsylvania Senate. He died in Selin's Grove soon after his sixtieth birthday.

SOWER, Christopher: clergyman, printer
Born Laasphe, Westphalia, Germany, September 26, 1721; son of Christopher and Maria (Christina) Sower; married Catharine Sharpnack, April 21, 1751; father of nine children (including Peter, Christopher, and Catharine); died August 26, 1784.

Arriving in the United States in 1724, Sower was the leader of the Dunken section of the German Baptist Brethren from circa 1753 until his death; he had been ordained a deacon in 1747 and an elder the next year. He was a founder of Germantown Academy.

Sower inherited his father's printing business in 1758 and published the second (1763) and third (1776) editions of the *Sower or Germantown Bible.* He built a paper mill on the Schuylkill River in Pennsylvania in 1773. Suspected of Loyalist sympathies in 1778, he was arrested and his property was confiscated. He died in Methatchen, Pennsylvania, at the age of sixty-two.

SOWER, Christopher: Loyalist
Born Germantown, Pennsylvania, January 27, 1754; son of Christopher and Catharine (Sharpnack) Sower; married Hannah Knorr, January 8, 1755; father of six children; died July 3, 1799.

Sower took charge of his father's Germantown printing firm, Christopher Sower and Son, in 1774, where he published the Loyalist newspaper *Die Germantowner Zeitung*

until 1777. He published the pro-British paper *Der Pennsylvanische, Staats Courier* in Philadelphia in 1777.

Sower formed Loyalist associations in Pennsylvania and New York while accompanying British forces in Philadelphia and New York City from 1778 to 1780. He advocated a loose imperial tie between England and the American colonies as a basis for peace. He went to England in 1781 and received indemnification for confiscated family properties in Pennsylvania.

Sower moved to New Brunswick, Canada, in 1785, where he served as postmaster and royal printer for the province. He died while visiting his brother's family in Baltimore.

SPANGENBERG, Augustus Gottlieb: Moravian bishop
Born Klettenburg, Prussia, July 15, 1704; son of George and Elizabeth (Nesen) Spangenberg; married Mrs. Eva (Ziegelbauer) Immig; second marriage to Mrs. Mary (Jaehne) Miksch, March 5, 1750; father of at least two children; died September 18, 1792.

Spangenberg graduated from the University of Jena (Germany) in 1726 with an M.A. in theology. He was a professor of religious education at the University of Halle in Germany about 1732–34 and was responsible for the establishment of Moravian missions in Surinam and in Georgia. He came to America in 1735 and participated in the founding of the Bethlehem, Pennsylvania, settlement. In 1741 he formed a group to seek the financial support of the Church of England for Moravian missions.

Consecrated a Moravian bishop in 1744, Spangenberg sailed for America again to become overseer of the Bethlehem settlement. He organized a new settlement on a large tract of land in North Carolina in 1757 and then returned to Herrnhut, Germany, in 1762.

An authority on Moravian missions, Spangenberg was the author of *Lebendes Herrn*

Nichlaus Ludwig Grafen und Herrn Zingendorf, three volumes, 1772–75, and *Idea Fidei Fratrum,* 1779. He died in Herrnhut at the age of eighty-eight.

STANSBURY, Joseph: alleged Loyalist, poet

Born London, England, January 9, 1740; son of Samuel and Sarah (Porter) Stansbury; married Sarah Ogler, April 2, 1765; father of nine children; died November 9, 1809.

Arriving in Philadelphia in 1767, Stansbury was an opponent of colonial independence. He wrote songs about race kinship during the Revolution, thus incurring suspicion as to his loyalty, and he was consequently arrested about 1780 for allegedly carrying on secret correspondence with the enemy. He carried Benedict Arnold's first proposals to British headquarters.

Stansbury moved to New York City in 1793 and served as secretary of the United Insurance Company for several years. A writer of poetry, his works were collected in *The Loyal Verses of Joseph Stansbury and Odell,* published in 1860. He died in New York City.

STIEGEL, Henry William (Baron von Stiegel): glassmaker, ironmaster

Born Cologne, Germany, May 13, 1729; son of John Frederick and Dorothea Elizabeth Stiegel; married Elizabeth Huber, November 7, 1752; second marriage to Elizabeth Holz, October 4, 1758; father of three children; died January 10, 1785.

Stiegel arrived in Philadelphia in 1750 and bought and added to his father-in-law's iron manufacturing business in 1758, naming it the Elizabeth Furnace. There he made six- and ten-plate stoves and kettles. He purchased a forge in Berks County, Pennsylvania, in 1760.

Stiegel acquired a third interest in 729 acres of land in Lancaster County from the Stedman brothers in 1762 and laid out the town of Manheim, where he built and sold houses. He brought skilled glassmakers from England during 1763–64 and began to build a glass factory in Manheim in 1764. He experimented in making bottles and window glass at the Elizabeth Furnace and built a second factory at Manheim, which became the American Flint Glass Manufacturing Company in 1772. In 1769 Stiegel glassware was being made at the Manheim works. Examples of his work are included in the Hunter Collection at the Metropolitan Museum of Art in New York City and also at the Pennsylvania Museum of Art.

Stiegel went bankrupt circa 1774 and became a country schoolmaster and music teacher in Brickerville and Schaefferstown in 1779. He was later a clerk at Reading Furnaces in Berks County. He died in Charming Forge, Berks County, and was buried in an unmarked grave.

SYNG, Philip: silversmith

Born Cork, Ireland, September 29, 1703; son of Philip and Abigail (Murdock) Syng; married Elizabeth Warner, February 5, 1729 or 1730; father of twelve children (including Philip); died May 8, 1789.

Syng came to Annapolis, Maryland, in 1714 and opened a shop in Philadelphia about 1720. His most famous silver creation was an inkstand made for the Pennsylvania Assembly in 1752 which was used at the signing of both the Declaration of Independence and the United States Constitution. He was a member of Benjamin Franklin's Junto and along with Franklin was one of the few serious experimenters in electricity in the 1740s. By 1747 Syng had invented a machine which aided in the generation of electricity.

Syng became a member of the American Philosophical Society and served as treasurer from 1769 to 1771. He was a grantee of a charter for the Philadelphia Library Company and a founding trustee of the College and Academy of Philadelphia (later a part of the University of Pennsylvania). Warden of Philadelphia in 1753, he was treasurer of the city from 1759 to 1769 and a member of the Pennsylvania Provincial Commission of Appeals and a signer of the Non-Importation Agreement in 1765. He died in Philadelphia.

★★★★★

TANNEBERGER, David: organ builder

Born Betheisdorf, Saxony, March 21, 1728; son of Johann and Judith (Nitschmann) Tanneberger; married Anna Rosina Kerner, June 15, 1749; second marriage to Anna Marie (Fisher) Hall, 1800; father of five children; died March 19, 1804.

Tanneberger, whose name was also spelled Tanneberg and Tannenberg, came to America in 1749 and settled in Bethlehem, Pennsylvania. In 1757 he learned the craft of building organs from John Gottlob Klemm and constructed organs in Bethlehem from 1760 to 1765. From 1765 until his death in 1804 he built organs in Lititz, Pennsylvania, for Moravian, Reformed, Lutheran, and Roman Catholic churches in places as far away as Albany, New York. Tanneberger died in York, Pennsylvania, and was buried there.

TANNEHILL, Adamson: congressman

Born Frederick County, Maryland, May 23, 1750; died December 23, 1820.

Tannehill, who received his education in public schools, served as a captain of riflemen in the Continental Army during the Revolutionary War. After the war he settled as a farmer near Pittsburgh, Pennsylvania. He held several local offices and served as brigadier general of the Pennsylvania Volunteers in the War of 1812.

In 1813 Tannehill was elected to represent Pennsylvania in the United States Congress and served for one term. He died near Pittsburgh and was buried in the churchyard of the First Presbyterian Church there. In 1849 he was reinterred in Pittsburgh's Allegheny Cemetery.

TAYLOR, George: Continental congressman

Born Northern Ireland, 1716; married Mrs. Anne Taylor Savage, 1742; second marriage to Naomi Smith; father of seven children; died February 23, 1781.

Taylor came to America around 1736 and settled in Pennsylvania, working as an ironmaster. He served as justice of the peace of Dearham, Northampton County, Pennsylvania, in 1757, 1761, and 1763, and from 1764 to 1772. He was a member of the Pennsylvania Provincial Assembly from 1764 to 1767 and again in 1775. During 1770 he served as a circuit court judge.

Taylor was quite active during the Revolutionary period, serving as a member of the Committee of Safety in 1775 and 1776. He was a delegate to the Continental Congress in 1776–77, and, on August 2, 1776, he signed the Declaration of Independence. The following year he was elected a representative from Northampton to the First Supreme Executive Council of Pennsylvania.

Taylor died in Easton, Pennsylvania, and was buried in St. John's Lutheran Church Cemetery there.

THOMAS, Richard: congressman

Born West Whiteland, Pennsylvania, December 30, 1744; died January 19, 1832.

Thomas, who was educated by private teachers, served as a colonel in the 1st Regiment of the Chester County Volunteers, Continental Army, during the American Revolution. A Federalist, from 1795 to 1801 he was a representative from Pennsylvania to the United States Congress. He died in Philadelphia and was buried in the Friends Western Burial Ground there.

THOMPSON, William: army officer

Born Ireland, 1736; died September 3, 1781.

At the age of twenty, Thompson came to America, settling in Carlisle, Pennsylvania, where he became a surveyor and a justice of the peace. He served as a captain during the French and Indian War and participated in John Armstrong's expedition against Kittanning.

In 1774 Thompson was elected to the Committee of Correspondence for Cumberland County, Pennsylvania; the following year he served on the Pennsylvania Committee of Safety, and also took command of a battalion of riflemen raised in the southeastern counties of Pennsylvania. He served in the 2nd Pennsylvania Regiment, the first body of men to reach Boston from the south, and he repulsed the attack on Lechmere Point.

In 1776 Thompson was commissioned a brigadier general in the Continental Army and was ordered to Canada in charge of a detachment of two thousand men. During that year he attempted to attack Three Rivers but failed because of treachery. Taken prisoner, he was exchanged four years later.

Thompson died in Carlisle and was buried there.

THOMSON, Charles: secretary of the Continental Congress

Born County Derry, Ireland, November 29, 1729; son of John Thomson; married Ruth Mather; second marriage to Hannah Harrison, September 1, 1774; died August 16, 1824.

Thomson came to America at the age of ten. In 1750 he was a tutor at the Philadelphia Academy. Seven years later he began a three-year term as master of the Latin school that later became William Penn Charter School, and in 1760 he became a merchant in Philadelphia.

Active in Pennsylvania politics in the years before the American Revolution, Thomson was one of the key members of the Sons of Liberty who persuaded Pennsylvania to support the Massachusetts position. He served as secretary of the Continental Congress from 1774 to 1789 and was the man who notified George Washington of his election as United States President.

Thomson published translations of the Septuagint and the New Testament under the title *The Holy Bible Containing the Old and New Covenant*, four volumes, 1808. His *Synopsis of the Four Evangelists* was published in 1815. He also wrote *Critical Annotations on Gilbert Wakefield's Works*. He received an LL.D. from Princeton in 1822, two years before his death in Lower Merion, Pennsylvania.

TILGHMAN, Edward: lawyer

Born Wyl, Maryland, February 22, 1751; son of Edward and Elizabeth (Chew) Tilghman; married Elizabeth Chew, May 26, 1774; father of four children (including Mary Anna); died November 1, 1815.

Tilghman graduated from the College of Philadelphia (now the University of Pennsylvania) in 1767 and entered Middle Temple in London, England, in 1772. Two years later he was admitted to the Philadelphia bar. He enlisted as a private during the Revolutionary War and rose to brigade major.

A leading lawyer in Philadelphia, Tilghman was known for his trial practice and procedure. He was an expert in the fields of contingent reminders and executory devices.

TILGHMAN, Tench: army officer

Born at the estate "Fausley," Talbot County, Maryland, December 25, 1744; son of James and Anna (Francis) Tilghman; married Anna Maria Tilghman (cousin), June 9, 1783; father of two children; died April 18, 1786.

Tilghman graduated from the College of Philadelphia (now the University of Pennsylvania) in 1761. For the next fourteen years he was a merchant in Philadelphia. In 1775 he was secretary and treasurer of the Continental Congress commissioners to the Iroquois.

Tilghman became captain of an independent company which joined the Flying Camp in 1776. From that year until 1781 he served as aide-de-camp and personal military secretary to General Washington. On Washington's recommendation, he was commissioned a lieutenant colonel in the Continental Army. In 1781 he was selected for the honor of carrying the message of Cornwallis's surrender to the Continental Congress.

Tilghman died in Baltimore and was buried in St. Paul's Churchyard there.

TILGHMAN, William: jurist
Born at the estate "Fausley," Talbot County, Maryland, August 12, 1756; son of James and Anna (Francis) Tilghman; married Margaret Elizabeth Allen, July 1, 1794; father of one child; died April 29, 1827.

Tilghman graduated from the College of Philadelphia (now the University of Pennsylvania) in 1772 and was admitted to the Maryland bar in 1783. From 1788 to 1791 he served in the Maryland Assembly. He was a delegate to the Maryland Convention to ratify the United States Constitution, and from 1791 to 1793 he was a member of the Maryland Senate.

In 1794 Tilghman was admitted to the Philadelphia bar. He served as chief judge of the 3rd United States Circuit Court of Pennsylvania in 1801–02. In 1805 he was appointed presiding judge of the Court of Common Pleas for the Philadelphia District and surrounding areas and as judge of the Pennsylvania High Court of Errors and Appeals.

Tilghman served as chief justice of the Pennsylvania Supreme Court from 1806 to 1827, during which time the court prepared for the legislature a report on the English statutes in force in Pennsylvania. His major contribution as chief justice was the incorporation of the principles of scientific equity into the law of Pennsylvania.

Tilghman was a trustee of the University of Pennsylvania from 1802 to 1827 and president of the American Philosophical Society from 1824 to 1827. He died in Philadelphia.

TOWER, John: ship owner, manufacturer
Born Philadelphia, Pennsylvania, September 10, 1758; married Susan Leake; died April 25, 1831.

Tower, an apprentice ship carpenter in Philadelphia in his youth, eventually became the owner of several ships, deriving the title "Captain" from his shipping interests. He constructed the first mill in Manayunk, Pennsylvania. During the Revolutionary War he served at the Battle of Trenton. In 1812 he entered into a manufacturing business in Germantown, Pennsylvania. He died in Manayunk nineteen years later.

TOWNE, Benjamin: printer, journalist
Born Lincolnshire, England; died July 8, 1793.

In 1766 Towne became a journeyman printer in Philadelphia and for the next four years was a partner in the *Pennsylvania Chronicle and Universal Advertiser.* He started his own print shop in 1774 and for the next ten years published the first evening newspaper in Philadelphia, the *Pennsylvania Evening Post.* The paper supported the Loyalist position during the British occupation of Philadelphia in 1775; later he was cited for high treason by the Supreme Executive Council of Pennsylvania, but the charges were dropped after he changed the content of his paper to express pro-Patriot sentiments. He died in Philadelphia.

TRUXTUN, Thomas: naval officer
Born Hempstead, Long Island, New York, February 17, 1755; son of Thomas and Sarah (Axtell) Truxtun; married Mary Fundran, May 27, 1775; father of thirteen children; died May 5, 1822.

Truxtun went to sea at the age of twelve and by the time he was twenty had become a ship's commander in the merchant service. He served as a lieutenant on the privateer *Congress* during the American Revolution, also commanding the ships *Independence* and *Mars.* In 1777 he captured many prizes while serving on or commanding other privateers.

Truxtun was later commissioned a captain in the United States Navy. In 1786 he took the first ship (the *Canton*) ever to sail from Philadelphia to China. He commanded the frigate *Constellation* and from 1798 to 1800 won two important engagements during the naval war with France. For these actions, Congress presented him a gold medal.

In 1801 Truxtun was commissioned to lead a squadron against Tripoli but withdrew because his flagship was not given a captain; a hostile administration considered his withdrawal a resignation. In 1806 he refused an offer of a naval command in Aaron Burr's western scheme. From 1816 to 1819 he was sheriff of Philadelphia, where he died in 1822. He was buried in Christ Churchyard there.

★★★★★

UDREE, Daniel: congressman, merchant
Born Philadelphia, Pennsylvania, August 5, 1751; died July 15, 1828.

Udree, who attended common schools, worked as a merchant in Berks County, Pennsylvania. He spent six years as a member of the Pennsylvania House of Representatives (1799–1805). A Democrat, he filled vacancies in the United States House of Representatives during the 13th Congress (October 12, 1813, to 1815), the 16th Congress (December 26, 1820, to 1821), and the 17th and 18th congresses (December 10, 1822, to 1825). He died in Reading, Pennsylvania, and was buried at the Oley (Pennsylvania) Cemetery.

★★★★★

VAN HORNE, Isaac: congressman
Born Tollbury Township, Bucks County, Pennsylvania, January 13, 1754; died February 2, 1834.

Van Horne was apprenticed as a carpenter and cabinetmaker. After becoming an ensign in a militia company in 1775, he was appointed an ensign in the Continental Army by the Committee of Safety and was assigned to Colonel Samuel McGaw's regiment in January 1776. In November of that same year he was taken prisoner and was held until his exchange in 1778. He then became a first lieutenant and later was commissioned a captain.

After the war, Van Horne held local office as justice of the peace of Tollbury Township for several years and as coroner of Bucks County for four years. He was a member of the Pennsylvania House of Representatives in 1796 and 1797 and served in the United States House of Representatives during the 7th and 8th congresses (1801–05). He moved to Zanesville, Ohio, in 1805 and served as receiver of land office from that year until 1826. He died in Zanesville and was buried in Woodlawn Cemetery.

★★★★★

WALKER, Jonathan Hoge: jurist
Born Hogestown, Pennsylvania, July 20, 1754; son of William and Elizabeth (Hoge) Walker; married Lucretia Duncan, circa 1788; father of two children (including Robert J.); died January 1824.

A 1787 graduate of Dickinson College, Walker was admitted to the Northumberland County, Pennsylvania, bar in 1790. He was president and judge of the 3rd Pennsylvania District from 1806 to 1818 and judge for the Western Pennsylvania District from 1818 to 1824. He died in Natchez, Mississippi.

WALLACE, James M.: congressman
Born Lancaster County, Pennsylvania, 1750; died December 17, 1823.

Wallace attended school in Philadelphia and saw service with various companies in the Revolution, rising to major of a battalion of Associators by war's end. He was commissioned a major in the Dauphin County militia in 1796.

A commissioner of Dauphin County from 1799 to 1801, Wallace served as a member of the Pennsylvania House of Representatives from 1806 to 1810 and was selected to fill a Pennsylvania vacancy in the United States House of Representatives on October 10, 1815; he served until 1821. He then retired to his farm and died soon afterward near Hummelstown, Pennsylvania. He was buried in Old Derry Church Graveyard in Derry (now Hershey), Pennsylvania.

WALN, Nicholas: lawyer, clergyman
Born Fair Hill, Pennsylvania, September 19, 1742; son of Nicholas and Mary (Shoemaker) Waln; mar-

ried Sarah Richardson, May 22, 1771; father of seven children; died September 29, 1813.

Admitted to the Pennsylvania bar in 1762, Waln became a member of the Society of Friends in 1772 and traveled to most of the centers of Quaker life and thought in America. He was clerk at a meeting of ministers and elders dealing with "Free Quakers" for supporting the Revolution with arms. He visited Quaker meetings and families in England from 1783 to 1785 and in Ireland in 1795. He was appointed chief official of the Philadelphia Yearly Meeting in 1789. A character in *Hugh Wynne*, a novel by Dr. S. Weir Mitchell, is based on his life.

WAYNE, Anthony: army officer
Born Waynesboro, Pennsylvania, January 1, 1745; son of Isaac and Elizabeth (Iddings) Wayne; married Mary Penrose, March 25, 1766; father of two children; died December 15, 1796.

Chairman of a Chester County (Pennsylvania) committee to frame resolutions of protest against the British in 1774, Wayne was a Chester County delegate to the Pennsylvania Provincial Assembly the following year. He was a colonel in a Chester County regiment sent with the Pennsylvania brigade to reinforce the Canadian expedition in 1776.

A brigadier general in the Continental Army, Wayne joined Washington at Morristown, New Jersey, in 1777 and took command of the Pennsylvania troops. He served in the battles of Brandywine and Germantown in 1777, was with Washington at Valley Forge during the winter of 1777–78, and served in the Battle of Monmouth in 1778. He received a medal from Congress for taking more than five hundred British prisoners and a large supply of munitions at Stony Point in 1779. He was sent to oppose the British, Loyalists, and hostile Indians in Georgia in 1781. He negotiated treaties of submission with the Creek and Cherokee Indians in the winter of 1782–83 and retired from active service in 1783 as brevet major general.

A Chester County representative in the Pennsylvania General Assembly in 1784 and 1785, Wayne was a Georgia delegate to the United States House of Representatives in 1791–92 (2nd Congress). He was a major general in command of the United States Legion in 1791 and defeated the Indians at Fallen Timbers on the Maumee River near what is now Toledo, Ohio. He died in Presque Isle (now Erie), Pennsylvania.

WEBSTER, Pelatiah: political economist
Born Lebanon, Connecticut, November 24, 1726; son of Pelatiah and Joanna (Crowfoot Smith) Webster; married Mrs. Ruth Kellogg, September 1750; second marriage to Rebecca Hunt, October 8, 1785; father of five children; died September 12, 1795.

A graduate of Yale in 1746, Webster was ordained a pastor and preached in Greenwich, Massachusetts, in 1749. He became a merchant in Philadelphia in 1755 and taught at the Germantown (Pennsylvania) Academy. He was taken prisoner by the British in 1777. He opposed the issue of paper money and advocated a national government with complete powers.

Webster was the author of a number of pieces dealing with the new government and with economics. They included *Remarks on the Address of Sixteen Members of the Assembly of Pennsylvania to their Constituents dated September 29, 1787*, 1787; *The Weakness of Brutus Exposed: or, Some Remarks in Vindication of the Constitution Proposed by the Late Federal Convention against the Objections and Gloomy Fears of that Writer*, 1787; *A Dissertation on the Political Union and Constitution of the Thirteen United States of North-America*, 1783; and *Political Essays on the Nature and Operation of Money, Public Finances, and Other Subjects; Published during the American War*, 1791 (in favor of a free trade policy and the support of war by taxation rather than by loans).

WETHERILL, Samuel: manufacturer, founder of religious society
Born near Burlington, New Jersey, April 12, 1736;

son of Christopher and Mary (Stockton) Wetherill; married Sarah Yarnall, April 5, 1762; father of at least one son (Samuel); died September 24, 1816.

Wetherill, a manufacturer, became a leader in the movement to make the colonies industrially independent of England. In 1775 he became a member of the United Company of Pennsylvania for the Establishment of American Manufacturing. A member of a group of Quakers who took an oath of allegiance to the colonies, he defended the right of American colonists to resist England with arms and consequently was deprived of his membership in the Society of Friends in 1777. In response he formed a society called the Free or Fighting Quakers.

Wetherill, with his son Samuel, established a chemical firm for the weaving and manufacturing of dye stuffs in 1785. He was the first manufacturer of white lead in the United States (1790) and erected a factory for producing it in 1804. He was vice president of the yellow fever committee in Philadelphia in 1793 and served on the Philadelphia City Council in 1802–03.

Wetherill was the author of *A Confutation of the Doctrines of Antinomianism,* 1790; *The Divinity of Jesus Christ Proved,* 1792; and *An Apology for the Religious Society, Called Free Quakers.* He died in Philadelphia.

WHARTON, Robert: mayor, merchant, sportsman

Born Southwark, Philadelphia, January 12, 1757; son of Joseph and Hannah (Owens Ogden) Wharton; married Salome Chancellor, December 17, 1789; father of two children; died March 7, 1834.

A wholesale grocer and flour merchant in Philadelphia, Wharton was a member of the Philadelphia Common Council from 1792 to 1795 and was appointed an alderman in 1796. He was instrumental in suppressing a riot by merchant men striking for higher wages. He served as mayor of Philadelphia in 1798–99, in 1806–07, in 1810, from 1814 to 1818, and from 1820 to 1824. After killing two mutinying convicts while in charge of

the Walnut Street Jail, he requested a grand jury investigation of the incident; the jury later ruled in his favor.

Wharton was a member of the Gloucester (New Jersey) Fox Hunting Club, serving as president from 1812 to 1818, and a member of the Schuylkill Fishing Company from 1790 to 1828. He joined the 1st Troop of the Philadelphia City Cavalry in 1798, was promoted to captain and then to colonel in 1810, and was commissioned a brigadier general in the 1st Brigade of the Pennsylvania militia in 1811. He died in Philadelphia.

WHARTON, Samuel: land speculator, Continental congressman

Born Philadelphia, Pennsylvania, May 3, 1732; son of Joseph and Hannah (Carpenter) Wharton; married Sarah Lewis, before 1775; father of six children; died March 1800.

Associated with the firm Baynton and Wharton (which became Baynton, Wharton and Morgan in 1763), Wharton was granted a large tract of land, the "Indiana Grant" (now in West Virginia), which was ceded to him by the Six Nations at Fort Stanwix in 1768. While in England to secure confirmation of the grant, some correspondence between him and Benjamin Franklin was discovered, and he was forced to flee with Franklin to France.

Wharton returned to Philadelphia in 1780 and was later an organizer of the Grand Ohio Company (generally known as the Walpole Company). He represented Delaware in the Continental Congress in 1782 and 1783. He was a justice of the peace in the Southwark (Pennsylvania) District from 1784 to 1786 and a judge of the Court of Common Pleas in 1790–91. He died in Philadelphia.

WHARTON, Thomas: merchant, chief executive of Pennsylvania

Born Chester County, Pennsylvania, 1735; son of John and Mary (Dobbins) Wharton; married Susannah Kearney, November 4, 1762; second marriage to

Elizabeth Fishbourne, December 7, 1774; father of eight children; died May 22, 1778.

A partner in the firm of Stocken and Wharton Exporters, Wharton attended the Pennsylvania Provincial Convention in 1774. He was a member of the Pennsylvania Provincial Committee of Safety in 1775, president of the Pennsylvania Council of Safety in 1776, and a councilor of Philadelphia in 1777. He served as president of Pennsylvania's Supreme Executive Council in 1777–78 and served as commander-in-chief of the forces of Pennsylvania. He died in Lancaster, Pennsylvania, and was buried with full military honors at Trinity Lutheran Church, in Lancaster.

WHITEHALL, John: congressman
Born Salisbury Township, Lancaster County, Pennsylvania, December 11, 1729; father of at least one son (James); died September 16, 1815.

Whitehall, after completing his law study, was admitted to the Pennsylvania bar and established a legal practice in Lancaster County. He accepted appointments as justice of the peace and justice of the Lancaster County Orphans Court in 1777. A member of the Pennsylvania House of Representatives from 1780 to 1782 and in 1793, he was also a member of the Pennsylvania Council of Censors in 1783 and a delegate to the Pennsylvania Supreme Executive Council in 1784. He was a member of the Pennsylvania Convention which ratified the United States Constitution in 1785.

Whitehall served as an associate judge of Lancaster County in 1791. Pennsylvania sent him to the United States House of Representatives for the 8th–9th congresses (1803–07). He died in Salisbury Township and was buried in the Pequea Presbyterian Church Cemetery there.

WHITEHALL, Robert: congressman
Born Lancaster County, Pennsylvania, July 21, 1738; son of James and Rachel (Cresswell) Whitehall; married Eleanor Reed, 1765; died April 7, 1813.

Whitehall attended the Pennsylvania convention that approved the Declaration of Independence in 1776. He served in the Pennsylvania Assembly from 1776 to 1778, from 1784 to 1787, and from 1797 to 1801. In addition he was a member of the Pennsylvania Council of Safety in 1777, of the Pennsylvania Supreme Executive Council from 1779 to 1781, and of the Pennsylvania Convention to consider ratification of the United States Constitution in 1787.

A delegate to the Pennsylvania Constitutional Convention in 1790, Whitehall sat in the Pennsylvania Senate from 1801 to 1805, serving as speaker in 1804. He was a Pennsylvania delegate to the United States House of Representatives and served from 1805 to 1813. He died in Cumberland County, Pennsylvania, and was buried in the Silver Spring Presbyterian Church Cemetery in Hampden Township.

WILLING, Thomas: banker, Continental congressman, mayor
Born Philadelphia, Pennsylvania, December 30, 1731; son of Charles and Anne (Shippen) Willing; married Anne McCall, June 9, 1763; father of thirteen children (including Anne [Willing] Bingham); died January 19, 1821.

At the age of eighteen, Willing entered his father's counting house, becoming a partner two years later; by 1754 he controlled the business. In the same year he formed a partnership in a Philadelphia mercantile firm called Willing, Morris and Company, and became assistant secretary to the Pennsylvania delegation at the Albany Congress. He was elected to the Common Council of Philadelphia in 1757.

Willing served as a Pennsylvania commissioner for trade with the Western Indians from 1758 to 1765 and also as a commissioner to supervise the surveying of the Pennsylvania-Maryland boundary line. From 1760 until 1791 he was a trustee of the Academy and Charitable School of the Province of Pennsylvania. He was appointed judge of the Orphans Court of Philadelphia in 1761.

In 1763 Willing was elected mayor of Philadelphia and the next year was elected to the Pennsylvania Provincial Assembly, serving in the latter body until 1767. He then became a justice of the Pennsylvania Provincial Supreme Court and sat for ten years, until 1777. A signer of the Non-Importation Agreement in 1765, he openly championed colonial rights during the years from 1774 to 1776. He was a president of the First Provincial Congress of Pennsylvania and, in 1775, a member of the Second Continental Congress.

Willing became president of the Bank of North America in 1781 and later was appointed by President Washington as a commissioner to receive subscriptions to the First Bank of the United States. He was president of this bank from 1791 until 1797. He died at age eighty-nine in Philadelphia.

WILSON, James: associate justice of the United States Supreme Court, Continental congressman

Born Carskerdo, Scotland, September 14, 1742; son of William and Aleson (Landale) Wilson; married Rachel Bird, November 5, 1771; second marriage to Hannah Gray, September 19, 1793; father of seven children (including Bird, a son); died August 21, 1798.

Following his education at three Scottish universities—St. Andrews from 1757 to 1759, Glasgow from 1759 to 1763, and Edinburgh from 1763 to 1765—Wilson came to America. He was admitted to the bar in 1767 and in 1776 received an honorary M.A. from the College of Philadelphia. In 1774 he was made head of the Committee of Correspondence in Carlisle, Pennsylvania. A proponent of loose imperial ties between England and the American colonies, he was elected to the First Pennsylvania Provincial Conference, which met in Philadelphia. He was elected a colonel in the 4th Battalion of the Cumberland County Associators in 1775.

Wilson was a Pennsylvania delegate to the Continental Congress in the years 1775–76, 1782–83, and 1785–87. He served as a member of committees to secure friendship with the Western Indians, voted for independence, and belonged to the Board of War, with quasi-judicial duties as chairman of the standing committee on appeals. He was a signer of the Declaration of Independence. A supporter of a strong federal government, he was one of the first to urge relinquishment of the western claims of states and to advocate revenue and taxation powers for Congress.

In 1787 Wilson was a delegate to the United States Constitutional Convention and the next year dominated the Pennsylvania Convention which ratified the United States Constitution. He sat as an associate justice of the United States Supreme Court from 1789 until his death in 1798, during which time (in 1793) he gave the majority opinion in the *Chisholm vs. Georgia* decision. Also during his Supreme Court tenure, in 1790, he became the first professor of law at the University of Pennsylvania. He was commissioned to make a digest of the laws of Pennsylvania.

Wilson died in Edenton, North Carolina, and was buried in Christ Church in Philadelphia.

WISTER, Sally: diarist

Born Philadelphia, Pennsylvania, July 20, 1761; daughter of Daniel and Lowry (Jones) Wister; never married; died April 21, 1804.

Sally Wister, who received only an informal education, began a journal at age sixteen, continuing the diary while her family lived near Philadelphia in 1777 and 1778. The journal survives as a historical document and an account of the life of a Quaker girl during the American Revolution. Miss Wister died in Germantown, Pennsylvania, at the age of forty-two.

WYNKOOP, Henry: congressman, Continental congressman

Born Northampton Township, Pennsylvania, March 2, 1737; died March 25, 1816.

Wynkoop sat as a member of the Pennsylvania Assembly in 1760 and 1761. He was an associate justice of the Bucks County Court from 1764 until 1777 and presiding judge of the court from 1777 to 1789. During the same time he was a member of the Committee of Observation (1774) and a delegate to the Pennsylvania provincial conferences of 1774 and 1775. He served as a major in the Bucks County Associated Battalions and in 1776–77 was a member of the General Committee of Safety.

Wynkoop represented Pennsylvania in the Continental Congress from 1779 until 1783, then became a justice of the Pennsylvania High Court of Errors and Appeals, serving until 1789. He sat in the 1st United States Congress (1789–91) as a Pennsylvania delegate to the House of Representatives. He then returned to his position as associate justice of Bucks County until his death in 1816. He was buried in the Low Dutch Reformed Church Graveyard in Richboro, Pennsylvania.

★★★★★

YEATES, Jasper: jurist

Born Philadelphia, Pennsylvania, April 17, 1745; son of John and Elizabeth (Sidebottom) Yeates; married Sarah Burd, December 30, 1767; father of at least four children; died March 14, 1817.

Yeates graduated from the College of Philadelphia (now the University of Pennsylvania) in 1761 and four years later was admitted to the Pennsylvania bar. He chaired the Lancaster County Committee of Correspondence in 1775 and favored reconciliation with England until the outbreak of the American Revolution. Circa 1776 the Continental Congress appointed him to the commission which negotiated the treaty with the Indians at Fort Pitt.

After the Revolutionary War, Yeates par-ticipated in the Pennsylvania Constitutional Convention in 1787. He held the office of associate justice of the state Supreme Court for many years (1791–1817). In 1794 President Washington appointed him to the commission which treated with the inhabitants of western Pennsylvania who took part in the Whiskey Rebellion. He died in Lancaster, Pennsylvania, and was buried in the St. James Episcopal Churchyard there.

★★★★★

ZIEGLER, David: army officer

Born Heidelberg, Palatinate (now part of Germany), July 13 or August 16, 1748; son of Johann Heinrich and Louise Fredericka (Kern) Ziegler; married Lucy Sheffield, February 22, 1789; died September 24, 1811.

After serving with the Russian Army against the Turks on the lower Danube and in the Crimea, Ziegler was promoted to the rank of a commissioned officer in 1768. Circa 1774 he came to the United States and settled in Carlisle, Pennsylvania. He served as a lieutenant in the Pennsylvania battalion of riflemen led by William Thompson in the siege of Boston in 1775 and fought at Long Island, Brandywine, Germantown, Paoli, and Monmouth. In 1778 he received a commission as captain in the Pennsylvania militia. Having served as commissary general for the Department of Pennsylvania (with headquarters at Waynesboro) in 1779–80, he moved to the regiment which joined General Lafayette in Virginia in 1781. The next year he was attached to General Nathanael Greene's Army in South Carolina.

Ziegler opened a grocery store in Carlisle in 1783. The following year he was commissioned a captain in Josiah Harmar's expeditions against the Indians and was stationed at Fort Mackintosh (Beaver, Pennsylvania), Fort Harmar (Marietta, Ohio), and Fort Washington (Cincinnati, Ohio). After rising to major in the 1st Infantry, he was sent to Marietta in 1790. Two years later he resigned from the army.

Ziegler then held several offices in Ohio: from 1802 to 1804 he was president of the Cincinnati City Council with the duties of chief magistrate; in 1803 he became the first marshal of the Ohio District; and in 1807 he was chosen adjutant general of Ohio. In the latter year he also was appointed surveyor of the Port of Cincinnati. He died at the age of sixty-three.

★★★★★★★★★★★★★

RHODE ISLAND

"Lieutenant-Colonel Barton, of Warren, in Rhode Island, is a young gentleman of about twenty-three or twenty-four years of age, of a martial and enterprising disposition, who has signalized himself on several occasions, particularly in attacking and driving the noted pirate, Wallace, and a party of his men, from an island near Newport, which they had been robbing and plundering; . . ."

PENNSYLVANIA EVENING POST, August 7, 1777

ANGELL, Israel: army officer
Born Providence, Rhode Island, August 24, 1740; son of Oliver and Naomi (Smith) Angell; married Martha Angell; second marriage to Susanne Wright; third marriage to Sarah Wood; father of seventeen children; died May 4, 1832.

Angell was commissioned a major in the Rhode Island Volunteers at the beginning of the Revolutionary War. He was commissioned a major with the 11th Continental Infantry in 1776; the following year he was promoted to lieutenant colonel and then to colonel of the 2nd Rhode Island Regiment. He served in the siege of Boston during 1775–76, at the battles of Brandywine and Red Bank (both 1777), at Monmouth (1778), and at Springfield (1780). He retired in 1781. He died in Smithfield, Rhode Island, at the age of ninety-one.

ARNOLD, Jonathan: physician, legislator
Born Providence, Rhode Island, December 3, 1741; son of Josiah and Amy (Phillips) Arnold; married Molly Burr; second marriage to Alice Crawford; third
marriage to Cynthia Hastings; father of nine children; died February 2, 1793.

Arnold became a member of the Rhode Island General Assembly in 1776 and worked for the repeal of the laws requiring oaths of allegiance to England. The same year he organized the Revolutionary Hospital of Rhode Island. After serving as a surgeon from 1776 to 1781, he represented Rhode Island at the Continental Congress during the years 1782–84.

Having founded the town of St. Johnsbury, Vermont, Arnold was judge in the Orange County Court from 1782 to 1793. During that period he attended the Vermont General Assembly, which voted to accept the United States Constitution in 1791, and was a trustee of the University of Vermont. He died in the town which he founded and was buried in Mount Pleasant Cemetery there.

ARNOLD, Peleg: Continental congressman
Born Smithfield, Rhode Island, June 10, 1751; died February 13, 1820.

After attending Brown University and studying law, Arnold was admitted to the bar and established a legal practice. He was elected deputy to the Rhode Island General Assembly for terms in 1777–78, 1782–83, and 1817–19. In 1790 he was assistant to the governor of Rhode Island and incorporator of the Providence Society for the Abolition of Slavery.

In addition to his political activities, Arnold served as a colonel in the 2nd Regiment of the Providence County militia during the years 1787–89 and as chief justice of the Rhode Island Supreme Court from 1795 to 1809 and then from 1810 to 1812. In the business arena, he was keeper of the Peleg Arnold Tavern in Smithfield and later, in 1803, became president of the Smithfield Union Bank. Seven years later he became president of Smithfield Academy.

Arnold died in his hometown and was buried in Union Cemetery, Union Village, near Woonsocket, Rhode Island.

★★★★★

BARTON, William: army officer
Born Warren, Rhode Island, May 26, 1748; son of Benjamin and Lydia Barton; married Rhoda Carver, 1770; died October 22, 1831.

Barton became a hatter in Rhode Island in 1770. Five years later he joined the Rhode Island militia as a captain, rising to major in 1776 and lieutenant colonel in 1777. The latter year, during the British occupation of the state, he conceived and executed the capture of Brigadier General Prescott by the Rhode Island militia. Congress awarded him a sword in recognition of this exploit.

In 1790 Barton participated in the Rhode Island Convention which adopted the United States Constitution. He died at the age of eighty-three and was buried in Providence.

BOURNE, Benjamin: congressman, jurist
Born Bristol, Rhode Island, December 9, 1755; son of Shearjashub and Ruth (Bosworth) Church Bourne;
married Hope (Child) Diman; father of four children; died September 17, 1808.

Bourne received an A.B. from Harvard in 1775 and an honorary A.M. in 1778. He became quartermaster of a company in the Rhode Island Regiment in 1776. Four years later he became a member of the Rhode Island Council of War and was elected to the Rhode Island legislature. Having attended the Rhode Island General Assembly from 1787 to 1790, he served in the United States House of Representatives for four terms, 1790–96 (1st–4th congresses).

In 1801 Bourne assumed the position of judge of the United States District Court for Rhode Island. He was influential in persuading Rhode Island to ratify the Constitution (the state was the last to ratify). He died in Bristol and was buried in Juniper Hill Cemetery there.

BOWLER, Metcalf: jurist
Born London, England, 1726; son of Charles Bowler; married Anne Fairchild; father of eleven children (including Bathsheba); died September 24, 1789.

Bowler came to American circa 1743 and settled in Newport, Rhode Island. He was a member of the Rhode Island General Assembly from 1767 to 1776. During that time (in 1768), he became an assistant judge in the state Supreme Court, rising to chief justice in 1776. He signed the Rhode Island Declaration of Independence on May 4, 1776. He wrote *Treatise on Agriculture and Practical Husbandry,* published in 1786. He died three years later.

BRADFORD, William: senator, lawyer
Born Plympton, Massachusetts, November 4, 1729; died July 6, 1808.

Bradford studied both medicine (in Hingham, Massachusetts) and law. He then practiced medicine in Warren, Rhode Island, and was later (1767) admitted to the bar and began the practice of law in Bristol, Rhode Island.

In 1764 and 1765 Bradford was speaker of the state House of Representatives, and in

1773 he became active on the Rhode Island Committee of Correspondence. Deputy governor of the state during the years 1775–78, he was later elected to the Continental Congress but did not serve. He was appointed to the United States Senate in 1793, serving briefly as president pro tem in 1797 before his resignation in October of that year.

Bradford died in Bristol and was buried in the East Burial Ground.

BROWN, John: merchant, congressman
Born January 27, 1736; son of James and Hope (Power) Brown; married Sarah Smith, November 27, 1760; father of six children; died September 20, 1803.

Brown was a member of the family mercantile firm of Nicholas Brown and Company in Providence until 1770, when he formed his own mercantile house. Having spoken out against the Stamp Act in 1765 while serving in the Rhode Island Assembly, seven years later he led the party which boarded and burned the H.M.S. *Gaspee* for her attempts to halt smuggling.

In 1775 Brown supported the Continental Association, and he profited greatly during the Revolutionary War by supplying the Continental Army and Navy and by building his own privateers. He was elected to the Continental Congress in 1784 but did not serve. After the war he entered into profitable trading ventures with the East and served as a Federalist from Rhode Island in the 6th Congress of the United States House of Representatives (1799–1801).

Brown aided in bringing Rhode Island College (now Brown University, named for his family) to Providence in 1770 and was a trustee for over a quarter of a century, from 1774 until 1803. He died in Providence and was buried in the North Burial Ground there.

BROWN, Moses: manufacturer, philanthropist
Born Providence, Rhode Island, September 23, 1738;
son of James and Hope (Power) Brown; married Anna Brown, 1764; second marriage to Mary Olney, 1779; third marriage to Phoebe Lockwood, 1799; father of three children (including Sarah and Obadiah); died September 7, 1836.

Brown was admitted to the firm of Nicholas Brown and Company in 1763 and retired from it ten years later. He was a member of the Rhode Island General Assembly from 1764 until 1771.

In 1770 Brown initiated a plan to move Rhode Island College from Warren to Providence and the following year gave one thousand dollars to the school. The college was later renamed Brown University because of his benefactions. In 1784 he became treasurer of the Friends School (now Moses Brown School).

Brown helped organize the Rhode Island Abolition Society in 1774 and founded many other societies, including the Providence Athenaeum Library, the Rhode Island Bible Society, and the Rhode Island Peace Society. He also belonged to the Rhode Island Historical Society. He died in Providence shortly before his ninety-eighth birthday.

BROWN, Nicholas: merchant
Born Providence, Rhode Island, August 8, 1729; son of James and Hope (Power) Brown; married Rhoda Jenckes, May 2, 1762; second marriage to Avis Binney, September 9, 1785; father of ten children (including Nicholas and Hope); died May 29, 1791.

Brown became an assistant and then a partner, along with his uncle and three brothers, in the firm Obadiah Brown and Company in Providence. Upon the death of his uncle in 1762 he changed the name of the firm to Nicholas Brown and Company.

Enterprising and innovative, Brown extended his firm's trade from the West Indies to Marseilles and Nantes in France as well as to Copenhagen, Hamburg, and London. He instigated the shifting of candle manufacture from home to factory in the Providence area and with his brothers was a leading figure in the United Company of Providence and Newport, which manufactured spermaceti candles and was the earliest monopoly in America. He established Furnace Hope, an iron manufacturing plant, in Scituate, Rhode Island, in 1764. He engaged in secret importation for the Continental Congress during the Revolution.

Brown, along with his brothers John and Moses, was influential in bringing Rhode Island College (now Brown University) to Providence in 1770. He was also a benefactor of the Baptist Society of Providence. He died at the age of sixty-one.

BROWN, Sylvanus: millwright, inventor
Born Valley Falls, Rhode Island, June 4, 1747; son of Philip and Priscilla (Carpenter) Brown; married Ruth Salisbury; father of James Salisbury; died July 30, 1824.

Brown, who learned the trade of millwright, served aboard the Continental Navy vessel *Alfred* at the beginning of the Revolutionary War. Besides working for the arsenal of the state of Rhode Island, he supervised the construction of several gristmills and sawmills in New Brunswick. After a short trip to Europe, he returned to Pawtucket, Rhode Island, and reestablished his machine shop.

In 1790 Brown assisted in the construction of the first practical power spinning wheel in America by turning Samuel Slater's memories of English spinning machines into a working model; Brown also designed a crucial part of the machine. He contributed a great deal to the profitable construction of textile machinery and was possibly the first to use the slide-crest lathe. From 1796 to 1801 he superintended furnaces in a cannon factory in Scituate, Rhode Island. He died in Pawtucket at the age of seventy-seven.

★★★★★

CARTER, John: journalist
Born Philadelphia, Pennsylvania, July 21, 1745; son of John and Elizabeth (Spriggs) Carter; married Amey Crawford, May 14, 1769; father of twelve children; died August 19, 1814.

After an apprenticeship to Benjamin Franklin, Carter became owner, editor, and printer of the *Providence Gazette* in 1768, remaining with the paper for forty-five years. The *Gazette* was greatly influential in Rhode Island affairs throughout the Revolutionary era. Carter was also a member of the Committee of Correspondence of Providence during the Revolutionary War. From 1772 to 1792 he was postmaster of Providence. He died in that city.

COLLINS, John: governor of Rhode Island, Continental congressman
Born Newport, Rhode Island, November 1, 1717; son of Samuel and Elizabeth Collins; married Mary Avery; died March 4, 1795.

Collins was a Rhode Island delegate to the Continental Congress for two terms, 1779–81 and 1782–83, and was a signer of the Articles of Confederation. He served as governor of Rhode Island from 1786 to 1790. He died in Newport, the town of his birth.

CORNELL, Ezekiel: army officer, Continental congressman
Born Scituate, Rhode Island, March 27, 1733; son of Richard and Content (Bronell) Cornell; married Rachel Wood, 1790; died April 25, 1800.

In 1776 Cornell was deputy adjutant general of the 11th Continental Infantry and the following year was commissioned commander of the Rhode Island Brigade with the rank of brigadier general. He served as a member of the Continental Congress from 1780 to 1783, in the meantime, in 1782, serving as inspector of the Continental Army under General Washington. He died in Milford, Massachusetts.

★★★★★

ELLERY, William: Continental congressman, jurist
Born Newport, Rhode Island, December 22, 1727; son of William and Elizabeth (Almy) Ellery; married Ann Remington, 1750; second marriage to Abigail Cary, 1767; died February 15, 1820.

Ellery, a graduate of Harvard, was an

original incorporator of Rhode Island College (now Brown University) in 1764. He was admitted to the Rhode Island bar in 1770.

A signer of the Declaration of Independence, Ellery was a member of the Continental Congress from 1776 to 1780. Among his later positions were chief justice of the Rhode Island Superior Court, commissioner of the Continental Loan Office for Rhode Island from 1786 to 1790, and customs collector for Newport District from 1790 until his death in 1820, at the age of ninety-two.

★★★★★

FENNER, Arthur: governor of Rhode Island

Born Providence, Rhode Island, December 10, 1745; son of Arthur and Mary (Olney) Fenner; married Amey Comstock; died October 15, 1805.

Fenner was appointed to the Committee of Inspectors of the Continental Congress in 1774. Later he became clerk of the Court of Common Pleas in Providence.

One of Fenner's first acts as governor of Rhode Island (1790–1805) was to convene the Rhode Island General Assembly in special session for the purpose of having all officers take an oath in support of the state constitution. An Anti-Federalist, he was strongly opposed to the adoption of the United States Constitution. He died in Providence.

FOSTER, Theodore: senator

Born Brookfield, Massachusetts, April 29, 1752; son of Jedidiah and Dorothy (Dwight) Foster; married Lydia Fenner, October 27, 1771; second marriage to Esther Millard, June 18, 1803; father of three children; died January 13, 1828.

Foster, a graduate of Rhode Island College (now Brown University), was admitted to the Rhode Island bar in 1770. He was deputy of the Rhode Island General Assembly, representing first Providence (1776–82), then Foster (1812–16), a town created in his honor in 1781. He was given an honorary Master of Arts degree from Dartmouth College in 1786 and served as a trustee of Brown University from 1794 to 1822. A Rhode Island delegate to the United States Senate from May 1790 until 1803, he supported Hamilton's financial policy and the Jay Treaty with Great Britain.

★★★★★

GANO, Stephen: clergyman

Born New York City, December 25, 1762; son of John and Sarah (Stites) Gano; married Cornelia Vavasour, October 25, 1782; second marriage to Polly Tallmadge, 1789; third marriage to Mary Brown, July 18, 1799; fourth marriage to Joanna Lattine, October 8, 1801; died August 18, 1828.

From 1779 to 1782 Gano was a surgeon's mate in the Continental Army. He practiced medicine in Tappan, New York, from 1782 to 1786 and in the latter year was ordained to the ministry of the Baptist Church. After a brief pastorate in Hudson, Ohio (1790–92), he moved to the First Baptist Church in Providence, Rhode Island, where he served for the remainder of his life.

In 1794 Gano became a member of the Providence School Committee and an overseer of Rhode Island College (now Brown University), continuing to hold these positions until his death in 1828. Brown awarded him an honorary A.M. in 1800. In addition to serving as moderator of the Warren Association of the Baptist Church from 1808 to 1828, he was a delegate to the Baptist Triennial Convention in Philadelphia. He died in Providence.

GARDINER, John: Continental congressman

Born South Kingstown, Rhode Island, 1747; died October 18, 1808.

Gardiner, who was engaged in agriculture in Narragansett, Rhode Island, served in the Revolutionary War as captain of the "Kingstown Reds" in 1775 and 1776. He was a Paper Money party representative to the General Assembly during 1786 and 1787 and a member of the Continental Congress in 1789. He became justice of the peace of South Kingstown in 1791. He died in that city.

GARDINER, Sylvester: colonial official, jurist

Born South Kingstown, Rhode Island, circa 1730; died 1803.

Gardiner was admitted a freeman from West Greenwich, Rhode Island, in 1757. He was commissioned a major for Kings County in 1769 and served until the following year. After a period as justice of the peace of North Kingstown, Rhode Island, in 1774, he became deputy from North Kingstown to the General Assembly in 1775, holding this office until 1778 and again in 1780–81 and 1790. In 1775 he also was appointed, along with others, to take account of powder, arms and ammunition and became a member of the committee which was to remove livestock. In 1780 he was appointed a major in the Kings County militia, becoming 6th assistant in 1781 and serving until 1783.

Gardiner was a justice in the Washington County Court of Common Pleas from 1781 to 1788 and was elected to the Continental Congress in 1787 but did not take his seat. In 1792 he became chief justice of the Court of Common Pleas. He died in North Kingstown.

GARDNER, Caleb: merchant, army officer

Born Newport, Rhode Island, January 24, 1739; son of William and Mary (Carr) Gardner; married Sarah Robinson, June 3, 1770; second marriage to Sarah Fowler, April 17, 1788; third marriage to Mary Collins, October 20, 1799; died December 24, 1806.

As a merchant marine, Gardner was connected with the slave trade. In 1775 he became a first captain in Colonel Richmond's Regiment of the Rhode Island militia; the following year he rose to major and then to lieutenant colonel in the 1st Rhode Island Regiment. He was elected to the Rhode Island General Assembly as deputy from Newport for terms in 1777 and 1779. Throughout the Revolutionary War he was adviser to the French officers in Rhode Island and to General Washington.

From 1777 to 1779 Gardner served on the Rhode Island Council of War; he is noted for piloting the French fleet into Newport in 1780. In that year he also was an assistant in the state General Assembly, returning for terms in 1787–90 and 1792. He also was a French vice consul, a bank president, and a warden at Trinity Church. He died in Newport.

GODDARD, John: cabinetmaker

Born Dartmouth, Massachusetts, January 9, 1724; son of Daniel and Mary (Tripp) Goddard; married Hannah Townsend, August 7, 1745; father of at least two sons (Stephen and Thomas); died July 1785.

After an apprenticeship to cabinetmaker Job Townsend in Newport, Rhode Island, Goddard became a freeman in the Rhode Island colony in 1745. By 1760 he was recognized as the leading cabinetmaker of Newport, his customers including such prominent men as Moses Brown of Providence and Governor Stephen Hopkins. The records of his work were lost during the American Revolution. In 1782 he became a partner in the firm of Goddard and Engs and opened a sales warehouse in Providence. He is identified with the block-front style in woodwork. He died in Newport.

GRAY, Robert: navigator

Born Tiverton, Rhode Island, May 10, 1755; son of Edward Gray; married Martha Atkins, February 3, 1794; father of four sons and one daughter; died 1806.

After fighting on the sea in the Revolutionary War, Gray made a voyage around the world during the years 1787–90. He began in the sloop *Washington,* of which he was in command, and then transferred to the *Columbia,* in which he completed the trip. From 1790 to 1793 he made a second trip around the world in the *Columbia.* During this voyage he discovered Gray's Harbor, which was named for him, and the Columbia River, which was named for his vessel, the first to enter the river. His discovery gave the United States a basis for later claims to Oregon. He died in Charleston, South Carolina.

GREENE, Christopher: army officer

Born Warwick, Rhode Island, May 12, 1737; son of Philip and Elizabeth (Wickes) Greene; married Ann Lippitt, January 6, 1757; father of several children; died May 14, 1781.

Greene was associated with relatives in the operation of extensive manufacturing works on the south branch of the Pawtuxet River. In 1759 he became a freeman in the colony of Rhode Island. During the years 1771–72 he was a member of the Rhode Island legislature from Warwick. In 1774 he was named a lieutenant in the Kentish Guards, established by the state legislature. The following year he was appointed a major in a regiment of the King's and Kent County militia under Colonel James Mitchell Varnum.

Greene was commissioned a lieutenant colonel in command of the 1st Battalion of the Rhode Island militia in Benedict Arnold's expedition to Canada (1775). He was captured and imprisoned in Quebec until his release in 1777; later that year he was promoted to colonel in the 1st Rhode Island Infantry and placed in command of Fort Mercer on the Delaware River. The Continental Congress voted to award him a sword for his gallant defense of the fort against Colonel (Count) Donop's troops. Transferred to Rhode Island in 1778, he took part in the Battle of Rhode Island by commanding a regiment of Negro troops recruited from slaves.

In 1781 Greene was transferred to Westchester County, New York, with headquarters on the Croton River. He was killed later that year.

GREENE, Nathanael: army officer

Born Warwick, Rhode Island, August 7, 1742; son of Nathanael and Mary (Mott) Greene; married Catharine Littlefield, July 20, 1774; father of George Washington, Martha Washington, Cornelia Mott, Nathanael Ray, and Louisa Catherine; died June 19, 1786.

Greene was elected a deputy to the Rhode Island General Assembly for terms in 1770–72 and 1775. In 1774 he organized the militia company known as the Kentish Guards and the following year was commissioned a brigadier general in the Continental Army. Present at the siege of Boston, he later (March 1776) commanded the army of occupation there. He then commanded Continental troops in New Jersey.

Promoted to major general, Greene took part in the fighting around New York in August 1776. He led the left wing of the American forces in the Battle of Trenton and then served at Valley Forge during 1777–78. He was promoted to quartermaster general in March 1778 and was placed in supreme command of the Continental Army during Washington's absence in September 1780. That same year he was president of the board which condemned Major John André to be hanged, was placed in command of the post at West Point (October), and then was put in command of the Army of the South. He is noted for his strategy in the Carolinas, which ultimately forced Cornwallis to Yorktown.

After the war, Greene lived on his plantation outside Savannah, Georgia. He died in Savannah and was buried in Christ Episcopal Church there.

GREENE, William: governor of Rhode Island

Born Warwick, Rhode Island, August 16, 1731; son of William and Catharine Greene; married Catharine Ray, 1758; father of four children (including Ray); died November 29, 1809.

Greene was a delegate from Warwick to the Rhode Island House of Delegates in 1773, 1774, 1776, and 1777, serving as speaker the latter year. He was a signer of the Declaration of Independence. In 1776 he also became first associate justice in the Superior Court of Rhode Island, rising to chief justice the next year. In 1777 he served as the Rhode Island commissioner to the commodity price regulation conference held by the northern states in New Haven, Connecticut. He was governor of Rhode Island from

1778 until 1786. He died in Warwick, the town of his birth.

★★★★★

HAZARD, Jonathan J.: Continental congressman

Born Newport, Rhode Island, 1744; son of Jonathan and Abigail (MacCoon) Hazard; married Patience Hazard; second marriage to Hannah Brown; third marriage to Marian Gage; died after 1824.

Hazard, who was referred to as "Bean Jonathan," was a member of the Rhode Island House of Representatives in 1776 and 1778 and from 1790 to 1805. He was paymaster of the Rhode Island Battalion of the Continental Army in 1777, joining George Washington's army later that same year. In 1778 he was a member of the Rhode Island Council of War.

From 1787 to 1789 Hazard was a member of the Continental Congress, representing Rhode Island. He was a delegate to the Rhode Island Convention at South Kingstown in 1790, where he opposed the ratification of the United States Constitution. He died on an estate in a Friends settlement at Verona, New York.

HAZARD, Thomas: abolitionist

Born Narragansett, Rhode Island, September 15, 1720; son of Robert and Sarah (Borden) Hazard; married Elizabeth Robinson, 1742; died August 26, 1798.

Hazard, who attended Yale, was one of the first members of the Society of Friends to take a stand against slavery. In 1774 he served on the committee of the Yearly Meeting which went to the Rhode Island General Assembly with a bill affirming personal freedom. He was also a member of a committee which brought to the General Assembly a petition for the abolition of slavery in 1783; this resulted in the abolition of slavery in that state the following year.

A founder of the Providence Society for Abolishing Slave Trade, Hazard was an incorporator of Rhode Island College (now Brown University) and a founder of the

Friends School in Providence, Rhode Island. He died at the age of seventy-seven.

HITCHCOCK, Enos: clergyman

Born Springfield, Massachusetts, March 7, 1744; son of Peletiah and Sara (Parsons) Hitchcock; married Achsah (Upham) Jordan, January 13, 1771; father of two daughters (one adopted); died February 26, 1803.

Four years after his graduation from Harvard in 1767, Hitchcock was ordained to the ministry of the Congregational Church. He served as a chaplain during the Revolutionary War and also preached in Beverly, Massachusetts, and Providence, Rhode Island, when not on duty. From 1783 to 1803 he was pastor of the Benevolent Congregational Church in Providence, Rhode Island. In 1785 he wrote *Discourse on Education,* a sermon which advocated free public schools.

HOPKINS, Esek: first commander-in-chief of the Continental Navy

Born Scituate, Rhode Island, April 26, 1718; son of William and Ruth (Wilkinson) Hopkins; married Desire Burroughs, November 28, 1741; father of ten children; died February 26, 1802.

A privateer during the French and Indian Wars, Hopkins was a brigadier general in charge of all the military forces of Rhode Island in 1775. He became commander-in-chief of the Continental Navy that same year, but he met with difficulties in equipping and manning the few American ships available. For these failures he was censured by Congress in 1776, suspended from his command in 1777, and dismissed in 1778. From 1779 to 1786 he was a deputy to the Rhode Island General Assembly; in 1783 a collector of imposts; and from 1782 to 1802 a trustee of Brown University. He died in North Providence, Rhode Island.

HOPKINS, John Burroughs: naval officer

Born Providence, Rhode Island, August 25, 1742; son of Esek and Desire (Burroughs) Hopkins; married Sarah Harris, October 2, 1768; died December 5, 1796.

Hopkins followed in his father's footsteps

by engaging in a naval career. He took part in the burning of the British ship *Gaspee* in 1772 and three years later was appointed captain of the ship *Cabot*. In 1777 he took command of the ship *Warren* and in 1779 captured the British ships *Jason* and *Hibernia*; he was dismissed from his command because of irregularities in his conduct on the latter cruise. From 1780 to 1781 he commanded privateers. He died at the age of fifty-four.

HOPKINS, Stephen: colonial governor, Continental congressman

Born Providence, Rhode Island, March 7, 1707; son of William and Ruth (Wilkinson) Hopkins; married Sarah Scott, 1726; second marriage to Anne Smith, 1755; father of seven children; died April 13, 1785.

At the age of twenty-four Hopkins laid out the town of Providence, serving as town clerk in 1732 and president of the town council in 1735. He attended several sessions of the Rhode Island General Assembly —1732–33, 1735–38, 1741–42, 1744–52, 1769–74, 1777—serving as speaker in 1742. He was an assistant justice of the Rhode Island Superior Court from 1747 to 1749 and held the position of chief justice from 1751 to 1755. He served as governor of Rhode Island in 1755–57, 1758–62, 1763–65, and 1767–68. He was a member of the General Colonial Congress in Albany in 1754, 1755, and 1757.

In 1762 Hopkins was a founder of the *Providence Gazette and Country Journal*. Two years later, he became the first chancellor of Rhode Island College (now Brown University). He was a delegate to the Continental Congress from 1774 to 1776 and again in 1778. On August 2, 1776, he signed the Declaration of Independence. In 1776 and 1780 he attended the conventions of the New England states.

Hopkins held membership in the Philosophical Society of Newport, Rhode Island. He wrote *The Rights of Colonies Examined*, 1756, and *The Grievances of the American Colonies Candidly Explained*, 1765. He died in Providence.

HOWELL, David: educator, Continental congressman, jurist

Born Morristown, New Jersey, January 1, 1747; son of Aaron and Sarah Howell; married Mary Brown, September 30, 1770; father of five children (including Jeremiah); died July 30, 1824.

Howell's education was quite extensive, beginning with his graduation from the College of New Jersey in 1766. He was granted an A. M. from Rhode Island College in 1769 and an A.M. from Philadelphia College that same year. He also held an A.M. from Yale, which he received in 1772, and an LL.D. from Rhode Island College, which he received in 1793.

From 1766 to 1769 Howell was a tutor at Brown University. He was also a member of the board of fellows, 1773–1824; secretary of the corporation, 1780–1806; professor of jurisprudence, 1790–1824; and president ad interim, 1791–92. In 1768 he was admitted to the Rhode Island bar. From 1782 to 1785 he served as a delegate from Rhode Island to the Continental Congress. In 1786–87 he was an associate justice in the Supreme Court of Rhode Island. He held the office of attorney general of Rhode Island in 1789. A boundary commissioner in connection with the Jay Treaty in 1794, he was a United States judge for Rhode Island from 1812 to 1824. He died in Providence.

HOWLAND, Benjamin: senator

Born Tiverton, Rhode Island, July 27, 1755; died May 1, 1821.

After attending common schools, Howland engaged in farming. He held several offices in Tiverton, including collector of taxes (1801), town auditor (1802), and town moderator (1805). A member of the Rhode Island House of Representatives in 1810, he served as a general in the Rhode Island militia during the War of 1812. A Democrat, he represented Rhode Island in the United States Senate from October 29, 1804, to 1809. He died in Tiverton and was buried in the family lot on his estate.

★★★★★

JOHNSTON, Augustus: colonial official, Loyalist

Born Perth Amboy, New Jersey, circa 1730; father of four children; died circa 1790.

Johnston moved to Newport, Rhode Island, circa 1750 and helped prepare bills for the Rhode Island General Assembly in 1754 and 1756. The latter year he served as a first lieutenant in a regiment which fought at Crown Point. From 1757 to 1766 he held the position of attorney general of the colony of Rhode Island.

In 1765, when he was stamp distributor, Johnston was forced to sign a paper stating that he would refrain from carrying out his duties; later that year, a mob attacked his house. In 1776 he refused to give an oath of allegiance to the colony and became a Loyalist; as a result, his property was confiscated.

JONES, William: army officer, governor of Rhode Island

Born Newport, Rhode Island, October 8, 1753; son of William and Elizabeth (Pearce) Jones; married Anne Dunn, February 28, 1787; father of Harriet; died April 9, 1822.

Jones received a commission as lieutenant from the Rhode Island General Assembly in 1776 and rose to captain later that year. In 1778 he served as captain of marines on the brig *Providence.*

After a period as justice of the peace in Providence, Jones was a delegate to the state General Assembly from 1807 to 1811, serving as speaker in 1809 and 1810. During his tenure in the Assembly he presented a petition against the Embargo Act (1808). From 1811 to 1817 he was governor of Rhode Island.

Jones was president of the Peace Society and belonged to the Rhode Island Bible Society and the American Bible Society. He also served as a trustee of Brown University. He died in Providence.

★★★★★

MALBONE, Francis: congressman, senator

Born Newport, Rhode Island, March 20, 1759; died June 4, 1809.

A merchant in Newport, Malbone was a colonel in the Newport Artillery from 1792 to 1809. A Federalist, he served in the United States House of Representatives as a delegate from Rhode Island in the 3rd and 4th congresses (1793–97). A member of the Rhode Island House of Representatives in 1807–08, he was elected to the United States Senate in 1809. He died on the steps of the Capitol and was buried in the Congressional Cemetery in Washington.

MANNING, James: clergyman, college president

Born Piscataway, New Jersey, October 22, 1735; son of James and Grace (Fitz-Randolph) Manning; married Margaret Stites, March 23, 1763; died July 29, 1791.

Manning, a 1762 graduate of the College of New Jersey, was licensed and ordained by the Scotch Plains Baptist Church in 1763. He was placed in charge of founding a Baptist-directed institution in Rhode Island and was a founder of Rhode Island College (now Brown University) in 1763. The school was granted a charter by the Rhode Island Assembly in 1765, and he became its first president and served as a professor of languages from 1765 to 1791.

Manning served as pastor of the First Baptist Church of Providence in 1771 and represented Rhode Island in the Congress of Confederation in 1786. He received an honorary D.D. from the University of Pennsylvania in 1785. A member of the Providence School Committee, in 1791 he drew up a report which recommended the establishment of free public schools.

MARCHANT, Henry: Continental congressman, jurist

Born Martha's Vineyard, Massachusetts, April 9, 1741; son of Hexford Marchant; married Rebecca Cooke, January 8, 1765; father of William; died August 30, 1796.

Marchant earned an A.M. from the College of Philadelphia in 1759. After reading law under Edmund Trowbridge, he was admitted to the Rhode Island bar around 1767 and established a legal practice in Newport. He served as attorney general of Rhode Island from 1771 to 1777.

During the years 1771–72 Marchant appeared before the Privy Council in England on private legal business and was designated joint colonial agent to obtain compensation for expenses incurred in the Crown Point campaign (1756). He accompanied Benjamin Franklin on a visit to Scotland and was a friend of radicals and nonconformists in Great Britain (called "Friends of America"). Upon his return to the United States he came under suspicion of accepting a retainer from a customs collector.

A member of the Rhode Island Committee of Correspondence in 1773, Marchant became a member of a committee to instruct delegates to the First Continental Congress in 1774. He represented Rhode Island in the Continental Congress from 1777 to 1779 and was a member of the standing committees on marine, appeals, treasury, and the Southern Department.

Marchant was a Newport delegate to the Rhode Island General Assembly from 1784 to 1790 and was a signer of a minority protest against the abstention of Rhode Island from the Philadelphia Convention of 1787. He was a delegate to the Rhode Island Convention which ratified the United States Constitution in 1790 and served as a judge of the United States District Court for Rhode Island from 1790 to 1796. He died in Newport and was buried in the Common Burial Ground there.

MILLER, Nathan: Continental congressman

Born Warren, Rhode Island, March 20, 1743; died May 20, 1790.

Miller attended a private school and became a merchant and ship-builder. He was a deputy to the Rhode Island General Assembly from 1772 to 1774 and in 1780, 1782, 1783, and 1790. He attained ranks to brigadier general in the Rhode Island militia from Newport and Bristol counties during the years 1772–78. A deputy to the Rhode Island Assembly for six years, he was a Rhode Island delegate to the Continental Congress in 1786; he was reelected but declined to take his seat. A member of the Rhode Island Constitutional Convention in 1790, Miller died in Warren later that year and was buried in Kickamuet Cemetery there.

MOWRY, Daniel, Jr.: Continental congressman

Born Smithfield, Rhode Island, August 17, 1729; son of Daniel Mowry; died July 6, 1806.

Mowry learned the cooper's trade. He served as town clerk of Smithfield from 1760 to 1780 and was a member of the Rhode Island General Assembly from 1766 to 1776. A judge of the Court of Common Pleas from 1776 to 1781, he represented Rhode Island in the Continental Congress from 1780 to 1782. He later engaged in farming. He died in Smithfield and was buried in a family cemetery in North Smithfield, Rhode Island.

★★★★★

PERRY, Christopher Raymond: naval officer

Born South Kingstown, Rhode Island, December 4, 1761; son of Freeman and Mercy (Hazard) Perry; married Sarah Wallace Alexander, August 1784; father of eight children (including Oliver Hazard, Matthew Calbraith, and Ann Maria); died June 1, 1818.

Perry served in several Continental privateers during the American Revolution. He was present at the siege of Charleston, South Carolina, and served on the *Trumbull* during the battle between that ship and the *Watt.* He was captured by the British four times.

After fourteen years as a captain in merchant service, Perry was commissioned a captain in the United States Navy in 1798. He commanded the ship *General Greene* in suppression of the pirates of Cuba and in escorting merchant vessels to the United States during the naval war with France.

Perry retired in 1801 but returned to the service eleven years later as commandant of the Charlestown (Massachusetts) Naval Yard. He died in Newport, Rhode Island.

POTTER, Elisha Reynolds: congressman
Born Little Rest (now Kingston), Rhode Island, November 5, 1764; died September 26, 1835.

As a young man Potter learned the blacksmith's trade, attended Plainfield Academy, and studied law. He served in the Revolutionary War as a private. He was admitted to the bar circa 1789 and began the practice of law in South Kingston Township, Rhode Island.

Potter was a member of the Rhode Island House of Representatives from 1793 to 1796, from 1798 to 1808, in 1816–17, and from 1819 to 1835; he was speaker in 1795–96, in 1802, and from 1806 to 1808. A Federalist, he was a delegate from Rhode Island to the United States House of Representatives from November 15, 1796, until his resignation in 1797, and again from 1809 to 1815. In 1818 he was an unsuccessful candidate for governor of Rhode Island.

Potter died in South Kingston, Rhode Island, and was buried in the family burial ground in Kingston.

POTTER, Samuel John: senator
Born South Kingston Township, Rhode Island, June 29, 1753; died October 14, 1804.

Potter, a lawyer by profession, was deputy governor of Rhode Island from 1790 to 1803. He was a presidential elector in 1792 and 1796 and a member of the United States Senate from Rhode Island in 1803 and 1804. He died in Washington, D.C., and was buried in the family burial ground in Kingston, Rhode Island.

★★★★★

REDWOOD, Abraham: merchant, philanthropist
Born on the island of Antigua, British West Indies, April 15, 1709; son of Abraham and Mehetable (Langford) Redwood; married Martha Coggeshall, March 6, 1726; father of six children; died March 8, 1788.

Redwood, who emigrated to the United States in 1711, developed one of the first botanical gardens in America, in Portsmouth, Rhode Island. He was a member of the Philosophical Society in Newport, Rhode Island, and a financial contributor to the founding of the Redwood Library there. This library building was one of the first in the United States to be designed by Peter Harrison.

Redwood helped to establish a Friends school in Newport, and he left 500 pounds in his will for the founding of a college in Rhode Island. He died in Newport.

ROBBINS, Asher: senator
Born Wethersfield, Connecticut, October 26, 1757; died February 25, 1845.

Robbins graduated from Yale in 1782 and studied law. For eight years after his graduation he was a tutor at Rhode Island College (now Brown University). He was admitted to the bar in 1792 and practiced law in Providence, Rhode Island. Three years later he moved to Newport, Rhode Island.

In 1812 Robbins was appointed United States district attorney. He was a member of the Rhode Island Assembly from 1818 to 1825 and in 1840–41. A Whig, he filled a vacancy in the United States Senate on October 31, 1825, serving until 1839. Two years later he became postmaster of Newport and served until his death. He was buried in the Burial Ground Common.

★★★★★

SCOTT, Job: clergyman
Born Providence, Rhode Island, October 18, 1751; son of John and Lydia (Comstock) Scott; married Eunice Anthony, June 1, 1780; father of six children; died November 22, 1793.

Scott conducted a Quaker school in Providence from 1774 until 1778, then was a teacher in Smithfield, Rhode Island, until 1783. He practiced medicine in Glocester, Rhode Island (1783–84) and made preaching pilgrimages to Vermont, New York, Pennsylvania, and New Jersey (1784–86). In 1789 he preached at Friends meetings along the Atlantic seaboard from Rhode Island to Georgia, and during 1792–93 he made a preaching tour of England and Ireland. He died in Ballitore, Ireland, in 1793.

Scott, a mystic, is an outstanding example of a quietist. He believed that if he completely suspended all his natural powers the divine spirit could work through him; he also held that messages received from the divine spirit within were more important than the scriptures. After the separation of the Quaker Church into the Orthodox and the Hicksite branches (1827–28), the Hicksites followed Scott's teachings.

STANTON, Joseph, Jr.: senator, congressman

Born Charlestown, Rhode Island, July 19, 1739; died 1807.

Stanton served in the expedition against Canada in 1759. He served in the Rhode Island House of Representatives from 1768 to 1774 and again from 1794 to 1800.

A colonel in the American army during the Revolution, Stanton was a delegate to the Rhode Island Constitutional Convention in 1790. A Democrat, he represented Rhode Island in the United States Senate from June 7, 1790, until 1793. He served in the United States House of Representatives during the 7th through the 9th congresses, (1801–07).

Stanton died in Charlestown and was buried in a family cemetery there.

★★★★★

TILLINGHAST, Thomas: congressman, jurist

Born East Greenwich, Rhode Island, August 21, 1742; died August 26, 1821.

Tillinghast received a preparatory education. He served as a member of the Rhode Island House of Representatives in 1772 and 1773 and from 1778 to 1780. He held several offices under the Revolutionary authorities. He served as judge of the Court of Common Pleas in 1779 and as a member of the Council of War.

From 1780 to 1797 Tillinghast was an associate justice of the Rhode Island Supreme Court. He filled a vacancy in the United States House of Representatives, serving from November 13, 1797, to 1799 and again from 1801 to 1803. He died in East Greenwich, the town of his birth.

★★★★★

VARNUM, James Mitchell: army officer, Continental congressman

Born Dracut, Massachusetts, December 17, 1748; son of Major Samuel and Hannah (Mitchell) Varnum; married Martha Child, February 8, 1770; no children; died January 10, 1789.

Varnum attended Harvard and graduated with honors from Rhode Island College (now Brown University) in 1769. After reading law in the office of Oliver Arnold in Rhode Island, he taught school and was admitted to the state bar in 1771. He received a commission as a colonel in the Kentish Guards in 1774 and became a colonel in the 1st Regiment of the Rhode Island Infantry (later the 9th Continental Infantry) the following year. He served in the siege of Boston and the battles of Long Island and White Plains. In 1776 he was commissioned a brigadier general in the Rhode Island militia and in the Continental Army (the latter commission was confirmed by George Washington). He wintered at Valley Forge with Washington in 1777–78.

In 1779 Varnum was appointed commander of the Rhode Island Department but resigned soon afterward to resume his law practice. However, he did serve as a major general in the Rhode Island militia from 1779 until 1788. He participated irregularly as a member of the Continental Congress during the years 1780–87. He was an early member of the Society of the Cincinnati and served as director of the Ohio Company of Associates. In 1788 he was appointed a United States judge for the Northwest Territory and assisted in drawing up territorial law. He served in this capacity until his death early the next year. He was buried in the Mound Cemetery in Rhode Island.

★★★★★

WANTON, Joseph: governor of Rhode Island

Born Rhode Island, August 15, 1705; son of William and Ruth (Bryant) Wanton; married Mary Winthrop, August 21, 1729; father of eight children (including Joseph and William); died July 19, 1780.

Admitted a freeman of Rhode Island in 1728, Wanton became deputy collector of customs at Newport, Rhode Island ten years later and held that post until 1748. He was a partner in the general merchandising firm of Joseph and William Wanton, exporters of fish, cheese, lumber, pork, mutton, and loaf sugar, from 1759 until his death.

Wanton was named governor of Rhode Island in 1769, serving until 1775. He remained loyal to England during the Revolution.

WARD, Samuel: colonial governor

Born Newport, Rhode Island, May 27, 1725; son of Richard and Mary (Tillinghast) Ward; married Anne Ray, 1745; father of eleven children; died March 26, 1776.

A deputy justice of Rhode Island in 1761–62, Ward signed the charter of Rhode Island College (now Brown University) in 1765 and was an original trustee. He held a meeting at his home to express indignation over the punishment of Boston after the Boston Tea Party. He was a delegate to the First and Second Continental congresses (1774–76) and proposed and helped secure the appointment of George Washington as commander-in-chief of the Continental Army. He died in Philadelphia and was buried in Old Cemetery in Newport.

WARD, Samuel: army officer, merchant

Born Westerly, Rhode Island, November 17, 1756; son of Governor Samuel and Ann (Ray) Ward; married Phoebe Green, March 8, 1778; father of ten children (including Samuel); died August 10, 1832.

Ward was a graduate of Rhode Island College (now Brown University) in 1771. Commissioned a captain in the 1st Rhode Island Regiment of the Continental Army in 1775, he was taken prisoner at the siege of Quebec that year but was released soon afterward. Becoming a major in 1777, he wintered at Valley Forge in 1777–78 and became a lieutenant colonel in 1779. He retired from the military in 1781.

Ward founded the firm of Samuel Ward and Brother in New York City and was one of the first Americans to visit the Far East. He was made a member of the Society of the Cincinnati in 1784 and was a delegate to the Annapolis Convention in 1786. He was president of the New York Marine Insurance Company from 1806 to 1808 and was a Rhode Island delegate to the Hartford Convention in 1814.

WEST, Benjamin: publisher

Born Rehoboth, Massachusetts, March 1730; son of John West; married Elizabeth Smith, June 7, 1753; father of eight children; died August 26, 1813.

West was a patriot and engaged in manufacturing clothes for the American troops throughout the Revolutionary War in Providence, Rhode Island. He received a number of degrees from American institutions, including M.A. (honorary), 1770, and LL.D. (honorary), 1792, Brown University; M.A. (honorary), 1770, Harvard; and M.A. (honorary), 1782, Dartmouth. He was a teacher at the Protestant Episcopal Academy in Philadelphia in 1787–88 and professor of mathematics and astronomy at Rhode Island College from 1786 to 1798.

West produced the first scientific publication in America, *An Almanack for the Year of Our Lord Christ, 1763,* which later became the *New-England Almanack or Lady's and Gentleman's Diary.* It was issued annually at Providence from 1765 to 1768, then published in Boston in 1769. He revived the name Isaac Bickerstaff (originated by Dean Swift in 1707) and issued *Bickerstaff's Boston Almanac for the Year of Our Lord, 1768.* The first illustrated almanac in Massachusetts, it continued annually through the issue of 1779 and was published again from 1783 to 1793. He was elected a fellow of the American Academy of Arts and Sciences in 1781.

West prepared the *North-American Calendar: or Rhode Island Almanac* from 1781 to 1787 and the *Rhode Island Almanac* from 1804 to 1806. He collaborated in the preparations for the observation of the transit of Venus in 1769 and wrote a pamphlet, *An Account of the Observation of Venus upon the Sun the Third Day of June, 1769.* He was a professor of mathematics and natural philosophy at Brown University in 1798–99 and served as postmaster of Providence from 1802 until his death.

WHIPPLE, Abraham: naval officer
Born Providence, Rhode Island, September 26, 1733; married Sarah Hopkins, August 2, 1761; father of three children; died May 27, 1819.

Whipple commanded the privateer *Gamecock* against the French in 1759–60. He was commissioned a captain in the Continental Navy in 1775. As commodore of several vessels, he captured and brought to port eight East Indiamen with cargoes worth more than one million dollars. He participated in the naval defense of Charleston, South Carolina, in 1779. He farmed in Ohio after the close of the Revolution and died in Marietta many years later.

WILKINSON, Jemima: religious leader
Born Cumberland, Rhode Island, November 29, 1752; daughter of Jeremiah and Elizabeth Amey (Whipple) Wilkinson; died July 1, 1819.

Following an illness circa 1774, Wilkinson believed she was possessed by a spirit from God and took the name of Public Universal Friend. She preached at revival meetings in Rhode Island and Connecticut, and from 1777 to 1782 she established churches in New Milford, Connecticut, and South Kingston and East Greenwich, Rhode Island. In 1784 she wrote *The Universal Friend's Advice to Those of the Same Religious Society, Recommended to Be Read in Their Public Meetings for Divine Worship.* Because of public hostility to her disparagement of the institution of marriage, she founded the colony of Jerusalem near Seneca Lake, New York, in 1790. She died twenty-nine years later.

WILKINSON, Jeremiah: manufacturer, inventor
Born Cumberland, Rhode Island, July 6, 1741; son of Jeremiah and Elizabeth Amey (Whipple) Wilkinson; married Hope Mosier; second marriage to Elizabeth Southwick; father of at least six children; died January 29, 1831.

As a youth, Wilkinson worked as a blacksmith and a silversmith. Around 1772 he began manufacturing hand cards for carding wool, and he developed a machine for shaping the iron wire used in the wool cards. He also invented a mill for grinding cornstalks. He manufactured pins and needles for a while and farmed in the Cumberland Valley throughout his life. He died at the age of eighty-nine.

★★★★★★★★★★★★★

SOUTH CAROLINA

"The Honorable William Henry Drayton, the worthy judge of the superior court, has made a treaty with the Cherokees to assist the inhabitants in case of necessity."

RIVINGTON'S GAZETTE, November 9, 1775

BARNWELL, Robert: Continental congressman

Born Beaufort, South Carolina, December 21, 1761; father of at least one son (Robert Woodward); died October 24, 1814.

Barnwell received his education from common schools and private tutors. At the age of sixteen he volunteered for military service in the Revolutionary War, later receiving seventeen wounds in the Battle of Johns Island, South Carolina. After his recovery he served as a lieutenant at the siege of Charleston in 1780, becoming a prisoner aboard the ship *Pack Horse* when the city fell. The next year he was released in a general exchange of prisoners.

As well as being the South Carolina delegate to the Continental Congress in 1788 and 1789, Barnwell participated in the South Carolina Convention to ratify the United States Constitution in 1788. A Federalist, he was a South Carolina delegate to the United States House of Representatives during the 2nd Congress (1791–93). He sat in the South Carolina House of Representatives during the years 1795–97, serving as speaker in 1795. He served in the state senate in 1805–06, holding the presidency of that body during the former year.

For many years Barnwell was president of the board of trustees of Beaufort College. He died in Beaufort and was buried in St. Helena's Churchyard.

BEE, Thomas: Continental congressman

Born Charleston, South Carolina, 1725; died February 18, 1812.

Bee was educated in Charleston and at Oxford University. After studying law, in 1761 he was admitted to the bar of the city of Charleston, where he established a legal practice. He also became a planter. He served in the Commons House of the Province of South Carolina as member for St. Pauls (1762–64), St. Peters (1765), and St. Andrews (1772–76). Having assumed the office of justice of the peace in 1775, he participated in the First and Second Provincial congresses (1775–76). He also served on the Council of Safety in 1775–76 and played an active part in the Revolutionary War.

Bee continued his legislative career with election to the South Carolina House of Representatives for the years 1776–79 and 1782, serving as speaker during the period from 1777 to 1779. From 1776 to 1778 he was both a member of the South Carolina Legislative Council and a judge. He held the lieutenant governorship of the state in 1779 and 1780, then served as a South Carolina delegate to the Continental Congress in 1780–82. President Washington appointed him judge of the United States Court for the District of South Carolina in 1790.

Bee published the reports of the district court of South Carolina in 1810. He died in Pendleton, South Carolina, and was buried in Woodstock Cemetery, Goose Creek, South Carolina.

BENTON, Lemuel: congressman, farmer
Born Granville County, North Carolina, 1754; died May 18, 1818.

After moving from Granville County to the Cheraw District, Benton became a planter and large landowner. He was elected major of the Cheraw Regiment in 1777, and served throughout the Revolutionary War. He was promoted to colonel in 1781 but resigned his commission in 1794.

Benton was elected to the South Carolina House of Representatives for the years 1781 through 1784 and in 1787. He participated in the South Carolina Convention which ratified the United States Constitution in 1788 and in the South Carolina Constitutional Convention in Columbia two years later. A Democrat, he was a South Carolina delegate to the 3rd through the 5th congresses of the United States House of Representatives (1793–99).

Benson also held several local positions, serving as justice of the Darlington County Court in 1785 and again in 1791; as escheator of the Cheraw District in 1787; and as sheriff of the Cheraw District in 1789 and 1791. He died in Darlington, South Carolina, and was buried on his estate "Stony Hill," near Darlington.

BERESFORD, Richard: Continental congressman
Born near Charleston, South Carolina, 1755; died February 6, 1803.

Educated in South Carolina and England, Beresford studied law at Middle Temple in London. He was admitted to the bar in 1773 and practiced in Charleston. He became a planter with extensive estates in Berkeley and Colleton counties, South Carolina, as well as in England.

Taking an active part in the Revolutionary War, Beresford served under General Huger in the 1778 Georgia campaign. He was captured at the fall of Charleston in 1780 and held prisoner at St. Augustine until his exchange in 1781. Later that year he became a member of the South Carolina House of Representatives, and the following year the state General Assembly elected him to the privy council.

Beresford was elected lieutenant governor of South Carolina and served in 1783, but resigned a short time later, next participating as a South Carolina delegate to the Continental Congress in 1783 and 1784. He was the author of *Vigil*, published in 1798. He died in Charleston.

BREVARD, Joseph: congressman, lawyer
Born Iredell, North Carolina, July 19, 1766; died October 11, 1821.

Brevard joined the Continental Army while still a boy, was commissioned lieutenant in the North Carolina militia in 1782, and served to the end of the Revolutionary War. He later moved to Camden, South Carolina, where he held the local offices of sheriff of Camden District (1789–91) and commissioner in equity (1791).

Brevard, who had earlier studied law, was admitted to the bar in 1792 and began a practice in Camden. During the years 1793–1815 he compiled the law report which bears his name. He was a judge in the state Supreme Court from 1801 to 1815, then represented South Carolina as a Whig in the United States House of Representatives during 1819–21 (16th Congress). He died in Camden and was buried in the Quaker Cemetery.

BULL, John: Continental congressman
Born Prince William's Parish, South Carolina, circa 1740; died 1802.

Bull served as a justice of the peace in Greenville County, South Carolina, before becoming a member of the Provincial House of Commons in 1772. Later that year he became secretary of the Province. He attended Provincial congresses in 1775 and 1776 and the first General Assembly of South Carolina in 1776. After serving in the state House of Representatives in the years 1778–81 and 1784, he represented his state in the Continental Congress from 1784 to 1787. He was elected to the South Carolina Senate in 1798. After his death he was buried in Prince William's Parish, Beaufort County, South Carolina.

BULL, William: colonial governor
Born Ashley Hall, South Carolina, September 24, 1710; son of William and Mary (Quintyne) Bull; married Hannah Beale, August 17, 1746; died July 4, 1791.

Bull received the M.D. from the University of Leyden in Holland and was thereby the first native American to earn the M.D. degree. He was a member of the South Carolina House of Commons in 1736–49, 1740–42 (during which time he was speaker), and 1744–49. He had taken a position on the Governor's Council in 1748 which he kept until 1759, when he became lieutenant governor of the state.

Bull served as acting governor of South Carolina for many years—1760–61, 1764–66, 1768, 1769–71, and 1773–75. In 1770 his plan for free public schools for the state was set aside because of the approaching Revolutionary War. A Loyalist, he departed from the United States in 1782 with British troops.

Bull contributed 150 pounds to the College of Philadelphia (now the University of Pennsylvania). He died in London, England.

BURKE, Aedanus: congressman, jurist
Born Galway, Ireland, June 16, 1743; never married; died March 30, 1802.

Burke studied theology in St.-Omer, France, and later, in 1769, studied law in Stafford County, Virginia. After a visit to the West Indies, he came to America and settled in South Carolina. In 1778 he resigned his commission as lieutenant in the 2nd South Carolina Continental Regiment. He held the position of judge in the state Supreme Court during the years 1778–80 and 1785–1802. From 1780 to 1782 he served as a captain in the Continental Army.

Burke was elected for several terms to the South Carolina House of Representatives, serving in 1781, 1782, and 1784–89; while there he advocated leniency for the Loyalists. In 1785 he became a commissioner to prepare a digest of the state laws. Three years later he attended the state convention to ratify the federal constitution, at which he opposed ratification unless an amendment was added restricting the President to one term. In further political activity, he went to the 1st Congress of the United States House of Representatives (1789–91), where he opposed the United States Bank and the excise tax and favored slavery and federal assumption of state debts. Later, from 1799 to 1802, he served as chancellor of the South Carolina Court of Equity.

Burke wrote a number of pamphlets, including *"An Address to the Freemen of South Carolina"* (1783) and *"Considerations on the Order of the Cincinnati"* (1783), which was translated into both French and German. He died in Charleston, South Carolina, and was buried at "Burnt Church," near Jacksonboro, South Carolina.

BUTLER, Pierce: senator
Born County Carlow, Ireland, July 11, 1744; son of Sir Richard and Henrietta (Percy) Butler; married Mary Middleton, January 10, 1771; died February 15, 1822.

Butler received a commission as major in Her Majesty's 9th Regiment. Having evidently changed allegiances, he later was elected a representative in the South Carolina legislature for the years 1778–79 and 1784–89. In 1779 he became adjutant general of the state and in 1786 was elected to fix the state's boundaries.

In 1787, as well as representing South Carolina at the Congress of Confederation, Butler attended the United States Constitutional Convention, at which he wrote the fugitive slave clause and advocated a strong central government with property as one of the main bases for representation. A Federalist, he was a member of the United States Senate in the years 1789–96 and 1802–04. He also was a director of the First and Second United States banks. He died in Philadelphia at the age of seventy-seven.

BUTLER, William: army officer, congressman

Born Prince William County, Virginia, December 17, 1759; son of James and Mary (Simpson) Butler; married Behethland Moore, June 3, 1784; father of James, Andrew, George, William, Frank, Pierce, Emmala, and Leontine; died September 23, 1821.

Butler became a commissioned officer in the South Carolina militia in 1781. He was elected to the South Carolina House of Representatives in 1786 and the following year attended the state convention to ratify the federal constitution, at which he voted against ratification. In 1791 he became sheriff of the 96th District. He received a commission as brigadier general and then as major general in the South Carolina militia in 1794. He served for six terms in the United States House of Representatives, from 1801 until 1813 (7th–12th congresses). He died in Columbia, South Carolina.

★★★★★

CALHOUN, Joseph: congressman
Born Staunton, Virginia, October 22, 1750; died April 14, 1817.

As a young man, Calhoun settled on a farm near the present town of Abbeville, South Carolina. He was a member of the South Carolina House of Representatives from 1804 to 1805. A Democrat, he filled a vacancy in the United States House of Representatives during the 10th and 11th congresses, serving from 1807 to 1811. He then returned to farming and milling.

Calhoun also served as a colonel in the South Carolina militia. He died in Calhoun Mills, Abbeville District, now known as Mount Carmel, McCormick County. He was buried in the family burying ground.

CASEY, Levi: congressman
Born South Carolina, circa 1752; died February 3, 1807.

Casey served with the Continental Army in the Revolutionary War and was elected brigadier general of the South Carolina militia. He was justice of the Newberry County Court in 1785. After serving in the South Carolina House of Representatives, he attended the United States House of Representatives during the 8th and 9th congresses (1803–07). Just before his death, he was reelected to the 10th Congress. He died in Washington, D.C., and was buried in the Congressional Cemetery.

COLHOUN, John Ewing: senator
Born Staunton, Augusta County, Virginia, 1750; died October 26, 1802.

At the age of twenty-four Colhoun graduated from Princeton and four years later became a member of the South Carolina House of Representatives, in which he served until 1800. In 1783 he was admitted to the bar and established a practice in Charleston, South Carolina. He later returned to the 96th District and became a farmer.

In 1785 Colhoun was elected to the Privy Council and became a commissioner of confiscated estates. In 1801 he served as a member of the South Carolina Senate; later that year he became a member of the United States Senate, in which he served as a member of the committee to report on modification of the judiciary system of the United

States. He died in Pendleton, South Carolina, and was buried in the Old Stone Churchyard.

COOPER, Thomas: scientist, college president

Born London, England, October 22, 1759; son of Thomas Cooper; married Alice Greenwood; second marriage to Elizabeth Hemming, 1811; father of eight children; died May 11, 1839.

Cooper entered Oxford University in 1779 and studied medicine in London and Manchester. He came to America in reaction to the conservative English policies in 1794. Although convicted, sentenced, and fined under the Sedition Act in 1800, he became commissioner in Luzerne County, Pennsylvania, the next year, serving until 1804.

After acting as a state judge in Pennsylvania for seven years (1804–11), Cooper was professor of chemistry at Dickinson College (1811–15). From 1816 to 1819 he was professor of applied chemistry and mineralogy at the University of Pennsylvania. He joined the faculty of the University of South Carolina as professor of chemistry in 1820 and became president of the university the following year, serving for thirteen years. At the end of that time (1834) the university awarded him an honorary LL.D.

Cooper was influential in establishing the first school of medicine and the first insane asylum in South Carolina and was a member of the American Philosophical Society. He was the author of *On the Constitution*, 1826, and *Lectures on Political Economy*, 1826. He edited *Thomson System of Chemistry*, four volumes, 1818, and *Statutes at Large of South Carolina*, five volumes, 1836–39. He died in Columbia, South Carolina, and was buried in Trinity Churchyard there.

CORAM, Thomas: artist

Born Bristol, England, April 25, 1757; died May 2, 1811.

Coram came to Charleston, South Carolina, in 1769. At the age of thirteen he took up engraving, and during the American Revolution he engraved bills of credit for the state of South Carolina. In 1784 he advertised as a drawing master. He died in Charleston.

★★★★★

De SAUSSURE, Henry William: legislator

Born Pocotaligo, South Carolina, August 16, 1763; son of Daniel and Mary (McPherson) De Saussure; married Eliza Ford, 1785; died March 29, 1839.

De Saussure, who saw a great deal of battle action in the American Revolution, was admitted to the Philadelphia bar in 1784. He was a member of the South Carolina Constitutional Convention in 1790 and served for several years in the lower house of the South Carolina General Assembly (1790–94, 1796–98, 1800–02, 1807–08). In 1795 he became the director of the United States Mint and in 1797–98 was intendant (administrator) of Charleston, South Carolina.

De Saussure, who was active in the establishment of South Carolina State University in Columbia in 1801, served as chancellor of South Carolina from 1808 to 1837. He died in Charleston.

DRAYTON, William: jurist

Born Ashley River, South Carolina, March 21, 1732; son of Thomas and Elizabeth (Bull) Drayton; married Mary Motte; second marriage to Mary Gates, 1780; father of ten children (including William); died May 18, 1790.

Drayton attended Middle Temple in London, England, from 1750 to 1754. After 1763 he went to East Florida and in 1767 was chief justice of the East Florida Province. He became a judge of the South Carolina Admiralty Court in 1780. In 1789 he was an associate justice of the South Carolina Supreme Court and the first judge of the United States Court for South Carolina. He died in South Carolina.

DRAYTON, William Henry: Continental congressman, jurist

Born at the estate "Drayton Hall," near Charleston, South Carolina, September 1742; son of John and

Charlotte (Bull) Drayton; married Dorothy Go-lightly, March 29, 1764; died September 3, 1779.

Drayton attended Westminster School and also Balliol College, Oxford University, England. After being admitted to the South Carolina bar in 1764, he became a member of the South Carolina Assembly the following year. In 1770 he was appointed privy councilor of South Carolina by King George III but was suspended for protesting the system of filling government positions with appointees from England.

Drayton was a member of the Governor's Council of the Province of South Carolina from 1772 to 1775, serving as president in 1775; he was suspended again for protesting the appointment system. In 1774–75 he was assistant judge of the Colony of South Carolina and president of the South Carolina Provincial Congress in 1775. In the summer of 1775, as commander of the armed ship *Prosper,* he actively engaged the British sloops *Tamar* and *Cherokee;* this action initiated hostilities in the South.

Drayton was chief justice of the South Carolina Supreme Court in 1776 and a member of the Continental Congress from South Carolina in 1778–79. In 1821 he wrote *A Memoir of the American Revolution from Its Commencement to the Year 1776 as Relating to South Carolina.* He died in Philadelphia and was buried in Christ Church Cemetery there.

★★★★★

EARLE, John Baylis: congressman, planter
Born near Landrum, Spartanburg County, South Carolina, October 23, 1766; died February 3, 1863.

Earle was nine years old when the Declaration of Independence was signed. During the Revolutionary War he participated as a drummer boy and as a soldier; more than thirty years later he took part in the War of 1812. He was a member of the United States House of Representatives from South Carolina during the 8th Congress (1803–05) and served as adjutant to the inspector general

of South Carolina for sixteen years. He was a member of the Nullification Convention during 1832–33. He died at the age of ninety-six and was buried on his plantation, "Silver Glade," in Anderson County, South Carolina.

EARLE, Samuel: congressman
Born Frederick County, Virginia, November 28, 1760; died November 24, 1833.

Earle fought in the Revolutionary War between the ages of sixteen and twenty-one, rising from ensign to captain of a company of rangers in the Continental Army. He was elected to the South Carolina House of Representatives in 1784, serving for four years. In 1788 he acted as a delegate to the South Carolina Convention which ratified the United States Constitution; the following year he was a delegate to the South Carolina Constitutional Convention. He was then elected to the United States House of Representatives from South Carolina during the 4th Congress (1795–97).

Earle died in Pendleton District, South Carolina, and was buried in Beaverdam Cemetery, Oconee County, South Carolina.

EVELEIGH, Nicholas: Continental congressman
Born Charleston, South Carolina, circa 1748; died April 16, 1791.

Eveleigh was educated in England. During the Revolution he was commissioned a captain in the 2nd South Carolina Regiment of the Continental Army, serving in battle against the British at Fort Moultrie in 1776. He was promoted to colonel, deputy adjutant general for South Carolina and Georgia, in 1778 and served in the Georgia campaign at Fort Tony in the same year.

Eveleigh was a delegate to the South Carolina House of Representatives in 1781. Later that year he became a member of the Continental Congress from South Carolina, serving until the following year. In 1783 he was a member of the South Carolina Legislative Council. He was the first comptroller of the United States Treasury, serving from 1789 until his death in 1791, in Philadelphia.

★★★★★

FARROW, Samuel: congressman
Born Virginia, 1759; died November 18, 1824.

Farrow was wounded while fighting in the Revolutionary War. After studying law, he was admitted to the bar in 1793 and began his law practice in Spartanburg, South Carolina. He also became engaged in agriculture near Cross Anchor, South Carolina.

Farrow served South Carolina in three political capacities: lieutenant governor from 1810 to 1812; a member of the United States House of Representatives as a War Democrat during the 13th Congress (1813–1815); and a member of the state House of Representatives from 1816 to 1821.

After his death in 1824, Farrow was interred in the family burial ground on his plantation near the battlefield of Musgrove Mill, in Spartanburg County, South Carolina.

FAYSSOUX, Peter: physician, surgeon
Born Charleston, South Carolina, 1745; stepson of Doctor James Hunter; married Sarah Wilson, January 29, 1772; second marriage to Ann Smith, March 1777; father of at least thirteen children; died February 1, 1795.

Fayssoux graduated from the University of Edinburgh, Scotland, in 1769. In 1773 he was elected curator of the first museum of natural history in America, in Charleston, South Carolina. In 1775 he was a member of a committee which collected signatures for the Patriots' Association. The following year his signature was used on South Carolina's paper money. He was a member of the South Carolina legislature and a member of the privy council of Governor Moultrie. In 1786 he incorporated the Santee Canal Company.

In the medical field, Fayssoux was a senior physician in the South Carolina militia, served under General Nathanael Greene in the Continental Army, and was appointed chief physician and surgeon of the hospital for the Southern Department in 1781. An organizer of the Medical Society of South Carolina in 1789, he was its first president, serving from 1790 to 1792.

FURMAN, Richard: clergyman, educator
Born Esopus, New York, October 9, 1755; son of Wood and Rachel (Brodhead) Furman; married Elizabeth Haynesworth, November 1775; second marriage to Dorothea Burn, May 5, 1789; died August 25, 1825.

Furman became an outstanding South Carolina Baptist leader after he was ordained as pastor of the Baptist Church in Esopus in 1774. Thirteen years later he became pastor of a Baptist Church in Charleston, South Carolina. He was an influential member of the South Carolina Constitutional Convention, and he produced a plan for the incorporation of the Charleston Baptist Association in 1785.

The first president of the South Carolina Baptist Convention in 1821, Furman was a leader in the plan for the Baptists of South Carolina and Georgia to unite in founding a collegiate institution (now known as Furman University) in Greenville, South Carolina. He was elected president of the Baptist Triennial Convention of the United States in 1814 and reelected in 1817. He was also a founder of George Washington University, Washington, D.C.

★★★★★

GADSDEN, Christopher: Continental congressman
Born Charleston, South Carolina, February 16, 1724; son of Thomas and Elizabeth Gadsden; married Jane Godfrey, August 28, 1746; second marriage to Mary Hassell, December 29, 1775; third marriage to Anne Wragg, 1776; father of at least one child; died August 28, 1805.

Gadsden served in the South Carolina Assembly from 1757 to 1784. By 1761 he had acquired a plantation, two stores in Charleston, and two stores in a rural area. He was a member of the Stamp Act Congress in 1765 and came to be a leader of radicals in South Carolina. He attended the First and Second Continental congresses in 1774 and 1775.

In 1776 Gadsden became the senior colonel in command of the South Carolina militia and was commissioned a brigadier general in the Continental Army. He was a delegate to state constitutional conventions in 1778 and 1790. From 1778 to 1780 he held the office of lieutenant governor of South Carolina; during this time he signed the surrender of Charleston to Sir Henry Clinton (1780), was imprisoned by the British, and then was exchanged in 1781.

After the war Gadsden participated in the South Carolina Convention which ratified the United States Constitution in 1788 and was a presidential elector the following year. He died in Charleston at the age of eighty-one.

GARDEN, Alexander: naturalist, physician
Born Aberdeenshire, Scotland, circa 1730; son of the Reverend Alexander Garden; married Elizabeth Peronneau, December 24, 1755; father of Major Alexander Garden; died April 15, 1791.

Garden earned an M.D. from Marischal College in Aberdeen, Scotland, in 1753 and came to America the next year, settling in Prince William Parish, South Carolina. He discovered the vermifugal properties of pinkroot *(Spigelia marilandica)* as well as the Congo snake and the mud eel. He corresponded with various American and European naturalists and was instrumental in sending the first electric eels to Europe.

Garden became a member of the Royal Society of Upsala (Sweden) in 1763 and ten years later became a fellow of the Royal Society of London. Having sided with the King during the American Revolution, he was banished and his property confiscated by the Act of February 26, 1782. Subsequently he was elected vice president of the Royal Society of England. The gardenia was named after him.

GARDEN, Alexander: army officer, author
Born Charleston, South Carolina, December 4, 1757; son of Alexander and Elizabeth (Peronneau) Garden; married Mary Anna Gibbes, 1784; father of one adopted child (Alester Gibbes); died February 24, 1829.

Garden received an M.A. from the University of Glasgow, Scotland, in 1779. He was commissioned a lieutenant in Lee's Legion of the Continental Army in 1780, and the following year he became aide-de-camp to General Nathanael Greene and was promoted to major. After the war, in 1784, he served in the South Carolina Assembly.

Garden became a member of the South Carolina Society of the Cincinnati in 1808, serving as vice president from 1814 to 1826 and as president from 1826 to 1829, the year of his death. He is best known for his accounts of the Revolution, which were published as *Anecdotes of the Revolutionary War in America* (1822) and *Anecdotes of the American Revolution, 2nd series* (1828).

GERVAIS, John Lewis: Continental congressman
Born probably in France; son of Huguenot parents; died August 18, 1798.

After being educated in Hanover, Germany, Gervais came to the United States, arriving in Charleston, South Carolina, in 1764, where he became a merchant planter and landowner. During 1775 and 1776 he was a delegate to the Provincial Convention and to the Provincial Congress and was a member of the Council of Safety, returning to it in 1781. Congress appointed him deputy postmaster general of South Carolina in 1778. He helped organize troops for the defense of Charleston in 1780.

A member of the South Carolina Senate in 1781–82, Gervais also served as its president during that time. He went to the Continental Congress during 1782–83, where he was on the committee to which were referred letters from United States representatives abroad. Later he was commissioner of public accounts for South Carolina (1794–95). He died in Charleston and was buried in St. Philip's Churchyard.

GIBBS, William Hasell: lawyer

Born Charleston, South Carolina, March 16, 1754; son of William and Elizabeth (Hasell) Gibbs; married Elizabeth Allston, August 29, 1772; second marriage to Mary Philip Wilson, January 21, 1808; father of at least ten children (including Robert W.); died February 13, 1834.

After reading law under John Rutledge, Gibbs attended Inner Temple in London in 1774. In the same year he signed a petition to the House of Commons protesting the Intolerable Acts. When the American Revolution began, he was refused a passport to America but managed to get to South Carolina. He received a commission as a captain lieutenant in the Ancient Artillery Company in Charleston, South Carolina, and served in the defense of Charleston and Savannah. In 1780 Cornwallis arrested him, and he was held prisoner for a time in St. Augustine, Florida.

Around 1782 Gibbs was admitted to the South Carolina bar. From 1783 to 1785 he was master in equity in South Carolina. The state legislature impeached him in 1811 on charges resulting from a sale of slaves, but a large majority acquitted him of all charges. He engaged in the private practice of law from 1825 until his death. He died in Charleston and was buried in St. Philip's Churchyard there.

GILLON, Alexander: naval officer, congressman

Born Rotterdam, Holland, August 13, 1741; son of Mary Gillon; married Mary Cripps, July 6, 1766; second marriage to Ann Purcell, February 10, 1789; father of one son and two daughters; died October 6, 1794.

In 1764 and 1765 Gillon commanded British merchant vessels headquartered in Charleston, South Carolina. In 1766 he began a ten-year engagement in trading enterprises. While a member of the South Carolina provincial congresses (1775–77), he strongly favored American independence.

Appointed a commodore in the navy of the state of South Carolina (1778), Gillon was sent to France as a financial agent to borrow money and purchase ships. In 1780 he obtained from Chevalier Luxembourg a frigate which he named the *South Carolina*. Taking command of the ship, he captured prizes in the North Sea in 1781 and the next year commanded the expedition that took the Bahamas. Unfortunately, his ship was captured by the British in 1782, and he lost money in the enterprise, as Luxembourg's claims for payment continued in the courts for many years.

After the war, Gillon served as a delegate to the Congress of Confederation (1784), a member of the South Carolina Assembly (1786–88), and a member of the United States House of Representatives during the 3rd Congress (1793–94). He died at his estate, "Gillon's Retreat."

GRIMKÉ, John Faucheraud: army officer, jurist

Born Charleston, South Carolina, December 16, 1752; son of John Paul and Mary (Faucheraud) Grimké; married Mary Smith, October 12, 1784; father of fourteen children (including Thomas Smith, Sarah Moore, and Angelina Emily); died August 9, 1819.

Grimké received an A.B. from Trinity College in 1774. In 1776 he was commissioned a captain in the South Carolina Artillery of the Continental Army and soon was promoted to lieutenant colonel. He served as deputy adjutant general for South Carolina and Georgia from 1776 until 1780, when he was imprisoned at the surrender of Charleston. Paroled in 1781, he was a member of the South Carolina House of Representatives from then until 1786.

Grimké participated in the South Carolina Convention which ratified the federal constitution in 1788. He was a presidential elector the following year. In 1799 he became a senior associate of the South Carolina Superior Court and served in this position until the year of his death. He died in Long Branch, New Jersey.

★★★★★

HAMILTON, Paul: governor of South Carolina, secretary of the navy

Born St. Paul's Parish, South Carolina, October 16, 1762; son of Archibald and Rebecca (Branford) Hamilton; married Mary Wilkinson, October 10, 1782; died June 30, 1816.

Hamilton, who fought in the Revolutionary War, became justice of the peace in St. Paul's Parish at the age of twenty-four. He was a member of the lower house of the South Carolina legislature from 1787 to 1789 and served in the South Carolina Senate in 1794 and 1798–99. From 1800 to 1804 he was comptroller of South Carolina. He acceded to the governorship of South Carolina in 1804 and served until 1806.

Hamilton, though a slave-owner himself, urged the South Carolina legislature to prohibit the African slave trade. Secretary of the navy from 1809 to 1813, he was hampered throughout his tenure by a lack of funds. He did help to secure an act for the construction of naval hospitals in 1811 and endeavored to enforce a government embargo policy at the beginning of the War of 1812. He died in Beaufort, South Carolina.

HAYNE, Isaac: planter, army officer

Born Colleton District, South Carolina, September 23, 1745; son of Isaac and Sarah (Williamson) Hayne; married Elizabeth Hutson, July 18, 1765; father of two children; died August 4, 1781.

Before the Revolution, Hayne was a planter and a breeder of fine horses in South Carolina. He served as a captain in the Colleton militia during the Revolutionary War. He swore allegiance to the Crown after the fall of Charleston, South Carolina, with the assurance that military service would not be required of him; however, he was later ordered to join the British Army. Considering this a release from his oath of allegiance, he joined the South Carolina militia and later captured General Andrew Williamson. He was captured by British Colonel Nisbet Balfour in July 1781 and hanged at Charleston.

HEWAT, Alexander: clergyman, historian

Born Scotland, 1745; married Eliza Barksdale; died 1829.

A graduate of the University of Edinburgh, Hewat came to America at the age of eighteen. In 1763 he became pastor of the First Presbyterian Church in Charleston, South Carolina, serving until 1775. He then traveled to England because of his Loyalist sympathies. He was a witness before the Royal Commission on the losses and services of the American Loyalists.

Hewat received an honorary D.D. from the University of Edinburgh in 1780. He was the author of *An Historical Account of the Rise and Progress of the Colonies of South Carolina and Georgia*, two volumes, published in 1799; this was the first history of South Carolina. He also wrote *Sermons*, two volumes, published in 1803–05. He died in London, England.

HEYWARD, Thomas: army officer, jurist

Born St. Helena's Parish, South Carolina, July 28, 1746; son of Daniel and Mary (Miles) Heyward; married Elizabeth Mathewes, April 20, 1773; second marriage to Susanna Savage, May 4, 1786; died March 6, 1809.

Heyward was admitted to the South Carolina bar in 1771 and was elected to the South Carolina House of Commons the following year. In 1774 he attended the South Carolina Provincial Convention in Charleston. In 1775 he was a member of the First and Second Provincial congresses in Charleston. A member of the South Carolina Council of Safety, he served on the Committee of Eleven, which prepared a constitution for South Carolina in 1776. From 1776 to 1778 he was a member of the

Second Continental Congress. He was a signer of the Declaration of Independence. He served as a circuit judge in 1778–79 and from 1784 to 1789.

Heyward, after serving in the Battle of Port Royal Island (1779) and in the defense of Charleston (1780), became a captain in an artillery battalion of the South Carolina militia in Charleston. He represented Charleston in the South Carolina legislature from 1782 to 1784. In 1785 he was a founder and the first president of the Agricultural Society of South Carolina. He died in St. Luke's Parish, South Carolina, and was buried there.

HOLCOMBE, Henry: clergyman
Born Prince Edward County, Virginia, September 22, 1762; son of Grimes and Elizabeth (Buzbee) Holcombe; married Frances Tanner, 1786; died May 22, 1824.

After serving in the Revolutionary War, Holcombe was ordained to the ministry of the Baptist Church in 1785. In 1788 he was a member of the South Carolina Convention which ratified the United States Constitution. He founded Beaufort College between 1795 and 1799 and the Savannah Female Asylum, an orphanage, in 1801. In 1800 he received an honorary D.D. and A.M. from Brown University; he also held an honorary D.D. from South Carolina College.

Holcombe was founder and editor of the *Analytical Repository* and helped found the Baptist Academy, Mount Enon, Burke County, Georgia, in 1804, and the Georgia Baptist Missionary Society in 1806. He originated a penitentiary system which abolished the death sentence for ordinary crimes and was the first clergyman to baptize a white person in Savannah, Georgia. He died in Philadelphia.

HUGER, Daniel: congressman
Born at the estate "Limerick," St. John's Parish, Berkeley County, South Carolina, February 20, 1742; children include Daniel Elliott; died July 6, 1799.

Huger attended school in Charleston,

South Carolina, and also in England. He served as a justice of the peace in 1755. In 1778–79 he held a seat in the South Carolina House of Representatives, and in 1780 he was a member of the South Carolina Governor's Council. He represented South Carolina in the Continental Congress from 1786 to 1788. He attended the 1st and 2nd congresses of the United States House of Representatives as a delegate from South Carolina (1789–93). He spent the remainder of his life managing his estates in South Carolina. He died in Charleston and was buried in the Western Churchyard of St. Philip's Church, in Charleston.

HUGER, Isaac: army officer
Born South Carolina, March 8, 1742; son of Daniel and Mary (Cordes) Huger; married Elizabeth Chalmers, March 23, 1762; father of eight children; died October 17, 1797.

Huger served in the South Carolina Provincial Congress in 1775 and again in 1778. He served as a lieutenant in the South Carolina militia during the Cherokee War (1760). A lieutenant colonel in the 1st Regiment of the Continental Army in 1775, the following year he became a colonel in the 5th Regiment. After becoming a brigadier general in the Southern Army in 1779, he fought at the battles of Stone Ferry, Charleston, Guilford Courthouse (in command of the Virginians), and Hobkirk's Hill. He was defeated by Tarleton and Webster at the Battle of Monk's Corner in 1780.

A member of the South Carolina General Assembly in 1782, Huger served as vice president of the South Carolina branch of the Society of the Cincinnati in 1783. He died in Charleston, South Carolina.

HUGER, John: Revolutionary patriot
Born Limerick Plantation, South Carolina, June 5, 1744; son of Daniel and Mary (Cordes) Huger; married Charlotte Motte, March 15, 1767; second marriage to Anne Broun, January 11, 1785; father of eight children (including Alfred); died January 22, 1804.

At the age of sixteen, Huger served as an ensign in the Cherokee War of 1760. In 1775 he held a seat in the Commons House of the Provincial Congress of South Carolina. A member of the South Carolina Council of Safety, he became the first secretary of state under the new South Carolina Constitution in 1776. From 1792 until his death in 1804 he was intendant of the city of Charleston, South Carolina.

HUNTER, John: senator, congressman
Born South Carolina, 1732; died 1802.

A farmer near Newberry, South Carolina, Hunter began an active political career by attending the South Carolina House of Representatives from 1786 to 1792. He was also a Federalist presidential elector in 1792. As a Federalist delegate from South Carolina, he attended the 3rd Congress of the United States House of Representatives (1793–95). He represented South Carolina in the United States Senate from December 8, 1796, to November 26, 1798. He then resumed farming. He was buried in the family plot in the Presbyterian Church Cemetery in Little River, South Carolina.

HUTSON, Richard: jurist, Continental congressman
Born Prince William Parish, South Carolina, July 9, 1748; son of the Reverend William and Mary (Ehardon) Hutson; died April 12, 1795.

Hutson received an A.B. from the College of New Jersey (now Princeton) in 1765 and an A.M. from that school in 1768. In 1776 he served on both the South Carolina Assembly and the South Carolina Legislative Council. In 1778–79 he was a delegate to the Continental Congress, and he was a signer of the Articles of Confederation.

In 1779 Hutson was a member of the lower house of the South Carolina Assembly, and he attended the South Carolina Assembly meeting at Jacksonborough in 1782. Later that year he was lieutenant governor of South Carolina, and the following year he was the first intendant of the City of

Charleston, South Carolina. He was elected one of the first chancellors of the South Carolina Equity Court in 1784, and served as senior judge from 1791 to 1793. He was a member of the 1787 South Carolina Convention which ratified the United States Constitution and a member of the South Carolina House of Representatives in 1789.

Hutson died in Charleston and was buried in the Independent Congregational Church Cemetery there.

HYRNE, Edmund Massingberd: army officer
Born January 14, 1748; son of Colonel Henry Hyrne; died December 1783.

Hyrne served as a captain in the 1st South Carolina Continental Regiment from 1775 until 1779, at which time he was promoted to major. From 1778 to 1783 he was deputy adjutant general of the Southern Department, receiving congressional notice for bravery in 1780. In 1781–82 he was aide-de-camp to General Nathanael Greene, and he was also a member of the Jacksonborough (South Carolina) legislature in 1782. He died on his plantation, "Ormsby," in St. Bartholomew's Parish, South Carolina.

★★★★★

IZARD, Ralph: diplomat, senator
Born Charleston, South Carolina, January 23, 1742; son of Henry and Margaret (Johnson) Izard; married Alice De Lancey, May 1, 1767; father of fourteen children; died May 30, 1804.

Izard graduated from Christ College, Cambridge University, England, in 1762. He was selected by the Continental Congress as commissioner to Tuscany in 1777. He began several years of service to his home state when he became a delegate to the Continental Congress from South Carolina in 1782. He also served in the South Carolina legislature and from 1789 to 1795 was a member of the United States Senate, acting as president pro tem in 1794 and 1795. He was a founder and trustee of the College of Charleston. He was buried at the Church of St. James in Goose Creek, South Carolina.

★★★★★

JASPER, William: patriot, army officer
Born probably Georgetown, South Carolina, circa 1750; died October 9, 1779.

Jasper enlisted as a sergeant in a company recruited by Francis Marion in 1775. He was assigned to Fort Johnson, South Carolina, later that year and then to Fort Sullivan (now Fort Moultrie) in 1776. Governor John Rutland awarded Jasper a sword for his bravery during a bombardment by the British fleet.

Jasper was later employed as a scout, making three trips behind British lines in Georgia and operating in the Black Swamp after the British capture of Savannah. He accompanied Benjamin Lincoln's assault on Savannah in 1779. He was killed while trying to plant the colors of the 2nd South Carolina Infantry on Spring Hill Redoubt.

★★★★★

KEAN, John: Continental congressman
Born Charleston, South Carolina, 1756; died May 4, 1795.

Kean, who was engaged in the mercantile business, was taken prisoner at the capture of Charleston by General Clinton in 1780. After his release General Washington appointed him to a commission to audit the accounts of the Continental Army. From 1785 to 1787 he represented South Carolina in the Continental Congress. President Washington then appointed him cashier of the Bank of the United States in Philadelphia, a position he held until 1795. He died that year in Philadelphia and was buried in St. John's Churchyard there.

KINLOCH, Francis: Continental congressman, army officer
Born Charleston, South Carolina, March 7, 1755; died February 8, 1826.

Kinloch graduated from Eton College in 1774, studied law at Lincoln's Inn in Lon-

don, and was admitted to the London bar. After traveling and studying in Paris and Geneva (1774–77), he volunteered to fight in the Revolutionary War, serving as a lieutenant and a captain during the years 1778–81. He participated in the Battle of Beaufort and in the defense of Charleston and was on the staffs of generals Moultrie and Huger and of Governor Rutledge. In 1779 he was wounded in an attack on Savannah.

In addition to serving in the South Carolina House of Representatives in 1779 and again from 1786 to 1788, Kinloch attended the Continental Congress in 1780–81. He became a rice planter at the estate "Kensington" in the Georgetown District of South Carolina. He attended the state ratification convention in 1788 and became both warden of the city of Charleston and justice of the peace and quorum in 1789. He also served that year on the South Carolina Legislative Council. In 1790 he participated in the state constitutional convention. He traveled in Europe in 1790 and again from 1802 to 1806.

Kinloch died in Charleston and was buried in St. Michael's Church Cemetery there.

★★★★★

LAURENS, Henry: Continental congressman, diplomat
Born Charleston, South Carolina, March 6, 1724; son of Jean Samuel and Esther (Grasset) Laurens; married Eleanor Ball, July 6, 1750; father of twelve children (including Henry, Martha, Eleanor, and John); died December 8, 1792.

Laurens was the owner of the largest export business in Charleston and the owner of plantations in Georgia and the Carolinas. From 1757 to 1776 he was a member of the South Carolina Provincial Commons House. In 1761 he served as a lieutenant colonel in the South Carolina militia.

Laurens was a member of South Carolina provincial congresses in 1774 and 1775, serving as president the latter year. In 1774 he was president of the Charleston Council of Safety, which drafted a form of association signed by those who favored independence. He was president of the Second Council of Safety and in 1775 president of the South Carolina Executive General Committee. In 1776 he served as vice president of the Executive Committee and helped draft a temporary constitution for South Carolina.

From 1777 to 1779 Laurens was a member of the Continental Congress, serving as its president in 1777 and 1778. In 1779 he was appointed United States minister to Holland; he was captured by the British en route to his post in 1780 and exchanged the next year. In 1782 he was appointed a peace commissioner and signed preliminaries of the treaty with England. He acted as an unofficial minister to Britain in 1782–83. He attended the United States Constitutional Convention in 1787.

Laurens died in Charleston and was buried on his estate "Mepkin," in South Carolina.

LAURENS, John: army officer, diplomat
Born Charleston, South Carolina, October 28, 1754; son of Henry and Eleanor (Ball) Laurens; married Martha Manning, September 16, 1776; died August 27, 1782.

At the age of seventeen Laurens was admitted to Middle Temple in London. In 1777 he joined Washington's staff as a volunteer aide and served in every battle that Washington engaged in, including Brandywine, Monmouth, Germantown, Savannah, and Charleston. He was later commissioned a lieutenant colonel by the Continental Congress.

Laurens was a member of the South Carolina Assembly in 1779. The next year Congress commissioned him an envoy extraordinary to France to obtain aid for the colonies. He helped organize a plan for the siege of Yorktown, and there, in 1781, he received Lord Cornwallis's sword.

In 1782 Laurens was a member of the Jacksonborough legislature. He died later that year, at the age of twenty-seven.

LOWNDES, Rawlins: colonial official
Born St. Kitts, British West Indies, January 1721; son of Charles and Ruth (Rawlins) Lowndes; married Amarinthia Elliott, August 15, 1748; second marriage to Mary Cartwright, December 23, 1751; third marriage to Sarah Jones, January 1773; father of twelve children (including William); died August 24, 1800.

From 1740 to 1752 Lowndes served as provost marshal of South Carolina. He was a member of the South Carolina legislature in 1749 (representing St. Paul's Parish), from 1751 to 1766, and from 1772 to 1775 (representing St. Bartholomew's Parish). He was speaker of the lower house from 1763 to 1765 and from 1772 to 1775. From 1766 to 1773 he was associate judge of the South Carolina Court of Common Pleas. He was a member of the South Carolina provincial congresses of 1775 and of the South Carolina Council of Safety.

After South Carolina declared independence from England, Lowndes became a member of the South Carolina Legislative Council in 1776. He was president of South Carolina in 1778–79 and a Charleston representative to the South Carolina Senate from 1782 to 1787. He opposed adoption of the United States Constitution. He died in Charleston.

LUCAS, Jonathan: millwright
Born Cumberland, England, 1754; son of John and Ann (Noble) Lucas; married Mary Cooke, May 22, 1774; second marriage to Ann Ashburn, between 1783 and 1786; father of five children (including Jonathan); died April 1, 1821.

Lucas, who moved to Charleston, South Carolina, in 1790, was the first to build a pounding mill driven by wind to remove husks from rice grain. He also built water mills for various plantations and constructed tide mills (mills powered by the movement of tides). He made the production of rice much more profitable for the

South. He was buried in St. Paul's Churchyard in Charleston.

LYNCH, Thomas: planter, Continental congressman

Born Berkeley County, South Carolina, 1727; son of Thomas and Sabena (Vanderhorst) Lynch; married Elizabeth Allston, September 5, 1745; second marriage to Hannah Motte, March 1755; father of four children (including Thomas and Elizabeth); died December 1776.

Lynch represented the Parish of St. James, Santee, in the South Carolina House of Commons in 1761–63, 1765, 1768, and 1772. He was a representative from South Carolina to the Stamp Act Congress in 1765 and chairman of the committee that drafted a petition to the House of Commons for the repeal of the Stamp Act.

From 1769 to 1774 Lynch was a member of the South Carolina General Committee. He was appointed to the Continental Congress by a popular convention in Charleston and served from 1774 to 1776. He was a delegate to South Carolina provincial congresses in 1775 and 1776; the latter year he was also a member of the first South Carolina General Assembly. He died in Annapolis, Maryland, and was buried in St. Anne's Churchyard there.

LYNCH, Thomas: Continental congressman

Born Prince George's Parish, Winyaw, South Carolina, August 5, 1749; son of Thomas and Elizabeth (Allston) Lynch; married Elizabeth Shubrick, May 14, 1772; died circa 1779.

Lynch graduated from Eton College and from Cambridge University in England, then was admitted to Middle Temple. He practiced law from 1764 to 1772. He was a member of South Carolina provincial congresses from 1774 to 1776; the latter year he also served as a member of the South Carolina Constitutional Committee. He served as a captain in the 1st South Carolina Regiment, then a part of the Continental Army, in 1775–76.

In 1776 Lynch was a member of the first South Carolina General Assembly. A member of the Second Continental Congress in 1776–77, he was a signer of the Declaration of Independence.

In 1779 Lynch went on a voyage to the West Indies and France because of illness; his ship was never heard from again.

★★★★★

McCREARY, John: congressman

Born near Fishing Creek, South Carolina, 1761; died November 4, 1833.

Educated privately, McCreary engaged in surveying and farming. He served in the Revolution and then became a member of the South Carolina House of Representatives and, later, of the South Carolina Senate. Sheriff of Chester District (now Chester County), South Carolina, for a time, he was elected to the United States House of Representatives from South Carolina for the 16th Congress (1819–21). He died in South Carolina and was buried in Richardson Church Cemetery in Chester County.

MANIGAULT, Peter: legislator, planter

Born Charleston, South Carolina, October 10, 1731; son of Gabriel and Ann (Ashby) Manigault; married Elizabeth Wragg, June 8, 1755; father of seven children; died November 12, 1773.

Educated in England, Manigault was called to the English bar in 1754 and then returned to South Carolina, where he served as a member of the Colonial Assembly from 1755 to 1772 (speaker, 1765–72). He opposed the Stamp Act. Owner of several acres of land in South Carolina, in 1763 he took over the management of plantations belonging to Ralph Izard. He later returned to England because of illness and died in London. He was buried in Charleston.

MARION, Francis: army officer

Born Berkeley County, South Carolina, 1732; son of Gabriel and Esther (Cordes) Marion; married Mary Videau, 1786; died February 27, 1795.

Marion purchased a plantation near

Eutaw Springs, South Carolina, in 1759. He served as a lieutenant in a Royal Scots Regiment in campaigns against the Cherokee Indians in 1761. In 1775 he was a member of the South Carolina Provincial Congress, representing St. John's Parish. That same year he was commissioned a captain in the 2nd South Carolina Regiment and served at the occupation of Fort Johnson. The next year he was commissioned a lieutenant colonel in the Continental Army, becoming a brigadier general in the South Carolina militia in 1780. He commanded the only Revolutionary forces in South Carolina during 1780 and 1781, continually disrupting British communication and preventing the organization of Loyalist forces by guerrilla-warfare methods. He was nicknamed "Swamp Fox" by British General Tarleton because of his tactic of hiding in the swamps between attacks. He served at the Battle of Eutaw Springs in 1781.

Marion was a member of the South Carolina Senate in 1781, 1782, and 1784. He attended the South Carolina Constitutional Convention of 1790 and was elected to fill an unexpired term in the South Carolina Senate in 1791. He died in St. John's Parish, South Carolina, and was buried on Belle Isle, in St. Stephen's Parish, Berkeley County.

MATHEWS, John: governor of South Carolina

Born Charleston, South Carolina, 1744; son of John and Sarah (Gibbes) Mathews; married Mary Wragg, December 1766; second marriage to Sarah Rutledge, May 5, 1799; died October 26, 1802.

Mathews, who served as an ensign and then as a lieutenant in an expedition against the Cherokee Indians in 1760, entered Middle Temple in London, England, in 1764 and was admitted to the South Carolina bar in 1766. He was a member of the South Carolina Provincial Congress from St. George's, Dorchester, in 1775, and was elected associate justice of the South Carolina Court of

General Sessions the following year. Speaker of the South Carolina General Assembly under the temporary constitution of 1776, he was the first speaker of the South Carolina House of Representatives under the Constitution of 1778.

Mathews attended the Continental Congress from 1778 to 1782 and was a signer of the Articles of Confederation. In 1782 he was elected governor of South Carolina by the Jonesborough Assembly, serving until the following year. Appointed a judge of the South Carolina Court of Chancery in 1784, he was named judge of the South Carolina Court of Equity in 1791.

Mathews was an original trustee of the College of Charleston. He died in Charleston.

MIDDLETON, Arthur: Continental congressman

Born Charleston, South Carolina, June 26, 1742; son of Henry and Mary (Williams) Middleton; married Mary Izard, August 19, 1764; father of nine children (including Isabella, Henry, and John Izard); died January 1, 1787.

After attending Middle Temple, London, England, from 1757 to 1763, Middleton returned to South Carolina, where he served as a justice of the peace in 1764 and a member of the House of Assembly from 1764 to 1768. He traveled in Europe with his family from 1768 to 1771, then served another year in the House of Assembly. In 1772 Middleton was a member of a special committee appointed after receipt of a letter from Arthur Lee in London mentioning the possibility of British instigation of slave insurrections in the colonies.

Middleton was a member of the First South Carolina Provincial Congress, a member of a general committee, and a member of a secret committee of five which arranged and directed the action of three parties of citizens who seized powder and weapons from public storehouses on April 21, 1776. In addition, Middleton became a member of the South Carolina Council of Safety in 1772, of the Council of Safety in the Second South Carolina Provincial Congress in 1775, and of the committee of eleven delegated to prepare the South Carolina Constitution in 1776. He served in the Continental Congress in 1776 and was a signer of the Declaration of Independence. During the Revolution he served with the South Carolina militia at the siege of Charleston, was taken prisoner, and was sent to St. Augustine, Florida, in 1780; he was exchanged in 1781.

After the war Middleton became a planter. He was a member of racing and hunting clubs in St. George's Parish, South Carolina, and was an original trustee of the College of Charleston. He died in Goose Creek, South Carolina, and was buried in a family mausoleum at "Middleton Place," near Charleston.

MIDDLETON, Henry: Continental congressman

Born Charleston, South Carolina, 1717; son of Arthur and Sarah (Amory) Middleton; married Mary Williams, 1741; second marriage to Maria Bull, 1762; third marriage to Lady Mary Mackenzie, January 1776; father of twelve children (including Arthur, Thomas, Henrietta, and Sarah); died June 13, 1784.

One of the most prominent landowners in South Carolina, Middleton was a justice of the peace and a member of the South Carolina House of Commons from 1742 to 1755, serving as speaker in 1747, 1754, and 1755. He was commissioner of Indian affairs in 1755 and a member of His Majesty's Council for South Carolina from 1755 to 1770.

A member of the Continental Congress from South Carolina from 1774 to 1776, Middleton was president of the congress from October 1774 to May 1775. He was president of the South Carolina Congress and a member of the Council of Safety after November 1775. Appointed to the committee to frame the temporary South Carolina Constitution in 1776, he became a member

of the legislative council and was named to the newly created South Carolina Senate in 1779.

Middleton died in Charleston and was buried at the Church of St. James Parish in Berkeley County, South Carolina.

MOORE, Thomas: congressman

Born Spartanburg District, South Carolina, 1759; died July 11, 1822.

Moore, a planter by trade, participated in the Battle of Cowpens during the Revolutionary War. He later co-founded the first high school in the Spartanburg District. He was elected a South Carolina delegate to the United States House of Representatives for the 7th–12th and 14th congresses (1801–13 and 1815–17). He served as a brigadier general in the War of 1812. After his last term in Congress, he resumed planting near Moores Station in Spartanburg County. He was buried in Moore's Burying Ground.

MOTTE, Isaac: Continental congressman

Born Charleston, South Carolina, December 8, 1738; died May 8, 1795.

Appointed an ensign in His Majesty's 60th Royal American Regiment in 1756, Motte was promoted to lieutenant in 1759. Having served in Canada during the French and Indian War in 1756, he later resigned from the military and returned to Charleston in 1766. A member of the South Carolina House of Commons in 1772, he was a delegate to the South Carolina provincial congresses in 1774, 1775, and 1776.

Motte was commissioned a lieutenant colonel in the 2nd South Carolina Regiment, Continental Army, in 1775 and participated in the defense of Fort Moultrie; he was promoted to colonel in 1776. He became a member of the South Carolina Privy Council and a member of the South Carolina Assembly from Charleston in 1779. A representative from South Carolina in the Continental Congress from 1780 to 1782, he was a delegate to the South Carolina Convention which ratified the United States Constitution in 1788.

Motte was appointed naval officer for the Port of Charleston by George Washington. He died in Charleston and was buried in St. Philip's Churchyard there.

MOULTRIE, John: physician, colonial official

Born Charleston, South Carolina, January 18, 1729; son of Dr. John and Lucretia (Cooper) Moultrie; married Dorothy (Dry) Morton, April 30, 1753; second marriage to Eleanor Austin, January 5, 1762; father of seven children; died March 19, 1798.

Moultrie received an M.D. from the University of Edinburgh in 1749. He served as a major in the militia in 1761 and was involved in the campaign against the Cherokees. A member of James Grant's council on East Florida in 1764, he became lieutenant governor of East Florida in 1771. A Loyalist, he went to England in 1784. He died in St. Andrews Parish, Shifnal, England, and was buried there.

MOULTRIE, William: army officer, governor of South Carolina

Born Charleston, South Carolina, November 23, 1730; son of Dr. John and Lucretia (Cooper) Moultrie; married Elizabeth Damares de St. Julien, December 10, 1749; second marriage to Hannah (Motte) Lynch, October 10, 1779; died September 27, 1805.

A member of the South Carolina Assembly from 1751 to 1771, Moultrie commanded a light infantry company against the Cherokees in 1761. He became a member of the South Carolina Provincial Congress at Charleston in 1775. From 1775 to 1780 he served concurrently on the South Carolina Legislative Council and in the South Carolina Senate.

A colonel in the 2nd Regiment of the Continental Army in 1776, Moultrie was promoted to brigadier general in 1777 and to major general in 1782. He served in the South Carolina House of Representatives in 1783 and acceded to the lieutenant governorship of South Carolina in 1784. He was elected governor of the state in 1785, serving until 1787 and again in 1792–94.

Moultrie presided over the South Carolina branch of the Society of the Cincinnati during the latter years of his life. He died in Charleston.

★★★★★

O'FALLON, James: army officer

Born Ireland, March 11, 1749; son of William and Anne (Eagan) O'Fallon; married Frances Clark, February 1791; father of John and Benjamin; died circa 1794.

After attending the University of Edinburgh in Scotland, O'Fallon came to America in 1774, where he served as a surgeon in the United States Army during the American Revolution. He was a member of the Charleston (South Carolina) Marine Anti-Britannic Society in 1785.

In 1790 O'Fallon became general agent of the South Carolina Yazoo Company. He then entered into a correspondence with the Spanish governor at New Orleans in which he claimed that the intention of the company was to break with the United States and form an independent government allied with Spain. He later wrote to President Washington representing the company in a more patriotic light and asking for the government's assistance. Washington soon discovered O'Fallon's true intentions and issued a public proclamation against American support for his plans in 1791.

Early in 1791 O'Fallon became an officer under George Rogers Clark (whose sister he married) but died soon afterward.

★★★★★

PARKER, John: Continental congressman

Born Charleston, South Carolina, June 24, 1759; died April 20, 1832.

After graduating from Middle Temple in London, England, Parker was admitted to the South Carolina bar in 1785. He established a legal practice in Charleston and engaged in rice planting, eventually becoming an executor of large rice estates.

Parker served as a member of the Continental Congress from South Carolina from 1786 to 1788. He was buried in the family burying ground at the estate "Hayes," near Charleston.

PICKENS, Andrew: army officer, congressman

Born Paxton, Pennsylvania, September 19, 1739; son of Andrew and Nancy Pickens; married Rebecca Calhoun, March 19, 1765; father of at least four children; died August 11, 1817.

Pickens fought against the Cherokee Indians in 1761. He served as a captain in the South Carolina militia in its first fight at Ninety-six Fort in 1775. Two years later he was commissioned a colonel; by 1780 he was a brigadier. He was made major general in the militia circa 1795 and later served in the War of 1812.

From 1781 to 1794 and from 1800 to 1812 Pickens was a member of the South Carolina House of Representatives. He attended the South Carolina Constitutional Convention in 1790 and was a delegate to the United States House of Representatives, 3rd Congress, from 1793 to 1795. He died in Pendleton District, South Carolina, and was buried at the Old Stone Church near there.

PINCKNEY, Charles: senator, governor of South Carolina, Continental congressman

Born Charleston, South Carolina, October 26, 1757; son of Colonel Charles and Frances (Brewton) Pinckney; married Mary Laurens, April 27, 1788; father of three children; died October 29, 1824.

After being admitted to the South Carolina bar in 1779, Pinckney enlisted in the Charleston Regiment of the South Carolina militia. He was captured by the British in 1780, remaining imprisoned nearly a year.

Pinckney served South Carolina in several political capacities for a total of more than forty-two years. He was a member of the South Carolina House of Representatives from 1779 to 1784 and again in 1786–89, 1792–96, 1805–06, and 1810–14. From 1784 to 1787 he was a member of the Continental Congress. A delegate to the United States Constitutional Convention in 1787, he submitted a proposed draft for a federal constitution, many provisions of which were incorporated into the finished document. The next year he was president of the South Carolina Convention that ratified the Constitution.

In 1790 Pinckney served as president of the South Carolina State Constitutional Convention. He was governor of the state from 1789 to 1792, from 1796 to 1798, and from 1806 to 1808. A Democrat, he represented South Carolina in the United States Senate from 1798 to 1805; during his tenure he also served as United States minister to Spain (1801–04). He was a member of the House of Representatives from 1819 to 1821.

Pinckney died in Charleston and was buried in St. Philip's Churchyard there.

PINCKNEY, Charles Cotesworth: diplomat, army officer

Born Charleston, South Carolina, February 25, 1746; son of Charles and Elizabeth (Lucas) Pinckney; married Sarah Middleton, September 28, 1773; second marriage to Mary Stead, June 23, 1786; father of three children; died August 16, 1825.

Pinckney, after graduating from Christ Church College in 1764, was admitted to Middle Temple. In 1769 he was admitted to the English bar and the next year to the South Carolina bar.

A ranking captain of the 1st Regiment of the South Carolina militia in 1775, Pinckney was appointed a colonel the next year. In 1777 he was made an aide to George Washington and served at the battles of Germantown and Brandywine. He commanded his regiment at the siege of Savannah and commanded Fort Moultrie during the attacks on Charleston. Taken prisoner by the British when Charleston fell, he was exchanged in 1782. In 1783 he was appointed a brigadier general in the Continental Army.

In 1769 and again in 1775 Pinckney was

a member of the South Carolina Provincial Assembly. In 1773 he was acting attorney general for Camden, Georgetown, and the Cheraw District. Five years later he was elected to the lower house of the South Carolina legislature and served again in 1782. In 1779 he was president of the South Carolina Senate.

In 1787 Pinckney served as a delegate to the United States Constitutional Convention and a year later as a member of the South Carolina Convention to ratify the United States Constitution. He was a member of the South Carolina Constitutional Convention in 1790. Six years later he was appointed United States minister to France; however, the French Directory, indignant over the Jay Treaty, which had recently been ratified by the United States Congress, refused to recognize his status. Pinckney then left Paris for Amsterdam, Holland.

Pinckney, John Marshall, and Elbridge Gerry were appointed as American representatives to France to negotiate the differences between the young republic and the Directory; a series of letters between Talleyrand's ministers and the three Americans precipitated the XYZ affair. Pinckney left Paris in 1798 and was appointed by Washington as commander of all forces and posts south of Maryland.

A Federalist, Pinckney was a candidate for the vice presidency in 1800 and for the presidency in 1804 and 1808. In 1810 he became the first president of the Charleston Bible Society. He died in Charleston.

PINCKNEY, Elizabeth Lucas: planter

Born Antigua, British West Indies, 1722; daughter of George Lucas; married Charles Pinckney, May 27, 1744; mother of at least three children (Charles Cotesworth, Thomas, and Mrs. Daniel Horry); died May 26, 1793.

Elizabeth Lucas came to America in 1738; a year later, at the age of seventeen, she took over the management of her father's three plantations in South Carolina. She was the first person to successfully raise indigo in South Carolina (1741–44).

After her marriage, Mrs. Pinckney revived the silk culture on her husband's plantation. Upon her husband's death in 1758, she came to own and manage several plantations in South Carolina. Mrs. Pinckney died in Philadelphia and was buried in St. Peter's Churchyard there.

PINCKNEY, Thomas: governor of South Carolina, diplomat

Born Charleston, South Carolina, October 23, 1750; son of Charles and Elizabeth (Lucas) Pinckney; married Elizabeth Motte, July 22, 1779; second marriage to Frances Motte, October 19, 1797; father of four children; died November 2, 1828.

After graduating from Oxford University, Pinckney studied at Middle Temple in London, England, in 1768. In 1774 he was admitted to both the English bar and the South Carolina bar.

Pinckney served as a captain in the 1st Regiment of the South Carolina militia in 1775 and three years later was promoted to major. He was a military aide to Count d'Estaing at Savannah, Georgia, and served under the Marquis de Lafayette at Yorktown.

Governor of South Carolina in 1787–88, Pinckney also served in the latter year as president of the South Carolina Convention to ratify the United States Constitution. In 1791 he was elected to the lower house of the South Carolina legislature.

In 1795 Pinckney was made a special commissioner to Spain; his negotiations with the Spanish government resulted in the Treaty of San Lorenzo el Real (also known as Pinckney's Treaty), by which Spain recognized the 31st parallel and the Mississippi River as the southern and western boundaries of the United States and gave the Americans free navigation of the Mississippi.

Pinckney, like his older brother Charles a member of the Federalist party, ran unsuccessfully for the vice presidency in 1796.

From 1797 to 1801 he was a delegate from South Carolina to the United States House of Representatives (5th and 6th congresses). During the War of 1812 he was a major general in the United States Volunteers in command of the district extending from North Carolina to the Mississippi River. In 1814 he negotiated the Treaty of Fort Jackson with the Creek Indian Nation, thus ending the Creek War.

Pinckney died in Charleston and was buried in St. Philip's Churchyard there.

PRINGLE, John Julius: state legislator
Born Charleston, South Carolina, July 22, 1753; son of Robert and Judith Mayrant (Bull) Pringle; married Susannah Reid, January 1, 1784; father of ten children; died March 17, 1843.

Pringle entered Middle Temple in London, England, in 1773, and was admitted to the Charleston bar in 1781. In 1778–79 he had been secretary to Ralph Izard, who was a commissioner to the Court of Tuscany, France. Pringle was a member of the South Carolina House of Representatives in 1785 and from 1786 to 1788, serving as speaker in 1787 and 1788. In 1788 he was also a member of the South Carolina Convention to ratify the United States Constitution and two years later a member of the South Carolina Constitutional Convention. He was United States district attorney from 1789 to 1792 and attorney general of South Carolina for the next sixteen years.

From 1796 to 1824 Pringle was a member of the board of trustees of the College of Charleston and served as president of the board from 1811 to 1815. He was president of the Charleston Library Society from 1812 to 1816 and chairman of the vestry at St. Michael's Church for several years. He died in Charleston.

★★★★★

RAMSAY, David: Continental congressman, physician, historian
Born Drumore Township, Lancaster County, Pennsylvania, April 2, 1749; son of James and Jane (Montgomery) Ramsay; married Sabina Ellis, February 1775; second marriage to Frances Witherspoon, 1783; third marriage to Martha Laurens, January 23, 1787; died May 8, 1815.

Ramsay graduated from Princeton at the age of sixteen, receiving his M.D. from the College of Pennsylvania in 1772. He was a member of the South Carolina legislature from 1776 to 1780, in 1781–82, and from 1784 to 1790. From 1782 to 1785 he served as a delegate to the Continental Congress. He was a delegate to and president of the South Carolina Senate in 1792, 1794, and 1796.

Ramsay wrote *Review of the Improvements, Progress, and State of Medicine in the XVIIIth Century.* In 1785 his *History of the Revolution of South Carolina* was published in two volumes, and four years later another two-volume work, *History of the American Revolution,* appeared. In 1809 the two-volume *History of South Carolina* was published, followed by the three-volume *The History of the United States,* published posthumously in 1816–17.

Ramsay died in Charleston, South Carolina.

READ, Jacob: Continental congressman, senator, army officer
Born Christ Church Parish, South Carolina, 1752; son of James and Rebecca (Bond) Read; married Catherine Van Horne, October 13, 1785; father of four children; died July 16, 1816.

In 1773 Read was admitted to the Georgia bar and to Gray's Inn in England. He was a signer of the petition of Americans in London protesting the Massachusetts Government Acts of 1774. He then journeyed to America, becoming a captain in the South Carolina militia in 1776.

In 1781 and 1782, and from 1789 to 1794, Read served as speaker of the South Carolina House of Representatives. He represented Charleston in the Jacksonborough Assembly of 1782 and the next year was a member of the South Carolina Privy Council. In 1783–84 he was a member of the

South Carolina Legislative Council and justice of quorum.

From 1783 to 1786 Read was a delegate from South Carolina to the Continental Congress. He then became a charter member of a company to build a canal from the Ashley River to the Edisto River. In 1788 he served as a member of the South Carolina Convention to ratify the United States Constitution.

In 1799 Read was admitted to the South Carolina bar. A Federalist, from 1795 to 1801 he represented South Carolina in the United States Senate. Commissioned a brigadier general in the South Carolina militia in 1808, he served as commanding officer of the 7th Brigade until his death eight years later. He died in Charleston and was buried in the Family Cemetery in Hobcaw, South Carolina.

RUTLEDGE, Edward: governor of South Carolina, Continental congressman
Born Christ Church Parish or Charleston, South Carolina, November 23, 1749; son of Dr. John and Sarah (Hext) Rutledge; married Henrietta Middleton, March 1, 1774; second marriage to Mary Shubrick Eveleigh, October 28, 1792; father of three children (including Henry Middleton); died January 23, 1800.

Rutledge was admitted to Middle Temple in London, England, in 1767 and in 1772 was called to the English bar. The following year he returned to South Carolina as a barrister. He served in the Continental Congress from 1774 to 1777 and was elected to serve in 1779 but did not reach Philadelphia because of ill health. He was a member of the first Board of War in 1776 and voted for the resolution of independence on July 2, 1776. In 1775–76 he was a member of the South Carolina provincial congresses.

Commissioned a captain in the South Carolina Artillery in 1776, Rutledge fought at Beaufort in 1779. In 1780 he was captured during the fall of Charleston and imprisoned by the British. He was one of the St.

Augustine "exiles" from September 1780 to July 1781.

A member of the South Carolina House of Representatives in 1782 and 1786 and from 1788 to 1792, Rutledge drew up a bill proposing confiscation of Loyalist properties in 1782. He was the author of an act abolishing the law of primogeniture in 1791.

Rutledge was an investor in plantations as a partner of his brother-in-law, Charles Cotesworth Pinckney. In 1788, 1792, and 1796 he was a Federalist presidential elector. He served as a member of the South Carolina Senate from Charleston in 1796 and in 1798. The latter year he became governor of South Carolina, an office his older brother John had held twenty years earlier. He died before the end of his term.

RUTLEDGE, John: governor of South Carolina, congressman, Continental congressman
Born Charleston, South Carolina, September 1739; son of Dr. John and Sarah (Hext) Rutledge; married Elizabeth Grimke, May 1, 1763; father of ten children; died July 23, 1800.

Rutledge studied at Middle Temple in London, England, then returned to the United States. From 1761 to 1776 he was a member of the South Carolina House of Commons. He served as attorney general pro tem of South Carolina in 1764–65. As a member of the Stamp Act Congress in 1765, he was chairman of a committee that wrote a memorial and petition to the House of Lords.

A member of the Continental Congress in 1774–76 and 1882–83, Rutledge led a successful fight to eliminate rice from the boycott list and advocated home rule in the colonies. In 1776 he served as a member of the South Carolina Council of Safety and was a writer of the South Carolina Constitution. He was president of the South Carolina General Assembly from 1776 to 1778, and he vetoed a new South Carolina Constitution that would have substituted a senate elected by the people for the legislative council.

Rutledge resigned his assembly seat in 1778 and became governor of South Carolina in 1779. During his three years as governor he was given emergency powers in times of invasion (1780), restored civil government (1781), issued a proclamation which suspended the use of currency, forbade suits for debts, and offered pardon to British supporters on the condition that they serve six months' militia duty.

Rutledge served in the South Carolina House of Representatives in 1781 and 1782. In 1784, after declining an appointment as United States minister to Holland, he became judge of the South Carolina Chancery Court. Later that year he was again elected to the South Carolina legislature, serving until 1790. He was a member of the United States Constitutional Convention in 1787 and served as chairman of the committee of detail. In 1788 he was a delegate to the South Carolina Convention to ratify the United States Constitution.

From 1789 to 1791 Rutledge was senior associate justice of the United States Supreme Court and for the next four years served as chief justice of the South Carolina Supreme Court. In 1795 he was nominated for the chief justiceship of the United States Supreme Court; he served during the August term, but the Senate later refused to confirm his appointment.

Rutledge died in Charleston—six months to the day after the death of his younger brother Edward—and was buried in St. Michael's Cemetery there.

★★★★★

SMITH, O'Brien: congressman
Born Ireland, circa 1756; died April 27, 1811.

Smith arrived in South Carolina just after the Revolution and took the oath of allegiance to the government of the United States in 1784. He became a member of the South Carolina Assembly in 1796 and of the state senate in 1803. South Carolina sent him to the United States House of Representatives for the 9th Congress (1805–07). He was buried in the burial ground of the Chapel of Ease, St. Bartholomew's Parish, in Colleton County, South Carolina.

SMITH, Robert: clergyman
Born Worstead, Norfolk, England, June 25, 1732; son of Stephen and Hannah (Press) Smith; married Elizabeth Pagett, July 9, 1758; second marriage to Sarah Shubrick, early 1774; third marriage to Anna Maria (Tilghman) Goldsborough, after 1779; father of three children; died October 28, 1801.

Smith received a B.A. degree from Gonville and Caius College at Cambridge University (England) in 1754 and became a fellow of the school in 1755. He was ordained a deacon of the Protestant Episcopal Church and became a priest in 1756. Arriving in Charleston, South Carolina, in 1757, he served as rector of St. Philip's Church from 1759 to 1775 and from 1783 to 1801.

In 1776 Smith served as chaplain of the 1st South Carolina Regiment and also of the Continental Hospital in Charleston. He was chaplain general of the Southern Department of the Continental Army circa 1778 and was imprisoned by the British in Charleston in 1780. Later banished to Philadelphia, he returned to Charleston in 1783, where he founded a school (known as the College of Charleston after 1790) circa 1785 and served as principal from 1790 to 1798.

Instrumental in summoning the South Carolina convention of the Protestant Episcopal Church which sent delegates to the General Convention in 1785, Smith was consecrated the first Protestant Episcopal bishop of South Carolina in 1795. He died in Charleston and was buried in St. Philip's Cemetery.

SMITH, William: senator, congressman
Born North Carolina, 1762; married Margaret Duff, 1781; father of one child; died June 26, 1840.

Smith graduated from Mount Zion Collegiate Institute in Winnsboro, South Carolina, in 1780 and was admitted to the South Carolina bar in 1784. A Democrat, he was a South Carolina delegate to the United States House of Representatives from 1797 to 1799 (5th Congress). He was a member of the South Carolina Senate from 1802 to 1808 and served as president from 1806 to 1808. He was a member of the United States Senate from 1817 to 1823 (twice elected president pro tem); he delivered his most important speech in the Missouri debates in 1820. He defended the Southern position in the Union and championed Southern rights. He again served in the Senate from 1826 to 1830.

Smith was a circuit judge from 1816 to 1823 and from 1826 to 1831. He served in the South Carolina House of Representatives from 1824 to 1826 and received Georgia's seven electoral votes for vice president in 1829. He was elected to the South Carolina Senate in 1831. After moving to Louisiana and then to Alabama in 1833, he served as a member of the lower house of the Alabama legislature from 1836 to 1840; he was a Jeffersonian Democrat. He died in Huntsville, Alabama.

SMITH, William Loughton: congressman, diplomat

Born Charleston, South Carolina, circa 1758; son of Benjamin and Anne (Loughton) Smith; married Charlotte Izard, May 1, 1786; second marriage to Charlotte Wragg, December 19, 1805; father of three children; died December 19, 1812.

In 1784 Smith was admitted to the South Carolina bar and became a member of the privy council. He was a member of the South Carolina House of Representatives from 1784 to 1788 and again in 1808.

Sent to the United States House of Representatives by South Carolina for the 1st through the 5th congresses (1789 to July 1797), Smith was then named minister to Portugal and Spain, serving from 1797 to 1801. He made an unsuccessful attempt to return to Congress in 1804. He served as a

lieutenant in the South Carolina militia in 1808 and later became president of the Santee Canal Company.

Smith was the author of several political pamphlets, including "The Politicks and Views of a Certain Party Displayed" (1792), an attack on Jefferson. He died in Charleston and was buried at St. Philip's Church.

STUART, John: army officer, superintendent of Indian affairs

Born Scotland, 1700; married Miss Fenwick, before 1759; father of at least one son (Lieutenant General Sir John); died March 25, 1779.

Stuart came to the United States about 1748 and served as a captain in the South Carolina provincial militia in 1757. He was superintendent of Indian affairs for the Southern District of South Carolina in 1762 and was responsible to the secretaries of state in England following the Proclamation of 1763.

In 1764 Stuart was named a member of the East Florida governing council by Governor James Grant. He gained imperial status for his department (responsible to the King rather than the secretaries of state) in 1765. He became a refugee in Florida in 1775 after his arrest was ordered by the South Carolina Assembly on the charge of attempting to incite the Catawba and Cherokee Indians in the British interest. He then organized three companies of refugees to further British interests in the South in 1778. He died in Pensacola, Florida, the following year.

SUMTER, Thomas: senator, congressman
Born Hanover County, Virginia, August 14, 1734; died June 1, 1832.

Sumter attended college for a time, then became a surveyor. He moved to South Carolina circa 1760, settling on a plantation near Stateburg. He entered military service as a lieutenant colonel in the 6th Continental Regiment of the Continental Army, then (in 1780) became a brigadier general in the South Carolina militia.

Sumter was elected to the South Carolina Senate in 1781 and to the privy council in 1782. He was a delegate to the South Carolina Convention to ratify the United States Constitution (which he opposed). He served as a South Carolina delegate to the United States House of Representatives from 1789 to 1793 and from 1797 until December 15, 1801, when he resigned to fill a vacant seat in the United States Senate. He resigned from the Senate on December 16, 1810.

Sumter was elected a delegate to the States' Rights and Free Trade Convention in Charleston, South Carolina, in 1832, but did not serve. He died on his plantation "South Mount" at the age of ninety-seven and was buried in a private burial ground on the estate.

★★★★★

THOMSON, William: army officer
Born Pennsylvania, January 16, 1727; son of Moses and Jane Thomson; married Eugenia Russell, August 14, 1755; father of twelve children; died November 2, 1796.

Thomson worked on his father's plantation in South Carolina and engaged in trade with the Indians. The South Carolina Assembly voted him a bonus and land for his service as a major in the South Carolina militia during the Cherokee War. At various times he was an indigo planter, a justice of the peace, and an enquirer and collector of taxes.

Thomson served as a member of the Georgia legislature and in 1772 as a commissioner to relocate the border between North and South Carolina. He was a member of the first Georgia Provincial Assembly.

After serving as a colonel in the Orangeburg militia, Thomson became a lieutenant-colonel-commandant in the Continental Army and in 1776 blocked the British attempt to land on Sullivan's Island, at the entrance to Charleston harbor. For this action he received congressional thanks and was promoted to colonel. He resigned from the army in 1778 and was imprisoned three years later by the British for having broken parole (a pledge by a prisoner of war not to bear arms until exchanged) following the capture of Charleston.

In 1788 Thomson served in the South Carolina Convention to ratify the United States Constitution. He died in Sweet Springs, Virginia.

TIMOTHY, Lewis: printer
No record of birth; married Elizabeth Timothy; father of six children (including Peter); died December 1738.

Timothy came to America in 1731 and settled in Philadelphia. In 1732 he did editorial work on Benjamin Franklin's *Philadelphische Zeitung,* the first German-language newspaper in America. In that year he was also librarian for the Philadelphia Library Society. In 1733 he became a journeyman printer for Benjamin Franklin and entered into a printing business with Franklin in Charleston, South Carolina.

In 1734 Timothy revived the *South Carolina Gazette* and printed official government documents. His most important work was *The Laws of the Province of South Carolina,* a two-volume work compiled by Nicholas Trott, LL.D., in 1736. Timothy printed only eighteen other pieces.

TRAPIER, Paul: Continental congressman
Born Prince George's Parish, Winyah (near Georgetown), South Carolina, 1749; died July 8, 1778.

Trapier was educated in England, attending Eton College from 1763 to 1765. He was admitted as a pensioner to St. John's College, Cambridge University, in 1766, and the next year was admitted to Middle Temple in London.

Trapier was a member of the Provincial Congress and a member of the Committee of Safety of Georgetown. In 1776 he served as a member of the South Carolina General Assembly and as a justice of the peace. During the Revolutionary War he served in the Continental Army as a captain in the Georgetown Artillery.

In 1777–78 Trapier was a member of the Continental Congress from South Carolina. He died near Georgetown and was buried in Prince George Churchyard in Winyah, South Carolina.

TUCKER, Thomas Tudor: United States treasurer, congressman, physician
Born Port Royal, Bermuda, June 25, 1745; died May 2, 1828.

After studying medicine at the University of Edinburgh, Scotland, Tucker moved to South Carolina to practice medicine. He served as a surgeon during the Revolutionary War. In 1787–88 he was a member of the Continental Congress from South Carolina. A Federalist, he was a South Carolina delegate to the United States House of Representatives during the 1st and 2nd congresses (1789–93). President Jefferson appointed him treasurer of the United States in 1801, and he served in that capacity until his death.

★★★★★

VESEY, Denmark: insurrectionist
Born Africa, 1767; died July 2, 1822.

Vesey was a slave who belonged to the slave dealer Captain Vesey from 1780 to 1800. He purchased his freedom with part of a $1,500 lottery prize won in 1800, then opened a carpenter shop in Charleston, South Carolina.

In 1817 Vesey was admitted to the Second Presbyterian Church in Charleston but soon afterward joined the African Methodist Congregation. During the years 1818–22 he planned a slave uprising intended to take over the city of Charleston, but the conspiracy collapsed when one of the participants betrayed the plot. A court of two magistrates and five freeholders convened as judge and jury to try the suspects. Vesey and thirty-five compatriots were hanged; thirty-four others were sent out of the state; sixty-one were acquitted; and four whites were fined for their part in the plot.

★★★★★

WALTER, Thomas: botanist
Born Hampshire, England, circa 1740; married Anne Lesesne, March 26, 1769; second marriage to Ann Peyre, March 20, 1777; third marriage to Dorothy Cooper, after 1780; father of three daughters (two by second marriage, one by third marriage); died January 17, 1789.

Walter attempted to introduce (with John Fraser) a native Carolina grass, *Agrostis perennans,* into general cultivation in England. He was the author of *Flora Caroliniana,* the sole record of his work, which described approximately 1,000 species of flowering plants from specimens collected in South Carolina, representing 435 genera.

An herbarium collected by Walter was presented to the Linnean Society of London in 1849 and acquired by the British Museum of Natural History in 1863. Walter was buried in a small botanical garden on a plantation located on the bank of the Santee River in South Carolina.

WELLS, William Charles: physician
Born Charleston, South Carolina, May 24, 1757; son of Robert and Mary Wells; never married; died September 18, 1817.

Wells, who had earned an M.D. from the University of Edinburgh (Scotland) in 1780, fled to England at the outbreak of the American Revolution. He served as a surgeon with a Scottish regiment in mercenary service with the Dutch in Europe in 1779. He returned to America in 1781 but went back to England three years later, practicing medicine in London from 1794 to 1817.

Wells became a licentiate of the Royal College of Physicians in 1788 and a member of the Royal Society in 1793. He was a pioneer in recognizing the principle of natural selection. He claimed to have been the first to experiment with the use of belladonna for the eyes and wrote an essay on single vision with two eyes. He also wrote an essay on the nature and quality of dew.

Wells died in London and was buried at the parish church of St. Brides there.

WILLIAMSON, Andrew: army officer
Born Scotland, circa 1730; married Eliza Tyler; father of four children; died March 21, 1786.

Having emigrated to Hard Labor Creek, near Savannah, Georgia, Williamson was well established as a planter there by 1765. He had been commissioned a lieutenant in the South Carolina militia in 1760 and was promoted to major in 1775, serving in the "Snow Campaign" the latter year. In 1776 he led the second Cherokee expedition, which was ambushed at Essenecca; in 1777 he signed a treaty which accepted a large land cession from the Indians. He was then promoted to colonel and later to brigadier general.

As commander of the South Carolina militia in Robert Howe's Florida expedition of 1778, Williamson shared blame for its failure. When it became obvious that the British would take Charleston in 1779, he sent the troops home. The city fell, and Williamson was accused of treason, a charge which was not proved. He died in St. Paul's Parish, near Charleston.

WINN, Richard: army officer, congressman
Born Fauquier County, Virginia, 1750; son of Minor and Margaret (O'Conner) Winn; married Priscilla McKinley; father of several children; died December 19, 1818.

Winn embarked on an army career with a commission as a first lieutenant in the 3rd South Carolina Regiment, Continental Army, in 1775; also that year he became a justice of the peace in South Carolina. He fought in the Battle of Fort Moultrie in 1776 and defended Fort McIntosh, Georgia, as the captain in command in 1777. He took part in the defense of Charleston in 1780, joining Thomas Sumter's guerrillas as a major. He served in the Jacksonborough Assembly in 1782. In 1783 he was commissioned a brigadier general in the South Carolina militia, later (1800) becoming a major general. Also in 1783 he surveyed the Camden District of South Carolina.

Interested in education of youth, Winn gave one hundred acres of land to the Mount Zion Society in 1785. He continued to serve South Carolina as a member of the South Carolina legislature and, in 1786, as a commissioner for buying (and later for selling) lands for the new state capital at Columbia. He was superintendent of Indian affairs for the Creek Nation in 1788.

Winn, a Democrat, had an extensive career in the United States House of Representatives; he sat in the 3rd and 4th congresses (1793–97) and in the 7th through 12th congresses (January 24, 1803, to 1813). He then moved to Tennessee and became a planter and merchant. He died in Duck River, Tennessee, and was buried in Winnsboro, South Carolina.

WRAGG, William: colonial official
Born South Carolina, 1714; son of Samuel and Marie (DuBose) Wragg; married Mary Wood; second marriage to Henrietta Wragg, February 5, 1769; father of two children; died September 2, 1777.

At the age of eleven in 1725 Wragg was admitted to Middle Temple in London, England, later (1733) gaining admission to the English bar. He returned to South Carolina circa 1734. He was a member of the South Carolina Governor's Council in 1753 and 1769 and a justice of the peace in 1756. From 1763 to 1768 he was a member of the South Carolina Assembly. He refused to sign the Articles of Non-Importation in 1769.

A leading landowner and man of affairs in South Carolina by 1776, Wragg was a supporter of royal authority in the colonies. In 1777 he was banished for his Loyalist attitudes and sailed for Amsterdam, Holland, in the ship *Commerce;* he died when the ship was wrecked off the coast of Holland on September 2 of that year.

★★★★★★★★★★★★★

VIRGINIA

ADAMS, Thomas: Continental congressman

Born New Kent County, Virginia, 1730; died August 1788.

Educated in common schools, Adams's first role in public life was as clerk of Henrico County. In 1762 he went to England to look after his extensive business interests and remained there for twelve years. After his return in 1774, he was elected to the Virginia House of Burgesses and signed the Articles of Association. That same year he became chairman of the New Kent County Committee of Safety. He was one of the Virginia delegates to the Continental Congress from 1778 to 1780 and was a signer of the Articles of Confederation. During the years 1783–86 he served in the Virginia Senate.

Adams moved to Augusta County, Virginia, in 1780, and died there on his estate, "Cowpasture."

ANDERSON, Richard Clough: army officer, pioneer

Born Hanover County, Virginia, January 12, 1750; son of Robert and Elizabeth (Clough) Anderson; married Elizabeth Clark, 1785; second marriage to Sarah Marshall, 1797; father of at least six children (Richard Clough, Larz, Robert, William Marshall, John, and Charles); died October 16, 1826.

Anderson was in Boston during the Boston Tea Party, in 1773. He was a captain in the Hanover County Company in the Revolutionary War; later, as a captain in the 5th Virginia Regiment of the Continental Army, he almost ruined George Washington's plans at Trenton by alarming the Hessians on the night before the battle. He fought at Germantown, Brandywine, and Monmouth and was commissioned a major in 1778. The following year he aided in the attempt to capture Savannah, where he was wounded.

While stationed at Charleston, South Carolina, Anderson was captured and held prisoner for nine months. After his release he joined General Daniel Morgan. He acted as messenger for the Marquis de Lafayette and later was sent to organize the Virginia militia. Toward the end of the war he was commissioned a lieutenant colonel.

In 1783 Anderson supervised a surveying crew that divided lands in the West which Virginia had reserved for her Continental troops. He then settled near Louisville, Kentucky, and in 1788 served as a member of the Kentucky Constitutional Convention. He died in Louisville.

★★★★★

BALLARD, Bland Williams: frontiersman
Born Fredericksburg, Virginia, October 16, 1759; son of Bland Ballard; married Elizabeth Williamson, 1783; second marriage to Diana Matthews, August 17, 1835; third marriage to Mrs. Elizabeth Garrett, October 28, 1841; died September 5, 1853.

Ballard, who received no formal education, was active in the war against the Indians in Kentucky during 1779 and 1780. He was with General George Rogers Clark in 1781 and 1782, took part in the war in the Pickaway towns in Ohio, and was with General Clark again in the expedition against the Indians on the Wabash River in 1787.

Ballard became a farmer in Shelbyville, Kentucky, and survived an Indian attack on his homestead in 1787. After participating in the Battle of Fallen Timbers in 1793, he served as a member of the Kentucky legislature for five terms between 1793 and 1810. He then returned to the battlefield, participating in the Battle of Tippecanoe in 1811 and serving with Colonel John Allen's Regiment in the War of 1812. The following year he fought at the Battle of Raisin River.

After his death in Shelbyville at the age of ninety-three, Ballard was buried in the State Cemetery in Frankfort, Kentucky.

BANISTER, John: Continental congressman, army officer
Born Bristol Parish, Virginia, December 26, 1734; son of John and Willmuth (or Wilmet, or Wilmette) Banister; married Patsy Bland; second marriage to Anne Blair; died September 30, 1788.

Banister became a member of Middle Temple in 1753. Having participated in the Virginia Convention in 1776, he became a member of the state's House of Burgesses the following year. Virginia sent him to the Continental Congress in 1778 and 1779, where he helped frame and signed the Articles of Confederation. He fought in the Revolutionary War as a lieutenant colonel in the Virginia Cavalry during the years 1778–81. He died at the age of fifty-three and was buried on the family estate at Hatcher's Run, near Petersburg, Virginia.

BAYLOR, George: army officer
Born Newmarket, Virginia, January 12, 1752; son of Colonel John and Fanny (Walker) Baylor; married Lucy Page; died March 1784.

Baylor was military aide to General Washington during the American Revolution, later gaining a promotion to colonel for his service in the Battle of Trenton. While commanding a regiment of cavalry, he was wounded when his encamped regiment was attacked by English troops under General Grey after the Battle of Monmouth in 1778. He died in Bridgetown, Barbados, six years later.

BLAIR, John: associate justice of the United States Supreme Court
Born Williamsburg, Virginia, 1732; son of John and Mary (Monro) Blair; married Jean Balfour; died August 31, 1800.

In 1755 Blair was admitted to Middle Temple in London, England. He served in the Virginia House of Burgesses from 1766 until 1770 and as clerk of the Virginia Council from 1770 to 1775. The next year he both participated in the Virginia Constitutional Convention and was active in the Virginia Privy Council.

After serving a tenure on the bench of the Virginia General Court (1778–80), Blair was a judge in the First Court of Appeals of Virginia from 1780 to 1789; during this period the court reviewed the case of *Commonwealth of Virginia vs. Caton,* which established the precedent of judiciary review of state legislation. A delegate to the United States Constitutional Convention in 1786, he believed firmly in the constitution and in a strong federal government.

In 1789 President Washington appointed him associate justice of the United States Supreme Court, where he remained until 1796. He died in Williamsburg four years later.

BLAND, Richard: Continental congressman

Born Williamsburg, Virginia, May 6, 1710; son of Richard and Elizabeth (Randolph) Bland; married Anne Poythress; second marriage to Martha Macon; third marriage to Elizabeth Blair; father of twelve children; died October 26, 1776.

After graduating from the College of William and Mary in 1730, Bland attended the University of Edinburgh. For thirty years, from 1745 to 1775, he was a member of the Virginia House of Burgesses from Prince George County, during which time (in the late 1740s) he was active on the committee which remonstrated with Parliament concerning taxation. He also signed the Non-Importation Agreement of 1769. He was a member of the Virginia Committee of Correspondence in 1773 and served as a delegate from Virginia to the Continental Congress in 1774 and 1775.

Bland wrote *Inquiry Into the Rights of British Colonies* (1776), which was the first published work stating the colonial position on taxation. He died in Williamsburg and was buried on the Jordan Point Plantation on the James River in Virginia.

BLAND, Theodorick: army officer, congressman, Continental congressman

Born Prince George County, Virginia, March 21, 1742; son of Theodorick and Frances (Bolling) Bland; married Martha Dangerfield; died June 1, 1790.

Bland received an M.D. from the University of Edinburgh, Scotland, in 1763. He was commissioned a captain in the 1st Troop of the Virginia Cavalry in 1776 and three years later was commissioned a colonel in the 1st Continental Dragoons.

Bland represented Virginia in the Continental Congress during the years 1780–83 and also served in the Virginia House of Delegates from 1786 to 1788. He ran unsuccessfully for governor of Virginia in 1786 and voted against ratification of the United States Constitution at the Virginia Convention two years later. He represented Virginia in the 1st Congress of the United States House of Representatives.

Bland died in New York City and was buried in Trinity Churchyard there.

BOONE, Daniel: Indian fighter, scout

Born Bucks County, Pennsylvania, February 11, 1735; son of Squire and Sarah (Morgan) Boone; married Rebeccah Bryan, August 14, 1756; father of nine children; died September 26, 1820.

After moving to North Carolina in 1750, Boone served as a wagoner in Braddock's unsuccessful expedition to Fort Duquesne in 1755; three years later he made a successful expedition to the fort under General John Forbes.

Boone began a deep and far-reaching relationship with Kentucky when he visited it for the first time on a hunting trip in 1767. He returned for a more thorough expedition in the company of his brother from 1769 to 1771; he was twice captured by Indians. In 1773 he made his first colonizing attempt in Kentucky, but he failed because of heavy Indian attacks. Two years later he returned to Kentucky with a group of men and established the Wilderness Trail over the Cumberland Gap through the Allegheny Mountains, founding Boonesborough (now Boonesboro) on the Kentucky River.

In 1776 Boone became a captain in the Virginia militia. Two years later he was captured by the Shawnee Indians and adopted by the tribe; however, he escaped and warned Boonesborough of an impending attack and aided in its defense. He was charged by some with disloyalty during this period, but was acquitted and returned to

North Carolina. Boone returned to Kentucky in 1779 and founded Boone's Station. He was a member of the Virginia legislature in 1780 and 1783, and sheriff, county lieutenant, and deputy surveyor of Fayette County, Virginia (now Kentucky), in 1782.

Boone was influential in American westward migration and in the defense of the Revolutionary frontier. He went to Missouri in 1799 and later had trouble with his land titles in both Kentucky and Missouri; part of his Missouri acreage was restored by Congressional intercession. He died in La Charette, Missouri, in 1820 and was returned to Frankfort, Kentucky, for burial.

BRADFORD, John: printer
Born Prince William, Virginia, June 6, 1749; son of Daniel and Alice Bradford; married Eliza James, 1771; father of at least one son (Daniel); died March 30, 1830.

After moving to Kentucky in 1779, Bradford took part in a survey of Kentucky County, Virginia, under George May. He was appointed by the third convention for the statehood of Kentucky to publish the *Kentucke Gazette* in 1787. (The spelling of the state name was changed to Kentucky in 1789.) He published the *Kentucke Almanac* in 1788, and the *Acts of the First Session of the Kentucky Legislature,* the first book printed in Kentucky, in 1792. He later published "Notes of Kentucky" in the *Kentucky Gazette* from 1826 to 1829.

Bradford served as a deputy under Colonel Thomas Marshall and was the first surveyor of Fayette County, Kentucky. He was clerk of the board of Transylvania Seminary until 1795. Four years later he founded Transylvania University and was the first chairman of the board. He helped found the Lexington, Kentucky, library and was a member of the Kentucky House of Representatives in 1797 and 1802.

BRAXTON, Carter: Continental congressman
Born Newington, Virginia, September 10, 1736; son of George and Mary (Carter) Braxton; married Judith Robinson, 1755; second marriage to Elizabeth Corbin, May 1761; father of sixteen children; died October 10, 1797.

Braxton was educated at the College of William and Mary. He was a member of the Virginia House of Burgesses for fourteen years (1761–75). During this time he also signed the Resolutions and the Non-Importation Agreement of 1769 and was a delegate to the Virginia Revolutionary conventions in 1774–76. He signed the Declaration of Independence and participated in the Continental Congress in the years 1775–76, 1777–83, and 1785. He also served on the Council of the State of Virginia from 1786 to 1794. He died at the age of sixty-one in Richmond, Virginia.

BROOKE, Francis Taliaferro: jurist
Born Smithfield, Virginia, August 27, 1763; son of Richard and Elizabeth (Taliaferro) Brooke; married Mary Randolph Spotswood, October 1791; second marriage to Mary Champe Carter, 1804; father of at least one son (Francis Jr.); died March 3, 1851.

Brooke studied medicine with his brother Lawrence and read law with his brother Robert. Commissioned a lieutenant in the Continental Army in 1780, he served under Lafayette the next year and later under General Greene.

After his admission to the Virginia bar in 1788, Brooke practiced law in Monongahela and Harrison counties. He was appointed attorney in the Virginia District Court and was elected to the state House of Delegates, where he served in 1794–95. He received a commission as a major in the Virginia militia in 1796 and moved to Fredericksburg later in the year. Six years afterward he was commissioned a brigadier general in the Virginia militia.

Brooke was elected to the state senate in 1800, serving as speaker in 1804. He was a longtime judge in the Virginia Supreme Court of Appeals, holding this position from 1811 until 1851, as well as serving as president of the court from 1824 to 1830. He also was a vice president of the Society of the Cincinnati. He died at the age of eighty-seven.

BROWN, John: senator, congressman, Continental congressman
Born Staunton, Virginia, September 12, 1757; son of John and Margaret (Preston) Brown; married Margaretta Mason, 1799; died August 29, 1837.

Brown was educated at Princeton and at the College of William and Mary, and he studied law under Thomas Jefferson. After fighting in the American Revolution he was admitted to the Virginia bar in 1782. He represented Kentucky in the Virginia legislature from 1784 to 1788. He was a delegate to the Continental Congress in 1787–88 and a member of the Kentucky Constitutional Convention in 1788. As a member of the Virginia Convention to ratify the United States Constitution in 1789, he voted against ratification.

Brown was a delegate from Virginia to the United States House of Representatives during the 1st and 2nd congresses. He spent the next thirteen years as a Kentucky delegate to the United States Senate; he was president pro tem in 1803 and 1804.

Brown's home, "Liberty Hall," in Frankfort, Kentucky, was designed by Thomas Jefferson. He died in Frankfort and was buried in the Frankfort Cemetery.

BROWN, William: physician
Born Haddingtonshire, Scotland, 1752; son of Richard and Helen (Bailey) Brown; married Catherine Scott; father of several children (including Gustavus Alexander); died January 11, 1792.

In 1770 Brown obtained an M.D. from the University of Edinburgh, Scotland. After being appointed a surgeon in the 2nd Virginia Regiment in 1776, he was promoted to surgeon general of the army hospital for the Middle Department of the Continental Army (1777–78) and then to physician general (1778–80). In 1778 he wrote the first

pharmacopeia published in the United States. He also served as chairman of the trustees of the Alexandria (Virginia) Academy. He died in 1792 and was buried at the Old Pohick Church in Alexandria.

BUFORD, Abraham: army officer
Born Culpeper County, Virginia, July 31, 1749; son of John and Judith Beauford; married Martha McDowell, October 1788; died June 30, 1833.

In 1774 Buford raised a company of Minutemen, who later helped in the expulsion of Governor Dunmore from Virginia. Commissioned a major in the 14th Virginia Regiment in 1776, the next year he was promoted to lieutenant colonel in the 5th Virginia Regiment. He was colonel in command of the 11th Virginia Regiment from 1778 until 1781, when he took command of the 3rd Virginia Regiment. After the Revolution he became a large landowner. He died in Georgetown, Kentucky, at the age of eighty-three.

★★★★★

CABELL, Samuel Jordan: congressman
Born Amherst County, Virginia, December 15, 1756; son of Colonel William and Margaret (Jordan) Cabell; married Sally Syme, 1781; died August 4, 1818.

Cabell was commissioned a major in the 6th Virginia Regiment in 1775 and served at Valley Forge and in Washington's campaigns of 1778. He was commissioned a lieutenant colonel in 1779. In 1784 he became a lieutenant in the Amherst County (Virginia) militia.

Cabell served in the Virginia legislature in 1785 and 1786 and was a member of the United States House of Representatives from Virginia during the 4th through the 7th congresses (1795—1803). He was an original member of the Virginia Society of the Cincinnati. He died in Nelson County, Virginia, and was buried in the family burial ground at "Soldiers' Joy" farm, in Norwood, Virginia.

CAMM, John: clergyman, college president
Born England, 1718; son of Thomas Camm; married Betsy Hansford, 1769; died 1778.

Camm, who attended Trinity College, Cambridge, Massachusetts, was ordained to the ministry of the Anglican Church of Newport Parish, Virginia, in 1745. He was a professor of divinity at the College of William and Mary from 1749 to 1756 and from 1760 to 1771. From 1771 to 1777 he was president of that school. He was also rector of Bruton Parish and a commissary of the Bishop of London.

Camm served for a time as a member of the Virginia Governor's Council. He was successful in 1759 in having the Two Penny Acts of 1755 and 1758 disallowed by the King in Council.

CAMPBELL, William: army officer
Born Augusta County, Virginia, 1745; son of Charles and (Miss Buchanan) Campbell; married Elizabeth Henry; died August 22, 1781.

Campbell compiled an impressive military and political record during his short life. Joining the Virginia militia as a captain, he saw considerable action as an Indian fighter. In 1773 he became justice of Fincastle County, Virginia. The following year he campaigned in Lord Dunmore's War and two years later led his company to Williamsburg to help expel Governor Dunmore. At the age of thirty-two he became a lieutenant colonel and a justice of Washington County, Virginia. In 1780 he was commissioned a full colonel; that same year he led four hundred men from Washington County to join Evan Shelby and John Sevier, and together they fought General Ferguson in the Carolinas. In 1781 he led the Virginia militia at the Battle of Guilford, after which he was voted a horse, a sword, and the thanks of the Continental Congress. He was appointed a brigadier general in the Virginia militia in 1781. He fought under the command of Lafayette in the Battle of Jamestown.

Campbell's involvement in politics began in 1775 with his signing of an address from Fincastle County, Virginia, to the Continental Congress declaring loyalty to the Crown and willingness to fight for "constitutional rights." In 1778 he became boundary commissioner between Virginia and the Cherokees. He also served briefly in the Virginia legislature.

Campbell died in Rocky Mills, Virginia.

CARRINGTON, Edward: Continental congressman
Born Goochland County, Virginia, February 11, 1748; died October 28, 1810.

During the Revolutionary War, Carrington saw considerable action with the Continental Army. He was commissioned a lieutenant colonel in the Artillery in 1776 and later served as quartermaster general on the staff of General Greene. He commanded the Artillery at the Battle of Hobkirks Hill, 1781, and also at Yorktown.

Carrington was a member of the Goochland County Committee in 1775–76. At the age of thirty-seven he became a member of the Continental Congress from Virginia and served for a year. President Washington appointed him marshal of Virginia in 1789. Later, in 1807, he acted as the foreman of the jury in the Aaron Burr treason trial.

Carrington died in Richmond, Virginia, and was buried in St. John's Cemetery.

CARRINGTON, Paul: jurist
Born Charlotte County, Virginia, March 16, 1733; son of George and Ann (Mayo) Carrington; married Margaret Read, October 1, 1755; second marriage to Priscilla Sims, 1793; died June 22, 1818.

Carrington graduated from the College of William and Mary in 1753. At the age of twenty-three he became the King's attorney for four counties. He was commissioned a major in the Virginia militia in 1761; three years later he was commissioned a full colonel. He later became county lieutenant of the Charlotte County militia.

Carrington's first juristic position was

presiding justice of Charlotte County (1765); later that year he was elected to the Virginia House of Burgesses, where he served for ten years. For three of those ten years, 1765–67, he was also a Charlotte County delegate to the Virginia Senate. A member of the Mercantile Association of 1770, he later served as chairman of the Revolutionary Committee of Charlotte County. In 1775–76 he was a member of the Virginia Committee of Safety.

Carrington served as chief justice of the Virginia General Court in 1780; later, in 1789, he began an eighteen-year career as a judge of the Virginia Court of Appeals. He died in Charlotte County, Virginia.

CARY, Archibald: planter, industrialist
Born Virginia, 1721; son of Henry and Anne (Edwards) Cary; married Mary Randolph, 1744; died September 1787.

Cary, educated at the College of William and Mary, was a mill operator and a cattle raiser. From 1747 to 1750 he was justice of the peace, burgess, and vestryman of Goochland and Cumberland counties, Virginia. In 1756 he became Chesterfield County's representative to the Virginia Assembly, a position he held for the remainder of his life. He served as chairman of the assembly's public claims committee in 1762 and as speaker of the assembly until 1787.

Cary was a member of the Committee of Correspondence in 1773. As chairman of the Committee of the Whole, he read Virginia's Resolution of Independence to the Second Virginia Convention of 1775–76. He died in Virginia.

CHRISTIAN, William: army officer
Born Berkeley County, Virginia, 1732; son of Israel and Elizabeth (Stark) Christian; married Anne Henry; died April 9, 1786.

Christian was commissioned a captain in Colonel William Byrd's Regiment in 1763. From 1773 to 1775 he represented Fincastle County in the lower house of the Virginia legislature. He was a member of the Virginia Committee of Safety in 1775. In 1776 he served Fincastle and Botetourt counties in the Virginia Senate; that same year he was commissioned a colonel in the Virginia militia by the Virginia Council of Defense. He served another term in the Senate from 1780 to 1783.

Christian was a member of the commission that negotiated the Cherokee treaty signed at Long Island on July 20, 1777. He was killed near Jeffersonville, Indiana, while leading a pursuit party against marauding Wabash Indians.

CLAIBORNE, Thomas: congressman
Born Brunswick County, Virginia, February 1, 1749; father of John and Thomas; died 1812.

Claiborne served as a member of the Virginia House of Delegates from 1783 to 1788. He was a member of the Virginia Senate from 1790 to 1792 and a member of the United States House of Representatives from Virginia during the 3rd, 4th, 5th, 7th, and 8th congresses (1793–99, 1801–05).

Claiborne was colonel in command of the Brunswick County militia in 1789 and served as sheriff of Brunswick County from 1789 to 1792. He died on his estate in Brunswick County.

CLARK, Christopher Henderson: congressman, lawyer
Born Albemarle County, Virginia, 1767; died November 21, 1828.

Clark was educated at Washington College (now Washington and Lee University) in Lexington, Virginia, and studied law in the office of Patrick Henry. Admitted to the Virginia bar in 1788, he began his practice of law in New London (now Bedford Springs), Virginia.

In 1790 Clark served as a delegate to the Virginia House of Delegates. A Jeffersonian Democrat, he filled a vacancy in the United States House of Representatives during the 8th and 9th congresses, from November 5, 1804, until July 1, 1806, at which time he resigned. He died near New London and was buried in a private cemetery at Old Lawyers Station, near Lynchburg, Virginia.

CLAY, Green: army officer, legislator
Born Powhatan County, Virginia, August 14, 1757; son of Charles Clay; married Sally Lewis; father of seven children (including Cassius Marcellus and Brutus J.); died October 31, 1826.

After coming to Kentucky circa 1777, Clay became deputy surveyor of Lincoln County, Kentucky, in 1781. After amassing a fortune by locating lands, he settled in Madison County, Kentucky. In 1787 he became a trustee of the town of Boonesborough. He spent the next two years as a member of the Virginia legislature. He was also a member of the lower house of the Kentucky legislature from Madison County in 1793 and 1794. He served in the Kentucky Senate from 1795 to 1798 and again in 1807, in the meantime (1799) representing Madison County at the convention to draft the second constitution for Kentucky.

Clay was commissioned a major general in the Kentucky militia and marched with three thousand state troops to relieve General Harrison at Fort Meigs. Clay County, Kentucky, is named in his honor. He died in Madison County.

CLAY, Matthew: congressman
Born Halifax County, Virginia, March 25, 1754; son of Charles and Martha (Green) Clay; married Polly Williams; second marriage to Miss Saunders; died May 27, 1815.

Clay was commissioned an ensign in the 9th Virginia Regiment in 1776, advancing to second lieutenant in 1777 and to first lieutenant in 1778. He was quartermaster of the 1st Virginia Regiment from 1778 to 1781.

After the war, Clay became involved in politics, serving in the Virginia House of Delegates from 1790 to 1794. He then represented Virginia in the United States House, attending the 4th through the 12th congresses (1795–1813) and the 14th (March 4, 1815, until his death). He died in the Halifax County Courthouse and was buried in the

family burying ground in Pittsylvania County, Virginia.

CLOPTON, John: congressman
Born St. Peter's Parish, New Kent County, Virginia, February 7, 1756; son of William Clopton; married Sarah Bacon; died September 11, 1816.

Clopton received his education at the University of Pennsylvania, graduating in 1776. From 1789 to 1791 he served in the Virginia House of Delegates. A delegate from Virginia to the United States House of Representatives, he attended the 4th through the 5th and the 7th through the 14th congresses (1795–99, 1801–16, respectively). In 1799 he served as a member of the Privy Council of Virginia.

Clopton died at his plantation near Turnstall, New Kent County, Virginia, and was buried there.

COLES, Isaac: congressman
Born Richmond, Virginia, March 2, 1747; father of at least one son (Walter); died June 3, 1813.

Coles, who attended the College of William and Mary, was a colonel of the militia in the Revolutionary War. He served in the Virginia House of Delegates from 1783 to 1787 and attended the Virginia Convention to ratify the United States Constitution in 1788. He was a member of the United States House of Representatives, as a delegate from Virginia, for the 1st, 3rd, and 4th congresses (1789–91, 1793–97).

During his political career Coles lived on his plantation, "Coles Ferry," on the Staunton River, Halifax County. In 1798 he moved to Pittsylvania County, Virginia. He died on his plantation, "Coles Hill," near Chatham, Virginia, and was buried in the family cemetery on the plantation.

CONNOLLY, John: army officer
Born Wright's Ferry, Pennsylvania, 1743; son of John and Susanna (Howard) Connolly; married Susanna Semple, before 1767; second marriage to Margaret Wellington; father of two children; died January 30, 1813.

A medical officer in the Pennsylvania militia in the Indian campaigns of 1762–64, Connolly studied Indian languages in Kaskaskia from 1767 to 1770. He practiced medicine in Pittsburgh for two years, 1770–72, then received a grant of land in Kentucky from Lord Dunmore, the governor of Virginia, and acted as Dunmore's agent in land speculation. That same year he was commissioned a captain in the Virginia militia and was appointed magistrate for the district of West Augusta. He attempted to recruit settlers in western Pennsylvania into the Virginia militia in 1774, and almost started a civil war between Pennsylvania and Virginia traders when he stopped Pennsylvania trade with the Indians and imposed a fur tax on Pittsburgh traders.

In 1775 Connolly made a treaty with the Iroquois and Delaware Indians wherein they agreed to support the British. That same year he was commissioned a lieutenant colonel in the British Army. While en route west to lead the British and Indian forces in 1776, he was captured by colonial forces and imprisoned until 1780. After his release he joined Lord Cornwallis at Yorktown and was again captured and imprisoned in 1781–82. Following his release he went to England, but returned in 1788 to serve as lieutenant governor of Detroit. He unsuccessfully attempted to persuade the leaders in Kentucky to shift allegiance to the British.

In 1799–1800 Connolly was deputy superintendent of Indian affairs. He died at the age of seventy.

CRAWFORD, William: army officer
Born Berkeley County, Virginia, 1732; died June 11, 1782.

Crawford served in the French and Indian War and, in 1755, was a captain and the leader of the scouts with General Braddock in the expedition against Fort Duquesne. In 1763–64 he served as a captain during the Pontiac War, and later became a justice in the Pennsylvania Court of Quarter Sessions.

In 1776 Crawford was commissioned a lieutenant colonel in the 5th Regiment of the Virginia militia; later that year he became a full colonel in the 7th Regiment. He participated in the battles of Long Island, Trenton, Princeton, Brandywine, and Germantown. In 1778 he was in charge of the Virginia frontier militia.

A commander of the expedition against the Wyandot and Delaware Indians in Ohio in 1782, Crawford was captured, tortured, and killed at "Battle Island," Wyandot County, Ohio.

★★★★★

DARKE, William: army officer
Born Philadelphia County, Pennsylvania, May 6, 1736; son of Joseph Darke; married Sarah Delayea; father of three sons (including Captain Joseph) and one daughter; died November 26, 1801.

Darke served as a corporal in the Rutherford Rangers during the French and Indian War, 1758–59. He became a captain in the Virginia Volunteers at the beginning of the Revolutionary War and was captured in 1777 at the Battle of Germantown. He remained aboard a prison ship in New York until 1780. The following year he recruited the Berkeley and Hampshire (Virginia) regiments. He served at the siege of Yorktown and retired as a lieutenant colonel.

In 1788 Darke was a member of the Virginia Convention to ratify the United States Constitution. Elected to the Virginia legislature in 1791, he served only three days, resigning to accept a commission under General Arthur St. Clair to fight Indians. He was wounded in a defeat at the hands of the Miami Indians in 1791. He was later promoted to brigadier general and given 8,000 acres of public lands for his military service. He died in Jefferson County, Virginia.

DAWSON, John: congressman
Born Virginia, 1762; son of the Reverend Musgrave and Mary (Waugh) Dawson; died March 30, 1814.

Dawson graduated from Harvard in 1782.

As a representative from Spotsylvania County, he served in the Virginia House of Delegates in 1786–87, 1787–88, and 1789. He was a member of the Virginia Convention that ratified the United States Constitution, a member of the Executive Council of Virginia, and (in 1793) a presidential elector. From 1797 to 1814 he served in the United States House of Representatives as a delegate from Virginia.

Dawson went to France as a bearer of the ratified Convention of 1800. He proposed the Twelfth Amendment to the Constitution, which provided for the separate election of the President and the vice president. During the War of 1812 he served as an aide to General Andrew Jackson. He died in Washington, D. C., two years later.

★★★★★

EDWARDS, John: planter, senator
Born Stafford County, Virginia, 1748; son of Hayden and Penelope (Sanford) Edwards; died 1837.

Edwards worked for the states of Virginia and Kentucky in several different political capacities. In Virginia he was a member of the House of Delegates from 1781 to 1783, in 1785–86, and in 1795. During this period he also served as a delegate to the Kentucky statehood conventions (1785–88) and participated in the Kentucky Constitutional Convention. He represented Kentucky in the United States Senate from 1791 to 1795. Following that term, he served in the Kentucky House of Representatives in 1795 and in the Kentucky Senate for the next four years.

Edwards died in Bourbon County, Kentucky, and was buried at his family estate near Paris, Kentucky.

EGGLESTON, Joseph: congressman
Born Middlesex County, Virginia, November 24, 1754; died February 13, 1811.

Eggleston, who graduated from William and Mary College, distinguished himself during the Battle of Guilford Courthouse and the capture of Augusta, Georgia, in 1781 while serving as a captain and then as a major in Lee's Lighthorse Cavalry of the Continental Army.

Eggleston's political career included membership in the Virginia House of Delegates (1785–88 and 1791–99), the Virginia Privy Council (1787), and the United States House of Representatives, in which he filled a Democratic vacancy during the 5th and 6th congresses (December 3, 1798, to 1801). He was also engaged in agriculture and spent ten years as a justice of the peace (1801–11).

After his death in Amelia County, Virginia, on February 13, 1811, Eggleston was buried in the Old Grubhill Church Cemetery, near Amelia Courthouse.

★★★★★

FAUQUIER, Francis: colonial official
Born England, circa 1704; son of Doctor John F. and Elizabeth (Chamberlayne) Fauquier; married Catharine Dalston; died March 3, 1768.

Fauquier became director of the South Sea Company in 1751, was elected a fellow of the Royal Society in 1753, and served as lieutenant governor of Virginia from 1758 to 1768. Forecasting the Revolutionary War, in 1760 he warned Pitt of colonial resistance if the policy of taxation was continued. Five years later, Fauquier dissolved the Virginia legislature for passing Patrick Henry's resolution against the Stamp Act. He died before the beginning of the Revolution.

FEBIGER, Christian: army officer
Born Funen, Denmark, 1746; married Elizabeth Carson; died September 20, 1796.

Febiger toured the American colonies in 1772, engaging in the lumber, fish, and horse trades. Soon afterward, he enlisted in the Essex and Middlesex Regiment of the Massachusetts militia, casting his fortune with the colonies.

While serving as a major in Benedict Arnold's brigade of the Continental Army, Febiger was taken prisoner in 1775. After regaining his freedom, he was commissioned a lieutenant colonel in the 11th Virginia Regiment in January 1777; he became a colonel later that year. George Washington chose Febiger to command one of the four light regiments for the storming of Stony Point in 1779. The following year, Febiger was an agent for obtaining and forwarding stores to the Southern Army under General Nathanael Greene.

In 1781 Febiger aided in suppressing the Loyalist insurrection in Hampshire County, Virginia, and served as the superintending officer of the Virginia militia. He was brevetted a brigadier general by the Continental Congress in 1783. For seven years he was treasurer of Philadelphia, serving until his death in 1796.

FILSON, John: explorer, historian
Born Chester County, Pennsylvania, circa 1747; son of Davidson Filson; died October 1788.

Filson was a literate explorer and historian of the Kentucky area. He recorded a narrative given by Daniel Boone of his expedition up the Chillicothe River in 1782. Filson also wrote a personal account of Daniel Boone. After conducting his own exploration along the Ohio River to Lexington, Kentucky, he acquired 12,000 acres of land in Fayette County, Kentucky. His explorations led to his creation of the first map of Kentucky.

Filson was the author of *Discovery, Settlement, and Present State of Kentucke,* the first history of Kentucky, the first edition of which was printed in 1784. He was also a backer of the founding of Cincinnati, Ohio. While surveying the Cincinnati area, he was killed by an Indian near Little Miami, Kentucky, in October 1788. The Filson Club, an historical society with its headquarters in Louisville, Kentucky, was later named in his honor.

FITZHUGH, William: Continental congressman
Born Eagles Nest, King George County, Virginia, August 24, 1741; died June 6, 1809.

Fitzhugh, who was privately educated, was a delegate to the Virginia Constitutional Convention in 1776 and served a number of terms in the Virginia House of Delegates (1776–77, 1780–81, and 1787–88). He attended the Continental Congress in 1779 and 1780 and was a member of the Virginia Senate from 1781 to 1785.

Fitzhugh, engaged in agriculture most of his life, died in Ravensworth, Virginia, and was buried in a private cemetery on his estate.

FLEMING, William: army officer, colonial official
Born Jedburgh, Scotland, February 18, 1729; son of Leonard and Dorothea Fleming; married Anne Christian, April 9, 1763; died August 5, 1795.

Fleming, who attended the University of Edinburgh in Scotland, came to Norfolk, Virginia, in 1755 and served as an ensign in a regiment under Colonel George Washington from that year until 1763. He was a colonel in the Botetourt Regiment at the Battle of Point Pleasant in 1774.

Fleming was a county lieutenant for Botetourt County, Virginia, in 1776. He served in the Virginia legislature from 1777 to 1779 and on the Virginia Council in 1780. He was acting governor of Virginia for twelve days (June 1–12, 1781) and in 1784 attended the Danville Convention for separate statehood for Kentucky.

FLEMING, William: Continental congressman, jurist
Born Cumberland County, Virginia, July 6, 1736; died February 15, 1824.

Fleming, after graduating from the College of William and Mary in 1763, was admitted to the bar and began a law practice. He was a member of the Virginia House of Burgesses from 1772 to 1775, then served as a delegate to the Revolutionary conventions in 1775 and 1776. He was a member of the Committee of Independence in 1776 and a delegate to the Virginia House of Delegates from 1776 to 1778. The following year he became a member of the Continental Congress, serving until 1781.

Fleming began his juristic career in 1788, sitting briefly as judge of the General Court before becoming a member of the First Supreme Court of Appeals, a position he held for thirty-five years (1789–1824). He served as president of the court in 1809.

After his death in 1824, Fleming was buried in the family cemetery on his estate, "Summerville."

FOWLER, John: congressman
Born Virginia, 1755; died August 22, 1840.

As a boy, Fowler attended common schools. He served as a captain in the Revolutionary War, entering politics at war's end as a member of the convention held at Danville, Virginia (now Kentucky), in 1787. That same year he was also a member of the Virginia House of Delegates, later attending the Virginia Convention which ratified the United States Constitution.

After moving to Lexington, Kentucky, Fowler became a member of the United States House of Representatives, serving during the 5th through the 9th congresses (1797–1807). He later served as postmaster of Lexington for eight years (1814–22). He died in Lexington and was buried in the Old Episcopal Cemetery.

FRY, Joshua: surveyor, educator
Born Crewkerne, England, circa 1700; son of Joseph Fry; married Mary (Micou) Hill, circa 1720; died May 31, 1754.

Soon after completing his education at Wadham College, Oxford University, England (1718), Fry came to Virginia. By 1731 he was professor of mathematics and natural philosophy at the College of William and Mary.

Fry was the first presiding justice of Albemarle County, justice of the Court Chancery, and county surveyor. He was a member of the House of Burgesses from Albemarle County until his death. After serving as county lieutenant in 1745, he became a mapmaker, drawing up a "Map of

the Inhabited Parts of Virginia" with Peter Jefferson. He and Jefferson also surveyed part of the Virginia-Carolina boundary in 1749. A commissioner to the Six Nations in 1752, Fry aided in drawing up the Treaty of Logstown.

As colonel and commander-in-chief of a regiment of the Virginia militia, Fry started for Ohio on an expedition against the French in 1754 but died en route at Fort Cumberland, Maryland. He was succeeded in his position by George Washington.

★★★★★

GARRARD, James: governor of Kentucky
Born Stafford County, Virginia, January 14, 1749; son of William Garrard; married Elizabeth Mountjoy, December 20, 1769; father of twelve children (including James); died January 19, 1822.

Garrard was a member of the Virginia House of Delegates in 1779, returning there in 1785. He received a commission as a colonel in the Stafford County Regiment of the Virginia militia in 1781. From 1784 to 1790 he represented Fayette and Bourbon counties in the conventions meeting to establish statehood for Kentucky. He also attended the first Kentucky Constitutional Convention and in 1787 helped organize Cooper's Run Church, near Mount Lebanon, Kentucky.

Garrard was governor of Kentucky from 1796 until 1804; during this period he used his influence to bring about the adoption of the Kentucky Resolutions of 1798. In 1803 he was expelled from the Baptist Church and the National Baptist Association for espousing Unitarian views. He died in Bourbon County.

GATES, Horatio: army officer
Born Maldon, Essex, England, circa 1728; son of Robert and Dorothy (Parker) Gates; married Elizabeth Phillips, October 20, 1754; second marriage to Mary Vallance, July 31, 1786; father of Robert (by first marriage); died April 10, 1806.

Gates, who had been a lieutenant in Nova Scotia during 1749–50, was commissioned a captain in the New York Independent Company of Foot in 1754. In subsequent service he was a captain with Braddock's army at Fort Duquesne in 1755 and served with General Nicholas Herkimer during the defense of Fort Herkimer against the French and the Indians in 1758 and with General Monckton in the expedition which took Martinique. In 1762 he received a commission as a major in the 45th Regiment. Later he became a lieutenant colonel in the Virginia militia.

In 1775 Gates was commissioned an adjutant general in the Continental Army with the rank of brigadier general; the next year he was promoted to major general. In late summer of 1777 he was placed in supreme command of the Northern Army, and it was he who was in charge of the Continental forces during the Saratoga campaign, which brought about the defeat of Burgoyne's army and which was a key factor in securing an alliance with France. He was implicated in the congressional conspiracy known as the Conway Cabal (a plot in which he was to replace George Washington as commander-in-chief).

Gates received a medal from Congress and became president of the Board of War, both in 1777. He took on the command of the Northern Department again in April 1778, moving to the Eastern Department in October 1778 and then to the Southern Department in 1780. Largely responsible for the American defeat at Camden in August 1780, he was relieved of his command later that year but rejoined the army two years later.

Gates became president of the New York Society of the Cincinnati in 1783 and served as a Whig in the New York legislature from 1800 to 1806, the year of his death.

GOODE, Samuel: congressman
Born at the estate "Whitby," Chesterfield County, Virginia, March 21, 1756; died November 14, 1822.

Goode, a lawyer, served as a lieutenant in the Chesterfield Troop of Horse and later as a colonel in the militia during the Revolutionary War. He was a member of the Virginia House of Delegates from 1778 to 1785 and served in the United States House of Representatives during the 6th Congress (1799–1801). He died in Invermay, Virginia, and was buried on his estate near there.

GOODWYN, Peterson: congressman
Born at the estate "Sweden," near Petersburg, Virginia, 1745; died February 21, 1818.

Goodwyn studied law, was admitted to the bar in 1776, and began the practice of law in Petersburg. In addition, he became engaged in planting.

During the Revolutionary War Goodwyn rose from captain to major, equipped his own company, and was promoted to colonel for the gallantry he displayed during the Battle of Smithfield. After serving in the Virginia House of Delegates from 1789 until 1802, Goodwyn was elected as a Democrat to several consecutive terms in the United States House of Representatives, from 1803 until 1818 (8th–15th congresses).

Goodwyn died at "Sweden" and was buried in the family burying ground there.

GRAY, Edwin: congressman
Born Southampton County, Virginia, July 18, 1743; no record of death.

Gray was educated at the College of William and Mary. In addition to serving for a number of years in the Virginia House of Burgesses (1769–75), he participated in the Virginia conventions in 1774, 1775, and 1786. He also was a member of the House of Delegates in 1776, 1779, 1787–88, and 1791. He went to the United States House of Representatives during the years 1799–1813 (6th–12th congresses).

GRAYSON, William: army officer, Continental congressman, senator
Born Prince William County, Virginia, 1736; son of Benjamin and Susanah (Monroe) Grayson; married Eleanor Smallwood; died March 12, 1790.

Grayson, who attended the College of Philadelphia (now the University of Pennsylvania), received a commission as a lieutenant colonel and was aide-de-camp to George Washington in 1776. The following year he was promoted to colonel and placed in command of a Virginia regiment. He took part in the battles of Long Island, White Plains, and Brandywine, and testified at the trial of Major General Charles Lee regarding the confusion prior to the Battle of Monmouth. In 1779 he retired from the army.

After a period as a member of the Board of War (1780–81), Grayson served in the Virginia House of Delegates in the years 1784–85 and 1788. He attended the Continental Congress from 1785 to 1787 and two years later became a United States Senator. In the Senate he was a strong supporter of Southern interests and was influential in securing the passage of the Ordinance of 1787. He died in Dumfries, Virginia.

GREENUP, Christopher: governor of Kentucky, congressman
Born Loudoun County, Virginia, circa 1750; married Mary Pope; died April 27, 1818.

Greenup served as a captain in the Revolutionary War. After his admission to the Virginia bar in 1783, he was a clerk at the Militia Convention in Danville, Kentucky, the following year. In 1785 he became a member of the Virginia legislature. He helped to secure statehood for Kentucky and attended conventions in Danville to consider separation from Virginia in 1785 and again in 1788. In 1787 he joined the Kentucky Society for Promoting Useful Knowledge and two years later helped organize the Kentucky Manufacturing Society.

Greenup was a delegate from Kentucky to the 2nd through the 4th congresses of the United States House of Representatives (1792–97). He was clerk of the Kentucky Senate from 1799 to 1802 and then governor of Kentucky from 1804 to 1808. In 1807 he became a director of the Bank of Kentucky. He also served as an original trustee of Transylvania University and was a member of the Danville Political Club. In 1812 he held the office of justice of the peace of Franklin County, Kentucky.

Greenup died in Blue Lick Springs, Kentucky, and was buried in the State Cemetery in Frankfort.

GRIFFIN, Cyrus: Continental congressman, jurist
Born Farnham Parish, Virginia, July 16, 1748; son of LeRoy and Mary Ann (Bertrand) Griffin; married Lady Christina Stuart, 1770; died December 14, 1810.

After studying law at Edinburgh University in Scotland, Griffin was admitted to Middle Temple in London, England; in 1774 he established a law practice in Virginia. In 1775 he addressed *Plan of Reconciliation between Great Britain and her Colonies* to the Earl of Dartmouth. In addition to serving in the Virginia legislature from Lancaster County in 1777 and 1778, he was a member of the Continental Congress in the years 1778–81, 1787–88, and 1788–89, presiding over the congress the latter two years.

From 1780 to 1787 Griffin was judge in the Court of Appeals in Cases of Capture (these cases helped to familiarize the public with the idea of some sort of superior federal judiciary). In 1789 he became a commissioner to attend the treaty between the Creek Indians and the state of Georgia. In the same year George Washington appointed him United States judge for the District of Virginia, a position he held until 1810; during this time (1807) he presided at Aaron Burr's trial. He died in Yorktown, Pennsylvania.

★★★★★

HADFIELD, George: architect
Born Leghorn, England, circa 1764; son of Charles and Isabella Hadfield; never married; died February 5, 1826.

Hadfield was educated at different schools of the Royal Academy of Art, by means of a traveling studentship. From 1795 to 1798 he was the superintendent of the construction of the Capitol building in Washington, D. C., but he was dismissed because of the controversy over his design and the actual superintendence of the work on the Capitol. He furnished the adopted design for the Treasury and Executive Offices, both of which were burned by the British in 1814.

In 1800 Hadfield patented the first machine for brickmaking in the United States. A councilman in Washington in 1803, he also designed the Washington Arsenal. Other buildings of his design include Commodore Porter's house, 1816–19; City Hall, 1820; Assembly Rooms, 1822; Branch Bank of the United States, 1824; and "Arlington," later the home of Robert E. Lee, and now preserved in the Arlington National Cemetery.

Hadfield died in Washington, D. C.

HALLET, Etienne Sulpice: architect

Born Paris, France, March 17, 1755; married Mary Gormain; father of three children; died February 1825.

Hallet came to America in 1786 as part of an attempt by Quesnay de Beaurepaire to found an Académie des Sciences et Beaux-Arts in Richmond, Virginia. In 1791 Hallet finished second to William Thorton of Philadelphia in a competition sponsored by Thomas Jefferson for the designing of the new Capitol building; Thorton's designs were later criticized, and Hallet was commissioned in 1793 to revise Thorton's plans and supervise the building. However, the following year he was dismissed in a controversy over the designs. He died in New Rochelle, New York.

HAMPTON, Wade: congressman, army officer, planter

Born Halifax County, Virginia, 1752; son of Anthony and Anne (Preston) Hampton; married Mrs. Martha Epps Howell, 1783; second marriage to Harriet Flud, 1786; third marriage to Mary Cantey, 1801; father of two children (including Wade); died February 4, 1835.

At the age of twenty-nine Hampton was commissioned a lieutenant colonel in the Continental Army and served with distinction under General Thomas Sumter in the Revolutionary War. From 1782 to 1792 he was a member of the Virginia legislature. Justice of the peace of Richmond County, he was a member of the Virginia Convention which ratified the United States Constitution in 1788. He was then sheriff of the Camden District. A Republican, he was a delegate from Virginia to the 4th Congress of the United States House of Representatives (1795–97); he also attended the 8th Congress (1803–05). In 1801 he was a presidential elector.

Commissioned a colonel in the United States Army in 1808, Hampton rose to brigadier general the following year and was in charge of the fortification of Norfolk, Virginia, in 1812–13. In 1813 he was commissioned a major general and placed in command of the army on Lake Champlain in Military District Nine. He was repulsed in the attack on Sir George Prevost at Chateaugay and in an expedition against Montreal in 1813.

Hampton was the owner of a cotton plantation in Richland County, South Carolina, and also of sugar plantations in Arkansas and Mississippi; he is reputed to have been the wealthiest planter in America at the time of his death. He died in Columbia, South Carolina, and was buried in Trinity Churchyard there.

HANCOCK, George: congressman

Born Chesterfield County, Virginia, June 13, 1754; died July 18, 1820.

Hancock served as a colonel of infantry in the Virginia Regiment of the Continental Army during the Revolutionary War. He was a member of the staff of Count Pulaski at the siege of Savannah, where he was taken captive and imprisoned for a time before gaining parole.

At the age of twenty Hancock was admitted to the Virginia bar and established a legal practice in Chesterfield County. He was appointed an ensign in Chesterfield County in 1776, then was promoted to captain. He then received an appointment as a colonel in the Botetourt County (Virginia) militia in 1785. He served as commonwealths attorney of Botetourt County from 1787 to 1789 and deputy state's attorney from 1789 to 1793. A Democrat, he was a Virginia delegate to the United States House of Representatives for the 3rd–4th congresses (1793–97).

Hancock died at the estate "Fotheringay," in Elliston Valley, Montgomery County, Virginia, and was buried in a tomb on the estate.

HARDY, Samuel: Continental congressman

Born Isle of Wight County, Virginia, 1758; son of Richard Hardy; died October 17, 1785.

Hardy graduated from the College of William and Mary at the age of twenty. He was admitted to the Virginia bar in 1781 and that same year was elected to the Virginia House of Delegates. In 1782 he was lieutenant governor of Virginia.

A delegate to the Continental Congress from 1783 to 1785, Hardy was effective in keeping the central government operating despite the weaknesses of the Articles of Confederation. He was a member of Phi Beta Kappa. He died in New York City and was buried at St. Paul's Church there.

HARRISON, Benjamin: governor of Virginia, Continental congressman

Born at the estate "Berkeley," Charles City County, Virginia, circa 1726; son of Benjamin and Anne (Carter) Harrison; married Elizabeth Bassett, circa 1745; father of Benjamin and William Henry; died April 24, 1791.

Harrison was educated at the College of William and Mary. He was a member of the Virginia House of Burgesses from 1749 to 1775, serving frequently as speaker. In 1764 he sat on the committee that drew up Virginia's protest to the Stamp Act, although he opposed Patrick Henry's resolutions. In 1775 he was a member of the Virginia Revolutionary Convention. From 1774 to 1778 he attended the Continental Congress as a delegate from Virginia; he was a member of the Board of War and Ordnance and also of the marine committee.

Harrison was a member of the Virginia House of Delegates from 1776 to 1782 and from 1784 to 1791, serving as speaker from 1778 to 1782 and in 1785–86. He was a signer of the Declaration of Independence in 1776 and the following year was a signer of the Articles of Confederation. He was governor of Virginia from 1782 to 1784 and a member of the Virginia Convention to ratify the United States Constitution, also in 1784. He died in Charles City, Virginia.

HARVIE, John: Continental congressman, mayor

Born Albemarle County, Virginia, 1742; son of John and Martha (Gaines) Harvie; married Margaret Jones; died February 6, 1807.

While engaged in the practice of law, Harvie was commissioned a colonel in the Virginia militia in 1776. He was a delegate to Virginia conventions in 1775 and 1776 and was a member of the committee to prepare a declaration of rights and a form of government. He received an appointment as commissioner for Indian affairs in 1776 and served in the Continental Congress from 1777 to 1779. He was a signer of the Articles of Confederation and a member of various committees for the provisioning of the army. He was the purchasing agent for Virginia and, in 1780, register for the Virginia Land Office. In 1785–86 he served as mayor of Richmond, Virginia. He died in that city.

HEATH, John: congressman

Born Wicomico Parish, Northumberland County, Virginia, May 8, 1758; died October 13, 1810.

Heath attended the College of William and Mary and was an organizer and first president of Phi Beta Kappa in 1776; this was the first Greek letter society established in an American college. After serving in the Revolutionary War, he was admitted to the Virginia bar and practiced law in Northumberland County. He was the commonwealth's attorney, 1781–84, 1787–93. He was a member of the Virginia Privy Council for several years and a member of the Virginia House of Delegates in 1782. A Republican, he served Virginia in the United States House of Representatives for the 3rd and 4th congresses (1793–97). He died in Richmond, Virginia.

HENRY, James: Continental congressman
Born Assomac County, Virginia, 1731; died December 9, 1804.

After studying law at the University of Edinburgh in Scotland, Henry was admitted to the bar and practiced law. He was a member of the Virginia House of Burgesses from 1772 to 1774 and of the Virginia House of Delegates in 1776, 1777, and 1779. In 1780–81 he represented Virginia in the Continental Congress. A judge in the Virginia Court of the Admiralty from 1782 to 1788, he served in the Virginia General Court from 1788 to 1800. He died at "Fleet Bay," in Northumberland County, Virginia.

HENRY, Patrick: governor of Virginia, Continental congressman
Born Hanover County, Virginia, May 29, 1736; son of John and Sarah (Winston) Henry; married Sarah Shelton, 1754; second marriage to Dorothea Dandridge, 1776; died June 6, 1799.

Henry was licensed to practice law at the age of twenty-four and was elected to the Virginia House of Burgesses six years later. Claiming independence for Virginia in his response to the Stamp Act of 1765, he gave one of his most famous speeches, which contained the declaration "If this be treason, make the most of it." With Thomas Jefferson and Richard Henry Lee, he organized the Committee of Correspondence in 1773.

Representing Virginia, Henry was a member of the First Continental Congress, 1774–75; at this congress he offered a resolution recommending that "this Colony be immediately put into a position of defense." This resolution also contained the famous phrase "Give me liberty or give me death." He took a seat in the Second Continental Congress on May 18, 1775, and participated in the legislation by which the Continental Army was organized. He resigned his commission as a colonel in the Virginia militia in 1776. That year he was elected to the Third Virginia Revolutionary Convention and took a decisive part in drafting the new Virginia Constitution. He also took part in urging the passage of the resolutions authorizing Congress to declare independence and to appeal to France for aid.

Henry was governor of Virginia for two terms, 1776–79 and 1784–86. He sent George Rogers Clark to expel the British from the Northwest Territory. In 1788 he was a delegate to the Virginia Convention to ratify the United States Constitution, where he opposed ratification. He was largely responsible for the addition of the Bill of Rights to the Constitution. A Federalist, he was elected to the Virginia House of Delegates in 1799 but died before taking office. He was buried on Red Hill Plantation on the Staunton River, in Virginia.

HOGE, Moses: clergyman, college president
Born Cedargrove, Virginia, February 15, 1752; son of James and Nancy (Griffiths) Hoge; married Elizabeth Poage, August 23, 1783; second marriage to Mrs. Susan (Watkins) Hunt, October 25, 1803; father of James and Samuel Davies; died July 5, 1820.

Hoge received his theological instruction from the Reverend James Waddel, "the blind preacher" immortalized by William Wirt, and later was awarded an honorary S. T. D. from the College of New Jersey (now Princeton). After fighting in the Revolutionary War, he was ordained to the ministry in the Presbyterian Church in Augusta, Virginia (now West Virginia), in 1782.

From 1791 to 1807 Hoge was a trustee of Washington College, and from 1807 to 1820 he was president of Hampden-Sydney College. He was the author of *Strictures on a Pamphlet by the Reverend Jeremiah Walker, entitled Fourfold Foundations of Calvinism Examined and Shaken,* 1793; *Christian Panoply: An Answer to Paine's Age of Reason,* 1799. He died in Philadelphia.

HOPKINS, Samuel: congressman, army
officer
Born Albemarle County, Virginia, April 9, 1753; son of Dr. Samuel and Isabella (Taylor) Hopkins; married Elizabeth Branch Bugg, January 18, 1783; died September 16, 1819.

During the American Revolution, Hopkins fought under George Washington at the battles of Trenton, Princeton, Monmouth, Brandywine, and Germantown. He served as a lieutenant colonel in the 10th Virginia Regiment at the siege of Charleston. He was an original member of the Society of the Cincinnati.

In 1796 Hopkins moved to Kentucky and from 1799 to 1801 was chief justice of the First Court of Criminal Common Law and Chancery Jurisdiction in Kentucky. He served several terms in the Kentucky House of Representatives—1800, 1801, 1803–06—and sat in the Kentucky Senate from 1809 to 1813. He was commissioned a major general in the United States Army in 1812, and rose to commander-in-chief of the western frontier later that year. He led two thousand volunteers against the Kickapoo Indian villages on the Illinois River in 1812.

From 1813 to 1815 Hopkins was a member of the United States House of Representatives as a delegate from Kentucky. He died in Henderson, Kentucky, and was buried in the family burial plot at "Spring Garden," near Henderson.

HORROCKS, James: clergyman, college
president
Born England, circa 1734; son of James Horrocks; died March 10, 1772.

Horrocks was granted a B.A. from Trinity College, Cambridge University, England, in 1755 and received an M.A. in 1758. Licensed to preach by the Church of England in 1761, he was sent to Virginia by the Bishop of London as master of the grammar school connected with the College of William and Mary; he held this position from 1762 to 1764. From 1764 to 1771 he was president of the College of William and Mary. By 1771 he was rector of Bruton Parish, the commissary of the Bishop of London, and a member of the Council of Virginia. He died in Oporta, Portugal.

HUNGERFORD, John Pratt: congressman
Born Leeds, Virginia, January 2, 1761; died December 21, 1833.

After completing his study of law, Hungerford was admitted to the bar and established a legal practice. He fought in the Revolutionary War. From 1797 to 1801, and again from 1823 to 1830, he was a member of the Virginia House of Delegates. He served in the Virginia Senate from 1801 to 1809.

Hungerford was a delegate from Virginia to the United States House of Representatives for the 13th–14th congresses (1813–17). He served as a brigadier general in the Virginia militia during the War of 1812. He died at the estate "Twilford," in Westmoreland County, Virginia, and was buried in Hungerford Cemetery in Leedstown, Virginia.

★★★★★

INNES, Harry: judge
Born Caroline County, Virginia, January 15, 1753; son of Robert and Catherine (Richards) Innes; married Elizabeth Calloway; second marriage to Mrs. Ann Shields; died September 20, 1816.

Innes was admitted to the Virginia bar in 1772; seven years later he was elected by the Virginia legislature to determine claims to unpatented lands in the district around Abingdon, Kentucky. That same year he was escheator of Bedford County, Kentucky. In 1782 he received an appointment as superintendent of the tax commissioners of six counties by Governor Benjamin Harrison.

Innes was elected by the Virginia legislature as attorney general for the Western District of Virginia in 1784, then served as United States district judge for Kentucky for twenty-seven years (1789–1816). He was also a trustee of Transylvania University. He died in Frankfort, Kentucky.

INNES, James: lawyer
Born Caroline County, Virginia, 1754; son of Robert and Catherine (Richards) Innes; married Elizabeth Cooke; father of Ann; died August 2, 1798.

After attending the College of William and Mary, Innes was commissioned a lieutenant colonel in the 15th Virginia Regiment. He was an aide to George Washington and in 1778 served as navy commissioner. Chairman of the Board of War for Virginia in 1779, he later held membership in the Virginia Assembly from James County and Williamsburg (1780–82). He was elected judge advocate of the Continental Army by Congress in 1782 and served as attorney general of Virginia in 1786.

Innes was well known as an orator and was selected to deliver the final speech for the adoption of the United States Constitution at the Virginia Constitutional Convention of 1788. He died in Philadelphia and was buried in Christ Church Burial Ground there.

★★★★★

JACKSON, George: congressman
Born Cecil County, Maryland, January 9, 1757; father of at least two sons (John George and Edward Brake); died May 17, 1831.

During the American Revolution, Jackson served in the army and rose to the rank of colonel. In 1787 he was admitted to the Virginia bar and established a legal practice in Clarksburg, Virginia (now West Virginia). He became a justice of the peace in 1784 and

the following year was elected to the Virginia House of Delegates, serving for the next seven years and again in 1794. In 1788 he participated in the Virginia Convention which ratified the federal constitution.

From 1799 to 1803 Jackson represented Virginia in the United States House of Representatives. About 1806 he moved to Zanesville, Ohio, and engaged in farming. He served in the Ohio House of Representatives (1809–12) and the Ohio Senate (1817–19). He died in Zanesville and was buried in Falls Township, near there.

JARRATT, Devereaux: clergyman
Born New Kent County, Virginia, January 17, 1733; son of Robert and Sarah (Bradley) Jarratt; married Martha Claiborne; died January 29, 1801.

Jarratt studied under Alexander Martin circa 1761 and became a tutor in the house of John Cannon. He sailed for England in 1762, and the following year was ordained a priest in the Presbyterian Church by the Bishop of Chester. He then returned to Virginia to become rector of Bath Parish in Dinwiddie County.

Jarratt proceeded to carry on reform work in other Virginia counties and in North Carolina. He assisted the Methodist preacher Robert Williams in 1773 and took a keen interest in and regularly attended Methodist conferences, despite his close association with the Episcopal (Presbyterian) Church.

Jarratt was the author of *A Brief Narrative of the Revival of Religion in Virginia in a Letter to a Friend* (1773), which he sent to John Wesley; *Thoughts on Some Capital Subjects in Divinity in a Series of Letters to a Friend* (1791); and *An Argument between an Anabaptist and a Methodist on the Subject and Mode of Baptism* (reprinted in 1814).

JEFFERSON, Martha Wayles
Born Charles City County, Virginia, October 19, 1748; daughter of John Wayles; married Bathurst Skelton; second marriage to Thomas Jefferson, 1772; died September 6, 1782.

Martha Wayles Jefferson inherited a large amount of property from her father as well as the estate of her first husband (in 1767). She was known as one of the most beautiful women in Virginia. Much of the time she suffered from ill health owing to the strain of managing her plantation, and Jefferson, her second husband, often turned down important positions in order to be near her. She died before he became President.

JEFFERSON, Thomas: third President of the United States

Born at the estate "Old Shadwell," Goochland (now Albemarle) County, Virginia, April 13, 1743; son of Peter and Jane (Randolph) Jefferson; married Martha Wayles Skelton, January 1, 1772; father of six children (of whom only Martha and Marie attained maturity); died July 4, 1826.

After attending the College of William and Mary from 1760 to 1762, Jefferson studied law under George Wythe. He became county lieutenant of Albemarle County in 1770 and county surveyor in 1773. In 1776 he gained admission to the bar.

Jefferson was a delegate to the House of Burgesses from 1769 to 1775 and was a member of the committee that created the Virginia Committee of Correspondence. He also introduced, with others, a resolution for a day of fasting in Virginia as a protest against the Boston Port Bill; the resolution resulted in the dissolution of the House of Burgesses. In 1774 he wrote *A Summary View of the Rights of British America,* but the Virginia house failed to adopt it. During 1775 and 1776 he was a member of the Continental Congress, where he served on the committee of five which was to draft the Declaration of Independence. He personally wrote the Declaration and was one of its signers. It underwent only minor changes by John Adams and Benjamin Franklin and by Congress.

After a term in the Virginia House of Delegates (1776–79), Jefferson became governor of Virginia, holding that office from 1779 to 1781. During his tenure he struck a blow at vested privilege by initiating the abolition of primogeniture (which was finally achieved in 1785) and of entail. He originated a bill to establish freedom of speech and religion, which was passed in 1786. He also urged the establishment of a public school system and a library system. A resolution calling for an inquiry into his military conduct as governor was found groundless by the House of Delegates, and a resolution of thanks was adopted instead.

Jefferson went into semi-retirement and finished his scientific work *Notes on the State of Virginia,* which was privately printed in 1785. After the death of his wife, he returned to the Continental Congress in 1783, drafting a committee report urging the adoption of the dollar as the unit of a monetary system based on decimal notation. In 1784 he drafted a resolution known as the Ordinance of 1784 which provided for a temporary government for the western territory. He also was named commissioner to help carry out his formula for negotiating treaties of commerce based on universal reciprocity. In 1785 he succeeded Benjamin Franklin as minister to France and served in that capacity until 1789.

Jefferson was the first secretary of state under the new constitution, serving from 1790 to 1793. During that period he was the chief architect of the policy of neutrality and became the leader of the Anti-Federalist (Republican) forces. In 1793 he retired to his home, Monticello. Three years later, however, he came out of retirement to become vice president of the United States, serving until 1801. During this time he wrote the Kentucky Resolutions (1798) in answer to the Alien and Sedition Acts, which had grown out of the trouble between America and France at the time.

In 1801 Jefferson was elected the third President of the United States. His first administration was marked by the Louisiana Purchase of 1803, which he commissioned

Lewis and Clark to explore. His second administration was beset by troubles stemming from wars between England and France on the European Continent. He maintained neutrality, largely through economic measures such as the Non-Importation Act (1806) and the Embargo Act (1807); however, economic distress forced him to partially ease the embargo by means of the Non-Intercourse Act in 1809. At the end of his second term he retired to Monticello for the remainder of his life.

An architect of renown, Jefferson had a hand in the planning of the city of Washington, D.C., and designed and built his home, Monticello. He was a principal founder of the University of Virginia, a member of that university's first board of visitors, and a rector (1819–26). In addition he conceived the university's distinctive architecture and educational perspective and personally compiled several thousand titles in all academic fields as a basis for its library. He was president of the American Philosophical Society from 1797 to 1815. He maintained many scientific interests which led him into studies and writings on paleontology, ethnology, geography, and botany. He also wrote *Manual of Parliamentary Practice* (1801), which was used thereafter in the United States Senate.

Jefferson is regarded as the first great shaper of an American democracy based on individual liberties and capabilities and on checks on federal power. He died on the fiftieth anniversary of the Declaration of Independence and was buried at Monticello.

JOHNSTON, Peter: army officer, jurist
Born Osborne's Landing, Virginia, January 6, 1763; son of Peter and Martha (Butler) Rogers Johnston; married Mary Wood, June 23, 1788; second marriage to Ann Bernard, December 13, 1828; father of ten children (including Joseph Eggleston); died December 8, 1831.

In 1781 Johnston received a commission as a lieutenant in a cavalry division of the Continental Army under the command of Lieutenant Colonel Henry Lee. He rose to adjutant and captain in a light corps and later to brigadier general in the militia.

In 1792 Johnston became a member of the Virginia legislature and in 1802 represented his state on the commission settling the boundary dispute with Tennessee. He served as speaker of the Virginia House of Delegates in the years 1805–06 and 1806–07. In 1811 he became a judge of the Virginia General Court.

JOHNSTON, Zachariah: legislator
Born near Staunton, Virginia, 1742; son of William Johnston; married Ann Robertson; died January 1800.

Johnston was commissioned a captain in the Virginia militia in 1776, serving in the campaign against the Indians in the west and in the defeat of Cornwallis in 1781. In 1778 he began a twenty-year tenure in the Virginia House of Delegates, representing Augusta County for fourteen years and Rockbridge County for six. During his time in the legislature he led in securing passage of the act establishing religious freedom in Virginia (1786) and participated in the Virginia Convention which adopted the federal constitution in 1788. He also worked on a scheme to connect the rivers of western Virginia with the Potomac navigation plan proposed by George Washington.

JONES, Gabriel: lawyer
Born Williamsburg, Virginia, May 17, 1724; son of John and Elizabeth Jones; married Margaret Morton, 1749; father of four children; died October 6, 1806.

After a law apprenticeship in London, Jones returned to America circa 1745 and settled in Virginia. He became King's attorney for Frederick and Augusta counties and held this office until 1775. He was a friend and mentor of George Washington during the 1750s and the 1760s, aiding Washington in his election to the Virginia House of Burgesses in 1758. Between 1774 and 1776 he had Loyalist sympathies, but he became an adherent of the American cause during the Revolution.

Jones served as prosecutor of Rockingham County, Virginia, from 1775 to circa 1780. The Virginia Assembly sent him as a commissioner to Fort Pitt on a diplomatic mission in 1777. He became a member of the Virginia House of Burgesses in 1783 and participated in the Virginia Conference which ratified the United States Constitution in 1788. An ardent Federalist, he favored the Constitution.

In 1804 Jones wrote a political pamphlet titled *A Refutation of the Charges . . .* He died in Frederick County, Virginia, two years later.

JONES, Joseph: Continental congressman
Born King George County, Virginia, 1727; son of James and Hester Jones; married Mary Taliaferro, before 1758; died October 28, 1805.

Jones was admitted to Inner Temple in 1749 and to Middle Temple in 1751; the latter year he was also called to the English bar. Three years later he became deputy attorney for the King of England.

In 1772 Jones served in the Virginia House of Burgesses. In 1774 he served as chairman of the King George County Committee of Correspondence; he was appointed to the Virginia Committee of Safety the following year and attended all Virginia revolutionary conventions. He was a member of the state House of Delegates in 1776, 1777, 1780, 1781, and 1783–85, serving on the committee which framed the Virginia Declaration of Rights and the Virginia Constitution in 1776. He was a delegate to the Continental Congress during the years 1777–78 and 1780–83 and participated in the convention that ratified the federal constitution in 1788.

Jones held the position of judge of the Virginia General Court from 1778 to 1783 and again from 1789 to 1805. He also served as a major general in the state militia. He died in Fredericksburg, Virginia.

JONES, Walter: physician, congressman
Born Williamsburg, Virginia, December 18, 1745; died December 31, 1815.

Jones, a 1760 graduate of the College of William and Mary, obtained an M.D. from the University of Edinburgh in 1770 and then began a practice of medicine in Northumberland County, Virginia. In 1777 he became physician general in the Middle Military Department.

Jones was elected to the Virginia House of Delegates for terms in 1785–87 and again in 1802–03 and attended the state constitutional convention in 1788. A Democrat, he was a delegate to the United States House of Representatives during the 5th Congress (1797–99) and the 8th through the 11th congresses (1803–11).

Jones died in Westmoreland County, Virginia, and was buried in the family burial ground on the estate "Hayfield," near Callo, Virginia.

JOUETT, John: state legislator
Born Albemarle County, Virginia, December 7, 1754; son of Captain John and Mourning (Harris) Jouett; married Sallie Robards, August 20, 1784; father of Matthew Harris; died March 1, 1822.

In 1779 Jouett signed an oath of allegiance to the Virginia Commonwealth. Serving around this time as a captain in the Virginia militia, he is remembered for his daring ride of more than forty miles to save Governor Jefferson and the Virginia legislature from capture. He represented Lincoln County in the Virginia Assembly in 1786–87 and Mercer County in 1787–88 and again in 1790.

A leading member of the Danville Convention, Jouett was influential in organizing Kentucky as a separate state. He was a member of the Kentucky legislature from Mercer County for one term and from Woodford County for three terms.

★★★★★

LEAR, Tobias: diplomat
Born Portsmouth, New Hampshire, September 19, 1762; son of Captain Tobias and Mary (Stilson)

Lear; married Mary Long, April 18, 1790; second marriage to Frances Bassett, August 22, 1795; third marriage to Frances Henley; died October 11, 1816.

Lear, who graduated from Harvard in 1783, was private secretary to George Washington from 1785 to 1792. He was elected president of the Potomac Canal Company in 1795. Three years later he was appointed by Washington as his military secretary with the rank of colonel.

In 1802 Thomas Jefferson appointed Lear consul in Santo Domingo. Lear served as consul general at Algiers from 1804 to 1811, and he negotiated the treaty with Tripoli that ended the exactment of tribute from American merchant vessels. For the last five years of his life he was an accountant with the War Department. He died in Washington, D.C.

LEE, Arthur: Continental congressman, diplomatic agent

Born at the estate "Stratford," Westmoreland County, Virginia, December 20, 1740; son of Thomas and Hannah (Ludwell) Lee; never married; died December 12, 1792.

In 1764 Lee received an M.D. from the University of Edinburgh in Scotland. He studied law at Lincoln's Inn and at Middle Temple in London, England, from 1766 to 1770. In 1766 he was elected a fellow of the Royal Society.

Lee wrote *Monitor's Letters* and, in 1769, *An Appeal to the English Nation*. In 1770 his *Junus Americasis*, written in support of the American colonies, was published in England.

In England and France, Lee, in association with Benjamin Franklin, acted as an agent for Massachusetts. He was admitted to the London bar in 1775, and in that year also became a confidential correspondent in London for the Continental Congress. In 1776 Lee, along with Benjamin Franklin and Silas Deane, was given the task of negotiating a treaty with France.

Lee was a commissioner to Spain in 1777. He served in the Virginia House of Delegates from 1781 to 1783 and again in 1785–86. From 1781 to 1784 he was a member of the Continental Congress. He negotiated the Indian treaty of Fort Stanwix in 1784 and of Fort McIntosh in 1785. In 1785 he was appointed by the Continental Congress to the board of the treasury, on which he served until 1789.

Lee died in Urbana, Virginia, and was buried at "Lansdowne," near Urbana.

LEE, Charles: army officer

Born Dernhall, Cheshire, England, 1731; son of John and Isabella (Bunbury) Lee; died October 2, 1782.

At the age of sixteen, Lee was an ensign in his father's regiment. Four years later he became a lieutenant with the 44th Regiment. He participated in General Braddock's expedition to Fort Duquesne in 1755 and served under Amherst in the capture of Montreal in 1760. The next year he became major of the 103rd Regiment and in 1762 advanced to lieutenant colonel.

In 1762 Lee served under Burgoyne in Portugal, in resistance to a Spanish invasion. Two years later he accompanied a Polish embassy to Turkey, and in 1769 he served as general and adjutant in the Polish Army. In 1773 he returned to America.

Lee wrote *Strictures on a Friendly Address to All Reasonable Americans,* an incitement to colonial rebellion, in 1774. In 1775 he acquired land in Berkeley County, Virginia (now West Virginia). He was commissioned a second major general in the Continental Army in 1775 and was put in command of the Southern Department the next year. He played a principal part in the American victory at Charleston and fought rear-guard action in Washington's retreat from New York City.

Ambitious to become commander-in-chief, Lee became a severe critic of Washington, most notably in a letter to General Gates. Lee was captured by the British in 1776 and while a prisoner submitted a secret plan to General Howe for defeating the

Americans. Two years after his capture he was released in a prisoner exchange and put in command of a planned attack on Monmouth. He retreated instead of attacking and was halted by the arrival of Washington, Greene, Von Steuben, and forces. He was court-martialed and found guilty of disobedience, misbehavior before the enemy, and disrespect to the commander-in-chief, which resulted in his suspension from command.

Lee continued his abuse of Washington and in 1780 was dismissed from the army. He died in Philadelphia and was buried in Christ Church Graveyard.

LEE, Charles: attorney general
Born Fauquier County, Virginia, July 1758; son of Henry and Lucy (Grymes) Lee; married Ann Lee, February 11, 1789; second marriage to Margaret (Scott) Peyton; father of nine children; died June 24, 1815.

In 1775 Lee received an A.B. from the College of New Jersey (now Princeton). He served as a naval officer of the South Potomac from 1777 to 1789. From 1789 to 1793 he was collector of the Port of Alexandria, Virginia. In 1794 he was admitted to the Pennsylvania bar. From 1793 to 1795 he was a member of the Virginia General Assembly from Fairfax County. He then entered the federal government, serving as United States attorney general for six years.

After the Judiciary Act of 1801, Lee became a judge in the newly created circuit courts. He was a leading lawyer in the Supreme Court bar and successfully pleaded *Marbury vs. Madison* before John Marshall. He defended Aaron Burr in his treason trial in Richmond, also before Marshall. He was a member of the defense staff in the impeachment of Judge Chase.

Lee died in Fauquier County.

LEE, Francis Lightfoot: Continental congressman
Born at the estate "Stratford," Westmoreland, Virginia, October 14, 1734; son of Thomas and Hannah (Ludwell) Lee; married Rebecca Tayloe, spring 1769; died January 11, 1797.

Lee was a member of the Virginia House of Burgesses for eighteen years, representing Loudoun County from 1758 to 1768 and Richmond County from 1769 to 1776. During this period, in 1766, he was a signer of the Westmoreland Association against the Stamp Act. In 1773 he was a member of the committee forming the Virginia Committee of Correspondence.

In 1774 Lee signed the call for the Virginia Convention and was a member of the convention in 1775. From 1775 to 1779 he was a delegate to the Continental Congress, signing the Declaration of Independence in 1776. He was a framer of the Articles of Confederation in 1777 and a member of the Virginia Senate from 1779 to 1782.

Lee died at his estate, "Menokin," in Richmond County, Virginia.

LEE, Henry (Light-Horse Harry): governor of Virginia, congressman, military officer
Born Dumfries, Virginia, January 29, 1756; son of Henry and Lucy (Grymes) Lee; married Matilda Lee, 1782; second marriage to Anne Hill Carter, June 18, 1793; father of seven children (including Robert E. and Henry); died March 25, 1818.

In 1773 Lee graduated from the College of New Jersey (now Princeton). Three years later he became a captain in Theodorick Bland's regiment of the Virginia Cavalry. He was major in charge of Lee's Legion, a cavalry corps which surprised the British garrison at Paulus Hook in 1779. For this attack he was awarded the gold medal by the Continental Congress. In 1780 he was commissioned a lieutenant colonel in the Continental Army. He served at the Battle of Guilford Courthouse and in 1781 besieged Augusta, Georgia.

Lee was a member of the Virginia House of Delegates in 1785 and from 1789 to 1791. In 1788 he served as a member of the Virginia Convention which ratified the United States Constitution. He was governor of

Virginia from 1792 to 1795, and in 1794 he commanded forces sent to suppress the Whiskey Insurrection in Pennsylvania. He served in the United States House of Representatives from 1799 to 1801.

Lee pronounced George Washington's funeral oration in 1799. His fortunes started to decline around the turn of the century, and in 1808 he was imprisoned for debt. Four years later he was injured by a mob while in prison for attempting to help a friend defend the press of the newspaper *Federal Republican* in Baltimore. He spent several years in the West Indies recovering his health.

Lee was the author of *Memoirs of the War in the Southern Department of the United States,* two volumes, published in 1812. He died and was buried on Cumberland Island, Georgia, but was reinterred in 1913 at Lee Chapel of Washington and Lee University.

LEE, Jesse: clergyman

Born Prince George County, Virginia, March 12, 1758; son of Nathaniel and Elizabeth Lee; died September 12, 1816.

From 1783 to 1789 Lee was a Methodist circuit preacher in Virginia, Maryland, and North Carolina. Ordained an elder in the Methodist Church in 1790, he was a pioneer in founding the Methodist Church in New England. He was an opponent of the hierarchical authority in the Methodist Council and Episcopate. From 1797 to 1800 he was assistant to Bishop Asbury and from 1801 to 1815 served as presiding elder of the Southern District of the Methodist Church in Virginia. He was chaplain of the United States House of Representatives from 1809 to 1813 and of the United States Senate in 1814. He was a presiding elder in Annapolis, Maryland, in 1816.

Lee wrote *A Short History of Methodism* (1807), the first history of the Methodist denomination published in the United States. In 1810 his *A Short History of the Methodists in the U.S.A.* was published. He died in Hills-

borough, Maryland, and was buried in the Mount Olivet Cemetery in Baltimore.

LEE, Richard Henry: senator

Born at the estate "Stratford," Westmoreland County, Virginia, January 20, 1732; son of Thomas and Hannah (Ludwell) Lee; married Ann Aylett, December 3, 1757; second marriage to Mrs. Anne Pinckard, 1769; father of six children; died June 19, 1794.

In 1757 Lee entered public life as justice of the peace of Westmoreland County. He then served as a member of the Virginia House of Burgesses for seventeen years (1758–75), during which time (1765–66) he helped to secure separation of the offices of speaker of the house and treasurer.

Lee was quite active in the furtherance of the American cause in the decade before the Revolutionary War. In 1764 he served on a committee to draw up an address to the King, and in 1765 he was head of an association to prevent the sale of stamped paper. In 1766 he formed the Westmoreland Association to boycott British goods. He suggested intercolonial corresponding societies in 1768; these were first used by Massachusetts and Virginia in 1773.

Lee engaged in the tobacco shipping business from 1768 to 1773. He was a delegate from Virginia to the Continental Congress from 1775 to 1779, where he was instructed to propose a general colonial independence. This action resulted in the Declaration of Independence, which Lee signed in 1776.

Lee attended the Virginia House of Delegates in 1777, 1780, and 1785. From 1784 to 1787 he was a delegate to the Congress of Confederation, serving as its president in 1784. He served as a delegate to the Virginia Convention to ratify the United States Constitution and from 1789 to October 8, 1792, represented Virginia in the United States Senate.

Lee died in Chantilly, Virginia, and was buried in the family burial ground at the estate "Mount Pleasant," in Virginia.

LEE, William: diplomat

Born at the estate "Stratford," Westmoreland County, Virginia, August 31, 1739; son of Thomas and Hannah (Ludwell) Lee; married Hannah Ludwell, March 7, 1769; died June 27, 1795.

Lee was one of only two Americans ever to hold the office of sheriff of London, England; he served as sheriff in 1773 and became an alderman of the city in 1775. In 1777 he was appointed by a secret committee of Congress as commercial agent in Nantes, France, where he became involved in the Lee-Deane controversy.

Lee negotiated a treaty of commerce between the Netherlands and America which, though never ratified, later became the ostensible cause of war between England and the Netherlands. As commissioner to Berlin and Vienna in 1777, he failed in his attempts to persuade Germany and Austria to recognize America.

Lee died near Williamsburg, Virginia.

L'ENFANT, Pierre Charles: army engineer, city planner

Born Paris, France, August 2, 1754; son of Pierre and Marie (Leullier) L'Enfant; died June 14, 1825.

L'Enfant was brevetted a lieutenant in the French Colonial Forces and in 1776 was commissioned a first lieutenant of engineers. He come to America with Lafayette in 1777 and joined the Continental Army; a year later he was commissioned a captain of engineers. In 1783 he was made a major by a special resolution of Congress.

A surveyor and planner of the new federal city of Washington, D.C., L'Enfant was forced to resign in 1792 because of the expense called for by his plans. (More than one hundred years later, in 1901, the government began remodeling the city along the lines of his original design.) He was employed to lay out the "Capital scene of manufactures" for the Society for Useful Manufactures in 1792. Two years later he served as a temporary engineer at Fort Mifflin on Mud Island in the Delaware River. In 1812 he was an engineer at Fort Washington on the Potomac River.

L'Enfant was a member of the Society of the Cincinnati. He died in Prince George County, Virginia, and was buried in Arlington National Cemetery.

LEWIS, Andrew: army officer

Born Donegal, Ireland, 1720; son of John and Margaret (Lynn) Lewis; married Elizabeth Givens; father of six children; died September 26, 1781.

Lewis served as a major in the Ohio campaigns commanded by Washington in 1754–55. He led the Sandy Creek expedition in 1756. He was county lieutenant of Augusta County, Virginia, a justice of the peace, and a representative of the Botetourt County legislature.

Lewis aided in the Indian treaty of Fort Stanwix and in 1774 defeated the Indians at the Battle of Point Pleasant in Lord Dunmore's War. In 1775 he was a member of the Revolutionary colonial conventions of Virginia. The next year he was commissioned a brigadier general in the Continental Army in command of American forces stationed at Williamsburg, Virginia. He defeated the British under Lord Dunmore at Gwynn's Island in 1776 and resigned from the Continental Army the next year.

From 1776 until his death in 1781 Lewis was a member of the Virginia Executive Council. He died in Bedford County, Virginia.

LEWIS, Fielding: planter, colonial official

Born Gloucester County, Virginia, July 7, 1725; son of John and Frances (Fielding) Lewis; married Catherine Washington, October 18, 1746; second marriage to Betty Washington, May 7, 1750; father of fourteen children (three by first marriage, eleven by second); died circa January 1782.

Lewis, a wealthy Virginia planter, was a longtime friend (as well as a brother-in-law) of George Washington and was associated with Washington's Dismal Swamp Company. For ten years he was a member of the Virginia House of Burgesses from Spotsylvania. He served as a member of the Committee of Correspondence and of the Spotsylvania County Committee. From 1775 to 1781 he was chief commissioner of a government arms factory in Fredericksburg, Virginia; he also donated part of his wealth to the factory.

LITTLEPAGE, Lewis: diplomat
Born Hanover County, Virginia, December 19, 1762; son of James and Elizabeth (Lewis) Littlepage; never married; died July 19, 1802.

Littlepage attended William and Mary College in 1778–79, and in 1780–81 he was a protégé of John Jay, who was serving as United States minister to Spain at that time. For the next two years he served with the Spanish Army. Throughout the early 1780s he was a secret Italian envoy to the French Court. From 1786 to 1798 he was chamberlain to King Stanislaus of Poland and served as Polish ambassador to Russia.

In the latter years of the century Littlepage engaged in various secret intrigues involving several European countries. He returned to the United States in 1801 and died in Fredericksburg, Virginia, the next year.

LOGAN, Benjamin: army officer, legislator
Born Augusta County, Virginia, 1743; son of David and Jane Logan; married Ann Montgomery, 1773 or 1774; father of eight children (including William); died December 11, 1802.

In 1764 Logan served as a sergeant in General Henry Bouquet's expedition against the Shawnee Indians. Ten years later he was commissioned lieutenant of a company of the Virginia militia. He served in Lincoln County, Virginia, as a county lieutenant in 1781. He was a Lincoln County representative to the Virginia General Assembly in 1781–82 and from 1785 to 1787.

In 1792 Logan was a member of the Kentucky Constitutional Convention. He was a member of the Board of War in the west and brigadier general of the Kentucky militia in 1790. In 1793–94 he served as a delegate from Lincoln County to the Kentucky

House of Representatives; in 1795 he represented Shelby County. He died seven years later and was buried in Shelbyville, Kentucky.

LYNCH, Charles: legislator
Born Chestnut Hill, Virginia, 1736; son of Charles and Sarah (Clark) Lynch; married Anna Yerrell, January 12, 1755; died October 29, 1796.

Lynch was justice of the peace of Bedford County, Virginia, in 1766. He was a member of the Virginia House of Burgesses from 1769 to 1776 and also a delegate to the Virginia Constitutional Convention the latter year. From 1776 to 1789 he helped mobilize Virginia for the Revolutionary War. During the war he presided over extralegal courts established in Bedford County, during which time he sentenced to death two members of a Loyalist conspiracy discovered in 1780. He was later exonerated for his part in the incident, but the terms "lynch law" and "lynching" have survived to this day to describe such vigilante acts.

From 1784 to 1789 Lynch served in the Virginia Senate. He died in Virginia.

LYONS, Peter: jurist
Born Cork County, Ireland, circa 1734; son of John and Catherine (Power) Lyons; married Mary Power; second marriage to Judith Bassett; died July 30, 1809.

Lyons read law with James Power and in 1756 was admitted to the Virginia bar. He was the plaintiff's attorney in the famous Parsons' Case in 1758. Twenty-one years later he served as judge of the General Court and of the Virginia Court of Appeals. He was president of the Virginia Court of Appeals from 1803 to 1807. He died in Hanover County, Virginia.

★★★★★

McCLURG, James: physician, army officer
Born Hampton, Virginia, circa 1746; son of Dr. Walter McClurg; married Elizabeth Selden, May 22, 1779; died July 9, 1823.

McClurg graduated from the College of William and Mary in 1762 and was awarded an M.D. by the University of Edinburgh in 1770. He published *Experiments upon the Human Bile and Reflections upon the Biliary Secretions* in 1772. He served as a surgeon in the Virginia militia and as physician general and director of hospitals in Virginia.

McClurg became a professor of anatomy and medicine at the College of William and Mary in 1779, serving there until 1783. He was a delegate to the United States Constitutional Convention in Philadelphia in 1787 and a member of the Virginia Executive Council in 1790. He served as president of the Virginia Medical Society in 1820 and 1821. He died in Richmond, Virginia.

McKENDREE, William: clergyman
Born William City, Virginia, July 6, 1757; son of John and Mary McKendree; died March 5, 1835.

McKendree, who served as an adjutant during the Revolution, converted to Methodism in 1787 and became a preacher the following year. Ordained a deacon in 1790, he was made an elder in 1791 and attended the General Conference of the Methodist Church in Baltimore the following year.

Presiding elder of the Richmond (Virginia) District from 1796 to 1799, McKendree was put in charge of missionary work in western Virginia, Ohio, and Kentucky, and in sections of Illinois, Tennessee, and Mississippi. In 1808 he was elected bishop at the General Conference, thus making him the first American-born bishop of the Methodist Episcopal Church. He inaugurated the practice of consultation with presiding elders in the making of appointments and gave 480 acres of land to the Lebanon (Illinois) Seminary.

McKendree died in Gallatin, Tennessee, and was buried in Sumner County, Tennessee. His remains were later reinterred on the campus of Vanderbilt University at Nashville.

MADISON, James: clergyman, college president
Born Staunton, Virginia, August 27, 1749; son of John and Agatha (Strother) Madison; married Sarah Tate, 1779; father of two children; died March 6, 1812.

A member of the Virginia bar, Madison was a professor of natural philosophy and mathematics at the College of William and Mary, Williamsburg, Virginia, from 1773 to 1789, also serving as a professor of natural and moral philosophy in 1784. He was president of the college from 1777 until his death. He was a captain in a militia company in 1777.

In 1776 Madison was ordained to the ministry of the Church of England (Protestant Episcopal Church) and played a prominent role in the formation of the Diocese of Virginia. He was president of the first convention of the church in 1785 and was elected the first bishop of the Protestant Episcopal Church in Virginia in 1790.

Madison was a member of a commission to define boundaries between Virginia and Pennsylvania in 1779. He was the author of "A Map of Virginia Formed from Actual Surveys." He was buried at the chapel of the College of William and Mary.

MADISON, James: fourth President of the United States
Born Port Conway, Virginia, March 16, 1751; son of James and Eleanor (Conway) Madison; married Dolly Payne Todd, September 15, 1794; no children; died June 28, 1836.

During his undergraduate days at the College of New Jersey (now Princeton), Madison was a founder of the American Whig Society (a debating club). He earned an A.B. from the school in 1771. He was then admitted to the Virginia bar and became a member of the Committee of Safety of Orange County, Virginia, in 1774. He served as a delegate to the Williamsburg Convention in 1776 and was a member of the committee which framed the constitution and declaration of rights for Virginia. He was a member of the First General Assembly of Virginia in 1776 and of the Virginia Executive Council in 1778.

A Virginia delegate to the Continental Congress from 1780 to 1783 and from 1786 to 1788, Madison kept notes on congressional debates in 1782–83 which have been useful as a supplement to the official journal. He advocated the raising of federal revenue by levying duties on imports for a period of twenty-five years; wrote instructions to John Jay, minister to Spain, concerning American rights to navigation of the Mississippi in 1780; and proposed the "3/5 Compromise" to Congress to break the deadlock on changing the basis of state contributions from land values to population by counting five slaves as three free people.

Madison returned to Virginia in 1783, where he began the study of law and natural history of the United States. He completed the disestablishment of the Anglican Church in Virginia (begun by Thomas Jefferson) in 1779 and served as a member of the Virginia House of Delegates from Orange County from 1783 to 1786. He favored the admission of Kentucky to statehood, inaugurated a series of surveys for improving transmountain communications, urged that Congress be granted the power to regulate commerce, and was a leader in effecting a series of interstate conferences.

Madison was a delegate from Virginia to the Annapolis Convention of 1786 and published *Vices of the Political System of the United States*. He made a number of proposals which were incorporated in the Virginia (or Randolph) Plan, including provisions for representation according to population, uniform national laws, a federal veto on state legislation, extension of national authority to a judiciary department, a two-house federal legislature with differing terms of office for each house, a national executive, an article guaranteeing the defense of the states by the federal government, and ratification of amendments to the Constitution by the people as well as by the legislature. De-

scribed as "the masterbuilder of the Constitution," he was a Virginia delegate to and chief recorder for the United States Constitutional Convention in 1787. He kept records which were published in the *Journal of the Federal Constitution* in 1840 and was associated with Alexander Hamilton and John Jay in writing the essays known as the *Federalist* papers (published under the signature "Publius" in 1788), which described the constitutional system of checks and balances and emphasized protection of private property. He was largely responsible for the ratification of the Constitution by Virginia in 1788.

A member of the United States House of Representatives from Virginia during the 1st-4th congresses (1789–97), Madison participated in passage of revenue legislation, creation of executive departments, and the framing of the Bill of Rights. He was a leader of the Democratic-Republican party, which opposed a pro-British policy and the creation of United States banks.

From August 24 through September 18, 1793, Madison published a series of letters under the name "Helvidius" in the *Gazette of the United States* which criticized George Washington's neutrality proclamations. He declined a mission to France and the post of secretary of state in 1794. He wrote the Virginia Resolutions against the Alien and Sedition Acts, expressing the opinion that states could declare acts of Congress unconstitutional.

Madison was Jefferson's secretary of state from 1801 to 1809. During those years he was faced with the problems of the Anglo-French war and sought peace with both countries. He protested the impressment of American sailors by England and supported Jefferson's Embargo Act of December 22, 1807 (the act was repealed March 1, 1809).

In 1808 Madison was elected the fourth President of the United States, defeating Charles Cotesworth Pinckney, and was inaugurated March 4, 1809; he was reelected in 1812.

Authorized by Congress to revive non-intercourse with either England or France, Madison was tricked by Napoleon Bonaparte and proclaimed non-intercourse against Great Britain on November 2, 1810. He feuded with his secretary of state, Robert Smith, in April 1811, dismissed him, and appointed James Monroe in his place. He declared war on Great Britain on June 18, 1812, because of that country's continuing impressment of American seamen, interference in American trade, and incitement of the Indians on American borders. He was forced to flee the White House when the British attacked and burned much of Washington, D.C., in 1812. He accepted an offer of mediation by the Russian Czar in 1813, but England rejected the offer. In 1814 he instructed American peace commissioners at Ghent to seek only the surrender to the United States of the territory occupied by the British; the Treaty of Ghent was signed December 24, 1814.

In 1816 Madison signed a bill providing for the Second Bank of the United States and a tariff act. That year he also enrolled in the Society for the Encouragement of American Manufacturers. He left office March 3, 1817, and became rector of the University of Virginia, succeeding Jefferson, in 1826. He was a delegate to the Virginia Constitutional Convention in 1829, after which he retired to his home, Montpellier, in Orange County. He was buried there.

MARSHALL, Humphrey: senator
Born Orlean, Virginia, 1760; son of John and Mary (Quisenberry) Marshall; married Anna Maria Marshall, September 18, 1784; father of three children (including Thomas Alexander and John Jay); died July 1, 1841.

Marshall served in the American Revolution from 1778 to 1781, advancing to the rank of captain-lieutenant of the Virginia Artillery. He moved to Kentucky in 1782

and became deputy surveyor for Fayette County; he also received a gift of 4,000 acres of land from Virginia during 1782 in recognition of his services during the war.

Marshall was a delegate to the Danville Convention to consider the separation of Kentucky from Virginia in 1787 and served as a member of the Virginia Convention (from Kentucky) to ratify the United States Constitution in 1788. He later moved to Woodford County, Kentucky, where he became county surveyor and served as a member of the Kentucky House of Representatives in 1793, 1794, 1807, 1808, 1809, and 1823.

Marshall served as a Kentucky delegate to the United States Senate from 1795 to 1801, during which time he voted for the Jay Treaty, an action which made him extremely unpopular with the people of Kentucky. Instrumental in exposing the conspiracy of Aaron Burr in 1806, he wrote articles in the paper *Western World,* under the name "Observer," to expose the conspirators and their plot with Spain. He was wounded in a duel with Henry Clay in 1809.

Marshall established the *American Republic* (the only Federalist newspaper in Kentucky) in 1810, later changing the name to *Harbinger* and publishing it until 1825. He was the author of *The History of Kentucky* (the first history of the state), published in one volume in 1812 and revised and republished in two volumes in 1824. He died in Lexington, Kentucky, and was buried at "Glen Willis," Leestown, Kentucky.

MARSHALL, James Markham: landowner
Born Fauquier County, Virginia, March 12, 1764; son of Thomas and Mary (Keith) Marshall; married Hester Morris, April 1795; father of six children; died April 26, 1848.

Marshall served with the 1st Virginia Artillery, Virginia militia, from 1779 to 1782 and moved to Kentucky in 1788, where he became active in Federalist politics and worked for statehood. He returned to Virginia about 1793 and soon afterward purchased (with his brother, John, and Raleigh Colston and Henry Lee) Fairfax lands in Virginia which amounted to approximately 180,000 acres. Marshall served as assistant judge of the District of Columbia in 1801–02, practiced law in Winchester, Virginia, after 1802, and was engaged in the management of land. He died in Winchester at the age of eighty-four.

MARSHALL, John: chief justice of the United States Supreme Court

Born Germantown, Virginia, September 24, 1755; son of Thomas and Mary (Keith) Marshall; married Mary Willis Ambler, January 3, 1783; father of ten children (including Thomas); died July 6, 1835.

Marshall was influenced by the writings of Alexander Pope, Adam Smith, and Edmund Burke in his early years. He served in the Revolution from 1775 to 1781, meanwhile, in May and June of 1780, attending the College of William and Mary. A lieutenant and then a captain in the 3rd Virginia Regiment (which later became part of the 11th Virginia Regiment) in 1777, he fought in the battles of Brandywine, Germantown, and Monmouth, and at Valley Forge.

Marshall was admitted to the bar of Fauquier County, Virginia, in 1780. A delegate to the Virginia House of Burgesses in 1780 and from 1782 to 1788, he was also a member of the Virginia Executive Council from 1782 to 1795. Marshall's father presented him with his Fauquier County estate.

Marshall served as city recorder of Richmond, Virginia, in 1783–85 and was a delegate to the Virginia Convention to ratify the United States Constitution in 1788. He was commissioned to purchase the Fairfax estate in 1793–94.

Marshall declined the post of attorney general of the United States in 1795, defended the Jay Treaty in 1795–96, and argued his only case before the Supreme Court *(Ware vs. Hylton)* in 1796. Declining the post of minister to France in 1796, he later served on the famous XYZ commission to France to demand redress and reparation for hostile actions in 1797–98; the mission failed when French agents asked for bribes.

Declining a seat on the Supreme Court in 1798, Marshall, a Federalist, served as a Virginia delegate to the United States House of Representatives from 1799 to June 7, 1800. He successfully defended John Adams on the charge of usurping judicial powers. He declined the post of secretary of war in 1800 but accepted an appointment as secretary of state later in the year.

Marshall was named chief justice of the Supreme Court in 1801 and served until his death. While on the bench he initiated a reform of the court system in the case of *Talbot vs. Seeman* (1801), in which the "unanimous court" procedure (having the chief justice speak on behalf of the entire court) was first used. He declared the "doctrine of judicial review" in the case *Marbury vs. Madison.* In 1807 he presided at the Aaron Burr trial and saved Burr from hanging. He ruled that the obligation of contract held even when it involved a dishonest act *(Fletcher vs. Peck,* 1810). He asserted the power of the Supreme Court over state courts whenever federal rights were involved *(Martin vs. Hunter's Lessee,* 1816, *Cohens vs. Virginia,* 1821). He maintained a charter of incorporation as a contract within the meaning of the Constitution *(Dartmouth College vs. Woodward,* 1819). In other decisions he ruled that the state of Maryland could not tax the Baltimore branch of the Bank of the United States and asserted the supremacy of the federal government over the states *(McCulloch vs. Maryland,* 1819). He issued 519 decisions out of 1,215 cases.

Marshall served as a member of the Virginia Constitutional Convention in 1829. The author of *The Life of George Washington,* in five volumes, 1804–07, he also prepared an autobiography for Delaplaine's Repository in 1818. He died in Philadelphia and was buried in the New Burying Ground, Richmond, Virginia.

MARSHALL, Thomas: surveyor;
Born Westmoreland County, Virginia, April 2, 1730; son of John and Elizabeth (Markham) Marshall; married Mary Keith, 1754; father of fifteen children (including Chief Justice John, James Markham, and Louis); died June 22, 1802.

Marshall began farming in Prince William County, Virginia, in 1754 and later became a land surveyor. A friend of George Washington, he helped survey Fairfax lands in Virginia. He served as a justice of the peace and a county surveyor in Fauquier County, Virginia, from 1759 to 1761 and lived at "Oak Hill" plantation in Fauquier County from 1773 to 1783.

A member of the Virginia House of Burgesses from 1761 to 1767, from 1769 to 1773, and in 1775, Marshall was sheriff of Fauquier County from 1767 to 1769. He served as a major in the 3rd Virginia Regiment in 1776 and as colonel in a regiment of the Virginia Artillery in the battles of Brandywine Creek and Trenton (1777–81).

Marshall served as a surveyor of Kentucky lands for the state of Virginia from 1781 to 1783 and moved to Woodford County, Kentucky, in 1783 where he purchased large tracts of land. He was surveyor of revenue for the District of Ohio circa 1787 to 1797. He died in Woodford County.

MASON, George: legislator
Born Doeg's Neck (now Mason's Neck), Virginia, 1725; son of George and Ann (Thompson) Mason; married Anne Eilbeck, April 4, 1750; second marriage to Sarah Brent, April 11, 1780; father of nine children; died October 7, 1792.

Mason was a trustee of Alexandria, Virginia, from 1754 to 1779 and treasurer of the Ohio Company from 1752 to 1773. He was the author of *Extracts from the Virginia Charters, with Some Remarks upon Them,* in 1733 and wrote the Fairfax Resolves of July 18, 1774.

Mason was a member of the Virginia House of Burgesses in 1759, a member of the First Virginia Convention in 1775, and a member of the Fifth Virginia Convention in 1776. In addition, he was a member of the Virginia Council of Safety in 1775. He was responsible for framing the Declaration of Rights and a major part of the Virginia Constitution during 1776.

An active organizer of military affairs, particularly in the West, Mason was partly responsible for fixing the British-American boundary at the Great Lakes rather than at the Ohio River in the Peace Treaty of 1783. He was Virginia's delegate to the Mount Vernon Meeting in 1785 and served as a member of the Virginia Assembly in 1786.

A delegate to the United States Constitutional Convention in 1787, Mason became the leader of the opposition to ratification in Virginia and refused to sign the Constitution. He wrote *Objections to the Federal Constitution* in 1787, insisting on the inclusion of a Bill of Rights and a condemnation of slavery.

Mason died in Gunston Hall, Virginia, at the age of sixty-seven.

MASON, Samuel: outlaw
Born Virginia, circa 1750; father of four sons; died July 1803.

After serving as a captain in the Ohio County (Virginia) militia during the Revolution, Mason turned outlaw, operating first in eastern Tennessee and later in Russellville and Henderson, Kentucky. With a band that included his sons, he attacked and robbed passing Mississippi rivermen in 1797. He continued his activities on the lower Mississippi and was later captured, along with his gang, by Spanish officials in Missouri. He escaped but was killed by his cohorts in 1803, who then attempted to collect a reward but were recognized and killed by federal officials in Old Greenville, Mississippi, in 1804.

MASON, Stevens Thomson: senator
Born Stafford County, Virginia, December 29, 1760; son of Thomas and Mary King (Barnes) Mason;

married Mary Elizabeth Armistead; father of Armistead and John; died May 10, 1803.

Mason, who attended the College of William and Mary, was a staff aide to General Washington during the Revolution. He was a member of the Virginia House of Delegates from 1783 to 1787 and of the Virginia Senate in 1787. He participated in the Virginia Convention to ratify the United States Constitution in 1788 and served as a United States Senator (Democrat) from Virginia from 1794 to 1803. He died in Philadelphia and was buried at "Raspberry Plain," Loudoun County, Virginia.

MASON, Thomson: legislator
Born Prince William County, Virginia, 1733; son of Colonel George and Ann (Thomson) Mason; married Mary Barnes, 1758; second marriage to Elizabeth Westwood; died February 26, 1785.

Admitted to Middle Temple, London, England, in 1751, Mason later returned to America, where he served as a member of the Virginia Assembly from Stafford County from 1758 to 1761 and from 1765 to 1772; from Loudoun County from 1772 to 1774 and in 1777–78; and from Elizabeth City County in 1779 and 1783. He was chairman of the committee on courts of justice and was author and chief supporter of a bill by which the Assembly organized the Northwest as the county of Illinois in 1778. He wrote a series of pamphlets signed "A British American" urging open resistance to England in 1774, and he served as a judge of the Virginia General Court in 1778. He died in Virginia at the age of fifty-two.

MAZZEI, Philip: wine merchant
Born Poggio-a-Caiano, Italy, December 25, 1730; son of Domenico and Eliszbetta Mazzei; married Marie Martin, 1774; married a second time, 1796; father of one child; died March 19, 1816.

Mazzei studied medicine at Santa Maria Nuova in Italy but went to London, England, in 1755, where he became a wine merchant. He arrived in Virginia to introduce the culture of grapes in 1773 and served during the Revolution as an agent to secure money for Virginia from the Grand Duke of Tuscany, from 1779 to 1784. Mazzei was "intelligencer" to the King of Poland in 1788 and was private adviser to Stanislas II of Poland in 1792.

Mazzei was the author of *Recherches historiques et politiques sur les Etats-Unis de l'Amérique septentrionale,* four volumes, 1788; and *Memorie della Vita e delle Pere grinazioni del Fiorentino Filippo Mazzei,* 1813. Mazzei died in Pisa, Italy, at the age of eighty-five.

MEADE, Richard Kidder: army officer
Born Nansemond County, Virginia, July 14, 1746; son of David and Susannah Meade; married Jane Randolph, 1765; second marriage to Mary Fitzhugh Grymes, 1780; father of four sons and four daughters; died February 9, 1805.

Meade served as a captain under Colonel Woodford at the Battle of Great Bridge in 1775 and was a lieutenant colonel and aide-de-camp to General Washington in 1777. He operated "Lucky Hit" farm in Frederick County, Virginia, after the Revolution.

MERCER, Hugh: army officer
Born Aberdeenshire, Scotland, circa 1721; son of the Reverend William and Anna (Munro) Mercer; married Isabella Gordon; father of four sons and one daughter; died January 12, 1777.

Assistant surgeon in Prince Charles Edward's Army at the Battle of Culloden in 1745, Mercer, who had been educated at Aberdeen University, served as a captain in the French and Indian War in 1755–56. He participated in the Battle of Monongahela in 1755, was commissioned a major and then a lieutenant colonel in 1758, and became a colonel in the 3rd Battalion, 5th Pennsylvania Regiment, in 1759. He was appointed commandant at Fort Pitt.

In 1775 Mercer was elected colonel of the Virginia Minutemen for Caroline, Stafford, King George, and Spotsylvania counties. In 1776 he organized and was elected colonel and then brigadier general of the 3rd Virginia Regiment. He served in the battles of Trenton in 1776 and Princeton in 1777.

Mercer was buried in Christ Churchyard in Philadelphia and was reinterred in Laurel Hill Cemetery in Philadelphia in 1840.

MERCER, James: Continental congressman
Born March 8, 1737; son of John and Catherine (Mason) Mercer; married Eleanor Dick, June 4, 1772; father of three children (including Charles Fenton and Mary Eleanor Dick); died October 31, 1793.

Mercer served as a captain in the Virginia militia during the French and Indian War and was commander of Fort Loudoun in Winchester, Virginia, in 1756. He was a member of the Virginia House of Burgesses from Hampshire County (now in West Virginia) from 1762 to 1776. He participated in the Virginia revolutionary conventions of 1774, 1775, and 1776, and was appointed a member of the Committee of Correspondence in 1774. He was a member of the first Virginia Committee of Safety in 1775.

Mercer was a member of the Virginia Constitutional Convention in 1776 and was sent to the Continental Congress from Virginia in 1779 and 1780. He was on the Virginia General Court in 1779 and was a trustee and president of Fredericksburg Academy from 1786 to 1790. He served as a judge of the Virginia Court of Appeals from 1789 until his death, in Richmond, Virginia. He was buried in St. John's Churchyard.

MONROE, James: fifth President of the United States
Born Westmoreland County, Virginia, April 28, 1758; son of Spence and Elizabeth (Jones) Monroe; married Eliza Kortright, February 1786; father of Eliza and Maria; died July 4, 1831.

Monroe attended the College of William and Mary from 1774 to 1776. Commissioned a lieutenant in the 3rd Virginia Regiment of the Continental Army in 1776, he served at the battles of Harlem, White Plains, and Trenton. He was promoted to major in 1777 and was an aide to the Earl of Stirling in 1777–78. He served in the battles of Brandywine, Germantown, and Monmouth. As military commissioner for Virginia, with the rank of lieutenant colonel, he visited the Southern Army in 1780.

A student of law under Thomas Jefferson from 1780 to 1783, Monroe attended the Virginia Assembly in 1782, 1786, and 1810–11. He was a Virginia delegate to the Continental Congress from 1783 to 1786. He was admitted to the Virginia bar in 1786 and attended the Annapolis Convention that year. A member of the Virginia Convention to ratify the United States Constitution in 1788, he represented Virginia in the United States Senate from November 9, 1790, to May 27, 1794. He was a member of the Senate committee to investigate Alexander Hamilton's handling of public funds in 1792. He was governor of Virginia from 1799 to 1802 and again in 1811.

Monroe carried out a number of diplomatic assignments prior to his own presidency. As United States minister plenipotentiary to France from 1794 to 1796, he was unable to establish friendly Franco-American relations owing to French anger over the Jay Treaty of 1794. He was appointed minister to France to arrange the terms of the Louisiana Purchase in 1803. Minister to England from 1803 to 1807, he was also an envoy to Spain in 1804. He served as secretary of state under President James Madison from 1811 to 1817 and gave tacit approval to General George Mathews's plans to invade Florida in 1811, withdrawing that support the following year. He served as secretary of war in 1814–15.

Monroe, a Democrat, was elected President of the United States in 1817 and served two terms. During his term of office he signed the treaty with Spain by which the United States received Florida in 1819 and signed the Missouri Compromise Bill in 1820. With his secretary of state, John Quincy Adams, he drafted the Monroe Doctrine in 1823, declaring that the new world was no longer open to European colonization.

Monroe was a member of the board of visitors of the University of Virginia from 1828 to 1831. He served as president of the Virginia Constitutional Convention in 1829. He died in New York City and was buried in Marble Cemetery there; his remains were reinterred in Hollywood Cemetery in Richmond, Virginia, in 1858.

MORGAN, Daniel: congressman, army officer

Born either Hunterdon County, New Jersey, or Bucks County, Pennsylvania, 1736; son of James and Eleanora Morgan; married Abigail Bailey; father of Nancy and Betty; died July 6, 1802.

Morgan worked in Bucks County, where his father was ironmaster of the Durham Iron Works. He quarreled with his father and moved to the Shenandoah Valley in Virginia, transporting supplies to frontier points of Virginia. He served as a lieutenant in Pontiac's War in 1774, accompanied Lord Dunmore's expedition to western Pennsylvania, and was commissioned captain of a company of riflemen from Virginia in 1775.

Morgan accompanied Benedict Arnold on the assault on Quebec and was captured in 1775. He was commissioned a colonel in the 11th Virginia Regiment in 1776 and brigadier general in the Continental Army in 1780. He joined General Nathaniel Gates and defeated the British in the Battle of Cowpens (North Carolina) in 1781.

Awarded a gold medal by the Continental Congress, Morgan retired to his estate in Virginia after the Revolution. He commanded the Virginia militia ordered by President Washington to suppress the Whiskey Rebellion in Pennsylvania in 1794. He was elected to the United States House of Representatives from Virginia for the 5th Congress (1797–99).

Morgan died in Winchester, Virginia, and was buried in Mount Hebron Cemetery there.

MOORE, Andrew: senator, congressman

Born at the estate "Cannicello," Rockbridge County, Virginia, 1752; son of David and Mary (Evans) Moore; married Sarah Reid, circa 1782; father of Samuel McDowell; died April 14, 1821.

Educated at Washington and Lee University, Moore read law under George Wythe and was admitted to the Virginia bar in 1774. He was head of a company in the 9th Virginia Regiment, Continental Army, and served as a lieutenant under General Gates at the Battle of Saratoga. Present at the surrender of Burgoyne, he later rose to major general in the Virginia militia.

Moore was a member of the Virginia House of Delegates from 1780 to 1783, 1785 to 1788, and in 1799–1800. A trustee of Washington and Lee University from 1782 to 1821, he was largely responsible for the permanent establishment of that school. He was a member of the Virginia Privy Council and a delegate to the Virginia Convention which ratified the United States Constitution in 1788. He was elected to the United States House of Representatives from Virginia for the 1st–4th and 8th congresses (1789–97 and from March 5 to August 11, 1804) and was a member of the Virginia Senate in 1800–01.

Moore was appointed United States marshal for the Western District of Virginia in 1801. He represented Virginia in the United States Senate from August 11, 1804, to 1809. He died in Lexington, Virginia, and was buried in Lexington Cemetery.

MUNFORD, Robert: army officer, dramatist

Born Prince George County, Virginia; son of Robert and Anna (Bland) Munford; married Anne Beverley; died 1784.

A captain in the 2nd Virginia Regiment during the French and Indian War, Munford was a member of the Virginia House of Burgesses from 1765 to 1775 and of the General Assembly in 1779 and 1780–81 and was a signer of the Williamsburg Association

(Non-Importation Agreement) June 22, 1770. He earned ranks to major in the Revolution. His writings are collected in the *Collection of Plays and Poems,* published posthumously in 1798.

★★★★★

NELSON, Thomas: governor of Virginia, Continental congressman

Born Yorktown, Virginia, December 26, 1738; son of William and Elizabeth (Burwell) Nelson; married Lucy Grymes, July 29, 1762; father of eleven children (including Hugh); died January 4, 1789.

Nelson, a 1761 graduate of Trinity College, Cambridge University, England, was a financier. He became a member of His Majesty's Council of Virginia in 1764. Ten years later he served in the Virginia House of Burgesses and was a delegate to the First Virginia Provincial Convention in Williamsburg. He was a member of the Continental Congress from 1775 to 1777, as well as of the Third Virginia Convention in Richmond in 1776; out of the latter body came the Virginia Resolutions, which later evolved into the Declaration of Independence. He was a signer of the Declaration.

In 1778 Nelson became a brigadier general and was commander-in-chief of the Virginia militia. During the next two years he was a member of the state assembly and in 1781 took office as governor of Virginia. That same year he took part in the Yorktown campaign as head of the state militia.

A statue of Nelson is located in Capital Park, in Richmond. He died in Hanover County in 1789 and was buried in Old Churchyard in Yorktown.

NELSON, William: merchant, planter, colonial legislator

Born Yorktown, Virginia, 1711; son of Thomas and Margaret (Reade) Nelson; married Elizabeth Burwell, 1738; father of six children (including Thomas); died November 19, 1772.

After becoming sheriff of York County, Virginia, in 1738, Nelson served as representative from York County in the Virginia House of Burgesses from 1742 to 1744. In the latter year he began a long term on the Virginia Council which lasted until 1772 and during which he also served as president of the council. During 1770 and 1771 he was ex officio governor of Virginia.

In addition, Nelson was a member of the Committee of Correspondence of the Virginia Assembly and a member of the board of visitors for the College of William and Mary. In 1763 he helped form the Dismal Swamp Company to drain Dismal Swamp. He died in Yorktown and was buried in the churchyard there.

NEVILLE, Joseph: congressman

Born 1730; died March 4, 1819.

Neville represented Hampshire County in the Virginia House of Burgesses from 1773 to 1776. He was a member of the conventions of December 1, 1775, and May 6, 1776. During the Revolutionary War he served with the Continental Army. He attended the Virginia House of Delegates in 1777, 1780, and 1781, and was involved in settling the Pennsylvania-Maryland boundary dispute in 1782. He represented Virginia in the United States House of Representatives during the 3rd Congress (1793–95). He died in Hardy County, Virginia.

NEW, Anthony: congressman

Born Gloucester County, Virginia, 1747; died March 2, 1833.

New studied law, was admitted to the Virginia bar, and established a legal practice. During the Revolutionary War he served as a colonel in the Continental Army. A Democrat, he was elected to serve Virginia in the United States House of Representatives for the 3rd through the 8th congresses (1793–1805). After moving to Elkton, Kentucky, he was elected to the 12th, 15th, and 17th congresses of the House (1811–13, 1817–19, and 1821–23). He was engaged in farming throughout his life. He died and was buried at the estate "Dunheath," near Elkton.

NICHOLAS, George: state official

Born Williamsburg, Virginia, 1755; son of Robert Carter and Anne (Cary) Nicholas; married Mary Smith, circa 1778; died June 1799.

Nicholas, a 1772 graduate of the College of William and Mary, served as a major in the 2nd Virginia Regiment in 1777 and later as a colonel. In 1787 he became a member of the Virginia House of Delegates and the next year participated in the state convention which adopted the United States Constitution. In 1792 he was a member of the first Kentucky Constitutional Convention.

Nicholas was the first attorney general of Kentucky. He helped to frame and was an advocate of Thomas Jefferson's Kentucky Resolutions of 1798, which were a response to the Alien and Sedition Acts of the same year. He died the following year.

NICHOLAS, Robert Carter: colonial official

Born Hanover, Virginia, January 28, 1728; son of Dr. George and Elizabeth (Carter) Burwell Nicholas; married Anne Cary, 1751; father of George, John, Wilson Cary, Philipe Norborne, and Elizabeth; died September 8, 1780.

Nicholas was educated at the College of William and Mary. He was a member of the Virginia House of Burgesses for twenty-one years (1756 to 1777). In 1765 he opposed Patrick Henry's Stamp Act Resolves, but he gradually came to favor the American cause. From 1766 to 1777 he served as treasurer of the state of Virginia and in 1773 was a member of the Committee of Correspondence. Although he opposed the assertion in the Declaration of Independence that all men are by nature equally free and independent, he was often appointed to committees to execute resolves of the patriots.

From 1777 to 1779 Nicholas was a member of the Virginia House of Delegates and in 1779 he became a judge in the Virginia High Court of Chancery. He died the following year in Hanover County, Virginia.

NICHOLAS, Wilson Cary: senator, congressman, governor of Virginia

Born Williamsburg, Virginia, January 31, 1761; son of Robert Carter and Anne (Cary) Nicholas; married Margaret Smith, circa 1781; father of four children; died October 10, 1820.

Nicholas graduated in 1774 from the College of William and Mary. He served in the Continental Army until 1783 and was a member of George Washington's Life Guard. From 1784 to 1788 he was a member of the Virginia House of Representatives, in the latter year also attending the Virginia Convention which ratified the United States Constitution.

Nicholas represented his state in the United States Senate from 1799 until March 22, 1804; in that year he became collector for the Port of Norfolk, holding that position until 1807, when he went to the United States House of Representatives. He served there during the 10th and 11th congresses, until November 27, 1809.

Nicholas was governor of Virginia from 1814 to 1817. He died at the estate "Tufton," near Charlottesville, Virginia, and was buried on the estate "Monticello," also near Charlottesville.

★★★★★

ORMSBY, Stephen: congressman

Born County Sligo, Ireland, 1759; died 1844.

After studying law, Ormsby came to America and settled in Philadelphia. He was admitted to the bar in 1786 and established a legal practice in Danville, Kentucky. He was deputy attorney general of Jefferson County, Kentucky, in 1787 and served as a brigadier general in the Indian wars under General Josiah Harmar in the campaign of 1790. The following year he was judge of the Jefferson County District Court.

A presidential elector in 1796, from 1802 to 1810 Ormsby was judge of the Circuit Court. A Democrat, he served in the United States House of Representatives for the 12th, 13th and 14th congresses. He was the first president of the Louisville (Kentucky) branch of the United States Bank in 1817.

Ormsby died near Louisville and was buried in Ormsby Burial Ground, Lyndon, Kentucky.

★★★★★

PAGE, Mann: Continental congressman

Born at the estate "Rosewell," Gloucester County, Virginia, 1749; died 1781.

Mann graduated from the College of William and Mary, studied law, was admitted to the Virginia bar, and established a legal practice; he later came to manage a large estate. After serving as a member of the Virginia House of Burgesses, he moved to Spotsylvania County, Virginia. In 1777 he represented Virginia in the Continental Congress. He died at the estate "Mansfield," near Fredericksburg, Virginia, and was buried near there.

PAGE, Robert: congressman

Born at the estate "North End," Gloucester County, Virginia, February 4, 1765; died December 8, 1840.

Before serving as a captain during the American Revolution, Robert Page attended William and Mary College and studied law. He was admitted to the Virginia bar and practiced in Frederick County.

Page was a member of the Virginia Council of State and became a member of the Virginia House of Delegates in 1795. A Federalist, he served in the United States House of Representatives during the 6th Congress (1799–1801). He died at the estate "Janesville," in Frederick County, and was buried in the Old Chapel Cemetery near Millwood, Virginia.

PARKER, Josiah: congressman

Born Isle of Wight County, Virginia, May 11, 1751; son of Nicholas and Ann (Copeland) Parker; married Mary Pierce Bridger, 1773; Died March 18, 1810.

In 1775 Parker became a member of the local Committee of Safety and a member of the Virginia Revolutionary Convention. In 1776 he was commissioned a major and served as lieutenant colonel of the 5th Virginia Regiment at the Battle of Trenton. A year later he was promoted to colonel.

Parker served as a member of the Virginia House of Delegates in 1780–81. From 1786 to 1788 he was a naval officer at the Port of Norfolk (Virginia). An Anti-Federalist, he served in the United States House of Representatives from Virginia in the 1st to the 6th congresses (1789–1801). He died in Isle of Wight County at the age of fifty-eight.

PATILLO, Henry: clergyman

Born Scotland, 1726; married Mary Anderson, July 23, 1758; died 1801.

Patillo was licensed to preach by the Presbytery of Hanover, Virginia, in 1757. He served pastorates at Willis Creek, Byrd, and Buck Island, Virginia, from 1758 to 1762. From 1764 to 1774 he served the North Carolina churches of Hawkfields and Little River. He spent the last twenty-seven years of his life as a pastor in Grassy Creek, North Carolina; while there he wrote *On the Divisions Among Christians* (1788) and *Geographical Catechism* (1796). He died in Dinwiddie County, Virginia.

PENDLETON, Edmund: Continental congressman, jurist

Born Caroline County, Virginia, September 9, 1721; son of Henry and Mary (Taylor) Pendleton; married Elizabeth Ray, 1742 (deceased same year); second marriage to Sarah Pollard, June 20, 1743; no children; died October 23, 1803.

Pendleton studied law under the clerk of the Caroline County Court; in 1740 he himself became clerk. He was admitted to practice by the local bar in 1741 and before the Virginia General Court in 1745. He served as justice of the peace of Caroline County in 1751, as a member of the Virginia House of Burgesses from 1752 to 1774, and as a member of the Committee of Correspondence in 1773. He was a member of the Virginia Convention and in 1774 served in the First Continental Congress. He was a member of all revolutionary conventions in Virginia. As president of the Virginia Committee of Safety from 1774 to 1776, he was in effect governor of the state. He served as lieutenant of Caroline County and in 1776–77 was a member of the Virginia House of Delegates, acting as speaker in 1776.

When the Boston Port Act was passed in 1776, the Virginia Convention was called, with Pendleton as its president. Its purpose was to draw up a resolution instructing Virginia delegates to the Continental Congress to propose independence. Pendleton was presiding judge of the First Virginia Court of Chancery and from 1779 to 1803 was president of the First Virginia Court of Appeals. In 1788 he was president of the Virginia Convention to ratify the United States Constitution.

Pendleton died in Richmond and was buried in the Bruton Parish Church Cemetery in Williamsburg.

POSEY, Thomas: army officer, senator
Born Fairfax County, Virginia, July 9, 1750; married Martha Matthews; second marriage to Mary Alexander Thornton; father of Mary; died March 19, 1818.

Posey served with the Virginia militia against the Indian tribes on the western frontier in 1774. At the beginning of the Revolutionary War he was commissioned a major in the 7th Virginia Regiment, gaining a promotion to lieutenant colonel in 1782 and to brigadier general in 1793.

Posey's early political activities included serving as a member of the Virginia Committee of Correspondence. He moved to Kentucky in 1794 and in 1805 and 1806 was a member and presiding officer of the Kentucky Senate. He served as lieutenant governor of Kentucky from 1805 to 1809. Also in 1809 he was commissioned a major general in the United States Volunteers.

After moving to Attakapas, Louisiana, Posey represented Louisiana in the United States Senate from October 1812 to February 1813. He was governor of the Indiana Territory from 1813 until it received statehood in 1816 and for the next two years served as Indian agent in the Illinois Territory. He died in Shawneetown, Illinois, and was buried in the Westwood Cemetery there.

POWELL, Levin: congressman
Born near Manassas, Prince William County, Virginia, 1737; father of at least one son (Cuthbert); died August 23, 1810.

Powell, who attended private schools, served as deputy sheriff of Prince William County before moving to Loudoun County in 1763. He then became engaged in mercantile activities. In the Revolutionary War he served as a major in the Continental Army in 1775 and a lieutenant colonel of the 16th Regiment in 1777–78.

Powell became a member of the Virginia House of Delegates in 1779 and served again in 1787–88 and 1791–92. He was a delegate to the Virginia Convention which ratified the United States Constitution in 1788 and a presidential elector in 1796. From 1799 to 1801 Powell, a Federalist, represented Virginia in the United States House of Representatives (6th Congress).

Powell was a builder of the turnpike from Alexandria, Virginia, to the upper country. He died in Bedford, Pennsylvania, and was buried in the Old Presbyterian Graveyard.

★★★★★

RANDOLPH, Beverley: governor of Virginia
Born Henrico County, Virginia, 1754; son of Colonel Peter and Lucy (Bolling) Randolph; died 1797.

At the age of seventeen Randolph graduated from the College of William and Mary. He was a member of the Virginia General Assembly at various times during the Revolutionary War. In 1784 he was on the board of visitors of the College of William and Mary. In 1787–88 he was president of the Virginia Executive Council.

Randolph became the first governor of the

State of Virginia under the United States Constitution. His term from 1788 to 1791 was marked by Indian trouble on the Virginia frontier and by controversy with Pennsylvania over the boundary of the two states. He died at "Green Creek," in Cumberland County, Virginia.

RANDOLPH, Edmund: secretary of state, governor of Virginia, Continental congressman

Born at the estate "Tazewell Hall," Williamsburg, Virginia, August 10, 1753; son of John and Ariana (Jenings) Randolph; married Elizabeth Nicholas, August 29, 1776; father of four children (including Peyton, Edmund, and Lucy [Randolph] Daniel); died September 12, 1813.

Randolph was educated at the College of William and Mary and in 1775–76 served as aide-de-camp to Washington. In 1776 he became the youngest member of the Virginia Constitutional Convention; in that year he also served as mayor of Williamsburg. He was attorney general of Virginia until circa 1782 and attended the Continental Congress from 1779 to 1782.

As governor of Virginia from 1786 to 1788, Randolph served as a delegate to the Annapolis Convention and to the Federal Convention of 1787, where he proposed the Virginia Plan. He declined to sign the United States Constitution because he feared the danger of a monarchy in the executive department, but in 1788 he advocated ratification of the Constitution in the Virginia Convention.

Randolph served as attorney general of the United States between 1789 and 1794. As secretary of state in 1795, he expelled the offensive French minister Edmond Charles Genet and advised Monroe on his negotiations with the French government. His conflict of opinion with the American envoys to England, John Jay and Alexander Hamilton, and with the envoy to France, James Monroe, resulted in an ineffectual term as secretary of state.

In 1795 Randolph wrote *A Vindication of Mr. Randolph's Resignation.* He was senior counsel for Aaron Burr in his treason trial. He died in Clarke County, Virginia.

RANDOLPH, John: colonial official

Born at the estate "Tazewell Hall," Williamsburg, Virginia, 1727 or 1728; son of Sir John and Susanna (Beverly) Randolph; married Ariana Jenings, circa 1752; father of Susanna, Ariana (Mrs. Wormley), and Edmund Jennings; died January 31, 1784.

Randolph graduated from the College of William and Mary and in 1750 was admitted to the bar. The next year he was a member of the Common Council of Williamsburg. From 1752 to 1756 he served as clerk of the Virginia House of Burgesses, and for the next nineteen years he was Virginia attorney general for the Crown.

A Loyalist during the Revolution, Randolph fled to England in 1775. He was granted a pension from the Crown and headed a movement of Loyalist refugees offering military service to the King to defend England against a feared invasion by France.

Randolph wrote the first book on gardening published in the colonies, *A Treatise on Gardening* (1793). He died in Brompton, England, his remains being returned to America for burial in the chapel of William and Mary College.

RANDOLPH, Peyton: president of the Continental Congress

Born at the estate "Tazewell Hall," Williamsburg, Virginia, September 1721; son of Sir John and Susanna (Beverly) Randolph; married Elizabeth Harrison, February 1746; died October 22, 1775.

Randolph was admitted to Middle Temple in London, England, in 1739, graduated from the College of William and Mary in 1742, and was admitted to the Virginia bar in 1744.

The most popular leader in Virginia during the decade before the Revolution, Randolph was the King's attorney for Virginia from 1748 to 1766 and served in the Virginia House of Burgesses for twenty-seven years, from 1748 to 1775. He was sent to England to oppose the governor's policy and to secure withdrawal of the land fee. He was chairman of the Virginia Committee of Correspondence in 1773. In 1774 and 1775 he presided over the revolutionary conventions of Virginia and served as president of the Continental Congress.

Randolph was also a member of the board of visitors of the College of William and Mary and provincial grand master of the Masonic Order in Williamsburg. He died in Philadelphia and was buried beneath the chapel of the College of William and Mary.

RICE, David: clergyman

Born Hanover County, Virginia, December 29, 1733; son of David Rice; married Mary Blair, 1763; father of eleven children; died June 18, 1816.

Rice graduated from the College of New Jersey (now Princeton) in 1761 and was licensed to preach by the Hanover Presbytery a year later; he was ordained in 1763. For the next five years he was a pastor in Hanover, Virginia. From 1769 to 1783 he served as a missionary in Bedford County, Virginia. He was co-founder of Hampden-Sydney College in 1775 and of Transylvania University in Lexington, Kentucky, in 1780.

An itinerant preacher from 1783 to 1798, Rice organized churches in Kentucky and Ohio. He was a member of the Kentucky Constitutional Convention in 1792. From 1798 to 1816 he served as a pastor in Green County, Kentucky. He was largely responsible for the establishment of Presbyterianism in Kentucky. In 1802 he gave the sermon at the founding of the Presbyterian Synod of Kentucky.

As an author, Rice was noted for *An Essay on Baptism* (1789) and for *Slavery Inconsistent with Justice and Good Policy* (1792). He also wrote *An Epistle to the Citizens of Kentucky Professing Christianity* (1805) and *Second Epistle* (1808).

ROANE, John: congressman

Born Uppowac, King William County, Virginia, February 9, 1766; father of at least one son (John Jones); died November 15, 1838.

Roane, who completed preparatory studies, was a presidential elector for Washington. He was a member of the Virginia House of Delegates from 1788 to 1790 and in 1792 and served in the Virginia Constitutional Convention in 1788. A Democrat, he served Virginia in the United States House of Representatives for the 11th through the 13th congresses (1809–15), the 20th and 21st congresses (1827–31), and the 24th Congress (1835–37). He became a farmer before his death at his home at Uppowac. He was buried in the old family burying ground in Rumford, Virginia.

RUMSEY, James: inventor

Born Bohemia Manor, Cecil County, Maryland, March 1743; son of Edward and Anna (Cowman) Rumsey; no record of first marriage; second marriage to Mary Morrow; father of three children; died December 20, 1792.

Rumsey began operating a gristmill at Sleepy Creek, Maryland, in 1782. With a friend he opened a general store, and he engaged in the building trade in Bath (now Berkley Springs), Virginia (now West Virginia), in 1783–84. The next year he accepted a position as superintendent of construction of canals with the Potomac Navigation Company.

In 1785 Rumsey began to experiment with a steam engine, having attempted to build a steamboat in 1783. In 1787 he exhibited on the Potomac River near Shepherdstown, West Virginia, a boat propelled by streams of water forced out through the stern, a steam engine being employed to operate the force pump.

The Rumseian Society was formed in 1781 to promote Rumsey's projects, which included an improved sawmill, an improved gristmill, and an improved steam boiler. The society sent Rumsey to England to patent his improvements and to interest English capital. In 1788 he secured English patents on his boiler and steamboat, and three years later he secured American patents. He died in London shortly before his second steamboat was completed and was buried in St. Margaret's Churchyard near Westminster, England.

RUTHERFORD, Robert: congressman
Born Scotland, October 20, 1728; died October 1803.

Rutherford attended the Royal College of Edinburgh in Scotland before coming to America. He settled in Berks County, Tennessee, and later moved to Virginia. From 1743 to 1744 he was high sheriff of Frederick County, Virginia. He held several local offices and was a delegate to the First Virginia Revolutionary Convention, held in Williamsburg in 1774, and the Second Virginia Revolutionary Convention, held in Richmond the following year.

From 1776 to 1790 Rutherford was a member of the Virginia Senate. From 1793 to 1797, during the 3rd and 4th congresses, he served as a delegate from Virginia to the United States House of Representatives. He later settled on the estate "Flowing Spring," near Charles Town, Virginia (now in West Virginia), where he died and was buried.

★★★★★

SCOTT, Charles: governor of Kentucky
Born Goochland County, Virginia, 1739; married Frances Sweeney, February 25, 1762; second marriage to Judith Cary (Bell) Gist, July 25, 1807; died October 22, 1813.

At the beginning of the Revolution, Scott raised the first companies of volunteers south of the James River. He was appointed a lieutenant colonel in the 2nd Virginia Regiment in 1776 and a colonel in the 3rd Regiment later the same year. He was commissioned a brigadier general in the Continental Army in 1777 and was captured at Charleston, South Carolina, three years later. In 1783 he was brevetted a major general.

Scott was an original member of the Society of the Cincinnati. In 1789 and 1790 he represented Woodford County (Kentucky) in the Virginia Assembly. In 1791 he became commandant of the Kentucky District with the rank of brigadier general and conducted an expedition against the Indians on the Wabash River. In 1792 Scott County, Kentucky, was named for him.

In 1794 Scott fought against the Indians with General Anthony Wayne at the Battle of Fallen Timbers. He was chosen a presidential elector from Kentucky in the elections of 1793, 1801, 1805, and 1809. From 1808 until 1812 he was governor of Kentucky. He died at the estate "Canewood" in Clark County, Kentucky, and was buried in the State Cemetery in Frankfort.

SEBASTIAN, Benjamin: jurist
Born 1745; father of at least one son (Charles); died March 1834.

In 1784 Sebastian moved to Jefferson County, Kentucky, and was admitted to the bar in Louisville. He was licensed an attorney two years later and joined the Political Club of Danville (Kentucky).

Sebastian, who advocated separation from Virginia and the establishment of Kentucky as a separate state, was suspected of negotiating with the Spanish to seek a means of making Kentucky subject to Spain. Appointed a judge in the Kentucky Appellate Court in 1792, he continued his correspondence with the Spanish and received a pension from Spain. The Federalist faction in Kentucky obtained a petition asking the legislature to investigate his activities with the Spanish, and his resignation in 1806 appears to have made his guilt certain.

Sebastian built a saw- and gristmill in 1810 and spent the remainder of his life engaged in general merchandising in Livingston, Kentucky. He lived to be nearly ninety years old.

SHELBY, Isaac: army officer, governor of Kentucky
Born North Mountain, Washington County, Maryland, December 11, 1750; son of Evan and Laetitia (Cox) Shelby; married Susannah Hart, April 19, 1783; father of eleven children; died July 18, 1826.

Shelby served as a lieutenant with the

Fincastle Company at the Battle of Point Pleasant (1774) and then commanded the garrison at Fort Blair during 1774–75. When the Long Island treaty was made with the Cherokee Indians, he attended the proceedings. He served in the Virginia legislature in 1779. In 1780 he became a colonel in the Sullivan County (North Carolina) militia and joined General McDowell at Cherokee Ford, South Carolina, with a force that he had organized. The same year he captured Fort Anderson on the headwaters of the Pacolet River. He went to the aid of General Greene in 1781 and became a member of the North Carolina legislature, to which he returned four years later.

In 1783 Shelby became a trustee of Transylvania Seminary (now Transylvania University). After serving on the Board of War for the District of Kentucky in 1791, he participated in the Kentucky Constitutional Convention the following year. He was the first governor of the state of Kentucky, serving from 1792 to 1796 and returning to serve as the fifth governor from 1812 until 1816. He assembled and led the Kentucky Volunteers who joined General Harrison in the northwest for the invasion of Canada.

Along with General Andrew Jackson, Shelby was appointed to make a treaty with the Chickasaw Indians for the purchase of lands west of the Tennessee River. In 1818 he declined an appointment as secretary of war. In 1819 he became chairman of the first board of trustees of Centre College, a position he held until 1826.

Counties in nine states were named after Shelby. He died at the age of seventy-five and was buried at the estate "Traveller's Rest," near Stanford, Kentucky.

SHORT, William: diplomat
Born at the estate "Spring Garden," Surry County, Virginia, September 30, 1759; son of William and Elizabeth (Skipwith) Short; died December 5, 1849.

Short, a 1779 graduate of the College of William and Mary, was a member of the Executive Council of Virginia in 1783–84. During the same years he was sent by Jefferson, Adams, and Franklin as a representative to negotiate a commercial treaty between Prussia and the United States with the Prussian envoy at The Hague. Circa 1786–89 he was Jefferson's private secretary in Paris, later serving as secretary of legation, and then as chargé d'affaires from 1789 to 1792. During the period 1792–93 he was United States minister at The Hague.

Short was a key figure in the drawing up of the Pinckney Treaty of 1795 between Spain and the United States, which had been under negotiation since 1793. In 1808 he was appointed minister to Russia, but the Senate rejected his appointment the following year. He died in Philadelphia at the age of ninety.

SMITH, John: congressman, army officer
Born Shooter's Hill, near Locust Hill, Middlesex County, Virginia, May 7, 1750; died March 15, 1836.

After moving to Frederick County, Virginia, in 1773, Smith became a planter at Hackwood, near Winchester, and acquired large land holdings. In 1773 the governor commissioned him one of the King's justices. Appointed a colonel by the Virginia Council of Safety in 1776, he was promoted to a lieutenant in the county militia by Governor Patrick Henry the following year.

After the Revolution, Smith rose further in the military. He was commissioned a lieutenant colonel commandant by Governor Henry Lee (1793), a brigadier general by Governor James Monroe (1801), and a major general of the 3rd Division of Virginia Troops (1811); he held the latter position until his death. During his career Smith served in Lord Dunmore's War with the Indians in 1774 and the War of 1812.

Smith also was active in politics. He was a member of the Virginia House of Delegates from 1779 to 1783 and a member of the Virginia Senate from 1792 to 1795 and again in 1796. A Democrat, he also served in the United States House of Representatives from 1801 until 1815 (7th–13th congresses). He died in Rockville, near Middletown, in Frederick County, and was buried in the family burying ground in Hackwood; he was reinterred in the Mount Hebron Cemetery in Winchester in 1890.

SMITH, John Blair: clergyman, college president

Born Pequea, Pennsylvania, June 12, 1756; son of the Reverend Robert and Elizabeth (Blair) Smith; married Elizabeth Nash, 1779; father of six children; died August 22, 1799.

In 1773 Smith graduated from the College of New Jersey (now Princeton). From 1775 to 1779 he was a tutor at Hampden-Sydney Academy (later rechartered as Hampden-Sydney College); he then served as president of the school until 1789. An early supporter of the movement for American independence, he became captain of a company of Hampden-Sydney students in the Virginia militia circa 1778.

Smith was ordained to the ministry of the Presbyterian Church in 1779 by the Hanover (Virginia) Presbytery. During the years 1789–91 he was a leader in the revival movement in Virginia. He then became pastor of the Third Presbyterian Church of Philadelphia, serving from 1791 to 1795 and returning in 1799. In the meanwhile he had held the position of president of Union College in Schenectady, New York (1795–99). He was elected president of the Presbyterian General Assembly in 1798. He died the following year in Philadelphia.

SMITH, Meriwether: Continental congressman

Born at the estate "Bathurst," Essex County, Virginia, 1730; son of Colonel Francis and Lucy (Meriwether) Smith; married Alice (Lee) Clarke, circa 1760; second marriage to Elizabeth Daingerfield, August 3, 1769; father of four children (including George William); died January 25, 1790.

A member of the Essex County Commit-

tee in 1774, Smith was a signer of the Westmoreland Association (in opposition to the Stamp Act) and a signer of the Williamsburg Association resolutions in 1776. He served as a member of the Virginia House of Burgesses in 1770, of the revolutionary conventions in 1775–76, and of the House of Delegates from 1776 to 1778, in 1781–82, and from 1785 to 1788. With Patrick Henry and Edmund Pendleton, he prepared a draft of resolutions of independence in 1776.

Smith was a delegate to the Continental Congress from 1778 to 1782, during which time (in 1781) he offered a plan of finance to Congress which was not accepted. He declined election to the Annapolis Convention in 1786 but became a member of the Virginia Convention which ratified the United States Constitution in 1788 (he opposed ratification). He died at the estate "Marigold," in Essex County.

STEPHENSON, James: congressman

Born Gettysburg, Pennsylvania, March 20, 1764; died August 7, 1833.

From Pennsylvania, Stephenson moved to Martinsburg, Virginia (now West Virginia). He served as a volunteer rifleman under General St. Clair in the Indian expedition of 1791 and as a brigade inspector. A member of the Virginia House of Delegates from 1800 to 1803 and again in 1806–07, Stephenson (a Federalist) was named to fill a vacant Virginia seat in the United States House of Representatives during the 8th (1803–05), 11th (1809–11), and 17th–18th (1822–25) congresses.

STOBO, Robert: army officer;

Born Glasgow, Scotland, 1727; son of William Stobo; died circa 1772.

Stobo, who attended the University of Glasgow circa 1742, served as a captain in the Virginia militia; he fought with George Washington at Fort Necessity in 1754 and was captured by the French. Tried for treason by the French in 1755, he was sentenced to execution; however, the sentence was never confirmed, and Stobo escaped down the St. Lawrence River in 1759. He received the gratitude of the Virginia House of Burgesses and a gift of 1,000 pounds.

Later a captain in Foot's 15th Regiment, Stobo's life served as the model for the character of Tismahago in Smollett's *The Expedition of Humphry Clinker.* Stobo was the author of *Memoirs of Major Robert Stobo of the Virginia Regiment,* published posthumously in 1800.

STUART, Archibald: legislator, jurist
Born Staunton, Virginia, March 19, 1757; son of Alexander and Mary (Patterson) Stuart; married Eleanor Briscoe, May 1791; father of Alexander Hugh Holmes; died July 11, 1832.

Stuart represented Botetourt County in the Virginia House of Delegates from 1783 to 1789 and was a leader in the ratification of the United States Constitution in 1788. He served as a member of the Virginia-Kentucky Boundary Commission in 1795 and was elected to the Virginia Senate in 1800, where he was a leader in the passage of the Virginia Resolutions.

A judge of the General Court of Virginia from 1800 until his death, Stuart was a leader of the conservative branch of the Jeffersonian Democrats in Virginia. He supported John Quincy Adams for the Presidency in 1828. He died in Staunton, the town of his birth.

★★★★★

TALIAFERRO, Richard: architect
No record of birth; died 1755.

Taliaferro practiced architecture in Virginia prior to the Revolutionary War. Although he was known as one of the ablest designers of his time, his only recorded work is the George Wythe house in Williamsburg, Virginia, which served as Washington's headquarters in 1781.

TAYLOR, John: frontier preacher
Born Fauquier County, Virginia, 1752; son of Lazarus and Anna (Bradford) Taylor; married Elizabeth Kavanaugh, 1782; died April 12, 1835.

Taylor preached among the scattered frontier settlements along the Shenandoah, the Potomac, the Monongahela, and the Green Briar rivers. He is one of the best examples of the farmer-preachers responsible for founding Baptist churches in western Virginia, North Carolina, Kentucky, and Tennessee.

Taylor was also a writer and in 1820 published a pamphlet titled *Thoughts on Missions* which attacked missionary societies for their mercenary objectives. In 1823 he related the story of his own pastoral activities in *A History of Ten Baptist Churches.* He died in Franklin County, Kentucky.

TAYLOR, John: senator, political writer
Born Caroline County, Virginia, May 17, 1753; son of James and Ann (Pollard) Taylor; married Lucy Penn, 1783; father of eight children; died August 20, 1824.

Known as John Taylor of Caroline, Taylor was admitted to the Virginia bar in 1774. During the Revolutionary War he served with the Continental Army and later (1781) became a lieutenant colonel in the Virginia militia. He was elected to several terms in the Virginia House of Delegates, serving from 1779 to 1785 and again from 1796 to 1800. He was a United States Senator from Virginia from 1792 to 1794, in 1803, and from 1822 to 1824.

In 1798 Taylor introduced the "Virginia Resolutions," which asserted the right of states to interpose authority in case of the overextension of federal powers. An opponent of the War of 1812, he took the stand that the war was an expansion of the powers of the central government. Taylor opposed permanent debt and was one of the first to present a well-developed view of states' rights. He held that Congress had no legitimate right to interfere with the institution of slavery established by law.

A political writer, in 1814 Taylor published *Inquiry into the Principles and Policy of the United States Government,* in which he refuted

John Adams's defense of the Constitution and the ideas of natural aristocracy. He wrote *Construction Construed and Constitutions Vindicated* in 1820, in which he argued for the unlimited right of the states to tax within their borders. That same year he attacked the protective tariff as a sectional device in *Tyranny Unmasked*. A proponent of the old agrarian order, he described his agricultural theories in *The Arator*.

Taylor died in Caroline County and was buried in Cadd, near Port Royal.

TAZEWELL, Henry: senator, jurist
Born Brunswick County, Virginia, November 15, 1753; son of Littleton and Mary (Gray) Tazewell; married Dorothy Waller, January 1774; father of Littleton Waller; died January 24, 1799.

Tazewell graduated from the College of William and Mary in 1772 and soon after embarked on a distinguished political and juristic career. Elected to the Virginia House of Burgesses in 1775, he served until 1778. From 1778 to 1785, he was a Williamsburg representative to Virginia's General Assembly. Elected to the Virginia Supreme Court in 1785, he served as chief justice in 1789. His term ended in 1793, at which time he was appointed judge of the Virginia High Court of Appeals.

An Anti-Federalist, Tazewell was elected to the United States Senate in 1794, serving as president pro tem in 1795. He was re-elected in 1796 and remained in office until his death in Philadelphia in 1799. He was buried in Christ Churchyard in that city.

THRUSTON, Buckner: senator, jurist
Born Petsoe Parish, Gloucester County, Virginia, February 9, 1764; died August 30, 1845.

Thruston graduated from William and Mary College in 1783, then studied law. In 1788 he moved to Lexington, in Fayette County, Virginia (now Kentucky), where he was admitted to the bar and began the practice of law.

In 1789 Thruston served as a member of the Virginia Assembly and in 1792 was elected clerk of the first Kentucky Senate. He was appointed a commissioner to settle the boundary dispute between Kentucky and Virginia. He was district judge of Kentucky in 1791 and judge of the circuit court in 1802–03. In 1804 he declined appointment as a United States judge of the court of the Territory of Orleans.

A Democrat, Thruston served in the United States Senate from 1805 until his resignation on December 18, 1809. From then until his death he served as a judge in the United States Circuit Court for the District of Columbia. He died in Washington, D.C., and was buried in the Congressional Cemetery.

TIMBERLAKE, Henry: army officer
Born Hanover County, Virginia, 1730; son of Francis and Sarah (Austin) Timberlake; died September 30, 1765.

In 1756 Timberlake joined the Patriot Blues under George Washington and fought against the French and the Indians. Two years later he was appointed to the regiment of William Byrd III in the campaign against the French at Fort Duquesne. In 1759 he was placed in command of Fort Necessity, Pennsylvania.

In 1761–62 Timberlake and Thomas Sumter made a twenty-two-day voyage to the Cherokee Indian villages and remained three months. In 1762 Timberlake accompanied a Cherokee chief and two warriors on a visit to England, and in 1764 he conducted another group of Cherokee warriors on an overseas journey. He was later commissioned a lieutenant for his services.

A valuable source for ethnologists is the *Memoirs of Henry Timberlake*, published in London in 1765. He died that year—at age thirty-five—in London.

TINGEY, Thomas: naval officer
Born London, England, September 11, 1750; married Margaret Murdoch, March 30, 1779; second marriage to Ann Bladen Dulany, December 9, 1812; third marriage to Ann Evelina Craven, May 19,

1817; father of three children; died February 23, 1829.

In 1778 Tingey commanded the brig *Lady Clausen,* sailing from St. Croix in the Virgin Islands to Europe. Serving in the American merchant marine after 1781, he was commissioned a captain in the United States Navy in 1798. During that year and the next he commanded three vessels in the Windward Passage and rejected the demand of the British frigate *Surprise* to have his crew examined for the presence of British seamen. He was a senior officer in the West Indies in 1799.

Tingey was an organizer of the Washington (D.C.) Navy Yard in 1800 and served as its commandant in that year and from 1804 to 1814. He served as superintendent of the yard from 1800 to 1803, as financial agent in 1803–04, and as naval agent from 1804 to 1814. When the British invaded in 1814, he burned the navy yard.

Tingey died in Washington and was buried in the Congressional Cemetery there.

TIPTON, John: army officer, state legislator
Born Baltimore County, Maryland, August 15, 1730; son of Jonathan and Elizabeth Tipton; married Mary Butler, circa 1753; second marriage to Martha Denton Moore, July 22, 1779; father of fifteen children; died August 1813.

Tipton was a founder of Woodstock in Dunmore (later Shenandoah) County, Virginia. He was a justice of the peace in Beckford Parish, Virginia, and an organizer and signer of the Independence Resolutions of Woodstock in 1774. He served as a recruiting officer and as a member of the Dunmore County Committee of Safety and Correspondence. From 1774 to 1781 he was a member of the Virginia House of Burgesses and in 1776 a representative to the Virginia Convention at Williamsburg. He was commissioned a lieutenant colonel in the Virginia militia and during the Revolutionary War served as high sheriff of Shenandoah County.

In 1785 Tipton was elected to the North Carolina Assembly in opposition to John Sevier, governor of the state of Franklin. Factions of Sevier and Tipton maintained separate courts and militias, and raiding parties from each side carried off court records and official papers of the other. There ensued a three-year civil war, ending in 1788 with a battle at Tipton's home near Jonesboro, Tennessee, in which Tipton was victorious.

In 1793 Tipton represented Washington County in the first Tennessee Assembly and served again in 1794–95. Also in 1795 he became a trustee of Washington College. He helped draft the Tennessee Constitution in 1796 and later was a member of the Tennessee Senate. He died in Sinking Creek, North Carolina.

TODD, Thomas: associate justice of the United States Supreme Court
Born King and Queen County, Virginia, January 23, 1765; son of Richard and Elizabeth (Richards) Todd; married Elizabeth Harris, 1788; second marriage to Lucy Payne, 1811; father of eight children (including Colonel Charles Stewart); died February 7, 1826.

After serving in the American Revolution, Todd was admitted in 1786 to the Kentucky bar. He was clerk of the United States Court for the Kentucky District circa 1787–92. From 1792 to 1801 he served as clerk of the Kentucky Court of Appeals, then became a judge. He was a clerk of the Kentucky House of Representatives in 1792.

As chief justice of the Kentucky Supreme Court in 1806, Todd wrote many decisions establishing a basis for land law in Kentucky. He was an associate justice of the United States Supreme Court from 1807 to 1826, serving on the Western Circuit. He died in Frankfort, Kentucky.

TRIGG, Abram: congressman, lawyer
Born near Old Liberty (now Bedford), Virginia, 1750; date of death unknown.

Trigg studied law and was admitted to the bar, then established a legal practice in

Montgomery County, Virginia. He lived on his estate, "Buchanan's Bottom," on the New River. He held various local offices, including clerk and judge of Montgomery County.

In 1782 Trigg served as a lieutenant colonel of militia in the Continental Army; later he was a general in the Virginia militia. He was a delegate to the Virginia Convention which ratified the United States Constitution in 1788. From 1797 to 1809 he represented Virginia in the United States House of Representatives.

Trigg died and was buried on the family estate.

TRIGG, John Johns: congressman
Born near Old Liberty (now Bedford), Virginia, 1748; died May 17, 1804.

Trigg received a liberal education, then became a farmer. In 1775 he raised a company of militia in Bedford County, Virginia. He was commissioned a captain in the Continental Army in 1778 and three years later was promoted to major. He served under General Washington at the siege of Yorktown. In 1791 he was a lieutenant colonel in the Virginia militia and two years later served as a major in the 2nd Battalion of the 10th Regiment of the Virginia militia.

In 1788 Trigg was a member of the Virginia Convention which ratified the United States Constitution. He served as a justice of the peace in Bedford County and, from 1784 to 1792, as a member of the Virginia House of Delegates. He was a member of the United States House of Representatives from Virginia from 1797 to 1804 (5th to 8th congresses).

Trigg died in Old Liberty and was buried on his estate.

TUCKER, St. George: army officer, jurist
Born Port Royal, Bermuda, July 10, 1752; son of Henry and Anne (Butterfield) Tucker; married Frances (Bland) Randolph, September 23, 1778; second marriage to Lelia (Skipworth) Carter, October 8, 1791; father of at least two sons (Nathaniel Beverley

and Henry St. George); died November 10, 1827.

After graduating from the College of William and Mary in 1772, Tucker was admitted to the Virginia bar. During the Revolutionary War he served as a colonel in the Chesterfield County (Virginia) militia and as a lieutenant colonel in the Virginia Cavalry. He served at the Battle of Guilford Courthouse and took part in the siege of Yorktown.

In 1786 Tucker became a commissioner at the Annapolis Convention. He sat as judge of the General Court of Virginia from 1788 to 1800, then taught at the College of William and Mary from 1800 to 1803 as professor of law. He was a judge in the Supreme Court of Appeals of Virginia from 1803 to 1811. In 1813 he became judge of the United States District Court for Virginia, serving until 1828. His opinion in *Kamper vs. Hawkins* held that the state constitution was a sovereign act of the people. In *Turpin vs. Locket* his opinion sustained the constitutionality of an 1802 act for relief of the poor.

Tucker was the author of a pamphet, *Dissertation on Slavery: with a Proposal for Its Gradual Abolition in Virginia,* published in 1796 and reprinted in 1861. He also published five volumes of an annotated edition of *Blackstone's Commentaries* in 1803. He wrote *Liberty, a Poem on the Independence of America* (1788) and *The Probationary Odes of Jonathan Pindar,* in two parts (1796). He died in Nelson County, Virginia.

TURNBULL, Andrew: physician, colonizer
Born circa 1718; married Maria Gracia Dura Bin; father of seven children (including Robert James); died March 13, 1792.

In 1766 Turnbull was granted by mandamus 20,000 acres of land in what is now Ponce de Leon, Florida. He returned to England in 1767 and the following year brought about 1,400 immigrants to America. He was a member and secretary of the Florida Provincial Council. As a result of his support of the American Revolution, Turnbull lost his land in Florida. He practiced medicine in Charleston, South Carolina, circa 1781 to 1792, the year of his death.

TYLER, John: governor, jurist
Born York County, Virginia, February 28, 1747; son of John and Anne (Contesse) Tyler; married Mary Armistead, 1776; father of at least two children (including John); died January 6, 1813.

Tyler attended the College of William and Mary. He was a member of the Charles City County (Virginia) Committee of Safety in 1774 and sat as judge of the High Court of Admiralty of Virginia in 1776. He served as Charles City County delegate to the Virginia House of Delegates from 1777 to 1788, holding the office of speaker from 1781 to 1784. He was a member of the Virginia Council of State in 1780 and 1781. In 1786 he presented a resolution calling for a federal convention which was to meet at Annapolis, Maryland. While vice president of the Virginia Convention of 1788, he opposed adoption of the United States Constitution.

From 1808 to 1811 Tyler was governor of Virginia. He sat as judge of the United States Circuit Court of Virginia from 1811 until 1813, when he died at the estate "Greenway," in Charles City County.

★★★★★

VENABLE, Abraham Bedford: senator, congressman
Born near Prince Edward Court House (now Worsham), Virginia, November 20, 1758; died December 26, 1811.

Venable attended Hampden-Sydney College in Virginia, graduated from Princeton in 1780, and studied law. He also became engaged in planting in Prince Edward County, Virginia. In 1784 he was admitted to the bar and began practicing law in the town of Prince Edward Court House.

Venable was a member of the United States House of Representatives from Virginia during the 2nd through the 5th congresses (1791–99) and served for a short while in the United States Senate, filling a vacancy on December 7, 1803, and resigning on June 7, 1804. In the latter year he became president of the first national bank organized in Virginia.

Venable died in a theater fire in Richmond; his ashes were buried along with those of the other fire victims under a stone in front of the altar in the Monumental Church in Richmond.

★★★★★

WADDEL, James: clergyman
Born Newry, Ireland, July 1739; son of Thomas Waddel; married Mary Gordon, 1768; father of ten children; died September 17, 1805.

Waddel arrived in America with his family in 1739. He attended the "Log College" of Samuel Finley in Nottingham, Pennsylvania. Later, in 1792, he received an honorary D.D. from Dickinson College.

After serving as a tutor at the "Log College," Waddel was licensed to preach by the Presbytery of Hanover, Virginia, in 1761. During the following year he served congregations in Northumberland and Lancaster counties in Virginia. He accepted a call from the Tinkling Spring congregation in Augusta County and served there in 1776–77, moving on to the Shenandoah Valley in 1778.

Waddel established a group of churches in Orange, Louisa, and Albemarle counties in Virginia. He died in Gordonsville, Virginia.

WALKER, David: congressman
Born Brunswick County, Virginia; died March 1, 1820.

Walker, who attended public and private schools, served as a private under General Lafayette during the Revolution and was present at the surrender of Cornwallis at Yorktown. After moving to Logan County, Kentucky, he became clerk of the county and circuit courts and served in the Kentucky House of Representatives from 1793 to 1796.

With the rank of major, Walker served on the staff of Governor Shelby of Kentucky in the Battle of Thames during the War of 1812. He was a Kentucky delegate to the United States House of Representatives from 1817 to 1820. He died in Washington, D.C., and was buried in the Congressional Cemetery.

WALKER, Francis: congressman

Born at the estate "Castle Hill," near Cobham, Albemarle County, Virginia, June 22, 1764; died March 1806.

Walker served as a magistrate of Albemarle County and as a colonel in the 88th Regiment of the Virginia militia. He attended the Virginia House of Delegates from 1788 to 1791 and from 1797 to 1801 and was sent to the United States House of Representatives from Virginia for the 3d Congress (1793–95). He died at "Castle Hill" and was buried in a family cemetery there.

WALKER, George: senator, lawyer

Born Culpeper County, Virginia, 1763; died 1819.

After attending common schools, Walker studied law. He served under Generals Greene and Morgan during the Revolution (1780–81) and was later admitted to the bar, establishing a law practice in Nicholasville, Kentucky, in 1799. A commissioner of the Kentucky River Company in 1801, he served in the Kentucky Senate from 1810 to 1814 and filled a vacant Kentucky seat in the United States Senate from August 30 to December 16, 1814. He died in Nicholasville and was buried on his nearby estate.

WALKER, Thomas: army officer, explorer

Born King and Queen County, Virginia, January 25, 1715; son of Thomas and Susanna (Peachy) Walker; married Mildred (Thornton) Meriwether, 1741; second marriage to Elizabeth Thornton, after 1778; father of twelve children (including Francis and John); died November 9, 1794.

Walker, who had studied medicine under his uncle, Dr. George Gilmer, in Williams-burg, Virginia, was chief agent of the Loyal Land Company in 1749. He held a number of legislative posts and appointments, including member of the Virginia House of Burgesses and deputy surveyor of Augusta County, Virginia, in 1752; commissary general to the Virginia militia in 1755; and member of the Virginia House of Burgesses from Hampshire County from 1756 to 1761 and from Albemarle County in 1761.

Walker was a commissioner selling lots in Charlottesville in 1763. He signed the Non-Importation Agreement in 1769 and became a member of the Virginia Committee of Safety in 1776. He served on Virginia's Executive Council in 1776, as a member of the Virginia Council in 1779, and on a committee to vindicate Virginia's claim to western lands.

Walker died at the estate "Castle Hill," in Albemarle County, Virginia.

WASHINGTON, Bushrod: associate justice of the United States Supreme Court

Born Westmoreland County, Virginia, June 5, 1762; son of John Augustine and Hannah (Bushrod) Washington; married Julia Ann Blackburn, 1785; no children; died November 26, 1829.

A nephew of George Washington, Bushrod Washington was a graduate of the College of William and Mary in 1778 and served as a private in the Revolutionary War. He was admitted to the Virginia bar and in 1787 was a member of the Virginia House of Delegates and a member of the Virginia Convention to ratify the United States Constitution.

Washington served as associate justice of the United States Supreme Court from 1798 until his death. He rendered a majority opinion in *Marine Insurance Company vs. Tucker,* 1806; *Eliason vs. Henshaw,* 1819; *Dartmouth College vs. Woodward,* 1819; *Green vs. Biddle,* 1823; *Thornton vs. Wynn,* 1827; *Ogden vs. Saunders,* 1827; *Buckner vs. Finley,* 1829; and *United States vs. Bright.*

Washington became the first president of

the American Colonization Society in 1816. Executor of his uncle George Washington's will, he inherited "Mount Vernon," the President's estate in Virginia. He died in Philadelphia and was buried at "Mount Vernon."

WASHINGTON, George: first President of the United States

Born Bridges Creek, Westmoreland County, Virginia, February 22, 1732; son of Augustine and Mary (Ball) Washington; married Mrs. Martha (Dandridge) Custis, January 6, 1759; father of two stepchildren; died December 14, 1799.

When he was sixteen, Washington, who had been educated privately, aided in the survey of the Shenandoah Valley in Virginia; the following year he was appointed county surveyor for Culpeper County, Virginia. He inherited his estate "Mount Vernon" from his half-brother, Lawrence, in 1752.

Washington was appointed district adjutant for Southern Virginia in 1752 by Governor Robert Dinwiddie, who also had him carry an ultimatum to the French to leave English lands in the Ohio country in 1753; an unconciliatory reply was received. He was also instructed to strengthen ties with the Six Nations, and his report to Dinwiddie was printed as the *Journal of Major George Washington* in 1754.

Commissioned a lieutenant colonel in the Virginia militia in 1754, Washington recommended the establishment of a post on the site of what is now Pittsburgh, but found the French entrenched there. He erected Fort Necessity at Great Meadow, Pennsylvania, and surprised and defeated a French force on May 27, 1754, obtaining generous terms in a parley with the French after a ten-hour battle on July 3, 1754. He served in the unsuccessful expedition under General Braddock against Fort Duquesne in 1755 and was appointed colonel and commander-in-chief of all Virginia forces that year. He was responsible for defending three hundred miles

of mountainous frontier with about three hundred men from 1755 to 1758. He accompanied the British under General Forbes, who occupied Fort Duquesne in 1758, and then resigned and became a gentleman farmer at "Mount Vernon" in 1759.

Washington was a contributor to educational institutions, including Washington College in Maryland and Liberty Hall in Lexington, Virginia. He urged the establishment of a national university in the nation's capital and provided an endowment for it in his will.

Washington attended the Virginia House of Burgesses from 1759 to 1774, also serving as justice of Fairfax County, Virginia. He was a leader of colonial opposition to British policies in America and acted as chairman of a meeting in Alexandria which adopted the Fairfax Resolutions on July 18, 1774. A member of the Continental Congress from Virginia in 1774–75, he served on a committee for drafting army regulations and planning the defense of New York City.

Elected commander-in-chief of the Continental Army on June 15, 1775, Washington took command at Cambridge, Massachusetts, on July 3 of that year. He forced the British evacuation of Boston on May 17, 1776, but was defeated at the Battle of Long Island in 1776. He made a Christmas-night crossing of the Delaware River and crushed the Hessians at the Battle of Trenton on December 26, 1776, thus dislocating the entire line of British posts along the river. He then won the Battle of Princeton, forcing the British to retire to Brunswick, New Jersey.

Although he sought the full cooperation of Congress in developing a regular Continental Army, Washington still was forced to rely on the militia to fill his ranks. He was defeated at the Battle of Brandywine on September 11, 1777, and lost the Battle of Germantown, October 3–4, 1777. He endured the hardships of the Valley Forge winter of 1777–78 with the Continental Army, after which the army emerged better trained and heartened by the French alliance of 1778.

Washington overtook the British at Monmouth, New Jersey, in 1778 and with the aid of the French under de Grasse and Rochambeau directed the siege of Yorktown, Virginia, which was brought to a successful conclusion on October 19, 1781. He held the army together until the British evacuated New York City on April 19, 1783. He bade his officers farewell at Fraunces Tavern in New York City on December 4, 1783, resigning his commission December 23. He then retired to "Mount Vernon."

Washington held a meeting at his estate on navigation rights on the Potomac River in 1785 which indirectly led to the United States Constitutional Convention. He served as president of the Constitutional Convention in Philadelphia in 1787 and was unanimously elected the first President of the United States under the new Constitution in 1788. He took the oath of office on the balcony of the United States Building in New York City (the site of the Washington statue, at the old Sub-Treasury Building), April 30, 1789.

Unopposed for reelection in 1792, Washington stated America's position regarding the French Revolutionary War in his Proclamation of Neutrality (issued in 1793). He was a strong nationalist and demonstrated the power of the United States Government by crushing the Indians and suppressing the Whiskey Rebellion. He firmly fixed governmental credit through Alexander Hamilton's policies. He felt it desirable for the United States to increase to a size befitting a world power. He backed the Pinckney Treaty with Spain and the Jay Treaty with Great Britain (1795), although he found neither to be completely satisfactory.

During his administration, certain fundamental patterns of American politics developed, including the formation of political parties (which he opposed), the establishment of basic functions and rights of the different branches of government (such as the method of treaty ratification and presidential consent for the use of executive documents in Congress), and the institutionalization of certain forms of patronage (such as having each major section of the country represented in the cabinet).

Washington gave his farewell address September 1796. He served as lieutenant general and commander-in-chief of the United States Army (raised in expectation of war with France) in 1798–99. He died at "Mount Vernon" and was buried there.

WASHINGTON, Martha Dandridge Custis: first lady of the United States
Born New Kent County, Virginia, June 2, 1732; married Daniel Parke Custis, 1749; mother of Martha (died at age seventeen), Colonel John Parke (died 1781), and two others who died in infancy; second marriage to George Washington, January 6, 1759; died 1802.

Characterized as "the prettiest and richest widow in Virginia" after Custis's death in 1757, Martha Custis married George Washington two years later. She managed Washington's plantations in his absence; visited him at Valley Forge, Newburgh, and other camps; and was a gracious hostess at official functions at the Washington mansion in New York City during her husband's Presidency. Mrs. Washington died three years after the death of her husband and was buried at "Mount Vernon."

WETZEL, Lewis: Indian fighter
Born probably Lancaster County, Pennsylvania, 1764; son of John and Mary (Bannett) Wetzel; died 1808.

Wetzel, who fought in the first siege at Wheeling, Virginia (now West Virginia), in 1777, served in several expeditions against the Indians in Ohio, notably against the Indian village on the site of the present town of Coshocton, Ohio, in 1781. Employed as a scout, he waylaid and killed a prominent Indian during negotiations with Ohio tribes at Fort Harmar; he escaped trial and punishment for the murder.

Wetzel County, Virginia (now West Virginia), is named for him. He died near Natchez, Tennessee.

WHITE, Alexander: congressman

Born Frederick County, Virginia, circa 1738; son of Robert and Margaret (Hoge) White; married Elizabeth Wood; second marriage to Sarah Hite; died September 19, 1804.

White attended the University of Edinburgh (Scotland) and studied at the Inner Temple and Gray's Inn in London in 1762–63. He became a member of the Virginia House of Burgesses from Hampshire County in 1772 and served as a member of the Virginia Assembly from 1782 to 1786 and again in 1788. The dominant leader of the Federalists in northwestern Virginia in 1788, he was a delegate to the Virginia Convention to ratify the United States Constitution that year.

White was elected to the United States House of Representatives from Virginia for the 1st–2nd congresses (1789–93) and was a member of the commission to lay out the new capital, Washington, D.C., from 1795 to 1802. He served in the Virginia Assembly from 1799 to 1801. He died in Frederick County and was buried at "Woodville," near Winchester, Virginia.

WICKHAM, John: lawyer

Born Southold, Long Island, New York, June 6, 1763; son of John and Hannah (Fanning) Wickham; married Mary Smith Fanning, December 24, 1791; second marriage to Elizabeth Selden McClurg; father of many children (including at least two sons); died January 22, 1839.

Wickham attended military school in Arras, France, and later studied law in Williamsburg, Virginia. After moving to Richmond, Virginia, in 1790, he was counsel for a British creditor in the case of *Ware vs. Hylton* (1793), in which he successfully contended that the Treaty of 1783 made the states responsible for debts incurred before the American Revolution. (The opposing lawyer in the case was John Marshall.) Wickham successfully defended Aaron Burr in his trial for treason in 1807.

WOODFORD, William: army officer

Born Caroline County, Virginia, October 6, 1734; son of Major William and Anne (Cocke) Woodford; married Mary Thornton, June 26, 1762; father of two children; died November 13, 1780.

Circa 1756–63 Woodford served as justice of the peace of Caroline County. In 1774 he was elected to the Committee of Correspondence of Caroline County, and in 1775 he sat as an alternate to Edmund Pendleton in the Virginia Convention. Also in 1775, as a colonel in the 3rd Virginia Regiment of the Continental Army, he defeated a British force of three hundred.

The Continental Congress made Woodford a colonel in the 2nd Virginia Regiment in 1776; he was commissioned a brigadier general in 1777. He fought at the battles of Brandywine, Germantown and Monmouth. At Washington's order, he relieved Charleston, South Carolina, in 1779; he besieged the British with seven hundred troops in 1780 but was made a prisoner when Clinton took the city. He was then taken to New York City.

Woodford County, Kentucky, is named for him. He died in New York City at age forty-six and was buried in Old Trinity Churchyard there.

WYTHE, George: jurist, Continental congressman

Born Elizabeth City County, Virginia, 1726; son of Thomas and Margaret (Walker) Wythe; married Ann Lewis, December 1747; second marriage to Elizabeth Taliaferro, 1755; father of one child; died June 8, 1806.

Having attended the College of William and Mary, Wythe studied law under Stephen Dewey in Prince George County, Virginia, and was admitted to the Virginia bar in 1746. He practiced law with John Lewis in Spotsylvania County, Virginia. In the absence of Peyton Randolph, he served as attorney general of Virginia in 1754. He was a member of the Virginia House of Burgesses in 1754–55 and from 1758 to 1768. The latter year he became mayor of Williamsburg. Again in the House of Burgesses from 1769 to 1775, he acted as clerk.

Wythe was a member of the Continental Congress in 1775–76 and signed the Declaration of Independence in 1776. He was speaker of the Virginia House of Delegates in 1777 and sat as judge of the Virginia High Court of Chancery in 1778. With Edmund Pendleton and Thomas Jefferson he revised the laws of Virginia in 1779. At the College of William and Mary in the same year he taught as professor of law and police, the first chair of law in America. He was also a member of the board of visitors.

As an ex officio member of the Virginia Supreme Court of Appeals in 1782, Wythe delivered the opinion in *Commonwealth vs. Caton.* He was a member of the Virginia Convention to ratify the United States Constitution in 1788. In 1790 he founded a small law school and in 1795 wrote *Decisions of Cases in Virginia.* He emancipated his Negro servants in his will.

Wythe was poisoned, along with a servant, by his grandnephew, George Wythe Sweeney, who hoped to gain his inheritance; however, he lived long enough to disinherit the grandnephew. He died at age eighty in Richmond and was buried in St. John's Churchyard there.

★★★★★★★★★★★★★★

FRONTIERSMEN AND FOREIGN NATIONALS

"A few days ago returned to New York from the eastward, Mr. William Goddard, who has been indefatigable in soliciting the establishment of post-offices on constitutional principles, in which he has at last succeeded."
NEW-YORK JOURNAL, June 15, 1775

BAILEY, Ann: frontier woman
Born Liverpool, England, 1742; daughter of Mr. Hennis; married Richard Trotter, circa 1762; second marriage to John Bailey, circa 1776; mother of one son; died November 22, 1825.

Bailey came to America in 1761 and married soon afterward. After her first husband was killed in a battle with Indians at Point Pleasant, Virginia, in 1774, she became a scout. Skilled in frontier life, she was known as the White Squaw of the Kanawha. Later, in 1791, when Fort Lee (which is near the present Charleston, West Virginia) was under siege by the Indians, she rode a hundred miles to Fort Lewis for gunpowder. After the death of her second husband she lived with her son in Gallia County, Ohio, where she died.

BANCROFT, Edward: inventor, British agent
Born Westfield, Massachusetts, January 9, 1744; died September 8, 1821.

Although Bancroft received no formal education, he went to England circa 1770 and became a contributor of articles on America to the *Monthly Review.* He became acquainted with Benjamin Franklin in London and served as an agent for him at the outbreak of the American Revolution. He served as an agent for American commissioner Silas Deane in France while in the pay of the British Government until 1783. He gave the British Government information regarding treaties and movements of troops and ships from France to America during the Revolution.

Bancroft lived in England after 1783 and invented dyes for use in textile manufacturing. He was a member of the Royal Society. He had written *Essay on the Natural History of Guiana* in 1769, and wrote *Experimental Researches Concerning the Philosophy of Permanent Colors* in 1794. He died in Margate, England, and was buried there.

BRANT, Joseph: Indian chief
Born Ohio River banks, 1742; died November 24, 1807.

Brant, whose Indian name was Thayendanegea, was educated at Moor's Charity School in Lebanon, Connecticut, and later became an Anglican convert. In 1774 he was secretary to the superintendent of Indian affairs and served as a captain in the British Army during the American Revolution. For many years chief of the Mohawk Indians, he directed the Cherry Valley massacre of 1778.

Brant had the distinction of being painted by Romney in his Mohawk regalia and was presented at court in England in 1785. The following year he built the first Episcopal Church erected in upper Canada. The King of England gave him an estate at the head of Lake Ontario. He died in Wellington Square, Canada.

★★★★★

CERRÉ, Jean Gabriel: merchant
Born Montreal, Quebec, Canada, August 23, 1734; son of Joseph and Marie (Picard) Cerré; married Catherine Giard, 1764; father of four children (including Marie Therese [Cerré] Chouteau); died April 4, 1805.

Cerré was a fur trader in Kaskaskia, Illinois, for twenty-four years (1755–79). He sent the first organized parties of hunters into the Missouri River country. He became one of the richest men in the Illinois area and gave money and provisions to George Rogers Clark and his men during the American Revolution. He moved to St. Louis, Missouri, in 1779 and became a member of the 1st Company of the St. Louis militia the following year. He was a founder of New Madrid in Spanish Louisiana (now Missouri) in 1780.

CHOUTEAU, Jean Pierre: fur trader, Indian agent
Born New Orleans, Louisiana, October 10, 1758; son of René Auguste and Marie Thérèse (Bourgeois) Chouteau; married Pelagie Kiersereau, July 26, 1783; second marriage to Brigitte Saucier, February 17, 1794; father of nine sons (including Auguste Pierre and Jean Pierre); died July 10, 1849.

Chouteau was stationed with the Osage Indians as commandant of Fort Carondele from 1794 to 1802. He established the first permanent white settlement (now Salina) in Oklahoma in 1796. After serving as United States agent for the Osage Indians in 1803, he became a founder of the St. Louis (Missouri) Fur Company (1809). He died near St. Louis.

CHOUTEAU, René: trader
Born New Orleans, Louisiana, September 7, 1749; son of René Auguste and Marie Thérèse (Bourgeois) Chouteau; married Marie Cerré, September 26, 1786; died February 24, 1829.

Chouteau accompanied the expedition of Pierre Laclede, his stepfather, in the founding of St. Louis in 1763. After acting as assistant to Laclede in various trading enterprises, he took over the business after Laclede's death in 1778. Chouteau obtained a monopoly on the Osage Indian trade near the Osage River in Missouri in 1794.

In 1804 Chouteau was appointed one of the first justices of the Court of the Louisiana Territory. Four years later he served as a colonel in the St. Louis militia. While a trader living in St. Louis after 1808, Chouteau served briefly as a federal pension agent for the Missouri Territory (1819–20). He died in St. Louis, where he was buried.

CLARK, George Rogers: army officer
Born near Charlottesville, Virginia, November 19, 1752; son of John and Ann (Rogers) Clark; died February 13, 1818.

Clark's military activities were preceded by minor exploring attempts on the Ohio River in 1772. He served as a captain in the Virginia militia in Dunmore's War, 1774. While a surveyor in Kentucky, he was the leader of the frontier defense against the British-supported Indian raids of 1776–77.

Clark set out to conquer Illinois, a mission largely under the auspices of Governor Patrick Henry of Virginia. He captured three key points, Kaskaskia, Cahokia, and Vincennes, and thus assured colonial control of both Kentucky and Illinois. Commissioned a brigadier general in the Virginia militia, from 1779 to 1783 he engaged in several battles and expeditions to protect the Northwest region.

Clark was a member of the board of commissioners which supervised the allotment of lands in the Illinois grant, and served on the commission making a treaty with the Indians of the Northwest. He set out on a retaliatory expedition against the Wabash tribe in 1786, a venture which was not wholly successful. Clark's political and economic fortunes declined toward the end of his life.

Clark was the author of *Memoir* in 1791. He died in Louisville, Kentucky, and was buried in Cave Hill Cemetery in Louisville. A memorial to him was erected in Vincennes, Indiana, by the United States Government in 1928.

CERACCHI, Guiseppe: sculptor
Born Rome, Italy, July 4, 1751; died January 30, 1802.

After studying under Tomaso Righi, Ceracchi went to England (1775) and soon became well known in London. After sculpting a bust of Sir Joshua Reynolds, he came to America in 1789 and attempted a statue entitled *Liberty*. The United States Congress refused to back it financially because of its expense. He did various busts, including Washington, Hamilton, and John Paul Jones, but he became discouraged by what he considered a lack of appreciation and went to France. There he joined a conspiracy against Napoleon Bonaparte, was captured, and died on the guillotine in Paris.

CONWAY, Thomas: army officer
Born Ireland, February 27, 1735; died 1800.

Conway was commissioned a brigadier general in the Continental Army on May 13, 1777. He was recommended for promotion to major general but was opposed by George Washington. As a result, Conway resigned; however, his resignation was not accepted, and he did become major general and inspector general on December 14, 1777. After serving in the battles of Germantown and Brandywine in 1777, he was an organizer of the Conway Cabal, a plot to replace General Washington with General Horatio Gates in 1778. This led to Conway's resignation from the Continental Army in 1778. He was badly wounded in a duel with General Cadwalader on July 4 of the same year.

Conway became governor general of the French possessions in India in 1787. He was named commander of the Order of St. Louis that year and given the name Count de Conway.

COOPER, Ezekiel: clergyman
Born Caroline County, Maryland, February 22, 1763; son of Richard and Ann Cooper; died February 21, 1847.

Cooper was admitted on trial to the ministry of the Methodist Church in 1785 and was ordained a deacon three years later. He served as pastor in several cities, including Long Island, New York; East Jersey and Trenton, New Jersey; Baltimore and Annapolis, Maryland; Alexandria, Virginia; Boston; New York City; Brooklyn; Philadelphia; and Wilmington, Delaware.

Cooper was an agent of the Methodist Book Concern from 1799 to 1808. He had previously (1790–91) written letters printed in the *Maryland Gazette*, the *Virginia Gazette*, and the *Maryland Journal* in which he advocated the abolition of slavery. He was also the author of *A Funeral Discourse on the Death of That Eminent Man, the Late John Dickins* (1799) and *The Substance of a Funeral Discourse . . . on the Death of the Reverend Francis Asbury* (1819).

CORNSTALK: Indian chief
Born Pennsylvania, 1720; died 1777.

Cornstalk, whose Indian name was Keigh-tugh-gua, was a Shawnee Indian chief and an ally of the French. He made his first attack on English settlers in Rockbridge County, Virginia, in 1759. An ally of Pontiac in 1763, he was taken hostage along with his brother Silver Heels and released on parole. He remained at peace with the settlers during the border skirmishes from 1764 to 1774.

FRONTIERSMEN AND FOREIGN NATIONALS

After he objected to authorities because his brother was maliciously shot and wounded, Lord Dunmore (then governor of Virginia) decided to settle the matter by force, beginning Lord Dunmore's War of 1764. This was ended by the Treaty of Camp Charlotte later the same year.

After being taken hostage at Fort Pitt while on a mission to warn settlers of an impending Shawnee uprising, Cornstalk was put to death along with other hostages in reprisal for the murder of a white soldier by a band of Indians.

★★★★★

De LANGLADE, Charles Michel: army officer

Born Mackinac, Canada, May 1729; son of Augustin Monet and Domitelle (an Ottawa Indian) De Langlade; married Charlotte Bourassa, 1754; father of several children; died 1801.

De Langlade was commissioned a cadet in the French Colonial Army in 1750, rising to ensign in 1755 and to lieutenant in 1760. He led the Indian allies in the battles at Lake Champlain, Fort William Henry, Quebec, and Montreal during the French and Indian War. In 1760 he became a British subject. As a captain in the British Army, he led the Indian auxiliaries against Colonel George Rogers Clark during the American Revolution. He was granted lands in Canada for his services to England. He died in Green Bay, Wisconsin.

De TOUSARD, A. Louis: army officer, diplomat

Born Paris, France, March 12, 1749; son of General Charles Germain and Antoinette de Poitevin (de la Croix) de Tousard; married Maria Francisca Joubert, January 1788; second marriage to Anna Maria Geddes, 1795; died May 8, 1817.

After graduating from Artillery School in Strasbourg, France, in 1769, de Tousard was commissioned a second lieutenant in the Royal Artillery Corps of the French Army. He arrived in Portsmouth, New Hampshire, in 1777 and took part in the battles of Brandywine and Germantown. He was brevetted a lieutenant colonel by Congress and voted a life pension for gallantry in 1778. He was decorated as chevalier of St. Louis, France, in 1779. The following year he was commissioned a major in the Provincial Regiment of Toul, France, and a lieutenant colonel of the Regiment du Cap in 1784.

De Tousard went to Santo Domingo in 1784, where he served with distinction against the Negro revolt. However, he was accused of possessing counterrevolutionary sentiments and resisting orders in 1792, and was arrested and sent to prison in France. He was released in 1793 and returned to the United States. He was reinstated in the United States Army in 1795 and was commissioned a major and then a colonel in the 2nd Artillery in 1800. He was promoted to inspector of the artillery that same year. He returned to Santo Domingo, and then to France in 1802.

In 1805 de Tousard was sent to America in charge of commercial relations at New Orleans. He moved to Philadelphia as vice consul, but was ordered to New Orleans as consul ad interim, 1811–16. He died in Paris.

DICKINS, John: clergyman

Born London, England, August 31, 1747; married Elizabeth Yancey; died September 27, 1798.

Dickins came to America circa 1770 and was converted to Methodism in 1774. He was an evangelist in North Carolina and Virginia from 1774 to 1781, having been admitted to the itinerant ministry in 1777. He was pastor of the John Street Church in New York City from 1783 to 1789, also serving the Bertie Circuit in North Carolina in 1785. He attended the Christmas Conference in Baltimore in 1784, which organized the Methodist Episcopal Church in America. He was ordained a deacon in 1784 and an elder in 1787. He attended the Conference of 1789.

Dickins may have financed the first *Methodist Book of Concern* in 1789. He was book steward from 1789 to 1798 and publisher of the *Arminian Magazine* (1789–90) and of the *Methodist Magazine* (1797–98). He was pastor of St. George's Church in Philadelphia circa 1789 to 1798. He died during the yellow fever epidemic in Philadelphia.

DUNBAR, William: planter, scientist
Born Elgin, Scotland, 1749; son of Sir Archibald Dunbar; father of seven children; died October 1810.

After arriving at Fort Pitt, Dunbar traded with the Indians from 1771 to 1773. He then became a partner with John Ross in a plantation in West Florida and founded a second plantation near Natchez, Mississippi, in 1792. In 1798 he was surveyor general of the District of Natchez, and the following year he conducted the first meteorological observations in the Mississippi Valley. He was a member of the American Philosophical Society and was delegated to explore the Hot Springs, Arkansas, area in 1804, and the Red River area in 1805.

Besides being a member of the territorial legislature in Mississippi, Dunbar also served as chief justice of the Court of Quarter Sessions. He was a contributor of numerous articles on natural and physical science to various journals, including the *Journal of the American Philosophical Society*. He died at "The Forest," near Natchez.

★★★★★

FARRAGUT, George: naval officer, army officer
Born Ciudadela, Minorca, September 29, 1755; son of Anthony and Juana (Mesquida) Farragut; married Elizabeth Shine, 1795; father of five children (including David Glasgow and William A. C.); died June 4, 1817.

Farragut began a long career on the sea when he joined the British merchant marine at the age of ten, sailing in the Mediterranean until he was seventeen. He then became a mariner in the American seas, trading chiefly between Havana, Cuba, and Veracruz, Mexico.

In 1776, when he was nearly twenty-one, Farragut came to America, where he joined the colonial cause as a lieutenant on a privateer. Two years later he was commissioned a first lieutenant in the South Carolina Navy. He served in the defense of Savannah, Georgia, in 1779, and during the siege of Charleston, South Carolina, in 1780. A volunteer for General Marion during the Battle of Cowpens (1780), he also served in the North Carolina Volunteer Artillery Company in the Battle of Beaufort Bridge. He then became captain of a cavalry troop which he had raised.

Following the Revolutionary War, Farragut served in the American merchant marine from 1783 to 1792. After becoming a sailing master in the United States Navy in 1807, he served as sailing master of an expedition dispatched by Governor William C. C. Claiborne of Louisiana to take from Spain the disputed Gulf Coast of Mississippi and the Louisiana Territory. He accompanied Andrew Jackson, his personal friend, on the 1813–14 Indian campaigns. He resigned from the United States Navy in 1814 and died three years later in Point Plaguet, Mississippi.

FIELD, Robert: painter, engraver
Born Gloucestershire, England, circa 1769; died August 9, 1819.

Field studied at the Royal Academy School in London before coming to the United States in 1794. He is famous for having engraved portraits of George Washington and Alexander Hamilton, as well as having painted an oil portrait of Martha Washington. In 1808 he moved to Halifax, Nova Scotia, and eight years later he went to Jamaica, British West Indies, where he died.

★★★★★

GIRTY, Simon: renegade
Born Pennsylvania, 1741; son of Simon and Mary (Newton) Girty; married Catharine Malott, 1784; died February 18, 1818.

Girty was held captive by Indians from

1756 until 1759; he then served as an interpreter at Fort Pitt, Pennsylvania, from 1759 to 1774. After a period as a scout in Lord Dunmore's War (1774–75), he was employed as an interpreter by the Continental Congress in 1776. Two years later he deserted and became an interpreter for the British at Fort Detroit, leading many Indian attacks on American settlers and gaining notoriety for the cruel tortures he and his Indian friends inflicted on their American victims.

Girty received a pension from the British and settled on a farm near Amherstburg, Ontario, in 1781. He continued to incite Indians to attack American settlers and led the Indians in their defeat of General Arthur St. Clair in 1791 and at the Battle of Fallen Timbers in 1794. He died in Amherstburg.

GIST, Christopher: explorer
Born Maryland, circa 1706; son of Richard and Zipporah (Murray) Gist; married Sarah Howard; father of five children; died 1759.

Having learned surveying from his father, Gist started from Cumberland, Maryland, in 1750 to explore the territory near the Ohio River for the Ohio Company. He passed through what is now Pittsburgh and explored as far as the mouth of the Scioto River. Then, exploring the country south of the Ohio River in 1752, he became the first American to explore southern Ohio and northeastern Kentucky from the Monongahela River to the Great Kanawha River.

In 1753 Gist started with George Washington on a journey to Fort Duquesne and twice saved Washington's life during their travels. He was with Washington at the surrender of Fort Necessity (near the present Uniontown, Pennsylvania) in 1754. After serving as a guide to General Braddock during the campaign of 1755, from 1756 to 1758 he was an Indian agent in what is now eastern Tennessee. It is believed that he died in Georgia.

GODDARD, William: printer, journalist
Born New London, Connecticut, 1740; son of Dr. Giles and Sarah (Updike) Goddard; married Abigail Angell, May 25, 1785; died December 23, 1817.

After an apprenticeship in 1755 to printer John Holt in New Haven, Connecticut, Goddard moved to James Parker's plant in New York City. He became a journeyman in New York City in 1761 and opened a printing office in Providence, Rhode Island, the next year. In 1762 he also founded the *Providence Gazette* and the *Country Journal* but suspended the latter owing to lack of support three years later. He was a partner with John Carter (an associate of Benjamin Franklin) in the years 1767–78.

Goddard published the *Constitutional Courant* in Woodbridge, New Jersey, in 1765. The following year he left his mother in charge of the *Providence Gazette* and went to Philadelphia to open a printery in partnership with Joseph Galloway and Thomas Wharton. From 1767 to 1774 he published the *Pennsylvania Chronicle and Universal Adviser,* at first with partners and then alone. He founded the *Maryland Journal and Baltimore Adviser* in Baltimore in 1773. During this time, he established an independent postal system which was later taken over by the Continental Congress. In 1793 he retired to Johnston, Rhode Island.

GRATIOT, Charles: fur trader
Born Lausanne, Switzerland, 1752; son of David and Marie (Bernard) Gratiot; married Victoire Chouteau, June 25, 1781; father of at least one son (Charles); died April 20, 1817.

Gratiot learned fur trading after coming to Montreal in 1769. In 1777 he joined the firm of David McCrae and Company and later in the year opened his own store in Cahokia, Illinois. He moved to St. Louis in 1781. In addition to working as a fur trader he operated a distillery, a tannery, and a salt works. The transfer of Upper Louisiana was made at his house in 1804.

Gratiot was the first presiding justice of

the Court of Quarter Sessions of St. Louis. He was elected a trustee when the town was incorporated in 1809. He was a close associate of George Rogers Clark.

★★★★★

HALLAM, Lewis: actor, theatrical manager
Born England, circa 1740; son of Lewis Hallam; no record of first marriage; second marriage to Miss Tuke, circa 1793; father of three children (including Mirvan); died November 1, 1808.

At the age of twelve, Hallam came to America with his parents, who were touring with an acting company, and made his first appearance on stage in *The Merchant of Venice,* Williamsburg, Virginia; he fled from the stage when he forgot his only line. He continued to travel with the company, however, playing in New York City and Philadelphia from 1752 to 1754 and in Jamaica from 1754 to 1758. When he returned to America, in 1758, he was the leading man of the company.

In 1775 Hallam sailed for England and appeared in Covent Garden, in London. He then returned to America as sole owner of the company, remaining in that position from the end of the Revolutionary War until 1797, when he became an actor in the company again. He died in Philadelphia.

HARDIN, John: army officer, Indian fighter
Born Fauquier County, Virginia, October 1, 1753; son of Martin Hardin; married Jane Davies, before 1786; father of at least one son (Martin D.); died April 1792.

An ensign in Dunmore's Indian campaign in 1774, Hardin served with Daniel Morgan's Riflemen at Saratoga during the Revolutionary War. He was a lieutenant colonel in the Kentucky militia in the Wabash expeditions led by George Rogers Clark in 1786. He then served with every American expedition into the Kentucky Indian territory except that of General Arthur St. Clair. He fought the Indians in western Pennsylvania from 1786 to 1792. He was colonel in charge of the Nelson County (Kentucky) militia in

1788 and 1789; he was then commissioned a brigadier general in the Kentucky militia.

Hardin County, Ohio, formed in 1792, was named in his honor, as was Hardin County, Kentucky. He was killed by Indians while on a peace mission to the Miami tribes in Hardin County, Ohio.

HARROD, James: frontiersman
Born Bedford County, Pennsylvania, 1742; married Anne; father of one daughter; died July 1793.

Harrod served until 1763 with General Forbes's forces in Pennsylvania during the French and Indian War. Ten years later he explored along the Ohio River as far as the site of present-day Louisville, Kentucky. In 1774 he founded the first settlement in Kentucky (which later became Harrodsburg) and lived there for the remainder of his life. In 1777, as a leader in the resistance to Indian attacks, he organized expeditions and participated in the Bowman expedition against Chillicothe. He was a member of George Rogers Clark's expedition to the Shawnee Territory in 1782.

Harrod served in the Virginia legislature in 1779. He is believed to have been murdered on an exploring expedition in Kentucky.

HECKEWELDER, John Gottlieb Ernestus: missionary
Born Bedford, England, March 12, 1743; son of the Reverend David Heckewelder; married Sarah Ohneberg, 1780; died January 31, 1823.

Heckewelder came to the United States in 1754. Between 1763 and 1777 he was occasionally dispatched as a messenger to the Indian settlement in Wyalusing, Pennsylvania, and to an Indian town on the west branch of the Susquehanna River, learning various Indian customs and languages. He began a regular mission service with the Moravian Christian Indians and guided them from the Susquehanna to Schoenbrunn and Gnadenhütten on the Muskingum River in Ohio in 1771.

In 1781 Heckewelder was captured by the

British and accused of being an American spy; however, he was later released to continue his missionary work. He was a member of the committee which arranged a peace treaty at Vincennes, Indiana, in 1792. He administered to the Indian "estate" on the Muskingum from 1801 to 1810. His writings include *Account of the History, Manners and Customs of the Indian Nations Who Once Inhabited Pennsylvania and the Neighboring States.* He died in Bethlehem, Pennsylvania.

HENRY, Alexander: fur trader

Born New Brunswick, New Jersey, August 1739; married the widow of John Kittson; father of four children (including William and Alexander); died April 4, 1824.

From 1760 to 1763, Henry was a merchant, trading between Albany, New York, and Michilimackinac (now Mackinac), Michigan. In 1763 he was captured by the Indians during the Pontiac Conspiracy but was saved by the French commandant at Michilimackinac. From 1764 to 1776 he was a fur trader in the Lake Superior area, during which time he discovered copper in the region. He went as far west as Saskatchewan in his fur trading expeditions.

After 1776 Henry lived in Montreal, Canada, where he served for a time as a captain in the militia. He was a charter member of the Beaver Club, an organization of men who had been fur traders in the old Northwest, in 1786. He wrote *Travels and Adventures of Alexander Henry* in 1809. He died in Montreal.

HENRY, John: actor, theatrical manager

Born Dublin, Ireland, circa 1746; married Maria Storer; died October 1794.

After his education at Trinity College in Dublin, Henry made his acting debut at Drury Lane in London in 1762; his American debut was at Southwark Theatre in Philadelphia on October 6, 1767. He adapted "The School for Soldiers; Or, The Deserter" for the Old American Company in 1782. From 1785 to 1791, in partnership with Lewis Hallam, he gained a monopoly in the American theater from New York to Annapolis, this despite the conflicting natures of the partners. Henry is considered one of the most accomplished performers of the early American theater. He died at sea.

HUTCHINS, Thomas: military engineer, geographer

Born Monmouth County, New Jersey, 1730; died April 28, 1789.

For two years (1757–59) Hutchins served as an officer in the Pennsylvania colonial militia. He was also the engineer at the military installations at Fort Pitt and at Pensacola, Florida. In 1772 he was elected to the American Philosophical Society.

Because of his refusal of the rank of major in a British regiment during the Revolutionary War, Hutchins was charged with treason and imprisoned by the British Government in 1779; he was released from jail the following year. He went to France, where he was recommended to Congress by Benjamin Franklin. In May 1781 he was appointed geographer of the Southern Army under General Greene; the title was changed to geographer to the United States in July of that year. In 1783 he was appointed to determine the boundary between Virginia and Pennsylvania. From 1785 to 1789 he was geographer in charge of surveying the western lands ceded by the states to Congress.

★★★★★

IMLAY, Gilbert: adventurer

Born Monmouth County, New Jersey, circa 1754; lived with Mary Wollstonecraft; father of Fanny; died November 20, 1828.

Imlay served as a first lieutenant in the Continental Army during the American Revolution in 1777–78 and later became a captain. He bought land and moved to Kentucky, where he became a deputy surveyor and speculated on land. Financial difficulties forced him to leave the country. He became important in French political councils which advised taking Louisiana in the early 1790s.

Imlay was the author of *A Topographical Description of the Western Territory of North America*, 1792; *The Emigrants*, 1793; and *Observations du Cap. Imlay*. He died on the island of Jersey and was buried at St. Brelade's.

★★★★★

JONES, John Paul: naval officer
Born Kirkcudbrightshire, Scotland, July 6, 1747; son of John and Jean (Macduff) Paul; died July 18, 1792.

Jones, who adopted his last name in 1773, was the most famous American naval commander of the Revolutionary War. His career began in 1766, when he became first mate on the slave ship *Two Friends*. He commanded the merchant ship *John* on two voyages to the West Indies in 1769 and 1770. In 1773 he became master of the ship *Betsey of London*. In 1775 he was commissioned a lieutenant and later in the year became a senior first lieutenant in the first Continental Navy, being the first-ranking officer in a list chosen from the colonies south of Pennsylvania.

When Jones hoisted the flag of colonial America on board the *Alfred* in 1775, it was the first time the flag had been displayed. He commanded the ship *Providence* and later was chosen captain. In 1777 he commanded the sloop *Ranger;* later that year he distinguished himself by capturing the British warship *Drake* during a successful offensive cruise around the British Isles. This marked the first time that a British warship had ever surrendered to a Continental vessel. He then commanded the forty-gun French ship *Duras,* which was renamed the *Bonhomme Richard* in 1779. It was in this vessel that he defeated the British ship *Serapis* on September 23, 1779. In 1781 he received the Cross of the Institution of Military Merit, which entitled him to be called "Chevalier." The same year he was unanimously elected to command the *America*.

Congress presented Jones with the gold medal in 1787. From 1788 to 1790 he served as a rear admiral with the Russian Navy on the Black Sea. During this time he was decorated with the Order of St. Ann.

In 1790 Jones moved to Paris, where he died two years later. In 1905 his remains were brought to the United States and buried at the United States Naval Academy in Annapolis, Maryland. He is remembered for the saying attributed to him when asked by an enemy officer if he wished to surrender: "Sir, I have not yet begun to fight!"

JUNGMAN, John George: missionary
Born Hockenheim, Baden, April 19, 1720; son of Johann Jungman; married Anna Bechtel Bütner, August 24, 1745; died July 17, 1808.

Jungman came to Philadelphia in 1732 and took his first holy communion at the Moravian Community in Bethlehem, Pennsylvania, in 1743. From 1746 to 1754 he was a Moravian missionary at Guadenhüton on the Mahoning, and from 1754 until his retirement in 1785 he served at Christiansbrunn, Schoenbrunn on the Muskingum, Detroit, and other locations. During this period, in 1781, he was captured by the English and sent to Detroit. He died at the age of eighty-eight.

★★★★★

KALB, Johann: army officer
Born Huttendorf, Bavaria, June 29, 1721; son of Johan Leonhard and Margarethe Seitz (Putz) Kalb; married Anna Van Robais, April 10, 1764; died August 19, 1780.

Known as Baron de Kalb, in 1747 Kalb served under the name "Jean de Kalb" as a lieutenant in Count Loewendal's regiment of the French Infantry. He rose to captain and adjutant officer of detail later the same year. In 1756, during the Seven Years' War, he was commissioned a major.

In 1768 Kalb became a French secret agent in America. In 1776 he joined the patriot cause, acceding to the rank of major general in the Continental Army and serving with Washington at Valley Forge. In 1780 he joined General Gates near Camden, South Carolina, and their combined forces attacked the British under Cornwallis and Rawdon in August; he died on the nineteenth of the month of a wound received in that battle.

KENTON, Simon: Indian fighter

Born Culpeper (now Fauquier) County, Virginia, April 3, 1755; son of Mark and Mary (Miller) Kenton; married Martha Dowden, February 15, 1787; second marriage to Elizabeth Jarboe, March 27, 1798; died April 29, 1836.

Kenton served as a scout in Lord Dunmore's War in 1774. Having been appointed a scout by Daniel Boone, he was a leading participant in encounters with Indians around Kentucky and Illinois. He helped to quell Indian riots in the Illinois region during the Revolutionary War (1777). As captain of a volunteer company, he helped drive the British and the Indians out of the Kentucky region in 1779.

After the war, in 1794, Kenton served as a major in Wayne's expedition. He became a brigadier general in the Ohio militia in 1805. During the War of 1812 he fought in Canada. A town in Ohio and a county in Kentucky are named after him. He died in Bellefontaine, Ohio, and was buried in Urbana, Ohio.

KOSCIUSZKO, Thaddeus (Tadeusz Andrzej Bonawentura): army officer, Polish patriot

Born Palatinate of Breescin, Grand Duchy of Lithuania, February 12, 1746; died October 15, 1817.

In 1769 Kosciuszko graduated with the rank of captain from the Royal School in Warsaw, Poland, and joined the Polish Army. He came to America in 1775 and was commissioned colonel of engineers in the Continental Army the next year. It was he who advised Horatio Gates to fortify Bemis Heights, an act which resulted in the victory of Saratoga.

From 1778 until 1780 Kosciuszko was in charge of building fortifications at the United States Military Academy; in 1779 he also was adjutant to George Washington. In 1781 he had charge of transportation during Greene's campaign in the South, and the Continental Congress appointed him a brigadier general two years later. He was one of the founders of the Society of the Cincinnati.

In 1789 Kosciuszko became a major general in the Polish Army. He is famous for his vow to fight to the death for Polish freedom from Russia. Toward this end, he headed the Polish Army's fight against the Russians (1792), led the rebellion of 1794, and was imprisoned for a time (1794–96). He continued his efforts for a free Poland until his death in 1817. He died in Switzerland and was buried in Cracow, Poland.

★★★★★

LACLEDE, Pierre Liguesle: fur trader

Born Bedous, France, 1724; father of three children; died June 20, 1778.

Laclede, whose real name was Pierre Laclede Liguesle, emigrated to New Orleans in 1755 and became associated with the trading establishment of Maxent, Laclede and Company. In 1763 he became an agent in the territory that is now Illinois.

After the eastern region came under British rule, Laclede went to the western bank of the Mississippi River. In 1764 he founded St. Louis, named in honor of Louis IX. He laid out the community and became its sole ruler. He died in 1778 near the mouth of the Arkansas River.

LAFAYETTE, Marquis de (Marie Joseph Paul Yves Roche Gilbert du Motier): army officer

Born Auvergne, France, September 6, 1757; son of Gilbert (Marquis de Lafayette) and Marie Louise Julie de la Riviere; married Marie Adrienne Françoise de Noailles, April 11, 1774; father of at least one son (George Washington); died May 20, 1834.

From 1768 to 1772 Lafayette attended the Collège du Plessis in Paris. He served with the 2nd Company of the King's Musketeers in the French Army from 1771 to 1773. He transferred to a regiment commanded by Louis, Vicomte de Noailles, became a second lieutenant in 1773, and was promoted to captain in 1774.

In 1777 Lafayette volunteered to enter the Continental Army at his own expense. He was commissioned a major general by a vote of the Continental Congress in July 1777 and was placed in command of a division of Virginia light troops by a vote of Congress in December of the same year. He spent his furlough in 1778–80 in France advancing the American cause.

Upon his return to the United States, Lafayette served in Virginia, taking part in the Battle of Yorktown in 1781. He became a member of the Society of the Cincinnati and was an intimate associate of George Washington. In December 1781 he returned to France, coming back to the United States for visits in 1784 and 1824–25.

In 1787 Lafayette became a member of the French Assembly of Notables and in 1789 a member of the French National Assembly. He was an organizer of the National Guard of France and a designer of the French tricolor flag. In 1790 he co-founded the Club of the Feuillants, a group of conservative liberals who wanted to establish a constitutional monarchy. The next year he commanded the French Army in the war with Austria.

Lafayette was declared a traitor by the National Assembly in 1792. He fled to Flanders, where he was captured and imprisoned by the Austrians. After seven years in exile, he returned to France in 1799. In 1815 and from 1818 to 1824 he served as a member of the Chamber of Deputies. He was a commander of the French National Guard in the July Revolution of 1830.

In 1794 the United States Congress voted $24,424 to Lafayette for his part in the American Revolution. He was given 11,520 acres of land in Louisiana in 1803, and he was named an honorary citizen of the United States. When Lafayette died, his grave in Picpus Cemetery in Paris was covered with earth from Bunker Hill.

LALOR, Alice (Mother Teresa): nun
Born Ireland, 1766; died September 9, 1846.

Mother Teresa came to America in 1795; two years later she served in Philadelphia during the yellow fever epidemic. In 1799 she went to Georgetown, D.C., with two widows, Mrs. McDermott and Mrs. Sharpe. She lived with a group of nuns called the Poor Clares and in 1816 founded the first convent of the Visitation Order of Nuns in America, with the help of the Reverend Leonard Neale and the group of nuns. She became a mother superior in 1816 and later founded houses in Mobile, Alabama (1832), St. Louis, Missouri (1833), and Baltimore (1837).

Mother Teresa died in Baltimore at the age of eighty.

LANDAIS, Pierre: naval officer
Born St. Malo, Brittany, France, 1731; died September 17, 1820.

Landais served as an officer in the French Navy and from 1766 to 1769 as a member of the French exploratory voyage around the world with Louis de Bougainville. He was commissioned a captain in the Continental Navy in 1777. He commanded the merchant ship *Flamand* and delivered supplies from France to Portsmouth, New Hampshire. In 1778 he commanded the frigate *Alliance.*

In 1778 Landais became a naturalized citizen of Massachusetts and the next year was assigned to the fleet of John Paul Jones. He was expelled from the United States Navy in 1781 after an incident that occurred during the battle with the British ship *Serapis,* which led to his conviction on a charge of insubordination.

Landais was commissioned a rear admiral in the French Navy in 1792 and five years later returned to New York, where he died at the age of eighty-nine.

LEAKE, Walter: senator, governor of Mississippi

Born Albemarle County, Virginia, May 25, 1762; died November 17, 1825.

After serving in the Revolutionary War, Leake was admitted to the bar and began to practice law. President Jefferson appointed him United States judge for the Mississippi Territory in 1807.

Leake represented Mississippi in the United States Senate from December 10, 1817, to May 15, 1820. In 1820 he was appointed United States marshal for the Mississippi District. He served as governor of Mississippi from 1821 to 1825. He died in Mount Salus, Mississippi.

LITTLE TURTLE: Miami chief

Born Eel River, Fort Wayne, Indiana, circa 1752; died July 14, 1812.

Little Turtle, whose Indian name was Michi Kini Kwa, led the slaughter of American troops under General Arthur St. Clair in Kentucky in 1791. He took over command of Indian forces in 1792 and two years later was soundly defeated at Fort Recovery (Ohio) by General Anthony Wayne. In 1795 he signed the Treaty of Greenville, the first of many treaties the Miami chief signed with the United States. He died in Fort Wayne.

LORIMIER, Pierre Louis: trader, interpreter

Born Lachine, Canada, March 1748; married Charlotte Pemanpieh Bougainville; second marriage to Marie Berthiaume; father of at least three children; died June 26, 1812.

Lorimier accompanied his father to the Miami River in Ohio in 1769 and established the post known as Lorimier's, which later became a rendezvous for the British during the Revolutionary War. A trader with the Indians and an interpreter of Indian dialects, he took part in several raids on American forces; on one of these raids he captured Daniel Boone.

Lorimier's post was destroyed by George Rogers Clark's expedition into Indiana and Illinois in 1782. Lorimier was driven to St. Mary's, Missouri, five years later by his creditors. He was appointed agent of Indian affairs and in 1808 became captain commandant of the Spanish militia in the Missouri District.

After the completion of the Louisiana Purchase, Lorimier was appointed by the United States Government as judge of the Missouri Territory Court of Common Pleas. He received many land concessions from the Spanish and developed these into districts that were later inhabited by Americans.

★★★★★

McGREADY, James: clergyman

Born western Pennsylvania, circa 1758; died February 1817.

Licensed to preach by the Presbytery of Redstone, Pennsylvania, in 1788, McGready served as pastor of a church in Orange County, North Carolina, in 1790. He had three small congregations in Logan County, Kentucky, in 1796. Responsible for revivals in 1797, 1798, and 1799 (which were forerunners of the Great Revival of 1800), McGready became allied with the Cumberland Presbytery in 1800 and was restored to the Orthodox Transylvania Presbytery. He was a pioneer preacher, founding churches in southern Indiana in 1811.

McGready was the author of *A Short Narrative of the Revival of Religion in Logan County in the State of Kentucky and the Adjacent Settlements in the State of Tennessee from May, 1797, until September, 1800.* He died in Henderson County, Kentucky.

MacKAY, James: explorer

Born Kildonan, County Sutherland, Scotland, 1759; son of George and Elizabeth (McDonald) MacKay; married Isabella Long, February 24, 1800; died March 16, 1822.

In 1776 MacKay arrived in Canada to explore for the British. He later moved to Louisiana, where he directed the third expedition sponsored by the Spanish Commercial

Company to explore the country on both sides of the Missouri River and across the continent to the Pacific. Along the way he supervised the construction of forts for the protection of Spanish trade. The mission resulted in peace between the Spanish and the Indians and among the tribes themselves.

MacKay had taken possession of the British fort at the Mandan village and prepared a map of the region he had explored. In 1797 he became deputy surveyor for the Spanish traders in America. Maps of his explorations were later used by the explorers Lewis and Clark between 1804 and 1806.

MacKay served as captain and later as major of the St. Louis County militia and as commandant of San Andres, Missouri. A judge of the Court of Quarter Sessions in the Missouri Territory in 1804, he became a member of the Missouri territorial legislature in 1816.

McLENE, Jeremiah: congressman
Born Cumberland County, Pennsylvania, 1767; died March 19, 1837.

McLene, who attended common schools, served as a major general in the Pennsylvania militia during the Revolution. He later moved to Ohio, settling in Chillicothe. A member of the Ohio House of Representatives in 1807–08, he served as secretary of state for Ohio from 1808 to 1831. He moved to Columbus, Ohio, in 1816. A Democrat, he was elected to serve Ohio in the United States House of Representatives from 1833 to 1837. He died in Washington, D.C., and was buried in the Congressional Cemetery.

MANN, James: physician
Born Wrentham, Massachusetts, July 22, 1759; son of David and Anna Mann; married Martha Tyler, December 12, 1788; father of five children; died November 7, 1832.

Mann graduated from Harvard in 1776, then studied with Doctor S. Danforth. He served as a surgeon with Colonel W. Shepard's 4th Massachusetts Regiment from 1779 to 1782, during which he was imprisoned by the British for two months in 1781. After the war he established a medical practice in New York City. He was awarded an honorary M.D. by Brown University in 1815.

Mann was head of the medical department of the United States Army on the northern frontier during the War of 1812. He was a senior hospital surgeon in Detroit from 1816 to 1818, a post surgeon from 1818 to 1821, and assistant surgeon from 1821 to 1832. He wrote *Medical Sketches of the Campaigns of 1812, 13, 14 to Which Are Added Surgical Cases, Observations on Military Hospitals; and Flying Hospitals Attached to a Moving Army, Also An Appendix* (1816).

MANSFIELD, Jared: surveyor general, educator
Born New Haven, Connecticut, May 23, 1759; son of Stephen and Hannah (Beach) Mansfield; married Elizabeth Phipps, March 2, 1800; father of Edward Deering; died February 3, 1830.

Mansfield, who graduated from Yale in 1777, became rector of Hopkins Grammar School in New Haven in 1786. The following year he was awarded an A.M. by his alma mater. In 1802 he was appointed a captain in the Engineers Corps of the United States Army by President Jefferson and became acting professor of mathematics at the United States Military Academy. In 1803 he was appointed surveyor general of the United States, with the rank of lieutenant colonel, to survey Ohio and the Northwest Territory; he served in this capacity until 1812, in the meantime gaining promotions to major in 1805 and to lieutenant colonel in 1808.

From 1812 to 1828 Mansfield was a professor of natural and experimental philosophy at the Military Academy. He was the author of *Essays, Mathematical and Physical*, 1801, and *Essays on Mathematics*, 1802. Mansfield, Ohio, is named for him. He died in New Haven and was buried in Grove Cemetery there.

MAXWELL, William: publisher
Born New York, circa 1755; son of William Maxwell; married Nancy Robbins; father of eight children; died 1809.

A printer in Lexington, Kentucky, in 1792–93, Maxwell founded the *Centinel of the Northwest Territory,* Cincinnati, which he published from 1793 to 1796. He served as postmaster of Cincinnati and published *Laws of the Territory of the United States Northwest of the Ohio,* the first book published in the Northwest Territory, in 1796.

Maxwell moved to Dayton and later, in 1799, to Hamilton County. He was a member of the first Ohio legislature and was the first associate judge of Greene County, both in 1803. Sheriff of Greene County from 1803 to 1807, he was also a captain in the Ohio militia from 1804 to 1806, gaining a promotion to colonel in 1806.

Maxwell died in Greene County and was buried on his farm there.

MENARD, Pierre: fur trader, legislator
Born St. Antoine, Quebec, Canada, October 7, 1766; son of Jean Baptiste and Marie (Ciree) Menard; married Therese Godin, June 13, 1792; second marriage to Angelique Saucier, September 22, 1806; father of ten children; died June 13, 1844.

Menard went to Vincennes, Indiana, to become a fur trader about 1787. He was appointed major in the Randolph County Regiment, Indiana militia, in 1795. Recommissioned in 1800, he was appointed lieutenant colonel and commanding officer in 1806.

A judge of the Court of Common Pleas from 1801 to 1811, Menard was an organizing partner of the St. Louis Missouri Fur Company. He served as an infantry captain on a fur company expedition which restored the Mandan chief Big White to his people in 1809. Elected to the first Illinois Senate in 1812, he served as its first president, 1812–18. He was the first lieutenant governor of Illinois in 1818. He served on a commission to treat with the Winnebagos at Prairie du Chien, Wisconsin, in 1828 and on a commission to treat with other tribes of the region in 1829.

MORGAN, George: land speculator, Indian agent
Born Philadelphia, Pennsylvania, February 14, 1743; son of Evan and Joanna (Biles) Morgan; married Mary Baynton, October 21, 1764; father of eleven children; died March 10, 1810.

Apprenticed to the Philadelphia mercantile firm Baynton and Wharton about 1756, Morgan became a full partner in 1763. He went to Illinois country in an effort to find trading opportunities for the firm in 1764. The firm later went into receivership, but its assets included a grant of land (approximately 2,800 acres in what is now West Virginia) from the 1768 Treaty of Fort Stanwix with the Six Nations.

Morgan became secretary general and superintendent of the newly formed Indiana Company in 1776. Virginia opposed the claims of the company, and Morgan was prevented from furthering his claim by the adoption of the Eleventh Amendment in 1798. He held the rank of colonel with duties as Indian agent and deputy commissary general for purchases during the Revolution.

Morgan resigned from the Continental Army in 1779 to become a farmer and landowner in New Jersey. He wrote scientific articles for various publications and helped found the colony of New Madrid in Spanish Louisiana (now Missouri). He declined Aaron Burr's attempt to enlist him in his western project.

Morgan died on his farm near Washington, Pennsylvania.

MULLANPHY, John: businessman
Born near Enniskillen, Fermanagh, Ireland, 1758; died August 29, 1833.

Having gone to France in 1778, Mullanphy served in the Irish Brigade and then returned to Ireland at the outbreak of the French Revolution. He came to the United States in 1792 and lived first in Philadelphia, then in Baltimore, and then in Frankfort, Kentucky. He settled in St. Louis in 1804, where he became a real-estate investor.

Mullanphy served under Andrew Jackson at New Orleans during the War of 1812 and made a fortune in cotton speculation during and after the war. He made many contributions to philanthropic causes during the last years of his life. He died in St. Louis.

★★★★★

NEWCOMER, Christian: clergyman

Born Lancaster County, Pennsylvania, February 1, 1750; son of Wolfgang and Elizabeth (Weller) Newcomer; married Elizabeth Baer, March 31, 1770; died March 12, 1830.

Newcomer entered the ministry in 1777. A leader in founding the Church of the United Brethren in Christ, he was especially active in missionary work west of the Alleghenies. From 1813 to 1829 he was a bishop. He wrote *Newcomer's Journal,* a diary which contains much early history of the United Brethren Church.

★★★★★

OCONOSTOTA: Indian chief

No record of birth; father of at least one child (Tuksi); died 1785.

Oconostota, chief of the Cherokee Indians, sided with the British during the French and Indian War. His tribe lent assistance to the Americans in their attack on Fort Duquesne in 1759; soon after, however, the Americans killed a number of the Cherokee warriors, leading Oconostota to make repeated attacks on frontier settlements in reprisal. These culminated in his massacre of the inhabitants of Fort Loudoun after they had surrendered to him in 1760.

In 1762 Oconostota went to England. Returning to America in 1768, he concluded a peace treaty with the Iroquois. At the outbreak of the Revolutionary War, he joined the British in the fight against the Americans. He resigned his chieftainship after signing peace treaties with the American states in 1782.

★★★★★

PIGGOTT, James: pioneer official in Illinois

Born Connecticut, circa 1739; no record of first marriage; second marriage to Francies James; father of eight children; died February 20, 1799.

Piggott was commissioned a captain from Westmoreland County in the Pennsylvania militia, serving under General Arthur St. Clair in 1776–77. He had command of Fort Jefferson, near the mouth of the Ohio River, during the 1780 siege by the Chickasaw Indians. A leader against the French in the area in 1787, he signed a contract delegating Bartholomew Tardiveau as agent to the United States Congress.

Piggott was appointed captain of the Illinois territorial militia and circa 1790 became a justice of the peace at Cahokia. In 1795 he served as judge of common pleas in Cahokia and the following year as judge of quarter sessions. He proclaimed the opening of the Orphans Court.

The nucleus of present-day East St. Louis, Illinois, is on the site of the buildings constructed by Piggott to house his ferrying business. He died in Kaskaskia, Illinois.

POLK, Charles Peale: artist

Born Maryland, March 17, 1767; died 1822.

In 1785 and from 1791 to 1793 Polk advertised in Baltimore as a portrait painter. In 1787 in Philadelphia he also advertised his skills as a house, ship, and sign painter. He sold copies of the portraits he painted of Washington, Franklin, and Lafayette; he also painted a portrait of Jefferson. After working in Richmond, Virginia, in 1799 and 1800, he became a clerk for the United States Government in Washington, D.C.

POLLOCK, Oliver: trader, planter, financier

Born Coleraine, Northern Ireland, 1737; son of Jaret Pollock; married Margaret O'Brien, 1770; second marriage to Mrs. Winifred Deady, November 2,

1805; father of eight children; died December 17, 1823.

Pollock came to Carlisle, Pennsylvania, circa 1760, and for eight years was a merchant in trade between Boston and Cuba. In 1768 he moved to New Orleans and the next year was granted freedom of trade in Louisiana by General Alexander O'Reilly for services to his army.

During the American Revolution, Pollock supplied ammunition and information to the American forces. He was a United States commercial agent in Louisiana from 1778 to 1783 and helped George Rogers Clark finance his western conquest. The United States drew supplies on Pollock's credit in excess of $300,000 during the war.

Pollock went to Havana in 1783 as a commercial agent for the United States; while there he was held in jail for eighteen months for failure to satisfy the claims of his creditors. He returned to Virginia circa 1796 and purchased an estate. He died in Pinckneyville, Mississippi.

POND, Peter: fur trader, explorer
Born Milford, Connecticut, January 18, 1740; son of Peter and Mary (Hubbard) Pond; married Susanna Newell sometime between 1761 and 1765; father of at least two children; died 1807.

At the age of nineteen Pond was a sergeant in the New York Regiment from Suffolk County and fought in the French and Indian War. In 1760 he was commissioned an officer under General Amherst at Montreal.

Pond was engaged in the western fur trade from 1765 to 1788, working out of Detroit from 1765 to 1770 and out of Mackinac from 1770 to 1775. He explored the Athabaska River in Canada and opened a rich fur region. He was a trader with the North West Company from 1775 to 1785 and a shareholder of the company from 1783 to 1785.

Pond presented to Congress a map of his voyages, which was later copied for the archives of Great Britain and France; he prepared a similar map for the Empress of Russia. He died in Boston.

POST, Christian Frederick: missionary
Born Conitz, East Prussia, circa 1710; married Rachel, 1743; second marriage to Agnes, 1747; third marriage to Mary Stadelman, August 27, 1763; died May 1, 1785.

Post came to Bethlehem, Pennsylvania, in 1742 and served as an itinerant Moravian missionary to various German groups. In 1743 he began missionary work among the Indians in the area between New York and Connecticut. When the Indian wars of 1744 forced him to leave, he went to live in Iroquois country among the Six Nations.

In 1758 Isaac Stille and Post held a conference on the Ohio River with members of the Delaware, Shawnee, and other tribes and persuaded the Indians to ally with the British. Faced with this alliance, the French abandoned Fort Duquesne later that year. Post founded a settlement near Bolivay in Ohio country in 1759.

PULASKI, Casimir: army officer
Born Podolia, Poland, March 4, 1748; son of Count Joseph Pulaski; died October 11, 1779.

Pulaski joined in an active rebellion to combat foreign domination of Poland through Stanislaus II in 1768. Four years later he fled to Turkey and for three years tried to incite Turkey to attack Russia. He left Turkey in 1775 and arrived in Boston the next year.

In the United States Pulaski served as a volunteer in the battles of Brandywine and Germantown. He commanded the cavalry at Trenton during the winter of 1777 and later at Flemington. He was commissioned by Congress to organize an independent cavalry corps in 1778 and was ordered to the support of General Lincoln in South Carolina the next year.

Pulaski was mortally wounded in the Battle of Charleston and died on board the *Wasp* off the Charleston coast.

PUTNAM, Rufus: army officer, surveyor general, pioneer

Born Sutton, Massachusetts, April 9, 1738; son of Elisha and Susanna (Fuller) Putnam; married Elizabeth Ayres, April 6, 1761; second marriage to Persis Rice, January 10, 1765; father of ten children; died May 4, 1824.

Putnam served as an ensign during the French and Indian War from 1757 to 1760. He was a member of a committee to explore and survey lands on the Mississippi River claimed as bounties for veterans of the French and Indian War in 1773; two years later he was commissioned a lieutenant colonel in the Continental Army. That year and the next he was in charge of the defensive works around Boston and New York City, during which time he became chief engineer with the rank of colonel. He served under Gates in the campaign against Burgoyne and in 1779 rebuilt fortifications at West Point. He was commissioned a brigadier general in 1783. As chairman of an officers' organization, he framed the Newburgh Petition on behalf of land bounties for Revolutionary veterans in 1783.

Putnam undertook the survey and sale of lands in Maine belonging to Massachusetts, and in 1785 he was a surveyor of western lands. He was an organizer of the Ohio Company, whose purpose it was to colonize the north bank of the Ohio River. He led a colony to Marietta, Ohio, in 1788 and laid out developmental plans for the town; this was the first organized territory of the Northwest.

From 1790 to 1796 Putnam served as a judge in the Northwest Territory. In 1792 he was commissioned a brigadier general in the United States Army and made a treaty at Vincennes with the lower Wabash Indian tribes. He took charge of important surveys in the neighborhood of Marietta circa 1794. From 1796 to 1803 he was surveyor general of the United States. He was a delegate to the Ohio Constitutional Convention in 1802. He died in Marietta.

★★★★★

QUESNAY, Alexandre-Marie: army officer

Born Saint-Germain-en-Viry, France, November 23, 1755; son of Blaise and Catherine (Deguillon) Quesnay; married Catherine Cadier; father of one son; died February 8, 1820.

After arriving in Virginia in 1777, Quesnay served as a captain in the Continental Army that year and the next. He then went to Philadelphia and conducted a school there during the period 1780–84. He produced the first French play to be given in America, *Eugénie,* by Beaumarchais. In 1786 he returned to France.

Quesnay later set forth a proposal for an Academy of the United States of America, which was to include an extensive system of schools and universities and a learned society for the advancement of art and science. President Jefferson rejected the plan because he felt the United States was too poor to support such a program.

Quesnay died in St. Maurice, France.

★★★★★

RED WING: Indian chief

Born probably Red Wing, Minnesota, circa 1750; died circa 1825.

Red Wing, whose Indian name was Tantagamini, was the chief and the most powerful leader of the Kehmnichan band of the Mdewakanton Sioux. He had a reputation as a seer. Siding with the British in the War of 1812, he participated in the attack on Fort Sandusky, Ohio, in 1813; in the capture of Fort Shelby, Prairie du Chien, Wisconsin, in 1814; and probably in a battle on Mackinac Island. He was later noted for his friendship with the whites.

ROCHAMBEAU, Jean Baptiste Donatien de Vimeur (Comte de): army officer

Born Vendôme, France, July 1, 1725; son of Joseph Charles (Comte de Rochambeau) and Claire (Bégon) de Vimeur; married Jeanne d'Acosta, December 1749; died May 10, 1807.

Rochambeau, who had attended the Collège de Vendôme, served in the War of Austrian Succession and in the Seven Years' War. In 1761 he was promoted to brigadier general and became inspector of cavalry. In 1776 he accepted an appointment as governor of Villefranche-en-Roussillon, France. He came to America in 1780 as commander of French troops in the American Revolution, sailing from Brest to Newport, Rhode Island, with 6,000 men. The next year he joined the Continental Army under Washington at White Plains, New York, and in October he besieged Cornwallis at Yorktown and aided in gaining his surrender. He returned to France in 1783.

Rochambeau became commander of an important military district with headquarters at Calais, France. He was an active member of the Society of the Cincinnati and was a member of the Second Assembly of Notables. He was made commander of the district of Alsace in France and then, in 1790, was placed in charge of the Northern Military Department. The next year he was created marshal of France.

Rochambeau was honored by Napoleon and was a member of the Legion of Honor. He wrote his *Memoirs,* which were published in Paris in 1809 and translated into English in 1838. He died in Alsace and was buried in Thoré, France.

ROGERS, Robert: army officer
Born Methuen, Massachusetts, November 7, 1731; son of James and Mary Rogers; married Elizabeth Browne, June 30, 1761; father of one child; died May 18, 1795.

Rogers entered the New Hampshire Regiment in 1755. He served as captain of William Johnson's Crown Point expedition and scouted enemy forces and positions. In 1756 he was appointed captain of an independent company of rangers. He served with General Loudon at Halifax in 1757, with General Abercrombie at Ticonderoga in 1758, and with General Amherst at Crown Point in 1759. The St. Francis Indians were destroyed in the raid at Crown Point.

Rogers served in the final Montreal campaign in 1760. The next year he served as captain of an independent company against the Cherokee Indians in South Carolina. He was superintendent of the Southern Indians and, in 1763, captain of a New York independent company. He aided in the defense of Detroit against Pontiac. He was involved in illicit trading with the Indians.

In 1765 Rogers sailed for England to solicit preferment. After returning to America, he was appointed to command Fort Michilimackinac. Arrested on a charge of treasonable dealings with the French, he was acquitted for lack of evidence. He then returned to England, where he spent some time in debtors' prison until he was rescued by his brother in 1769.

Rogers returned to America in 1775 and the next year was imprisoned by George Washington for alleged spy activities. He escaped to the British and in 1780 fled to England. A journal kept by him from September 21, 1766, to July 3, 1767 was printed by William L. Clements in the *Proceedings of the American Antiquarian Society* in October 1918. Rogers died in London and was buried at St. Mary's in Newington, England.

★★★★★

SARGENT, Winthrop: territorial governor
Born Gloucester, Massachusetts, May 1, 1753; son of Winthrop and Judith (Saunders) Sargent; married Rowena Tupper, February 9, 1789; second marriage to Mary (McIntosh) Williams, October 24, 1798; father of three sons; died June 3, 1820.

After graduating from Harvard in 1771, Sargent joined the Continental Army in 1775; he was brevetted a major in 1781. In 1786 he became a surveyor on the Seven Ranges in Ohio and an original member of the Ohio Company, of which he was elected secretary the following year. He helped found the Marietta (Ohio) Company in 1788. Congress appointed him secretary of the territory northwest of the Ohio River in 1787, and he retained this position until 1798.

Sargent served as adjutant general to General Arthur St. Clair during the latter's expedition against the Indians. While acting as governor of the territory northwest of the Ohio River, he organized a militia to repel anticipated Indian attacks (1791). He then became the first governor of the Mississippi Territory, holding this office from 1798 until 1801.

In other activities, Sargent belonged to the American Philosophical Society, the Society of the Cincinnati, the American Academy of Arts and Sciences, and the Massachusetts Historical Society. With Benjamin Smith he published *Papers Relative to Certain American Antiquities.* In 1803 he wrote a poem titled "Boston." He died in New Orleans, Louisiana.

SCHÖPF, Johann David: physician, scientist
Born Wunsiedel, Germany, March 8, 1752; died September 10, 1800.

Schöpf studied medicine and natural sciences at the University of Erlangen in Germany during the period 1770–73 and received an M.D. in 1776. The following year he began a six-year term of service as a surgeon in a German regiment assigned to the British Army in New York. After his service ended, in 1783 and 1784 he traveled throughout the eastern United States and the Bahamas. In 1795 he became president of the Ansbach Medicinal-Collegium in Prussia.

Schöpf was the author of the first systematic work on American geology, *Beyträge zur Mineralogischen Kenntniss des Ostlichen Theils von Nordamerika und seiner Gebürge* (1787). In 1788 he wrote his two-volume masterpiece, *Reise durch einige der mittlern und südlichen vereinigten nordamerikanischen Staaten nach Ost-Florida und den Bahama-Inseln.* He also wrote papers on the climate and diseases of America and was the author of the first papers ever written on American ichthyology and American frogs and turtles. Other publications of his were *Materia Medica Americana, Potissimum Regni Vegetabilis* (1787) and *Historia Testitudinum, Iconibus Illustrata* (Fasc. I–VI, Erlangen, 1792–1801).

SIBLEY, John: physician, Indian agent
Born Sutton, Massachusetts, May 19, 1757; son of Timothy and Ann (Waite) Sibley; married Elizabeth Hopkins, 1780; second marriage to Mrs. Mary White Winslow, November 10, 1791; third marriage to Eudalie Malique, 1813; father of George Champlain; died April 8, 1837.

Sibley established the *Fayetteville* (North Carolina) *Gazette* circa 1785. In 1803 he became contract surgeon to the United States Army in the Orleans Territory. From 1805 until 1814, as Indian agent for the Orleans Territory, he gathered vocabularies of the tribes within the territory; his reports to Jefferson are a valuable source of knowledge about Louisiana in this period.

Sibley served in the Louisiana legislature for many years, was a colonel in the state militia, and served with Colonel James Long during the latter's raid on Texas in 1819. Circa 1819 he became a member of the supreme council governing the military post of Nacogdoches, Texas. He owned a cotton plantation, "Grand Encore," near Natchitoches, Louisiana. He was seventy-nine when he died.

SMITH, John: senator, clergyman
Born Hamilton County, Ohio, circa 1735; died circa 1824.

In 1790 Smith became a minister to a Baptist congregation in West Virginia. He was a member of the first Legislative Assembly of the Northwest Territory from 1799 to 1803 and then represented Ohio in the United States Senate from April 1, 1803, until April 25, 1809. His association with Aaron Burr during 1805 and 1806 resulted in his being suspected in 1806 of complicity with Burr. When Burr's plans were threatened, Smith contributed provisions and credit to keep the Ohio militia in the field. He was able to explain most of the charges against him acceptably but was unable to clear himself of the suspicion that he knew of Burr's plans.

The Senate censure of his activities failed to pass, but he resigned his seat. He died in Hamilton County.

★★★★★

TAMMANY: Indian chief
Born along the Delaware River, Bucks County, Pennsylvania; no record of death.

Tammany was chief of the Lenni-Lenape (or Delaware) Indians. At a council of Pennsylvania colonists and Indians in 1694, he spoke in favor of friendship with the settlers.

Although few records of his activities exist, it is clear that he had become a symbol of American resistance to British tyranny by the time of the advent of the Revolutionary War. After the war, Tammany became a symbol of democracy versus aristocracy. His name was adopted by the New York City Society of Tammany, founded by William Mooney in 1786.

TENNENT, John: physician
Born England, circa 1700; married Dorothy Paul, 1730; second marriage to Mrs. Hanger, November 8, 1741; died circa 1760.

Tennent came to America in 1725 and ten years later developed a treatment for pleurisy using rattlesnake root. Returning to England in 1739, he met with little success in securing recognition for his treatment, which he claimed would cure pleurisy, gout, rheumatism, dropsy, and nervous disorders.

In 1724 Tennent published *Every Man His Own Doctor* (second edition), which advocated the use of medicines grown in America. He published "Essay on the Pleurisy" in 1736 and *Detection of a Conspiracy . . . The Singular Case of John Tennent*, a defense of his career, in 1743.

THAYER, John: missionary
Born Boston, Massachusetts, May 15, 1758; son of Cornelius and Sarah (Plaisted) Thayer; died February 17, 1815.

Thayer was licensed a Congregational minister circa 1778 and received an honorary degree from Yale in 1779. For the next two years he served as chaplain under John Hancock at Castle William. In 1783 Thayer chose to enter the Roman Catholic Church and four years later was ordained a priest. This same year he wrote *The Conversion of John Thayer . . . Written by Himself.* Holding services in Alexandria, Virginia, he prepared to build a church in that city in 1793.

An abolitionist, Thayer went to assist Stephen Theodore Badin as a Kentucky missionary in 1799. Also as a missionary, he went to Limerick, Ireland, in 1803, where he died in 1815.

Thayer left a legacy which enabled several postulants to go to Three Rivers, Quebec, Canada, in 1817. On completion of their novitiate they established a house in Boston in 1819 which became the nucleus of the Ursuline Convent in Charlestown, Massachusetts.

TRENT, William: Indian trader
Born Philadelphia, February 13, 1715; son of William and Mary (Coddington) Trent; married Sarah Wilkins, 1752; father of six children; died 1787.

In 1746 Trent was appointed a captain in the Pennsylvania militia. From 1749 to 1754 he and a partner, George Croghan, engaged in Indian trade along the Ohio River. He attended councils with the Indians in 1752, 1757, and 1759. He was an agent for Virginia in charge of an expedition transporting gifts to the Miami Indians in 1752.

Trent began construction of a fort on the Ohio River in 1754; the post was captured by the French, completed, and named Fort Duquesne. In 1758 he was a member of the American expedition that recaptured the fort.

From 1760 to 1763 Trent was a member of Simon, Trent, Levy and Franks, traders. In 1768 he bought from Six Nations a large tract of land on the Ohio River that later became most of Indiana. He merged the tract with the Vandalia project in 1769 but was unsuccessful in his attempts to obtain

Royal or, later, congressional confirmation of the grant.

Trent died in Philadelphia.

TRUTEAU, Jean Baptiste: Indian trader, explorer, schoolmaster

Born Montreal, Quebec, Canada, December 11, 1748; son of Joseph and Catherine (Menard) Truteau; married Madeleine (LeRoy) Bellhomme, May 1, 1781; died circa January 30, 1827.

From 1774 to 1827 Truteau taught school in the village of St. Louis. During part of this time (1794–97) he was engaged by the Missouri Trading Company to lead an exploration expedition. In 1794 and 1795 he began a journal which became a valuable contribution to knowledge of the Upper Missouri River and its Indian tribes. He gave money to aid Spain in war. Truteau died near St. Louis and was buried in Carondelet, Missouri.

★★★★★

VAN HAGEN, Peter Albrecht: composer

Born Holland; married; father of at least one son (Peter); no record of death.

Van Hagen came to America and became a music teacher in Charleston, South Carolina, in 1774. In 1789 he began teaching in New York City. Together with his wife and son he gave numerous concerts. He moved to Boston in 1796. He is the composer of "Federal Overture" (1797) and "Funeral Dirge for George Washington" (1800) as well as of much theatrical music.

VIGO, Joseph Maria Francesco: army officer, fur trader

Born Mondoni, Piedmont, Italy, December 3, 1747; son of Matheo and Maria Magdalena (Iugalibus) Vigo; married Elizabeth Shannon, before 1783; died March 22, 1836.

Vigo, known in America as Francis Vigo, was engaged in the New Orleans–St. Louis fur trade. He reached the trading post at St. Louis and ultimately formed a secret partnership with Fernando de Leyba, the Spanish governor of St. Louis. Twice he journeyed to Kaskaskia from St. Louis to give assistance to George Rogers Clark during the Revolutionary War. In 1780 he was named executor under the will of Governor de Leyba.

Vigo County, Indiana, is named for him. He died in Vincennes, Indiana, and was buried in the Protestant Cemetery there.

VILLERÉ, Jacques Philippe: governor of Louisiana

Born Parish of St. John the Baptist, Louisiana, April 28, 1761; son of Joseph Roy and Louise Marguerite (de la Chaise) Villeré; married Jeanne Henriette Fazende, 1784; died March 7, 1830.

Villeré served as lieutenant of artillery in Santo Domingo and later (in 1815) was commissioned a major general in the Louisiana militia. In the meantime he had become a leading sugar planter in New Orleans and in 1812 had attended the Louisiana Constitutional Convention, which framed the first constitution for the state.

Villeré was governor of Louisiana from 1816 to 1820, the first Creole to hold that position. He advanced the opinion that yellow fever was not due directly to climate, for, as he observed, Louisiana prisoners segregated from the city did not fall victim to it. During his administration the state debt was paid off and a surplus of $40,000 was accumulated. He died on his plantation outside New Orleans.

VON STEUBEN, Friedrich Wilhelm Ludolf Gerhard Augustin (Baron): army officer

Born Magdeburg, Prussia, Germany, September 17, 1730; son of Wilhelm Augustin and Maria Dorothea (von Jagow) von Steuben; died November 28, 1794.

Von Steuben served as a staff officer with the rank of captain under Frederick the Great in the Seven Years' War. Benjamin Franklin and French officials recommended him as a military expert to the American Government. After his arrival in Portsmouth, New Hampshire, in 1777, the Continental Congress directed him to serve under George Washington at Valley Forge. As acting inspector general of the Continental Army, he was highly successful in drilling the army and was appointed inspector general with the rank of major general in 1778. He fought with distinction at the Battle of Monmouth.

During the winter of 1778–79 von Steuben wrote a drill manual, *Regulations for the Order and Discipline of the Troops of the United States,* which was invaluable for training American volunteers and which was immediately adopted by the Continental Army. The next winter he was General Washington's representative to the Continental Congress during its efforts to reorganize the army. During 1780–81 he was in command in Virginia under General Greene, and in 1781 he commanded a division at the Battle of Yorktown. He served as Washington's aide in military planning, helping to prepare plans for the future defense of the United States and for the demobilization of the Continental Army in the spring of 1783. He was honorably discharged the next year.

The legislatures of Pennsylvania and New York made von Steuben an American citizen in 1783 and 1786, respectively. He was a prominent founder of the Society of the Cincinnati and served as president of the New York branch. He also served as president of the German Society and was elected a regent of the University of the State of New York in 1787. He died in Utica, New York, at the age of sixty-four.

★★★★★

WARD, Nancy: Indian leader
Born circa 1740; no record of death.

A Cherokee Indian, Nancy Ward was called "Beloved Woman" or "Pretty Woman" by her people. She enjoyed the privilege of sitting on the tribal council and the right to revoke, at her will alone, any tribal sentence of punishment or death. She is credited with giving aid to frontiersmen

and supplying the Americans with beef cattle from her own large herd during the Revolution. She introduced Negro slavery and the use of cattle to the Cherokee tribe.

WHITAKER, Nathaniel: clergyman
Born Huntington, Long Island, New York, November 1730; son of Jonathan and Elizabeth (Jervis) Whitaker; married Sarah Smith; father of five children; died January 26, 1795.

A graduate of Princeton in 1752, Whitaker studied for the Presbyterian ministry. He was licensed to preach by the New York Presbytery about 1752 and served as minister of the Presbyterian Church in Woodbridge, New Jersey, from 1755 to 1760 and of the Sixth Parish in Norwich, Connecticut, from 1760 to 1765.

Whitaker traveled to England with the Reverend Samson Occom to collect funds for educating American Indians in 1765; they obtained 12,000 pounds. While in England he received an honorary D.D. from St. Andrew's University. He returned to America to serve as minister of the Third Church of Salem, Massachusetts, from 1769 to 1784 and of the Presbyterian Church, Skowhegan, Maine, from 1785 to 1790. He died in Hampton, Virginia.

WHITE EYES: Indian chief
No record of birth; died 1778.

Chief sachem of the Delaware tribe of Indians in Ohio in 1776, White Eyes had been responsible for his tribe's peaceful acceptance of the white man and had led his people to neutrality in Lord Dunmore's War of 1774 (the war in which the Shawnee Indians were completely defeated). He committed his tribe to the American cause with the Treaty of Fort Pitt in 1775 but was deceived into signing a treaty of alliance with the American Confederation in 1778. He led General Lachlin McIntosh's troops in an unsuccessful attempt to capture Detroit from the British in 1778; he was murdered by American soldiers during this attack.

WOODMAN, John: reformer

Born Anococas (now Rancocas), New Jersey, October 19, 1720; son of Samuel and Elizabeth (Burr) Woodman; married Sarah Ellis, October 18, 1749; died October 7, 1772.

A tailor by trade, Woodman was an itinerant Quaker preacher from 1743 to 1772, speaking in all of the colonies and in England. He inveighed against slavery and is best known as a pioneer advocate of its abolition. He also opposed conscription. He was active in Indian conversions and preached to Indians in the Wyoming region in 1763. In 1772 he went to England, where he also established a reputation as an abolitionist.

Woodman based his slavery writings on visits to slave-trading centers throughout the United States, especially in the South. He was the author of *Some Considerations on the Keeping of Negroes* (1754) and *A Plea for the Poor* (1763). Published posthumously were *Serious Consideration, with Some of His Dying Expressions* (1773) and his *Journal* (1774). He died in York, England.

★★★★★

ZANE, Ebenezer: pioneer

Born Hardy County, West Virginia, October 7, 1747; married Elizabeth McCulloch; father of thirteen children; died November 19, 1812.

In 1769 Zane and his brothers claimed land at the mouth of Wheeling Creek in Ohio. He served as a colonel in the Virginia militia in Dunmore's War and helped repel the sieges of Fort Henry in 1777 and 1782.

After the Revolutionary War, Zane obtained permission from Congress to build a road from Wheeling to Limestone, Kentucky. In 1796 he also received grants of mile-square plots of land where the road crossed the Muckingum, Hocking, and Scioto rivers. The town of Zanesville was founded on the first plot in 1799 and the town of Lancaster on the second plot the following year. Zane died twelve years later and was buried in the family plot in Martin's Ferry, Ohio.

ZEISBERGER, David: missionary

Born April 11, 1721; son of David and Rosina Zeisberger; married Susan Lecron, June 4, 1781; died November 17, 1808.

Zeisberger joined the Moravian colony in Pennsylvania circa 1740. Having helped arrange the treaty allying the Six Nations during the period from 1745 to 1763, in the latter year he lived with the Delaware Indians. In 1771 he established the Christian Indian settlement at Schoenbrunn in the Tuscarawas Valley and built the first church and school west of the Ohio River. He also helped to establish settlements at New Salem, Ohio, and Fairfield, Canada, during the years 1786–98. He died at the age of eighty-seven.

★★★★★★★★★★★★★